ANNUAL REVIEW OF ANTHROPOLOGY

EDITORIAL COMMITTEE (1994)

ANNUAL REVIEW OF ANTHROPOLOGY

VOLUME 23, 1994

WILLIAM H. DURHAM, *Editor*
Stanford University

E. VALENTINE DANIEL, *Associate Editor*
University of Michigan

BAMBI SCHIEFFELIN, *Associate Editor*
New York University

ANNUAL REVIEWS INC.   4139 EL CAMINO WAY   P.O. BOX 10139   PALO ALTO, CALIFORNIA   94303-0139

ANNUAL REVIEWS INC.
Palo Alto, California, USA

International Standard Serial Number: 0084-6570
International Standard Book Number: 0-8243-1923-0
Library of Congress Catalog Card Number: 72-821360

Annual Review and publication titles are registered trademarks of Annual Reviews Inc.

The paper used in this publication meets the minimum requirements of American National Standards for Information Sciences—Permanence of Paper for Printed Library Materials, ANZI Z39.48-1984

Annual Reviews Inc. and the Editors of its publications assume no responsibility for the statements expressed by the contributors to this *Review*.

Typesetting by Ruth McCue-Saavedra and the Annual Reviews Inc. Editorial Staff

PRINTED AND BOUND IN THE UNITED STATES OF AMERICA

PREFACE

In the past decade, personal computer technology has increasingly affected the way we do anthropology. Many among us now store and retrieve field notes, quantitative data, geographic information, and bibliographic entries by PC. We do much of our writing via word processing programs and now we use e-mail for much of our correspondence, even gossip. But new technologies are beginning to affect the way we read anthropology as well. There are growing numbers of on-line journals and newsletters, and before long some major publications will surely become available by electronic network distribution and CD-ROM. The *Annual Review of Anthropology* (*ARA*) is already included in a computer-based preprint and reprint delivery service, and in a cumulative 10-year index on diskette (for details, contact Annual Reviews Customer Service).

We at the *ARA* are interested to hear reactions from readers and subscribers to the new distribution technologies. To that end, we include with this volume a questionnaire that we hope you will use to share your views on three related subjects. First, please tell us how you currently receive and use the *ARA,* and how we might better serve your needs using our existing distribution technology. Second, please give us your suggestions about which of the new media options would improve the accessibility and value of the *ARA* both in the United States and abroad. Finally, we are keenly interested in your perceptions of the impact of the new technologies on the nature and pursuit of knowledge in the discipline. How does electronic production affect our work, our lives, and our influence as anthropologists? We hope you will take a few minutes to share your views on these matters using the enclosed questionnaire and return envelope. We look forward to hearing from you.

Other changes underway at the *ARA* this year include the appointment of our first International Correspondents, Dr. Veena Das of the Department of Sociology at the University of Delhi, India, and Dr. Alcida Rita Ramos at the Institute of Human Sciences at the University of Brasilia, Brazil. We welcome Drs. Das and Ramos and thank them cordially for their ongoing contributions to the *ARA* process. We are also pleased to announce that, beginning with Volume 24 next year, each issue of the *ARA* will include reviews from a number of perspectives on selected special themes in addition to our standard coverage. Next year's special themes will be "Border Issues" and "Gender."

William H. Durham
Editor

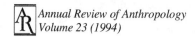
Annual Review of Anthropology
Volume 23 (1994)

CONTENTS

SOME RELATED ARTICLES IN OTHER *ANNUAL REVIEWS*

From the *Annual Review of Ecology and Systematics*, Volume 25 (1994)

> *The Evolutionary Biology of Human Immunodeficiency Virus*, Andrew J. Leigh Brown and Edward C. Holmes

From the *Annual Review of Energy and the Environment*, Volume 19 (1994)

> *The Economics of Sustainable Development*, D. W. Pearce, G. D. Atkinson, and W. R. Dubourg
> *Disseminating Renewable Energy Technologies in Sub-Saharan Africa*, S. Karekezi

From the *Annual Review of Nutrition*, Volume 14 (1994)

> *Childhood Malnutrition in Developing Nations: Looking Back and Looking Forward*, J. C. Waterlow

From the *Annual Review of Psychology*, Volume 45 (1994)

> *The Self in Social Contexts*, Mahzarin R. Banaji and Deborah A. Prentice
> *Color Appearance: On Seeing Red—Or Yellow, Or Green, Or Blue*, Israel Abramov and James Gordon

From the *Annual Review of Sociology*, Volume 20 (1994)

> *Sociobiology and Sociology*, François Nielsen
> *Why Fertility Changes*, Charles Hirschman
> *Women, Family, and Class*, Annemette Sørensen
> *Comparative Studies in Class Structure*, John Myles and Adnan Turegun
> *The Sociology of Ethnic Conflicts: Comparative International Perspectives*, Robin M. Williams, Jr.
> *Aging and Generational Relations: A Historical and Life Course Perspective*, Tamara K. Hareven

Annu. Rev. Anthropol. 1994. 23:1–23

DIGGING ON: A Personal Record and Appraisal of Archaeological Research in Africa and Elsewhere

J. Desmond Clark

Department of Anthropology, University of California, Berkeley, California 94720

KEY WORDS: archaeology training, early experience in Africa, first concepts, modern developments, African archaeology

INTRODUCTION

I first began working in Africa fifty-six years ago and am lucky enough to have been able to do fieldwork there ever since. My involvement in the better understanding of the past record of human endeavor and achievement there has remained as stimulating and exciting to me today as it was on January 6, 1938, when I first set foot in Livingstone in what was then Northern Rhodesia (now Zambia). It gives me the greatest satisfaction to see how archaeology and the study of African prehistory have developed since those early days before World War II and how the record of the human past in Africa has received the recognition it deserves from not only the international world of paleoanthropologists, archaeologists, and historians, but also from the interested public in many different countries and walks of life. The greater part of the long record of the biological, intellectual, and technological evolution of humankind is to be found in Africa until the movement into Eurasia one million or more years ago. I have found it especially valuable, therefore, to have been privileged to work in parts of Asia—Syria, India, and China. This has allowed a more balanced assessment of Africa's contribution to the historical record. This record shows humankind's pathways to biological and cultural evolution, with its increasingly ingenious intensity in the use of natural resources. Archae-

0084-6570/94/1015-0001$05.00

1

ological understanding provides much of the basic source data for writing the early history of the many diverse populations originating in Africa. That I was able to work in Asia as well as in Africa has been mostly the result of accidental and fortuitous circumstances and the generous invitations that have come my way, and not to any particular planning on my part. From the start, circumstances frequently offered new opportunities, some of which I was wise—or foolish—enough to take.

EARLY DAYS IN PREHISTORY

I became seriously involved with prehistory in my last year at Cambridge when I did the "Arch. and Anth." Tripos (honors exams) and was lucky enough to have two of the best teachers I have known—Miles Burkitt and Grahame (now Sir Grahame) Clark. My abiding interest in archaeology received its focus from the enthusiasm and skills they shared with their students. Miles Burkitt began teaching prehistory at Cambridge in 1919 and was an inspiring teacher for those with the good fortune to attend his lectures and supervisions. The supervisions in particular were a pleasure never to be missed. They were held in his house in Grantchester, about two miles out of Cambridge. After a formal tea around the dining table at which his wife, Peggy, presided, the six or seven of us (in 1937) trooped into Miles' study where we were instructed in the intricacies of the Paleolithic through the Neolithic with the aid of artifacts and photographs passed around for us to handle. Facing Miles, who always sat with his back to the embers, on a high, leather-padded fire screen, we listened to him. He had dug at Castillo with Hugo Obermaier and Henri Breuil and was well acquainted with the French and Spanish *savants,* landowners, antiquarians, and prehistorians, in particular with those working on the Paleolithic. His witty and interesting anecdotes about his colleagues and their discoveries helped us to retain the essential data. In those days it was possible to buy artifacts from amateur collectors and Miles' collection of European and African specimens was an inestimable adjunct to his teaching and to our learning about tools and their manufacture. When he died in the 1960s he left two thirds of his collection to the Museum of Archaeology and Anthropology in Cambridge and one third to me. I was then teaching Old World Prehistory at the University of California, Berkeley, and here and elsewhere we continue to make very good use of the collection.

In Miles' study we learned the difference between a *bec de perroquet* and a *burin busqué,* and much other typology besides, since this was all important in the 1930s. We also tried to understand the sequence of climatic events and technological innovations, as well as the Abbé Breuil's complex interpretations of the sedimentary history in the Somme terraces. I later found that many professionals also had difficulty understanding the Abbé's masterly interpretations, which were published in his papers in *L'Anthropologie,* and which are still an important part of the European prehistoric archives. The preoccupation with various taxonomic systems remained for a long time in Europe because this was the only way to establish a relative chronology for Lower Paleolithic assemblages in peri-glacial high latitudes. Some thought that the same criteria for estimating age in Europe could equally be applied in Africa and I remember the Abbé saying that he could tell me which stages of the Acheulian (1–7 in the Somme) I was finding in the Zambezi Valley simply by feeling, with eyes shut, the degree of abrasion each biface exhibited. It is hard to realize today that such subjective ordering was possible and acceptable in the 1930s but subjective reasoning was with us—and is still very much alive—until radiometric dating became available to prehistorians.

My other teacher at Cambridge, Grahame Clark, had joined Miles two years earlier to begin the systematic teaching of prehistory, in which Cambridge still leads in Britain. Grahame's speciality was in Mesolithic and Neolithic prehistory—designations that do not mean as much now as they did then. Grahame gave us the depth of understanding and the rigor of the scientific manner that is still so all-important. Grahame has remained an intellectual giant who, stressing human paleo-ecology, has left an indelible record of outstanding research and teaching. He was a close friend of C. W. Phillips, the excavator of Sutton Hoo and a fairly regular visitor at supervisions. Grahame and Miles stressed the overriding importance of rigorous excavation and recording methods, so I was sent to join Sir Mortimer Wheeler's excavations at Maiden Castle in Dorset. This huge Iron Age hill camp had fallen to Vespasion's legions during the Roman invasion of Britain in A.D. 43, and the last defenders killed in the storming of the east gate were buried where they fell in the breastworks. The two seasons I spent there gave me the training in field methods that has been the basis for all later refinements. Wheeler was a superb organizer; his excavations were run with almost military precision. This did not suit some people, but it provided the outstanding site report that his volume on Maiden Castle remains (18). I had two excellent site supervisors on this dig, Molly Cotton and John Waechter, who both went on to distinguished careers in archaeology. They shared with us the personal kindness, encouragement, and humor that I have always tried to provide for my own field teams.

I took the Tripos in the spring of 1937 and did better than I had expected. I was also awarded an Honorary Bachelor Scholarship at my college (Christ's). The scholarship carried no financial support, so I looked for a job that would enable me to continue with archaeology. For three or four months I did voluntary work under Mortimer Wheeler at the London Museum (then in Lancaster House). I learned how to draw sections of Iron Age pottery with John Ward-Perkins, later Director of the British School in Rome, and catalogued large numbers of Acheulian bifaces from Thames gravel terraces.

Ward-Perkins taught me to purchase a set-square calibrated in cm and mm from the base—set-squares and rulers with markings that start part way up the edge are a nuisance. This tool has been invaluable ever since and was indispensable last season (November/December 1993) in the Ethiopian Rift.

JOB PROSPECTS

In 1937 there were only two universities in Britain where prehistory was taught—Cambridge and Edinburgh. There was a position for an Archaeology Officer in the Ordinance Survey, but that was held by O. G. S. Crawford, who was a pioneer of air photography for archaeology. So, one applied for museum positions, which were not easy to come by. Some, like the British Museum, were prestigious and financially adequate but most were county or city/town museums, where the average stipend was 135 pounds (about $540) per year. Archaeologists were thought to be amateurs who did archaeology in their spare time, so these jobs were not expected to provide major financial support. The core of professional archaeologists were highly successful, respected doctors, chemists, lawyers, and farmers, among others, until after the war, when universities began to provide more opportunities for training and appointments in archaeology and prehistory. I applied for a vacancy in the British and Mediaeval Antiquities Department of the British Museum. The only question I can remember having been asked at the interview was how good was my knowledge of Byzantine art and antiquities as the department had quite a lot of Byzantine material. I was not offered the position because my knowledge stretched no further than an interest in the later Byzantine Empire's successful intrigues in stemming Islamic invasion for several hundred years, an interest I acquired while at Cambridge. I have always been grateful that I did not get this or one of the other museum positions for which I applied. Toward the end of 1937 I was offered a position by Sir Hubert Young, the Governor of Northern Rhodesia. He had started a museum and expanded it to include a social-anthropological institute, six miles from the Victoria Falls in Livingstone, almost on the Zambezi River. The town was full of empty houses and other buildings because the government seat had been moved from there in 1935 to the more centrally located Lusaka. So I became Curator of the David Livingstone Memorial Museum and Secretary of the Rhodes-Livingstone Institute for Social Anthropology. What I knew about Northern Rhodesia was limited, but encouraging, mostly concerned with the discovery in 1922 of *Homo rhodesiensis* in the Broken Hill (now Kabwe) mine. They wanted me out there as soon as possible, so I left England on December 17 on an Intermediate Union Castle boat bound for Cape Town via Las Palmas and St. Helena. The journey to Cape Town took about two weeks and from there to Livingstone on the South African and Rhodesia Railways took three and a half days. I arrived in Livingstone at 8 P.M. during the rains. I experienced for the first time the exotic scents of the tropical vegetation in the humid time of the year—the heady aromas of the *Bauhinias, Cassias,* Flamboyants, and African Violet trees that still bring back good memories of the twenty-three years when Livingstone was our home.

These were the "bad old days" of colonial rule when most people in Zambia, black and white, got by, were assured of the essentials of life, and lived in peace. Colonialism, as we know now, was not good for the indigenous peoples, but it was the best thing at the time, and it was certainly better than what had gone before. I don't know if Northern Rhodesia's colonial administration was better than others, but the men who were appointed to the Provincial Administration were some of the most unbiased, hard working, and concerned people I have known. They were responsible for seeing that the Africans in their districts were looked after fairly with the means at their disposal. Some of these men were fine scholars in their own right—classicists, ornithologists, linguists—and all District Officers had to learn at least one local language so communication could be direct and not just through interpreters. All the younger men spent half of most months on tour in the villages and our first knowledge of likely archaeological sites in the country often came from the records of caves, rock paintings, and engravings they wrote about in the District Notebooks. Many of these men and some of their wives held bachelor's degrees, and Miles Burkitt taught several of them in the post-graduate year the Colonial Office gave them before they were posted overseas. One such man was F. D. Macrae, who had carried out the first archaeological excavation in Northern Rhodesia in the Mumbwa Caves in 1924. Another was Vernon Brelsford, trained at Oxford, and who later went on to write a definitive monograph for the Rhodes-Livingstone Institute on the peoples of the Bangweulu Swamps (2). Vernon had been seconded to Livingstone to write a handbook for the collections that Hubert Young, through the Provincial Administration, had asked District Officers to put together and send down to the Museum. This collection of ethnographic material culture formed an important nucleus for the expanding museum. Vernon's handbook (1) is an invaluable record of everyday life, ceremony and ritual in tribal villages, and a testimonial to the cultural variability of local people who spoke seven main languages and some sixty-three dialects. This book, now long out of print, was a fine compilation based on district notes and firsthand knowledge of the people and objects themselves. When I first arrived in Livingstone I overlapped for three days with Vernon before he left for a long leave in England; I was then on my own.

The Museum and the Institute's offices were housed in what had been the United Services Club. This single story building had an imposing facade and, inside, three main display rooms with smaller ancillary buildings, all of which had more than their share of termites against which a perpetual war was waged with "dip" to keep them at bay. The Museum also housed a collection of relics connected with David Livingstone, who discovered and named the Victoria Falls in 1855 and whose watercolor sketchbook of his trans-Africa journey was placed on permanent loan by his grandson, Dr. Hubert Wilson, whom I later had the privilege of counting among my highly respected friends.

Hubert Young had also been interested in early African explorers ("first tourists" as some would call them today) and the cartographic development that can be seen in the changing maps of Africa. The Museum had the nucleus of a fine collection of such maps, originally bought and presented by the Governor's friends and acquaintances and to which we later added significantly. I have retained to this day my interest in the early cartographers and historians of Africa—Pigafetta, Senuto, Ogilby, Linschoten, Hondius, d'Almeida. The names and notes on some of these maps provide the first written record of a people, a chieftainship, or a trading center, and the geographic context in which they occurred.

My colleagues at the Rhodes-Livingstone Institute were Godfrey and Monica Wilson, who had recently completed several years' work among the Nyakusa in southern Tanganyika (Tanzania). They were later joined by Max Gluckman, who worked with the Barotse. The Wilsons' friendship and intellectual stimulus were invaluable in my first two years in Livingstone. During my last year at Cambridge I had become engaged to a Modern Languages scholar at Newnham. Betty came out to Livingstone shortly after I arrived there and we were married in April 1938. She has remained a vital linch-pin and support ever since. Those were exciting and enjoyable days even though we had to watch the pennies. My salary was 400 pounds (about $1600) per year—lavish by what a young archaeologist could expect in England but exiguous in Africa. We were still careful, though. A bottle of Scotch cost only 10 shillings (about $2), but we had to make one last a month! The Zambezi and the Victoria Falls were 3–6 miles away and stone artifacts had been found at the Falls since the 1920s. A canal for a hydroelectric scheme had been dug a year before my arrival and the sediments exposed in the canal and in storm drains provided the first evidence of a stratigraphic sequence of artifacts and cultural remains in geological context in the Valley. My first paper was published in 1939, with Basil Cooke, who had been on a visit to the Falls and described the elephant remains I had found in these excavations (5). The survey of this part of the Zambezi Valley up and down stream from the Victoria Falls was extended with invaluable help from the geologist Frank Dixey, who transferred from Nyasaland (Malawi) to Northern Rhodesia to start the Geological Survey in Lusaka. In its upper course above the Victoria Falls, the Zambezi cut through thick expanses of what were, and probably still are, called "Kalahari Sands." These sands represent a record of greatly ex-

tended desertic conditions in the later Tertiary, stretching westward and northward even across the lower reaches of the Congo River, and the subsequent
redistributions in later climatic episodes during the Pleistocene. The Zambezi
survey and excavation work correlated the fluvial sedimentary geology with
the episodes of redeposition of the Kalahari-type sands and the cultural sequence they, and the river terraces, contained.

ARCHAEOLOGICAL RESEARCH ON THE CONTINENT

I have already written about the state of archaeological research in the Continent when I first started to work in Africa (4), and it can best be understood
from *A History of African Archaeology,* edited by Robertshaw (16). I speak
here only of those who were valued friends and colleagues for me. These
include two of Miles Burkitt's best known students, John Goodwin and Louis
Leakey. John, the founder of systematic, archaeological research in South
Africa, began teaching prehistory at the University of Cape Town in the 1920s.
Another fine colleague and friend was "Peter" Van Riet Lowe in Johannesburg, a civil engineer turned professional archaeologist. He was closely associated with Goodwin in establishing in 1929 the chronological sequence, terminology, and methodology for the Stone Age in South Africa, a framework that
was used extensively, and still is more generally, in Africa south of the Sahara
(11). Goodwin was the moving force in establishing prehistory as a science in
southern Africa as demonstrated by his handbooks, *Method in Prehistory* (9)
and *The Loom of Prehistory* (10), his founding of the South African Archaeological Society, his editorship of the society *Bulletin,* and his leading the first
systematic excavation of a cave site, Oakhurst Shelter (8). Mary Leakey,
coming to South Africa on her way to East Africa in 1935 says she was deeply
impressed by John's excavation and recording methods during the weeks she
spent digging with him at Oakhurst (15:51).

Goodwin was at the Cape, Van Riet Lowe with Berry Malan in Johannesburg, and the only possible communication was by mail, although after the war
we had overseas leave to England when we traveled by sea via the Cape. On
our return we would bring back a new car to the Cape and drive it to Northern
Rhodesia visiting friends and sites en route. Fortunately, 300 miles to the south
was Neville Jones, a Methodist missionary turned professional archaeologist
and a Keeper at the National Museum of Southern Rhodesia in Bulawayo. Our
all too infrequent visits helped stimulate my investigation of the prehistory of
Northern Rhodesia.

My contract with the Institute trustees was for three years, with an option
for long-term renewal and overseas leave of six months every three and later
every two and a half years. When not on leave I was expected to stay in the
country. I was especially lucky in having the Zambezi Valley research at my

doorstep, and because there were no funds for archaeological fieldwork in the Institute, I had to use my own car and equipment. In 1939, wishing to do more work at Mumbwa and in the Lusaka area, I was given 15 pounds (about $60) to help with this new venture. Roads were bad and it took three days by car to get to Mumbwa, but it was an enjoyable trip and there was much to learn and see: new people and cultural behavior, and new terrain—vegetation, animals, and the different habitats to which they were adapted. Mumbwa was a successful dig and enabled me to define the Middle and Later Stone Age assemblages in the Kafue Basin. I was also able to make some suggestions about the seasonal movements of the prehistoric hunter-gatherers because the site was in the ecotone between the grasslands of the Kafue Flats and the savanna woodlands.

The outbreak of World War II put a stop to field research and in January 1941 I joined the Field Ambulance Unit of the Northern Rhodesia Regiment and left for the war against the Italians in Ethiopia and Somalia. I suppose most wars involve times when little or nothing happens and others of more intense, often unpleasant activity. The war in the Horn was no exception, so I was able to do some archaeological surveying, which resulted in the volume, *The Prehistoric Cultures of the Horn of Africa* (3). It was not until the early 1980s that Steven Brandt was able to continue the work in Somalia and to produce the first radiometric dates for the prehistoric cultures there.

I always went to see Louis and Mary Leakey on my way through Nairobi, which was the Headquarters of the British East Africa Command. We would visit their sites in the Kenya Rift and have lively discussions about collections and correlations using fauna and artifacts because radiocarbon dating wasn't yet available. I learned a great deal from these meetings. The opportunity to visit key sites and to handle artifacts provided the basic understanding that, for me, any amount of reading or photographs do not. Because archaeologists are essentially concerned with artifacts of one kind or another and the contexts in which they occur, I have always considered hands-on laboratory and fieldwork the basis for a comprehensive understanding of the archaeology of a region.

In 1946, after two years in the Military Administration of Somalia, I was discharged from the army and returned to the Museum, which my wife had administered during my absence. At this time, the Institute and Museum were separated, with the former moving to Lusaka, the capital. The Museum was renamed The Rhodes-Livingstone Museum and plans were formed for a new building in a new location in town. We were overdue for leave and I had a number of months coming to me from my time in the army, so I was able to spend an academic year back in Cambridge, to add to the two years spent away on fieldwork for my doctorate. We spent the latter part of 1946 and much of 1947 in a rented cottage in Grantchester, while I worked on the collections I had brought back and wrote my dissertation. Returning to Livingstone and to new prospects for development and a new building, I continued to work in Africa from then until 1961, when I left for a teaching position at the University of California, Berkeley.

In 1947 Louis Leakey organized the first Pan-African Congress on Prehistory and Related Studies in Nairobi. Louis was well aware of the need for dialogue and interaction among the prehistorians, archaeologists, physical anthropologists, and quaternary geologists, and he was able to get most of those working in northern and sub-Saharan Africa to meet in Nairobi. This was the first time that such an international forum on Africa had been possible, and it began what has become an invaluable meeting ground for the exchange of new information and the critical examination of regional collections and sites through organized excursions all followed up by discussions and future planning. There have been nine of these Congresses and it is a pleasure to record that, after a lapse of twelve years, the tenth is expected to meet in Harare, Zimbabwe, in 1995.

Back in Livingstone, the new Museum was built and opened in 1951 and the scientific staff were increased and expanded to include an ethnographer, an archaeologist specializing in the Iron Age (a period that had been largely neglected up to then), and a Technical Officer. A new ordinance was established in 1951, protecting antiquities (sites and relics) and sites of natural significance and beauty, and an inspector was appointed to ensure compliance. My own research had extended beyond the boundaries of Northern Rhodesia to include Malawi as well as Angola, where large open excavations for diamonds exposed great thicknesses of Kalahari Sand and fluvial sequences with large numbers of stone artifacts, notably the fine lanceolates and core-axes of the Middle Stone Age Lupemban Culture Complex. This work was undertaken at the invitation of Diamang, the Portuguese Diamond Company operating in Lunda, Northeast Angola. These were most enjoyable visits, the last in 1968, and resulted in several monographs published by the Company.

After the war, it was easier to attend scientific meetings in South Africa and Zimbabwe. Those of the South African Archaeological Society and the Museums Association of Southern Africa stand out—in particular, one excursion from Windhoek to central and northern Namibia, and especially those to the sites and rock paintings in the Erongo and Brandberg Mountains. Dialogue with colleagues was important to me because archaeology was developing quickly and important new sites were being excavated. There were new findings from the southern African Australopithecine cave sites around Krugersdorp and at Makapan. Revil Mason excavated the Cave of Hearths. Another *Homo rhodesiensis* partial cranium had been found with bifaces in the western Cape. C. K. Cooke carried out important excavations of Later and Middle Stone Age stratified sequences in the Matopos. And a team of Roger Summers, Keith Robinson, and Tony Whitty re-excavated at Great Zimbabwe after

Gertrude Caton Thomson's classic study in 1929. Raymond Inskeep became the first Keeper in Archaeology at the Rhodes-Livingstone Museum, followed by, Brian Fagan, both of them remaining firm friends and esteemed colleagues of mine. With Raymond, Brian, Barrie Reynolds as Keeper of Ethnography, and Clayton Holliday as Technical Officer, we established and ran successfully for several years a Winter School for Archaeology. This was held in July when the climate of Livingstone was superb. Specialists were invited to supplement the talks and hands-on lab and fieldwork. At least a dozen amateurs with archaeological interests, mostly from South Africa and Rhodesia, came to share with us and local Africans a week to ten days of lab and fieldwork on a Stone or Iron Age site in the Livingstone Area. Each year was more enjoyable and rewarding than the preceding one and many professional anthropologists and archaeologists have told me subsequently that they first became interested in the profession through the Winter School.

Until another archaeologist was appointed to the Museum, I had to try covering the full range of prehistoric research in Northern Rhodesia. Unfortunately, I was not able to do this too successfully, especially when it came to the Iron Age, because my training and experience had been almost entirely with the Stone Age and this continued to occupy most of my time available for research. Iron Age archaeology in Zambia made great advances under Inskeep, Fagan, and later, David Phillipson and Joseph Vogel, and it has been of major importance for writing the early history of the Zambian peoples. I am glad to say that I have been able to maintain an interest in both time periods. Today, with the increasing amount of literature produced, it is not always easy to keep up with new discoveries and developments in Iron Age research, though the connections that are evident between the past and the ethnic present make it important to do so. Our overseas leaves were especially important for keeping abreast of recent advances in concepts and methodology as they developed. We would rent a cottage not far from Cambridge, renew old friendships, make new ones, read and generally catch up with current ways of understanding the meaning of archaeological residues.

POST-WAR PROGRESS

Some major developments took place in the early years after the war. Everything from an excavation was now kept and not simply the *belles pièces*. Prehistorians began to use statistics and associated faunal remains to determine what assemblages meant in terms of ecology, seasonality, hunting abilities, and the importance of change. Artifact assemblages were no longer looked upon primarily as subjects to be categorized taxonomically, with emphasis on the *fossiles directeurs* (type-fossil), nor were the typological and technological changes seen in a stratigraphic sequence always interpreted as the outcome of population migration. There was a refreshing return to the days when the early antiquarians looked at prehistoric tools as the products of human hands and studied the processes involved in their manufacture, use, and life history. The development of radiocarbon dating in 1950, followed by potassium argon dating not long afterward, encouraged this renewed focus on understanding the behavior behind assemblages. These methods and others released the archaeologist and paleoanthropologist from the confining taxonomic straitjacket and opened up new horizons for recognizing behavioral activities in the archaeological residues. This was epecially important for showing the time-depth for hominid evolution and for the Iron Age in Africa. At the same time, Mary Leakey's pioneering excavations at Olorgesailie and Olduvai in the later 1940s and 1950s showed that old land surfaces with minimally disturbed archaeological assemblages were preserved in long sequences of fine-grained sedimentary strata that contained a unique record of early hominid activities. The context of the finds became much more important for the record they showed of the natural and cultural processes involved in the site formation. Increasingly rigorous methods of excavation, recording, and analysis have developed over the years and input from the natural, earth, and behavioral sciences now provides a sophisticated range of techniques and methods of extracting data from the archaeology in context. These innovations have revolutionized studies of the Paleolithic and have made archaeological fieldwork a team and no longer a one-person project.

A turning point in my career as an archaeologist began in 1955 when we held the Third Pan-African Congress on Prehistory in Livingstone. The conference was well-attended, with participants from most parts of the Continent and from overseas. Some major discoveries were made known, new behavioral scenarios were put forward (e.g. Raymond Dart's Australopithecine osteodontokeratic culture), and the unreliability of the Pluvial/Interpluvial hypothesis was first recognized. There were also three excellent field excursions to sites in Southern Rhodesia, Northern Rhodesia, and in the Katanga (now Shaba) Province of the Belgian Congo (Zaire). These excursions provided an understanding of the regional archaeology not previously possible and laid the basis for interregional collaboration.

It was at this time that I first met Sherwood Washburn and several other American anthropologists who became long-time friends of mine. Sherry was studying the baboons at the Victoria Falls and the Wankie Game Reserve and we both acknowledge our indebtedness to Paul Fejos, the Director of the Wenner-Gren Foundation, for the support we received for our fieldwork. Not often does one get a letter asking, "Would your work benefit from the use of a large American car?"

BERKELEY DAYS

After taking up a professorship at the University of California at Berkeley, Sherry started a program in paleoanthropology and in 1960 the Anthropology Department asked me if I would like to join them to teach Old World Prehistory with an emphasis on Africa. I was around 45 at the time—an age when one begins to wonder if one should continue to do what one is doing or change to something else—and this invitation seemed to come from out of the blue. Even though I had not done regular teaching before, we decided to move, so in the fall of 1961 we started our new lives in Berkeley. We have never regretted the move even though some of the happiest days of our lives were spent in Livingstone. The important persuasive factor, besides working with Sherry and Ted McCown, was the expectation of obtaining funds for continued fieldwork in Africa. In this I have never been disappointed, and the greatest pleasure of all has been the opportunity Berkeley has given me to help train many excellent students, several of whom are now at the top of their profession. Berkeley was a great place to be from the 1960s until the mid-1980s, when there was special interest in human origins and the evidence being produced in East and South Africa, particularly in the Eastern Rift from southwest Ethiopia to northern Tanzania.

Glynn Isaac joined us in 1966 and we had seventeen superb years together to learn more and to teach about human origins and the biological and cultural evolution of our own species. Glynn was unique in having been trained in part as a natural scientist when at Cape Town. This training resulted in his innovative ways of looking at archaeological assemblages. His scenarios for interpreting a set of residues were the incentive to develop a new kind of data—so-called actualistic data—that provided the basis for comparing and assessing the meaning of missing or misplaced elements in the surviving archaeological record. This new approach has proved important in the way that faunal residues and artifact assemblages are treated and how they are associated today. Many field and lab studies now reveal the taphonomic history of a carcass and the agencies that have worked on it. Similarly, experimental replication, debitage, and refitting studies of flaking waste from stone tool manufacture offer alternative behavioral explanations for a set of artifacts and fossil faunal remains in juxtaposition. By comparing the data recovered from controlled field and lab experiments, it is possible to show how water, wind, or animals can distort the residues on an archaeological horizon/activity area. Many of these new approaches, some developed by ex-Berkeley students, are providing a much more reliable and realistic explanation of the history and behavioral implications of archaeological occurrences. It is a source of great pleasure to have had a chance to share and pass on some of the enjoyment and enthusiasm that I still retain for African prehistory. Our students worked in what Glynn and I and our wives sought to make a congenial, critical, provoking, and for most, I trust, a companionable and exciting milieu during their preparation for the professional career. We always emphasized the recovery of the hard data by rigorous fieldwork and publication. This is the basis from which new understanding develops and is the material on which hypotheses are made and scenarios constructed. We used a scientific approach for tackling problems— exploration and experimentation, followed by hypothesis and proposition forming, with further testing of the premise.

FIELDWORK

Most of my own work in Africa has been on the Paleolithic, but there are exceptions. For example, in the 1960s I was involved in Keith Radcliffe Robinson's pioneering studies of the Iron Age in northern and central Malawi. Robinson's eagle eye could see an Iron Age settlement area with unerring accuracy and his publications are the foundation on which the late pre- and protohistoric sequence in Malawi is firmly based. I also worked on team studies at the Kalambo Falls prehistoric site, which was found in 1953 near the southeast end of Lake Tanganyika. The long sequence there from the late Middle Pleistocene (Acheulian) to the later Iron Age indicates almost continuous occupation of this small basin and the significant cultural, climatic, and environmental changes that took place in what was the ecotone between the woodland savanna and the evergreen forest of Equatoria.

Since 1974 our fieldwork in Africa has been mostly in Ethiopia, in Lower and Middle Pleistocene contexts and at late Pleistocene and Holocene localities that were valuable training grounds for graduates. The Ethiopian work continues with increased input from professional Ethiopian paleoanthropologists and archaeologists. Such collaboration between African and expatriate professionals is a reflection of archaeology in most of the African continent today, and it has only been possible with the help of funding agencies like the National Science Foundation, the Wenner-Gren Foundation, and the Leakey Foundation.

I gain much more from examining a site in person and handling the finds than in any other way, and I have been fortunate to be able to work in or visit much of the Continent, thus gaining a broader perspective on African archaeology. A special privilege was spending over a month in the central Sahara with a British expedition to the Air massif and Adrar Bous. We found a rich prehistoric record in the desert, but this work also focused my attention on the importance of the Sahara as the major influence controlling the movement of human and animal populations between sub-Saharan Africa and the Mediterranean. The record of past changes in climate and environment is becoming increasingly well known and dated in the desert and shows the extent to which the Sahara was at times a major deterrent or barrier to movement. At other times, under increased precipitation when streams and lakes again filled with water, the desert became a welcoming and favored habitat for penetration and settlement by human populations and the large Ethiopian mammalian fauna. Not only could the Sahara have been a controlling factor over movement north and south within the Continent, but also for peoples and animals moving in and out of Africa linked, as Saharan climates must have been, with similar ecological changes in the Arabian peninsula, the Levant, and northwestern India. When more reliable methods for dating and correlating become available, beyond the lower limits of the radiocarbon method, we will have a better understanding of the significance of desertic climatic events and the causes and incentives for movement out of Africa into Eurasia in the earlier Pleistocene and again at the time of the spread of anatomically Modern humans.

It was all the more gratifying, therefore, to have the opportunity to do fieldwork in Syria in 1964 and 1965, in India in 1980–1982, and in China in 1989–1992. This work was immensely valuable for comparative purposes and it allowed me to look at the African field with a more balanced perspective on the similarities, differences, and the *raisons d'etre* behind the prehistoric past in those countries. The distinctiveness of the Acheulian techno-complex has become much more apparent, and the alternative hypotheses explaining its absence from so much of Eurasia, where only the core/chopper and flake complex occurs, have been expanded and now need systematic testing. Much less systematic research has been carried out in Asia, but this is changing. There has been a renewal of research in places that, for one reason or another, have been closed to this kind of work for some time. In some countries, such as India and Pakistan, research has been going on for many years. In others, modern field and laboratory methods and input from the sciences is just getting under way. It will probably be from systematic work in Asia that a number of the key questions and problems in human evolution will be solved.

My time spent with colleagues in many parts of Eurasia, in particular in India and China, as well as with long-time African colleagues and friends, has been more rewarding than I can ever say. It has taught me to appreciate the uniqueness of the cultural diversity, antiquity, and richness of Indian and Chinese civilizations and their evolving village farming antecedents. This is where Africa's contribution to the cultural record is complementary and unequaled, partly for the evolutionary history of the human race preserved there, but more importantly for the continued existence of ecosystems, not necessarily in the same place as they once were, that still preserve the evidence of past landscapes, flora, and fauna. These ecosystems provide us with windows into the past that in many other parts of the world have long since disappeared because of increasing over-use of the land.

Looking back on the naive, subjective interpretations and limited methods of recovery and insight that were available when I began work and the outstanding advances that have been made during the last twenty-five years as the result of science-based archaeology, I am amazed and impressed. This has been an unparalleled time for an archaeologist to have lived and, with the molecular input shortly to become available from DNA through the Human Genome Program, a whole new spectrum of data and pronouncements can be expected. It has been a great privilege and an abiding pleasure to have been able to add my bit to the structure and content of African archaeology and Paleolithic studies.

AFRICAN ARCHAEOLOGY TODAY

There are still two major divisions in African archaeology today: historic and prehistoric. In those African countries where early literate societies flourished, as in the Nile Valley in Egypt and in the Sudan, prehistory is the Cinderella among national researchers. The emphasis in professional training and finance is on the Dynastic periods and prehistoric research is generally left to overseas professionals—often with outstanding success. There is room for change. Historic archaeology had never had a place in the meetings of the Pan-African Congress on Prehistory and Related Studies until Neville Chittick introduced it at the 9th Congress in Nairobi in 1977. One can hardly believe this, but at the 8th Congress in Addis Ababa in 1971, there were no sessions or papers on the Axumite Civilization nor any excursions arranged to the historic places of Ethiopia. Although historic archaeology today has its foot in the door in connection with the Islamic settlements along the East African coast, the classical colonization of the Mediterranean coast and hinterland, the Axumite civilization of Ethiopia, and the pre-Colonial history of European settlement and interaction with indigenous peoples in South Africa, an expanded forum clearly is needed, where historic archaeologists can interact with prehistorians to great mutual benefit. I think this kind of forum exists only in South Africa; Ethiopia, now that the war is over; and perhaps in the Maghreb.

During the past fifty years, we have been concerned with prehistoric archaeology for obvious reasons. The volume and intensity of research and the number of trained professionals have grown significantly from the pre–World War II days when there were only a few professional archaeologists and huge areas of the African continent remained archaeologically unknown. After World War II and the abandonment of the taxonomic approach to archaeology, a more relativistic approach was taken, in which ideologies were constructed to answer questions about the social, economic, and political meaning of the archaeological data. This approach initially was a product of the founders of so-called New (or Processual) Archaeology, such as Grahame Clark, Gordon

Childe, and Gordon Willey. But it has sometimes been taken to extremes. As Bruce Trigger has said, "Although hyper-relativism is intellectually challenging, its principal effect is to undermine an independent role for archaeology as a source of insight into human history and behavior and to reduce the social sciences to the same level as works of fiction or political advocacy (which lack systematization and verifiability, although they may provide significant insights into human behavior)" (17:309). Fortunately, for the most part, this hyper-relativism is not strong in African archaeology, where most professional researchers recognize that the value of a constructed model is only as good as the data on which it is based.

Since the late 1950s and 1960s, when most African colonial countries became independent, the number of professionals has increased greatly and continues to do so, but in the last decade the number of significant new published works coming from institutions in Sub-Saharan Africa has not shown a similar increase, perhaps for logistical reasons, largely financial.

Studies of human origins and Early *Homo* studies cover more than five million years, and if the Miocene apes are included, it would be fifteen million years. During the past thirty years, research interests have focused on where we all came from—the why, when, and where of biological, behavioral and psychological evolution of the human lineage as shown by the social, economic, and technological changes seen in the archaeological record. Today there is little doubt that our own lineage—the Hominidae—evolved in Africa and that it was somewhere in the dryer, tropical savanna regions that the first tool-makers, the first hominids with enlarged brains, evolved two to two-and-a-half million years ago. The impetus given by natural and earth scientists working with the archaeologists and physical anthropologists has contributed immeasurably to the understanding of when, where, and how this biological and cultural evolution came about, over a time-depth stretching between five million or more to less than half a million years ago. This understanding has been made possible by the development of various dating techniques (e.g. radiometric, isotopic, and paleomagnetic reversal methods) and by increasing amounts of paleoanthropological data. Such data are interpreted in the context of present climates and habitats as well as behavioral changes induced by environmental fluctuations, which are reflected in the geological record, or by human influence on the environment. The so-called actualistic studies that came about as a result of Glynn Isaac's and Lewis Binford's pioneering work introduced the cautionary approaches to the study of site formation and alteration. Taphonomic and archaeological residues are now being identified and interpreted in the light of the controls that these studies of present-day behavior and processes are making available.

Although the hard data are becoming increasingly more abundant, they are still pitifully few and almost every time a significant new find is made—such as the robust Australopithecine "Black Skull" or the *H. erectus* skeleton from Nariakotome (both in northern Kenya)—new interpretations of the evolutionary model become essential. As a result, possibly the most important advance in archaeological research is the realization that systematic searches are needed to find new and more complete fossil and cultural remains in sealed contexts that can be reliably dated by the methods available today.

Hominidae continued to evolve in Africa until about one million or more years ago when there was an exodus, first into western and tropical Asia, and then into more temperate Eurasia. But an intriguing new development has arisen to make us look more carefully at this scenario. *Homo erectus* remains have been dated to 1.6 to 1.8 million years ago in Africa and to around 1.0 million years ago or less in southeast Asia. This seems to confirm what was expected, but in 1989 a *H. erectus* jaw was found in Georgia that, on the basis of the associated fauna, is thought to be 1.5 million years old. This may not present a problem and the definitive reports are awaited. However, the earliest recognized tool-makers in Africa belong to the grade of *H. habilis,* makers of the Oldowan Industrial Complex, the dates for which are around 2.3 to 1.6 million years ago. This leaves very little or no time for *H. erectus* to have evolved from *H. habilis.* What are the alternatives? The *H. habilis* fossils may represent more than one species and one or none may be a direct ancestor of *H. erectus,* which might again come from another, as yet unrecognized, African ancestor. For many, the African *H. erectus* fossils are sufficiently distinctive to be placed in their own taxon, *Homo ergaster* (19). Or the dates could be unreliable and *H. erectus* may have evolved in Asia and migrated into Africa. These are some of the hypotheses that need to be investigated by paleoanthropologists, again emphasizing the need for ever more systematic fieldwork and the recovery of more hard data.

In 1984 the focus on human origins was readjusted when molecular biologists announced that the mutational clock and history of mitochondrial DNA (the stuff from which genes are made) showed that the first anatomically Modern humans had also evolved in Africa sometime between 200 and 100 thousand years ago. Physical anthropologists and archaeological and human fossil discoveries in sealed and dated contexts supported the geneticists. The original data have now been challenged, so the origin and spread of anatomically Modern humans remains one of the hottest topics in world prehistory today. As a result, emphasis is now placed on a time period that previously had attracted little attention. The Middle Stone Age/Middle Paleolithic, dated by various methods to between ±150,000 and ±35,000 years ago, saw the extinction of the Neanderthals and all other archaic hominid populations and their replacement by anatomically and psychologically Modern humans with regionally diverse technology. This research is being undertaken by African nationals and expatriates collaborating in field and laboratory studies, with funding coming from outside the Continent, except in South Africa, Kenya, and Ethiopia, where laboratory resources already exist.

Research on Early *Homo* and Modern human origins is pursued actively in those African countries where the record is preserved in sealed contexts: south of the Sahara in Kenya, Tanzania, Uganda, Malawi, Ethiopia, South Africa, Botswana, Namibia, and Angola; and north of the desert in Morocco, Algeria, Tunisia, Egypt, and in the Sahara as well. The work is undertaken by nationals working alone or in teams with expatriates. The preparatory and analysis work in the laboratory generally is carried out in the country concerned, but except in South Africa, much of the specialized technical work (e.g. various kinds of dating and carbon isotope work or comparative studies with DNA research or comparative research on fossil hominids) is done in laboratories overseas. In Sub-Saharan Africa the funding comes essentially from outside the Continent. Whether this support will remain at its present, relatively high level will depend on the continuation and extension of collaborative teamwork for the recovery of new archaeological and paleontological data and the continued field and laboratory studies of animal and plant behavior, cultural residues in ethnoarchaeological contexts, and land formation processes. The interest is world-wide and is also of great practical value for African museums, universities, and individual scientists by providing funding for research.

The knowledge stemming from work on the recent archaeology of the African continent, in particular of those countries south of the Sahara, is probably contributing more to our understanding the antecedents and history of the indigenous peoples there than is any other single source of history. After independence, the support afforded by the new African nations to archaeological research in all its forms was immediate and important. The abundance of remains (in the form of ceramics, metallurgical objects, and evidence of settlements and social and agricultural systems in well-dated contexts) helped extend the history of the peoples of the new states back some two thousand years or, in some regions, infinitely further into the past. Moreover, this past has become visible in the monuments, reconstructed remains, and the interpretations presented in museums and preserved by National Monuments Commissions.

The evidence, and so the approaches and methodology used, are often different from one region to another because protohistory can include studies of the Meroitic Civilization in the Sudan, of the coastal trading centers along the east African coast, or the rise of pre-Islamic urban centers in West Africa. Protohistory is concerned with the interaction between stone-using foragers, Neolithic farmers, and metal-using food-producers as well as the ethnic and economic changes that came about as a result of the movement of Bantu-speaking agriculturalists into the sub-continent. But protohistory is not just the antecedent of history. It covers a wide range of knowledge that varies consid-

erably in time and cultural content from one part of Africa to another. Protohistoric research in Africa began in the early years of this century and since
then a great deal of work has been carried out in all regions of the Continent.
The development of radiocarbon dating in 1950 gave tremendous new impetus
to African protohistoric research. As a result, in southern, western, and eastern
Africa, a new interest in the Iron Age began to grow where previously the
emphasis had been on the earlier periods.

Researchers began to undertake studies of ceramics, metallurgical practices, the origins and spread of food production, short and long distance
exchange systems, and the origins and development of urban centers and
markets. By the 1970s Iron Age studies had made considerable progress. The
Iron Age has the advantage that the later the time period, the greater and more
complete are the surviving archaeological residues and other sources and,
therefore, the greater the opportunity for establishing continuity between an
extant ethnic population and its past. The input here from ethnoarchaeology is
considerable, through the links with ethnography that provide the means of
checking the interpretative models presented by archaeological residues. Protohistory can be seen as the product of using documentary, oral, and archaeological sources as well as the resulting insights of cultural and social anthropology to reconstruct the history of indigenous peoples before and after European contact. One of the most successful studies that comes to mind is the
reconstruction of the Zulu royal settlements in Natal. Another is the spread of
pastoral and mixed farming peoples to Botswana (6, 12:136–138).

Pioneering studies by Lee & DeVore, Silberbauer, Yellen, Teleki, and
others on the San foragers in the Kalahari, and studies by French and American researchers on the Efe and other Pygmy groups in forested Equatoria, have
developed immeasurably our understanding of the hunter-gatherer way of life
in two very different kinds of habitat. At the same time, recent research
emphasizing the temporal changes this way of life has undergone as a result of
long-time interaction with cultivators and pastoralists provides a cautionary
warning against hasty, uncritical use of such analogs in reconstructing the
behavior patterns of prehistoric foragers.

Some of the most impressive work on the Neolithic and Iron Age south of
the Sahara is that being pursued actively by Francophone and Anglophone
archaeologists, paleontologists, and ecologists in northern and western
Equatoria. Until about fifteen years ago this region had not been worked in any
systematic way. The work done by de Maret and his Cameronian colleagues in
that country, the region that linguists accept as having been the heartland of the
Bantu language family, is uncovering a chronological and cultural record that
goes deep into the later Pleistocene. In Gabon and Congo Brazzaville, the
work of Lanfranchi, Clist, Schmidt, and Denbow (in Zaire), is one of the most
exciting advances in pre- and protohistoric archaeology today. The volumes

Paysages Quaternaires de l'Afrique centrale atlantique and *Aux Origines de l'Afrique central,* edited by Lanfranchi, Schwartz, and Clist, are major reference works and milestones in synthesis and presentation of new data (13, 14)

FUTURE PROSPECTS

As with human origins research, more hard factual data in well-dated contexts are essential. For example, major research programs are required for understanding the domestication and spread of indigenous food plants of Ethiopia and West Africa south of the Sahara. New stimulus is needed here in identifying and dating cause and effect and in understanding the disappearance of the pastoral Neolithic populations of the Sahara. New, interdisciplinary teams of ecologists, climatologists, botanists, and agronomists as well as linguists, geneticists, and faunal experts working closely with archaeologists in the field can be expected to clarify our understanding of these events, which played such an important part in initiating change in the lifeways of peoples living in tropical Africa. The recent discovery of DNA in human bones at least 5000 years old and claims for DNA from bones as early as Neanderthal fossils opens up a whole new field of research on ethnic relationships between families, clans, and so-called tribal peoples in Africa. As far as I know, genetic studies of this kind have been confined to those of San and Pygmy populations and to Egyptian mummies.

This emphasis on the later time range is understandable because the later prehistory and protohistory are more directly related to the interests of the indigenous African peoples. Archaeology alone can often provide the framework for economic and technological developments that took place in earlier time periods. This framework can be related directly to existing populations, giving them the stability that comes from a long cultural history. This concept was realized by some of the colonial powers through their establishment of museums, research institutes, and antiquities services. But significant expansion only took place after independence and with the pressing need for the training of African professionals. In some countries (e.g. Ghana and Nigeria) training came about through the establishment of universities with archaeology departments. In other cases, archaeology is sometimes taught in a history department. An increasing number of African students have worked or are working toward a degree in archaeology in overseas universities in Europe, America, India, and elsewhere. Those who return to their own country after completion of their studies usually have a hard row to hoe. Many of the Sub-Saharan African countries are weak economically, which means that funding is no longer as adequate as it once was. To counteract the lack of local financial support for research, for expanding facilities at museums, for exhibitions and other visual media, and for adequate documentation of all this, it is necessary to develop strong public relations to encourage funding from commercial and industrial sources within the country as well as to seek funding and equipment from overseas. But, obtaining overseas funding from domestic and international sources is not easy.

Another problem that strikes at the heart of the matter is the need for contact and interaction with fellow archaeologists and those working in related disciplines. It is not easy for young scientists to leave their own country unless they receive grants to attend a conference or other meeting. Regular interaction and discussions are essential if knowledge of current research is to be maintained and if enthusiasm and enterprise are not to be dampened. This, I believe, is one of the most important problems that exists today in African archaeology. In the past, and still in some parts today, regional association meetings or conferences are held concerning special topics or more general exchange of information and discussion. In other regions the archaeologist or antiquities officer has to go it alone.

Considerable intellectual stimulus comes from joint research programs between African institutions or individuals and research teams from overseas. These researchers often come from universities or museums in America or Europe and they provide the funding and equipment for the programs, which often lead to fellowships for further training overseas and regular visits to the overseas host institution. This, I feel, is the most practical way to help the African national institutions and professionals. Another way, which has varying success, is overseas funding for Africans to attend conferences or seminars. Some will benefit greatly from such attendance, others not at all, and with the increasing number of young professionals being trained and the reduction of research funds in Western nations in general, there is likely to be less money available for attending conferences unless participants have important contributions to make. One way this isolation can be reduced is through regular regional meetings and the establishment of staff exchanges between particular institutions overseas. In Africa, where visiting faculty can teach and undertake fieldwork with local student participants, this can do much to help broaden understanding of recent developments in the host institution and country. Collaborative field projects, which are fairly universal these days, are another way to maintain regular contact and they often result in exchange visits for laboratory and other studies.

Another matter deserving attention is the need for regular and prompt publication of research results, in particular, in international peer review journals. There has not been much of this outside East and South Africa and I do not understand why. Clearly, there are some difficulties in the provision of funds for printing and publication of journals and newsletters in Sub-Saharan Africa, which is frustrating. Publication is, however, the best way to let others know of work being done and it is essential when seeking funds for further work. Just as a faculty member's publication record in a European or American university is, perhaps, the most important part of a regular promotion and the funding of research proposals, it might be expected to be the case in Africa. Such visibility is an important step in obtaining support for new work.

The Pan-African Congress on Prehistory and Related Studies, or a similar forum for international and interdisciplinary exchange of information and discussion at regular intervals, needs to be revived. All Africanists must explore possibilities and develop ways to diminish the near isolation from on-going research in which so many African archaeologists are working today. Regular interaction and collaborative training programs at institutions of higher learning within the Continent can be the best immediate way to advance the progress of archaeological research in Africa today and to realign its potential for understanding the origins of Africa's ethnic diversity. As T.S.Eliot (7) said:

> Time present and time past
> Are both present in time future
> And time future contained in time past.

Any *Annual Review* chapter, as well as any article cited in an *Annual Review* chapter, may be purchased from the Annual Reviews Preprints and Reprints service.
1-800-347-8007; 415-259-5017; email: arpr@class.org

Literature Cited

1. Brelsford WV. 1938. *Handbook of the David Livingstone Memorial Museum*. Lusaka: The Government Printer
2. Brelsford WV. 1946. *The Fishermen of the Bangweulu Swamps*. Rhodes-Livingstone Pap., No. 12. Oxford: Oxford Univ. Press
3. Clark JD. 1954. *The Prehistoric Cultures of the Horn of Africa*. Cambridge: Cambridge Univ. Press
4. Clark JD. 1986. Archaeological retrospect 10. *Antiquity* 60:179–88
5. Cooke HBS, Clark JD. 1939. New fossil elephant remains from the Victoria Falls, Northern Rhodesia and a preliminary note on the geology and archaeology of the deposits. *Trans. R. Soc. S. Afr.* 27:287–319
6. Denbow JR. 1982. The Toutswe tradition: a study in socioeconomic change. In *Settlement in Botswana*, ed. RR Hitchcock, MR Smith, pp. 73–86. Johannesburg: Heinemann
7. Eliot TS. 1943. *Four Quartets, Burnt Norton*. In *Oxford Dictionary of Quotations*, p. 202. London: Faber & Faber. 3rd ed.
8. Goodwin AJH. 1938. Archaeology of the Oakhurst Shelter, George. *Trans. R. Soc. S. Afr.* 25:229–324
9. Goodwin AJH. 1945. *Method in Prehistory*. S. Afr. Archaeol. Soc., Handb. No. 1. Wynberg: Rustica
10. Goodwin AJH. 1946. *The Loom of Prehistory*. S. Afr. Archaeol. Soc., Handb. No. 2. Wynberg: Rustica
11. Goodwin AJH, Van Riet Lowe C. 1929. The Stone Age cultures of South Africa. *Ann. S. Afr. Mus.* Vol. 27. Edinburgh: Neil
12. Hall M. 1987. *The Changing Past: Farmers, Kings and Traders in South Africa, 200–1860*. Cape Town: Philip
13. Lanfranchi R, Clist B. 1991. *Aux Origines de l'Afrique Centrale*. Centres Culturels Français d'Afrique Centrale/Centre International des Civilisations Bantu. Paris: Libreville
14. Lanfranchi R, Schwartz D. 1990. *Paysages Quaternaires de l'Afrique Centrale Atlantique*. Paris: ORSTOM
15. Leakey MD. 1984. *Mary Leakey: Disclosing the Past*. New York: Doubleday
16. Robertshaw P, ed. 1990. *A History of African Archaeology*. London: Currey

17. Trigger BG. 1990. The history of African archaeology in world perspective. In *A History of African Archaeology,* ed. P Robertshaw, pp. 309–19. London: Currey
18. Wheeler REM. 1943. *Maiden Castle, Dorset.* Rep. Res. Comm. Soc. Antiq. London, No. 12. Oxford: Oxford Univ. Press
19. Wood BA. 1992. Origin and evolution of the genus *Homo. Nature* 355:783–90

Annu. Rev. Anthropol. 1994. 23:25–53

MUSIC AND LANGUAGE

Steven Feld and Aaron A. Fox

Department of Anthropology, The University of Texas at Austin, Austin, Texas 78712

KEY WORDS: ethnomusicology, poetics, song, lament, voice

TOWARD A MUSICO-LINGUISTIC ANTHROPOLOGY[1]

In recent years, work in ethnomusicology has moved decisively toward a fully anthropological perspective. Rhetorically evolving from an anthropology of music (229) to a musical anthropology (297), from the study of music *and* or *in* culture, society, and history to the study of music *as* culture, society, and history (28, 34, 35, 70, 91, 116, 127, 230, 250, 265, 268, 272, 298, 346, 347), ethnomusicological perspectives are increasingly social, linking the structure and practice of musical performances and styles with music's deep embeddedness in local and translocal forms of social imagination, activity, and experience. These shifts parallel similar movements in linguistic anthropology that emphasize the social, pragmatic, and emotional constitution of linguistic structures emerging in discourse, performance, textuality, and poetics. Although these latter shifts have been well chronicled recently (e.g. 17, 18, 25, 47, 99, 109, 119, 217, 218, 354), it has been twenty years since the last review of developments in ethnomusicology and musical anthropology appeared in this journal (227).

In that review, McLeod predicted that the relationship between musical and linguistic approaches to culture would be crucial to a future of more rigorously contextualized ethnographic descriptions of musical behavior. The descriptive and analytic issues she raised, however, have developed both beyond and

---

1

    This review treats only English language sources. The large and important literature on music and language in French and German would require a separate paper to survey.

counter to her focus on the application of formal linguistic models to musical analysis. This review focuses on these new developments and their historical antecedents to suggest the outlines of a more complexly integrated musico-linguistic anthropology of sound communication. In doing so, we seek to link two discourses on voice. One is a phenomenological concern with voice as the embodiment of spoken and sung performance, and the other is a more metaphoric sense of voice as a key representational trope for social position and power (14).

The relationship of music to language is an enormously broad area of research. Ethnomusicological surveys (88, 243, 261) and substantial musical, linguistic, and literary dissertations (124, 150, 255) indicate how this vast interdisciplinary literature links research in musicology, acoustics, linguistics, literary studies, philosophy, psychology, and anthropology, and continues to inspire conferences, symposia, and research across these disciplines. We begin this review by tracing historical trajectories of thought about language and music in terms of four major predications: music as language, language in music, music in language, and language about music.[2] Next, we discuss attempts to integrate these four arenas through semiotics and sociomusicology, prominent themes in 1980s ethnomusicology. Finally, we examine recent trends in monographic writing and genre analysis, which demonstrate the empirical complexity and theoretical potential of the ethnographic approach to intersections of language and music. This ethnographic literature in particular demonstrates the relevance of a refigured anthropology of the speaking and singing voice to key issues in contemporary social theory.

MUSIC AND LANGUAGE: HISTORICAL TRAJECTORIES AND MAJOR ISSUES

Radically divergent perspectives and courses of development mark the literature on the relationship of music and language. But taken as a whole, the literature has tended toward programmatic speculation and suggestive analogies directed from linguistic structures to musical ones (e.g. the language of music, musical syntax, the grammar of a particular musical style, or the identification of deep and surface structures in a particular music genre). This approach follows trends evident in the social sciences, where linguistics has often been idealized as a source of methodological rigor, discovery procedures, and formal models (61, 88, 195:54–96, 197:138–47, 222, 242). Many

---

2

Of course, these predications do not capture the total range of concerns linking music and language, such as the relatively smaller literatures on linguistic-musical analogs in diffusion (143), bi- and multilingualism and musicality (318), and the intertwined biological origins of language and music (198, 261).

approaches to music have been predicated on a linguistic analogy where musical sound is viewed as an autonomous formal domain, abstractable as hierarchical structure or cognitive process. Musical structures are thus taken as generally analogous to grammatical categories or processes that can be analyzed using linguistic approaches to syntax, morphology, and phonology. We consider these analogies under the heading of "music as language."

Critiques of formal cognitive and structuralist models in linguistics and linguistic anthropology are clearly evident in the growth of discourse-centered (354) and pragmatic (314) approaches, the ethnography of speaking (19, 20, 153), performance studies (16), sociolinguistics (82), ethnopoetics (154, 312, 336), and studies of language socialization (254). At some historical distance, these critiques have also been registered in ethnomusicological approaches (28, 30, 31, 94, 296, 297). Following from these developments, perspectives on "language in music" contrast a more empirical functionalism to the formalist cognitivism of the "music as language" research. Concerns with language in music focus on the phenomenological intertwining of language and music in verbal art, song texts, and musical performance. Emphases on "music in language" focus on the musical dimensions of prosody and paralanguage (e.g. voice quality, dynamics, and tempo). "Language about music" calls attention to the omnipresence of aesthetic and technical discourses about music. These three perspectives embrace both contrasts and interfaces between the communicative and social functions of musical and verbal discourse.

These approaches can also be set in a larger ethnomusicological context of research on indexical and isomorphic relationships between musical genres, forms, and performance styles and their directly associated social categories and institutions, including gender (128, 184, 289), social class (221, 259, 332, 361), and ethnicity (36, 177, 319). Such analyses of concrete social correlations are in places theoretically or methodologically analogous to a variety of approaches in linguistic pragmatics and sociolinguistics (319), even when they don't substantively explore music-language relationships or matters of musical semantics.

From a broader perspective, the formal parallelism and informational redundancy of musical structures, musically structured song texts, performances, and musically structured kinesic forms such as dance (163–166, 199, 213, 248, 253, 260, 322) exemplify and expand what Jakobson (157) called the poetic and metalinguistic functions in language (153, 219). In this view, musically structured communication suppresses verbal referentiality in order to reveal the formal and pragmatic ordering of messages, codes, and communicative contexts. Music's formal redundancy and auto-referentiality heighten poetic texts and produce a musical metalanguage (15, 94, 142, 209). The extension from discourse structures to social function draws on Prague School poetics (157–159, 255), especially as mediated through the ethnography of speaking.

It draws as well on the Boasian tradition in both language and music studies as represented by Sapir and Herzog (133–136, 284–287). This metasemiotic perspective, analogous to the ethnography of speaking and the discourse-centered approach in linguistics (309, 310, 312, 354), brings together formal and functional analysis and implies attention to the entire range of communicative modalities and genres in a particular society.

Related to divisions between cognitivist formalism and phenomenological functionalism, the music and language literature also represents a wide range of opinions on the nature and accessibility of musical meaning. The entrenched theoretical division between absolutist and referentialist positions is a frequently recurring theme (67, 90, 93, 137, 233). Absolutist views, deeply rooted in Western musical aesthetics, stress music's non-referentiality and locate musical meaning in an individual listener's cognitive processing of implicative patterns of musical form (10, 194, 233, 235, 236, 267). Such views, which claim that musical meaning is strictly syntactic, have been compatible with formal cognitivist linguistic models (81, 267, 276, 320). The absolutist perspective has been only minimally concerned with fundamentally social aspects of musical meaning (137, 305).

Referentialist views hold that music symbolizes extramusical (i.e. linguistically translatable) concepts, objects, or affects, implying the possibility of a musical semantics (203). Both absolutists and referentialists may or may not also hold the expressionist position, which holds that music communicates (whether syntactically or referentially) within the domain of human emotion, by contrast with language's capacity to communicate about conceptualization (66, 137, 233, 285, 299). As a Western folk-theory of musical meaning, expressionism is a common feature of many otherwise fundamentally divergent theories of musical significance. The distinction between musically encoded feeling and linguistically encoded thought, with its concomitant claim that musical meaning is somehow ineffable, is frequently advanced in both cognitive and social accounts of the music-language relationship.

From a cross-cultural and ethnographic perspective, the main positions in the musical meaning debate oversimplify the communicational complexity and interpretive density of real verbal and musical experience (137, 178, 203). Absolutist positions on musical meaning are typically falsified by the ubiquitous intertwining of musical and verbal communication in song texts (31, 358), by prosodics (136), or by discourse about music (90, 357). Another important base for critique is philosophical and anthropological work problematizing the cross-cultural validity of Western models of emotion and strict opposition between cognition and affect that underlies these positions (52, 137, 218). And as a further example of complex empirical challenges, we could ask how typifications provided in the absolutist-referentialist-expressionist scheme could begin to account for meaning production in musical speech surrogates

(37, 53, 56, 64, 71, 135, 252, 256, 263, 325, 350, 351, 363:189–96). These phenomena, which might warrant a fifth predication of "music about language," involve the transposition of linguistic tonal and temporal contours to surrogate articulatory modes, like humming or whistling, or musical media, like drums or flutes. Abridging systems, where a limited array of phonemic elements are imitated by the surrogate, and logographic or ideographic systems, where the surrogate sound symbolizes a concept without an intermediary connection to the phonemic structure of the base language, are both well described (252, 325, 350). Surrogates may alternate between a signal mode, where texts are more formulaic or stereotypic, and a speech mode, where more novel utterances are produced. They may also alternate with a variety of musical modes. Hence, surrogate media may easily mix referential and non-referential messages with a complex interplay of metalingual and metamusical signs.

MUSIC AS LANGUAGE: LANGUAGE MODELS

Previous reviews (51, 88, 120, 261) have observed a duality in the music-language literature. On the one hand, the research literature emphasizes application of formal analytic linguistic models to music. On the other hand, it emphasizes research into the phenomenological intertwining of musical and linguistic phenomena in four areas: musical speech surrogates, the musical structuring of linguistic supra-segmentals, verbal discourse about musical meaning, and song texts. From the first perspective, music is considered amenable to the analytic techniques and models developed for linguistic phonology and syntax. This position is often sustained by analogies between the distributional organization of musical pitch and the phonetic organization of language (61, 62, 149, 150, 160, 242, 244, 245, 249, 280, 323). Analogies between the harmonic or metrical or motivic organization of musical works and the syntactic organization of language, deeply rooted in Western musical theory (241, 261), have been the basis for the enormous influence of generative syntactic theory on cognitivist music theory and ethnomusicology. Work in this tradition has produced numerous musical grammars, or formal descriptions of the phrasal, harmonic, and metric syntax of musical pieces and styles (22, 28, 38, 62, 63, 68, 81, 83, 125, 144, 151, 182, 194, 201, 204, 264, 267, 280, 288, 315, 331). Lerdahl & Jackendoff's (194) work, with its provocative claims about universals, musical competence, and the hierarchical and language-like nature of musical cognition, intuition, and information processing, has been particularly influential in setting agendas for generative analyses of musical form.

Both distributional and generative structural approaches have been criticized from the perspective of an anthropological approach to music, for their reification of musical sound structure as a decontextualized code (27, 31, 88, 90, 121) and for their bias toward the hierarchical, architectonic, and metrically regular art music traditions of Western Europe and, to a lesser extent, other stratified complex societies (261). They have also been criticized for their emphasis on discrete, macro-syntactic (melody, rhythm, tonality, mode), score-centric, and transcribed/transcribable dimensions of musical products while excluding gradient, nuanced, emergent, oral/aural, or micro-parameters of musical process like pitch, texture, timbre, tempo, dynamics, and performance (40, 121, 172, 178, 202, 267, 302, 304). Additionally, these critiques of textual reification have called attention to the individualistic conception of musical competence and socialization in cognitive modeling (27, 31, 90, 220, 305).

Despite criticisms, generative musical syntax has stimulated a reemergent psychomusicology focused on the cognitive bases of musical knowledge, understanding, and composition (190, 191, 267, 300, 327). Psychomusicology explores questions about ineffability of musical experience as compared to linguistic knowledge and communication, and about the cognitive processes that give rise to (one kind of) musical meaning. This perspective has suggested empirical approaches to problems that are central to the tradition of philosophical musical aesthetics (52, 67, 113, 137, 189, 233, 379). Such problems, when refigured in social terms, remain significant for musical anthropology as it grapples with the particular cultural functions of music in relation to language and other communicative modalities.

Cognitivist perspectives have tried to approach the question of uniquely musical forms of consciousness and experience. Despite this potential relevance, cognitivist approaches to music are somewhat removed from engagement with ethnomusicology and anthropology, and from the empirical complexity of real musical discourse. This follows a similar divergence between cognitive and social perspectives on language. An important agenda for contemporary musical anthropology is the reintegration of sophisticated cognitivist approaches with grounded social investigation (11, 12, 29, 32, 81, 182).

MUSIC IN LANGUAGE AND LANGUAGE IN MUSIC

An alternative strand in the history of discussions of music and language involves empirical inquiry into the phenomenological intertwining of musical and linguistic parameters in situated acts of communication. This view has focused on the cross-cultural ubiquity of texted vocal music (210), on musical speech surrogates (325, 350), on intermediate poetic and performative forms and genres, and on means of articulation that call attention to the boundaries of speech and song (93, 126, 207), such as chant, recitative, *sprechgesang* (sung speech), *sprechstimme* (dynamically, rhythmically, and intonationally heightened speech), preaching, and lamentation.

Some key areas of empirical research have included the comparative phonetics of spoken and sung genres (62, 142, 328, 329, 364, 372, 373); issues of voice quality and the acoustics of the singing voice (102, 162, 277–279, 303, 329, 330, 337); complex forms like Swiss yodel (376, 377), Tibetan and Mongolian biphonic overtone singing (258, 321, 343, 378), and Inuit vocal games (21, 59, 244); comparisons between the poetic organization of song texts and the musical structure of their settings; and the linkage of text and tune in compositional formulae (4, 43, 79:47–58; 136, 138, 215, 246, 311, 372, 373). Other issues include distinctions and continua between semantically meaningful song texts and the various uses of meaningless vocables (105, 141, 142, 224), and the mutual influences of musical and linguistic structures (83, 142, 215, 277, 278). Especially important are determinate relationships between speech intonation and musical melody, for example, in the song and instrumental traditions of societies with tonal languages (4, 58, 133, 193, 206, 252, 269, 281, 290, 371) or in Native South American microtonal pitch rising (139, 297).

This empirical, form and function approach to language in music is perhaps the most important historical antecedent for contemporary musico-linguistic ethnography. Among other aspects, this rubric subsumes the study of the meaning and structure of song texts, arguably the most widely used musical data throughout the social sciences. Although countless ethnographers, sociologists, and cultural critics have referred to the verbal content of sung texts as evocative poetic performances, these verbal texts have been especially important for anthropologists working from the perspective of contemporary cultural poetics (1, 2, 46, 48, 97, 100, 131, 185, 186, 219, 220, 301, 344, 345, 365), and for bridging textual and musical dimensions in cultural studies approaches to contemporary popular music (103, 108, 112, 123, 225, 304, 361).

Ethnographic treatments of song texts have tended to treat songs as verbal art, and to background the question of why and how certain texts are sung (14, 108, 209, 304). A central focus for the language in music perspective is the question of how a particular expressive economy models distinctions and continua between speech and song styles, or between song-speech genres and their functions and contexts (69, 70, 94, 95, 103, 115, 142, 155, 295–297, 311, 352, 358, 359). Issues include the relative stability of song forms and topics (142, 229:187ff, 297); the selection and alteration of spoken language in song (94, 103, 142, 297, 352); the social indexing of gender, authority, age, and class through speech and song genres (1, 94, 115, 123, 175, 177, 272, 273, 297, 306, 307, 352); and the role of song in language-learning and pedagogy (220, 297, 370).

Another perspective on language and music, which we would label a music in language approach, comes from linguists and literary theorists working with discourse prosodics, stylistics, and the (ethno)poetics of verbal art. Here the focus is on the musical—that is, suprasegmental, iconic, or non-discrete—dimensions of spoken discourse. These include rhythm, meter, pausing, and other durational and stress phenomena in speech and verbal art (62, 73, 87, 142, 144, 156, 181, 294, 306, 308, 336, 368, 369), as well as issues of voice quality and timbre (73, 192, 238, 352). Linguistic work has also focused on the continua of relative tonal stability and contour stylization which cross-cut speech intonation and sung melody (39–41, 43, 76, 110, 187, 364), linking musical melody and linguistic intonation to an iconic, emotional level of meaning that is complexly interwoven with discrete, segmentable, conventional levels of linguistic organization (40, 42, 187, 188, 226, 366). Other researchers have looked at phonological modifications of vowel quality in sung versus spoken articulation (50, 94, 142, 328, 330), and at phenomena of phonaesthesia and phonetic sound symbolism, again emphasizing an iconic, gradient stratum of linguistic meaning that tends to be heightened in poetic and sung discourse (15, 42, 94, 105, 161, 273, 340, 366). Whether oriented to social and functionalist concerns (73, 75, 142, 226, 368, 369) or to cognitivist perspectives (87, 144, 156), the variety of empirical work in discourse prosodics suggests the importance of music in language approaches to a reintegration of linguistic and musical research.

LANGUAGE ABOUT MUSIC

Since the late 1970s an additional perspective on the language and music relationship has emerged in ethnomusicology, to some extent circumventing the earlier debates about form and function, cognition and feeling, linguistic models, and the prosodics and poetics of speech and song. Though strongly influenced by earlier developments in ethnosemantics and cognitive anthropology, this work has emphasized the social indexicality and cultural symbolism of discourse about music, rather than abstract cognitive semantic domains. Perspectives that focus on functional or formal oppositions between speech and music may obscure the poetic and pragmatic connections between the two modalities. By contrast, the language about music perspective is predicated on the fact that people talk about music, and that music interacts with naturally occurring verbal discourse, not only in song texts, verbal art, and the prosodic, musical structuring of speech, but also in the interpretive, theoretical, and evaluative discourses surrounding musical experiences.

Ethnomusicologists and philosophers have often stressed the difficulty of translating musical meaning into verbal analytic discourse (31, 90, 125, 299, 302, 357). Recent approaches have focused on spontaneous or elicited oral discourse about music, often in small-scale societies, where there was no prior investigation of culturally specific music theories (89, 94, 173, 180, 262, 282, 297, 326, 335, 374, 375). Zemp analyzes how such oral discourse may encode remarkably complex technical systems of theoretical knowledge about musical structures and compositional principles in the instrumental (panpipe) music of a Solomon Islands society (374, 375). Extending this perspective to vocal and instrumental music, Feld analyzes the technical and metaphoric discourse linking musical practices to other forms of social and ecological knowledge in a Papua New Guinea rainforest community (89, 92, 94, 96). Turning to complex social formations, Kingsbury (180) demonstrates the pragmatic social efficacy of verbal evaluations that ostensibly are detached judgments of musical talent in an American music conservatory. Finally, interviews conducted by the Music in Daily Life project (72) indicate an enormous range of idiocultural diversity in verbal engagement and reflection on American musical experiences. These analyses argue for the abstract and pragmatic ways music and verbal experience are intertwined in the dialectical processes of emergence, maintenance, and change in social life.

SEMIOTICS AND SOCIOMUSICOLOGY

Since the 1970s two convergent perspectives have pursued integrations of form and function in musico-linguistic analysis. The first follows from developments in Saussurian and Peircian semiotics (90, 245, 324, 334). The second, dubbed sociomusicology by Keil in the early 1960s (229:221ff), developed distinctly in the early 1980s (91, 174, 272). Musical semiotics emerged with a predominantly musicological orientation, and like linguistic semiotics it developed the kinds of formalist, cognitive, and structural biases discussed in our music as language section above. Nattiez (242, 243, 245) stresses the possibility of a neutral segmentation of musical sound structure, abstracted from social and cognitive contexts of musical production and reception (88, 90, 121, 202). Nattiez's more recent work (243, 245) invokes the Peircian semiotic concept of multiple interpretants, and rhetorically stresses the importance of modeling musical meaning from the neutral level to the levels of creation (poeisis) and reception (esthesis), even arguing for a semiotics of discourse about music. But Nattiez's empirical analyses remain focused on the distributional properties of a limited number of sonic parameters in prescriptively notated scores of Western art musics (179). Inspired by Peircian semiotics, Boilés (38) and Karbusicky (168, 169) have offered more processual accounts of the sign typologies implicated in varieties of musical meaning. With Nattiez, these accounts share an emphasis on terminological definitions and abstraction, as do even more explicitly sociological and historical semiotic perspectives (122, 333).

By contrast, a more eclectic blend of semiotic concepts has emerged in recent ethnographic work. Peirce's second trichotomy, which delineates iconic, indexical, or symbolic relationships between signs and objects, has stimulated research bringing together sign-object-interpretant relationships with issues of semiotic function within and across expressive genres (231, 316). The concept of semiotic iconicity, for example, posits a formal resemblance between sign and object. This notion has been applied to the study of tropes of repetition, coherence, and naturalization across musical, linguistic, visual, and kinesic modalities. Iconicity has been shown to create stylistic cultural linkages between experience, knowledge, and interpretation (23, 92, 96, 173, 175, 219, 273, 344).

Drawing on semiotics to develop a discourse-centered perspective on culture, Urban (352–354) stresses that discourse styles are both objective arrangements of sign-object relations and conceptual arrangements of interpretants. His work shows how native Brazilian speech styles with multiple social indexical meanings are iconically represented in other musical and linguistic genres and styles. These icons meta-semiotically reframe their prior indexical meanings, to create, challenge, and restore sociability. Urban's Peircian perspective seems especially well-suited for formally describing the varieties of musical and linguistic signification inherent in natural discourse, including syntactic, mimetic, ostensive, associational, evocative, and referential meanings (90, 313).

Studies of musical symbolism rarely invoke the Peircian trichotomy; however, they often trace interactions between the concrete semiotic mechanics of musical and linguistic discourse (especially indexical and iconic relationships), and generalized and abstracted concepts and affects (symbols). Ethnographers have attended to the processes by which concrete acoustic signs (e.g. musical pieces, forms, techniques, styles, tones of voice, phonetic and instrumental icons of natural or mythic sounds, and sonic poetic tropes) become public, articulate, and powerful symbolic condensations of diffuse or inchoate social sentiments and identities (15, 92, 94, 96, 97, 173, 176, 177, 228a, 273, 297, 348).

Music is often invoked as a key metaphor for the symbolic in philosophical and anthropological approaches to the social and cultural significance of aesthetics (111:11, 137, 189, 196, 291, 360, 379). This is because of music's association with ritual and performative contexts, its informational redundancy, its poetic intensification of verbal texts, its formalization of bodily movements in dance, and its social and temporal coordination of participants in music-making. Here semiotics, via semantics and pragmatics, finds its common ground with a comparative, cross-cultural sociomusicology. Feld (91) and Roseman (272) take up this trajectory by suggesting six areas of inquiry that might serve as a comparative matrix for analyzing the social structuring of musical symbols in classless societies: competence, form, per-formance, environment, theory, and social value/equality. These rubrics, in parallel to similar proposals in sociolinguistics (153), probe the interface be-tween forms of linguistic and musical expression, forms of social organization, the social organization of musical production, and cultural ideologies of knowledge, value, and power.

Fused with other concerns from practice theory (44, 45) these rubrics have been brought to bear on the social functions of music in a variety of social formations: as an emblem of social identity (97, 123, 348, 362, 363), as a medium for socialization (28, 219, 296, 297, 370), as a site of material and ideological production (180, 225, 304, 361), as a model for social under-standings and evocations of place and history (94, 273), as a modality for the construction and critique of gender and class relations (45, 69, 70, 94, 95, 103, 115, 225, 362, 363), and as an idiom for metaphysical experience (15, 94, 273, 338).

FROM ACOUSTICS TO ETHNOGRAPHY: REFIGURING SONG AND SPEECH

The significance of music and language interactions can also be traced through a more specific historical trajectory that led to the development of a new genre of musico-linguistic ethnography in the 1980s. Thirty years earlier, speech and song were implicitly assumed to be normative poles of a single objective continuum of sonic communication, bounded on one end by the notion of sound as articulated sense, and on the other end by the notion of sound as pure tone. Toward the pole of maximum sense one might imagine more deliberate, projected, and articulate varieties of staged formal speech, sliding toward variants of informal, conversational, and more intonationally dynamic speech. From here the continuum moves toward sung speech and then merges into song forms. The most basic of these forms is typically syllabic song, charac-terized by one melodic tone and one rhythmic pulse per verbal syllable. The next contrast is with melismatic song, where more than one tone and pulse are articulated for each or any syllable. At the final, maximally song pole of the continuum, one finds vocables or other forms of vocalization with little or no linguistically referential, even if phonologically conventional, material. In this general scheme referentiality serves as the bottom line in the distinction be-tween speech and song. This scheme paralleled larger 1950s philosophical or information-cybernetic preoccupations with logical communicational models of music and language (234:5–21; 239), musicological distinctions between musical feeling and referential intellection (299), and linguistic and stylistic concerns with the gradience between expression and reference (292).

List's (207) analysis of speech and song boundaries moved beyond these bipolar models by proposing a hemispheric map, overlaid by a diamond with speech and song as north and south poles, and monotone and *sprechstimme* as east and west poles. Tracing four routes from these ideal points, List proposed that from the north to the east, speech travels a continuum that passes through recitation to monotone by decreasing intonational dynamics. Continuing from east to south, expansion of scalar structure moves monotone through chant and on toward song. In parallel, at the other side of the diamond, from north to west speech travels a continuum that passes through intoned recitation to *sprechstimme* by increasing intonational dynamics. And from the west to the south pole, stability of pitch moves from *sprechstimme* through intonational chant to song. To exemplify the classificatory and analytic ideal types and particular points along these continua, List provided both sonographic pitch tracks and conventional musical transcriptions.

Although List recognized problems adapting his framework to sung forms in tonal languages, he did not consider other problems inherent in focusing entirely on acoustic common denominators of melody and pitch. Prominently absent here is any mapping of sounds in time, examining the interaction of melody and pitch with rhythm (237). Also absent is any discussion of prosody, voice quality, timbre, texture, grain, (65, 86, 317), or other dimensions of vocal performance that intersect both the tonal and temporal planes, fundamentally adding significant features that differentiate or link speech and song.

Searching for another kind of taxonomy, one open to additional levels of acoustic and expressive patterning, Lomax (209–211) looked beyond linguistics to music's analogs with paralinguistic phenomena (26, 342). With his cantometrics song measures, Lomax focused not on acoustic ideal types but on properties of singing styles. Coding 37 levels of musical behavior in a sample of over 400 musical traditions, Lomax attempted to correlate the most highly patterned and redundant song performance features with HRAF data on social structure as well as economic and political institutions for the same groups. With his provocative claim that song be viewed as danced speech (209), and his later forays into choreometrics (213) and parlametrics (212), Lomax placed speech-song forms in an even more ambitious framework of the evolutionary taxonomy of expressive culture (214), recently integrated into a computer database called Global Jukebox. For many researchers, Lomax's most interesting contribution is his exploration of how redundancy underlies song's power to create consensus and solidarity in ritual interactions (142, 227). Ideas of this sort overshadow cantometrics' many methodological problems, which include conflation of sample time depths, compatibility of song coding and HRAF societal data, inferential history by reading correlation as causation, and lack of concern with intracultural and areal variation (85, 91).

These taxonomic and classificatory urges to normatively define and measure speech, song, or in-between forms on the basis of formal and gradient acoustic regularities were not the unique preserve of ethnomusicologists or linguists in the 1960s. Their work took place in the broader context of scientific invention and experimentation with sound analysis and synthesis (78, 145, 205). But the first generation of speech and music synthesis also yielded other kinds of research documents. At the same moment speech scientists programmed their synthesizers to articulate the difference between "recognize speech" and "wreck a nice beach," sound-poets taught theirs to playfully transform Professor Henry Higgins' perfectly enunciated "Why can't the English teach their children how to speak?" into the mangled cyber-slur "Why can't the linguists teach their computers not to lisp?" In an experiment no less intellectually engaging than the Bell Telephone Laboratories 1962 effort to have a synthesizer sing "A Bicycle Built for Two," Dodge (80) used early synthesis technology to manipulate sounds from monotone to melodic expansion and back, recitation to sung-speech and back, free rhythm to metrics and back, in each case stopping at numerous articulatory points along the way. "Speech Songs," his exploration of synthesis as analysis, has the synthesizer alternating monotonic and melodic zigzags of syllabic cybersong beginning with the phrase of Mark Strand's poem "When I am with you I am two places at once." One quickly senses that Dodge's "two places at once" are speech and song, text and tune, melody and monotone, sound and meaning, form and content, reference and expression.

Dodge's exploration of these "two places" also resonates both with Lévi-Strauss' mythic dictum that the proof of the analysis is in the synthesis, and with an earlier Boasian-Sapirian concern with the simultaneously material-physical and aesthetic-emotive basis of poesis and aesthetics. These ideas were developed in Herzog's empirical work on text and tune (133, 134), his masterful survey of song (136), and Jakobson's concern with sound shape, parallelism, and markedness (158, 159, 161). Particularly significant to both Herzog and Jakobson was the coincident parallelism of textual and melodic stanzas, and the parallel organization of the foot of poetic meter and the measure of musical rhythm. As early as 1932 Jakobson took an interest in the universal analogy between a phoneme and the articulatory phonetic realizations it takes in speech, and a musical tone value and its potential pitch realizations (160). Herzog (136) likewise insisted on the universality of the line or phrase as the basic principle of textual and musical sub-division. Recognizing that these line or phrase sub-divisions may be marked either by formal structures of closure (grammatical or melodic-cadential) or by breath pause, Herzog even seems to have anticipated the important contemporary discussion between Hymes (154) and Tedlock (336) concerning the relative significance of textual-grammatical vs oral-performative markers of structure in ethnopoetic (and by extension, ethnomusicological) translation and representation (308, 368).

Many of Herzog's and Jakobson's concerns were reincarnated in the ethnomusicological research of the 1970s and 1980s. Like ethnography generally, this work began to draw on eclectic mixes of cognitive, structuralist, semiotic, symbolic, hermeneutic, historical, and praxis approaches in cultural and social theory. As approaches to language had become more deeply constituted in ethnographic studies of speaking and verbal art as performance, approaches to speech-song intersections likewise shifted toward the ethnography of musical performance (24, 228). Blacking's *How Musical is Man?* (28) cleverly attempted to capture this motion linking form and pragmatics by parallel chapter title shifts. For example, "Music in Culture and Society" became "Society and Culture in Music," and "Humanly Organized Sound" became "Soundly Organized Humanity." In short, ethnomusicology through the 1970s and 1980s moved from asking how sound reflects social structure to how musical performance embodies and articulates social imagination and practices, how sonic organizations are total social facts, saturated with messages about time, place, feeling, style, belonging, and identity.

The maturation of this interdisciplinary trend can be seen in the increasing blend and synthesis of musical and linguistic research in ethnographic monographs (e.g. 15, 94, 173, 185, 273, 297, 338). These monographs rely on the complexity of the worlds they seek to interpret to create the terms of an emerging genre, one that brings phenomenological premises about the creative and expressive nature of experience together with ethnographic exploration that makes no technical or analytic compromise on musical and linguistic detail. Each monograph stretches previous conceptions of how language and music might be related in local performance practices, and explores problems of musico-linguistic representation and evocation. For example, Basso links the processual and performative dimensions of Kalapalo (Brazil) myth and ritual through the power of sound symbolism (15). Roseman demonstrates how Temiar (penisular Malaysia) trance healing emerges as a fusion of medical and musical imagination and gendered practice (273). Kratz analyzes structural and temporal alternations of speech and song in Okiek (Kenya) women's initiation ceremonies, showing how affect and persuasion are forged in ritual (185). Titon analyzes the full array of speech, chant, and song practices in a Appalachian Baptist church (Virginia), interpreting how the efficacy of their performances constitutes religious belief and community consciousness (338). Seeger shows the multiple ways Suyá (Brazil) discourse genres of speech, instruction, and song are interrelated in ceremonial performance (297). Feld shows how Kaluli (Papua New Guinea) lament, poetics, and song are complexly related to their natural historical and cosmological origins in bird voice symbolism (94). Finally, Keil's search for the significance of Tiv (Nigeria) song led to a critique of aesthetic theory and evocation of the material and performed expressions of Tiv being and energy (173). In these writings, the emergent focus on transformative and affecting powers of ritual performance moves earlier music-language questions forcefully toward a processual symbology and hermeneutics of voice, self, and action. Likewise, the focus on sound and synesthesia (interactions across visual-sonic-movement modes) further relocates music-language concerns in an anthropology of the senses and of sensual experience. In these ways musico-linguistic ethnography participates fully in the recent trends in ethnographic writing to forcefully link voice, experience, self, body, gender, and agency.

STYLIZING SUNG-SPOKEN INTERSECTIONS: THE LAMENT GENRE

Current developments in the analysis of speech-song interactions also can be scrutinized through refigurations of genre studies. The lamentation genre includes verbal-vocal (and occasionally verbal-vocal-instrumental; e.g. 5, 251) performances typically labeled lament, ritual wailing, sung-texted-weeping, keen, mourning song, dirge, eulogy, and elegy. Approaches to understanding the structure and significance of forms within the lamentation genre have brought together a variety of anthropological, musical, linguistic, and folkloristic issues. These concern oral and literate traditions, performance of verbal arts, gendering of genre, fixity-plasticity-hybridity of genres, and interpenetrations of speech and song, as well textual history, improvisation, memorization, and oral formulae (6, 7, 60, 62, 94, 95, 115, 130, 146, 147, 171, 247, 307, 339, 352). Lament varieties are reported throughout many regions of the world, and in some cases have a long history of comparative analysis, for example, in European folklore and ethnomusicology (148, 170, 208). Newer comparative questions about semiotic universals and the cultural specificity of the ritual wailing variants of the genre have also been raised (50, 94, 95, 115, 353). Yet the overwhelming significance of lamentation is hardly confined to issues about intersecting musical and linguistic codes, folkloric genres, or comparison. Lament stylizations performatively embody and express complex social issues connecting largely female gendered discourses on death, morality, and memory to aesthetic and political thematization of loss and pain, resistance and social reproduction, and to ritual performance of emotion (1, 3, 49, 50, 54, 55, 94, 95, 117, 132, 146, 167, 301, 340, 341, 344).

With the possible exception of certain forms of religious discourse, notably sermon preaching performances (77, 104, 274, 283, 338), lament is the most prominent and widespread discourse genre where one can comparatively study stylized progressions moving back and forth on all continua relating the speaking and singing voice. This alone makes lamentation an important locus of research on questions of the boundaries of speech and song, in both genre-specific and performance-specific terms. But to make matters even more complex, many forms of lament simultaneously move along a continuum from relatively cried semi-melodic fragments with vocables or text, to more texted recitation and/or singing while continuously or intermittently weeping. The continua of tuneful and textual performance in lamentation are often further stylized together with "icons of crying" like voiced inhalation, cry breaks or sobs, falsetto vowels, and creaky voice, features that are linked indexically to the emotional states and affective projection of lament performance (353, 354). Across these stylistic variations, lamentation performances are occasion-specific to funerals or contexts of loss (including, importantly, marriages); thus, they are universally charged with evocative and emotive significance, albeit often producing highly specific local discourses on abandonment, transition, and renewal that are aesthetically central to distinct social constructions of memory.

Lamentation forms can be placed in the broader social and cultural framework of the anthropology of mortuary rituals. Contemporary anthologies, syntheses, ethnographies, and critiques on this topic (33, 57, 74, 76a, 152, 183, 232, 257, 271, 275) grapple with how "death provides occasions and materials for a symbolic discourse on life" (152:9). This perspective follows the insights of several theorists; the early progression is Hertz (129), van Gennep (355), Durkheim (84), Radcliffe-Brown (266), Mauss (223). Later theorists (114, 349) developed and extended Hertz's often cited admonition that "death must be given its due if it is not to continue its ravages within the group" (129:51). This due, as Hertz emphasized, is the force of social obligation compelling the collectivity to participate in compulsory acts that mark and honor the social nature of death. Mortuary activities thus involve expressive and physical actions to remove the presence of death while inventing the tone of the deceased's memory projection for the future. Performed acts of remembering oppose the imagined horror of forgetting. They simultaneously renew and potentially amplify both the sociability and solidarity forged by participation, and the emotional exhaustion, enmity, and antipathy forged by contemplating loss.

Despite the theoretical and ethnographic sophistication of this line of social and cultural inquiry, the actual discursive means (i.e. the laments) constituting these symbolic discourses on life have not been fully described or analyzed in the mortuary ritual literature. Even when texts are presented and analyzed, weeping and wailing references are often entirely casual. The terms *cry, wail,* and *lamentation* are often found interchangeably, usually with no mention of what is or isn't sung or texted, what these expressions are locally called, and how obligatory or socially significant they are. Crying is often represented as an obvious and natural occurrence, which in many cases makes it uncritically gendered as female (cf. 216). Much of the social anthropological literature lacks a view of the discursive materials and performative display of lamentation as part of, and not superfluous to, the ritually gendered production and circulation of memory and emotion.

Lamentation can be approached as an interpenetration of the full range of possibilities for the vocal stylization of affective performance (3, 50, 95, 132, 167, 340, 341, 367). In this respect lamentation is distinct from other vocal-verbal performance genres and from other kinds of cried responses to pain or distress. Musical features that participate in lament stylizations include pitch selection and range, stylization of melody contour and metric and rhythmic groups, correspondence of phrase group and breath point, degree of phrasal and sub-phrasal repetition, and amount of improvisation. Linguistic features that participate in this stylization range from pure sound vocalizations to the use of conventional well-formed words, and from ellipsis and formulaic phrases to full syntactic constructions. Additional structural variables include line length and format; phonological, syntactic, and semantic micro- and macro-parallelism; and correspondence of line and sub-line units with breath points and melodic contours. Sung-texted lamentations are characterized by intersections of melodic and rhythmic aspects of tune with phonological and syntactic aspects of text, mostly marked in the organization of phrases, breath groups, and lines.

These sung-texted dimensions are further stylized by the kinds of crying that bracket or bundle with the verbal-vocal articulation. Urban (353, 354) has isolated four "icons of crying" found in ritual wailing: the cry break, the voiced inhalation, creaky voice, and the falsetto vowel. These involve performative stylizations of voice qualities, which articulate and embody heightened emotional states.

These dimensions of stylization in the lament form take on a great cultural variety of performative manifestations. Some forms are more clearly spoken, narrated, or recited strictly in a speaking voice, often with a highly stylized intonational contour. Others are more sung and marked by a stylization of melodic contour and rhythmic formula. Others are more principally cried, and thus stylistically marked by a distinctly non-speaking and non-singing voice. Cross-cutting dimensions of voice modality, some lament texts are more improvised, formulaic, or composed-in-performance, while others are more fixed, pre-composed, and/or memorized. Thus, laments need also be scrutinized for the extent to which they uphold or challenge assumptions within oral-formulaic theory about variable texts and authentic versions. Likewise, laments can be scrutinized for the extent to which they are occasion-dependent and composed in performance rather than memorized or composed prior to performance (98, 101).

Some varieties of lament have no referential content at all but are enunciated as phonologically conventional vocables (115). Others are in conversational everyday speech (95) and still others use more formal speech registers, marked by formal metric schemes (167). Ethnographic accounts that closely examine the metalinguistics and etymologies of lamentation also reveal ways these genres are marked in relation to other speech or song forms, or marked for gender, for affective and emotional voice qualities, or other indications of local associations relating sadness and emotion to human expressive sound (3, 50, 95, 132, 340, 354).

Although lamentation forms are locally considered as distinct types of vocalization and expression, studies have begun to explore complex interactions of stylized weeping signals and other dimensions of lamentation as they intersect or appear within other genres, like narrative (117, 140) and song (9, 94). The necessity of understanding the complementarity of lamentation with other speech and song genres has been taken up by several authors (3, 115, 146, 352).

Another trend in recent analyses of lament concerns the value of acoustic transcription and micro-analysis of performance to understanding the intersection of affective and aesthetic vocal signals. Urban (353, 354), Briggs (50), Tolbert (340), and Vaughan (356) use a variety of recent digitizing, spectrographic, and pitch-tracking technologies to examine details of lament vocalization. Adding to Urban's characterization of the crying voice, Tolbert (340) and Vaughan (356) show how increased vibrato, changes in pitch, phrase length, and rhythmic density map into the temporal progression of Karelian (Finland) lament, heightening affective dimensions of performance. Briggs (50) raises additional questions about iconic and indexical dimensions of affecting performance and gendered expression in the dialogic interaction of Warao (Venezuela) vocal tempo, pitch, and timbre.

Many lament forms are principally monophonic, maximizing the social distinctiveness of a solo voice performing a personal text. But recent attention has turned to cases where members of a group lament simultaneously, typically in heterophony (simultaneous performances involving different texts vocalized to variations of a single melody), or in more structured polyphonic, responsorial, or antiphonal forms. In these cases distinct melodic and textual parts are performed in dialogic patterns of multi-voice alternation, or leader-chorus alternation, or alternation with vocal overlap. Other variants of this pattern involve additional dialogic complexities in the interaction of overlapping or interlocking voices. Patterns of multi-voice performance, regardless of musical or textual complexities, produce possibilities for performed intertextuality, where the spatio-temporal character of multiple voice utterances is indexical to a process of emergence as a cohesive, jointly produced text. Intertextuality points to the process of simultaneously cooperative or competitive production of texts (50, 95, 132).

Recent studies by Briggs (49, 50), Feld (95), and Serematakis (301) analyze how complexities of gendered participation relationship in lament performance are simultaneously encoded through polyphony and intertextuality. Within and across performances, the continual alternating and overlapping of voices in Warao, Kaluli, and Maniat (Greece) women's sung-texted-weeping interlock to produce a layered musicality matched by a layered intertextuality. Even though each voice laments distinctly, the cumulative interaction between voices draws the temporal process of the mourning event and its participants into a more dialogic arena. Intertextuality thereby links unique and distinct voices thematizing highly salient personal, collective, emotional, and social concerns. As might be expected, these texts draw significantly on highly affect-laden lexical or discourse areas (e.g. place names; personal names and relationship terms; rhetorical questions to the deceased or audience; accusations; remembrance formulae; allegorical, metaphorical, or veiled speech; indirectness; social criticism and transgressive commentary; and appropriation or recontextualization of prior discourses). Vocal polyphony and intertextuality reveal the power of spontaneous joint performance to co-articulate personal and collective biography and memory.

CONCLUSION

Trends toward ethnographic studies of the interpenetration of music and language contribute strongly to the developing emphasis in sociocultural anthropology on the poetics and pragmatics of expressive performance (18). At the same time, detailed musico-linguistic ethnographies offer a critique of certain trends in both sociocultural and linguistic anthropology toward an over-textualized conception of voice and an overly discursive conception of the social construction of meaning. This critique traces the consequences of music's phenomenological distinctiveness from language, leading toward deeper exploration of polysemous, associative, iconic, presentational, ostensive, reflexive, ludic, emotive, and embodied dimensions of sociability. Music's poetic de-referentializing of language heightens the symbolic efficacy of its affecting discourse, making it a sensitive gauge of both traditional and emergent forms of sociability and identity, and a key resource in both the construction and the critical inversion of social order (8, 15, 50, 69, 70, 92, 142, 173, 174, 178). Perhaps this is why Lévi-Strauss' *The Raw and the Cooked* (196) is the only anthropological work audacious enough ever to bear the dedication "To Music." Ironically, when all is said and sung, it was the structuralist tradition that made anthropology and linguistics pay attention to the social immanence of

music's supreme mystery, the grooving redundancy of elegant structuring that
affectively connects the singularity of form to the multiplicity of sense.

ACKNOWLEDGMENTS
For years of dialogue on many of the issues discussed here we thank Joel
Sherzer and Greg Urban. We also thank Cindie McLemore and Tony Woodbury for coaching us on recent linguistic research in discourse prosodics and
intonation, but don't hold them responsible for our lack of comprehensivness
in this area.

Literature Cited

1. Abu-Lughod L. 1986. *Veiled Sentiments: Honor and Poetry in a Bedouin Society.* Berkeley: Univ. Calif. Press
2. Abu-Lughod L. 1990. Shifting politics in Bedouin love poetry. See Ref. 217, pp. 24–45
3. Abu-Lughod L. 1993. Islam and the gendered discourses of death. *Int. J. Mid. East. Stud.* 25:187–205
4. Agawu VK. 1984. The impact of language on musical composition in Ghana: an introduction to the compositional style of Ephraim Amu. *Ethnomusicology* 28(1):37–74
5. Agawu VK. 1988. Music in the funeral traditions of the Akpafu. *Ethnomusicology* 32(1):75–105
6. Ajuwon B. 1981. Lament for the dead as a universal folk tradition. *Fabula* 22:272–80
7. Alexiou M. 1974. *The Ritual Lament in Greek Tradition.* Cambridge: Cambridge Univ. Press
8. Attali J. 1985. *Noise: The Political Economy of Music.* Minneapolis: Univ. Minn. Press
9. Auerbach S. 1987. From singing to lamenting: women's musical role in a Greek village. See Ref. 184, pp. 25–43
10. Austerlitz R. 1983. Meaning in music: Is music like a language and if so, how? *Am. J. Semiot.* 2(3):1–11
11. Baily J. 1985. Music structure and human movement. In *Musical Structure and Cognition,* ed. P Howell, I Cross, R West, pp. 237–58. London: Academic
12. Baily J. 1988. Anthropological and psychological approaches to the study of music

theory and musical cognition. *Yearb. Tradit. Music* 20:114–24
13. Barnouw E. 1989. *International Encyclopedia of Communication,* ed. E Barnouw, Vol. 1–4. Philadelphia: Univ. Penn. Press
14. Barthes R. 1977. The grain of the voice. In *Image—Music—Text,* pp. 179–89. London: Fontana
15. Basso EB. 1985. *A Musical View of the Universe: Kalapalo Myth and Ritual Performances.* Philadelphia: Univ. Penn. Press
16. Bauman R. 1977. *Verbal Art as Performance.* Prospect Heights, IL: Waveland
17. Bauman R, ed. 1992. *Folklore, Cultural Performances, and Popular Entertainments: A Communications-Centered Handbook.* New York: Oxford Univ. Press
18. Bauman R, Briggs CL. 1990. Poetics and performance as critical perspectives on language and social life. *Annu. Rev. Anthropol.* 19:59–88
19. Bauman R, Sherzer J. 1975. The ethnography of speaking. *Annu. Rev. Anthropol.* 4:95–119
20. Bauman R, Sherzer J, eds. 1989. *Explorations in the Ethnography of Speaking.* New York: Cambridge Univ. Press. 2nd ed.
21. Beaudry N. 1978. Toward transcription and analysis of Inuit throat-games: macrostructure. *Ethnomusicology* 22(2):261–73
22. Becker A, Becker J. 1979. A grammar of the musical genre *srepegan. J. Music Theory* 23(1):1–43
23. Becker J, Becker A. 1981. A musical icon: power and meaning in Javanese gamelan music. See Ref. 324, pp. 203–16
24. Béhague G, ed. 1984. *Performance Practice.* New York: Greenwood

MUSIC AND LANGUAGE   45

25. Besnier N. 1990. Language and affect. *Annu. Rev. Anthropol.* 19:419–52
26. Birdwhistell R. 1970. *Kinesics and Context.* Philadelphia: Univ. Penn. Press
27. Blacking J. 1971. Deep and surface structures in Venda music. *Yearb. Int. Folk Music Counc.* 3:91–108
28. Blacking J. 1973. *How Musical Is Man?* Seattle: Univ. Wash. Press
29. Blacking J, ed. 1977. *The Anthropology of the Body.* London: Academic
30. Blacking J. 1981. The problem of 'ethnic' perceptions in the semiotics of music. See Ref. 324, pp. 184–94
31. Blacking J. 1982. The structure of musical discourse: the problem of the song text. *Yearb. Tradit. Music* 14:15–23
32. Blacking J. 1992. The biology of music making. See Ref. 240, pp. 301–14
33. Bloch M, Parry J, eds. 1982. *Death and the Regeneration of Life.* Cambridge: Cambridge Univ. Press
34. Blum S. 1975. Toward a social history of musicological technique. *Ethnomusicology* 19(2):207–32
35. Blum S, Bohlman PV, Neuman DM, eds. 1991. *Ethnomusicology and Modern Music History.* Urbana: Univ. Ill. Press
36. Bohlman PV. 1988. *The Study of Folk Music in the Modern World.* Bloomington: Ind. Univ. Press
37. Boilés C. 1967. Tepehua thought-song: a case of semantic signalling. *Ethnomusicology* 11(3):267–91
38. Boilés C. 1982. Processes of musical semiosis. *Yearb. Tradit. Music* 14:24–44
39. Bolinger D. 1978. Intonation across languages. In *Universals of Human Language.* Vol. 2: *Phonology,* ed. J Greenberg, pp. 471–524. Stanford, CA: Stanford Univ. Press
40. Bolinger D. 1986. *Intonation and its Parts: Melody in Spoken English.* Stanford, CA: Stanford Univ. Press
41. Bolinger D. 1989. *Intonation and its Uses.* Stanford, CA: Stanford Univ. Press
42. Bolinger D. 1992. Sound symbolism. In *International Encyclopedia of Linguistics,* ed. W Bright, 4:28–30. Cambridge: Cambridge Univ. Press
43. Boswell G. 1977. Pitch: musical and verbal in folksong. *Yearb. Tradit. Music* 9:80–88
44. Bourdieu P. 1977. *Outline of a Theory of Practice.* Cambridge: Cambridge Univ. Press
45. Bourdieu P. 1984. *Distinction: A Social Critique of the Judgment of Taste.* Cambridge, MA: Harvard Univ. Press
46. Brenneis DL. 1987. Performing passions: aesthetics and politics in an occasionally egalitarian community. *Am. Ethnol.* 14(2):236–50
47. Brenneis DL. 1988. Language and disputing. *Annu. Rev. Anthropol.* 17:221–38
48. Briggs CL. 1988. *Competence in Performance: The Creativity of Tradition in Mexicano Verbal Art.* Philadelphia: Univ. Penn. Press
49. Briggs CL. 1992. Since I am a woman I will chastise my relatives: gender, reported speech, and the (re)production of social relations in Warao ritual wailing. *Am. Ethnol.* 19(2):337–61
50. Briggs CL. 1993. Personal sentiments and polyphonic voices in Warao women's ritual wailing: music and poetics in a critical and collective discourse. *Am. Anthropol.* 95(4):929–57
51. Bright W. 1963. Language and music: areas for cooperation. *Ethnomusicology* 7(1):23–32
52. Burrows D. 1990. *Sound, Speech and Music.* Amherst: Univ. Mass. Press
53. Busnel RG. 1966. Information in the human whistled language and sea mammal whistling. In *Whales, Dolphins, and Porpoises,* ed. K Norris, pp. 544–68. Berkeley: Univ. Calif. Press
54. Caraveli A. 1986. The bitter wounding: the lament as social protest in rural Greece. In *Gender and Power in Rural Greece,* ed. J Dubisch, pp. 169–94. Princeton, NJ: Princeton Univ. Press
55. Caraveli-Chaves A. 1980. Bridge between worlds: the Greek women's lament as communicative event. *J. Am. Folklore* 93:129–57
56. Carrington J. 1971. The talking drums of Africa. *Sci. Am.* 225(6):90–94
57. Cederroth S, Corlin C, Lindstrom J, eds. 1988. *On the Meaning of Death: Essays on Mortuary Rituals and Eschatological Beliefs. Uppsala Stud. Cult. Anthropol.* 8. Stockholm: Almqvist & Wiksell
58. Chao YR. 1956. Tones, intonation, singsong, chanting, recitative, tonal composition, and atonal composition in Chinese. See Ref. 118, pp. 52–59
59. Charron C. 1978. Toward transcription and analysis of Inuit throat-games: micro-structure. *Ethnomusicology* 22(2):245–59
60. Chenoweth V. 1968. Managalasi mourning songs. *Ethnomusicology* 12(3):415–18
61. Chenoweth V. 1972. *Melodic Perception and Analysis.* Papua New Guinea: Summer Inst. Linguist.
62. Chenoweth V. 1979. *The Usarufas and their music.* Summer Inst. Ling. Mus. Anthropol., Dallas, Texas
63. Chenoweth V, Bee D. 1971. Comparative-generative models of a New Guinea melodic structure. *Am. Anthropol.* 73:773–82
64. Chernoff JM. 1979. *African Rhythm and African Sensibility.* Chicago: Univ. Chicago Press
65. Cogan R, Escot P. 1976. *Sonic Design: The*

Nature of Sound and Music. Englewood Cliffs, NJ: Prentice-Hall
66. Coker W. 1972. *Music and Meaning.* New York: Free Press
67. Cooke D. 1959. *The Language of Music.* London: Oxford Univ. Press
68. Cooper R. 1977. Abstract structure and the Indian raga system. *Ethnomusicology* 21(1):1–32
69. Coplan D. 1987. Eloquent knowledge: Lesotho migrants' songs and the anthropology of experience. *Am. Ethnol.* 14(3):413–33
70. Coplan D. 1988. Musical understanding: the ethnoaesthetics of migrant workers' poetic song in Lesotho. *Ethnomusicology* 32(3):337–68
71. Cowan GM. 1948. Mazateco whistle speech. *Language* 24:280–86
72. Crafts S, Cavicchi D, Keil C. 1993. *My Music.* Hanover, NH: Wesleyan Univ. Press
73. Crystal D. 1971. Prosodic and paralinguistic correlates of social categories. In *Social Anthropology and Language,* ed. E Ardener, pp. 185–206. ASA Monogr. London: Tavistock
74. Damon F, Wagner R, eds. 1989. *Death Rituals and Life in Societies of the Kula Ring.* DeKalb: N. Ill. Univ. Press
75. Danes F. 1960. Sentence intonation from a functional point of view. *Word* 16:34–54
76. Danes F. 1984. Review of Gardiner. *Lang. Soc.* 13(1):113–17
76a. Danforth LM. 1982. *The Death Rituals of Rural Greece.* Princeton, NJ: Princeton Univ. Press
77. Davis GL. 1985. *I Got the Word in Me and I Can Sing It, You Know: A Study of the Performed African-American Sermon.* Philadelphia: Univ. Penn. Press
78. Deutsch HA. 1976. *Synthesis: An Introduction to the History, Theory, and Practice of Electronic Music.* New York: Alfred
79. Dixon RMW. 1980. *The Languages of Australia.* Cambridge: Cambridge Univ. Press
80. Dodge C. 1980. Speech songs. In *Text-Sound Texts,* ed. R Kostelanetz, pp. 362–64. New York: Morrow
81. Dowling WJ, Harwood DL. 1986. *Music Cognition.* Orlando, FL: Academic
82. Duranti A. 1988. Ethnography of speaking: toward a linguistics of the praxis. In *Linguistics: The Cambridge Survey.* Vol. 4: *Language: The Socio-Cultural Context,* ed. FJ Newmeyer, pp. 210–28. Cambridge: Cambridge Univ. Press
83. Durbin MA. 1971. Transformational models applied to musical analysis: theoretical possibilities. *Ethnomusicology* 15(3):353–62
84. Durkheim E. 1965. *The Elementary Forms of the Religious Life.* New York: Free Press
85. Erickson E. 1976. Tradition and evolution

in song style. *Behav. Sci. Res.* 11(1):277–308
86. Erickson R. 1975. *Sound Structure in Music.* Berkeley: Univ. Calif. Press
87. Evans JR, Clynes M, eds. 1986. *Rhythm in Psychological, Linguistic, and Musical Processes.* Springfield, IL: Thomas
88. Feld S. 1974. Linguistic models in ethnomusicology. *Ethnomusicology* 18(2): 197–217
89. Feld S. 1981. 'Flow like a waterfall': the metaphors of Kaluli musical theory. *Yearb. Tradit. Music* 13:22–47
90. Feld S. 1984. Communication, music, and speech about music. *Yearb. Tradit. Music* 16:1–18
91. Feld S. 1984. Sound structure as social structure. *Ethnomusicology* 28(3):383–409
92. Feld S. 1988. Aesthetics as iconicity of style, or 'lift-up-over sounding': getting into the Kaluli groove. *Yearb. Tradit. Music* 20:74–113
93. Feld S. 1989. Sound. See Ref. 13, 4:101–7
94. Feld S. 1990. *Sound and Sentiment: Birds, Weeping, Poetics and Song in Kaluli Expression.* Philadelphia: Univ. Penn. Press. 2nd ed.
95. Feld S. 1990. Wept thoughts: the voicing of Kaluli memories. *Oral Tradit.* 5(2–3):241–66
96. Feld S. 1991. Sound as a symbolic system: the Kaluli drum. In *The Varieties of Sensory Experience: A Sourcebook in the Anthropology of the Senses,* ed. D Howes, pp. 79–99. Toronto: Univ. Toronto Press
97. Fernandez JW. 1986. Syllogisms of association: some modern extensions of Asturian deepsong. In *Persuasions and Performances: The Play of Tropes in Culture,* ed. J Fernandez, pp. 103–28. Bloomington: Ind. Univ. Press
98. Finnegan R. 1988. *Literacy and Orality.* Oxford: Blackwell
99. Finnegan R. 1992. *Oral Traditions and the Verbal Arts: A Guide to Research Practices.* London: Routledge
100. Firth R, with McLean M. 1990. *Tikopia Songs: Poetic and Musical Art of a Polynesian People of the Solomon Islands.* Cambridge: Cambridge Univ. Press
101. Foley JM. 1988. *The Theory of Oral Composition.* Bloomington: Ind. Univ. Press
102. Fonagy I. 1981. Emotions, voice, and music. In *Research Aspects of Singing,* 3:51–79. Royal Swedish Academy of Music
103. Fox A. 1992. The jukebox of history: narratives of loss and desire in the discourse of country music. *Pop. Music* 11(1):53–72
104. Franklin CL. 1989. *Give Me This Mountain: Life History and Selected Sermons,* ed. JT Titon. Urbana: Univ. Ill. Press
105. Frisbie C. 1980. Vocables in Navajo cere-

monial music. *Ethnomusicology* 24(3): 347–92
106. Frisbie C, ed. 1980. *Southwestern Indian Ritual Drama*. Albuquerque: Univ. N. Mex. Press
107. Frisbie C, ed. 1986. *Explorations in Ethnomusicology: Essays in Honor of David P. McAllester*. Detroit: Detroit Monogr. Musicol.
108. Frith S. 1988. Why do songs have words? In *Music for Pleasure*, ed. S Frith, pp. 105–28. London: Routledge
109. Gal S. 1989. Language and political economy. *Annu. Rev. Anthropol.* 18:345–67
110. Gardiner DB. 1980. *Intonation and Music: The Semantics of Czech Prosody*. Bloomington, IN: Physsardt
111. Geertz C. 1973. *The Interpretation of Cultures*. New York: Basic
112. Gilroy P. 1991. *'There Ain't No Black in the Union Jack': The Cultural Politics of Race and Nation*. Chicago: Univ. Chicago Press
113. Goodman N. 1976. *Languages of Art*. Indianapolis: Hackett. 2nd ed.
114. Goody J. 1962. *Death, Property, and the Ancestors*. Stanford, CA: Stanford Univ. Press
115. Graham L. 1986. Three modes of Shavante vocal expression: wailing, collective singing, and political oratory. See Ref. 310, pp. 83–118
116. Grenier L, Guibault J. 1990. 'Authority' revisited: the 'other' in anthropology and popular music studies. *Ethnomusicology* 34(3):381–98
117. Grima B. 1992. *The Performance of Emotion Among Paxtun Women*. Austin: Univ. Texas Press
118. Halle M, Lunt HG, McLean H, Van Schooneveld CH, eds. 1956. For *Roman Jakobson: Essays on the Occasion of His Sixtieth Birthday*. The Hague: Mouton
119. Hanks W. 1989. Text and textuality. *Annu. Rev. Anthropol.* 18:95–127
120. Harweg R. 1968. Language and music: an immanent and sign theoretic approach. *Found. Lang.* 4:270–81
121. Hatten RS. 1980. Nattiez's semiology of music: flaws in the new science. *Semiotica* 31(1–2):139–55
122. Hatten RS. 1987. Style, motivation, and markedness. See Ref. 293, pp. 408–29
123. Hebdige D. 1979. *Subculture: The Meaning of Style*. New York: Methuen
124. Henrotte GA. 1988. *Language, linguistics, and music: a source study*. PhD thesis. Univ. Calif., Berkeley
125. Herndon M. 1974. Analysis: the herding of sacred cows? *Ethnomusicology* 18:219–62
126. Herndon M. 1989. Song. See Ref. 13, 4:98–101
127. Herndon M, McLeod N. 1979. *Music as Culture*. Norwood, PA: Norwood
128. Herndon M, Ziegler S, eds. 1990. *Music, Gender, and Culture*. Wilhelmshaven: Florian Noetzel Verlag
129. Hertz R. 1960. A contribution to the study of the collective representation of death. In *Death and the Right Hand*, ed. R Hertz, pp. 27–86. New Yorkt: Free Press
130. Herzfeld M. 1981. Performative categories and symbols of passage in rural Greece. *J. Am. Folklore* 94:44–57
131. Herzfeld M. 1985. *The Poetics of Manhood: Contest and Identity in a Cretan Mountain Village*. Princeton, NJ: Princeton Univ. Press
132. Herzfeld M. 1993. In defiance of destiny: the management of time and gender at a Cretan funeral. *Am. Ethnol.* 20(2):241–255
133. Herzog G. 1934. Speech melody and primitive music. *Music Q.* 20:452–66
134. Herzog G. 1942. Text and melody in primitive music. *Bull. Am. Musicol. Soc.* 6:10–11
135. Herzog G. 1945. Drum signalling in a West African tribe. *Word* 1:217–38
136. Herzog G. 1950. Song. In *Funk & Wagnall's Dictionary of Folklore, Mythology and Legend*, ed. M Leach, 2:1032–50. New York: Funk & Wagnall's
137. Higgins KM. 1991. *The Music of Our Lives*. Philadelphia: Temple Univ. Press
138. Hill CA, Podstavsky S. 1976. The interfacing of language and music in Hausa praise-singing. *Ethnomusicology* 20(3): 535–40
139. Hill JD. 1993. *Keepers of the Sacred Chants: The Poetics of Ritual Power in an Amazonian Society*. Tucson: Univ. Ariz. Press
140. Hill JH. 1990. Weeping as a meta-signal in a Mexicano woman's narrative. In *Native Latin American Cultures Through Their Discourse*, ed. EB Basso, pp. 29–49. Bloomington: Folklore Inst., Indiana Univ.
141. Hinton L. 1980. Vocables in Havasupai song. See Ref. 106, pp. 275–305
142. Hinton L. 1984. *Havasupai Songs: A Linguistic Perspective*. Tübingen: Gunter Narr Verlag
143. Hinton L. 1986. Musical diffusion and linguistic diffusion. See Ref. 107, pp. 11–24
144. Hinton L. 1990. Song metrics. In *Berkeley Linguistics Society: Proc. 16th Annu. Meet., Special Session on General Topics in Am. Indian Ling.*, pp. 51–60. Berkeley: Dept. Ling., Univ. Calif., Berkeley
145. Holmes JD. 1985. *Electronic and Experimental Music*. New York: Scribners
146. Holst-Warhaft G. 1992. *Dangerous Voices: Women's Laments and Greek Literature*. New York: Routledge
147. Honko L. 1974. Balto-Finnic lament poetry. *Stud. Fennica* 17:9–61
148. Honko L. 1980. The lament: problems of genre, structure, and reproduction. In

Genre, Structure and Reproduction in Oral Literature, ed. L Honko, V Voigt, pp. 21–40. Budapest: Akademiai Kiado

149. Hosokawa S. 1984. How Saussurian is music? In *Musical Grammars and Computer Analysis*, ed. M Baroni, L Callegari, pp. 155–63. Firenze: Olschki

150. Houghton C. 1984. *Structure in language and music: a linguistic approach*. PhD thesis. Stanford Univ.

151. Hughes DW. 1988. Deep structure and surface structure in Javanese music: a grammar of *gendhing lampah*. *Ethnomusicology* 32(1):23–74

152. Humphreys SC, King H, eds. 1981. *Mortality and Immortality: The Anthropology and Archeology of Death*. London: Academic

153. Hymes D. 1974. *Foundations of Sociolinguistics*. Philadelphia: Univ. Penn. Press

154. Hymes D. 1981. *'In Vain I Tried to Tell You': Essays in Native American Ethnopoetics*. Philadelphia: Univ. Penn. Press

155. Irvine J. 1990. Registering affect: heteroglossia in the linguistic expresssion of emotion. See Ref. 217, pp. 126–61

156. Jackendoff R. 1989. A comparison of rhythmic structures in music and language. See Ref. 181, pp. 15–44

157. Jakobson R. 1960. Concluding statement: linguistics and poetics. See Ref. 292, pp. 350–77

158. Jakobson R. 1985. *Verbal Art, Verbal Sign, Verbal Time*, ed. K Pomorska, S Rudy. Oxford: Blackwell

159. Jakobson R. 1987. *Language in Literature*, ed. K Pomorska, S Rudy. Cambridge, MA: Belknap

160. Jakobson R. 1987. Musicology and linguistics. See Ref. 159, pp. 455–57

161. Jakobson R, Waugh LR. 1979. *The Sound Shape of Language*. Bloomington: Ind. Univ. Press

162. Johnson A. 1984. Voice physiology and ethnomusicology: physiological and acoustical studies of the Swedish herding song. *Yearb. Tradit. Music* 16:42–66

163. Kaeppler A. 1978. Dance in anthropological perspective. *Annu. Rev. Anthropol.* 7: 31–49

164. Kaeppler A. 1986. Cultural analysis, linguistic analogies, and the study of dance in anthropological perspective. See Ref. 107, pp. 25–34

165. Kaeppler A. 1989. Dance. See Ref. 13, 1:450–54

166. Kaeppler A. 1991. American approaches to the study of dance. *Yearb. Tradit. Music* 23:11–22

167. Kaeppler A. 1993. Poetics and politics of Tongan laments and eulogies. *Am. Ethnol.* 20(3):474–501

168. Karbusicky V. 1987. The index sign in music. *Semiotica* 66(1–3):22–36

169. Karbusicky V. 1987. Signification in music: a metaphor? See Ref. 293, pp. 430–44

170. Kaufman N. 1990. Lamentations from four continents, after materials from Europe, Asia, Africa, and America. *Int. Folklore Rev.* 7:22–29

171. Kaufman N, Kaufman D. 1988. *Funeral and Other Lamentations in Bulgaria*. Sofia: Bulgarian Acad. Sci. (In Bulgarian with English précis)

172. Keil C. 1966. Motion and feeling through music. *J. Aesthet. Art Crit.* 24:337–49

173. Keil C. 1979. *Tiv Song*. Chicago: Univ. Chicago Press

174. Keil C. 1984. Response to Feld and Roseman. *Ethnomusicology* 28(3):446–49

175. Keil C. 1985. People's music comparatively: style and stereotype, class and hegemony. *Dialect. Anthropol.* 10:119–30

176. Keil C. 1987. Participatory discrepancies and the power of music. *Cult. Anthropol.* 2(3):275–83

177. Keil C. 1991. *Urban Blues*. Chicago: Univ. Chicago Press. 2nd ed.

178. Keil C, Feld S. 1994. *Music Grooves*. Chicago: Univ. Chicago Press

179. Keiler A. 1981. Two views of musical semiotics. See Ref. 324, pp. 138–68

180. Kingsbury H. 1988. *Music, Talent and Performance: A Conservatory Cultural System*. Philadelphia: Temple Univ. Press

181. Kiparsky P, Youmans G, eds. 1989. *Phonetics and Phonology*. Vol. 1: *Rhythm and Meter*. San Diego: Academic

182. Kippen J. 1987. An ethnomusicological approach to the analysis of musical cognition. *Music Percept.* 5(2):173–96

183. Kligman G. 1988. *The Wedding of the Dead: Ritual, Poetics, and Popular Culture in Transylvania*. Berkeley: Univ. Calif. Press

184. Koskoff E, ed. 1987. *Women and Music in Cross-Cultural Perspective*. New York: Greenwood

185. Kratz CA. 1994. *Affecting Performance: Meaning, Movement, and Experience in Okiek Women's Initiation*. Washington, DC: Smithsonian Inst. Press

186. Kuipers J. 1990. *Power in Performance: The Creation of Textual Authority in Weyewa Ritual Speech*. Philadelphia: Univ. Penn. Press

187. Ladd DR. 1980. *The Structure of Intonational Meaning: Evidence From English*. Bloomington: Ind. Univ. Press

188. Ladd DR. 1990. Intonation: emotion vs. grammar. *Language* 66(4):806–16

189. Langer S. 1957. *Philosophy in a New Key: A Study in the Symbolism of Reason, Rite, and Art*. Cambridge, MA: Harvard Univ. Press. 3rd ed.

190. Laske O. 1977. *Music, Memory, and Thought: Explorations in Cognitive Musi-*

cology. Pittsburgh: Music Dept., Univ. Pittsburgh
191. Laske O, ed. 1986. Cognitive musicology. Special Issue of *J. Integr. Stud. Artif. Intell. Cogn. Sci. Appl. Epistemol.* 3(3)
192. Laver J. 1980. *The Phonetic Description of Voice Quality.* Cambridge: Cambridge Univ. Press
193. Leben WR. 1985. On the correspondence between linguistic tone and musical melody. In *African Linguistics: Essays in Memory of M.W.K. Semikenke,* ed. DL Goyvaerts, pp. 335–43. Amsterdam: Benjamins
194. Lerdahl F, Jackendoff R. 1983. *A Generative Theory of Tonal Music.* Cambridge, MA: MIT Press
195. Lévi-Strauss C. 1963. *Structural Anthropology.* New York: Doubleday
196. Lévi-Strauss C. 1969. *The Raw and the Cooked.* New York: Harper
197. Lévi-Strauss C. 1985. *The View From Afar.* New York: Basic
198. Levman B. 1992. The genesis of music and language. *Ethnomusicology* 36(2):147–70
199. Lewis JL. 1992. *Ring of Liberation.* Chicago: Univ. Chicago Press
200. Liberman M, McLemore C, eds. 1992. *Proceedings of the IRCS Workshop on Prosody in Natural Speech.* IRCS Report No. 92–37. Philadelphia: Inst. Res. Cogn. Sci., Univ. Penn.
201. Lidov D. 1975. *On the Musical Phrase.* Monogr. sémiol. anal. music., No. 1. Montréal: Groupe Rech. Semiol. Music., Univ. Montréal
202. Lidov D. 1977. Nattiez's semiotics of music. *Can. J. Res. Semiotics* 5(2):13–54
203. Lidov D. 1980. Musical and verbal semantics. *Semiotica* 31(3/4):369–91
204. Lindblom B, Sundberg J. 1975. A generative theory of Swedish nursery tunes. *Actes du 1er congres international de sémiotique musicale,* pp. 111–24. Pesaro: Cent. Iniziative Cult.
205. Linggard R. 1985. *Electronic Synthesis of Speech.* Cambridge: Cambridge Univ. Press
206. List G. 1961. Speech melody and song melody in central Thailand. *Ethnomusicology* 5:16–32
207. List G. 1963. The boundaries of speech and song. *Ethnomusicology* 7(1):1–16
208. Lloyd AL. 1980. Lament. In *New Grove Dictionary of Music and Musicians,* ed. S Sadie, pp. 407–10. London: Macmillan
209. Lomax A. 1967. Special features of the sung communication. In *Essays on the Verbal and Visual Arts: Proc. 1966 Annu. Spring Meet. Am. Ethnol. Soc.,* ed. J Helm, pp. 109–27. Seattle: Univ. Wash. Press
210. Lomax A. 1968. *Folk Song Style and Cul-*

ture. Washington, DC: Am. Acad. Advance. Sci.
211. Lomax A. 1977. *Cantometrics: An Approach to the Anthropology of Music.* Berkeley: Univ. Calif. Extension Media Center
212. Lomax A. 1977. A stylistic analysis of speaking. *Lang. Soc.* 6(1):5–36
213. Lomax A, Bartenieff I, Paulay F. 1969. Choreometrics: a method for the study of cross-cultural pattern in film. *Res. Film* 6(6):505–17
214. Lomax A, Berkowitz N. 1972. An evolutionary taxonomy of culture. *Science* 177: 228–39
215. Longacre RE, Chenoweth V. 1986. Discourse as music. *Word* 37(1):125–39
216. Lutz C. 1988. *Unnatural Emotions.* Chicago: Univ. Chicago Press
217. Lutz C, Abu-Lughod L, eds. 1990. *Language and the Politics of Emotion.* New York: Cambridge Univ Press
218. Lutz C, White GM. 1986. The anthropology of emotions. *Annu. Rev. Anthropol.* 15:405–36
219. Mannheim B. 1986. Popular song and popular grammar, poetry and metalanguage. *Word* 37(1–2):45–75
220. Mannheim B. 1987. Couplets and oblique contexts: the social organization of a folksong. *Text* 7(3):265–88
221. Marothy J. 1974. *Music and the Bourgeois, Music and the Proletariat.* Budapest: Akademiai Kiado
222. Matthews PH. 1982. Formalization. In *Linguistic Controversies: Essays in Linguistic Theory and Practice in Honor of F.R. Palmer,* ed. D Crystal, pp. 1–15. London: Arnold
223. Mauss M. 1979. The physical effect on the individual of the idea of death suggested by the collectivity. In *Sociology and Psychology,* ed. M Mauss, pp. 35–56. London: Routledge & Kegan Paul
224. McAllester DP. 1954. *Enemy way music.* Pap. Peabody Mus. Am. Archaeol. Ethnol. 41(3). Cambridge, MA: Peabody Mus., Harvard Univ.
225. McClary S. 1991. *Feminine Endings: Music, Gender, and Sexuality.* Minneapolis: Univ. Minn. Press
226. McLemore CA. 1991. *The pragmatic interpretation of English intonation: sorority speech.* PhD thesis. Univ. Texas, Austin
227. McLeod N. 1974. Ethnomusicological research and anthropology. *Annu. Rev. Anthropol.* 3:99–115
228. McLeod N, Herndon M, eds. 1980. *The Ethnography of Musical Performance.* Norwood, PA: Norwood
228a. Meintjes L. 1990. Paul Simon's Graceland, South Africa, and the mediation of musical meaning. *Ethnomusicology* 34(1):37–73

229. Merriam A. 1964. *The Anthropology of Music*. Evanston, IL: Northwestern Univ. Press
230. Merriam A. 1975. Ethnomusicology today. *Curr. Musicol.* 20:50–66
231. Mertz E, Parmentier R, eds. 1985. *Semiotic Mediation: Sociocultural and Psychological Perspectives*. Orlando, FL: Academic
232. Metcalf P, Huntington R. 1991. *Celebrations of Death: The Anthropology of Mortuary Ritual*. Cambridge: Cambridge Univ. Press. 2nd ed.
233. Meyer L. 1956. *Emotion and Meaning in Music*. Chicago: Univ. Chicago Press
234. Meyer L. 1967. Meaning in music and information theory. In *Music, the Arts, and Ideas*, ed. L Meyer, pp. 5–21. Chicago: Univ. Chicago Press
235. Meyer L. 1973. *Explaining Music*. Chicago: Univ. Chicago Press
236. Meyer L. 1989. *Style in Music*. Philadelphia: Univ. Penn. Press
237. Meyer L, Cooper G. 1960. *The Rhythmic Structure of Music*. Chicago: Univ. Chicago Press
238. Miller CA. 1992. Prosodic aspects of M.L. King's 'I Have A Dream' speech. See Ref. 200, pp. 129–37
239. Moles A. 1968. *Information Theory and Esthetic Perception*. Urbana: Univ. Ill. Press
240. Myers H, ed. 1992. *Ethnomusicology: An Introduction*. New York: Norton
241. Narmour E. 1977. *Beyond Schenkerism*. Chicago: Univ. Chicago Press
242. Nattiez JJ. 1972. Linguistics: a new approach for musical analysis? *Int. Rev. Aesthet. Sociol. Music* 4(1):51–67
243. Nattiez JJ. 1977. The contribution of musical semiotics to the semiotic discussion in general. In *A Perfusion of Signs*, ed. TA Sebeok, pp. 121–42. Bloomington: Ind. Univ. Press
244. Nattiez JJ. 1983. Some aspects of Inuit vocal games. *Ethnomusicology* 27(3):457–75
245. Nattiez JJ. 1990. *Music and Discourse: Toward a Semiology of Music*. Princeton, NJ: Princeton Univ. Press
246. Nelson K. 1985. *The Art of Reciting Qur'an*. Austin: Univ. Texas Press
247. Nenola-Kallio A. 1982. *Studies in Ingrian Laments. Folklore Fellows Communication 234.* Helsinki: Suomalainen Tiedeakatemia
248. Ness SA. 1992. *Body, Movement, and Culture*. Philadelphia: Univ. Penn. Press
249. Nettl B. 1958. Some linguistic approaches to musical analysis. *J. Int. Folk Music Counc.* 10:37–41
250. Nettl B, Bohlman PV, eds. 1991. *Comparative Musicology and the Anthropology of Music: Essays on the History of Ethnomusicology*. Chicago: Univ. Chicago Press

251. Nketia JHK. 1969. *Funeral Dirges of the Akan People*. New York: Greenwood
252. Nketia JHK. 1971. Surrogate languages of Africa. In *Current Trends in Linguistics*, ed. TA Sebeok, 7:699–732. The Hague: Mouton
253. Novack CJ. 1990. *Sharing the Dance: Contact Improvisation and American Culture*. Madison: Univ. Wisc. Press
254. Ochs E, Schieffelin B. 1984. Language acquisition and socialization: three developmental stories and their implications. In *Culture Theory: Essays on Mind, Self, and Emotion*, ed. RA Shweder, RA LeVine, pp. 276–320. Cambridge: Cambridge Univ. Press
255. Oliva J. 1977. *Structure of music and structure of language: a semiotic study.* PhD thesis. State Univ. NY, Buffalo
256. Ong W. 1977. African talking drums and oral noetics. *New Lit. Hist.* 8(3):411–29
257. Palgi P, Abramovitch H. 1984. Death: a cross-cultural perspective. *Annu. Rev. Anthropol.* 13:385–417
258. Pegg C. 1992. Mongolian conceptualizations of overtone singing (*xöömii*). *Br. J. Ethnomusicol.* 1:31–54
259. Peña M. 1985. *The Texas-Mexican Conjunto: History of a Working-Class Music*. Austin: Univ. Texas Press
260. Pierce A. 1987. Music and movement. See Ref. 293, pp. 514–35
261. Powers HS. 1980. Language models and musical analysis. *Ethnomusicology* 24(1):1–61
262. Powers WK. 1980. Oglala song terminology. *Sel. Rep. Ethnomusicol.* 3(2):23–41
263. Pugh-Kitingan J. 1977. Huli language and instrumental performance. *Ethnomusicology* 21(2):205–32
264. Prociuk P. 1981. The deep structure of Ukrainian hardship songs. *Yearb. Tradit. Music* 13:82–96
265. Qureshi R. 1987. Musical sound and contextual input: a performance model for musical analysis. *Ethnomusicology* 31(1):56–86
266. Radcliffe-Brown AR. 1964. *The Andaman Islanders*. New York: Free Press
267. Raffman D. 1990. *Language, Music, and Mind*. Cambridge, MA: MIT Press
268. Rice T. 1987. Toward the remodeling of ethnomusicology, and responses. *Ethnomusicology* 31(3):469–16
269. Richards P. 1972. A quantitative analysis of the relationship between speech tone and melody in a Hausa song. *Afr. Lang. Stud.* 13:137–61
270. Richman B. 1980. Did human speech originate in coordinated vocal music? *Semiotica* 32(3/4):233–44
271. Rosaldo R. 1984. Grief and the headhunter's rage: on the cultural force of emotions. In *Text, Play and Story: The Con-*

struction and Reconstruction of Self and Society, ed. E Bruner, pp. 178–95. Washington, DC: Am. Ethnol. Soc.

272. Roseman M. 1984. The social structuring of sound among the Temiar of Peninsular Malaysia. Ethnomusicology 28(3):411–45

273. Roseman M. 1991. Healing Sounds from the Malaysian Rainforest: Temiar Music and Medicine. Berkeley: Univ. Calif Press

274. Rosenberg B. 1970. The Art of the American Folk Preacher. New York: Oxford Univ. Press

275. Rosenblatt P, Walsh R, Jackson A. 1976. Grief and Mourning in Cross-Cultural Perspective. New Haven, CT: HRAF Press

276. Rosner B, Meyer L. 1986. The perceptual roles of melodic process, contour and form. Music Percept. 4:1–39

277. Rouget G. 1966. African traditional nonprose forms: reciting, declaiming, singing, and strophic structures. In Proc. Conf. Afr. Lang. Lit., April 28–30, pp. 45–58. Evanston, IL: Northwestern Univ. Press

278. Rouget G. 1971. Court songs and traditional history in the ancient kingdoms of Porto-Novo and Abomey. In Essays on Music and History in Africa, ed. K Wachsmann, pp. 27–64. Evanston, IL: Northwestern Univ. Press

279. Rouget G. 1977. Retrieving the world's disappearing music. CNRS Res. 5:38–48

280. Ruwet N. 1967. Linguistics and musicology. Int. Soc. Sci. J. 19:79–87

281. Rycroft DK. 1983. The relationship between speech-tone and melody in Southern African music. In South African Music Encyclopedia, Vol. 2, ed. K Wachsmann, pp. 301–14. Cape Town: Cape Town/Oxford Univ. Press

282. Sakata HL. 1983. Music in the Mind: The Concepts of Music and Musician in Afghanistan. Kent, OH: Kent State Univ. Press

283. Samarin W. 1972. Tongues of Men and Angels: The Religious Language of Pentecostalism. New York: Macmillan

284. Sapir E. 1910. Song recitative in Paiute mythology. J. Am. Folklore 23:455–72

285. Sapir E. 1918. Representative music. Music. Q. 4:161–67

286. Sapir E. 1921. The musical foundations of verse. J. Engl. Germ. Philol. 20:213–28

287. Sapir E. 1925. The sound patterns in language. Language 1:37–51

288. Sapir JD. 1969. Diola-Fogny funeral songs and the native critic. Afr. Lang. Rev. 8:176–91

289. Sarkissian M. 1992. Gender and music. See Ref. 240, pp. 337–48

290. Schneider M. 1961. Tone and tune in West African music. Ethnomusicology 5(3):204–15

291. Schutz A. 1951. Making music together: a study in social relationship. Soc. Res. 18(1):76–97

292. Sebeok T, ed. 1960. Style in Language. Cambridge, MA: MIT Press

293. Sebeok T, Umiker-Sebeok DJ, eds. 1987. The Semiotic Web 1986. Berlin: Mouton de Gruyter

294. Sedelow WA, Sedelow SY, eds. 1983. Computers in Language Research. Vol. 2: Notating the Language of Music and the (Pause) Rhythms of Speech. Trends Ling. Stud. Monogr. 19. Berlin: Mouton de Gruyter

295. Seeger A. 1980. 'Sing for your sister': the structure and performance of Suyá akia. See Ref. 228, pp. 7–42

296. Seeger A. 1986. Oratory is spoken, myth is told, and song is sung, but they are all music to my ears. See Ref. 310, pp. 59–82

297. Seeger A. 1987. Why Suyá Sing: A Musical Anthropology of an Amazonian People. Cambridge: Cambridge Univ. Press

298. Seeger A. 1992. Ethnography of music. See Ref. 240, pp. 88–109

299. Seeger C. 1977. Speech, music, and speech about music. In Studies in Musicology, 1935–1975, ed. C Seeger, pp. 16–30. Berkeley: Univ. Calif. Press

300. Serafine ML. 1988. Music as Cognition: The Development of Thought in Sound. New York: Columbia Univ. Press

301. Serematakis CN. 1991. The Last Word: Women, Death, and Divination in Inner Mani. Chicago: Univ. Chicago Press

302. Shepherd J. 1977. The 'meaning' of music. See Ref. 305, pp. 53–68

303. Shepherd J. 1987. Music and male hegemony. In Music and Society, ed. R Leppert, S McClary, pp. 151–72. Cambridge: Cambridge Univ. Press

304. Shepherd J. 1991. Music as Social Text. Cambridge, UK: Polity

305. Shepherd J, Virden P, Vulliamy G, Wishart T. 1977. Whose Music? A Sociology of Musical Languages. London: Latimer

306. Sherzer J. 1983. Kuna Ways of Speaking: An Ethnographic Perspective. Austin: Univ. Texas Press

307. Sherzer J. 1987. A diversity of voices: men's and women's speech in ethnographic perspective. In Language, Gender and Sex in Comparative Perspective, ed. SU Philips, S Steele, C Tanz, pp. 95–120. Cambridge: Cambridge Univ. Press

308. Sherzer J. 1987. Poetic structuring of Kuna discourse: the line. See Ref. 312, pp. 103–39

309. Sherzer J. 1987. A discourse-centered approach to language and culture. Am. Anthropol. 89(2):295–309

310. Sherzer J, Urban G, eds. 1986. Native South American Discourse. Berlin: Mouton de Gruyter

311. Sherzer J, Wicks SA. 1982. The intersec-

tion of music and language in Kuna discourse. *Latin Am. Music Rev.* 3(2):147–64

312. Sherzer J, Woodbury A, eds. 1987. *Native American Discourse: Poetics and Rhetoric.* Cambridge: Cambridge Univ. Press

313. Silverstein M. 1976. Shifters, linguistic categories, and cultural description. In *Meaning in Anthropology,* ed. KH Basso, H Selby, pp. 11–55. Albuquerque: Univ. N. Mex. Press

314. Silverstein M. 1979. Language structure and linguistic ideology. In *The Elements: A Parasession On Linguistic Units and Levels,* ed. P Clyne, W Hanks, C Hofbauer, pp. 193–247. Chicago: Univ. Chicago Press

315. Singer A. 1974. The metrical structure of Macedonian dance. *Ethnomusicology* 18(3):379–404

316. Singer M. 1984. *Man's Glassy Essence: Explorations in Semiotic Anthropology.* Bloomington: Ind. Univ. Press

317. Slawson W. 1985. *Sound Color.* Berkeley: Univ. Calif. Press

318. Slobin M. 1986. Multilingualism in folk music cultures. See Ref. 107, pp. 3–10

319. Slobin M. 1993. *Subcultural Sounds: Micromusics of the West.* Hanover, NH: Wesleyan Univ. Press

320. Sloboda JA. 1985. *The Musical Mind.* Oxford: Oxford Univ. Press

321. Smith H, Stevens K. 1967. Unique vocal abilities of certain Tibetan lamas. *Am. Anthropol.* 69:209–12

322. Spencer P. 1985. *Society and the Dance.* Cambridge: Cambridge Univ. Press

323. Springer G. 1956. Language and music: parallels and divergences. See Ref. 118, pp. 504–13

324. Steiner W, ed. 1981. *The Sign in Music and Literature.* Austin: Univ. Texas Press

325. Stern T. 1957. Drum and whistle languages: an analysis of speech surrogates. *Am. Anthropol.* 59:487–506

326. Stone R. 1981. Toward a Kpelle conceptualization of music performance. *J. Am. Folklore* 94(372):188–206

327. Storr A. 1992. *Music and the Mind.* New York: Free Press

328. Sundberg J. 1969. Articulatory differences between spoken and sung vowels. *Speech Transmission Lab. Q. Progr. Status Rep.* 1:33–46. Stockholm: Royal Inst. Technol.

329. Sundberg J. 1977. The acoustics of the singing voice. *Sci. Am.* 231(3):82–91

330. Sundberg J. 1987. *The Science of the Singing Voice.* Dekalb: N. Ill. Univ. Press

331. Sundberg J, Lindblom B. 1976. Generative theories in language and music descriptions. *Cognition* 4(1):99–122

332. Supicic I. 1987. *Music and Society: A Guide to the Sociology of Music.* New York: Pendragon

333. Tagg P. 1982. Analysing popular music: theory, method, and practice. *Pop. Music* 2:37–68

334. Tarasti E. 1987. Basic concepts of studies in musical signification: a report on a new international research project in semiotics of music. See Ref. 293, pp. 405–584

335. Tedlock B. 1980. Songs of the Zuni Kachina Society: composition, rehearsal, and performance. See Ref. 106, pp. 7–35

336. Tedlock D. 1983. *The Spoken Word and the Work of Interpretation.* Philadelphia: Univ. Penn. Press

337. Titon JT. 1977. *Early Downhome Blues: A Musical and Cultural Analysis.* Urbana: Univ. Ill. Press

338. Titon JT. 1988. *Powerhouse for God: Speech, Chant and Song in an Appalachian Baptist Church.* Austin: Univ. Texas Press

339. Tiwary KM. 1978. Tuneful weeping: a mode of communication. *Frontiers* 3(3): 24–27

340. Tolbert E. 1990. Women cry with words: symbolization of affect in the Karelian lament. *Yearb. Tradit. Music* 22:80–105

341. Tolbert E. 1990. Magico-religious power and gender in the Karelian lament. See Ref. 128, pp. 41–56

342. Trager GL. 1958. Paralanguage: a first approximation. *Stud. Ling.* 13:1–12

343. Tran Quang H, Guillou D. 1980. Original research and acoustical analysis in connection with the *xöömij* style of biphonic singing. In *Musical Voices of Asia,* ed. R Emmert, Y Minegishi, pp. 162–73. Tokyo: Heibonsha

344. Trawick M. 1986. Iconicity in Paraiyar crying songs. In *Another Harmony: New Essays on the Folklore of India,* ed. AK Ramanujan, S Blackburn, pp. 294–344. Berkeley: Univ. Calif. Press

345. Trawick M. 1990. *Notes on Love in a Tamil Family.* Berkeley: Univ. Calif. Press

346. Turino T. 1989. The coherence of social style and musical creation among the Aymara in Southern Peru. *Ethnomusicology* 33(1):1–30

347. Turino T. 1990. Structure, context, and strategy in musical ethnography. *Ethnomusicology* 34(3):399–412

348. Turino T. 1993. *Moving Away from Silence: Music of the Peruvian Altiplano and the Experience of Urban Migration.* Chicago: Univ. Chicago Press

349. Turner V. 1969. *The Ritual Process.* Chicago: Aldine

350. Umiker DJ. 1974. Speech surrogates: drum and whistle systems. In *Current Trends in Linguistics,* ed. TA Sebeok, 12:497–536. The Hague: Mouton

351. Umiker-Sebeok DJ, Sebeok TA, eds. 1976. *Speech Surrogates: Drum and Whistle Languages,* Vols. 1–2. The Hague: Mouton

352. Urban G. 1985. The semiotics of two

speech styles in Shokleng. See Ref. 231, pp. 311–29

353. Urban G. 1988. Ritual wailing in Amerindian Brazil. *Am. Anthropol.* 90:385–400

354. Urban G. 1991. *A Discourse-Centered Approach to Culture.* Austin: Univ. Texas Press

355. van Gennep A. 1960. *The Rites of Passage.* Chicago: Univ. Chicago Press

356. Vaughan K. 1990. Exploring emotion in sub-structural aspects of Karelian lament: application of time series analysis to digitized melody. *Yearb. Tradit. Music* 22:106–22

357. Wachsmann K. 1982. The changeability of musical experience. *Ethnomusicology* 26(2):197–216

358. Wade B. 1976. Prolegomenon to the study of song texts. *Yearb. Int. Folk Music Counc.* 8:73–88

359. Wadley S. 1991. Why does Ram Swarup sing? Song and speech in the North Indian epic *Dhola.* In *Gender, Genre, and Power in South Asian Expressive Traditions,* ed. A Appadurai, F Korom, M Mills, pp. 210–23. Philadelphia: Univ. Penn. Press

360. Wagner R. 1986. *Symbols That Stand for Themselves.* Chicago: Univ. Chicago Press

361. Walser R. 1993. *Running With the Devil: Power, Gender, and Madness in Heavy Metal Music.* Hanover, NH: Wesleyan Univ. Press

362. Waterman CA. 1990. 'Our tradition is a very modern tradition': popular music and the construction of pan-Yoruba identity. *Ethnomusicology* 34(3):367–80

363. Waterman CA. 1990. *Jùjú: A Social History and Ethnography of an African Popular Music.* Chicago: Univ. Chicago Press

364. Waugh L, Van Schooneveld CH, eds. 1980. *The Melody of Language.* Baltimore: Univ. Park Press

365. Weiner J. 1991. *The Empty Place.* Bloomington: Ind. Univ. Press

366. Wescott RW. 1980. *Sound and Sense: Linguistic Essays on Phonosemic Subjects.* Lake Bluff, IL: Jupiter

367. Wickett E. 1993. *For our destinies: the funerary laments of Upper Egypt.* PhD thesis. Univ. Penn.

368. Woodbury AC. 1987. Rhetorical structure in a Central Alaskan Yupik Eskimo traditional narrative. See Ref. 312, pp. 176–239

369. Woodbury AC. 1992. Prosodic elements and prosodic structures in natural discourse. See Ref. 200, pp. 241–53

370. Yamada Y. 1983. Musical performance as a means of socialization among the Iatmoi. *Bikmaus* 4(3):2–16

371. Yung B. 1983. Creative process in Cantonese opera. I: The role of linguistic tones. *Ethnomusicology* 27(1):29–48

372. Yung B. 1983. Creative process in Cantonese opera. II: The process of *t'ien tz'u* (textsetting). *Ethnomusicology* 27(2):297–318

373. Yung B. 1983. Creative process in Cantonese opera. III: The role of padding syllables. *Ethnomusicology* 27(3):439–56

374. Zemp H. 1978. 'Are'are classification of musical types and instruments. *Ethnomusicology* 22(1):37–67

375. Zemp H. 1979. Aspects of 'Are'are musical theory. *Ethnomusicology* 23(1):5–48

376. Zemp H. 1987. *Head voice, chest voice.* Meudon: CNRS Audiovisuel. (Film)

377. Zemp H. 1990. Visualizing music structure through animation: the making of the film *Head voice, chest voice. Vis. Anthropol.* 3:65–79

378. Zemp H, Tran Quang H. 1989. *The song of harmonics.* Meudon: CNRS Audiovisuel (Film)

379. Zuckerkandl V. 1956. *Sound and Symbol: Music and the External World.* Princeton, NJ: Princeton Univ. Press

Annu. Rev. Anthropol. 1994. 23:55–82

LANGUAGE IDEOLOGY

Kathryn A. Woolard

Department of Sociology, University of California, San Diego, La Jolla, California 92093

Bambi B. Schieffelin

Department of Anthropology, New York University, New York, New York 10003

KEY WORDS: language politics, literacy, language and colonialism, language contact, linguistics

INTRODUCTION

The terms *ideology* and *language* have appeared together frequently in recent anthropology, sociolinguistics, and cultural studies, sometimes joined by *and,* sometimes by *in,* sometimes by a comma in a trinity of nouns. We have had analyses, some of them very influential, of cultural and political ideologies as constituted, encoded, or enacted in language (100, 239, 298). This review is differently, and (on the surface) more narrowly, conceived: our topic is ideologies *of* language, an area of scholarly inquiry just beginning to coalesce (185). There is as much cultural variation in ideas about speech as there is in speech forms themselves (158). Notions of how communication works as a social process, and to what purpose, are culturally variable and need to be discovered rather than simply assumed (22:16). We review here selected research on cultural conceptions of language—its nature, structure, and use—and on conceptions of communicative behavior as an enactment of a collective order (277:1–2). Although there are varying concerns behind the studies reviewed, we emphasize language ideology as a mediating link between social structures and forms of talk.

Ideologies of language are significant for social as well as linguistic analysis because they are not only about language. Rather, such ideologies envision and enact links of language to group and personal identity, to aesthetics, to morality, and to epistemology (41, 104, 186). Through such linkages, they often underpin fundamental social institutions. Inequality among groups of speakers, and colonial encounters *par excellence,* throw language ideology into high relief. As R. Williams observed, "a definition of language is always, implicitly or explicitly, a definition of human beings in the world" (320:21). Not only linguistic forms but social institutions such as the nation-state, schooling, gender, dispute settlement, and law hinge on the ideologization of language use. Research on gender and legal institutions has contributed important and particularly pointed studies of language ideology, but they are reviewed elsewhere (see 81, 213).

Heath (135) observed that social scientists have resisted examining language ideology because it represents an indeterminate area of investigation with no apparent bounds, and as reviewers we note this with wry appreciation even as we find that the resistance has worn down. Although there have been recent efforts to delimit language ideology (138a, 327), there is no single core literature. Moreover, linguistic ideology, language ideology, and ideologies of language are all terms currently in play. Although different emphases are sometimes signaled by the different terms, with the first focusing more on formal linguistic structures[1] and the last on representations of a collective order, the fit of terms to distinctive perspectives is not perfect, and we use them interchangeably here.

At least three scholarly discussions, by no means restricted to anthropology, explicitly invoke language or linguistic ideology, often in seeming mutual unawareness. One such group of studies concerns contact between languages or language varieties (118, 133, 135, 152, 219, 249, 285). The recently burgeoning historiography of linguistics and public discourses on language has produced a second explicit focus on language ideologies, including scientific ideologies (173, 256, 268). Finally, there is a significant, theoretically coherent body of work on linguistic ideology concentrating on its relation to linguistic structures (214, 237, 258, 275). Beyond research that explicitly invokes the term ideology are numerous studies that address cultural conceptions of language, in the guise of metalinguistics, attitudes, prestige, standards, aesthetics, hegemony, etc. There is an emerging consensus that what people think, or take for granted, about language and communication is a topic that rewards investigation, and the area of study is in need of some coordination.

We note a particularly acute irony in our task of delimiting this emerging field. One point of the comparative study of language ideology is to show the cultural and historical specificity of visions of language, yet as reviewers we

---

[1]
   See Silverstein (279:312, footnote) for an account of why this should be.

must decide what counts as language. We run the risk of excluding work in which language does not seem focal precisely because the group studied does not compartmentalize and reify social practices of communicating, does not turn Humboldt's *energeia* (activity) of language into *ergon* (product) as does the European-American tradition (41, 155, 198, 203, 258). Our purpose is not to distinguish ideology of language from ideology in other domains of human activity. Rather, the point is to focus the attention of anthropological scholars of language on the ideological dimension, and to sharpen the understanding of linguistic issues among students of ideology, discourse, and social domination.

WHAT IS LINGUISTIC IDEOLOGY?

Linguistic/language ideologies have been defined as "sets of beliefs about language articulated by users as a rationalization or justification of perceived language structure and use" (275:193); with a greater social emphasis as "self-evident ideas and objectives a group holds concerning roles of language in the social experiences of members as they contribute to the expression of the group" (135:53) and "the cultural system of ideas about social and linguistic relationships, together with their loading of moral and political interests" (162:255); and most broadly as "shared bodies of commonsense notions about the nature of language in the world" (258:346). Some of the differences among these definitions come from debates about the concept of ideology itself. Those debates have been well reviewed elsewhere (9, 31, 78, 100, 298, 327), but it is worthwhile to mention some of the key dimensions of difference.

The basic division in studies of ideology is between neutral and critical values of the term. The former usually encompasses all cultural systems of representation; the latter is reserved for only some aspects of representation and social cognition, with particular social origins or functional or formal characteristics. Rumsey's definition of linguistic ideology is neutral (258). For Silverstein, rationalization marks linguistic ideology within the more general category of metalinguistics, pointing toward the secondary derivation of ideologies, their social-cognitive function, and thus the possibility of distortion (275). Ideological distortion in this view comes from inherent limitations on awareness of semiotic process and from the fact that speech is formulated by its users as purposive activity in the sphere of interested human social action. In critical studies of ideology, distortion is viewed as mystification and is further traced to the legitimation of social domination. This critical stance often characterizes studies of language politics and of language and social class.

A second division is the siting of ideology. Some researchers may read linguistic ideology from linguistic usage, but others insist that the two must be carefully differentiated (164). While metalinguistic discourse, as Silverstein suggested, is a sufficient condition for identifying ideology, Rumsey's "commonsense notions" (258) and Heath's "self-evident ideas" (135) may well be unstated assumptions of cultural orthodoxy, difficult to elicit directly. Although ideology in general is often taken as explicitly discursive, influential theorists have seen it as behavioral, pre-reflective, or structural, that is, an organization of signifying practices not in consciousness but in lived relations (see 78 for a review). An alertness to the different sites of ideology may resolve some apparent controversies over its relevance to the explanation of social or linguistic phenomena.

The work we review here includes the full range of scholars' notions of ideology: from seemingly neutral cultural conceptions of language to strategies for maintaining social power, from unconscious ideology read from speech practices by analysts to the most conscious native-speaker explanations of appropriate language behavior. What most researchers share, and what makes the term useful in spite of its problems, is a view of ideology as rooted in or responsive to the experience of a particular social position, a facet indicated by Heath's (135) and Irvine's (162) definitions. This recognition of the social derivation of representations does not simply invalidate them if we recognize that there is no privileged knowledge, including the scientific, that escapes grounding in social life (205). Nonetheless, the term ideology reminds us that the cultural conceptions we study are partial, contestable and contested, and interest-laden (151:382). A naturalizing move that drains the conceptual of its historical content, making it seem universally and/or timelessly true, is often seen as key to ideological process. The emphasis of ideological analysis on the social and experiential origins of systems of signification counters this naturalization of the cultural, in which anthropology ironically has participated (9). Some of the work reviewed here may seem to be simply what anthropology "has always been talking about anyway" as culture now in the guise of ideology (31:26), but the reconceptualization implies a methodological stance (279). The term ideology reminds analysts that cultural frames have social histories and it signals a commitment to address the relevance of power relations to the nature of cultural forms and ask how essential meanings about language are socially produced as effective and powerful (9, 78, 241).

APPROACHES TO LANGUAGE IDEOLOGY

Language ideology has been received principally as an epiphenomenon, an overlay of secondary and tertiary responses (34, 36), possibly intriguing but relatively inconsequential for the fundamental questions of both anthropology and linguistics. But several methodological traditions and topical foci have encouraged attention to cultural conceptions of language. We review work in several areas: ethnography of speaking; politics of multilingualism; literacy studies; historiography of linguistics and public discourse on language; and metapragmatics and linguistic structure. There are many connections among these, but the work tends to form different conversations, varying in the social and linguistic themes they foreground. Our bibliography is a representative sampling of the research done in these areas. To illustrate some of the social variation in conceptions of language, and in the institutions and interests to which they are tied, we reach back to earlier studies that were not conceived in the frame of ideological analysis, but which we believe can be rethought profitably in relation to the concerns outlined above.

ETHNOGRAPHY OF SPEAKING

The ethnography of speaking has long given attention to ideology as neutral, cultural conceptions of language, primarily through description of vernacular speech taxonomies and metalinguistics (24, 121, 242). The ethnography of speaking was chartered to study ways of speaking from the point of view of events, acts, and styles, but Hymes (158) suggested that an alternative focus on beliefs, values and attitudes, or on contexts and institutions would make a different contribution. This alternative enterprise has been taken up more recently. Language ideology has been made increasingly explicit as a force shaping the understanding of verbal practices (21, 46, 91, 138b, 210, 272, 303). Genres are now viewed not as sets of discourse features, but rather as "orienting frameworks, interpretive procedures, and sets of expectations" (128:670; see also 23, 42, 43). Local conceptions of talk as self-reflexive action have been explored for a variety of genres such as oratory (210), disputes (38, 116, 186, 188, 196), conflict management (253, 315), and also as the foundation of aesthetics in such areas as music (90).

Ethnographers of speaking have studied the grounding of language beliefs in other cultural and social forms. For example, language socialization studies have demonstrated connections among folk theories of language acquisition, linguistic practices, and key cultural ideas about personhood (49, 63, 138, 187, 217, 231–234, 262, 267, 284).

The eventual critical response of the ethnography of speaking (158) to speech act theory (13, 270) stimulated thought about linguistic ideology. Speech act theory is grounded in an English linguistic ideology, a privatized view of language emphasizing the psychological state of the speaker while downplaying the social consequences of speech (308:22; cf 244, 255, 275). This recognition triggered taxonomic studies of conceptualizations of speech acts in specific linguistic communities (308, 318), research on metapragmatic universals (309, 310), and numerous ethnographic challenges to the key assumptions of speech act theory (74, 150, 178, 221). Ethnographers of Pacific societies identified the centrality of intention to speech act theory as rooted in Western conceptions of the self, and argued that its application to other societies obscures local methods of producing meaning (75, 76, 230, 292a).

As is true of cultural anthropology in general, ethnographers of speaking have increasingly incorporated considerations of power in their analyses, again leading to a more explicit focus on linguistic ideology. Bauman's (22) historical ethnography of language and silence in Quaker ideology was an important development, because it addressed a more formal, conscious, and politically strategic form of ideology. Silence has been recognized as carrying a paradoxical potential for power that depends greatly on its varying ideologization within and across communities (103). Advocating a view of linguistic ideology as interactional resource rather than shared cultural background, Briggs finds social power achieved through the strategic use not just of particular discursive genres, but of talk about such genres and their appropriate use (41). Speakers in multilingual communities have marshaled purist language ideologies to similar interactional ends (146; see discussion of purism below.) Ethnographers have also seen the role of language ideology in creating power in other guises and moments: the display of gender and/or affect (26, 28, 143, 163, 175, 188, 232), the strategic deployment of honorifics (3), the regulation of marriage choices (167), and the display of powerful new social affiliations and identities introduced through missionization (187, 254, 314).

LANGUAGE CONTACT, COMPETITION, AND POLITICS

Research on self-conscious struggles over language in class-stratified and especially multilingual communities has treated language ideologies as socially, politically, and/or linguistically significant, even when the researcher's primary interest may be in debunking such ideologies (64, 84, 277).

The identification of a language with a people has been given the most attention (95, 160, 302). It is a truism that the equation of language and nation is a historical, ideological construct (61, 69, 118, 127, 201), conventionally dated to Herder and eighteenth century German romanticism, although the famous characterization of language as the genius of a people can be traced to the French Enlightenment and specifically Condillac (1, 179, 235). Exported through colonialism to become a dominant model around the world today, the nationalist ideology of language structures state politics, challenges multilingual states, and underpins ethnic struggles to such an extent that the absence of a distinct language can cast doubt on the legitimacy of claims to nationhood (33:359; 4, 32, 51, 61, 87, 95, 115, 140, 171, 176, 202, 238, 243, 299, 305, 307, 317, 319, 323, 325).

Ironically, movements to save minority languages are often structured around the same notions of language that have led to their oppression and/or suppression (5, 6, 32, 80, 169, 206, 305), although traditional or emergent views that resist this hegemonic construction have been documented (10, 57, 105, 306). The equation of one language/one people, the Western insistence on the authenticity and moral significance of the mother tongue, and associated assumptions about the importance of purist language loyalty for the maintenance of minority languages have all been criticized as ideological red herrings, particularly in settings where multilingualism is more typical and where a fluid or complex linguistic repertoire is valued (10, 176, 194, 206, 238, 273, 282). Modern linguistic theory itself has been seen as framed and constrained by the one language/one people assumption (194).

Although the validity of the nationalist ideology of language has often been debated or debunked, less attention traditionally has been given to understanding how the view of language as symbolic of self and community has taken hold in so many different settings. Where linguistic variation appears to be simply a diagram of social differentiation, the analyst needs to identify the ideological production of that diagram (162). Recent studies of language politics have begun to examine specifically the content and signifying structure of nationalist language ideologies (127, 277, 285, 326).

Peirce's semiotic categories have been used to analyze the processes by which chunks of linguistic material gain significance as representations of particular populations (104). Researchers have distinguished language as an index of group identity from language as a metalinguistically created symbol of identity, more explicitly ideologized in discourse (105, 168, 302). Irvine (162) finds that Wolof villagers construe linguistic differentiation as iconically related to social differentiation, distinguishing inter- and intra-lingual variation and devising a migration history for a particular caste to match their linguistic difference. Here we see how linguistic ideology can affect the interpretation of social relations.

Mannheim (204) also notes different cultural ideologies of different kinds of linguistic variation in southern Peru. Endogenous variation in Quechua, which is seen simply as natural human speech, is not socially evaluated by speakers. But in Spanish, which is regarded as pure artifice, phonological markers and stereotypes are common and lead to hypercorrection among second-language speakers. In this case, linguistic ideology drives linguistic change along different paths.

Language varieties that are regularly associated with (and thus index) particular speakers are often revalorized—or misrecognized (37)—not just as symbols of group identity, but as emblems of political allegiance or of social, intellectual, or moral worth (37, 72, 79, 101, 102, 120, 149, 195, 207, 277, 325). Although the extensive body of research on linguistic prestige and language attitudes grew up in a social psychological framework (109), the intrapersonal attitude can be recast as a socially-derived intellectualized or behavioral ideology (Bourdieu's *habitus*) (37, 107, 119, 144, 149, 153, 200, 251, 311, 324, 325, 328). Such meanings affect patterns of language acquisition, style-switching, shift, change, and policy (120, 251). Moreover, symbolic revalorization often makes discrimination on linguistic grounds publicly acceptable, whereas the corresponding ethnic or racial discrimination is not (156, 193, 197, 219, 326). However, simply asserting that struggles over language are really about racism does not constitute analysis. Such a tearing aside of the curtain of mystification in a "Wizard of Oz theory of ideology" (9) begs the question of how and why language comes to stand for social groups in a manner that is socially both comprehensible and acceptable. The current program of research is to address both the semiotic and the social process.

Communities not only evaluate but may appropriate some part of the linguistic resources of groups with whom they are in contact and in tension, refiguring and incorporating linguistic structures in ways that reveal linguistic and social ideologies (146). Linguistic borrowing might appear superficially to indicate speakers' high regard for the donor language. But Hill (148) argues that socially-grounded linguistic analysis of Anglo-American borrowings and humorous misrenderings of Spanish reveals them as racist distancing strategies that reduce complex Latino experience to a subordinated, commodity identity. The commodification of ethnolinguistic stereotypes, ostensibly positive, is also seen in the use of foreign languages in Japanese television advertising (124). The appropriation of creole speech, music, and dress by white adolescents in South London, who see only matters of style (again, commodified), is in tension with black adolescent views of these codes as part of their distinctive identity (143). Basso (20) classically describes a Western Apache metalinguistic joking genre that uses English to parody "Whiteman" conversational pragmatics, in a representation of and comment on ethnolinguistic differences and their role in unequal relations. In the Javanese view, learning to translate (into high Javanese from low) is the essence of becoming a true adult and a real language speaker, and Siegel (273) argues that Javanese metaphorically incorporates foreign languages into itself by treating other languages as if they were low Javanese. Whether a code is a language or not depends on whether its speakers act like speakers of Javanese. Encounters with the languages of others may trigger recognition of the opacity of language and concern for delineating and characterizing a distinctive community language (259).

Linguistic ideology is not a predictable, automatic reflex of the social experience of multilingualism in which it is rooted; it makes its own contribution as an interpretive filter in the relationship of language and society (211). The failure to transmit vernaculars intergenerationally may be rationalized in various ways, depending on how speakers conceptualize the links of language, cognition, and social life. For example, Nova Scotian parents actively discourage children from acquiring a subordinated vernacular, because they believe it will somehow mark their English (211); Gapun parents blame their children's dissatisfaction and aggression as the roots of the loss of the vernacular (187); and Haitian parents in New York City believe their children will speak Kreyòl regardless of the input language (263; cf 329).

Beliefs about what is or is not a real language, and underlying these beliefs, the notion that there are distinctly identifiable languages that can be isolated, named, and counted, enter into strategies of social domination. Such beliefs, and related schemata for ranking languages as more or less evolved, have contributed to profound decisions about, for example, the civility or even the humanity of subjects of colonial domination (93, 166, 204, 216, 236). They also qualify or disqualify speech varieties from certain institutional uses and their speakers from access to domains of privilege (37, 57, 68, 120, 191, 288). Language mixing, codeswitching, and creoles are often evaluated as indicating less than full linguistic capabilities, revealing assumptions about the nature of language implicitly based in literate standards and a pervasive tenet that equates change with decay (25, 120, 127, 174, 224, 251, 265). Written form, lexical elaboration, rules for word formation, and historical derivation are often seized on in diagnosing real language and ranking the candidates (111, 165, 235, 287). Grammatical variability and the question of whether a variety has a grammar play an important part (80). The extension of the notion of grammar from the explicitly artifactual product of scholarly intervention to an abstract underlying system has done nothing to mute the polemics (222).

Language Policy

Macrosocial research on language planning and policy has traced distinctive ideological assumptions about the role of language in civic and human life (2, 18, 19, 33, 228, 285, 322, 326) and distinctive stances toward the state regulation of language, for example, between England and France (65, 118, 136, 139, 201). Cobarrubias has sketched a taxonomy of language ideologies underlying planning efforts: assimilation, pluralism, vernacularization, and internationalization (4, 51). At an even more fundamental level, Ruiz (257) distinguishes three fundamental orientations to language as resource, problem, or right (see also 152), and commentators on bilingual and immigrant education have noted such orientations conflated within these programs (117, 135). The model of development is pervasive in post-colonial language planning, with paradoxical ideological implications that condemn languages, like societies, to perennial status as underdeveloped (32, 87, 110).

DOCTRINES OF CORRECTNESS, STANDARDIZATION, AND PURISM

Since Dante's time, the selection and elaboration of a linguistic standard has stood for a complex of issues about language, politics, and power (289). The existence of a language is always a discursive project rather than an established fact (259). Standard languages and/or their formation had been studied earlier by philologists, Prague School functional linguists, and applied linguists (52, 96, 134), but the emphasis on the ideological dimension has given rise to new analyses of language standardization (172), with the concept of a standard treated more as ideological process than as empirical linguistic fact (16, 65, 112, 194, 219).

Notions of better and worse speech have been claimed to exist in every linguistic community (35), but this claim has been disputed (132). There is more agreement that codified, superposed standard languages are tied not only to writing and its associated hegemonic institutions, but to specifically European forms of these institutions (35, 131, 132, 172, 219, 277, 286). In the vernacular belief system of Western culture, language standards are not recognized as human artifacts, but are naturalized by metaphors such as that of the free market (172, 277). Ideological analysis addresses questions such as how doctrines of linguistic correctness and incorrectness are rationalized or how they are related to doctrines of the inherent representational power, beauty, and expressiveness of language as a valued mode of action (276:223; 18). Moral indignation over nonstandard forms derives from ideological associations of the standard with the qualities valued within the culture, such as clarity or truthfulness (70, 118, 145, 172, 276:241; 293).

Purist doctrines of linguistic correctness close off non-native sources of innovation, but usually selectively, targeting only languages construed as threats (316; cf 142, 297). The linguistic effects of purism are not predictable, and similarly, its social meaning and strategic use are not transparent (99, 171). An apparently purist linguistic conservatism among the Tewa may derive not from resistance to contact phenomena at all, but from the strength of theocratic institutions and of ritual linguistic forms as models for other domains of interaction (182, 183, 184). In contrast, an ideology of the sanctity of language in an ultraorthodox Jewish community leads to the restriction of the Hebrew language to sacred contexts (113). Mexicano vernacular purist ideologies are deployed paradoxically to enhance the authority of those who are least immersed in the vernacular and most enmeshed with the larger economy (146, 149). Some Spanish loanwords sound more authentic to non-elite members of the Gallego speech community in Spain, who dissociate themselves from the linguistically pure forms that smack of institutional minority politics (5, 6). Such complex relations among social position, linguistic practice, and purist ideologies illustrate the importance of problematizing ideology rather than assuming that it can be read from one of the other two elements.

Orthography

In countries where identity and nationhood are under negotiation, every aspect of language, including its phonological description and forms of graphic representation can be contested (226, 265). Even where nationhood is as classically well-established as it is in France, orthographic battles flare. Thus, orthographic systems cannot be conceptualized simply as reducing speech to writing, but rather they are symbols that carry historical, cultural, and political meanings (62, 96, 154, 169, 300). In some creoles, for example, supporters of etymological orthographies appeal to an historical connection to the prestige of the colonizing language. Those favoring a phonemic approach argue that a more objective mode of representing the sounds allows wider access to literacy and helps establish the language as respectable in its own right (44, 141, 199, 265, 321).

LITERACY

Ideologies of literacy have complex relations to ideologies of speech and can play distinctive, crucial roles in social institutions. Even the conceptualization of the printed word can differ importantly from that of the written (7, 313). Derrida's (71) deconstruction of a Western view of speech as natural, authentic, and prior to the mere lifeless inscriptions of alien, arbitrary writing, has brought considerable attention to ideas about the spoken and written word. Eighteenth century Japanese elite notions of language also included a phonocentric ideology stressing the primacy, immediacy, and transparency of speech over writing (259). Javanese do not share the view of the original voice as the authentic (273). Not all commentators on Western ideology find the oral bias Derrida describes. Harris (131) argues that a scriptism founded in European literate experience is smuggled into the apparent oral bias of contemporary linguistic concepts, from the sentence through the word to the phoneme. Mignolo (216) asserts that the supremacy of the oral in Plato's *Phaedrus* was inverted and the ideology of the alphabetic letter was established in Renaissance Europe. Tyler (301) sees a Western visualist ideological emphasis on transparent, referential discourse as rooted in the primacy of text and the suppression of speech.

Anthropological studies of literacy (e.g. its introduction in oral societies or its use in schooling) recognized belatedly that it is not an autonomous, neutral technology, but rather is culturally organized, ideologically grounded, and historically contingent, shaped by political, social, and economic forces (53, 56, 58, 60, 97, 138, 161, 223, 266, 269, 290–292). Research now emphasizes the diversity of ways in which communities "take up" literacy, sometimes altering local forms of communication or fundamental concepts of identity (15, 27, 29, 30, 37a, 77, 88, 114, 138, 214a, 252, 264). Considerations of power significantly affect literacy strategies. In Gapun, views of language as a powerful means to transform the world are extended to literacy in Tok Pisin, which is thought to enable acquisition of valuable cargo (189). In contrast, Yekuana do not extend their view of speech to literacy. Spoken words are transformative and magical, but inscription destroys their power (122). For Chambri (108) and Yekuana, "fixity" in writing is the source of danger; printed words are not responsive to social circumstances. Maori convictions that there is an authoritative oral text captured only weakly by a written treaty are an ironic Platonic counterpoint to European-origin New Zealanders' search for a true text among multiple written translations of the treaty in which the government is rooted (208). Textual exegesis depends fundamentally on ideologies of language, or ideas about the ways texts are created and are to be understood. Contrasting approaches to locating scriptural truth can be found within the Judeo-Christian religious tradition (170).

The definition of what is and what is not literacy is always a profoundly political matter. Historical studies of the emergence of schooled literacy and school English show the association between symbolically valued literate traditions and mechanisms of social control (56, 60, 137). Analyses of classroom interaction further demonstrate how implicit expectations about written language shape discriminatory judgments about spoken language and student performance (37, 55, 215). The nineteenth century foundation of English as a university discipline created a distinction between reading as aristocratic and leisurely and writing as work. Composition as skill training for employment is the dirty work of English departments, with consequences for gender politics (58).

Transcription, or the written representation of speech, within academic disciplines and law, for example, relies on and reinforces ideological conceptions of language (73:71; 83, 120, 159, 262, 295). In studies of child language, for example, use of standard orthography forces a literal interpretation on utterances that might otherwise be seen as objects of phonological manipulation (229). On the other hand, folklorists and sociolinguists who have recorded dialects of English reveal their linguistic biases when they use non-standard orthography (sometimes called eye dialect) to represent the speech of blacks and Appalachians more than that of other groups. Given the ideology of the value of the letter, non-standard speakers thus appear less intelligent (82, 245, 246). In the American legal system the verbatim record is an idealist construction, prepared according to the court reporter's model of English, against which incoming speech is filtered, evaluated, and interpreted. It is considered information if a witness speaks ungrammatically, but not if lawyers do, and editing is applied accordingly (312).

HISTORICAL STUDIES

Although there has been a notable linguistic turn in historical studies in recent decades, Bauman noted that much of the work was linguistically naive and not grounded in an investigation of the social and ideological significance of language in people's own conceptions of the nature of language and its use (22:16). Since then, there has been a wave of historical examinations of ideologies of language, including dominant national ideologies, elite debates, and colonial expressions. Western states, and particularly France, England, and the United States, predominate in this literature, but there also has been some attention to Asia (16, 18, 65, 94, 98, 173, 180, 218, 219, 259, 281, 283). Closely linked are critical histories of linguistics and of the philosophy of language (8, 45, 106, 280), which join more traditional intellectual histories (1).

In the late eighteenth through the mid-nineteenth century in Western Europe, language became the object of civil concern as new notions of public discourse and forms of participation (and exclusion) were formulated by new participants in the public sphere (17, 22, 65, 67, 69, 118, 126, 145, 192, 276, 313). Much of the historical research focuses on normative ideas about rhetoric rather than grammar, but demonstrates how closely linked these topics were. Political conceptualizations of language rather than meditations on an autonomous language dominated French and American debates in the seventeenth through the nineteenth century (8, 12). Hegemonic English ideology drew its political and social effectiveness from a presupposition that language revealed the mind, and civilization was largely a linguistic concept (283, 294). The nineteenth century debate over language in the United States essentially was a fight over what kind of personality was needed to sustain democracy (50). The emergence of a compartmentalized democratic personality corresponded to the acceptance of style-shifting and a range of linguistic registers (see also 14, 18, 94, 123, 180, 281).

Colonial Linguistics

"Language has always been the companion of empire," asserted the sixteenth century Spanish grammarian Nebrija (161, 225). Some of the most provocative recent work on linguistic ideology, clearly tracing the links among linguistic, ideological, and social forms, comes from studies of colonialism. Which language(s) to use in colonial administration was not always obvious, and each choice had its own ideological motivations and practical consequences. An indigenous vernacular might be selected, for example, to protect the language of the colonizers from non-native versions considered distasteful (272).

European missionization and colonization of other continents entailed control of speakers and their vernaculars. Recent research on colonial linguistic description and translation has addressed the ideological dimension of dictionaries, grammars, and language guides, demonstrating that what was conceived as a neutral scientific endeavor was very much a political one (248).

In what Mignolo (216) calls the colonization of language, Europeans brought to their tasks ideas about language prevalent in the metropole, and these ideas, though themselves shifting in different historical moments, blinkered them to indigenous conceptualizations and sociolinguistic arrangements (165, 177, 216, 260). As with many other colonial phenomena, linguists constructed rather than discovered distinctive varieties (166), as Fabian (89) argues for Swahili and Harries (130) for Tsonga. Cohn argues that British grammars, dictionaries, and translations of the languages of India created the discourse of Orientalism and converted Indian forms of knowledge into European objects (54:282–283; cf 224).

Perceived linguistic structure can always have political meaning in the colonial encounter. Functional or formal inadequacy of indigenous languages and, therefore, of indigenous mind or civilization was often alleged to justify European tutelage (89). On the other hand, a sixteenth century grammar asserted that Quechua was so similar to Latin and Castilian that it was "like a prediction that the Spaniards will possess it" (216:305; see also 166, 248).

Because of the availability of documents, much of this historical research has explored the linguistic ideologies of colonizers rather than of indigenous populations. But some work seeks to capture the contradictions and interactions of the two (59, 128, 204, 216). Tongan metapragmatics of speech levels indicate a reanalysis of society that incorporates European-derived institutional complexes into Tongan constructions of social hierarchy (240). The structure and focus of a seventeenth century instructional manual on Castilian written by a Tagalog printer contrast sharply with Spanish missionaries' grammars of Tagalog, showing the different political interests behind translation for the Spanish and indigenous Filipinos (247).

Historiography of Linguistics

The close intertwining of public and scholarly conceptualizations of language in the West and its colonies through the nineteenth century leads directly to critical studies of Western philosophy of language and of the emergence of professional linguistics (1, 45, 98). Contributors to Joseph & Taylor's collection (173) examine intellectual as well as political prejudices that framed the growth of linguistic theory, from Locke through Saussure to Chomsky, and the role of linguistic ideas in specific social struggles (cf 227). Of particular relevance to our topic, Attridge (11) deconstructs Saussure's linguistics as hostile to and suppressing evidence that the language user and language community intervene, consciously or unconsciously, to alter the language system. Attridge suggests that Saussure sees language as open to external change by humanly uncontrollable forces, but rejects the influence of history as intellectual construct. A number of studies of the nineteenth century show how philology and emerging linguistics contributed to religious, class, and/or nationalist projects (65, 67, 235).

Professional, scientific linguistics in the twentieth century has nearly uniformly rejected prescriptivism, but many authors argue that this rejection hides a smuggled dependence on and complicity with prescriptive institutions for the very subject matter of the field. Rather than registering a unitary language, linguists helped to form one (66:48; 131, 132). Sankoff (261) argues that contemporary positivist linguistic methodologies that invoke a scientific rationale are imposed ideologically by the same interests that propagate normativism and prescriptivism. The idealism of modern autonomous linguistics has come under concerted ideological scrutiny (37, 157, 173, 320; cf 68, 227).

More anthropologically-oriented linguistics also has been analyzed ideologically. For example, the concept of diglossia has been criticized as an ideological naturalization of sociolinguistic arrangements (205a). Rossi-Landi (256) critiques linguistic relativism as bourgeois ideology, seeing in the theory a manifestation of guilt for the savage destruction of American Indians. The idealism of linguistic relativity transforms linguistic producers into consumers, and enables the illusion that the theoretical exhibition of the structures of a language saves the world view of the extinct linguistic workers (cf 57, 151). Schultz (268) argues that contradictory strategies in Whorf's writings arose in response to the constraint of the American folk ideology of free speech. Although his ideas paralleled those of Bakhtin, Whorf had to first convince his audience that linguistic censorship existed.

IDEOLOGY, LINGUISTIC STRUCTURE, AND LANGUAGE CHANGE

As noted earlier, modern linguistics has generally held that linguistic ideology and prescriptive norms have little significant—or, paradoxically, only pernicious—effect on speech forms (although they may have some less negligible effect on writing) (35; cf 84, 92, 125, 181). Prescriptivism does not directly transform language, but it does have an effect. Silverstein argues that a grasp of language ideology is essential for understanding the evolution of linguistic structure (276:220). Important sociolinguistic changes can be set off by ideological interpretation of language use, although because they derive only from a larger social dialectic, such changes are likely to take an unintended direction, as in the historical case of second person pronoun shift in English. To the extent that speakers conceptualize language as socially purposive action, we must look at their ideas about the meaning, function, and value of language in order to understand the extent and degree of systematicity in empirically occuring linguistic forms (cf 47, 129, 209, 212).

In analyses of gender in English, T/V pronoun shift, and Javanese speech levels, Silverstein shows that rationalization not only explains but actually affects linguistic structure, or rationalizes it by making it more regular. To understand one's own linguistic usage is potentially to change it (275:233). Imperfect, limited awareness of linguistic structures, some of which are more available to conscious reflection than are others, leads speakers to make generalizations that they then impose on a broader category of phenomena, changing those phenomena (see also 181). Structure conditions ideology, which then reinforces and expands the original structure, distorting language in the name of making it more like itself (37, 258).

Errington (86) observes that although it is standard in sociolinguistic analysis to look for relations between structural change and communicative function, it is more controversial to invoke a notion of native speaker awareness as an explanatory link. Labov differentiates mechanisms of change from below and above the level of speakers' awareness. He argues that subconscious changes are extensive and systematic, while conscious self-correction, which he labels ideology, leads to sporadic and haphazard effects on linguistic forms (190:329). But several authors note that correlational sociolinguistic models gloss over the actual motivating force of linguistic change, which often lies in social evaluations of language (85, 162, 261).

Errington (86) argues that Labov's generalization is most applicable to phonological variation, which may not be mediated by speakers' understandings of their conscious communicative projects. More pragmatically salient classes of variables are recognized by speakers as crucial linguistic mediators of social relations, and speakers' awareness makes these variables more susceptible to rationalization and strategic use (85, 240). Because such awareness and use drive linguistic change, these variables require a fundamentally different, participant-oriented analysis (86).

Irvine (162) notes that the formal linguistic characteristics of Hallidayan anti-languages, such as inversion, are not arbitrary and that they suggest the mediation of ideological conceptualizations of linguistic structures. Similarly, subordinate languages in contact situations can acquire both functional and formal properties of anti-languages. Speakers of moribund varieties of Xinca, for example, go "hog-wild" with glottalized consonants, which are exotic from the point of view of the dominant Spanish language (48). This is a Silversteinian distortion that makes a code more like itself, in this case, importantly, a self that is most distinctive from its socially dominant counterpart.

Silverstein and others give examples from European languages, especially English, that reveal a tendency to see propositionality as the essence of language, to confuse the indexical function of language with the referential function, and to assume that the divisions and structures of language should—and in the best circumstances do—transparently fit the structures of the real world (39, 162, 181, 212, 237, 250, 274, 275, 278). A focus on the surface segmentable aspects of language, a conception of language focusing on words and expressions that denote, is widely attested (32, 57, 112, 220, 277). But Rumsey (258) argues that it is not characteristic of Australian aboriginal cultures, which do not dichotomize talk and action or words and things, and Rosaldo (255) similarly asserts that Ilongots think of language in terms of action rather than reference. Hill (147) describes a counter-hegemonic ideology of language among Mexicano women that emphasizes not reference but performance and the proper accomplishment of human relationships through dialogue. See reference 151 for further discussion.

VARIATION AND CONTESTATION IN IDEOLOGY

Therborn (296:viii) characterizes ideology as a social process, not a possession, more like "the cacaphony of sounds and signs of a big city street than...the text serenely communicating with the solitary reader or the teacher...addressing a quiet, domesticated audience." The new direction in research on linguistic ideology has also moved away from seeing ideology as a homogeneous cultural template, now treating it as a process involving struggles among multiple conceptualizations and demanding the recognition of variation and contestation within a community as well as contradictions within individuals (104, 258, 279, 308). Warao strategically deploy conflicting models for language use as resources for interactional power (40, 41). German speakers in Hungary frame language and identity differently at different moments, to resist also-changing official state ideologies (105). English has an entirely different significance to New York Puerto Ricans depending on whether they think of it as spoken by white Americans, by black Americans, or by Puerto Ricans (304). Where casual generalization contrasts English and French linguistic attitudes as if they were uniform cultural attributes inhering at the state and individual level, historical studies show that such apparently characteristic national stances emerge conjuncturally from struggles among competing ideological positions (139, 201, 249).

CONCLUSION

It is paradoxical that at the same time that language and discourse have become central topics across the social sciences and humanities, linguistic anthropologists have bemoaned the marginalization of the subdiscipline from the larger field of anthropology. The topic of language ideology is a much-needed bridge between linguistic and social theory, because it relates the microculture of communicative action to political economic considerations of power and social inequality, confronting macrosocial constraints on language behavior (P Kroskrity, personal communication). It is also a potential means of deepening a sometimes superficial understanding of linguistic form and its cultural variability in political economic studies of discourse.

Many populations around the world, in multifarious ways, posit fundamental linkages among such apparently diverse cultural categories as language, spelling, grammar, nation, gender, simplicity, intentionality, authenticity, knowledge, development, power, and tradition (104). But our professional attention has only begun to turn to understanding when and how those links are forged—whether by lay participants or their expert analysts—and what their consequences might be for linguistic and social life. A wealth of public problems hinge on language ideology. Examples from the headlines of United States newspapers include bilingual policy and the official English movement; questions of free speech and harassment; the meaning of multiculturalism in schools and texts; the exclusion of jurors who might rely on their own native-speaker understanding of non-English testimony; and the question of journalists' responsibilities and the truthful representation of direct speech. Coming to grips with such public issues means coming to grips with the nature and working of language ideology.

Research on topics such as pronouns, politeness, and purism has begun the difficult program of considering whose interests are served by linguistic ideology taking the form that it does, relating notions of linguistic ideology as rooted in linguistic structure and cognitive limitations to understandings of ideology as rooted in social practices and interests (258:356). It is the attempt to link these two aspects of ideology, and to tie social and linguistic forms together through ideology, that is both most provocative and most challenging.

ACKNOWLEDGMENTS

We thank Susan Gal for encouragement to write this essay. We also wish to thank participants in the session on Language Ideologies at the 1991 American Anthropological Association Meeting and members of the Center for Transcultural Studies Working Group on Language. Their research and conversations helped shape our vision of the field. Kathryn Woolard is grateful to the National Endowment for the Humanities and the Spencer Foundation for support while preparing the review, and to Alex Halkias, Natasha Unger, and Begoña Echeverria, who helped with bibliographic work in various stages. Bambi Schieffelin thanks Paul Garrett for bibliographic assistance and Molly

Mitchell for editorial help. This essay is dedicated to Ben, whose wonderful sense of time helped organize this project.

Any *Annual Review* chapter, as well as any article cited in an *Annual Review* chapter, may be purchased from the Annual Reviews Preprints and Reprints service. 1-800-347-8007; 415-259-5017; email: arpr@class.org

Literature Cited

1. Aarsleff H. 1982. *From Locke to Saussure: Essays on the Study of Language and Intellectual History.* Minneapolis: Univ. Minn. Press
2. Adams KL, Brink DT, eds. 1990. *Perspectives on Official English: The Campaign for English as the Official Language in the USA.* Berlin: Mouton de Gruyter
3. Agha A. 1994. Honorification. *Annu. Rev. Anthropol.* 23:277–302
4. Akinnaso FN. 1991. Toward the development of a multilingual language policy in Nigeria. *Appl. Linguist.* 12(1):29–61
5. Alvarez C. 1990. *The institutionalization of Galician: linguistic practices, power and ideology in public discourse.* PhD thesis. Univ. Calif., Berkeley
6. Alvarez-Cáccamo C. 1993. The pigeon house, the octopus and the people: the ideologization of linguistic practices in Galiza. *Plurilinguismes* 6:1–26
7. Anderson B. 1983. *Imagined Communities: Reflections on the Origin and Spread of Nationalism.* London: Verso
8. Andresen J. 1990. *Linguistics in America 1769–1924: A Critical History.* London: Routledge
9. Asad T. 1979. Anthropology and the analysis of ideology. *Man* 14:607–27
10. Attinasi JJ. 1983. Language attitudes and working class ideology in a Puerto Rican barrio of New York. *Ethnic Groups* 5(1–2):55–78
11. Attridge D. 1988. *Peculiar Language.* London: Methuen
12. Auroux S. 1986. Le sujet de la langue: la conception politique de la langue sous l'ancien régime et la révolution. See Ref. 45, pp. 259–78
13. Austin JL. 1962. *How To Do Things with Words.* Cambridge, MA: Harvard Univ. Press
14. Bailey RW. 1991. *Images of English: A Cultural History of the Language.* Ann Arbor: Univ. Mich. Press
15. Baker C, Freebody P. 1986. Representations of questioning and answering in children's first school books. *Lang. Soc.* 15:451–84
16. Balibar R. 1991. La révolution française et l'universalisation du français national en France. *Hist. Eur. Ideas* 13(1/2):89–95
17. Balibar R, Laporte D. 1984. *Le français national.* Paris: Hachette
18. Baron DE. 1982. *Grammar and Good Taste: Reforming the American Language.* New Haven, CT: Yale Univ. Press
19. Baron DE. 1990. *The English Only Question: An Official Language for Americans?* New Haven, CT: Yale Univ. Press
20. Basso K. 1979. *Portraits of "the Whiteman": Linguistic Play and Cultural Symbols Among the Western Apache.* Cambridge: Cambridge Univ. Press
21. Basso K. 1988. Speaking with names. *Cult. Anthropol.* 3(2):99–131
22. Bauman R. 1983. *Let Your Words Be Few: Symbolism of Speaking and Silence Among Seventeenth-Century Quakers.* New York: Cambridge Univ. Press
23. Bauman R, Briggs CL. 1990. Poetics and performance as critical perspectives on language and social life. *Annu. Rev. Anthropol.* 19:59–88
24. Bauman R, Sherzer J, eds. 1974. *Explorations in the Ethnography of Speaking.* Cambridge: Cambridge Univ. Press
25. Bébel-Gisler D. 1981. *La langue créole force jugulée.* Paris: L'Harmattan
26. Bell AR. 1990. Separate people: speaking of Creek men and women. *Am. Anthropol.* 92(2):332–45
27. Besnier N. 1989. Literacy and feelings: the encoding of affect in Nukulaelae letters. *Text* 9(1):69–92
28. Besnier N. 1990. Language and affect. *Annu. Rev. Anthropol.* 19:419–51
29. Besnier N. 1991. Literacy and the notion of person on Nukulaelae Atoll. *Am. Anthropol.* 93(2):570–87
30. Bledsoe CH, Robey KM. 1993. Arabic literacy and secrecy among the Mende of Sierra Leone. See Ref. 291, pp. 110–34
31. Bloch M. 1985. From cognition to ideology. In *Power and Knowledge,* ed. R Fardon, pp. 21–48. Edinburgh: Scottish Academic Press
32. Blommaert J. 1994. The metaphors of de-

velopment and modernization in Tanzanian language policy and research. In *African Languages, Development and the State,* ed. R Fardon, G Furniss, pp. 213–26. London: Routledge

33. Blommaert J, Verschueren J. 1992. The role of language in European nationalist ideologies. See Ref. 185, pp. 355–75
34. Bloomfield L. 1944. Secondary and tertiary responses to language. *Language* 20:44–55
35. Bloomfield L. 1970. Literate and illiterate speech. In *A Bloomfield Anthology,* ed. C Hockett, pp. 147–56. Bloomington: Ind. Univ. Press
36. Boas F. 1911. Introduction to the Handbook of American Indian Languages. In *Bulletin of the Bureau of American Ethnology,* ed. F Boas, pp. 1–83. Washington, DC: Gov. Print. Off.
37. Bourdieu P. 1991. *Language and Symbolic Power.* Cambridge, MA: Harvard Univ. Press
37a. Boyarin J, ed. 1993. *The Ethnography of Reading.* Berkeley: Univ. Calif. Press
38. Brenneis D, Myers F, eds. 1984. *Dangerous Words: Language and Politics in the Pacific.* New York: New York Univ. Press
39. Briggs CL. 1986. *Learning How to Ask: A Sociolinguistic Appraisal of the Role of the Interview in Social Science Research.* Cambridge: Cambridge Univ. Press
40. Briggs CL. 1988. Disorderly dialogues in ritual impositions of order: the role of metapragmatics in Warao dispute mediation. *Anthropol. Linguist.* 30:448–91
41. Briggs CL. 1992. Linguistic ideologies and the naturalization of power in Warao discourse. See Ref. 185, pp. 387–404
42. Briggs CL. 1993. Genric versus metapragmatic dimensions of Warao narratives: Who regiments performance? In *Reflexive Language: Reported Speech and Metapragmatics,* ed. JA Lucy, pp. 179–212. Cambridge: Cambridge Univ. Press
43. Briggs CL, Bauman R. 1992. Genre, intertextuality, and social power. *J. Linguist. Anthropol.* 2(2):131–72
44. Brown B. 1993. The social consequences of writing Louisiana French. *Lang. Soc.* 22:67–101
45. Busse W, Trabant J, eds. 1986. *Les idéologues. Sémiotique, théories et politiques linguistiques pendant la révolution française.* Amsterdam: John Benjamins
46. Calame-Griaule G. 1986. *Words and the Dogon World.* Philadelphia: Inst. Stud. Human Issues
47. Cameron D. 1990. Demythologizing sociolinguistics: why language does not reflect society. See Ref. 173, pp. 79–96
48. Campbell L, Muntzel MC. 1989. The structural consequences of language death. See Ref. 72, pp. 181–96
49. Clancy P. 1986. The acquisition of communicative style in Japanese. In *Language Socialization across Cultures,* ed. BB Schieffelin, E Ochs, pp. 213–50. New York: Cambridge Univ. Press
50. Cmiel K. 1990. *Democratic Eloquence: The Fight Over Popular Speech in Nineteenth Century America.* Berkeley: Univ. Calif. Press
51. Cobarrubias J. 1983. Ethical issues in status planning. See Ref. 52, pp. 41–86
52. Cobarrubias J, Fishman JA, eds. 1983. *Progress in Language Planning: International Perspectives.* Berlin: Mouton de Gruyter
53. Cochran-Smith M. 1984. *The Making of a Reader.* Norwood, NJ: Ablex
54. Cohn B. 1985. The command of language and the language of command. *Subaltern Stud.* 4:276–329
55. Collins J. 1986. Differential treatment in reading instruction. In *The Social Construction of Literacy,* ed. J Cook-Gumperz, pp. 117–37. Cambridge: Cambridge Univ Press
56. Collins J. 1991. Hegemonic practice: literacy and standard language in public education. In *Rewriting Literacy: Culture and the Discourse of the Other,* ed. C Mitchell, K Wesler, pp. 229–53. New York: Bergin & Garvey
57. Collins J. 1992. Our ideologies and theirs. See Ref. 185, pp. 405–16
58. Collins J. 1993. The troubled text: history and language in basic writing programs. In *Knowledge, Culture and Power: International Perspectives on Literacy Policies and Practices,* ed. P Freebody, A Welch, pp. 162–86. Pittsburgh: Univ Pittsburgh Press
59. Comaroff J, Comaroff J. 1991. *Of Revolution and Revelation: Christianity, Colonialism and Consciousness in South Africa,* Vol. 1. Chicago: Univ. Chicago Press
60. Cook-Gumperz J. 1986. Schooling and literacy: an unchanging equation? In *The Social Construction of Literacy,* ed. J Cook-Gumperz, pp. 16–44. Cambridge: Cambridge Univ Press
61. Coulmas F, ed. 1988. *With Forked Tongues: What Are National Languages Good For?* Ann Arbor, MI: Karoma
62. Coulmas F. 1990. Language adaptation in Meiji Japan. See Ref. 317, pp. 69–86
63. Crago M. 1988. *Cultural context in communicative interaction of Inuit children.* PhD thesis. McGill Univ., Montreal
64. Crawford J. 1992. *Hold Your Tongue: Bilingualism and the Politics of "English Only."* Reading, MA: Addison-Wesley
65. Crowley T. 1989. *Standard English and the Politics of Language.* Urbana: Univ. Ill. Press
66. Crowley T. 1990. That obscure object of desire: a science of language. See Ref. 173, pp. 27–50

67. Crowley T. 1991. *Proper English? Readings in Language, History and Cultural Identity.* London: Routledge
68. Davies A. 1984. Idealization in sociolinguistics: the choice of the standard dialect. In *Georgetown University Round Table on Languages and Linguistics 1984,* ed. D Schiffrin, pp. 229–39. Washington, DC: Georgetown Univ. Press
69. de Certeau M, Julia D, Revel J. 1975. *Une politique de la langue: la révolution française et les patois.* Paris: Gallimard
70. Decrosse A. 1986. Généologie du français: purism et langue savante. In *Etats de langue,* ed. M-P Gruenais, pp. 161–200. Paris: Fondation Diderot/Fayard
71. Derrida J. 1974. *Of Grammatology.* Transl. GC Spivak. Baltimore: Johns Hopkins Univ. Press
72. Dorian NC, ed. 1989. *Investigating Obsolescence: Studies in Language Contraction and Death.* Cambridge: Cambridge Univ. Press
73. Du Bois JW. 1991. Transcription design principles for spoken discourse research. *Pragmatics* 1(1):71–106
74. Du Bois JW. 1992. Meaning without intention: lessons from divination. In *Responsibility and Evidence in Oral Discourse,* ed. JH Hill, JT Irvine, pp. 48–71. Cambridge: Cambridge Univ. Press
75. Duranti A. 1992. Intentions, self and responsibility. In *Responsibility and Evidence in Oral Discourse,* ed. JA Hill, JT Irvine, pp. 24–47. Cambridge: Cambridge Univ. Press
76. Duranti A. 1993. Intentionality and truth: an ethnographic critique. *Cult. Anthropol.* 8(2):214–45
77. Duranti A, Ochs E. 1986. Literacy instruction in a Samoan village. See Ref. 266, pp. 213–32
78. Eagleton T. 1991. *Ideology: An Introduction.* London: Verso
79. Eckert P. 1980. Diglossia: separate and unequal. *Linguistics* 18:156–64
80. Eckert P. 1983. The paradox of national language movements. *J. Multiling. Multicult. Dev.* 4(4):289–300
81. Eckert P, McConnell-Ginet S. 1992. Think practically and look locally: language and gender as community-based practice. *Annu. Rev. Anthropol.* 21:461–90
82. Edwards J. 1992. Transcription of discourse. In *International Encyclopedia of Linguistics,* ed. W Bright, pp. 367–71. New York: Oxford Univ. Press
83. Edwards J, Lampert MD, eds. 1993. *Talking Data: Transcription and Coding in Discourse Research.* Hillsdale, NJ: Erlbaum
84. Emonds J. 1985. Grammatically deviant prestige dialect constructions. In *A Festschrift for Sol Saporta,* ed. M Brame, H Contreras, F Newmeyer, pp. 93–129. Seattle: Noit Amrofer
85. Errington JJ. 1985. On the nature of the sociolinguistic sign: describing the Javanese speech levels. See Ref. 214, pp. 287–310
86. Errington JJ. 1988. *Structure and Style in Javanese: A Semiotic View of Linguistic Etiquette.* Philadelphia: Univ. Penn. Press
87. Errington JJ. 1992. On the ideology of Indonesian language development: the state of a language of state. See Ref. 185, pp. 417–26
88. Ewald J. 1988. Speaking, writing and authority: explorations in and from the kingdom of Taqali. *Comp. Stud. Soc. Hist.* 39:199–223
89. Fabian J. 1986. *Language and Colonial Power: The Appropriation of Swahili in the Former Belgian Congo 1880–1938.* Cambridge: Cambridge Univ. Press
90. Feld S, Fox A. 1994. Music and language. *Annu. Rev. Anthropol.* 23:25–53
91. Feld S, Schieffelin BB. 1981. Hard words: a functional basis for Kaluli discourse. In *Georgetown University Round Table on Languages and Linguistics 1981,* ed. D Tannen, pp. 350–70. Washington, DC: Georgetown Univ. Press
92. Ferguson CA. 1983. Language planning and language change. See Ref. 52, pp. 29–40
93. Filgueira Alvado A. 1979. Capacidad intelectual y actitud del indio ante el castellano. *Rev. Indias* 39:163–85
94. Finegan E. 1980. *Attitudes Towards Language Usage: A History of the War of Words.* New York: Teacher's College Press
95. Fishman JA. 1989. *Language and Ethnicity in Minority Sociolinguistic Perspective.* Clevedon, England: Multilingual Matters
96. Fodor I, Hagège C, eds. 1983–1990. *Language Reform: History and Future in 5 Volumes.* Hamburg: Buske Verlag
97. Forstorp P-A. 1990. Receiving and responding: ways of taking from the Bible. In *Bible Reading in Sweden: Studies Related to the Translation of the New Testament 1981,* ed. G Hansson, pp. 149–69. Uppsala: Almqvist & Wiksell
98. Foucault M. 1970. *The Order of Things.* New York: Random House
99. Frangoudaki A. 1992. Diglossia and the present language situation in Greece. *Lang. Soc.* 21(3):365–81
100. Friedrich P. 1989. Language, ideology and political economy. *Am. Anthropol.* 91(2):295–312
101. Gal S. 1987. Codeswitching and consciousness in the European periphery. *Am. Ethnol.* 14(4):637–53
102. Gal S. 1989. Language and political economy. *Annu. Rev. Anthropol.* 18:345–67
103. Gal S. 1991. Between speech and silence:

the problematics of research on language and gender. In *Gender at the Crossroads of Knowledge*, ed. M di Leonardo, pp. 175–203. Berkeley: Univ. Calif. Press

104. Gal S. 1992. Multiplicity and contention among ideologies. See Ref. 185, pp. 445–50

105. Gal S. 1993. Diversity and contestation in linguistic ideologies: German speakers in Hungary. *Lang. Soc.* 22(3):337–359

106. Gal S. 1993. *Lost in a Slavic sea: linguistic theories and expert knowledge in the making of Hungarian identity*. Presented at 92nd Annu. Meet. Am. Anthropol. Assoc., Washington, DC

107. Garcia O, Evangelista I. 1988. Spanish language use and attitudes: a study of two New York City communities. *Lang. Soc.* 17(4):475–511

108. Gewertz D, Errington F. 1991. *Twisted Histories, Altered Contexts*. Cambridge: Cambridge Univ. Press

109. Giles H, Hewstone M, Ryan EB, Johnson P. 1987. Research on language attitudes. In *Sociolinguistics: An International Handbook of the Science of Language and Society*, ed. U Ammon, 1:585–97. Berlin: Mouton de Gruyter

110. Gilliam AM. 1984. Language and "development" in Papua New Guinea. *Dialect. Anthropol.* 8(4):303–18

111. Gilman S. 1986. *Jewish Self-Hatred: Anti-Semitism and the Hidden Language of the Jews*. Baltimore: Johns Hopkins Univ. Press

112. Glinert L. 1991. The "back-to-the future" syndrome in language planning: the case of modern Hebrew. In *Language Planning: Focusschrift in Honor of Joshua A. Fishman*, ed. DF Marshall, pp. 215–43. Amsterdam: Benjamins

113. Glinert L, Shilhav Y. 1991. Holy land, holy language: a study of an ultraorthodox Jewish ideology. *Lang. Soc.* 20(1):59–86

114. Goddard C. 1990. Emergent genres of reportage and advocacy in Pitjantjatjara print media. *Aust. Aborig. Stud.* 2:27–47

115. Gold DL. 1989. A sketch of the linguistic situation in Israel today. *Lang. Soc.* 18: 361–88

116. Goldman L. 1983. *Talk Never Dies: The Language of Huli Disputes*. London: Tavistock

117. Grillo RD. 1985. *Ideologies & Institutions in Urban France: The Representation of Immigrants*. Cambridge: Cambridge Univ. Press

118. Grillo RD. 1989. *Dominant Languages: Language and Hierarchy in Britain and France*. New York: Cambridge Univ. Press

119. Gross JE. 1993. The politics of unofficial language use: Walloon in Belgium, Tamazight in Morocco. *Crit. Anthropol.* 13(2): 177–208

120. Gumperz JJ. 1982. *Discourse Strategies*. Cambridge: Cambridge Univ. Press

121. Gumperz JJ, Hymes D, eds. 1972. *Directions in Sociolinguistics: The Ethnography of Communication*. New York: Holt, Rinehart & Winston

122. Guss D. 1986. Keeping it oral: a Yekuana ethnology. *Am. Ethnol.* 13(3):413–29

123. Gustafson T. 1992. *Representative Words: Politics, Literature and the American Language 1776–1865*. Cambridge: Cambridge Univ. Press

124. Haarman H. 1989. *Symbolic Values of Foreign Language Use: From the Japanese Case to a General Sociolinguistic Perspective*. Berlin: Mouton de Gruyter

125. Haas W. 1982. On the normative character of language. In *Standard Languages: Spoken and Written*, ed. W Haas, pp. 1–36. Manchester, UK: Manchester Univ. Press

126. Habermas J. 1989. *The Structural Transformation of the Public Sphere*. Transl. T Burger. Cambridge, MA: MIT Press

127. Handler R. 1988. *Nationalism and the Politics of Culture in Quebec*. Madison: Univ. Wisc. Press

128. Hanks WF. 1987. Discourse genres in a theory of practice. *Am. Ethnol.* 14(4):668–92

129. Hanks WF. 1993. Metalanguage and pragmatics of deixis. In *Reflexive Language*, ed. JA Lucy, pp. 91–126. Cambridge: Cambridge Univ. Press

130. Harries P. 1988. The roots of ethnicity: discourse and the politics of language construction in South-East Africa. *Afr. Affairs* 87(346):25–52

131. Harris R. 1980. *The Language Makers*. London: Duckworth

132. Harris R. 1987. *The Language Machine*. London: Duckworth

133. Haviland JB. 1989. Mixtecs, migrants, multilingualism, and murder. *Work. Pap. Proc. Cent. Psychosoc. Stud.* 25. Chicago: Cent. Transcult. Stud.

134. Havranek B. 1964. The functional differentiation of the standard language. In *A Prague School Reader on Esthetics, Literary Structure, and Style*, ed. PL Garvin, pp. 3–16. Washington, DC: Georgetown Univ. Press

135. Heath SB. 1977. Social history. In *Bilingual Education: Current Perspectives*. Vol. 1: *Social Science*, pp. 53–72. Arlington, VA: Cent. Appl. Linguist.

136. Heath SB. 1980. Standard English: biography of a symbol. In *Standards and Dialects in English*, ed. T Shopen, J Williams, pp. 3–31. Cambridge, MA: Winthrop

137. Heath SB. 1981. Toward an ethnohistory of writing in American education. In *Writing: The Nature, Development and Teaching of Written Communication*, ed. MF Whiteman, 1:25—45. Hillsdale, NJ: Erlbaum

138. Heath SB. 1983. *Ways with Words.* Cambridge: Cambridge Univ. Press
138a. Heath SB. 1989. Language ideology. In *International Encyclopedia of Communications,* 2:393–95. New York: Oxford Univ. Press
138b. Heath SB. 1991. Women in conversation: covert models in American language ideology. In *The Influence of Language on Culture and Thought,* ed. R Cooper, B Spolsky, pp. 199–218. Berlin: Mouton de Gruyter
139. Heath SB, Mandabach F. 1983. Language status decisions and the law in the United States. See Ref. 52, pp. 87–105
140. Heller M. 1985. Ethnic relations and language use in Montreal. See Ref. 323, pp. 75–90
141. Hellinger M. 1986. On writing English-related Creoles in the Caribbean. In *Focus on the Caribbean,* ed. M Gorlach, J Holm, pp. 53–70. Amsterdam: Benjamins
142. Herzfeld M. 1982. *Ours Once More: Folklore, Ideology, and the Making of Modern Greece.* Austin: Univ. Texas Press
143. Hewitt R. 1986. *White Talk Black Talk.* Cambridge: Cambridge Univ Press
144. Hidalgo M. 1986. Language contact, language loyalty, and language prejudice on the Mexican border. *Lang. Soc.* 15(2):193–220
145. Higonnet P. 1980. The politics of linguistic terrorism and grammatical hegemony during the French revolution. *Soc. Hist.* 5(1):41–69
146. Hill JH. 1985. The grammar of consciousness and the consciousness of grammar. *Am. Ethnol.* 12(4):725–37
147. Hill JH. 1992. "Today there is no respect": nostalgia, "respect" and oppositional discourse in Mexicano (Nahuatl) language ideology. See Ref. 185, pp. 263–80
148. Hill JH. 1993. Hasta la vista, baby: Anglo Spanish in the American Southwest. *Crit. Anthropol.* 13:145–76
149. Hill JH, Hill KC. 1986. *Speaking Mexicano: Dynamics of Syncretic Language in Central Mexico.* Tucson: Univ. Ariz. Press
150. Hill JH, Irvine JT. 1992. Introduction. In *Responsibility and Evidence in Oral Discourse,* ed. JH Hill, JT Irvine, pp. 1–23. Cambridge: Cambridge Univ. Press
151. Hill JH, Mannheim B. 1992. Language and world view. *Annu. Rev. Anthropol.* 21:381–406
152. Hornberger N. 1988. Language planning orientations and bilingual education in Peru. *Lang. Probl. Lang. Plan.* 12(1):14–29
153. Hornberger N. 1988. Language ideology in Quechua communities of Puno, Peru. *Anthropol. Linguist.* 30(2):214–35
154. Hornberger N. 1994. Five vowels or three?: Linguistics and politics in Quechua language planning in Peru. In *Language Pol-*

icy and Language Education, ed. JW Tollefson. Cambridge: Cambridge Univ. Press. In press
155. Humboldt W. 1988. *On Language.* Transl. P Heath. Cambridge: Cambridge Univ. Press
156. Hurtado A, Rodriguez R. 1989. Language as a social problem: the repression of Spanish in South Texas. *J. Multiling. Multicult. Dev.* 10(5):401–19
157. Hymes D. 1971. On linguistic theory, communicative competence, and the education of disadvantaged children. In *Anthropological Perspectives on Education,* ed. M Wax, SA Diamond, FO Gearing, pp. 51–66. New York: Basic
158. Hymes D. 1974. *Foundations in Sociolinguistics: An Ethnographic Approach.* Philadelphia: Univ. Penn. Press
159. Hymes D. 1981. *"In Vain I Tried to Tell You."* Philadelphia: Univ. Penn. Press
160. Hymes D. 1984. Linguistic problems in defining the concept of "tribe." In *Language in Use,* ed. J Baugh, J Sherzer, pp. 7–27. Englewood Cliffs, NJ: Prentice-Hall
161. Illich I, Sanders B. 1988. *ABC: The Alphabetization of the Popular Mind.* San Francisco: North Point
162. Irvine JT. 1989. When talk isn't cheap: language and political economy. *Am. Ethnol.* 16(2):248–67
163. Irvine JT. 1990. Registering affect: heteroglossia in the linguistic expression of emotion. In *Language and the Politics of Emotion,* ed. CA Lutz, L Abu-Lughod, pp. 126–61. Cambridge: Cambridge Univ. Press
164. Irvine JT. 1992. Ideologies of honorific language. See Ref. 185, pp. 251–62
165. Irvine JT. 1993. Mastering African languages: the politics of linguistics in nineteenth-century Senegal. *Soc. Anal.* 34:27–46
166. Irvine JT. 1993. *The family romance of colonial linguistics: gender in 19th-century representations of African languages.* Presented at 92nd Annu. Meet. Am. Anthropol. Assoc., Washington, DC
167. Jackson JE. 1983. *The Fish People: Linguistic Exogamy and Tukanoan Identity in Northwest Amazonia.* Cambridge: Cambridge Univ. Press
168. Jacquemet M. 1992. "If he speaks Italian, it's better": metapragmatics in court. *Pragmatics* 2(2):111–26
169. Jaffe A. 1993. Obligation, error, and authenticity: competing cultural principles in the teaching of Corsican. *J. Linguist. Anthropol.* 3(1):99–114
170. Janowitz N. 1993. Re-creating Genesis: the metapragmatics of divine speech. In *Reflexive Language,* ed. JA Lucy, pp. 393–405. Cambridge: Cambridge Univ Press.
171. Jernudd BH, Shapiro MJ, eds. 1989. *The*

Politics of Language Purism. Berlin: Mouton de Gruyter
172. Joseph JE. 1987. *Eloquence and Power: The Rise of Language Standards and Standard Languages.* New York: Basil Blackwell
173. Joseph JE, Taylor TJ, eds. 1990. *Ideologies of Language.* New York: Routledge
174. Jourdan C. 1991. Pidgins and creoles: the blurring of categories. *Annu. Rev. Anthropol.* 20:187–209
175. Katriel T. 1986. *Talking Straight: Dugri Speech in Israeli Sabra Culture.* New York: Cambridge Univ. Press
176. Khubchandani LM. 1983. *Plural Languages, Plural Cultures: Communication, Identity, and Sociopolitical Change in Contemporary India.* Honolulu: Univ. Hawaii Press
177. Klor de Alva JJ. 1989. Language, politics and translation: colonial discourse and classic Nahuatl in New Spain. In *The Art of Translation: Voices from the Field,* ed. R Warren, pp. 143–62. Boston: Northeastern Univ. Press
178. Kochman T. 1986. Strategic ambiguity in black speech genres. *Text* 6(2):153–70
179. Koepke W, ed. 1990. *Johann Gottfried Herder: Language, History and the Enlightenment.* Columbia, SC: Camden House
180. Kramer MP. 1992. *Imagining Language in America: From the Revolution to the Civil War.* Princeton, NJ: Princeton Univ. Press
181. Kroch AS, Small C. 1978. Grammatical ideology and its effect on speech. In *Linguistic Variation: Models and Methods,* ed. D Sankoff, pp. 45–55. New York: Academic
182. Kroskrity PV. 1992. Arizona Tewa Kiva speech as a manifestation of linguistic ideology. See Ref. 185, pp. 297–310
183. Kroskrity PV. 1994. Arizona Tewa public announcements: form, function, linguistic ideology. *Anthropol. Linguist.* 35:In press
184. Kroskrity PV. 1993. *Language, History, and Identity: Ethnolinguistic Studies of the Arizona Tewa.* Tucson: Univ. Ariz. Press
185. Kroskrity PV, Schieffelin BB, Woolard KA, eds. 1992. Special Issue on Language Ideologies. *Pragmatics* 2(3):235–453
186. Kulick D. 1992. Anger, gender, language shift and the politics of revelation in a Papua New Guinean village. See Ref. 185, pp. 281–96
187. Kulick D. 1992. *Language Shift and Cultural Reproduction: Socialization, Self and Syncretism in a Papua New Guinean Village.* Cambridge: Cambridge Univ. Press
188. Kulick D. 1993. Speaking as a woman: structure and gender in domestic arguments in a New Guinea village. *Cult. Anthropol.* 8(4):510–41

189. Kulick D, Stroud C. 1990. Christianity, cargo and ideas of self. *Man* (NS) 25:70–88
190. Labov W. 1979. Locating the frontier between social and psychological factors in linguistic variation. In *Individual Differences in Language Ability and Language Behavior,* ed. CJ Fillmore, D Kempler, WS-Y Wang, pp. 327–39. New York: Academic
191. Labov W. 1982. Objectivity and commitment in linguistic evidence. *Lang. Soc.* 11:165–201
192. Landes JB. 1988. *Women and the Public Sphere in the Age of the French Revolution.* Ithaca, NY: Cornell Univ. Press
193. Leibowitz AH. 1976. Language and the law: the exercise of political power through the official designation of language. In *Language and Politics,* ed. W O'Barr, J O'Barr, pp. 449–66. The Hague: Mouton de Gruyter
194. Le Page RB. 1988. Some premises concerning the standardization of languages, with special reference to Caribbean Creole English. *Int. J. Sociol. Lang.* 71:25–36
195. Limón J. 1982. El meeting: history, folk Spanish and ethnic nationalism in a Chicano student community. In *Spanish in the United States,* ed. J Amastae, L Elías-Olivares, pp. 301–32. New York: Cambridge Univ. Press
196. Lindstrom L. 1992. Context contests: debatable truth statements on Tanna (Vanuatu). In *Rethinking Context,* ed. A Duranti, C Goodwin, pp. 101–24. Cambridge Univ. Press: Cambridge
197. Lopez DE. 1991. The emergence of language minorities in the United States. In *Language and Ethnicity: Focusschrift in Honor of Joshua A. Fishman,* ed. JR Dow, pp. 131–44. Amsterdam: Benjamins
198. Lucy JA. 1993. Reflexive language and the human disciplines. In *Reflexive Language: Reported Speech and Metapragmatics,* ed. JA Lucy, pp. 9–32. Cambridge: Cambridge Univ. Press
199. Ludwig R, ed. 1989. *Les créoles français entre l'oral et l'écrit.* Tübingen, Germany: Gunter Narr Verlag
200. Luhman R. 1990. Appalachian English stereotypes: language attitudes in Kentucky. *Lang. Soc.* 19:331–48
201. Mackey W. 1991. Language and the sovereign state. *Hist. Eur. Ideas* 13(1/2):51–61
202. Maguire G. 1991. *Our Own Language: An Irish Initiative.* Philadelphia: Multilingual Matters
203. Mannheim B. 1986. Popular song and popular grammar, poetry and metalanguage. *Word* 37(1–2):45–75
204. Mannheim B. 1991. *The Language of the Inka Since the European Invasion.* Austin, TX: Univ. Texas Press
205. Mannheim K. 1985. *Ideology and Utopia: An Introduction to the Sociology of Knowl-*

edge. San Diego: Harcourt, Brace, Jovanovich

205a. Martin-Jones M. 1989. Language, power and linguistic minorities: the need for an alternative approach to bilingualism, language maintenance and shift. In *Social Anthropology and the Politics of Language*, ed. RD Girllo, pp. 106–25. London: Routledge

206. McDonald M. 1989. *We are not French: Language, Culture, and Identity in Brittany.* London: Routledge

207. McDonogh G. 1993. Stop making sense: language, humor and the nation-state in transitional Spain. *Crit. Anthropol.* 13(2): 177–208

208. McKenzie DF. 1987. The sociology of a text: oral culture, literacy and print in early New Zealand. In *The Social History of Language*, ed. P Burke, R Porter, pp. 161–97. Cambridge: Cambridge Univ. Press

209. Meeuwis M, Brisard F. 1993. *Time and the Diagnosis of Language Change.* Antwerp Pap. Linguist. 72. Antwerp: Univ. Antwerp

210. Merlan F, Rumsey A. 1991. *Ku Waru: Language and Segmentary Politics in the Western Nebilyer Valley, Papua New Guinea.* Cambridge: Cambridge Univ. Press

211. Mertz E. 1989. Sociolinguistic creativity: Cape Breton Gaelic's linguistic "tip." See Ref. 72, pp. 103–16

212. Mertz E. 1993. Learning what to ask: metapragmatic factors and methodological reification. In *Reflexive Language: Reported Speech and Metapragmatics*, ed. JA Lucy, pp. 159–74. Cambridge: Cambridge Univ. Press

213 Mertz E. 1994. Legal language: pragmatics, poetics and social power. *Annu. Rev. Anthropol.* 23:435–55

214. Mertz E, Parmentier RJ, eds. 1985. *Semiotic Mediation: Sociocultural and Psychological Perspectives.* Orlando, FL: Academic

214a.Messick B. 1993. *The Caligraphic State: Textual Domination and History in a Muslim Society.* Berkeley: Univ. Calif. Press

215. Michaels S, Cazden C. 1986. Teacher/child collaboration as oral preparation for literacy. See Ref. 266, pp. 132–54

216. Mignolo WD. 1992. On the colonization of Amerindian languages and memories: Renaissance theories of writing and the discontinuity of the classical tradition. *Comp. Stud. Soc. Hist.* 34(2):301–30

217. Miller PJ, Potts R, Fung H, Hoogstra L, Mintz J. 1990. Narrative practices and the social construction of self in childhood. *Am. Ethnol.* 17(2):292–311

218. Miller RA. 1982. *Japan's Modern Myth: The Language and Beyond.* New York: Weatherhill

219. Milroy J, Milroy L. 1985. *Authority in Language: Investigating Language Prescription and Standardisation.* London: Routledge & Kegan Paul

220. Moore RE. 1993. Performance form and the voices of characters in five versions of the Wasco Coyote Cycle. In *Reflexive Language*, ed. JA Lucy, pp. 213–40. Cambridge Univ. Press

221. Morgan MH. 1991. Indirectness and interpretation in African American women's discourse. *Pragmatics* 1(4):421–51

222. Morgan MH. 1994. Theoretical and political arguments in African American English. *Annu. Rev. Anthropol.* 23:325–45

223. Mühlhäusler P. 1990. 'Reducing' Pacific languages to writing. See Ref. 173, pp. 189–205

224. Musa M. 1989. Purism and correctness in the Bengali speech community. See Ref. 171, pp. 105–12

225. Nebrija A. 1946. *Gramatica Castellana.* Madrid: Edic. Junta Centenario

226. Neu-Altenheimer I, Marimoutou J, Baggioni D. 1987. Névrose diglossique et choix graphiques. *Lengas* 22:33–57

227. Newmeyer FJ. 1986. *The Politics of Linguistics.* Chicago: Univ. Chicago Press

228. Nunberg G. 1989. Linguists and the official language movement. *Language* 65(3): 579–87

229. Ochs E. 1979. Transcription as theory. In *Developmental Pragmatics*, ed. E Ochs, BB Schieffelin, pp. 43–72. New York: Academic

230. Ochs E. 1984. Clarification and culture. In *Georgetown University Round Table on Languages and Linguistics 1984*, ed. D Schiffrin, pp. 325–41. Washington, DC: Georgetown Univ. Press

231. Ochs E. 1988. *Culture and Language Development.* Cambridge: Cambridge Univ. Press

232. Ochs E. 1992. Indexing gender. In *Rethinking Context*, ed. A Duranti, C Goodwin, pp. 335–58. Cambridge: Cambridge Univ. Press

233. Ochs E, Schieffelin BB. 1984. Language acquisition and socialization: three developmental stories and their implications. In *Culture Theory: Essays on Mind, Self and Emotion*, ed. R Shweder, R Levine, pp. 276–320. Cambridge: Cambridge Univ. Press

234. Ochs E, Schieffelin BB. 1994. The impact of language socialization on grammatical development. In *Handbook of Child Language*, ed. P Fletcher, B MacWhinney. New York: Basil Blackwell. In press

235. Olender M. 1992. *The Languages of Paradise: Race, Religion, and Philology in the Nineteenth Century.* Cambridge, MA: Harvard Univ. Press

236. Pagden A. 1993. *European Encounters*

with the New World: From Renaissance to Romanticism. New Haven, CT: Yale Univ. Press

237. Parmentier RJ. 1986. Puffery and pragmatics, regulation and reference. Work. Pap. Proc. Cent. Psychosoc. Stud. 4. Chicago: Cent. Transcult. Stud.

238. Pattanayak DP. 1988. Monolingual myopia and the petals of the Indian lotus: do many languages divide or unite a language? In Minority Education: From Shame to Struggle, ed. T Skutnabb-Kangas, J Cummins, pp. 379–89. Clevedon, England: Multilingual Matters

239. Pecheux M. 1982. Language, Semantics and Ideology. London: Macmillan

240. Philips S. 1991. Tongan speech levels: practice and talk about practice in the cultural construction of social hierarchy. Pac. Linguist. Ser. C 117:369–82

241. Philips S. 1992. A Marx-influenced approach to ideology and language: comments. See Ref. 185, pp. 377–86

242. Philipsen G, Carbaugh D. 1986. A bibliography of fieldwork in the ethnography of communication. Lang. Soc. 15:387–98

243. Posner R. 1993. Language conflict in Romance. In Trends in Romance Linguistics and Philology, Vol. 5: Bilingualism and Linguistic Conflict in Romance, ed. R Posner, JN Green, pp. 41–76. Berlin: Mouton de Gruyter

244. Pratt ML. 1981. The ideology of speech-act theory. Centrum (NS) 1:5–18

245. Preston DR. 1982. 'Ritin fowklower daun 'rong. J. Am. Folk. 95(377):304–26

246. Preston DR. 1985. The Li'l Abner syndrome: written representations of speech. Am. Speech 60(4):328–36

247. Rafael V. 1988. Contracting Colonialism: Translation and Christian Conversion in Tagalog Society under early Spanish Rule. Ithaca, NY: Cornell Univ. Press

248. Raison-Jourde F. 1977. L'échange inégal de la langue: La pénétration des techniques linguistiques dans une civilisation de l'oral. Annales 32:639–69

249. Reagan TG. 1986. 'Language ideology' in the language planning process: two African case studies. S. Afr. J. Afr. Lang. 6(2): 94–97

250. Reddy MJ. 1979. The conduit metaphor: a case of frame conflict in our language about language. In Metaphor and Thought, ed. A Ortony, pp. 284–324. New York: Cambridge Univ. Press

251. Rickford J. 1985. Standard and non-standard language attitudes in a creole continuum. See Ref. 323, pp. 145–60

252. Rockhill K. 1993. Gender, language, and the politics of literacy. See Ref. 291, pp. 156–75

253. Rodman WL. 1991. When questions are answers. Am. Anthropol. 93(2):421–34

254. Rosaldo MZ. 1973. I have nothing to hide: the language of Ilongot oratory. Lang. Soc. 2(2):193–223

255. Rosaldo MZ. 1982. The things we do with words: Ilongot speech acts and speech act theory in philosophy. Lang. Soc. 11: 203–37

256. Rossi-Landi F. 1973. Ideologies of Linguistic Relativity. The Hague: Mouton de Gruyter

257. Ruiz R. 1984. Orientations in language planning. Natl. Assoc. Biling. Educ. J. 8(2):15–34

258. Rumsey A. 1990. Wording, meaning and linguistic ideology. Am. Anthropol. 92(2):346–61

259. Sakai N. 1991. Voices of the Past: The Status of Language in Eighteenth-Century Japanese Discourse. Ithaca, NY: Cornell Univ. Press

260. Samarin WJ. 1984. The linguistic world of field colonialism. Lang. Soc. 13:435–53

261. Sankoff D. 1988. Sociolinguistics and syntactic variation. In Linguistics: The Cambridge Survey, Vol. IV: Language: The Socio-cultural Context, ed. FJ Newmeyer, pp. 140–61. Cambridge: Cambridge Univ. Press

262. Schieffelin BB. 1990. The Give and Take of Everyday Life: Language Socialization of Kaluli Children. New York: Cambridge Univ. Press

263. Schieffelin BB. 1994. Codeswitching and language socialization: some probable relationships. In Pragmatics: From Theory to Practice, ed. JF Duchan, LE Hewitt, RM Sonnenmeier, pp. 20–42. New York: Prentice Hall

264. Schieffelin BB, Cochran-Smith M. 1984. Learning to read culturally. In Awakening to Literacy, ed. H Goelman, A Oberg, F Smith, pp. 3–23. Exeter, NH: Heinemann Educ.

265. Schieffelin BB, Doucet RC. 1994. The "real" Haitian Creole: ideology, metalinguistics and orthographic choice. Am. Ethnol. 21(1):177–201

266. Schieffelin BB, Gilmore P, eds. 1986. The Acquisition of Literacy: Ethnographic Perspectives. Norwood, NJ: Ablex

267. Schieffelin BB, Ochs E. 1986. Language socialization. Annu. Rev. Anthropol. 15: 163–91

268. Schultz EA. 1990. Dialogue at the Margins: Whorf, Bakhtin, and Linguistic Relativity. Madison: Univ. Wisc. Press

269. Scollon R, Scollon SB. 1981. Narrative, Literacy and Face in Interethnic Communication. Norwood, NJ: Ablex

270. Searle J. 1969. Speech Acts: An Essay in the Philosophy of Language. Cambridge: Cambridge Univ. Press

271. Deleted in proof

272. Siegel J. 1987. Language Contact in a

LANGUAGE IDEOLOGY 81

Plantation Environment: A Sociolinguistic History of Fiji. Cambridge: Cambridge Univ. Press

273. Siegel JT. 1986. *Solo in the New Order: Language and Hierarchy in an Indonesian City.* Princeton: Princeton Univ. Press

274. Silverstein M. 1976. Shifters, linguistic categories, and cultural description. In *Meaning in Anthropology,* ed. KH Basso, HA Selby, pp. 11–55. Albuquerque: Univ. N. Mex. Press

275. Silverstein M. 1979. Language structure and linguistic ideology. In *The Elements: A Parasession on Linguistic Units and Levels,* ed. R Clyne, W Hanks, C Hofbauer, pp. 193–247. Chicago: Chicago Linguist. Soc.

276. Silverstein M. 1985. Language and the culture of gender: at the intersection of structure, usage and ideology. See Ref. 214, pp. 219–59

277. Silverstein M. 1987. Monoglot "standard" in America. *Work. Pap. Proc. Cent. Psychosoc. Stud.* 13. Chicago: Cent. Transcult. Stud.

278. Silverstein M. 1990. *The skin of our teeth: registers, poetics, and the first amendment.* Presented at 89th Annu. Meet. Am. Anthropol. Assoc., New Orleans

279. Silverstein M. 1992. The uses and utility of ideology: some reflections. See Ref. 185, pp. 311–24

280. Silverstein M. 1993. *From the meaning of meaning to the empires of the mind: Ogdon's orthological English.* Presented at 92nd Annu. Meet. Am. Anthropol. Assoc., Washington, DC

281. Simpson D. 1988. *The Politics of American English 1776–1850.* Oxford: Oxford Univ. Press

282. Skutnabb-Kangas T, Phillipson R. 1989. "Mother tongue": the theoretical and sociopolitical construction of a concept. In *Status and Function of Languages and Language Varieties,* ed. U Ammon, pp. 450–77. Berlin: de Gruyter

283. Smith O. 1984. *The Politics of Language 1791–1819.* New York: Oxford Univ. Press

284. Smith-Hefner NJ. 1988. The linguistic socialization of Javanese children in two communities. *Anthropol. Linguist.* 30(2): 166–98

285. Sonntag SK, Pool J. 1987. Linguistic denial and linguistic self-denial: American ideologies of language. *Lang. Probl. Lang. Plan.* 11(1):46–65

286. Southworth FC. 1985. The social context of language standardization in India. See Ref. 323, pp. 225–39

287. Speicher BL, McMahon SM. 1992. Some African-American perspectives on Black English vernacular. *Lang. Soc.* 21(3):383–408

288. Spitulnik D. 1992. Radio time sharing and the negotiation of linguistic pluralism in Zambia. See Ref. 185, pp. 335–54

289. Steinberg J. 1987. The historian and the Questione della Lingua. In *The Social History of Language,* ed. P Burke, R Porter, pp. 198–209. Cambridge: Cambridge Univ. Press

290. Street BV. 1984. *Literacy in Theory and Practice.* New York: Cambridge Univ. Press

291. Street BV, ed. 1993. *Cross-cultural Approaches to Literacy.* Cambridge: Cambridge Univ. Press

292. Street BV, Besnier N. 1994. Aspects of literacy. In *Companion Encyclopedia of Anthropology,* ed. T Ingold, pp. 527–62. London: Routledge

292a.Stroud C. 1992. The problem of intention and meaning in code-switching. *Text* 12(1): 127–55

293. Swiggers P. 1990. Ideology and the 'clarity' of French. See Ref. 173, pp. 112–30

294. Taylor C. 1987. Language and human nature. In *Interpreting Politics,* ed. MT Gibbons, pp. 101–32. New York: New York Univ. Press

295. Tedlock D. 1983. *The Spoken Word and the Work of Interpretation.* Philadelphia: Univ. Penn. Press

296. Therborn G. 1980. *The Ideology of Power and the Power of Ideology.* London: Verso

297. Thomas G. 1991. *Linguistic Purism.* London: Longman

298. Thompson JB. 1984. *Studies in the Theory of Ideology.* Cambridge: Polity

299. Trosset CS. 1986. The social identity of Welsh learners. *Lang. Soc.* 15:165–92

300. Twine N. 1991. *Language and the Modern State: The Reform of Written Japanese.* New York: Routledge

301. Tyler SA. 1987. *The Unspeakable: Discourse, Dialogue and Rhetoric in the Postmodern World.* Madison: Univ. Wisc. Press

302. Urban G. 1991. The semiotics of state-Indian linguistic relationships: Peru, Paraguay, and Brazil. In *Nation-States and Indians in Latin America,* ed. G Urban, J Sherzer, pp. 307–30. Austin: Univ. Texas Press

303. Urban G. 1993. The represented functions of speech in Shokleng myth. In *Reflexive Language,* ed. JA Lucy, pp. 241–86. Austin: Univ. Texas Press

304. Urciuoli B. 1991. The political topography of Spanish and English: the view from a New York Puerto Rican neighborhood. *Am. Ethnol.* 18(2):295–310

305. Urla J. 1988. Ethnic protest and social planning: a look at Basque language revival. *Cult. Anthropol.* 1(4):379–94

306. Urla J. 1993. Contesting modernities: language standardization and the production of an ancient/modern Basque culture. *Crit. Anthropol.* 13(2):101–18

307. Urla J. 1993. Cultural politics in an age of statistics: numbers, nations and the making of Basque identity. *Am. Ethnol.* 20(4):818–43

308. Verschueren J. 1985. *What People Say They Do With Words: Prolegomena to an Empirical-Conceptual Approach to Linguistic Action.* Norwood, NJ: Ablex

309. Verschueren J, ed. 1987. *Linguistic Action: Some Empirical-Conceptual Studies.* Norwood, NJ: Ablex

310. Verschueren J. 1989. Language on language: toward metapragmatic universals. *Pap. Pragmat.* 3(2):1–44

311. Wald B. 1985. Vernacular and standard Swahili as seen by members of the Mombasa Swahili speech community. See Ref. 323, pp. 123–44

312. Walker A. 1986. The verbatim record. In *Discourse and Institutional Authority,* ed. S Fisher, A Todd, pp. 205–22. Norwood, NJ: Ablex

313. Warner M. 1990. *The Letters of the Republic: Publication and the Public Sphere in Eighteenth-Century America.* Cambridge, MA: Harvard Univ. Press

314. Watson-Gegeo KA, Gegeo D. 1991. The impact of church affiliation on language change in Kwara'ae (Solomon Islands). *Lang. Soc.* 26(4):533–55

315. Watson-Gegeo KA, White GM, eds. 1990. *Disentangling: Conflict Discourse in Pacific Societies.* Stanford, CA: Stanford Univ. Press

316. Weinstein B. 1989. Francophonie: purism at the international level. See Ref. 171, pp. 53–80

317. Weinstein B, ed. 1990. *Language Policy and Political Development.* Norwood, NJ: Ablex

318. Wierzbicka A. 1985. A semantic metalanguage for a crosscultural comparison of speech acts and speech genres. *Lang. Soc.* 14:491–514

319. Williams G. 1988. Discourse on language and ethnicity. In *Styles of Discourse,* ed. N Coupland, pp. 254–93. London: Croom Helm

320. Williams R. 1977. *Marxism and Literature.* Oxford: Oxford Univ. Press

321. Winer L. 1990. Orthographic standardisation for Trinidad and Tobago: linguistic and sociopolitical consideration in an English Creole community. *Lang. Probl. Lang. Plan.* 14(3):237–68

322. Wodak R, ed. 1989. *Language, Power, and Ideology: Studies in Political Discourse.* Philadelphia: Benjamins

323. Wolfson N, Manes J, eds. 1985. *Language of Inequality.* Berlin: Mouton de Gruyter

324. Woolard KA. 1985. Language variation and cultural hegemony: towards an integration of sociolinguistic and social theory. *Am. Ethnol.* 12(4):738–48

325. Woolard KA. 1989. *Double Talk: Bilingualism and the Politics of Ethnicity in Catalonia.* Stanford, CA: Stanford Univ. Press

326. Woolard KA. 1989. Sentences in the language prison: the rhetorical structuring of an American language policy debate. *Am. Ethnol.* 16(2):268–78

327. Woolard KA. 1992. Language ideology: issues and approaches. See Ref. 185, pp. 235–50

328. Woolard KA, Gahng T-J. 1990. Changing language policies and attitudes in autonomous Catalonia. *Lang. Soc.* 19:311–30

329. Zentella AC. 1994. *Growing Up Bilingual in El Barrio.* Cambridge, MA: Basil Blackwell. In press

Annu. Rev. Anthropol. 1994. 23:83–108

PREHISTORIC DESERT FARMERS OF THE SOUTHWEST

Suzanne K. Fish and Paul R. Fish

Arizona State Museum, University of Arizona, Tucson, Arizona 85721

KEY WORDS: Southwest United States, prehistoric agriculture, desert environment, subsistence
systems, irrigation

INTRODUCTION

The fact and intensity of their commitment to agriculture is a foremost characteristic that distinguished the prehistoric farmers of the Greater Southwest (82)
from their contemporaries to the east, north, and west. As the ultimate members of a continuum of agricultural peoples stretching north from Mesoamerica, pottery-making cultivators in the southwestern United States and
adjacent northwestern Mexico (see Figure 1) formed an agricultural peninsula
with constantly shifting boundaries among North American groups who were
predominantly hunters and gatherers. To understand the environmental context
and social role of agriculture, then, is to understand the most essential factors
that differentiated the Southwest as a culture area and distinctively shaped the
lifeways of its inhabitants. This review explores recent advances in the effort
to understand the relationship between society and agriculture in southwestern
archaeology.

To those whose perceptions are conditioned by temperate climates and
technology of the industrial era, the original occupants of arid southwestern
basins, plateaus, and mountains faced daunting challenges to an agricultural
lifestyle. Concepts concerning agricultural marginality have played a central
role in the study of societal forms and dynamics, as can be seen in current
analytical approaches and interpretive frameworks favored by southwestern
archaeologists. As Kohler observes (85), "the effectiveness of various ecologi-

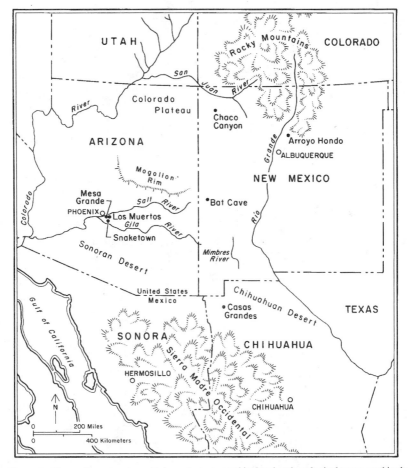

Figure 1   The southwest region with important geographical and archaeological terms used in the text.

cal approaches for understanding culture change in these environments (which, on a large scale of comparison, are marginal for agriculture and sensitive to climatically induced change and human impact) has allowed these positions to remain more dominant than they are, for example, in Europe."

FIRST FARMERS

New findings about initial transitions to agriculture have led to dramatic reformulations of southwestern culture history. An erroneous age of 5000 years for corn at Bat Cave in west-central New Mexico created the impression that there had been a lapse of 3000 years before cultigens began to support instances of village life and farming economies. Agricultural marginality was implicated in the apparent delay between the appearance of cultigens and visible effects on regional societies. Proposed deterrents to an immediate impact included low yielding types of early corn, the lack of varieties adapted to conditions outside the presumed locale of entry in the relatively cool and moist Mogollon highlands, and the mobility of populations in the Late Archaic period between approximately 2000 B.C. and A.D. 1 (68, 107). According to Wills (173), Late Archaic planting was pursued despite very modest returns because small, predictable harvests allowed activities that in turn improved foraging success.

Re-dating of the earliest Mesoamerican corn from the Tehuacan Valley (95) within a few centuries of the original dates from Bat Cave reveals a new timing of northward transmittal. However, skepticism regarding the existing set of earliest southwestern corn dates (9), and the re-study of Bat Cave (173) had already laid the groundwork for revised models of the southwestern transition. A proliferation of evidence for Late Archaic cultigens has provided further impetus for currently changing ideas.

Late Archaic Cultivators

The widespread distribution of Late Archaic farmers in the Southwest is now supported by the recovery of corn in unexpected locations (e.g. 34, 44, 145, 172) as well as through focused Archaic investigations (e.g. 76, 146, 163) and comprehensive regional sampling (e.g. 64:109–113, 99, 147). Site types yielding these materials range from isolated features to rock shelters to small pithouse villages with substantial middens and numerous burials. Early dates on corn at about 3000 B.P. occur in widely separated locales in the Mogollon highlands, Sonoran and Chihuahuan desert basins, and the Colorado plateaus (176). The early corn is usually described, if at all, as resembling modern Chapalote, although a second variety has been reported in one case (163).

One of the largest and most coherent bodies of information pertaining to Late Archaic farmers comes from the Tucson Basin and adjoining areas in southeastern Arizona (48, 76, 176). Extensive excavations over the last ten years have documented cultigens dated between 3000 and 2000 B.P. at more than fifteen widespread locations. In well studied village sites among these, flotation analyses reveal a ubiquity of corn in the range of later Hohokam settlements (76), and settlement patterns also appear to parallel those of ceramic times (48).

Based on evidence for a pre-ceramic Basketmaker II reliance on crops and close stylistic similarities in projectile points and a few other elements of material culture with Late Archaic manifestations in southern Arizona, Matson (98, see also 9) favors a northward migration of southern cultivators to the

Colorado plateaus. His model posits an initial suitability of the low elevation desert basins for the biological requisites of corn and farming techniques originating in Mexico, followed by a further transmission after the development of adaptations to northern conditions. Equally early dates for corn of similar morphology in a variety of southwestern locations and environments (see 76, 146, 147, 163, 173) brings this scheme into question, however.

Alternative models for the adoption of cultigens, emphasizing evidence from other southwestern regions, feature longer periods of minor incorporation into primarily foraging orientations (e.g. 110, 145, 146, 173). The degree of dietary reliance and commitment to agriculture are difficult to determine even with the fuller record of ceramic times, but secure storage of seed in addition to consumable supplies is mandatory at any level of cropping. Pre-ceramic technology for storage in the form of large, often bell-shaped pits is common at sites yielding cultigens, both with and without indications of extended residence (e.g. 76, 98, 145, 146, 173).

It is doubtful that any single model of transition will prove adequate, given the environmental and probable Archaic cultural diversity of the Southwest. Indeed, the historic period, harboring contemporary groups whose practices ranged from mobile foraging to intensive irrigation, is a reminder that the transition was never geographically uniform, completed, or irreversible. The notably low visibility of Late Archaic populations before the appearance of cultigens and the virtual absence of knowledge about their modes of subsistence are major obstacles to reconstructing processes and rates of incorporation. The influence of cultigen donor groups is also unknown in the absence of archaeological investigations in northern Mexico for the period when domesticates first appeared in the Southwest.

The recent demonstration of extensive manipulation and unequivocal cultivation of local species in the eastern United States long before the advent of Mesoamerican crops (148) should serve as a caution against the automatic assumption that a residentially mobile seasonal round of hunting and gathering constituted the sole Late Archaic strategy throughout the west. Ethnographically recorded practices provide possible analogs for similar, pre-agricultural interventions to increase the yields from wild plants. Groups on the southwestern fringes such as the Paiute, Cahuilla, and Washoe used a variety of techniques for sowing, transplanting, tending, irrigating, and otherwise heightening the productivity and predictability of native species (e.g. 6, 38, 144, 151). A few sites with pit house structures (e.g. 122) predate the known entry of Mesoamerican cultigens by many centuries, and village settlements in southern Arizona are approximately as old as the oldest well-replicated dates for southwestern corn. Determining the combinations of environmental, demographic, cultural, and economic factors that would have facilitated or inhibited the adoption of farming lifestyles in different sectors of the Southwest (47,

175) and identifying their consequences in the archaeological record are priorities for future research on the transition to agriculture.

Early Ceramic Farmers

Differential rates and mechanisms of cultigen incorporation in Late Archaic times involve many of the same issues of current interest in the archaeology of ensuing ceramic sequences (e.g. the degree of dietary reliance on crops and residential mobility). It is now apparent that residential sites associated with the earliest regional ceramics (by about A.D. 200 to 300) in many parts of the Southwest are not the first farming villages, but this temporal threshold marks a change in the visibility of cultivators and undoubtedly in key aspects of behavior other than pottery use. For the first time, data are sufficient to address effectively the relationships between organization and subsistence. However, as with Late Archaic methods of agriculture, the technologies that supported these settlements are still inferred exclusively from locational correlates. In terms of developmental timespans, the interval between the earliest record of dietary importance for cultigens (e.g. as early as 800 B.C. in southern Arizona) and the appearance of pottery in the same southwestern region is almost as long as the ensuing ceramic sequence.

Estimates of agricultural commitment figure prominently in interpretations of cultural variability in Basketmaker and earliest Mogollon sequences. Both weak and strong commitments are suggested on the basis of site types and the distribution of cultigen remains within settlement patterns (64, 145, 147), organization of architecture and storage (128:185, 174:173), groundstone attributes (66), and the regional availability of natural resources (9, 55, 98, 146, 177). A limited number of studies that attempt quantitative assessment of subsistence for the Four Corners area (the intersection of Arizona, New Mexico, Utah, and Colorado) show high proportions of cultigens (e.g. 31, 99, 109).

Many archaeologists see an increase in regional differentiation across the upland Southwest within several hundred years of the earliest plain ceramics, although prior to the adoption of pottery, broad Basketmaker II divisions are also defined on nonceramic stylistic grounds (e.g. 98, 165). More geographically limited stylistic zones are linked to a decreasing scale of routine interaction and to the adoption of designs that signal social identities (14, 128:189), processes stemming from increasing sedentism and territorial delimitation among agriculturalists.

A more unified pattern emerges for Hohokam and nearby portions of the southern Southwest during early ceramic times. A widespread horizon of brownwares similar to initial northern and eastern ceramics has been identified recently as preceding decorated styles (e.g. 18, 40, 77, 93). Analyses of subsistence remains for most well-sampled early ceramic occupations reveal almost every cultigen in quantities comparable to representation in later prehistoric times (e.g. 8, 20, 49, 65). The array of settlement locations strongly suggests a variety of surface runoff, floodwater, and irrigation strategies, and large Phoenix canals can be dated as early as A.D. 450 (2). Although these findings indicate that sedentism and agricultural commitment should have been relatively strong and pervasive in the southern Southwest, regional differentiation in early decorated ceramics and architectural styles has not been as readily distinguished as it has been in the north.

ENVIRONMENT, AGRICULTURE, AND CULTURE CHANGE

Environmental variables critical for agricultural success are regionally and topographically diverse. Separate weather systems produce winter dominant precipitation to the west and summer dominant moisture to the east. The timing of adequate rainfall is balanced against spring and fall frosts at upper elevations and withering summer heat in low basins. Average precipitation ranges from barely sufficient amounts for rain-fed farming at upper elevations in some regions to several orders of magnitude less than is necessary for direct rainfall agriculture in the hottest, driest sectors. All regions are subject to significant seasonal and annual variability. The consequences of marginality, a unifying theme throughout southwestern archaeology, are most commonly conceptualized as a dependent relationship between culture change and climatic trends of regional or subregional extent.

Response to Climate

The ability to rigorously examine climate and, in the broader sense, environment as a causal force in southwestern prehistory is largely attributable to the quantity and precision of combined climatic and chronological information from tree-ring studies. Plog (128:194) notes that when this information is compared to temporally coarser reconstructions of culture history, it will always be possible to find climatic fluctuations that are roughly contemporaneous with episodes of culture change. Although a response to climate is one of the most common explanations for cultural change in the southwestern archaeological literature, an explicit or well-supported linking argument is not always supplied.

Archaeologists of the upland Southwest have also produced highly refined and sophisticated treatments of relationships between environment and culture, as reflected in the exigencies of arid land farming. A series of multidisciplinary studies of the western Anasazi in northeastern Arizona is a prime example (29, 63, 64). Environmental processes are analyzed in terms of low frequency (periodicities of more than 25 years or one generation) and high frequency (periodicities less than 25 years) categories that are meaningful in terms of human perception and response. A long-term developmental scheme for the region is developed through correlations between multiple measures of environment and changing cultural patterns (summarized in 41, 64). A plausible and painstakingly documented connection is formulated between climatic events, corresponding hydrological and geomorphological effects on agricultural locations and production, and the implications for settlement and other societal patterns. A second set of exemplary multidisciplinary studies used a similar framework of low and high frequency periodicity with tree-ring and pollen data for the Anasazi of the Mesa Verde region in the Four Corners area. Investigators examined linkages among the movements of farmers, the form of successive dispersed or aggregated settlement patterns at varying scales, and climatic fluctuations in precipitation and temperature (125, 141). Values for intermediary variables such as agricultural yields, costs, and surpluses were also considered in determining whether aggregation, complexity, conflict, or other societal processes tended to occur in conjunction with particular kinds of climatic trends (16, 124).

   Two recent versions of the developmental trajectory for Chaco Canyon in northwestern New Mexico illustrate the point that the juxtaposition of precise climatic measures and intensively studied archaeological remains does not guarantee consensus on the manner in which agricultural response to climate operated as a contributing factor. R. Vivian (165) sees an expansion of agriculturally-based settlements by the aggregated builders of great houses within the Chacoan core and then outward during favorable climatic episodes, thus accounting for their culturally distinctive sites connected by roads among surrounding dispersed populations of different origin. Deteriorating conditions later forced the carriers of the great house tradition from the core and truncated development there. In L. Sebastian's (142) reconstruction, early great houses are associated with favored agricultural locations near Chaco side canyons at a time when corn production would have been low elsewhere. When climate and productivity improved, now-established leaders in the canyon controlled greater surpluses with which they underwrote competitive construction, both internally and among more distant client groups. A final climatic downturn again figures in the ultimate collapse outward from Chaco Canyon.

   The ability to evaluate climatic influence in the low southern deserts by methods other than long-range projection (e.g. 97:215, 216; 167) is constrained by the rarity in structures of conifer beams suitable for tree-ring analysis. Graybill overcame this limitation in a pioneering interpolation with explicit consequences for the study of Hohokam irrigators in the Phoenix Basin (59). Using modern calibrations, he reconstructed annual streamflow, including disruptive floods, from tree-ring records in the upland watersheds of the Salt and Gila Rivers that flow into the deserts. Archaeologists have also applied this reconstruction in the Tonto Basin, another region supplied by the Salt River system (5, 22:27).

Two floods of maximal scale coincided with an earlier interval of significant culture change in the Hohokam sequence near A.D. 900 and a subsequent interval of transition between early and late divisions of the Classic period, respectively (59). Erosion following the later flood may have precluded repairs of canal intakes in a locality where several lines headed (61:184–186), although canals headed there again historically. The timing of this second flood at A.D. 1358 and the presumed agricultural crisis that it generated fits what some scholars see as the approximate onset of collapse of the first Classic peak in organizational complexity. This catastrophic flood fed by winter precipitation might be implicated in downturns in Phoenix or Tonto Basin trajectories. The summer rainfall critical for agriculture along the hydrologically dissimilar Hohokam drainages to the south, however, varied little during the same years (60:12). Thus, the same climatic phenomenon cannot be directly invoked to account for generally synchronous expressions of cultural trend in these parts of the Hohokam tradition that would not experience flooding or be affected agriculturally in an equivalent manner.

Calculation and Quantification of Agricultural Variables

Climatic data in combination with other factors influencing agricultural production and consumption provide a means for deriving measures of variables immediately affecting human behavior. In a pioneering example of such quantification, Wetterstrom (168) considered climatic fluctuations, amounts of arable land and crop harvests, yields from wild plants and animals, and satisfaction of nutritional requirements in her investigation of demographic and subsistence stress at Arroyo Hondo in north-central New Mexico. Other studies in the Four Corners area build upon annual climate and yields from carefully specified acreage to reconstruct storage values, capacities for population support in relation to demographic change, and the interplay between risks, costs, and production in land-extensive agricultural systems (16, 87, 164). Hegmon (70) drew upon coordinated historic values for Hopi climate, fields, and yields to simulate different patterns of household sharing and the implications of these patterns for optimal organization and behavior in counteracting agricultural risks.

AGRICULTURAL LANDSCAPES

Non-climatic elements figure in the basic relationships between environment and agriculture that underlie the broadest southwestern cultural divisions. A dichotomy can be drawn between plateaus of the north and southern desert basins, a contrast that holds to a lesser degree between upper and lower elevation landforms throughout. Higher upland precipitation and greater numbers of mountain-fed drainages in the north, coupled with relatively widespread domestic water sources, imparted greater flexibility in field location. Where agriculture was supplied by direct rainfall or clear mountain streams, fertility sometimes may have declined with continued use (140), but cultivation required minor ancillary effort. Settlements could be readily relocated, a factor in land tenure and territoriality. Farming locations in the low deserts of the south, on the other hand, were more restricted by the scarcity of seasonally prolonged domestic water and situations that insured supplemental moisture for fields. Structural improvements for water delivery required investment by cultivators, after which plentiful suspended nutrients in soil-laden flows repetitively renewed the fields (113). Options and agricultural inducements for relocation were correspondingly few.

Resource Depletion

North-south contrasts for prehistoric agriculturalists are reflected in the analytical interests of regional archaeologists. The issue of depletion of critical resources has drawn most attention in the upland Southwest. Retrodicted magnitudes of decline in soil fertility (e.g. 7, 126, 140) remain problematic without supporting observations of decline in different soil types under indigenous cultivation techniques (see 100:258, 86:539 for evidence suggesting persistent fertility); likewise, swidden-like practices in response to this problem (86, 100, 152, 155) are plausible but as yet unconfirmed through archaeological indications such as lenses or pockets of ash in prehistoric fields. Most quantified studies of depletion focus on natural resources consumed by cultivators over time, based on species composition and relative quantities of biological remains and estimated use rates, rather than on the exhaustion of an area by farming per se.

The reduction of woody growth for fuel and construction has been examined on various scales with regard to limits on residential duration, increased costs of supply, and alternative uses. Changes in charcoal of more and less desirable fuel species indicate a resort to alternative trees and woody shrubs over the course of occupations in a number of disparate locales (e.g. 86, 106). Fuel depletion may have been a factor in sequential short-term occupations where cold temperatures created high demands and where alternative arable locations were still plentiful relative to farmers. Simultaneous depletion of pinyon nut sources in these same situations was serious for subsistence systems that depended on substantial increments from gathering (52). In the long-term and densely settled occupation of Chaco Canyon, inhabitants appear to have decimated trees on a regional scale (139) and ultimately recycled structural timbers for fuel (178). Certainly, substantial distances had to be traversed to acquire the many timbers in the unusually elaborate Chacoan edifices (10) and in most similar examples of massive communal constructions elsewhere in the Southwest. Localized depletion of particular kinds of trees probably also resulted from timber consumption in settlement patterns composed of more ordinary modes of Puebloan ceremonial and residential architecture (73).

The extermination of game in the vicinity of agricultural settlements is one form of depletion registered in faunal analyses of both upland plateaus and desert basins. Earlier proportions of large mammals, often deer, gave way to smaller species commonly dominated by rabbits (78, 123, 143, 152, 157). A shift to animals favoring open habitats and secondary vegetation is also a common finding (120, 152, 157) after natural vegetation was progressively cleared. Even farmers in settlements with great time depth may have achieved some degree of compensation in their overall protein supply by the convenient hunting of animals attracted to fields and the other anthropogenic habitats of agrarian landscapes.

Mechanisms for Balance and Sustainability

If recent publications on southwestern archaeology are indicative, it is easier to investigate and reconstruct the mechanisms through which prehistoric agriculturalists depleted their environments than those through which they maintained balances permitting residential stability. Natural resource pressure was undoubtedly greatest in instances of aggregated and persistent settlement patterns in the northern Southwest and in a broader variety of enduring southern occupations tied to circumscribed water sources and investments in delivery structures. However, depletion of soils, native plants, and animals is but one aspect of the culturally modified environments created by prehistoric southwestern farmers.

In an influential articulation of the holistic effects of farming in early agricultural occupations, Ford (55) noted that resource predictability and available edible biomass were enhanced in agricultural contexts through the cumulative productivity of crops, weedy plants, and game drawn to fields. The proliferation and subsistence contribution of successional species is now often treated as a separate interpretive category in archaeobotanical analyses. Carbonized seeds and pollen reveal rich weedy floras in agricultural environs that included abundant resource species (e.g 7, 51, 55, 58, 105, 168:55–60). In seasons lacking sufficient precipitation for successful crops, these hardier southwestern native taxa may have provided the major returns from cultivated land. The management of anthropogenic environments toward greater productivity represents an ancillary subsistence strategy, and probably included an enhanced diversity of harvestable flora and fauna in hedgerows, along canals, and in other differentiated habitats of cultivated landscapes (e.g. 114, 133, 134, 143).

The ethnographic literature of the Greater Southwest records a variety of behaviors aimed at guaranteeing or augmenting densities of resource species in anthropogenic vegetation (e.g. 17, 23, 53:190, 170). Morphological attributes believed to be associated with human selection or manipulation and anomalous archaeological distributions (summaries in 13, 51) suggest active intervention, transplantation, and even cultivation of nondomesticates (e.g. cholla and little barley) that were not formerly thought to be potential cultigens. A significant breakthrough of this sort is the compilation of evidence for agave as a cultigen among the Hohokam and its subsequent documentation as a major crop in southern Arizona (50, 51, 56).

Compensation for some aspects of depletion or scarcity involved long distance solutions. Aquisition methods may be uncertain, as in the case of fuel consumed in firing the impressive quantities of Hohokam pottery at Snaketown (69:192), a relatively large site occupied continuously for more than 700 years in an environment with sparse and highly localized trees. In other cases, as with the timbers in Chacoan edifices and large Hohokam adobe structures, aggregated agriculturalists clearly bore the transport costs of obtaining distant supplies. Other examples of organizational solutions and attendant costs include episodic communal hunting of large game that was depleted in the vicinity of farming settlements (149), regular trade with hunters and gatherers as in eastern Pueblos-Plains exchange (150), and the possible existence of extractive specialists.

MOBILITY, SEDENTISM, AND COMMITMENT

Sedentism, mobility, and agricultural commitment are important, interrelated issues in current southwestern archaeology. Perhaps one of the most important outcomes of re-examining assumptions about these topics is a heightened awareness of the range of potential patterns and combinations of relevant variables. Villages may have been permanent over many years, occupied year-round for a few years, occupied seasonally, reoccupied at intervals in either of the two preceding cases, or may have encompassed different mobility patterns among member households (81, 86, 100, 115).

The manner in which southwestern scholars interpret the duration of residential settlements and reliance on agriculture is undergoing scrutiny. Most archaeologists have advanced arguments in terms of features, structure types, or diversity in residential architecture (e.g. 32, 57, 103, 129, 174), and artifact attributes and assemblages (e.g. 66, 112, 117, 118), rather than by prehistoric evidence for agricultural activities or products. Explicit expectations for distributions or proportions of subsistence remains and their identification in the archaeological record have played a relatively minor part in these discussions.

Agricultural variables and farming behavior enter the equation primarily through ethnographic analogy. The western Apache and a few other comparatively mobile groups such as the Navajo and Tohono O'odham furnish the models for subsistence practices of prehistoric groups with high mobility and low commitment to agriculture (e.g. 18; 88; 110:130–132; 173). In addition to animal transport, herding, armed warfare, and other post-contact factors in mobility options, these southwestern groups maintained strong economic ties with committed neighboring farmers, regularly exchanging for agricultural products and replenishing vital seed after episodes of lapsed planting or crop failure. Thus, these analogies may be misleading unless qualified by similar prehistoric interdependencies. Models featuring mobility during the growing season are also questionable where immediate manipulation of fleeting storm runoff, diversion of channelized flow, or irrigation was critical to crop success.

Interpretations emphasizing appreciable mobility and low commitment tend to be correlated with cases involving little or no archaeological evidence for agricultural locations and techniques. It is probably no coincidence that greater potential for mobility is disproportionately associated with rain-fed cropping and a lack of investment in durable constructions. Earlier records of agricultural features in the southern Southwest support the previously discussed environmental inducements for settlement stability among low basin farmers. Moreover, proposed archaeological signatures for mobility and low commitment such as pithouse residence cannot necessarily be extended to the intensive farmers of the Hohokam tradition, as illustrated by the co-occurrence of pithouses and massive canals used for hundreds of years.

As with most topics in archaeology, a consideration of scale provides alternative perspectives on relationships between agriculture and residential duration. For example, house clusters of Hohokam floodwater farmers might come and go with changes in hydrological processes on individual alluvial fans, while settlement was continuous across the larger topographic zone composed of these landforms. Phase to phase continuity in residence and farming for up to 600 years on an optimal alluvial fan and for more than 1500 years at a zonal scale (from Late Archaic to late ceramic times) can be documented in Hohokam basins (49). In southwestern Colorado prior to A.D. 1000, rain-fed cultivators with land-extensive practices occupied small settlements briefly while slowly regenerating resources were consumed. They resettled successively until entire locales were abandoned. On an expanded temporal and spatial scale, however, these systems were sustained over a prolonged period as this kind of land-use cycled through successive locales across a larger regional segment (83:241).

Wide variability in mobility and agricultural dependence is a characteristic of southwestern agriculturalists at any point in time. In an insightful study of the Tarahumara, Hard & Merrill (67) describe differential residential movement among households in the same settlement, reflecting individual responses to social and economic factors. Simultaneous variation among ethnic groups is illustrated dramatically in the historic period when economic orientations ranged from mobile foraging to fully sedentary and intensive cultivation, often within the same region. Degrees of mobility and agricultural commitment were clearly reversible among historic populations, and some archaeologists see reversals periodically and at regional scales in the past (127, 154, 162). Seasonal and year-round occupations at contemporary small Pueblo II Anasazi sites (81) typify the prehistoric diversity in synchronous patterns that archaeologists are more likely to recognize as the result of recent attention.

FOOD STRESSES AND HEALTH

Food stress resulting from agricultural failure or an imbalance between population and productive limits, particularly under conditions of aggregation and intensification, is an important topic. Although the detection of stress has been the focus of much research (12, 108, 123, 168), unequivocal and replicable criteria for demonstrating its occurrence have seldom been sought through the quantified study of botanical and faunal remains alone. Conclusions from recent, regionally diverse human skeletal studies involving bone chemistry, pathologies, developmental deficiencies, and demographic indices have emphasized dietary stress and low levels of health in the most densely settled areas of the Southwest (e.g. 96, 104, 116, 153). Better nutrition and longer life expectancy among limited social groups at Chaco Canyon and Casas Grandes in northern Chihuahua suggest differential access to food, but such indications are rare in studies of human biology (116). A comprehensive examination of health and nutrition among worldwide Neolithic populations in temperate and tropical as well as arid environments is needed to determine the uniqueness or comparative significance of southwestern dietary stress.

SCALES OF ANALYSIS

Studies at different cultural and geographic scales reveal different facets of the relationship between agriculture and society. Cumulative effects of variables and processes at smaller scales may be inadequate to account for more widespread social responses. Common micro-, meso-, and macro-scales of analysis in southwestern archaeology focus on individual settlements and their components, interrelated settlements in a region, and associated sets of regionally interlinked settlements.

Micro-scale Studies

Southwestern archaeologists have devoted appreciable effort to defining the households or groupings of households that compose individual settlements. In most parts of the Southwest, these are the basic units in what is seen as a modular series. Criteria for discriminating social units involve the function and orientation of rooms and structures and the distribution of shared facilities. Modules of Anasazi and Mogollon affiliation include a structure with communal functions, the kiva, within most multiple household units; the Hohokam lack an equivalent feature. Successively inclusive combinations are often identified as the building blocks of even the largest sites. Village modules are primary objects of investigation for questions concerning social organization and the production and consumption of durable items, but only occasionally are they analyzed in terms of farming requisites and strategies.

With a few exceptions, the occurrence of isolated structures in settlement patterns is attributed to seasonal fieldside residence (e.g. 166). Several authors (84, 131, 156) view these field houses as establishing claims on prime land in addition to reducing travel time to fields distant from a home village. Preucel (130, 131) associates the appearance and proliferation of field houses with population growth and agricultural intensification. Kohler (84:625, 626) outlines linkages with longer term occupations, formalized systems of inheritance, a corresponding potential for inequality in productive access, and heightened agricultural risk in situations of intensified land use. Ownership under intensive practice is illustrated by the apparently contemporary, regular spacing of ephemeral field houses along the canals in a small central Arizona system (42). This example suggests that field houses may have also been convenient residences for timely distribution of water and for assuring fair allotments in irrigation.

A few authors relate household size and composition to agricultural concerns. The appearance of integrated Hohokam households, indicated by groups of structures sharing courtyards, has been correlated with the rise of corporate groups in response to the cooperative demands of irrigated agriculture (71:124–127). The ability of the head of such a household to successfully schedule its labor would add to household size, cohesion, and prestige through the generation of socially manipulable surplus (35). Greater household size in turn increases the possibility for simultaneous tasks and would be beneficial in diversified productive systems. Environmental uncertainty is another proposed factor in large household size because greater risks would inhibit the establishment of independent new households.

Wills' (175) conclusion that production shifted from a communal mode to a household mode during early ceramic times is based on the contrast between publicly visible storage facilities at an earlier Chaco Canyon pithouse village, and storage within structures at a somewhat later village in the Mogollon Highlands. This proposed change to a household mode occurred in conjunction with increasing sedentism and a risk-prone strategy of temporally focused subsistence production, including wild resources and crops, in relatively favorable environments. Hegmon (70) examines the effects of resource sharing and agricultural risk in her simulation of pooling among Hopi households. Heightened survival rates through limited sharing of surplus defined an optimal pooling group of about five households under modern conditions of fluctuation in annual climate and observed field production.

Current attempts to investigate prehistoric land rights coincide with reevaluations of corporate control as the overriding principle in post-contact Puebloan access to productive land (e.g. 90, 169). Furthermore, rules varied historically, as in the different use rights for favorable locales of long-term farming at Zuni and unclaimed land at a distance (27). Reconstructions of corporate tenure have been extended to the Hohokam (e.g. 71), although Piman successors gained access to irrigated land through participation in the original construction of canals rather than through kinship status (19:126, 127; 138:88). Household control of land, intensive practices, and investment in farming improvements tend to be correlated (119). Even in the extensive floodwater systems of northern Sonora, cultivators incrementally established and improved large series of contiguous fields over time (36).

Many researchers see a connection between agricultural conditions and the number of households or multi-household units in a single settlement. The most common and straightforward example is an increase in the number of units per settlement following an environmental deterioration that reduces the overall availability of farmable land (21). This process is the most frequent explanation for late prehistoric aggregation across the Southwest. Variations on the theme include an accretion of units into larger settlements to avoid conflicts over agricultural land that might arise among dispersed populations (124) and the emergence within sites of larger co-residential, land-holding units in tandem with agricultural intensification and greater potential for resource imbalance (4). An alternative relationship between aggregation or settlement size and agriculture is the simple coincidence of larger sites with large expanses of optimal farm land (160).

Meso-scale Studies

The term *community* is often used in southwestern archaeology to denote a configuration of interrelated settlements that includes a central site containing the most elaborated communal architecture and a series of other, usually smaller sites. Such multi-site communites are subjects of meso-scale analysis. Agricultural topics figure broadly in discussions of community form and function, but they are most fully explored in the literature dealing with the Hohokam and Chaco Canyon.

The community concept is particularly prominent in Hohokam archaeology because the well-mapped canal networks along the Salt and Gila Rivers graphically define sets of interconnected sites and simultaneously provide a rationale for cooperation and coordination (39). A single central site with associated lesser settlements occurs along smaller networks, while several such community units occur along larger ones. The fairly regular spacing of central sites and communities along canals and central tendencies in community size and amount of irrigable land probably reflect magnitudes attuned to regular communication concerning irrigation, labor mobilization, and transport of agricultural products (24:155–158; 49:99, 100; 62:383). Integrative mechanisms spanning separate networks after A.D. 1100 have been suggested on the basis of cross cutting canals (121) and the expansion of the total system to the limits of river capacity (75). Communities and sets of communities with primary interconnections ascribed to irrigation are also located in the Tonto Basin (22:29, 30; 180) and possibly in the Mimbres Valley (72) and the southern Tucson Basin (35, 49:101).

Even in the core area of large-scale riverine irrigation, Hohokam communities integrated ancillary environmental zones with different productive potential and agricultural technologies (e.g. 24, 74, 111). Zonally differentiated land-use, however, was at the heart of the territorial and productive organization of Hohokam communities away from the perennial Salt and Gila Rivers. In Hohokam communities elsewhere, canals were constructed along favorable stretches of the intermittent or ephemeral watercourses, but technological mixes in a single community could also include floodwater diversion on alluvial fans, rockpile complexes (stone features supplied by surface runoff) on mid-basin slopes, checkdams, and contour terraces on upper slopes, bottomland farming in large arroyos, and hillside masonry terraces (49). Productive specialization is most clearly illustrated by the localized distribution of rockpile complexes producing agave. The size of the zonally extensive Hohokam communities, up to 150 sq km, was several times the average size of individual Salt and Gila communities with massive irrigation (49:99).

Communities and their environmentally and technologically differentiated territories have been defined in widely separated sectors of the Southwest, including the San Juan Basin in northwestern New Mexico (15), the Casas Grandes region of northern Chihuahua (33), and the Tonto Basin of eastern Arizona (136, 180). Descriptions of such productively diversified entities will be refined and the roster will continue to grow as attention is devoted to recording the impressive variety of prehistoric technologies (45, 97, 101, 179, 181) and specifying their territorial and societal contexts.

Several roles for agriculture are cited with regard to the integrative rationale and structure of productively diversified communities. Reid & Whittlesey (135) observe that differentiated settlement patterns might develop in the absence of overall integration as the result of population growth, when smaller sites are established near limited or marginal acreage following the initial occupation of large sites near prime land. The incorporation and pooling of localized risks is a primary benefit of community organization to the degree that members participate in compensatory exchange. Exchange relationships are likely between sites with complementary patterns of risk (132). Reciprocal elevational and topographic risks are offset where territorial boundaries encompass both settlements near irrigated bottomlands and higher elevation fields; an enlarged labor force is concomitantly achieved for necessarily rapid canal repairs during the agricultural season (1, 94).

Central sites and public architecture are loci of integrative ideologies and processes that foster the circulation of harvests and other subsistence resources among the differentiated sectors of a community in many interpretive schemes. Although not always articulated in detail, these processes are often perceived as involving communal consumption and ritualized exchange among relatively equal social components in the manner of the historic pueblos (3, 11, 54). A major role in the circulation of subsistence goods is also ascribed to central site leaders, particularly in view of evidence for substantial storage and preeminence in other kinds of exchange (e.g. 39, 46, 92, 137). Models highlighting the control of surpluses and their redistribution, including kin-based organizational hierarchies in the manner of a chiefdom (136), are typically associated with Chacoan, Hohokam, and Casas Grandes manifestations that exhibit maximum southwestern complexity.

Macro-scale Studies

Interpretations of the relationship between agriculture and societal organization for Chaco Canyon and its larger regional system span meso- and macro-scales of analysis. The level and significance of subsistence transfer in different schemes reflects differing assessments of whether agricultural production in Chaco Canyon and its surroundings was insufficient for supporting the resident population (80), sufficient during a majority of the occupational interval (165), or at times capable of producing surpluses for exterior expansion and integration (142). Likewise, centralized storage facilities and formal roads enhancing transport might function in the regularized movement of staples (80) or the occasional transfer of emergency supplies to counteract serious agricultural failures (159). Elite exchange and a unifying ideology expressed in the elaborated public architecture of Chacoan centers and outliers maintained connections among these nodes according to various versions of subsistence interdependency (summaries in 26).

Upham (161) formulated a framework for macro-scale subsistence exchange from the clustered distributions of large, fourteenth century western Anasazi pueblos on the southern Colorado Plateau. Average spacing between his clusters converges with the 50 km distance that he identified as the maximum for efficient food transport (91). The 50 km spacing also would have permitted practicable exchange within the clusters. Similar spatial clusterings are suggested to have occurred more widely in the the Southwest (79). The regional system, marked by broadly shared ideology and ceramic and architectural styles that emerged under increasing aggregation and agricultural intensification, represents another model for macro-scale networks of a size sufficient to ameliorate periodic food shortages among members (e.g. 3, 25, 89, 171). Regional inequalities in the environmental potential for agricultural production were the basis for other kinds of subsistence relations between large sectors of prehistoric population. Examples are the exchange of eastern Pueblo crops for Plains buffalo products (150), the exchange of Papaguerian shell for Hohokam crops from the Phoenix Basin (102), and the possible exchange of seasonal agricultural labor by resident Yumans (158:131) for a share of Hohokam irrigated yields in a parallel to historic Tohono O'odham-Pima interchanges.

CONCLUSION: TEMPORAL TRENDS AND TERMINAL SCENARIOS

An integral relationship between regional abandonments and aggregated configurations began to develop before the thirteenth century and then became expressed widely in late prehistoric times. Maps of the Greater Southwest (see Figure 2) illustrate broad-brush patterns of settlement at two successive intervals (43). These distributions contrast with generally uninterrupted occupations across the Southwest at A.D. 1100. Early Pueblo III patterns at approximately A.D. 1275 to 1300 and those of the mid-Pueblo IV period, about A.D. 1400 to 1425, can be compared to locations of historic irrigation in the earliest part of this century, when gravity systems resembling prehistoric technologies were predominant and few dams were in place. A general congruence can be seen between late prehistoric processes of aggregation and irrigable situations (43).

Late prehistoric abandonments have been treated primarily from the point of view of negative climatic conditions (21). However, the timing of agriculturally critical rainfall and other limiting factors are not uniform across southwestern regions and cannot account for all aspects of this phenomenon. By A.D. 1000, agriculturalists were experimenting with denser populations, intensified production, and more integrated territorial units in a few areas such as Chaco Canyon and the Phoenix Basin. Natural or cultural limits that were eventually exceeded may have challenged the stability of aggregated populations in particular times and places. Nevertheless, because organizational modes and structures that facilitated aggregation were cumulative over time, successive entities could build on the organizational innovations and productively intensified techniques of predecessors. Such solutions necessarily included the means to provide the members of increasingly heterogenous populations with access to land and water, to use the expanded labor pool to support

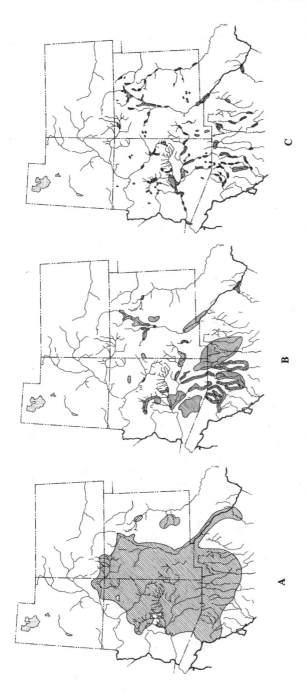

Figure 2   Comparison of prehistoric agricultural occupations during two successive intervals and the distribution of historic gravity irrigation in the Greater Southwest. (Adapted from 43) A. Approximate outlines of southwestern agricultural occupation during the Pueblo III interval between A.D. 1275 and 1300. B. Approximate outlines of southwestern agricultural occupations during the Pueblo IV interval between A.D. 1400 and 1425. C. Distribution of historic gravity irrigation agriculture prior to A.D. 1900.

higher population totals, and to assign and mediate social roles amenable to aggregated modes of interaction.

During the fifteenth century, areas with the densest regional populations, the most interlinked productive technologies, and the strongest evidence for well-integrated territorial configurations (most notably Casas Grandes and sites such as Mesa Grande and Los Muertos in the Phoenix Basin) experienced disruption. However, it is difficult to document end points in these sequences. Recent reanalysis of absolute dates suggests that terminal occupations approaching A.D. 1500 are plausible (28, 30), permitting an increasingly realistic consideration of roles for disease and other vectors of European contact.

The recurrent theme of agricultural marginality plays a central role in scenarios for the terminal era of southwestern prehistory. One polar position advocates absolute environmental constraints on the size and complexity of southwestern societies. A corollary is the notion that the organizational range in the ethnographic record is closely adapted to southwestern limitations, and more hierarchical structures represented inherently unlikely and unsustainable divergences. The opposite view is that European intrusion truncated a still-viable trajectory of cultural evolution that had produced late prehistoric hierarchical societies exceeding the complexity of any found in the historic period.

Concepts of environmental constraint minimally must be tempered for the Hohokam, who constructed more massive irrigation networks than those in Mesoamerica or any other part of North America north of Peru (37). An appreciable if less impressive irrigated core also marks Casas Grandes, another peak of complexity in southwestern cultural expressions. The location of the relatively early Chacoan development in the less hydrologically favored San Juan Basin is instructive by contrast. It is a reminder that, rather than simply being the bearers of a marginal but enduring agrarian tradition, the desert farmers of the Southwest were also the formulators of cultural trajectories that successfully challenged their difficult southwestern environment in accordance with the changing objectives of prehistoric economy and society.

Literature Cited

1. Abbruzzi W. 1989. Ecology, resource redistribution, and Mormon settlement in northeastern Arizona. *Am. Anthropol.* 91(3):642–55

2. Ackerly N, Henderson T. 1989. *Prehistoric Agricultural Activities on the Lehi-Mesa Terrace: Perspectives on Hohokam Irrigation Cycles.* Flagstaff, AZ: Northland Res.

3. Adams E. 1991. *The Origin and Development of the Pueblo Katsina Cult.* Tucson: Univ. Ariz. Press

4. Adler M. 1990. *Communities of soil and stone: an archaeological investigation of population aggregation among the Mesa Verde Anasazi, A.D. 900–1300.* PhD thesis. Univ. Mich., Ann Arbor. 455 pp.

5. Altschul J, Van West C. 1992. Agricultural productivity estimates for the Tonto Basin, A.D. 740–1370. In *Proc. 2nd Salado Conf.*, ed. R Lange, S Germick, pp. 172–82. Phoenix: Ariz. Archaeol. Soc.
6. Bean L, Saubel K. 1972. *Tempalpakh: Cahuila Indian Knowledge Usage of Plants.* Banning: Malki Mus.
7. Berlin G, Salas D, Geib P. 1990. A prehistoric Sinagua agricultural field in the ashfall zone of Sunset Crater, Arizona. *J. Field Archaeol.* 17:1–16
8. Bernard-Shaw M. 1990. *Archaeological Investigations at the Lonetree Site, AZ AA:12:120 (ASM), in the Northern Tucson Basin,* Tech. Rep. No. 90–1. Tucson: Cent. Desert Archaeol.
9. Berry M. 1982. *Time, Space, and Transition in Anasazi Prehistory.* Salt Lake City: Univ. Utah Press
10. Betancourt J, Dean J, Hull H. 1986. Prehistoric long-distance transport of construction beams, Chaco Canyon, New Mexico. *Am. Antiq.* 51(3):370–75
11. Blinman E. 1989. Potluck in the protokiva: ceramics and ceremonialism in Pueblo I villages. In *The Architecture of Social Integration in Prehistoric Pueblos,* Occas. Pap. No. 1, ed. W Lipe, M Hegmon, pp. 113–24. Cortez: Crow Canyon Archaeol. Cent.
12. Bohrer V. 1970. Ethnobotanical aspects of Snaketown: a Hohokam village in southern Arizona. *Am. Antiq.* 35(3):413–30
13. Bohrer V. 1991. Recently recognized cultivated and encouraged plants among the Hohokam. *Kiva* 56(3):227–36
14. Braun D, Plog S. 1982. Evolution of "tribal" social networks: theory and prehistoric North American evidence. *Am. Antiq.* 47(3):504–25
15. Breternitz C, Doyel D, Marshall M. 1982. *Bis sa'ani: A Late Bonito Phase Community on Escavada Wash, Northwest New Mexico,* Anthropol. Pap. No. 14. Window Rock, AZ: Navajo Nation
16. Burns B. 1983. *Simulated Anasazi storage behavior using crop yields reconstructed from tree-rings: A.D. 652–1968.* PhD thesis. Univ. Ariz., Tucson. 756 pp.
17. Bye R. 1979. Incipient domestication of mustards in northwestern Mexico. *Kiva* 44(4):237–36
18. Cable J, Doyel D. 1987. Pioneer Period village structure and settlement pattern in the Phoenix Basin. In *The Hohokam Village: Site Structure and Organization,* ed. D Doyel, pp. 21–70. Glenwood Springs, CO: Am. Assoc. Adv. Sci.
19. Castetter E, Bell W. 1942. *Pima and Papago Indian Agriculture.* Albuquerque: Univ. N. Mex. Press
20. Chenault M, Ahlstrom R, Motsinger T. 1992. *In the Shadow of South Mountain: The Pre-Classic Hohokam of La Ciudad de Los Hornos.* Tucson, AZ: SWCA Environ. Consult.
21. Cordell L, Gumerman G. 1989. Cultural interaction in the prehistoric Southwest. See Ref. 21a, pp. 1–18
21a. Cordell L, Gumerman G, eds. 1989. *Dynamics of Southwest Prehistory.* Washington, DC: Smithsonian Inst. Press
22. Craig D, Elson M, Wood J. 1992. The growth and development of a platform mound community in the eastern Tonto Basin. In *Proc. 2nd Salado Conf.,* ed. R Lange, S Germick, pp. 22–30. Phoenix: Ariz. Archaeol. Soc.
23. Crosswhite F. 1981. Desert plants, habitat, and agriculture in relation to the major pattern of cultural differentiation in the O'Odham people of southern Arizona. *Desert Plants* 3(1):47–76
24. Crown P. 1987. Classic Period Hohokam settlement and land use in the Casa Grande Ruin area, Arizona. *J. Field Archaeol.* 14(2):147–62
25. Crown P. 1994. *Expressions of Change: The Salado Polychromes in Southwestern Prehistory.* Albuquerque: Univ. N. Mex. Press
26. Crown P, Judge J, eds. 1991. *Chaco and Hohokam: Prehistoric Regional Systems in the American Southwest.* Santa Fe, NM: School Am. Res.
27. Cushing F. 1920. *Zuni Breadstuff.* New York: Mus. Am. Indian, Heye Found.
28. Dean J. 1991. Thoughts on Hohokam chronology. In *Exploring the Hohokam: Prehistoric Desert People in the American Southwest,* ed. G Gumerman, pp. 61–150. Albuquerque: Univ. N. Mex. Press
29. Dean J, Euler R, Gumerman G, Plog F, Hevly R, Karlstrom T. 1985. Human behavior, demography, and paleoenvironment on the Colorado Plateaus. *Am. Antiq.* 50(3):537–54
30. Dean J, Ravesloot J. 1994. The chronology of cultural interaction in the Gran Chichimeca. In *Culture and Contact: Charles Di Peso's Gran Chichimeca,* ed. A Woosley, J Ravesloot, pp. 83–103. Albuquerque: Univ N. Mex. Press
31. Decker K, Tiezen L. 1989. Isotopic reconstruction of Mesa Verde diet from Basketmaker III to Pueblo III. *Kiva* 55(1):33–47
32. Diehl M. 1992. Architecture as a material correlate of mobility strategies: some implications for archaeological research. *Behav. Sci. Res.* 26(1):1–33
33. Di Peso C. 1984. The structure of the 11th century Casas Grandes agricultural system. See Ref. 45, pp. 261–70
34. Doelle W. 1985. *Excavations at the Valencia Site: A Preclassic Hohokam Village in the Southern Tucson Basin,* No. 3. Tucson, AZ: Inst. Am. Res.
35. Doelle W, Huntington F, Wallace H. 1987.

Rincon phase reorganization in the Tucson Basin. In *The Hohokam Village: Site Structure and Organization,* ed. D Doyel, pp. 71–96. Glenwood Springs, CO: Am. Assoc. Adv. Sci.

36. Doolittle W. 1984. Agricultural change as incremental process. *Ann. Assoc. Am. Geogr.* 74(1):124–37

37. Doolittle W. 1990. *Canal Irrigation in Prehistoric Mexico: The Sequence of Technological Change.* Austin: Univ. Texas Press

38. Downs J. 1966. The significance of environmental manipulation in the Great Basin cultural development. In *The Current Status of Anthropological Research in the Great Basin,* Tech. Rep. No. 1, ed. W d'Azevedo, pp. 29–56. Reno, NV: Desert Res. Inst.

39. Doyel D. 1980. Hohokam social organization and the Sedentary to Classic transition. In *Current Issues in Hohokam Prehistory,* Anthropol. Res. Pap. No. 23, ed. D Doyel, F Plog, pp. 23–40. Tempe: Ariz. State Univ. Press

40. Elson M, Stark M, Heidke J. 1992. Prelude to Salado: Preclassic Period settlement in the upper Tonto Basin. In *Proc. 2nd Salado Conf.,* ed. R Lange, S Germick, pp. 274–85. Phoenix: Ariz. Archaeol. Soc.

41. Euler R, Gumerman G, Karlstrom T, Dean J, Hevly R. 1979. The Colorado Plateaus: cultural dynamics and paleoenvironment. *Science* 205:1089–91

42. Fish P, Fish S. 1984. Agricultural maximization in the Sacred Mountain basin. See Ref. 45, pp. 147–60

43. Fish P, Fish S, Gumerman G, Reid J. 1994. Towards an explanation of Southwestern abandonments. In *Themes in Southwestern Prehistory: Grand Patterns and Local Variations in Culture Change,* ed. G Gumerman, M Gell-Mann. Santa Fe, NM: School Am. Res. In press

44. Fish P, Fish S, Long A, Miksicek C. 1986. Early corn remains from Tumamoc Hill, southern Arizona. *Am. Antiq.* 51(3):563–72

45. Fish S, Fish P, eds. 1984. *Prehistoric Agricultural Strategies in the Southwest,* Anthropol. Res. Pap. 33. Tempe: Ariz. State Univ. Press

46. Fish S, Fish P. 1990. An archaeological assessment of ecosystem in the Tucson Basin of southern Arizona. In *The Ecosystem Concept in Anthropology,* ed. E Moran, pp. 159–90. Ann Arbor: Univ. Mich. Press

47. Fish S, Fish P. 1991. Comparative aspects of paradigms for the Neolithic transition in the Levant and the American Southwest. In *Perspectives on the Past: Theoretical Biases in Meditrranean Hunter-Gatherer Research,* ed. G Clark, pp. 396–410. Philadelphia: Univ. Penn. Press

48. Fish S, Fish P, Madsen J. 1990. Sedentism and settlement mobility in the Tucson Basin

prior to A.D. 1000. See Ref. 110a, pp. 76–91

49. Fish S, Fish P, Madsen J. 1992. *The Marana Community in the Hohokam World,* Anthropol. Res. Pap. No. 56. Tucson: Univ. Ariz. Press

50. Fish S, Fish P, Miksicek C, Madsen J. 1985. Largescale prehistoric agave cultivation in southern Arizona. *Desert Plants* 7(1):107–12

51. Fish S, Nabhan G. 1991. Desert as context: the Hohokam environment. In *Exploring the Hohokam: Prehistoric Desert People of the American Southwest,* ed. G Gumerman, pp. 29–60. Albuquerque: Univ. N. Mex. Press

52. Floyd M, Kohler T. 1990. Current productivity and prehistoric use of piñon (*Pinus edulis,* Pinaceae) in the Dolores Archaeological Project area, southwest Colorado. *Econ. Bot.* 44(2):142–56

53. Ford R. 1968. *An ecological analysis involving the population of San Juan Pueblo, New Mexico.* PhD thesis. Univ. Mich., Ann Arbor. 331 pp.

54. Ford R. 1972. An ecological perspective on the Eastern Pueblos. In *New Perspectives on the Pueblos,* ed. A Ortiz, pp. 1–17. Albuquerque: Univ. N. Mex. Press

55. Ford R. 1984. Ecological consequences of early agriculture in the Southwest. In *Papers on the Archaeology of Black Mesa,* ed. S Plog, S Powell, 2:127–38. Carbondale: Univ. S. Ill. Press

56. Gasser R, Kwiatkowski S. 1991. Food for thought: recognizing patterns in Hohokam subsistence. In *Exploring the Hohokam: Prehistoric Desert Peoples of the American Southwest,* ed. G Gumerman, pp. 417–60. Albuquerque: Univ. N. Mex. Press

57. Gilman P. 1987. Architecture as artifact: pit structures and pueblos in the American Southwest. *Am. Antiq.* 52(4):538–64

58. Gish J. 1991. Current perceptions, recent discoveries, and future discoveries in Hohokam palynology. *Kiva* 56(3):237–54

59. Graybill D. 1989. The reconstruction of the prehistoric Salt River streamflow. In *The 1982–1984 Excavations at Las Colinas: Environment and Subsistence,* Archaeol. Ser. No. 162, ed. L Teague, W Deaver, pp. 25–38. Tucson: Ariz. State Mus., Univ. Ariz.

60. Graybill D, Nials F. 1989. Aspects of climate, streamflow, and geomorphology affecting irrigation systems in the Salt River Valley. In *The 1982–1984 Excavations at Las Colinas: Environment and Subsistence,* Archaeol. Ser. No. 162, ed. L Teague, W Deaver, pp. 5–24. Tucson: Ariz. State Mus., Univ. Ariz.

61. Gregory D. 1991. Form and variation in

Hohokam settlement patterns. See Ref. 26, pp. 159–94

62. Gregory D, Nials F. 1985. Observations concerning the distribution of Classic period Hohokam platform mounds. In *Proc. 1983 Hohokam Symp.*, ed. A Dittert, D Dove, pp. 373–88. Phoenix: Ariz. Archaeol. Soc.

63. Gumerman G, ed. 1988. *The Anasazi in a Changing Environment.* Cambridge: Cambridge Univ. Press

64. Gumerman G, Dean J. 1989. Prehistoric cooperation and competition in the western Anasazi area. See Ref. 21a, pp. 99–148

65. Hackbarth M. 1992. *Prehistoric and Historic Occupation of the Lower Verde River Valley: The State Route 87 Verde Bridge Project.* Flagstaff, AZ: Northland Res.

66. Hard R. 1990. Agricultural dependence in the Mountain Mogollon. See Ref. 110a, pp. 135–49

67. Hard R, Merrill W. 1992. Mobile agriculturalists and the emergence of sedentism: perspectives from northern Mexico. *Am. Anthropol.* 94(4):601–20

68. Haury E. 1962. The Greater American Southwest. In *Courses Toward Urban Life,* ed. R Braidwood, G Willey, pp. 106–31. Chicago: Univ. Chicago Press

69. Haury E. 1976. *The Hohokam: Desert Farmers and Craftsmen.* Tucson: Univ. Ariz. Press

70. Hegmon M. 1989. Risk reduction and variation in agricultural economies: a computer simulation of Hopi agriculture. *Res. Econ. Anthropol.* 11:89–121

71. Henderson K. 1987. *Structure and Organization at La Ciudad,* Field Stud. No. 18. Tempe: Ariz. State Univ. Press

72. Herrington L, Creel D. 1991. Treasure Hill: an agricultural center and type site revisited. In *Mogollon V,* ed. P Beckett, pp. 50–61. Las Cruces, NM: COAS

73. Honezak M. 1992. *Contruction timber economics at Sand Canyon Pueblo.* MA thesis. Northern Ariz. Univ., Flagstaff. 225 pp.

74. Howard J. 1987. The Lehi canal system: organization of a Classic period community. In *The Hohokam Village: Site Structure and Organization,* ed. D Doyel, pp. 211–22. Glenwood Springs, CO: Am. Assoc. Adv. Sci.

75. Howard J. 1993. A paleohydraulic approach to examining agricultural intensification in Hohokam irrigation systems. *Res. Econ. Anthropol.* 7:231–322

76. Huckell B. 1990. *Agriculture and late Archaic settlements in the river valleys of southeastern Arizona.* PhD thesis. Univ. Ariz., Tucson. 409 pp.

77. Huckell B, Tagg M, Huckell L. 1987. *The Corona de Tucson Project: Prehistoric Use of a Bajada Environment,* Archaeol. Ser.

No. 174. Tucson: Ariz. State Mus., Univ. Ariz.

78. James S. 1990. Monitoring archaeofaunal changes during the transition to agriculture. *Kiva* 56(1):25–43

79. Jewitt R. 1989. Distance, interaction, and complexity: the spatial organization of pan-regional settlement clusters in the American Southwest. In *The Sociopolitical Structure of Prehistoric Southwestern Societies,* ed. S Upham, K Lightfoot, R Jewett, pp. 363–88. Boulder, CO: Westview

80. Judge J. 1984. New light on Chaco Canyon. In *New Light on Chaco Canyon,* ed. D Noble, pp. 1–12. Santa Fe, NM: School Am. Res.

81. Kent S. 1992. Studying variability in the archaeological record: an ethnoarchaeological model for distinguishing mobility patterns. *Am. Antiq.* 57(4):635–60

82. Kirchoff P. 1954. Gatherers and farmers of the Greater Southwest. *Am. Anthropol.* 56(4):539–50

83. Kohler T. 1992. Guest editorial: the prehistory of sustainability. *Popul. Environ.* 13(4):237–42

84. Kohler T. 1992. Field houses, villages, and the tragedy of the commons in the early northern Anasazi Southwest. *Am. Antiq.* 57(4):617–35

85. Kohler T. 1994. News from the North American Southwest: prehistory on the edge of chaos. *J. Archaeol. Res.* 1(4):In press

86. Kohler T, Matthews M. 1988. Long-term Anasazi land-use and forest reduction: a case study from southwest Colorado. *Am. Antiq.* 53(3):537–64

87. Kohler T, Orcutt J, Blinman E, Petersen K. 1986. Anasazi spreadsheets: the cost of doing business in prehistoric Dolores. In *Dolores Archaeological Program: Final Synthetic Report,* ed. D Breternitz, C Robinson, T Gross, pp. 525–38. Denver: US Bur. Reclam.

88. Lekson S. 1989. Regional systematics in later prehistory of southern New Mexico. In *4th Jornada Mogollon Conf.,* ed. M Duran, K Laumbach, pp. 1–37. Las Cruces, NM: Human Syst. Res.

89. Lekson S. 1991. Settlement patterns and the Chaco region. See Ref. pp. 31–56

90. Levy J. 1992. *Orayvi Revisited.* Tucson: Univ. Ariz. Press

91. Lightfoot K. 1979. Food redistribution among prehistoric Pueblo groups. *Kiva* 44(4):319–39

92. Lightfoot K. 1984. *Prehistoric Political Dynamics: A Case Study from the American Southwest.* Dekalb: N. Ill. Univ. Press

93. Lightfoot K. 1984. *The Duncan Project: A Study of the Occupation Duration of an Early Mogollon Pithouse Village,*

Field Stud. No. 6. Tempe: Ariz. State Univ. Press

94. Lightfoot K, Plog F. 1984. Intensification along the north side of the Mogollon Rim. See Ref. 45, pp. 179–95

95. Long A, Benz B, Donahue D, Jull A, Toolin L. 1989. First direct AMS dates on early maize from Tehuacan, Mexico. *Radiocarbon* 31(3):1035–40

96. Martin D, Goodman G, Armelagos G, Magennis A. 1991. *Black Mesa Anasazi Health: Reconstructing Life from Patterns of Death and Disease*, Pap. No. 14. Carbondale: Cent. Archaeol. Inv., S. Ill. Univ.

97. Masse W. 1991. The quest for subsistence sufficiency and civilization in the Sonoran Desert. See Ref. 26, pp. 195–224

98. Matson R. 1991. *The Origins of Southwestern Agriculture*. Tucson: Univ. Ariz. Press

99. Matson R, Chisholm B. 1991. Basketmaker II subsistence: carbon isotopes and other dietary indicators from Cedar Mesa, Utah. *Am. Antiq.* 56(3):444–59

100. Matson R, Lipe W, Haase W. 1988. Adaptation continuities and occupational discontinuities: the Cedar Mesa Anasazi. *J. Field Archaeol.* 15(2):245–64

101. Maxwell T, Anschuetz K. 1992. The Southwestern ethnographic record and prehistoric agricultural diversity. In *Gardens of Prehistory*, ed. T Killion, pp. 35–68. Tuscaloosa: Univ. Ala. Press

102. McGuire R, Howard A. 1987. The structure and organization of Hohokam exchange. *Kiva* 52(2):113–46

103. McGuire R, Schiffer M. 1983. A theory of architectural design. *J. Anthropol. Archaeol.* 2:277–303

104. Merbs C. 1989. Patterns of health and sickness in the precontact Southwest. In *Columbian Consequences*, Vol. 1. *Archaeological and Historical Perspectives on the Spanish Borderlands West*, ed. D Thomas, pp. 41–55. Washington, DC: Smithsonian Inst. Press

105. Miksicek C. 1988. Rethinking Hohokam paleoethnobotanical assemblages. In *Recent Research on Tucson Basin Prehistory*, ed. W Doelle, P Fish, pp. 47–56. Tucson, AZ: Inst. Am. Res.

106. Minnis P. 1979. Paleoethnobotanical indicators of prehistoric environmental disturbance. In *The Nature and Status of Ethnobotany*, Pap. No. 67, ed. R Ford, pp. 347–66. Ann Arbor: Univ. Mich. Mus. Anthropol.

107. Minnis P. 1985. Domesticating people and plants in the Greater Southwest. In *Prehistoric Food Production in North America*, Pap. No. 75, ed. R Ford, pp. 309–40. Ann Arbor: Univ. Mich. Mus. Anthropol.

108. Minnis P. 1985. *Social Adaptation to Food Stress: A Prehistoric Southwestern Example*. Chicago: Univ. Chicago Press

109. Minnis P. 1989. Prehistoric diet in the northern Southwest: macroplant remains from Four Corner's feces. *Am. Antiq.* 54(3):543–63

110. Minnis P. 1992. Earliest plant cultivation in the desert borderlands of North America. In *The Origins of Agriculture*, C Cowan, P Watson, pp. 121–42. Washington, DC: Smithsonian Inst. Press

110a. Minnis P, Redman C, eds. 1990. *Perspectives on Southwest Prehistory*. Boulder, CO: Westview

111. Mitchell D. 1988. La Lomita Pequeña: relationships between plant resource variability and settlement patterns in the Phoenix Basin. *Kiva* 54(2):127–46

112. Morris D. 1990. Changes in groundstone following the introduction of maize into the American Southwest. *J. Anthropol. Res.* 46(2):177–94

113. Nabhan G. 1986. Ak-chin "arroyo-mouth" and the environmental setting of Papago Indian Fields in the Sonoran Desert. *Appl. Geogr.* 6:61–75

114. Nabhan G, Rea A, Reichhardt K, Mellink E, Hutchinson C. 1983. Papago influences on habitat and biotic diversity: Quitovac oasis ethnoecology. *J. Ethnobiol.* 2(2): 124–43

115. Nelson B, LeBlanc S. 1986. *Short-term Sedentism in the American Southwest*. Albuquerque: Univ. N. Mex. Press

116. Nelson B, Martin D, Swedlund A, Fish P, Armelagos, G. 1994. Studies in disruption: demography and health in the prehistoric American Southwest. In *Understanding Complexity in the Prehistoric Southwest*, ed. G Gumerman, M Gell-Mann. Boston: Addison-Wesley. In press

117. Nelson M. 1990. Comments: sedentism, mobility, and regional assemblages: problems posed in the analysis of Southwestern prehistory. See Ref. 110a, pp. 150–56

118. Nelson M. 1991. The study of technological organization. In *Advances in Archaeological Method and Theory* 3:57–100. Tucson: Univ. Ariz. Press

119. Netting RM. 1993. *Smallholders, Householders: Farm Families and the Ecology of Intensive, Sustainable Agriculture*. Stanford, CA: Stanford Univ. Press

120. Neusius S, Gold M. 1988. Faunal remains: implications for Dolores Anasazi adaptions. In *Dolores Archaeological Program: Anasazi Communities of Dolores*, ed. W Lipe, J Morris, T Kohler, pp. 1049–136. Denver, CO: US Bur. Reclam.

121. Nicholas L, Feinman G. 1989. A regional perspective on Hohokam irrigation in the lower Salt River Valley, Arizona. In *The Sociopolitical Structure of Prehistoric Southwestern Societies*, ed. S Upham, K

Lightfoot, R Jewett, pp. 199–236. Boulder, CO: Westview
122. O'Laughlin T. 1980. *The Keystone Dam Site and Other Archaic and Formative Sites in Northwest El Paso, Texas*, Rep. No. 8. El Paso: Texas Centennial Mus.
123. Olsen J. 1990. *Vertebrate Faunal Remains from Grasshopper Pueblo, Arizona*, Pap. No. 83. Ann Arbor: Univ. Mich. Mus. Anthropol.
124. Orcutt J, Blinman E, Kohler T. 1990. Explanations of population aggregation in the Mesa Verde region prior to A.D. 900. See Ref. 110a, pp. 196–212
125. Peterson K. 1988. *Climate and the Dolores River Anasazi*, Anthropol. Pap. No. 113. Salt Lake City: Univ. Utah Press
126. Pilles P. 1978. The field house and Sinagua demography. In *Limited Activity and Occupations Sites*, ed. A Ward, pp. 119–33. Albuquerque: Cent. Anthropol. Stud.
127. Plog F. 1989. The Sinagua and their relations. See Ref. 21a, pp. 263–92
128. Plog S. 1990. Agriculture, sedentism, and environment in the evolution of political systems. In *The Evolution of Political Systems*, ed. S Upham, pp. 177–202. Cambridge: Cambridge Univ. Press
129. Powell S. 1990. Sedentism and mobility: what do the data say? What did the Anasazi do? See Ref. 110a, pp. 92–102
130. Preucel R. 1987. Settlement succession on the Pajarito Plateau, New Mexico. *Kiva* 53(1):3–34
131. Preucel R. 1988. *Seasonal agricultural circulation and residential mobility: a prehistoric example from the Pajarito Plateau, New Mexico*. PhD thesis. Univ. Calif., Los Angeles. 356 pp.
132. Rautman A. 1993. Resource variability, risk, and the structure of social networks: an example from the prehistoric Southwest. *Am. Antiq.* 58(3):403–24
133. Rea A. 1981. The ecology of Pima fields. *Environ. Southwest* 484:8–15
134. Rea A. 1983. *Once a River: Bird Life and Habitat Changes on the Middle Gila River.* Tucson: Univ. Ariz. Press
135. Reid J, Whittlesey S. 1990. The complicated and the complex: observations on the archaeological record of large pueblos. See Ref. 110a, pp. 184–95
136. Rice G. 1990. *A Design for Salado Research*, Anthropol. Field Stud. No. 22. Tempe: Ariz. State Univ. Press
137. Rice G, Redman C. 1993. Platform mounds of the Arizona desert. *Expedition* 35(1):53–63
138. Russell F. 1975. *The Pima Indians*. Tucson: Univ. Ariz. Press
139. Samuels ML, Betancourt JL. 1982. Modeling the long-term effects of fuelwood harvests on pinon-juniper woodlands. *Environ. Manage.* 6(6):505–15

140. Sandor J, Gersper P. 1988. Evaluation of soil productivity in some prehistoric agricultural terraces in New Mexico. *Agron. J.* 80:846–50
141. Schlanger S. 1988. Patterns of population movement and long-term population growth in southwestern Colorado. *Am. Antiq.* 53(3):460–74
142. Sebastian L. 1992. *The Chaco Anasazi: Sociopolitical Evolution in the Prehistoric Southwest.* Cambridge: Cambridge Univ. Press
143. Seme M. 1984. The effects of agricultural fields on faunal assemblage variation. In *Papers on the Archaeology of Black Mesa, Arizona*, ed. S Plog, S Powell, 2:139–57. Carbondale: Univ. S. Ill. Press
144. Shipek F. 1989. An example of intensive plant husbandry: the Kumeyaay of southern California. In *Foraging and Farming: The Evolution of Plant Exploitation*, ed. D Harris, G Hillmann, pp. 159–70. London: Unwin Hyman
145. Simmons A. 1982. Modeling Archaic adaptive behavior in the Chaco region. In *Prehistoric Adaptive Strategies in the Chaco Canyon Region, Northwestern New Mexico*, Anthropol. Pap. No. 9, ed. A Simmons, pp. 731–80. Window Rock, AZ: Navajo Nation
146. Simmons A. 1986. New evidence for the early use of cultigens in the American Southwest. *Am. Antiq.* 51(1):73–88
147. Smiley F. 1985. *Chronometrics and the Lolomai farmer/hunter gatherers of Black Mesa: approaches to the interpretation of radiocarbon determinations.* PhD thesis. Univ. Mich., Ann Arbor. 520 pp.
148. Smith BD. 1989. Origins of agriculture in the eastern United States. *Science* 246:1566–71
149. Speth J, Scott S. 1989. Horticulture and large mammal hunting. In *Farmers as Hunters: The Implications of Sedentism*, ed. S Kent, pp. 71–79. Cambridge: Cambridge Univ. Press
150. Spielmann K, Schoeninger M, Moore K. 1990. Plains-pueblo interdependence and human diet at Pecos Pueblo, New Mexico. *Am. Antiq.* 55(4):745–65
151. Steward J. 1929. Irrigation without agriculture. *Pap. Mich. Acad. Sci. Arts Lett.* 22:149–56
152. Stiger M. 1979. Mesa Verde subsistence patterns from Basketmaker to Pueblo III. *Kiva* 44(2):133–44
153. Stodder A, Martin D. 1991. Native health and disease in the American Southwest before and after Spanish contact. In *Disease and Demography in the Americas*, ed. J Verano, D Ubelaker, pp. 55–73. Washington, DC: Smithsonian Inst. Press
154. Stuart D, Gautier R. 1981. *Prehistoric New*

Mexico: Background for Survey. Santa Fe, NM: Hist. Preserv. Bur.

155. Sullivan A. 1982. Mogollon agrarian ecology. *Kiva* 48(1):1–15

156. Sullivan A, Downum C. 1991. Aridity, activity, and volcanic ash agriculture. *World Archaeol.* 22(3):271–86

157. Szuter C, Bayham F. 1989. Sedentism and animal procurement among desert horticulturalists of the North American Southwest. In *Farmers as Hunters: The Implications of Sedentism,* ed. S Kent, pp. 80–95. Cambridge: Cambridge Univ. Press

158. Teague L. 1988. The history of occupation at Las Colinas. In *The 1982–1984 Excavations at Las Colinas: The Site and Its Features,* Archaeol. Ser. No. 162, ed. D Gregory, pp. 121–52. Tucson: Ariz. State Mus., Univ. Ariz.

159. Toll W. 1991. Material distributions and exchange in the Chaco system. See Ref. 26, pp. 77–108

160. Tuggle D, Reid J, Cole R. 1984. Fourteenth century Mogollon agriculture in the Grasshopper region of Arizona. See Ref. 45, pp. 101–10

161. Upham S. 1982. *Polities and Power: An Economic and Political History of the Western Pueblo.* New York: Academic

162. Upham S. 1992. Interaction and isolation: the empty spaces in panregional political and economic systems. In *Resources, Power, and Interregional Interaction,* ed. E Schortman, P Urban, pp. 139–52. New York: Plenum

163. Upham S, MacNeish R, Galinat W, Stevenson C. 1987. Evidence concerning the origin of *Maiz de Ocho. Am. Anthropol.* 89(2):410–19

164. Van West C. 1990. *Modeling prehistoric climatic variability and agricultural production in the Dolores area, Southwest Colorado.* PhD thesis. Wash. State Univ., Pullman. 123 pp.

165. Vivian R. 1990. *The Chacoan Prehistory of the San Juan Basin, New Mexico.* San Diego: Academic

166. Ward A, ed. 1978. *Limited Activity and Occupation Sites,* Contr. No. 1. Albuquerque: Cent. Anthropol. Stud.

167. Weaver D. 1972. A cultural-ecological model for the Classic Hohokam Period in the lower Salt River Valley, Arizona. *Kiva* 38(1):43–52

168. Wetterstrom W. 1986. *Food, Diet, and Population at Prehistoric Arroyo Hondo Pueblo, New Mexico.* Santa Fe, NM:

School Am. Res.

169. Whitely P. 1988. *Deliberate Acts.* Tucson: Univ. Ariz. Press

170. Whiting A. 1939. *The Ethnobotany of the Hopi,* Bull. 15. Flagstaff: Mus. N. Ariz.

171. Wilcox D, Sterberg C. 1983. *Hohokam Ballcourts and Their Interpretation,* Archaeol. Ser. No. 160. Tucson: Ariz. State Mus., Univ. Ariz.

172. Wilde J, Newman D. 1989. Late Archaic corn in the eastern Great Basin. *Am. Anthropol.* 91(3):712–19

173. Wills W. 1988. *The Agricultural Transition in the American Southwest.* Santa Fe, NM: School Am. Res.

174. Wills W. 1991. Organizational strategies and the emergence of prehistoric villages in the American Southwest. In *Between Bands and States,* ed. S Gregg, pp. 161–80. Carbondale: Cent. Archaeol. Invest., Univ. S. Ill.

175. Wills W. 1992. Foraging systems and plant cultivation during the emergence of agricultural economies in the prehistoric American Southwest. In *Transitions to Agriculture in Prehistory,* ed. A Gebauer, T Price, pp. 153–76. Madison, WI: Prehistory

176. Wills W, Huckell B. 1994. Economic implications of changing landuse patterns in the Late Archaic. In *Themes in Southwestern Prehistory: Grand Patterns and Local Variations in Culture Change,* ed. G Gumerman, M Gell-Mann. Santa Fe, NM: School Am. Res. In press

177. Wills W, Windes T. 1989. Evidence for population aggregation and dispersal during the Basketmaker III Period in Chaco Canyon, New Mexico. *Am. Antiq.* 53(2):347–69

178. Windes T. 1987. *Investigations at the Pueblo Alto Complex, Chaco Canyon,* Vol. 1. Santa Fe, NM: Natl. Park Serv.

179. Winter J. 1978. Anasazi agriculture at Hovenweep. In *Limited Activity and Occupation Sites,* ed. A Ward, pp. 83–98. Albuquerque: Cent. Anthropol. Stud.

180. Wood J, Rice G, Jacobs D. 1992. Factors affecting prehistoric Salado irrigation in the Tonto Basin. In *Developing Perspectives on Tonto Basin Prehistory,* Anthropol. Field Stud. No. 26, ed. C Redman, G Rice, K Pedrick, pp. 27–32. Tempe: Ariz. State Univ. Press

181. Woosley A. 1980. Agricultural diversity in the prehistoric Southwest. *Kiva* 45(4):315–35

Annu. Rev. Anthropol. 1994. 23:109–36

VIOLENCE, TERROR, AND THE CRISIS OF THE STATE

Carole Nagengast

Department of Anthropology, University of New Mexico, Albuquerque, New Mexico 87131

KEY WORDS: violence, state, dissidence, human rights

INTRODUCTION

Among the primary goals of the modern, post-Enlightenment state are assimilation, homogenization, and conformity within a fairly narrow ethnic and political range, as well as the creation of societal agreement about the kinds of people there are and the kinds there ought to be. The ideal state is one in which the illusion of a single nation-state is created and maintained and in which resistance is managed so that profound social upheaval, separatist activity, revolution, and *coups d'etat* are unthinkable for most people most of the time. The state thus attempts to ensure conformity to encompassing unitary images through diverse cultural forms and an array of institutions and activities that, taken together, help determine the range of available social, political, ethnic, and national identities (2, 12, 66).

The crisis of the contemporary state springs from its differentially successful monopolization of power and the contradiction between it and the demands of peripheralized people(s) who through resistance have created new subject positions that challenge fundamentally the definitions of who and what ought to be repressed. To phrase it differently, the ways in which nation and state are constructed and the manner in which those constructions enter into social knowledge have to do with consensus about what is and what is not legitimate. When consensus fails, ethnic or political opposition, which is otherwise suppressed or subtle, becomes overt. The state, of course, cannot allow this to happen. As Claestres (49:110) phrases it, "The refusal of multiplicity, the dread of difference—ethnocidal violence—[is] the very essence of the state."

Since the Berlin Wall fell in 1989, twenty-two new *global communities* have been created, fifteen from the remains of the Soviet Union alone, but the phenomenon is not restricted to that part of the world. There are over fifty ethnic conflicts now taking place, mostly within the confines of diverse nation-states—a veritable explosion of violence with the state lending the force of arms to one side or the other. Geographers predict that there will be twenty-five additional new states by 1996, even more in the twenty-first century (260), all forged, some violently and some by agreement, from the territory and peoples of existing states. In addition to Abkhazians in Georgia and Armenians in Nagorno-Karabakh, Tibetans, Quebequois, Kurds, Tamils, and Basques are among others seeking their own version of a nation-state.

At the same time there is an apparently contradictory trend, namely the globalization of capitalist economy and culture. These two trends—the fragmenting of illusory nation-states and the simultaneous homogenization of culture—may only appear contradictory; the latter may be driving the former. The nation-state has long been the vehicle, the ideological justification, and the political legitimation for liberal rational forms of political and cultural unity and economic homogeneity. Although the social organization and economic achievements of a market economy are goals toward which many new entities are striving, especially those of the former Soviet Union and East Central Europe, their prospects for retracing the trajectory of nineteenth and twentieth century bourgeois capitalism are slight. The potential and reality of additional ethnic and nationalist violence are enormous as dissidents challenge the prevailing and approaching order and existing states struggle to implement new distributions of power and capital, to suppress internal movements for political change, especially autonomy and self-determination, and to stave off external threats to newly established borders.

Until relatively recently, few anthropologists examined violence and conflict between groups and the state and among groups within states, especially violence rooted in ethnicity, nationalism, bids for autonomy and self-determination, and political demands for fundamental change. Some have looked primarily at the invention and reinvention of categorical differences inflected by language, culture, and history in colonial and post-colonial societies (101, 102, 109, 117, 135, 209). An emerging project to rethink violence and social theory at the level of the imagining of the state and the role of the anthropologist in this project is suggested by the work of Coronil (64), Feldman (84a), Gordon (109), Isbell (138–140), Taussig (240, 241), Poole & Renique (198), recent collections of Carmack (37), Downing & Kushner (74, 75), Nordstrom & Martin (192), Warren (253), and others (29, 65, 230). This review places the

existing literature within a theoretical perspective that considers both the ethnography of the state and the ethnography of violence, but we must first
consider some terms of the discussion.

VIOLENCE, TERRORISM, AND TORTURE

Violence is often reified, taken as a characteristic or category that is either
present or absent within a society or group, making it difficult to examine the
role it plays in social relations or to examine it as an alternative people use to
deal with human predicaments. Going beyond the mere presence or absence of
violence challenges us to locate it within a set of practices, discourses, and
ideologies (137), to examine it as a way to deploy power within differential
social and political relations (30), or as a means that states use to buttress
themselves and to maintain power (132).

Scholars do not agree on exactly what constitutes violence. Noting that it
permeates daily life in many parts of the modern world, Williams (256) selects
violence as a keyword, denoting a concept that in his estimation significantly
reflects ideas and values that often characterize general discussions of contemporary society. He identifies seven senses of violence: aggressive behavior,
vehement conduct, infringement of property or dignity, the use of physical
force, and threat, or dramatic portrayal of any of the above. Riches (204)
argues that what is generally called violence can be practical or symbolic,
visible or invisible (as in witchcraft), physical or emotional, and can stem from
a perpetrator's personal capacity or from the forces of society. He gives
precedence to the first in each of these dichotomies, restricting the use of the
term *violence* to practical, physical, visible, and personal physical force that
people use to achieve goals. In this instrumental view, interactions in which
physical hurt is either absent or not readily apparent, even if it may have been
intended or implicit, is not violence.

Bourdieu, on the other hand, includes the symbolic "censored" and
"euphemized" but "socially recognized violence" embedded in everyday,
hegemonic practice in "disguised and transfigured" form (30:191), a totalizing
vision partially challenged by Comaroff (56). Feminist scholarship in particular (177, 228, 235) and that of subordinate peoples in general (45, 63) insists
that symbolic violence is important in the structuring and ordering of relations
of domination and subordination, though critics caution that state regimes
everywhere justify their own violence as a reaction to the (symbolic) violence
implicit in opposition itself. The very presence of opposition is read by the
state as violence subject to suppression (192). This review addresses both
physical and symbolic violence.

ANTHROPOLOGICAL STUDIES OF VIOLENCE

Anthropologists who have considered violence primarily in its practical, physical, and visible manifestations have juxtaposed "violent" societies [e.g. the Yanomami (42, 43), the Kiowa (178), or the Kohistani of Pakistan (147)] with those said to be peaceful [e.g. the !Kung (157, 169), the Semai (72, 204–207), the Innuit (32–34), the Buid of the Philippines (104), and the Xinguanos of the Brazilian Amazon (114)], as though they were mirror-images. No single explanation has been found for the variance in the degree to which people use violence to solve differences. Biological explanations are far from a dead letter in psychological and genetic studies, especially as they are viewed in popular culture (245), but biology is rarely cited as a single cause explanation in anthropology (41–43, 76, 97, 115). A large literature has emerged on other causes of violence [e.g. material, ecological, psychological, and historical (38, 39, 85, 87–89, 103, 104, 114)].

Historically, anthropology has been concerned mostly with so-called sub-state or pre-state societies—the tribal zone (91). Here, people condone, even encourage violence as a social and cultural resource for a variety of reasons. For the Maori and indigenous people of the Northwest Coast of North America, it is a means to material rewards and a way to maintain a trade advantage (86, 247). The Yanomami use it to protect valued resources (42, 43), the Kohistani as part of a religious code involving honor or vengeance (147), and the Ilongot to assuage grief (210). Anthropology has not been in the forefront of the study of collective violence, terrorism, and especially violence in state societies, in part because its methods and theory depend on months or years in the field, until recently defined as a relatively small, self-contained community that did not include the state. Also, prolonged research in a local community is difficult or impossible in times of violent strife and it is risky business to appear to take sides in situations in which the state resorts to torture, terrorism, and disappearances and in which armed opposition groups operate in a similar manner. Even studies of violence in the tribal zone, however, are rarely contextualized in a matrix of regional, state, or global economic and political systems, nor are they always well placed in historic perspective, though this is changing gradually (91), especially with respect to complex societies (37, 112, 192, 253).

Political, economic, and historical correctives to the more egregious representations of the colonial subject as either inherently violent or innately peaceful have appeared (109, 181). Gibson (104) discusses the historical circumstances in which the Semai, Buid, and Bataak of Southeast Asia were taken as slaves by the Sulu sultanate of eighteenth and nineteenth century Philippines. They responded by retreating deep into the forest and elaborating a cultural complex of peace and non-violence. Several restudies of the Yanomami indicate that much of their violent activity coincides with contact with settlers, petrochemical industries, and institutions of the state (68, 90, 108). Gordon (109) places the "Bushmen" of southern Africa, the quintessential harmless people, in the context of the colonial project to simultaneously subdue and domesticate them on the one hand and to define them as "vermin of the veldt" on the other, a strategy of containment the United States found enormously successful in "taming" North American indigenous peoples.

Social scientists who address collective violence in complex state societies (37, 105, 121, 192, 243, 244, 253) examine the culture, economics, politics, or sociolinguistics of components of those societies from points of view that may, for example, explore local culture as it is embedded in the structure and institution of the state (224), but they do not necessarily theorize those structures and institutions (62, 63, 126, 195, 200) or the nature of the state itself. Others more successfully address historical representations of the violent Other (239–241) and take up the violence that arises within the context of decolonization, political and cultural struggles for independence from colonial rule, and the continued domination of former colonial powers (24, 45, 118, 149). Das (67b), Guidieri et al (117) and Horowitz (136) address ethnic conflict within the boundaries of a state and Glenny (106), Magas (165), and Poulton (199) are among those who examine the breakup of the Yugoslav state, though they do so with varying degrees of even-handedness, Magas being the most obviously partisan.

A number of anthropologists have studied warfare in pre-state and archaeologically known societies (87, 91, 99, 120, 258). War between states as a special kind of collective violence, its reasons and its meanings, and especially the national character of the enemies of the United States were early taken up as anthropological phenomena by North American scholars, partly in response to the needs of the United States War Department (22, 110) and in support of the United States in World War II. Since the notorious involvement of anthropologists in counter-insurgency in Thailand in the 1960s (251), anthropologists have avoided direct involvement in war related research.

Anthropological perspectives on the origins of warfare are more or less the same as for violence: they encompass the cultural (137), social and cultural (113), economic and political (248), and scarce resources arguments (92). Others take a political economy approach (18, 47, 259) or a purely historical one (171). Explanations for maintenance or continuation of war include resistance and rebellion on the part of indigenous or other oppressed people (91) and revenge, which in state societies may be couched in religious, ethnic, and ideological language (e.g. "Remember the Alamo" or "Kill a Commie for Christ"). Revenge is often deeply personalized—the images of Saddam Hussein the assassin in the Gulf War of 1990, the World War I specter of the bloodthirsty Hun, World War II and Cold War enemies as insects, pigs, and beasts of various kinds are commonplace (146). Cohn (54) discusses the imagery of sex and death among nuclear defense technicians, and other articles in a edited volume (182) reveal the triumph of image over reality and the social, economic, and political context of media coverage of the Gulf War throughout the Middle East, Asia, and Europe. Sex and masculinity are often aspects of the representation of warfare, but Elshtain (79) casts considerable doubt on gendered myths that depict men as makers of war and women as simultaneously conciliators and socializers of warriors.

The continuation of war may also be justified in official circles as a rational, common sense strategy of deterring force with equal or greater force. Finally, a warrior class or group has an interest in maintaining war or its threat (171). These last two explanations are especially characteristic of state societies with well-developed departments of defense and standing armies, but numerous non-state societies also have permanent warrior classes and measured responses to violent incursions from the outside (91).

POLITICAL VIOLENCE

Political violence encompasses overt state-sponsored or tolerated violence in all of Williams' senses, (coercion or the threat of it, bodily harm, etc) but may also include actions taken or not by the state or its agents with the express intent of realizing certain social, ethnic, economic, and political goals in the realm of public affairs, especially affairs of the state or even of social life in general. These may or may not be direct violence. For example, ferocity between Hutus and Tutsi in Rwanda and Burundi (158, 166, 167, 173); between Tamils and Sinhalese in Sri Lanka (142, 215, 228a, 236–238); between Ladinos and indigenous peoples in Guatemala (37, 168, 246, 253); between Israelis and Palestinians in Israel, the West Bank, and Gaza Strip (227); or among Croats, Serbs, and Muslims in the Balkans (106, 125, 165, 199), insofar as it is tolerated or encouraged by states in order to create, justify, excuse, explain, or enforce hierarchies of difference and relations of inequality, are acts of state violence, even though states themselves may not appear on the surface to be primary agents (cf 133). Moreover, the deliberate acts of agents of the state in, for example, the Soviet Union in the 1930s, which caused mass starvation in the countryside (13, 14, 164), and similar economic or political deeds elsewhere in the world that result in widespread deaths (226) and often huge numbers of political refugees (67a, 84, 124, 262) also qualify as political violence, terror, even genocide (151, 160).

Terrorism is, according to the dictionary, "the policy of using acts inspiring great fear as a method of ruling or of conducting political opposition," and may include violence in all of its senses including torture or its threat. It "is not so much the exploitation of the other as much as the mere consciousness of the possibility," said Simmel (quoted in 192:8) of domination. Clearly the same must be even more true of torture. Torture—the very term evokes images of a distant, less civilized past, of dark cellars, of both the tortured and torturers radically different from ourselves. Nonetheless torture perpetrated by states and their agents is commonplace, documented in scores of countries around the world (9). As for terror, academics, politicians, and popular pundits usually reserve the label for political opposition movements or figures (155), only rarely applying it to states (29, 46, 132, 156). Violence and terror are highly politicized terms embraced and elaborated by victims and avoided by perpetrators, especially if the perpetrator is a state. In fact, state leaders everywhere claim respect for universal human rights and deny that their acts constitute torture, violence, or terror, preferring to characterize them as necessary measures to insure order and respect for the law. Nonetheless, the state is often the instigator of cycles of violent human rights abuses as it seeks to suppress change and prevent opposition movements from undermining its legitimacy (9, 69).

Discussions and explanations of torture, other violence, and terrorism within state society center on the purported need of societies to modernize quickly at all costs (197, 202), to coordinate knowledge with systems of social control (93), and to legitimate the rule of the state (202). Legitimacy is always a central concern in the sense that violence is only violence by definition if the perpetrators fail to establish the legitimacy of their acts against claims of others that it is illegitimate (203). Consider the case of a California woman who shot dead, in the very courtroom in which he was being tried, the man accused of sodomizing her son. In the eyes of her supporters, she was justified in killing the man who, just before the shooting, allegedly smirked at her terrified son, whom he had earlier threatened with death if he, the child, ever told anyone about his sexual abuse. The woman's supporters do not define her act as violence. Similarly, the person who bombs an office building or hijacks an airplane is not considered a terrorist by those who believe that the workers in the building are part of a military and industrial complex that threatens world peace or that their political cause will somehow be advanced by the hijacking.

States as well as political opposition movements also take this instrumental view as justification for tactical preemption in which they gain advantage over opponents by forestalling with violent measures possible action by opponents or by taking revenge for acts completed. They present their actions as both unavoidable and necessary to prevent what would otherwise be inevitable and unavoidable deeds of their targets (203). For the most part, the public has learned to find such official measures justified, that is to say, legitimate by definition. But the public does not accept as readily the structurally similar acts of foreign nationals targeting civilian centers or vigilante justice of the sort meted out to the alleged sodomizer.

THE STATE

Conventional social science theories of the state, drawn largely from utilitarian and Weberian analyses of legitimacy and political power, objectify and endow the state with institutions with law-making and enforcing capabilities that may be more or less democratic, more or less brutal, more or less violent. Insofar as anthropology has dealt with the state, it has taken it as an unanalyzed given or posited a stage, implicitly the final one, in the evolution of political and cultural organization. In this view, the state is manifest as the political management of a specified geographic territory and its inhabitants through the mechanism of centralized government institutions staffed and controlled by a small number of specialists (51, 221). State structures and practices are the cumulative effect of a social contract in which the public has ostensibly agreed that the state has a monopoly on force, and therefore it and only it can legitimately constrain and coerce people. According to conflict theory, the state emerged in order to allow an elite class to obtain and maintain power over subordinates, thereby managing class conflict through force and by means of the control of ideology (99; cf 48, 152). In a benign view of origins, the state provides the stability needed for increasing complexity and presumably desirable and beneficial overall growth and development (39, 51), a utopian bias that has been implicated in the ongoing critique of colonialism and its projects (188, 216; cf 222). Recent debate in other social sciences about the nature of the state (21, 35, 40, 83, 100, 141, 179, 211, 223) and analyses that interrogate the state as ethnographic subject are not as commonplace in anthropology, although that is changing slowly (1, 10, 52, 71, 250).

To be sure, there is an autonomous and extraordinarily powerful entity called the state. According to Abrams, one measure of its powerfulness is its ability to thwart attempts to unmask that power (2:63). But the state is not just a set of institutions staffed by bureaucrats who serve public interest. It also incorporates cultural and political forms, representations, discourse, practices and activities, and specific technologies and organizations of power that, taken together, help to define public interest, establish meaning, and define and naturalize available social identities (2, 12, 53, 66, 79, 94–96, 185, 186, 190, 193). These identities are located within both the domain of state apparatuses and so-called civil society, often glossed as public versus private, a distinction that renders opaque the state's daily intrusions into peoples' lives, their employment, their bodies, "through a plurality of qualities and statuses which are the predicate of the subject 'I'" (3:42). Abrams, for example, characterizes the state as an ideological project, "an exercise in legitimation of that which would be illegitimate if seen directly and as itself, an unacceptable domination" (2:76). He advocates a shift to analysis of social subordination, the legitimating of the illegitimate, and to the hegemonic fields in which power relations play themselves out. Integral to this view is Gramsci's (111) theory of hegemony, especially transformative hegemony (58, 255, 256).

It has become an anthropological commonplace to note that arbitrary symbolic systems are created in a dialectic of official hegemony and popular resistance that both divide and unite and that are naturalized so that they are both part of taken-for-granted daily life and flexible enough to respond to changing political and economic circumstances (35, 66). The agreed upon identities imply closure on other modes of being by disrupting, diluting, sometimes even denying the possibility of alternatives. The state promotes and enforces that consensus in a dialectical relationship with the intelligentsia (31) even as external relations change. This is not a totally transparent process of course, as Stuart Hall (122:44) reminds us:

> Ruling or dominant conceptions of the world [may] not directly prescribe the mental content of...the heads of the dominated classes. But the circle of dominant ideas does accumulate the symbolic power to map or classify the world for others; its classifications do acquire not only the constraining power of dominance over other modes of thought but also the inertial authority of habit and instinct. It becomes the horizon of the taken for granted: what the world is and how it works, for all practical purposes. Ruling ideas may dominate other conceptions of the social world by setting the limit to what will appear as rational, reasonable, credible, indeed sayable or thinkable, within the given vocabularies of motive and action available to us.

In most states, the struggle for consensus is not ordinarily contested in the realm of politics but rather in that of social life where consensus is built. It is the deviants and resisters of all kinds who are subject to the state's violence. Although there is a danger that the state as ideological project becomes a mechanical device to explain all limitations to human freedom, proponents maintain that that project is a dialogue between destruction and preservation, prohibition and enabling, and it illuminates how people contest, negotiate, learn, and ultimately internalize identities.

THE NATION

We cannot speak of the state without also discussing nation and nationalism as hegemonic ideas that inflect the behavior of those who engage in violent action against a perceived Other. There are two views of nation, the first of which is that nations existed naturally before the emergence of states; that they are unique, distinctive units distinguishable from all others; that language, culture, or religious differences may even be manifest in physical singularity;

and that they are unambiguously based on shared history, values, and/or territory (23, 27). In this Herderian view, nationalism is the spiritual, ideological,
and political expression of objective reality and must coincide with a political
state and a specific territory. The second, more generally held view, among
scholars at least, is that a nation is constructed initially by subjective self-
awareness by virtue of its presumed members bringing to consciousness a
sense of commonality and collective will (12, 58, 60, 61, 100, 134, 145, 225,
237, 237a). Moreover, nations do not produce states, but rather states produce
nations through "the artefact, invention, and social engineering of nations"
(134:10). In short, the integrative needs of the modern state produced nationalist ideology, which created the nation, "sometimes tak[ing] pre-existing cultures and turn[ing] them into nations, sometimes invent[ing] them, and often
obliterat[ing] pre-existing cultures" (100:48, 49), a dynamic relationship recognized and elaborated by nationalist leaders of the late nineteenth and early
twentieth centuries, among them Pilsudski of Poland (185, 208) and Mazzini
of Italy (111). Those who discuss nationalism solely as an instrument of
intellectuals and activists (261), however, must explain how it becomes the
lived reality of everyone else who then act upon it, and acknowledge that
intellectual ideology is not transformed into folk culture unproblematically
unless the ideas of intellectuals are a reflection of an already hegemonic
popular culture.

The liberal intelligentsias of the nineteenth century, leaders of nationalist
movements in Poland, Italy, Germany, Serbia, Romania, Belgium, and elsewhere had to codify one of a number of dialects, almost always that of the
elite, into national languages and privilege or invent common histories in order
to bind people together around loyalty to a new political form that in Europe,
North America, and their colonies had a decidedly economic rationale (148).
Elites, national leaders, and educators did not apologize for this cultural re-
packaging but rather celebrated what they saw as rational, democratic movements toward modernity and capitalism. It was progress (145; cf 45) and
subordinate atavistic identities and people had to be submerged and homogenized, sometimes disappearing altogether, sometimes retaining an identity as a
minority or an indigenous people. At best subordinate languages, cultures, and
ways of life are elaborated as national symbols of the past, often converted into
tourist attractions for domestic and foreign consumption (186). At worst they
are suppressed violently as threats to national unity and territorial integrity.
Sometimes, as in Guatemala, both strategies are mobilized (37, 168, 188).

Nation and nationalism are in Europe and North America terms of modernity, offspring of the Enlightenment, colonial expansion, religious wars, ra-
tionalism, and liberal capitalism that serve as ideological justification and
political legitimation for certain notions of territorial, political, and cultural
unity enforced by the hegemony of liberal thought and organization. The

vision of shared nationality as routine lived reality usually masks the hidden presence of class and other power relations of modern states, including those of parts of socialist East Central Europe and the Soviet Union, which were constructed of similar raw materials (185, 249). Other literature that defines nation and state broadly include Malkki's (167) account of the manner in which maps and scholarly studies of refugees contribute to the definition of that which roots people in specific bits of soil. Malkki invokes the "territorializing concepts of identity" (167:25) in describing desecrated graves in a Jewish cemetery in France and the recently buried corpse that was disinterred and impaled on an umbrella. The corpse could not, in the estimation of the desecrators, be simultaneously Jewish and of the French nation and therefore had to be taken out of its soil, lest it *root* there. Borneman (28) takes up the constructions of national and nationalist narratives and conversations among states and citizens as a means of legitimating both the division and ultimately the reunification of Berlin, and Dominquez (73) discusses the politics of heritage as Ashkenazim and Sepharadim contest the cultural contents of the Israeli state.

Some scholars of the post-colonial world insist that the content of nationalism in the southern hemisphere has logical and theoretical implications not derived from western, rational thought but rather is a discourse that emerged in dialogue with colonialism. Insofar as it is able to reject colonial rule as an "almost palpable historical truth," so is this nationalist discourse able to construct and assert new political possibilities (45:40, 41). Chatterjee presumes that these possibilities, though still encompassing discourses of power, are capable of perceiving, revising, and rejecting the imperatives of capitalism, the hegemony of the liberal rationalist state, and the moral leadership of an intelligentsia derived from elite classes.

Not only has nation been conceptually delinked from state, but there is a growing literature on deterritorialized spatial possibilities in which nations are deployed in transnational communities of various kinds (15, 107, 143, 144, 212, 213). Gupta (119) offers the non-aligned movement and the European Community as communities that transgress expectable spatial arrangements. Violence in the name of keeping some people out, however, is still a means of enforcing definitions of the nation-state and class and power relations appropriate to capitalist production, as many Mexican and Central American farm worker migrants to California and the Southwest well-know (187, 254).

THE STATE, THE NATION, AND HEGEMONY

The numbers of people worldwide subjected to the violence of their own states are staggering. More than a quarter of a million Kurds and Turks in Turkey have been beaten or tortured by the military, police, and prison guards since 1980; tens of thousands of indigenous people in Peru and Guatemala (8), street children in Brazil and Guatemala, Palestinians in Kuwait, Kurds in Iraq, and Muslim women and girls in Bosnia have been similarly treated (9). Mutilated bodies turn up somewhere every day. Some 6000 people in dozens of counties were legally shot, hung, electrocuted, gassed, or stoned to death by their respective states between 1985 and 1992 for political misdeeds: criticism of the state, membership in banned political parties or groups, or for adherence to the "wrong" religion; for moral deeds: adultery, prostitution, homosexuality, sodomy, or alcohol and drug use; for economic offenses: burglary, embezzling, and corruption; and for violent crimes: rape, assault, and murder (5, 7, 9).

Lyotard (163:46) describes the postmodern as "the presentation of the unpresentable," its translation into recognizable and acceptable myths and discourses. For a state, the unpresentable is that which is improper, unthinkable under the requirements of its formal presentation of itself. It is formally unthinkable that a state would typically and openly exercise its power through violence, even torture and terrorism (248). If torture is unimaginable in unmediated form, unpresentable for what it is, its representation must be fit into existing, acceptable discourses: patriotism, retaliation for real and imagined past injustices, separatism, terrorism, communism, subversion, anarchy, the need to preserve the state's territorial integrity, the need to protect the nation from subversion through ethnic cleansing, the fight against crime, the war on drugs (172).

All peoples, to a certain extent, take myth as reality (142, 239, 240). Essential to myth is a process in which "one immunizes the contents of the collective imagination by means of a small inoculation of acknowledged evil; thus protecting it against the risk of a generalized subversion" (20:150). A single or a few separatists, communists, or dissidents of other sorts is sufficient to inoculate a shaky social order with evil, first justifying the torture or killing of all separatists, then anyone who knows a separatist, those who are friends or family to those who know separatists, and so forth. The social order, of course, need not be objectively precarious for the heavy hand of the state to be felt. Andersen (11) argues that Argentina's generals fabricated a threat from armed leftists in the 1970s as pretext for their own seizure of power and for the "dirty war" that cost eight to ten thousand people their lives because they "might have had" leftist sympathies. Inoculations of evil become part of social knowledge that enter public discourse and inflect the building of consensus around categories of dissidence and the state's control of them. The repression of the real or imagined violence of dissidents is also justified and enters into the hegemonic field through the violence of representation in popular culture, the media, television, films, the theater, and music (e.g., 17, 116, 123, 127, 128, 214; cf 180).

"We only beat bad people," said a prison official in Turkey in 1984.[1] "They are no good, they are worthless bums, they are subversives who think that communism will relieve them of the necessity of working." The warden revealed with apparent pride that he had "given orders that all prisoners should be struck with a truncheon below the waist on the rude parts and warned not to come to prison again." "My aim," he said, "is to ensure discipline. That's not torture, for it is only the lazy, the idle, the vagabonds, the communists, the murderers who come to prison." "Communism is against the law here, so is separatism," said another, referring to the Kurdish movement for independence. During the "dirty war" in Argentina, a general is reported to have said that "Democracy must be protected for wrong ideas spread like a cancer through the society if they are not excised." One is reminded of the announcement that Joao Baptista Figueriredo, President of Brazil, made after his election in 1979: "I intend," he said, "to open this country up to democracy and anyone who is against that, I will jail, I will crush" (quoted in 201:304).

Torture is in part an expedient, a means of squeezing information or confessions from suspected criminals, subversives, traitors, terrorists. Women in several countries have been raped and otherwise sexually abused by guards, sometimes in the presence of their husbands or parents as a means of extracting information from witnesses. This form of violence, a commonplace in Bosnia-Herzegovina during the war of the 1990s, is particularly diabolical in societies where women are more often assigned responsibility for sexual transgressions than are men and in which rape is a means by which the men of one faction humiliate those of another. Rape both creates and punishes Otherness. Turkish guards have reportedly raped men with truncheons (6, 129), a significant symbolic act linked to the stigma assigned in Islamic societies to acts attributed stereotypically to the passive partner in a homosexual encounter. General Turgut Sunalp, a candidate for Prime Minister in 1983, scoffed at allegations of sexual torture of prisoners, but added his claim for the normality of soldiers, saying in effect that if the point was to rape, soldiers are healthy young men with more pleasurable "tools" at their disposal, so why would they use truncheons. As for the men who claimed they had been raped, he said that "if such prisoners had any character at all, they would have committed suicide" (translation of remarks reported in Turkish newsmagazine *Notka*, personal communication). The conflation of the penis as an object of the victim's

---

[1]
    Between 1982 and 1987, I headed a group in Amnesty International, USA that coordinated all Amnesty International's work on human rights abuses in Turkey. During that time, I came into contact, both through correspondence and in person, with a number of people who had been imprisoned, sometimes tortured, for their political beliefs or activities, often only because they were suspected of subversive activities. Consequently, I have a large store of quotes and comments from former prisoners and from Turkish officials. It serves no interests to name names, especially since torture is still daily fare in Turkey (see 6, 129, 130, 174–176).

pain and the torturer's pleasure suggests the often sadomasochistic nature of the relationship. But a number of researchers (93, 170, 217) remind us that the goal of state violence is not to inflict pain; it is the social project of creating punishable categories of people, forging and maintaining boundaries among them, and building the consensus around those categories that specifies and enforces behavioral norms and legitimates and de-legitimates specific groups. Torture has another, only partially successful function—to terrorize people into conformity.

In 1984, the then Turkish Ambassador to the United States insisted to me that Turks who claim they were tortured were really "just" members of unlawful political organizations. He meant Kurdish separatist groups and several opposition political parties. He explained that they were agitators, ignorant peasants and workers manipulated by communist infiltrators. And because they were common workers and peasants, they had probably been beaten before and could not have been surprised when they were struck by prison guards. "They are calling it torture in order to influence world opinion and discredit the Turkish state," the Ambassador said. He did not mention the students, professors, doctors, publishers, lawyers, and politicians who were among the tortured but invited my complicity in his claim for the radical Otherness of the tortured with his confidential tone of voice, adding that Turkish police, prison guards, and soldiers were mostly poor peasants with little education. He claimed that brutality was part of their culture, and sometimes the guards were overzealous, but they were true patriots, true enemies of communism and other threats to the Turkish state. Not only must the torturer and his apologist assign the status of Other to the condemned, the specification of the kind of differentness the tortured symbolizes must conform to dominant representations of the vile and worthless, a vileness that has mythical status as something to be found lurking everywhere, a constant threat to the accepted order (109, 183, 240). It is largely underclass status that makes certain people(s) susceptible to violent abuses and it is their ambiguity—as both less-than-human brutes and super-humans capable of undermining the accepted order of society—that allows elites to crystallize the myths about the evil they represent, hence, justifying the violence perpetrated against them.

Depending on the success or failure of their cause, survivors of state violence often need to conquer the impulse to reciprocate, even the hidden transcripts of power that Scott describes as used by slaves, serfs, and minorities held in contempt (55, 219), for the terror of the survivor may be complete and social disapprobation may be more or less total. Some survivors speak of the guilt and shame they feel as well as of the refusal of people to believe their stories of abuse and of the persistent questioning about what they had done to get themselves arrested in the first place (159, 234). Just as Jews have been held responsible for anti-Semitism (183), women for misogyny (70), Latinos and African-Americans in the United States for racism, so too have those who have suffered torture been blamed for their own oppression. Survivors often suffer total social, political, and psychological isolation, and suicide is common. Having been tortured by the state may be the ultimate form of distinction (31).

Research suggests that torturers are ordinary people. The techniques of training them, best known to human rights monitors from the experiences of the military police in Greece during the dictatorship of the early 1970s, do brutalize young men. More importantly, they are taught, through the manipulation of symbols, that they are "just doing their jobs," as one former torturer put it in a rare depiction of the voice of the violent in the documentary film "Your Neighbor's Son: The Making of a Torturer" (196). This is a process common to military recruits the world over (36, 146, 162). The very phraseology of police or soldiers "doing their jobs," the above quoted Turkish general's use of the metaphor of the penis as a tool of the trade of torture, so to speak, an emblem of his work in mastering the world, the once High Executioner of Great Britain's remark that he didn't think executions prevented crime, but that he did what he was hired to do, that it was a matter of sacred duty to him (229:24–28), all suggest that the discourse of work has historically been an effective instrument of state control, an instrument whereby certain sectors of society have been deprived of essential aspects of their humanity through the work of others.

At the core of the social contract theory of the state—its surface appearance—is Locke's (161) contention that "through work, man embarked on a voyage of exploration whose ultimate goal is the discovery of man; through work man becomes master of the world; through a community of work, society comes into being" (see also 50). The unproblematized equation in the capitalist world of work with society and culture entails a compulsion to represent political, cultural, or ethnically subordinate dissidents as the negation of the proper working self. So represented, we cannot help but take their Otherness personally. Thus, the natives discovered and described by early colonists, missionaries, and ethnographers were depicted as savages, prone to mindless violence, dirty, and without material or symbolic goods (25, 109). Most of all, they were categorized as lazy and shiftless and as such were said to be without rationality, without culture. Their life styles violated colonial mores and European notions of progress and civilization, which by the beginning of the seventeenth century centered increasingly upon the discipline of work (58, 59). Work discipline is an integral principle upon which the institutions of private property and law-and-order were founded and are central to the project of the state in the liberal bourgeois world order. Certainly the most chilling and supremely ironic expression of the relationship between work and national purity was the slogan *Arbeit mach frei* (Work Makes One Free) over the entrance to Auschwitz.

Non-work in the sense of labor will not do, of course, but neither will work that undermines the disciplining of the labor force and the proper order of things. The state must be a state of mind that divides people into the purified and honest who do legitimate work and a politically suspect or criminal, deviant underworld of aliens, communists, loafers, delinquents, even thieves, killers, and drug lords who do not. The violent dissident must be positioned and repositioned as necessary, "in a negative relationship with middle-class rational masculinity, a model that ensures a relationship of dominance and subordination...by locking the two into a mutually defining relationship" (16:15, 21). In the United States, the presumed idleness of the unemployed, the poverty-stricken, the drug user or gang member, the single parent, gay man or lesbian woman (all the latter with overtones of promiscuity and contagious disease) is also seen as violence against the social body. It cannot be just any old work; it must be work that contributes to what dominant groups have defined as the common good (153).

The hegemony of respectable culture and good taste and the denigration of what is represented as the disgusting, degenerate, worthless, criminal lower parts of the social body is so strong that, according to a poll conducted by the *Washington Post* and ABC News in September 1989, 66% of those surveyed favored random searches of peoples' houses, cars, and personal belongings, even if the police had no suspicion of any wrongdoing. Seventy-two percent said they approved of censorship of any film depicting illegal drug use. People have been so inoculated with the fear of evil and with the myth of an essential relationship of repression to the cure of society, that they are willing to give up some of their own rights for what has been defined as the good of the social body. When William Bennett, the so-called drug czar until 1990, said he saw nothing wrong with beheading drug offenders, his audience applauded wildly.

An anthropological task for the 1990s and beyond is to continue to uncover the ways in which identities that entail inequalities are historically constructed, ascertain how those identities become deployed in time and space, determine under what circumstances people do or do not internalize and subjectify them, and how they are dismantled, disorganized, and redefined through the redistribution of people in different spaces at other times. In other words, what are the circumstances and the means through which people create identities and have them created for them? How are these identities then normalized so that resistance is domesticated or failing that, crushed by violent means that meet with general social approval? Finally, how do people generate oppositional identities, a sense of self that rejects subordination and repression, how do they achieve autonomy?

Resistance to the project of the state is understood by some scholars as a manifestation of class struggle, especially against capitalist relations of production (189, 194, 240). Others examine resistance in the context of colonialism (58, 233, 241), or view it as a result of competition for scarce resources among ethnic groups (136, 190, 238). Finally, theorists of "new social movements" (4, 77, 81, 82, 232) describe the deliberate appropriation and incorporation of montages of diverse cultural forms into local resistance movements (55, 154, 220, 252). Sometimes these movements mobilize people in the name of loyalty to an existing nation-state (98, 100, 142, 236), but increasingly they are couched in terms of self-determination and the dismantling of those same nation-states.

SELF DETERMINATION, NATION-STATES, AND HUMAN RIGHTS

Some scholars conclude that while nationalism and human rights are compatible, self-determination is not a human right (148). Others (23) are convinced that self-determination is the highest right of all. Yelena Bonner, the respected Russian human rights activist, is but one proponent of the view that "self-determination is the essence of human rights...self-determination for every people, for every nationality, a state" (27). These statements raise two sets of questions as peoples who live or once lived within the confines of another state or empire struggle to assert their autonomy. What if self-determination claims on the part of one nation mean that the individual and collective human rights of another are violated? What happens if one side is coincidentally more powerful militarily than the other, or if there is cheap high-powered and sophisticated weaponry readily available to the highest bidder? Battles raging in the Caucasus, Tadzhikistan, Bosnia-Herzegovina, and Croatia center on definitions of nation, state, minority group, and peoples, and on the assumption of state power by a new set of elites or in some cases old elites in new guises. The other set of questions focuses on the kind of future newly emerging elites imagine in a world order in which the possibilities for recapitulating the trajectory of the west is unlikely, where socialism has been discredited, and where there are no other alternatives on the horizon. How, under these circumstances, will new constellations of power and social knowledge emerge and be channeled?

In the contemporary post-colonial world left by the demise of communism, the predominate discourse invokes the paradigmatic liberal ideas of democracy, reason, and progress toward capitalism. At the same time, local populations seek to recover their histories and traditions. In contradictory national situations in which an emergent bourgeoisie cannot, in the absence of appropriate social conditions, establish adequate hegemonic domination over a newly constituted nation (which is clearly the case for many nascent or hopeful new states), it may resort to what Gramsci (111:181, 182) called passive revolution, the transformation of once dominant classes into partners in a configuration that replaces the structure of colonial power with a different order, that of national power. This translates into the creation of states capable of transforming the economy while at the same time suppressing or submerging the interests of subordinate groups.

Those subordinate groups often constitute power groups challenging similarly constituted rivals or the state itself. Many are the historical victims of colonization, internal or external, or a result of the way colonial empires were carved up. Their claims may be couched in the language of human, minority, or indigenous rights. For their part, states often attempt to absorb subalterns in a process benignly described as assimilation or acculturation, and less benignly as ethnocide (231:91), a dialectic between state and nation, peoples and minorities, which often results in violent suppression, even genocide (26, 44, 150). Since 1945, state-sponsored violence toward ethnic and political groups has caused more deaths, injuries, and general human suffering than "all other forms of deadly conflict, including international wars and colonial and civil wars" (231:76). Other costs are incalculable: extinction of languages, cultures, and ways of life; destruction of ethnographic and historical treasures; and loss or damage to residences, industry, and commerce.

The Universal Declaration of Human Rights (UDHR) and the covenants and treaties that give them the force of law in the United Nations (UN) are designed to protect people from the excesses of the state, including torture and other forms of cruel, inhuman, and degrading treatment, and are intended to be universal (131, 257). Self-determination is another basic right regarded as so essential it appears as Article One in both covenants to the UDHR:

> All peoples have the right of self-determination. By virtue of that right, they freely determine their political status and freely pursue their economic, social and cultural development.

Although this seems on the face of it an unambiguous statement, its interpretation in the UN has been problematic. The definition of peoples itself is both contested and confused with other categories, such as minorities. Member states define a minority as "a group numerically inferior to the rest of the population of a state, in a non-dominant position, whose members...possess ethnic, religious, or linguistic characteristics differing from those of the rest of the population, and show, if only implicitly, a sense of solidarity directed towards preserving their culture, traditions, religions, or language" (Capotorti quoted in 231:59). For some purposes, states consider refugees and indigenous peoples minorities as well as those in the numerical majority who are legislatively or practically prevented from full participation in the rights of citizenship (e.g. the indigenous peoples of Peru, Bolivia, and Guatemala; Blacks in South Africa; and Palestinians in the Occupied Territories). Finally, most of the world's five to eight thousand ethnic groups are considered minorities by their own states. The United Nations has carefully and deliberately avoided defining *peoples* even though it allows them certain rights (80). Peoples are generally to be understood not in an ethnic sense but as the inhabitants of a specific territory, and international law is to be understood as applicable to peoples but not to minorities. Peoples can claim self-determination; minorities cannot (231:60-70).

Except for cases of colonialism and recent occupations, even peoples must meet minimum requirements in order to claim self-determination leading to independence (78). First, they must be clearly differentiated in key aspects from the dominant population in the country concerned. Ethnic, cultural, or linguistic differences are not sufficient if there is no clear territorial division. When group members are geographically spread out among other populations, the UN will not usually recognize a self-determination claim. The principle of territorial integrity, an important aspect of the principle of sovereignty, normally overrides a claim of self-determination, which is another aspect of sovereignty. Thus, a people can claim independence only if they are under military occupation, have historically formed a nation-state of its own, or were once part of a different state, *and* occupy a clearly defined territory. The drafters of Article 1 of the UDHR had in mind independence for various African, Asian, and Caribbean colonies, a goal that has been long since realized. Aside from the successor states of East Central Europe and the former Soviet Union, which by and large met the criteria above, the Security Council and the General Assembly are not likely to recognize self-determination demands of regional or local ethnic groups, indigenous peoples, or minorities of any kind.

Minorities with aspirations to independence were not satisfied to be told that those aspirations could never be considered collective human rights and that "whatever depredations are inflicted upon [minorities], they must attempt to find justice within the boundaries of existing states and be reconciled with them. Since self determination in the sense of independence is not a right of minorities, they must look instead to individual human rights [standards]" (242:5). As a result of subsequent activism by minorities and indigenous peoples, the international community has been forced to recognize some rights of minorities to internal self-determination, that is within the boundaries of existing states (231). This means the right to control some aspects of education, social affairs, welfare, and culture while defense, international trade relations, and diplomatic affairs are left to the central state. Indigenous peoples, for example, often demand internal autonomy or access to land that was once theirs as well as other social rights (67, 184).

The message of the UN is that states should avoid interfering with the sovereign decisions of other states about who does or does not constitute a people. This is hardly surprising since the UN comprises states that presumably would be disinclined to entertain independence movements within their own borders. As far as the UN is concerned, maintaining the existing territorial integrity of member states trumps any nascent disposition toward self-determination on the part of self-described nations, ethnic groups, or indigenous peoples (136, 231, 261). Moreover, the commitment to the sovereignty of existing states in their bureaucratic and administrative roles also takes precedence over, in almost all cases, the sovereignty of the individual. Individuals can bring legal suit against their own government or that of another state for human rights violations through the UN Human Rights Commission but the process is cumbersome, lengthy, and generally unsatisfactory (190).

Historically, the states of the UN have shown themselves willing to commit troops to the principle of state sovereignty and territorial integrity. This is the version of the state, however, that is in crisis in this the last dance of the twentieth century. Consensus about the virtual inviolability of the state is unraveling as conflicts over nationalism, ethnicity, and paradoxically a dialectic between individual and collective human rights threaten the given order of the world, as formerly powerless individuals are able to call on allies around the world (e.g. Amnesty International and the Watch Commmittees) to defend them from their own states, and as historically peripheralized peoples assert autonomy and demand self-determination. The sanctity of the individual person who has a set of specific rights recognized by virtue of common humanity, rather than entitlements to be petitioned for from one's state, has entered the lexicon, if not the practice of the community of nations (191). Although the process is less than satisfactory, states no longer enjoy absolute impunity.

It is perhaps indicative of the crisis of the state that the universality of human rights came under attack at the 1993 UN World Conference on Human Rights, an attack led for the most part by China and other states that have most openly failed to make consensus prevail over coercion and that have records of especially egregious human rights abuses against both individuals and peoples. China's record in suppressing students and Tibetans, for example, needs no rehearsal here. Nonetheless, China, Singapore, and other less well-developed states invoked cultural relativity to justify torture and mistreatment. Cultural relativity is now code in some circles for permission to oppress people and peoples and to maintain women as second and third class citizens in the name of ostensible tradition (186) and lack of cultural equivalence (218). The world community staved off threats to the universality concept, but the attack suggests the complexity of the terrain faced by anthropologists concerned with many voices and many modalities (19, 75).

Some politicians are sanguine about the continued development of a new hierarchy of governance, not only established state governments, but also regional associations like the European Community, the North American Free Trade Association, and global federation under the UN. Others are less optimistic as the UN founders in Somalia, as the war in the Balkans continues, and as violence flares in Chiapas and elsewhere. As one scholar said as recently as December 1992, "The world is...in transition from strict acceptance of sovereign jurisdiction and non-intervention to more and more readiness to undertake...action, up to and including military action, that would in the past have been considered intervention in domestic affairs" (Sonnenfeldt quoted in 260:21). Is the world moving away from the nation-state as the key unit and toward some kind of world government? Probably not. It is more likely that a multitude of new linguistically and ethnically based nation-states will emerge, even though the salient differences of languages and ethnicities must be ever created and recreated, and that their legitimacy might have to be maintained at least in the short run through violence and terrorism.

Literature Cited

1. Abercrombie N, Hill S, Turner B. 1980. *The Dominant Ideology Thesis*. Boston: Allen & Unwin
2. Abrams P. 1988. Notes on the difficulty of studying the state. *J. Hist. Sociol.* 1(1):58–89
3. Alonso AM. 1988. The effects of truth: re-presentations of the past and the imagining community. *J. Hist. Sociol.* 1(1):31–57
4. Alvarez S. 1990. *Engendering Democracy in Brazil's Women's Movements in Transition Politics*. Princeton: Princeton Univ. Press
5. Amnesty International. 1983. *Political Killings by Governments*. London: Amnesty Int. Publ.
6. Amnesty International. 1985. *Turkey: Testimony on Torture*. London: Amnesty Int. Publ.
7. Amnesty International. 1989. *When the State Kills*. London: Amnesty Int. Publ.
8. Amnesty International. 1992. *The Americas: Human Rights Violations Against Indigenous Peoples*. New York: Amnesty Int. Publ.
9. Amnesty International. 1993. *Annual Report*. London: Amnesty Int. Publ.
10. Anagnost A. 1993. The politicized body. *Stanford Humanities Rev.* 2(1):86–102
11. Andersen MA. 1993. *Dossier Secreto: Argentina's Desaparecidos and the Myth of the "Dirty War."* Boulder, CO: Westview
12. Anderson B. 1983. *Imagined Communities*. London: Verso
13. Antonov-Ovseyenko A. 1981. *The Time of Stalin: Portrait of a Tyranny*. Transl. G Saunders. New York: Harper & Row
14. Antonov-Ovseyenko A. 1990. The time of Stalin. See Ref. 44, pp. 305–11
15. Appadurai A. 1991. Global ethnoscapes: notes and queries for a transnational anthropology. In *Recapturing Anthropology*, ed. RG Fox, pp. 191–210. Santa Fe: School Am. Res. Press
16. Armstrong N, Tennenhouse L, eds. 1989. *The Violence of Representation: Literature and the History of Violence*. London: Routledge
17. Aronowitz S. 1989. Working class identity and celluloid fantasies in the electronic age. In *Popular Culture: Schooling and Everyday Life*, ed. H Giroux, R Simon, and contributors, pp. 197–217. South Hadley, MA: Bergin & Garvey

18. Balandier G. 1986. An anthropology of violence and war. *Int. Soc. Sci. J.* 110:499–511
19. Barnett CR. 1988. Is there a scientific basis in anthropology for the ethics of human rights? See Ref. 75, pp. 21–26
20. Barthes R. 1972. *Mythologies.* Transl. A Lavers. New York: Noonday
21. Beetham D. 1973. *Max Weber and the Theory of Modern Politics.* London: Allen & Unwin
22. Benedict R. 1946. *The Chrysanthemum and the Sword.* Boston: Houghton Mifflin
23. Berlin I. 1991. Return of the Volkgeist. *New Perspect. Q.* 8(4):4–10
24. Bhabha H. 1990. DissemiNation: time, narrative, and the margins of modern nation. In *Nation and Narration,* ed. H Bhabha, pp. 291–322. London: Routledge
25. Bodley J. 1975. *Victims of Progress.* Menlo Park, CA: Cummings
26. Bodley J. 1992. Anthropology and the politics of genocide. See Ref. 192, pp. 37–51
27. Bonner Y. 1991. For every nationality, a state. *New Perspect. Q.* 8(4):15–17
28. Borneman J. 1992. State, territory, and identity formation in the postwar Berlins, 1945–1989. *Cult. Anthropol.* 7(1):45–62
29. Borque SC, Warren K. 1989. Democracy without peace: the cultural politics of terror in Peru. *Latin Am. Res. Rev.* 24(1):7–34
30. Bourdieu P. 1977. *Outline of a Theory of Practice.* Cambridge: Cambridge Univ. Press
31. Bourdieu P. 1984. *Distinction: A Social Critique of the Judgment of Taste.* Cambridge, MA: Harvard Univ. Press
32. Briggs JL. 1970. *Never in Anger: Portrait of an Eskimo Family.* Cambridge, MA: Harvard Univ. Press
33. Briggs JL. 1978. The origins of non-violence: Innuit management of aggression. In *Learning Non-Aggression,* ed. A Montague, pp. 54–93. Oxford: Oxford Univ. Press
34. Briggs JL. 1982. Living dangerously: the contradictory foundations of value in Canadian Innuit society. In *Politics and History in Band Societies,* ed. E Leacock, R Lee, pp. 109–31. Cambridge: Cambridge Univ. Press
35. Bright C, Harding S, eds. 1984. *State Making and Social Movements.* Ann Arbor: Univ. Mich. Press
36. Browning C. 1992. *Ordinary Men: Reserve Police Battalion 101 and the Final Solution in Poland.* New York: Harper Collins
37. Carmack RM, ed. 1988. *Harvest of Violence: The Mayan Indians and the Guatemalan Crisis.* Norman: Univ. Okla. Press
38. Carneiro RL. 1970. A theory of the origin of the state. *Science* 169:733–38
39. Carniero RL. 1978. Political expansion as an expression of the principle of competitive exclusion. See Ref. 51, pp. 205–24
40. Carnoy M. 1984. *The State and Political Theory.* Princeton: Princeton Univ. Press
41. Chagnon N. 1980. Kin selection theory, kinship, marriage, and fitness among the Yanomamo Indians. In *Sociobiology: Beyond Nature/Nurture,* ed. G Barlow, J Silverberg, pp. 545–71. Boulder, CO: Westview
42. Chagnon N. 1983. *The Fierce People.* New York: Holt, Rinehart & Winston. 3rd ed.
43. Chagnon N. 1990. Reproductive and somatic conflicts of interest in the genesis of violence and warfare among tribesmen. See Ref. 121, pp. 77–104
44. Chalk F, Jonassohn K, eds. 1990. *The History and Sociology of Genocide.* New Haven, CT: Yale Univ. Press
45. Chatterjee P. 1986. *Nationalist Thought and the Colonial World—A Derivative Discourse.* London: Zed
46. Chomsky N. 1988. *The Culture of Terrorism.* Boston: South End
47. Chomsky N, Herman ES. 1979. *After the Cataclysm: Postwar Indochina and the Reconstruction of Imperial Ideology.* Boston: South End
48. Claessen HJM. 1993. *Ideology and state formation.* Presented at 13th Int. Cong. Anthropol. Ethnol. Sciences, Mexico City
49. Clastres P. 1974. De l'ethnocide. *L'Homme* 14(3–4):101–10
50. Coetzee JM. 1989. Idleness in South Africa. See Ref. 16, pp. 119–39
51. Cohen R, Service ER, eds. 1978. *Origins of the State: The Anthropology of Political Evolution.* Philadelphia: Inst. Study Human Issues
52. Cohen R, Toland JD, eds. 1988. *State Formation and Political Legitimacy.* New Brunswick, NJ: Transaction Books
53. Cohn BS, Dirks NB. 1988. Beyond the fringe: the nationstate, colonialism, and the technologies of power. *J. Hist. Sociol.* 1(2):224–29
54. Cohn C. 1987. Sex and death in the rational world of defense intellectuals. *Signs* 12:687–718
55. Colburn FD, ed. 1990. *Everyday Forms of Resistance.* Armonk, NY: Sharpe
56. Comaroff J. 1985. *Body of Power, Spirit of Resistance: The Culture and History of a South African People.* Chicago: Univ. Chicago Press
57. Comaroff J, Comaroff JL. 1991. *Of Revelation and Revolution: Christianity and Colonialism in South Africa.* Chicago: Univ. Chicago Press
58. Comaroff JL. 1987. Of totemism and ethnicity. *Ethnos* 52(3–4):301–23
59. Comaroff JL, Comaroff J. 1987. The madman and the migrant: work and labour in the historical consciousness of a South African people. *Am. Ethnol.* 14(2):191–209
60. Comaroff JL, Comaroff J. 1989. The colo-

nization of consciousness in South Africa. *Econ. Soc.* 18:267–95

61. Comaroff JL, Comaroff J. 1992. *Ethnography and the Historical Imagination.* Boulder, CO: Westview

62. Corbin J. 1977. An anthropological perspective on violence. *Int. J. Environ. Stud.* 10:107–11

63. Corbin J. 1986. Insurrections in Spain: Casas Viejas 1933 and Madrid 1981. See Ref. 203a, pp. 28–49

64. Coronil F. 1988. *The Magical State: History and Illusion in the Appearance of Venezuelan Democracy.* Notre Dame, IN: Helen Kellogg Inst. Int. Stud.

65. Coronil F, Skurski J. 1991. Dismembering and remembering the nation: the semantics of political violence in Venezuela. *Comp. Stud. Soc. Hist.* 33(2):288–337

66. Corrigan P, Sayer D. 1985. *The Great Arch: English State Formation as Cultural Revolution.* Oxford: Blackwell

67. Daes EA. 1989. On the relation between indigenous peoples and states. *Without Prejudice: EAFORD Int. Rev. Racial Discrimination* 2(2):41–52

67a. Daniel EV, Knudsen, eds. 1994. *The Mistrust of Refugees.* Los Angeles: Univ. Calif. Press

67b. Das V, ed. 1990. *Mirrors of Violence: Communities, Riots and Survivors in South Asia.* Delhi: Oxford Univ. Press

68. Davis SH. 1976. The Yanamamo: ethnographic images and anthropological responsibilities. In *The Geological Imperative: Anthropology and Development in the Amazon Basin,* ed. S Davis, R Matthews, pp. 7–23. Cambridge: Anthropol. Resour. Cent.

69. Davis SH. 1988. Introduction: sowing the seeds of violence. See Ref. 37, pp. 3–38

70. De Lauretis T. 1989. The violence of rhetoric: consideration on representation and gender. See Ref. 16, pp. 239–58

71. DeSoto HG, Anderson DG. 1993. *The Curtain Rises: Rethinking Culture, Ideology and the State in Eastern Europe.* Atlantic Highlands, NJ: Humanities

72. Dentan R. 1978. Notes on childhood in a non-violent context: the Semai case. In *Learning Non-Aggression,* ed. A Montague, pp. 94–133. Oxford: Oxford Univ. Press

73. Dominquez VR. 1990. Politics of heritage in Israel. See Ref. 98a, pp. 130–47

74. Downing TE. 1988. Human rights research: the challenge for anthropologists. See Ref. 75, pp. 1–8

75. Downing TE, Kushner G, eds. 1988. *Human Rights and Anthropology.* Cambridge, MA: Cultural Survival

76. Dyson-Hudson R, Smith E. 1978. Human territoriality: an ecological reassessment. *Am. Anthropol.* 80:21–41

77. Eckstein S. 1989. *Power and Popular Protest: Latin American Social Movements.* Berkeley: Univ. Calif. Press

78. Eide A. 1990. The Universal Declaration in time and space. In *Human Rights in a Pluralist World,* ed. J Berting, PR Baehr, JH Burger, et al, pp. 15–32. London: Mercker

79. Elshtain JB. 1987. *Women and War.* New York: Basic

80. Ennals M. 1988. Ethnic rights and the rights of minorities. In *Human Rights,* ed. P Davies, pp. 111–19. London: Routledge

81. Escobar A. 1992. Culture, practice, and politics: anthropology and the study of social movements. *Crit. Anthropol.* 12(4):395–432

82. Escobar A, Alvarez S. 1992. *The Making of Social Movements in Latin America: Identity, Strategy and Democracy.* Boulder, CO: Westview

83. Evans P, Rueschemeyer D, Skocpol T, eds. 1985. *Bringing the State Back In.* Cambridge: Cambridge Univ. Press

84. Falla R. 1988. Struggle for survival in the mountains: hunger and other privations inflicted on internal refugees from the Central Highlands. See Ref. 37, pp. 235–55

84a. Feldman A. 1991. *Formations of Violence: The Narrative of the Body and Political Terror in Northern Ireland.* Chicago: Univ. Chicago Press

85. Ferguson RB. 1983. Warfare and redistributive exchange on the Northwest Coast. In *The Development of Political Organizations in Native North America: 1979 Proceedings of the American Ethnological Society,* ed. E Tooker, pp. 133–47. Washington, DC: Am. Ethnol. Soc.

86. Ferguson RB. 1984. A reexamination of the causes of Northwest Coast warfare. In *Warfare, Culture, and Environment,* ed. RB Ferguson, pp. 267–328. Orlando, FL: Academic

87. Ferguson RB. 1984. Introduction: studying war. In *Warfare, Culture, and Environment,* ed. RB Ferguson, pp. 1–81. Orlando, FL: Academic

88. Ferguson RB. 1989. Anthropology and war: theory, politics, ethics. In *The Anthropology of War and Peace,* ed. D Pitt, P Turner, pp. 141–59. South Hadley, MA: Bergin & Garvey

89. Ferguson RB. 1990. Blood of the leviathan: western contact and warfare in Amazonia. *Am. Ethnol.* 17:237–57

90. Ferguson RB. 1992. A savage encounter. See Ref. 91, pp. 199–228

91. Ferguson RB, Whitehead NL. 1992. *War in the Tribal Zone.* Santa Fe, NM: School Am. Res. Press

92. Foster M, Rubinstein R, eds. 1986. *Peace and War: Cross Cultural Perspectives.* New Brunswick, NJ: Transaction Books

93. Foucault M. 1977. *Discipline and Punish: The Birth of the Prison.* New York: Vintage
94. Foucault M. 1980. *Power/Knowledge.* New York: Pantheon
95. Foucault M. 1980. *The History of Sexuality.* Vol. 1, *An Introduction.* New York: Vintage
96. Foucault M. 1985. *The History of Sexuality.* Vol. 2, *The Use of Pleasure.* New York: Pantheon
97. Fox R. 1977. The inherent rules of violence. In *Social Rules and Social Behaviour,* ed. P Collett, pp. 132–49. Oxford: Blackwell
98. Fox RG. 1990. Hindu nationalism in the making or the rise of the hindian. See Ref. 98a, pp. 63–80
98a. Fox RG, ed. 1990. *Nationalist Ideologies and the Production of National Culture.* *Am. Ethnol. Monogr. Ser.,* No. 2. Washington, DC: Am. Ethnol. Monogr. Soc.
99. Fried M, Harris M, Murphy R, eds. 1967. *War: The Anthropology of Armed Conflict and Aggression.* Garden City, NJ: Nat. Hist.
100. Gellner E. 1983. *Nations and Nationalism.* Ithaca, NY: Cornell Univ. Press
101. Geertz C. 1973. *The Interpretation of Culture.* New York: Basic
102. Geertz C. 1983. *Local Knowledge: Further Essays in Interpretive Anthropology.* New York: Basic
103. Gibson T. 1986. *Sacrifice and Sharing in the Philippine Highlands: Religion and Society Among the Buid of Mindoro.* London: Athlone
104. Gibson T. 1990. Raiding, trading and tribal autonomy in insular Southeast Asia. See Ref. 121, pp. 125–45
105. Giddens A. 1985. *The Nation-state and Violence: Volume Two of a Contemporary Critique of Historical Materialism.* Berkeley: Univ. Calif. Press
106. Glenny M. 1992. *The Fall of Yugoslavia: The Third Balkan War.* New York: Penguin
107. Glick Schiller N, Basch L, Blanc-Szanton C, eds. 1992. *Towards a Transnational Migration Perspective on Migration.* New York: NY Acad. Sci.
108. Good K. 1989. *Yanomami hunting patterns: trekking and garden relocation as an adaptation to game availability in Amazonia, Venezuela.* PhD dissertation, Univ. Fla., Gainesville
109. Gordon RJ. 1992. *The Bushman Myth: The Making of a Namibian Underclass.* Boulder, CO: Westview
110. Gorer G. 1943. Themes in Japanese culture. *Trans. NY Acad. Sci. Ser. II,* 5:106–24
111. Gramsci A. 1971. *Selections from Prison Notebooks,* ed./transl. H Hoare, G Smith. New York: Int. Publ.
112. Greenberg JB. 1989. *Blood Ties: Life and Violence in Rural Mexico.* Tucson: Univ. Ariz. Press

113. Greenhouse C. 1987. Cultural perspectives on war. In *The Quest for Peace: Transcending Collective Violence and War among Societies, Cultures and States,* ed. R. Varynen, pp. 32–47. Beverly Hills, CA: Sage
114. Gregor T. 1990. Uneasy peace: intertribal relations in Brazil's Upper Xingu. See Ref. 121, pp. 105–24
115. Groebel J, Hinde RA. 1989. *Aggression and War: Their Biological and Social Bases.* Cambridge: Cambridge Univ. Press
116. Grossberg L. 1989. Pedagogy in the present: politics, postmodernity, and the popular. In *Popular Culture: Schooling and Everyday Life,* ed. H Giroux, R Simon, and contributors, pp. 91–115. South Hadley, MA: Bergin & Garvey
117. Guidieri R, Pellizzi F, Tambiah S, eds. 1988. *Ethnicities and Nations: Processes of Interethnic Relations in Latin America, Southeast Asia, and the Pacific.* Austin: Univ. Texas Press
118. Guha R, Spivak GC, eds. 1988. *Selected Subaltern Studies.* London: Oxford Univ. Press
119. Gupta A. 1992. Song of the non-aligned world: transnational identities and the reinscription of space in late capitalism. *Cult. Anthropol.* 7(1):63–79
120. Haas J. 1990. Warfare and the evolution of tribal politics in the prehistoric Southwest. See Ref. 121, pp. 171–89
121. Haas J, ed. 1990. *The Anthropology of War.* Cambridge: Cambridge Univ. Press
122. Hall S. 1988. The toad in the garden: Thatcherism among the theorists. In *Marxism and the Interpretation of Culture,* ed. C Nelson, L Grossberg, pp. 35–57. Urbana: Univ. Ill. Press
123. Hall S, Jefferson T, eds. 1976. *Resistance Through Rituals: Youth Subcultures in Post-war Britain.* London: Hutchinson
124. Hamilton V, Frelik B, eds. 1991. *World Refugee Survey.* Washington, DC: U.S. Comm. Refugees, Am. Counc. Nationalities
125. Hayden R. 1992. Yugoslavia: where self-determination meets ethnic cleansing. *New Perspect. Q.* 9(4):41–46
126. Heald S. 1986. The ritual use of violence. See Ref. 203a, pp. 70–85
127. Hebdige D. 1979. *Subculture: The Meaning of Style.* London: Routledge
128. Hebdige D. 1988. *Hiding in the Light.* London: Routledge
129. Helsinki Watch. 1987. *State of Flux: Human Rights in Turkey.* New York: Helsinki Watch
130. Helsinki Watch. 1988. *Destroying Ethnic Identity: The Kurds of Turkey.* New York: Helsinki Watch
131. Henkin L. 1989. The universality of the

concept of human rights. *Ann. Am. Acad. Polit. Soc. Sci.* 506:10–29

132. Herman ES. 1982. *The Real Terror Network: Terrorism in Fact and Propaganda.* Boston: South End

133. Hinshaw RE. 1988. Tourist town amid the violence: Panajachel. See Ref. 37, pp. 195–205

134. Hobsbawm E. 1990. *Nations and Nationalism Since 1780.* Cambridge: Cambridge Univ. Press

135. Hobsbawm E, Ranger T, eds. 1983. *The Invention of Culture.* Cambridge: Cambridge Univ. Press.

136. Horowitz D. 1985. *Ethnic Groups in Conflict.* Berkeley: Univ. Calif. Press

137. Howell S, Willis R, eds. 1989. *Societies at Peace: Anthropological Perspectives.* London: Routledge

138. Isbell BJ. 1977. *To Defend Ourselves: Ecology and Ritual in an Andean Village.* Austin: Univ. Texas Press

139. Isbell BJ 1985. *To Defend Ourselves: Ecology and Ritual in an Andean Village.* Prospect Heights, IL: Waveland

140. Isbell BJ. 1990. *The Texts and Contexts of Terror in Peru.* New York: The Consortium

141. Jessop B. 1983. *Theories of the State.* New York: Univ. Press

142. Kapferer B. 1988. *Legends of People, Myths of State: Violence, Intolerance, and Political Culture in Sri Lanka and Australia.* Washington, DC: Smithsonian Inst. Press

143. Kearney M. 1991. Borders and boundaries of state and self at the end of empire. *J. Hist. Sociol.* 4:52–74

144. Kearney M, Nagengast C. 1990. *Anthropological Perspectives on Transnational Communities in Rural California.* Davis, CA: Calif. Inst. Rural Stud.

145. Kedourie E. 1985. *Nationalism.* London: Hutchinson

146. Keen S. 1986. *Faces of the Enemy: Reflections of the Hostile Imagination.* New York: Harper & Row

147. Keiser L. 1991. *Friend by Day, Enemy by Night.* New York: Holt, Rinehart & Winston

148. Kiss E. 1992. *Is nationalism compatible with human rights? Reflections on East-Central Europe.* Presented at Natl. Acad. Sci. Conf., Moscow

149. Klor de Alva JJ. 1992. Colonialism and postcolonialism as (Latin) American mirages. *Col. Latin Am. Rev.* 1(1–2):3–23

150. Kuper L. 1981. *Genocide.* Hammondsport, NY: Penguin

151. Kuper L. 1990. The genocidal state: an overview. See Ref. 246, pp. 19–52

152. Kurtz DV. 1993. *The ideology of work and the political economy of state formation.*

Presented at 13th Int. Cong. Anthropol. Ethnol. Sci., Mexico City

153. Lafferty W. 1989. Work as a source of political learning among wage laborers and lower level employees. In *Political Learning in Adulthood: A Sourcebook of Theory and Research,* ed. RS Sigel, pp. 89–101. Chicago: Univ. Chicago Press

154. Lan D. 1985. *Guns and Rain: Guerrillas and Spirit Mediums in Zimbabwe.* Berkeley: Univ. Calif. Press

155. Laqueur W. 1977. *Terrorism.* Boston: Little Brown

156. Leach E. 1977. *Custom, Law and Terrorist Violence.* Edinburgh: Univ. Edinburgh Press

157. Lee R. 1984. *The Dobe !Kung.* New York: Holt, Rinehart & Winston

158. Lemarchand R. 1990. Burundi: ethnicity and the genocidal state. See Ref. 246, pp. 89–112

159. Levi P. 1988. *The Drowned and the Saved,* Transl. R Rosenthal. New York: Summit

160. Lifton RJ, Markuson E. 1990. *The Genocidal Mentality.* New York: Basic

161. Locke J. 1960. *Two Treatises of Government,* Cambridge: Cambridge Univ. Press

162. Lovell JP, Stihm JH. 1989. Military service and political socialization. In *Political Learning in Adulthood: A Sourcebook of Theory and Research,* ed. RS Sigel, pp. 172–202. Chicago: Univ. Chicago Press

163. Lyotard JF. 1993. Answering the question: "What is postmodernism," In *Postmodernism: A Reader,* ed. T Docherty, pp. 38–46. New York: Columbia Univ. Press

164. Mace J. 1990. Genocide by famine: Ukraine in 1932–1933. See Ref. 246, pp. 53–72

165. Magas B. 1993. *The Destruction of Yugoslavia.* London: Verso

166. Malkki L. 1990. Context and consciousness: local conditions for the production of historical and national thought among Hutu refugees in Tanzania. See Ref. 98a, pp. 32–62

167. Malkki L. 1992. *National Geographic*: the rooting of peoples and the territorialization of national identity among scholars and refugees. *Cult. Anthropol.* 7(1):24–44

168. Manz B. 1988. *Refugees of a Hidden War: The Aftermath of Counterinsurgency in Guatemala.* Albany: State Univ. NY Press

169. Marshall E. 1959. *The Harmless People.* New York: Knopf

170. Martin E. 1987. *The Women in the Body.* Boston: Beacon

171. McCauley C. 1990. Conference overview. See Ref. 121, pp. 1–25

172. McGowen R. 1989. Punishing violence, sentencing crime. See Ref. 16, pp. 140–56

173. Meisler S. 1990. Holocaust in Burundi. See Ref. 44, pp. 384–93

134 NAGENGAST

174. MERIP Middle East Report. 1981. *The Generals Take Over,* No. 93, January
175. MERIP Middle East Report. 1984. *State Terror in Turkey,* No. 121, February
176. MERIP Middle East Report. 1984. *Turkey Under Military Rule,* No. 122, March–April
177. Minh-ha TT. 1989. *Woman, Native, Other: Writing Postcoloniality and Feminism.* Bloomington: Ind. Univ. Press
178. Mishkin B. 1940. *Rank and Warfare Among the Plains Indians.* Seattle: Univ. Wash. Press
179. Moore B. 1966. *The Social Origins of Dictatorship and Democracy.* Boston: Beacon
180. Moore SF. 1989. The production of cultural pluralism as a process. *Public Cult.* 12(2):26–48
181. Morphy H, Morphy F. 1984. The 'myths' of Ngalakan history: ideology and images of the past. *Man* 19(3):459–78
182. Mowlana H, Gerbner S, Schiller H. 1992. *Triumph of the Image: The Media's War in the Persian Gulf—A Global Perspective.* Boulder, CO: Westview
183. Muller-Hill B. 1988. *Murderous Science: The Elimination by Scientific Selection of Jews, Gypsies, and Others, Germany 1933–1945.* Oxford: Oxford Univ. Press
184. Muntarbhorn V. 1989. Realizing indigenous social rights. *Without Prejudice: EAFORD Int. Rev. Racial Discrim.* 2(2):7–26
185. Nagengast C. 1991. *Reluctant Socialists, Rural Entrepreneurs: Class, Culture, and the Polish State.* Boulder, CO: Westview
186. Nagengast C, Kearney M. 1990. Mixtec ethnicity: social identity, political consciousness, and political activism. *Latin Am. Res. Rev.* 25(1):61–91
187. Nagengast C, Stavenhagen R, Kearney M. 1992. *Human Rights and Indigenous Workers: The Mixtecs in Mexico and the United States.* San Diego: Univ. Calif., Cent. U. S. Mex. Stud.
188. Nandy A. 1992. The state. In *The Development Dictionary: A Guide to Knowledge and Power,* ed. W Sachs, pp. 264–74. London: Zed
189. Nash JC. 1970. *We Eat the Mines and the Mines Eat Us: Dependency and Exploitation in Bolivian Tin Mines.* New York: Columbia Univ. Press
190. Newman F, Weissbrodt D. 1990. *International Human Rights, Law, Policy and Process.* Cincinnati, OH: Anderson
191. Newman S. 1991. Does modernism breed ethnic political conflict? *World Polit.* 43:451–78
192. Nordstrom C, Martin J, eds. 1992. *The Paths to Domination, Resistance, and Terror.* Berkeley: Univ. Calif. Press
193. Nugent D. 1988. Rural revolt in Mexico, Mexican nationalism and the state and forms of U. S. intervention. In *Rural Revolt in Mexico and U. S. Intervention,* ed. D Nugent, pp. 1–21. San Diego: Univ. Calif., Cent. U. S. Mex. Stud.
194. Ong A. 1987. *Spirits of Resistance and Capitalist Discipline: Factory Women in Malaysia.* Albany: State Univ. NY Press
195. Overing J. 1986. Images of cannibalism, death and domination in a 'non-violent' society. See Ref. 203a, pp. 103–17
196. Pedersen JF, Stephensen E, directors. 1982. *Your Neighbor's Son: The Making of a Torturer.* Prod. Ebbe Preisher Film, eps TV, Stockholm, Sweden
197. Peters E. 1985. *Torture.* Oxford: Blackwell
198. Poole D, Renique G. 1992. *Peru: Time of Fear.* New York: Monthly Review
199. Poulton H. 1991. *Balkans: Minorities and States in Conflict.* London: Minority Rights
200. Rapport N. 1987. *Talking Violence: An Anthropological Interpretation of Conversation in the City.* Social and Economic Stud. No. 34. Newfoundland: Memorial Univ., Inst. Soc. Econ. Res.
201. Rawson H. 1981. *A Dictionary of Euphemisms & Other Doubletalk.* New York: Crown
202. Rejali DM. 1993. *Torture and Modernity: Self, Society, and State in Modern Iran.* Boulder, CO: Westview
203. Riches D. 1986. The phenomenon of violence. See Ref. 203a, pp. 1–27
203a. Riches D, ed. 1986. *The Anthropology of Violence.* New York: Blackwell
204. Robarchek C. 1977. Frustration, aggression, and the non-violent Semai. *Am. Ethnol.* 4:762–79
205. Robarchek C. 1979. Conflict, emotion, and abreaction: resolution of conflict among the Semai Senoi. *Ethnos* 7:104–23
206. Robarchek C. 1979. Learning to fear. *Am. Ethnol.* 6:555–67
207. Robarchek C. 1990. Motivations and material causes: on the explanation of conflict and war. See Ref. 121, pp. 56–76
208. Roos H. 1966. *A History of Poland.* Transl. J Foster. New York: Knopf
209. Roosens E. 1989. *Creating Ethnicity: The Process of Ethnogenesis.* Newbury Park, CA: Sage
210. Rosaldo R. 1984. Grief and a headhunter's rage: on the cultural force of emotions. In *Text, Play and Story: The Construction and Reconstruction of Self and Society,* ed. S Plattner, E Bruner, pp. 178–95. Washington, DC: Am. Ethnol. Soc.
211. Rosenblum N. 1978. *Bentham's Theory of the Modern State.* Cambridge, MA: Harvard Univ. Press
212. Rouse R. 1989. *Mexican migration to the U. S.: family relations in the development of a transnational migrant circuit.* PhD thesis. Stanford Univ.
213. Rouse R. 1992. Making sense of settlement: class transformation, cultural strug-

gle, and transnationalism among Mexican migrants in the United States. See Ref. 107, pp. 25–52

214. Rowe JC. 1989. Bringing it all back home: American recycling of the Vietnam War. See Ref. 16, pp. 197–218

215. Sabaratnam L. 1990. Sri Lanka: the lion and the tiger in the ethnic archipelago. See Ref. 246, pp. 187–220

216. Sachs W, ed. 1992. *The Development Dictionary: A Guide to Knowledge and Power.* London: Zed

217. Scarry E. 1985. *The Body in Pain: The Making and Unmaking of the World.* Oxford: Oxford Univ. Press

218. Schirmer J. 1988. The dilemma of cultural diversity and equivalency in universal human rights standards. See Ref. 75, pp. 91–106

219. Scott J. 1992. Domination, acting and fantasy. See Ref. 192, pp. 55–84

220. Scott J. 1985. *Weapons of the Weak.* New Haven, CT: Yale Univ. Press

221. Service E. 1975. *Origins of the State and Civilization: The Process of Cultural Evolution.* New York: Norton

222. Seymour-Smith C. 1986. *Dictionary of Anthropology.* Boston: Hall

223. Skocpol T. 1979. *States and Social Revolutions.* Chicago: Univ. Chicago Press

224. Sluka JA. 1989. *Hearts and Minds, Water and Fish: Support for the IRA and INLA in a Northern Irish Ghetto.* Greenwich, CT: JAI

225. Smith AD. 1987. *The Ethnic Origin of Nations.* New York: Blackwell

226. Smith CA. 1988. Destruction of the material basis for Indian culture: economic changes in Totonicapan. See Ref. 37, pp. 206–31

227. Smooha S. 1990. Israel's options for handling the Palestinians in the West Bank and Gaza Strip. See Ref. 246, pp. 143–86

228. Spivak GC. 1992. *Thinking Academic Freedom in Gendered Post-coloniality.* Cape Town: Univ. Cape Town Press

228a. Spencer J, ed. 1990. *Sri Lanka: History and the Roots of Conflict.* London: Routledge

229. Stanley I, Grey M. 1989. *A Punishment in Search of a Crime.* New York: Avon

230. Starn O. 1991. Missing the revolution: anthropologists and the war in Peru. *Cult. Anthropol.* 6(1):63–91

231. Stavenhagen R. 1990. *The Ethnic Question: Conflict, Development and Human Rights.* Tokyo: United Nations Univ. Press

232. Stephen L, Dow J. 1990. *Class, Politics and Popular Religion in Mexico and Central America.* Washington, DC: Soc. Latin Am. Anthropol, Am. Anthropol. Assoc.

233. Stoler A. 1985. *Capitalism and Confrontation in Sumatra's Plantation Belt, 1870–1979.* New Haven, CT: Yale Univ. Press

234. Suárez-Orozco M. 1992. A grammar of terror: psychological responses to state terrorism in dirty war and post-dirty war Argentina. See Ref. 192, pp. 219–59

235. Sutton C. ed. 1993. *Feminism, Nationalism and Militarism.* Washington, DC: Am. Anthropol. Assoc.

236. Tambiah S. 1986. *Sri Lanka: Ethnic Fratricide and the Dismantling of Democracy.* Chicago: Univ. Chicago Press

237. Tambiah S. 1988. Forward. See Ref. 117, pp. 1–6

237a. Tambiah S. 1988. Ethnic fratricide in Sri Lanka: an update. See Ref. 117, pp. 293–319

238. Tambiah S. 1990. Reflections on communal violence in South Asia. *J. Afr. Stud.* 49(4):741–760

239. Taussig M. 1980. *The Devil and Commodity Fetishism in South America.* Chapel Hill: Univ. NC Press

240. Taussig M. 1984. Culture of terror, space of death. Roger Casement and the explanation of torture. *Comp. Stud. Soc. Hist.* 26:467–97

241. Taussig M. 1987. *Shamanism, Colonialism, and the Wild Man: A Study in Terror and Healing.* Chicago: Univ. Chicago Press

242. Thornberry P. 1987. *Minorities and Human Rights Law.* Rep. No. 7. London: Minorities Rights Group

243. Tilly C. 1978. *From Mobilization to Revolution.* Reading, MA: Addison-Wesley

244. Tilly C. 1985. War making and state making as organized crime. See Ref. 83, pp. 169–91

245. Toufexis A. 1993. Seeking the roots of violence. *Time* April 19, pp. 52–53

246. Van den Berghe P, ed. 1990. *State Violence and Ethnicity.* Boulder: Univ. Colo. Press

247. Vayda A. 1976. *War in Ecological Perspective: Persistence, Change, and Adaptive Process in Three Oceanian Societies.* New York: Plenum

248. Vayrynen R. 1987. Global power dynamics and collective violence. In *The Quest for Peace,* ed. R Vayrynen with D Senghaas and C Schmidt, pp. 80–96. London: Sage

249. Verdery K. 1991. *National Ideology Under Socialism: Identity and Cultural Politics in Ceausescu's Romania.* Berkeley: Univ. Calif. Press

250. Vincent J. 1990. *Anthropology and Politics: Visions, Traditions, and Trends.* Tuscon: Univ. Ariz. Press

251. Wakin E. 1992. *Anthropology Goes to War: Professional Ethics and Counterinsurgency in Thailand.* Madison: Univ. Wisc. Cent. SE Asian Stud., Monogr. No. 7

252. Warren K. 1989. *The Symbolism of Subordination: Indian Identity in a Guatemalan Town.* Austin: Univ. Texas Press

253. Warren K, ed. 1993. *The Violence Within:*

Cultural and Political Opposition in Divided Nations. Boulder, CO: Westview

254. Weaver T. 1988. The human rights of undocumented workers in the United States-Mexico border region. See Ref. 75, pp. 73–90

255. Williams B. 1991. *Stains on My Name, War in My Veins: Guyana and the Politics of Cultural Struggle.* Durham, NC: Duke Univ. Press

256. Williams R. 1976. *Keywords.* Oxford: Oxford Univ. Press

257. Winston ME, ed. 1989. *The Philosophy of Human Rights.* Belmont, CA: Wadsworth

258. Wolf E. 1969. *Peasant Wars of the Twentieth Century.* New York: Harper & Row

259. Worsley P. 1986. The superpowers and the tribes. See Ref. 92, pp. 293–306

260. Wright R. 1992. U. N.: Latest missions reflect changing rules. *Los Angeles Times* Dec. 27, pp. A21–22

261. Young C, Turner T. 1985. *The Rise and Fall of the Zairian State.* Madison: Univ. Wisc. Press

262. Zolberg A, Sahrke A, Aguayo S. 1989. *Escape from Violence: Conflict and the Refugee Crisis in the Developing World.* New York: Oxford Univ. Press

Annu. Rev. Anthropol. 1994. 23:137–58

OLD AGE: Cultural and Critical Perspectives

Lawrence Cohen

Department of Anthropology, University of California, Berkeley, California 94720

KEY WORDS: old age, gerontology, generation, critical gerontology, aging

INTRODUCTION

Despite numerous review articles and programmatic essays surveying the social and cultural anthropology of old age (2, 13, 14, 41, 47, 53, 55, 79, 82, 99, 102, 103), a theme in many of them is the relative paucity of anthropological attention to the topic. In 1967 Clark made the classic observation that "if one is to judge from typical anthropological accounts, the span of years between the achievement of adult status and one's funerary rites is either an ethnographic vacuum or a vast monotonous plateau of invariable behavior" (13). Clark's criticism, opening anthropology's future while closing its past to old age, was soon routinized into a requisite lament preceding many essays on the anthropology of aging (79).

This gerontological lament did not, however, correlate with the writing of actual monographs. In 1980, after thirteen years and much productive research by many scholars, Fry could still begin her edited anthology by noting that "anthropology has a long history of being interested in age, but not in aging or the aged" (41). Similarly, in 1981 Amoss & Harrell offered an anthology to "help to remedy a massive neglect of old age by the discipline of anthropology" (2); and in 1984 Keith & Kertzer began their introduction to another anthology by again drawing attention to the need in anthropology to "pay more systematic attention to the role of age in human societies and cultural sys-

0084-6570/94/1015-0137$05.00

tems." What was at stake for the authors was perhaps summed up in the first sentence: "This book admittedly aims to proselytize" (58).

An abundance of writing about an apparent lack of writing presents an interesting contradiction, and it forces us to rethink what this writing—all these reviews that by their own accounts survey and signify an absence—might then be about. Why, it might be asked, were so many reviews and assessments produced that share the sense that there isn't much to review? In dwelling on the contradictions and paradoxes of this emergent discourse of geroanthropology[1] (84), I want to offer a heretical reading of its narrative claims of a salvatory future against a blighted past. Heresy seems to me a necessary response to the language of mission and conversion ubiquitous to the field, Kertzer & Keith's will to proselytize. Yet if the review article is itself somewhat of an instantiating genre within geroanthropology, legitimating in its frequent reiteration this enforced youth with its Golden Future and Leaden Past, then any new review must tread carefully if it would claim to do otherwise. Rather than reiterate the few oases in the imagined desert [classically, the work of Simmons (100)] or chronicle the important achievements of the new geroanthropology—which have been carefully documented in the review literature cited above—I want to frame another past and another present, both to focus on the kind of questions geroanthropology has not tended to ask and to reread the ethnographic vacuum taken by now as an unquestioned part of geroanthropological prehistory.

This review makes no claim to be a comprehensive review of all significant ethnographically or cross-culturally defined work in gerontology. The several published bibliographies of old age, anthropology, and ethnicity indicate that such work numbers in the thousands of articles, books, and films (40, 97). It eschews reproducing the standard categories of cross-cultural gerontology, such as life history, life span and life course, age stratification, grandparenthood, modernization and disengagement theories and challenges to them, caregiving, chronicity, and most recently, critical gerontology. Each of these perspectives and debates engages important questions, but their separation as independent areas of inquiry with reliable and clear-cut methodologies and boundaries may have more to do with the funding structure of much American gerontological work and its relationship to biomedical authority than with their stated objects. To borrow a phrase of Strathern, what is of concern here is the methodological rhetoric involved in "the manufacture of a subdiscipline" (108).

---

[1]
Several disciplinary labels have appeared to describe the subdiscipline. *The anthropology of aging* is perhaps the most common, but it is less about aging from birth to death than about old age, and the euphemism is significant. *Gerontology and anthropology* is also common, perhaps because it leaves open whether the disciplinary commitment of the researcher is primarily to one or the other field or to both. I use *geroanthropology* because it is, quite blessedly, the shortest.

This second point is best illustrated by example. One of the characteristics of geroanthropology is its rapid alchemy of theoretical perspective into scientistic and pseudo-operationalizable jargon. Even Luborsky & Sankar's critical geroanthropological essay (68), which parallels some of the concerns of this review, ironically conjoins a critical sociology of science to a far less critical mystification of the authors' method. Luborsky & Sankar claim to utilize Frankfort School sociology to apply "critical theory" to gerontological research agendas. As anthropologists, they are concerned specifically with adding "culture" to what has become known as the Critical Gerontology perspective (3, 75). But their discussion of critical theory is vague and limited to the assertion that "scientific and philosophical constructs are enmeshed in and serve to recreate the wider socio-historical settings." The term *critical* is taken as a monolithic and unambiguous signifier of method. The text's referent is ultimately not the Continental tradition that it invokes yet never engages, but rather a simulacrum of that tradition used to mark subdisciplinary boundaries.

Luborsky & Sankar move immediately from the invocation of critique to the naturalization of their approach as CG (Critical Geronotology) and CG Studies. Culture, when added to CG, generates extended CG. Along with a scientific-sounding nomenclature, an operationalizable method is offered, promising "the systematic pursuit of a set of clearly articulated questions" through a quantifiable set of components. Over and over, the language of hard science and real results is proffered: the considerable irony and rapidity of this move from critical stance to positivist rhetoric goes unnoticed.

A related concern raised by the authors' invocation of critical theory is the seldom articulated relationship between sociological and anthropological theory in gerontological social science. The authors' appeal to a sociological framework for a critical theory and their mechanistic use of culture as something one can insert into an analysis recapitulate the institutional history of professional gerontology and its embeddedness in ideologies of applied sociology and social work. With such a dearth of anthropological theory in gerontological settings, the term *anthropology* becomes less an epistemological than a professional marker, and the term *culture*—elsewhere an increasingly treacherous foundation for the anthropologist's practice—is proudly displayed as disciplinary icon.

The Luborsky & Sankar essay is state-of-the-art gerontological anthropology. I cite it at the beginning of this review to stress what is at stake in the debate I hope to engender. In short: Where is contemporary anthropological theory in the contemporary anthropology of old age? Why is it represented but seldom engaged? Is a genuinely critical gerontology possible within the parameters of the subfield? If we are to avoid, paraphrasing Clark, either a theoretical vacuum or a vast monotonous plateau of invariable "culture," how must we renegotiate a history?

THE EPISTEMOLOGY OF GEROANTHROPOLOGY

In the 1980s, disciplinary lament slowly shifted to cries of victory: American geroanthropological narratives of mission among the unbelievers gave way to those of successful conversion. In 1981, Nydegger contrasted the dearth of work in the anthropological past with an emerging shift: "...interest is accelerating. Anthropological gerontology is shaping itself into a distinct speciality" (82). By 1990 Sokolovsky confirmed the strength of an "important new specialty" and offered several more names for it: comparative sociogerontology, ethnogerontology, and the anthropology of aging (102). Professional structures emerged: a coterie of leaders, including many of the editors of the anthologies cited above; an organization, the Association of Anthropology and Gerontology (AAGE); and a journal, the *Journal of Cross-Cultural Gerontology*. Group rituals and narratives appeared, for example, centered around the scramble to attend the often conflicting meetings of the Gerontological Society of America (GSA) and the American Anthropological Association (AAA). By 1992, Keith (54) could declare triumphantly, at the GSA meetings in Washington, DC, that the battle for the inclusion and serious consideration of old age within anthropology had been won. But the language of unending mission still dominated her remarks, through its inversion. Now that gerontology has conquered anthropology, Keith suggested, the new task is the spreading of the anthropological gospel within gerontology. No rest for the faithful.

There are two possible approaches to the pervasiveness of this explicit and apparently unceasing language of conversion in geroanthropology. One is a hermeneutic of generosity reading it as the necessary accompaniment of a paradigm shift in a passively but pervasively ageist discipline. The other is a hermeneutic of suspicion taking the sheer quantity and force of this language seriously in asking what else might be at stake for the architects of discourse, particularly in terms of their relationship to old persons, the disciplinary object.

Both approaches are necessary. Ageist language and potentially dehumanizing assumptions continue to influence anthropological work, often in very subtle ways. A recent anthology of feminist anthropology begins in the editor's acknowledgements with a reminder of gendered difference in the extraprofessional pressures placed upon academics: "This project was uniquely arduous, in part for a gendered reason. Most of the contributors (and I) are women in 'sandwich generation' positions...my thanks to contributors who made valiant efforts in hard times" (25). The authors' dilemma as women taking care of teenagers and elderly parents is quite real, and is inarguably gendered. But the sandwich generation as a construction of a middle aged and middle class authorial voice draws its irony not from the expected burden of college-aged children but from the other source of pressure—the inherently difficult and here dangerously naturalized burden of older parents. The elaboration of middle-aged experience as a series of arduous and valiant efforts assumes an unquestioned sense of the burdensomeness of old people. Links and bridges to women older than the volume's contributors are effectively denied in this reduction of older persons to nameless pressures. That the reference is situated within a text otherwise carefully attentive to the politics of difference and their representation suggests the continued invisibility of the representational politics of generation and old age in anthropological writing.

Yet the example of feminist anthropology is instructive in a second sense. Whereas this field is constituted in terms of questions of women both as authors and as subjects of anthropological discourse, geroanthropology is not primarily or even partially a movement generated by old anthropologists. Old persons remain distinctly the Other. Given the extent of geroanthropology's construction as an unrepentant heterology, I adopt the latter hermeneutic, of suspicion, in reviewing its claims to knowledge. Specifically, I challenge both geroanthropology's paradigmatic novelty and its anti-ageist self-construction, drawing on the critical approaches Luborsky & Sankar describe and in particular on Estes' now classic analyses (27–30).

Estes chronicles the paradox of gerontology as a growing service industry that dedicates itself to preserving and protecting the independence and normality of old persons yet requires their dependence and marginality to survive. I have elsewhere built upon her analysis in a critique of international gerontology (16). Estes' *The Aging Enterprise* is about the "programs, organizations, bureaucracies, interest groups, trade associations, providers, industries, and professionals that serve the aged in one capacity or another" (27). Both the book and Estes' follow-up article a decade and a half later (29) focus on the relationship between old age as service industry and the articulation of policy. In extending the critique to the sociology of knowledge, I foreground an anthropological concern with local epistemologies.

Like critical gerontology, Estes' own practice is an ironic site of gerontology as aging enterprise. "The Aging Enterprise Revisited" was delivered as the 1992 Kent Lecture at the GSA meetings in Washington, DC, the same meetings where Keith renewed the call to mission. In front of several thousand gerontologists, the aging enterprise incarnate, Estes invoked Maggie Kuhn and the Gray Panthers and other signifiers of an activist gerontology articulated by and for older persons. But the gap between the vision of the Gray Panthers and the constitution of the gerontological audience, who through Estes' powerful speech could erase all generational difference and envision themselves as fellow travelers, mirrored the gap between critical theory and CG studies: again, politics as representation.

Geroanthropology, like gerontology as a whole, fails to articulate an internal politics or hermeneutics of generational difference, and disguises this difference through the language of conversion and the trope of anger that underlies it ("no one here cares about old age") and through the language of exploration ("old age is *terra incognita,* awaiting our discovery"). The language of conversion is ubiquitous in gerontological and geriatric writing. For the World Assembly on Aging in Vienna in 1982, the United States Department of State (110) produced a document summarizing the history of American gerontology, which from the outset is framed as a missionary speciality. Thus the report notes that in the 1950s an "Inter-University Council on Social Gerontology [met to] further professional training" through "two month-long indoctrination programs for 75 college and university faculty members who had developed an interest in aging."

By a trope of anger, I mean that writing in gerontology and geriatrics frequently takes the narrative form: "Old people are neglected. No one appears to realize this unpleasant fact. I [the author] do; I hope to convince you. Together we can make old age a good age." Nascher, the New York physician who coined the term *geriatrics* in 1909, in later life offered a classic conversion narrative (quoted in 109) explaining his founding of the field. Early in his medical training in the 1880s, Nascher was struck by the frequency with which physicians used the rationale of "it's just old age" to avoid disentangling the complex medical problems of elderly patients. Nascher retells the birth of geriatrics as an epiphany: visiting a slum workhouse with mostly elderly inhabitants, young Nascher and his medical preceptor are accosted by an old woman complaining of her pain. "It's just old age," Nascher is told. Suddenly he realizes that it is not just old age, but rather disease. In the declaration of old age's normality and the refusal of others to see, Nascher has the vision of geriatrics. He composes a monumental text, *Geriatrics* (81), drawing on contemporary debate on the line between the normal and the pathological in medicine (9, 10) both to assert the normality of old age and to declare that in old age, the distinction between normal and pathological is lost. The contradiction in this foundational text continues to suffuse geriatric and gerontological practice and theory. A discipline is articulated to demonstrate the normality of old age by segregating its study and treatment from that of young and middle adulthood.

De Beauvoir's 1970 *La Vieillesse (The Coming of Age)* (24) is rooted in this trope of anger, as are other classic works of the 1970s. The titles of Butler's *Why Survive? Being Old in America* (8), Curtin's *Nobody Ever Died of Old Age: In Praise of Old People, In Outrage at their Loneliness* (22), and in anthropology, Kayser-Jones' *Old, Alone, and Neglected: Care of the Aged in the United States and Scotland* (52) convey a sense of old age as a state of misery and offer gerontology and politically engaged fieldwork as responses. The generational location of the author is seldom taken as relevant to these politics, save when, like young Nascher, youth sees through the denials of middle age to the truths of the old. De Beauvoir (24) likewise concludes: "The young man dreads this machine that is about to seize hold of him, and sometimes he tries to defend himself by throwing half-bricks; the old man, rejected by it, exhausted and naked, has nothing left but his eyes to weep with. Between youth and age there turns the machine."

The language of exploration similarly maintains a distinction between the young or ageless author and the old subject. Kaufman begins her important study, *The Ageless Self: Sources of Meaning in Late Life* (51), with an appeal to demographic urgency—"how to cope with an aging population"—and follows with an appeal to exploring "meaning" in old age:

> The research upon which this book is based grew out of my awareness of this gap [between the added years of life and our knowledge of how best to spend them], the uncharted territory in which we find ourselves both as aging individuals and as an aging nation. In order to improve the quality of life experience for those in their later years, we must understand what it means to be old.... For only by first knowing how the elderly view themselves, their lives, and the nature of old age can we hope to fashion a meaningful present and future for them and for those who follow (p. 4).

Katz (50) has called attention to such uses of alarmist demography, and from the beginning old age is framed in a split fashion in *The Ageless Self*, as the aged Other presenting a threat and the aging Self who is threatened. The latter is the explorer, adrift in "uncharted territory," the heart of darkness of old age where we encounter the natives in classic anthropological fashion: "for only by first knowing how the elderly view themselves, their lives, and the nature of old age can we hope to fashion a meaningful present and future for them and for those who follow." We fashion for them, and what is exchanged in this colonial encounter is meaning. We lack it, and search among them for "what it means to be old"; then we extract this meaning like Indian cotton to Manchester mills and refashion it, for both them and, ultimately, us. Meaning circulates within the exploratory text much as politics circulate within the gerontological polemic.

THE TROPE OF AMBIGUITY

There is a third form of circulating argument in gerontology and geroanthropology, which I call a trope of ambiguity. For Minois, ambiguity is a phenomenological universal of old age, a time both of maximal experience and of maximal debility, simultaneously vaunted and evaded. Minois looks for and finds this ambiguity "throughout the whole of history" (74:18); the fairly exhaustive text proceeds from period to period over millennia, evaluating whether old age was more gerontophobic or gerontophilic in each.

Minois' history deals in the murky currency of "attitudes" toward old age; history for him is a cyclical narrative of their oscillation. The book is a response both to aging and modernization theory accounts that posit a law of the diminishing status of old persons with industrialization (20, 21) and to revisionist accounts that place the decline prior (32) or subsequent (1) to industrialization or that challenge the possibility of a decline (62, 88). Minois suggests that the image of old age has always shifted around the fundamental ambiguity at its core.

Cole's *The Journey of Life: A Cultural History of Aging in America* provides a far more nuanced history (18), yet the ambiguity of aging remains the central insight offered. For Cole, ambiguity is not the slightly ironic fact that it appears to be for Minois, but a lost truth about aging that "postmodern culture" can help us recover:

> We need to revive existentially nourishing views of aging that address its paradoxical nature. Aging, like illness and death, reveals the most fundamental conflict of the human condition: the tension between infinite ambitions, dreams, and desires on the one hand, and vulnerable, limited, decaying physical existence on the other—the tragic and ineradicable conflict between spirit and body. This paradox cannot be eradicated by the wonders of modern medicine or by positive attitudes toward growing old. Hence the wisdom of traditions that consider old age both a blessing and a curse (p. 239).

Cole here notes the ironic ageism of gerontological ideology in its denial of old age as a time of inevitable suffering, but he is specific in placing the blame far earlier, with the Victorians. *The Journey of Life* is ultimately an appeal to an awkwardly romanticized and thinly contextualized Puritan ideology. Cole closes by invoking a Lyotardian postmodernism as metaphor for a return to an invented tradition of gerontological ambiguity.

Cole's argument, that "the wisdom of traditions" successfully negotiates the ambiguity of old age by accepting it, is a key theme of Myerhoff's classic ethnography *Number Our Days* (77) and the genre it spawned. Myerhoff's brilliantly constructed work on Jewish members of a senior center in Venice Beach, Los Angeles, came more than any other to define the potential for an anthropology of old age, as Kaminsky (49) and others have noted. Myerhoff utilized Turner's processual and performative analyses of social systems and developed a sophisticated interpretive methodology, transforming the ethnography of communal and institutional old age in the United States from the more static and skeletal accounts that preceded her work (44, 46, 48).

Like the aging and modernization literature of the 1960s and 1970s, with its normative focus on whether old age is better now or then, here or there (83), Myerhoff's work centers on sets of fundamentally moral oppositions: success or failure, joy or pain, independence or dependency, and continuity or disruption. But whereas in the aging and modernization paradigm the central question is in which society or period is old age better, for Myerhoff the poignancy of old age lies in its comprehending both poles of each of these oppositional frames. The power of the work lies in its reconstruction of informants' lives as momentous struggles for dignity, survival, autonomy, continuity, and joy within such an oppositional universe. Like the Huichol Indians on pilgrimage in Myerhoff's earlier work, the old people of Venice Beach are liminal figures, here not the ritually created liminality of the pilgrimage but the existential condition of old age. Ritual, in the senior center, is articulated by the elders to maintain a sense of continuity and *communitas,* binding together the oppositions that frame their old age against a dissolution into meaninglessness. Culture—the center's rituals, the heretic Shmuel's wisdom, the fashioning of everyday life—manages ambiguity.

A danger in this approach is its use of culture and ritual as inherently holistic. Myerhoff's romanticization of Yiddishkeit as authentic culture healing the Eriksonian crises of late life has been taken to task by Kaminsky in an introduction (49) to his edited collection of Myerhoff's essays (78). Kaminsky points out Myerhoff's deemphasis of the class location and the cohort experience of the Venice Beach elders in the labor movement, her insistence on culture as a totalizing construct, and her unacknowledged reworking of the biographies of the book's *dramatis personae* to achieve her desired effects. The closing of analysis to other axes of social difference and the emphasis on culture as a response to existential ambiguity are not limited to Myerhoff but characterize the genre of institutional and community studies that build on her text. Kugelmass chronicles the life of a synagogue and its elderly members in the South Bronx (59); like Myerhoff's work, his ethnography offers a powerful narrative of survival and a testimony to the healing miracles of ritual and myth. Shield examines "daily life in an American nursing home," using a similar focus on liminality and culture (98). The nursing home Shield studies is the inverse of Myerhoff's senior center, a total institution represented as lacking ritual and culture and thus lacking the possibility of a response to generational and institutional ambiguity. Each of these ethnographies examines complex questions of class and racial boundaries and the relation of everyday experience to the state and the aging enterprise; but in each, Turnerian tools of liminality, ritual process, and social drama are used to construct what Vesperi criticizes as an "ethnographic present" (111) in which the everyday relevance of the macrosocial world is sidelined to give way to the morality play of old age, in triumph and in pathos.

The liminality of old age may often be more rooted in generational politics than existential conditions; the trope of ambiguity tends to obscure this difference. Vesperi's study of old age, local communities, and the state in St. Petersburg, Florida (111) marks a radical break from the trope. *City of Green Benches* weaves together macrosocial issues—national advertising campaigns, local and state business interests, representations by gerontologists—with a complex ethnography that resists situating old persons within a single institution, includes gerontological professionals as ethnographic subjects, and draws on the lifelong and ongoing construction of race and class in the constitution of old age. Culture and ritual do not serve as the totalizing constructs that they do in the Myerhoff genre of ethnography; local knowledge is often distorted within the politics of social interaction. Like other anthropologists of aging who focus on class (6, 15, 48, 104, 105), Vesperi relies primarily on interactionist—sociological and social psychological—frameworks of analysis, but here they are thickened through a more sophisticated use of ethnographic and macrosocial data.

Neither interactionist nor Turnerian studies attempt an integration of their respective foci on class and culture; concurrent and subsequent debates on practice theory, on *habitus*, and on hegemony, ideology, and culture seem far removed from most geroanthropological concerns. The subdiscipline crystallizes around an academic aging enterprise and its associated incitements to speak of old age in moral, oppositional terms: it is as much about a fantasized uncharted territory of Old Age as about the everyday lives of older persons. Through the mobilization of anger and ambiguity, a disciplinary ethos emerges that envisions itself as mission practice against an empty past and writes itself through a mix of applied sociology and romanticized narrative. To reintroduce anthropological theory into and to write against the geroanthropological enterprise, it may be time to reappropriate an anthropological past.

FRAZER AND THE SYMBOLIC CONSTRUCTION OF GENERATION

A cultural anthropology of old age might begin its genealogy with Frazer's repudiated classic, *The Golden Bough* (39), organized around the figure of the hunted, killed, and regenerated king or god. Frazer is read in at least three ways; I suggest a fourth. Within anthropology's own narrative of its emergence into cultural particularism, Frazer is represented as the archetypical armchair anthropologist brandishing a theory of primitive error, here that of sympathetic magic. A Freudian appropriation takes the deep meaning of the violence as Oedipal conflict, and neglects Frazer's focus on magic as socially constituted reality. A reading that draws on Joseph Conrad centers on the social (particularly the colonial and gendered) constitution of the text's regicidal violence but downplays the generational specificity of *The Golden Bough*.

The reduction of Frazer to a theory of primitive error is premature. Like Robertson Smith (101), Frazer grapples with Christianity and prefigures a much later celebration of anthropology as cultural critique (70). The implicit and ultimate referent of the dying god is Christ, and the scope of sympathetic irrationality implicitly encompasses contemporary European civilization. Errors of sympathetic magic for Frazer raise the question of the social construction of reality for both primitives and moderns. Magic, which in this extended sense encompasses most of civilization, is what a subsequent anthropology would call the symbolic. In asking how generations magically reconstitute themselves, Frazer is concerned primarily with the symbolic reproduction of the body in time.

Kings and human representatives of the divine are put to death, Frazer argues in his introduction to the third volume of the work, "to arrest the forces of decomposition in nature by retrenching with ruthless hand the first ominous symptoms of decay" (39:v–vi). Sickness and particularly old age are signs of enfeeblement and of death, and are perceived as challenges to the body not only of the individual but of the community and the state. The continuity of the social body is challenged by the potential degeneration of each successive generation. Symbolically, continuity is maintained by preventing the degeneration of charismatic authority vested in the king or god, through the circulation of charisma in a series of youthful bodies. Generations must replicate themselves: "no amount of care and precaution will prevent the man-god from growing old and feeble" (p. 9). Aging is a challenge not only to individual lives but to the possibility of social meaning, to culture. The hegemonic location of dominant bodies in society is achieved by and through their identification with the social body; Frazer recognizes aging in later life as a challenge to the seamless constitution of the hegemonic.

At stake is not only the particular interests of age groups—a reduction of Frazer by Radcliffe-Brown, maintained in most subsequent work on generation—but the very possibility of hegemony in itself. Thus the patriarchal body in decline central to the text presents a problem in signification: it forces the question of the continuity of the Symbolic—in Lacanian terms the Law of the Father—in a world full of ruptures in lived experience, a world where fathers and mothers and other embodiments of the hegemonic grow old and die. By reading a violent act at the core of culture, Frazer does not just open the way for psychodynamic hearts of darkness, but grounds a symbolic theory of generational difference and particularly of the construction of old age within a crisis of meaning. *The Golden Bough* concerns itself at length not only with questions of the politics of debility (When do societies mark the powerful body as senescent?) and of the means of destruction (How do societies disassociate the individual from the social body?), but with the semiotics of exchange (How is a new body seamlessly enabled to become the social body?).

Frazer's emphasis on the integrity of violence and culture differentiates the position of intergenerational conflict in *The Golden Bough* from the less meaning-centered and more social structural analyses of generational conflict of Radcliffe-Brown and his successors, of the French structural Marxists, of the theorists of the domestic cycle, and of the age stratification theorists in sociology and their anthropological proponents. Central for Frazer is the relationship between debility and the impossibility of magical, or symbolic, representation, reframing Clark's question of why anthropology has erased the period between marriage and funerary rites. Instead, we are pushed to asked what is it about local constructions of middle and late adulthood that may or may not resist certain modes of representation. Geroanthropology, born of the bureaucratic construction of old age and its particular moral imperative, cannot see crises of meaning in such absences. It must, endlessly, produce the requisite old body to be simultaneously romanticized and fixed, like the realist aesthetic of the old bodies that each month adorn the cover of *The Gerontologist.*

Work on generation from Radcliffe-Brown through the domestic cycle literature fails to take up the symbolic dimension of Frazer's work; yet, this literature is still more relevant to a contemporary anthropology of old age than geroanthropology is sometimes willing to consider. Radcliffe-Brown's famous essays on joking relationships present a second moment in a provisional genealogy (90, 91). Like de Beauvoir, Radcliffe-Brown shifts a two-generational model of the politics of aging, the old being replaced by their children, into a three-generational model, the old and young in conjunctive joking alliance with each other and in an asymmetric disciplinary relationship with the intermediate generation. Intergenerational joking relationships, for Radcliffe-Brown, are again structural responses to the predicament of social and cultural reproduction: "The social tradition is handed down from one generation to the next. For the tradition to be maintained it must have authority behind it. The authority is therefore normally recognized as possessed by members of the preceding generation and it is they who exercise discipline." In contrast, "grandparents and their grandchildren are grouped together in the social structure in opposition to their children and parents. An important clue to the understanding of the subject is the fact that in the flow of social life through time, in which men are born, become mature and die, the grandchildren replace their grandparents" (90).

The Frazerian concern with symbolic action has given way to a functionalism that foreshadows future gerontological analysis. Yet Radcliffe-Brown merits closer attention. Social reproduction is twofold: parents hand down tradition to children; grandparents are replaced by grandchildren. Two processes are detailed: an assymetrical and contractual gifting of culture and a symmetrical and informal circulation of bodies and roles. Both are explained, in the contemporary fashion of the discipline, as responses to the problem of social reproduction. The old attempt to discipline and are marginalized by their children, like Frazer's dying king. For the successive generation of grandchildren, however, grandparents are not a threatening body of decrepitude but a source of support and alliance and meaning in their own agonal struggles with parents. Multiple threats and threatening bodies emerge, as do multiple constructions of old age, middle age, and youth. The political landscape of generational analysis thickens, if not its symbolic terrain.

Two avenues of contemporary geroanthropological interest draw upon these responses to questions of social reproduction: the study of formalized age groups and age stratification theory. The first of these subfields never became central to geroanthropological self-construction. Rooted in a sense of its connectedness to social anthropology and resistant to the incitement to name and isolate old age central to the subdiscipline, age set research shares few of the epistemological concerns detailed above. The field therefore does not share geroanthropology's amnesic tendencies but constructs a genealogy for itself. In Bernardi's literature review (5), "the first interpretive scheme for the cultural and social significance of age" is Schurtz's (96) 1902 *Alterklasses und Männerbünde*. For Schurtz, men's age-specific groups are formed as secret societies to wrest societal control from the primeval matriarchy. Bernardi passes on quickly to Webster's 1932 study of postpubertal male institutions (112) and the work of Radcliffe-Brown (89), Lowie (66), and Evans-Pritchard (31), but despite Schurtz's specific emphasis on the destruction of the matriarchy, he offers an early argument for the close relationship of the politics of gender and generation, an idea later elaborated by Meillassoux (73).

There are two types of traditional anthropological work on age sets or age classes: 1. monographs concerned with their particularities as social institutions and 2. those concerned with the integrated analysis of age sets and other forms of age grades and age stratification. The former include classic ethnographies—e.g. Spencer's work on gerontocracy among the Samburu (106), Wilson's work on Nyakyusa age-villages (113), Maybury-Lewis' study of Shavante age sets (71), and Legesse's (63) work on the Boran *gada*—as well as attempts like Bernardi's to construct broader theories and typologies of age sets (4, 56, 67, 72, 107). The latter, like Radcliffe-Brown, see formal age sets and age grades on a continuum of social organization, and take as their focus either the totality of the system or the dynamics between age groups. Systemic approaches stress either functional or symbolic integrity. Eisenstadt offers a Parsonian typology of age groups (26). Maybury-Lewis, in a comparison of Brazilian and African age group systems, develops a meaning-centered alternative that sees the essence of age group structure not in the utility of its social functions but in age as both ideology and principal of organization (72). He suggests applying a meaning-centered analysis of age as category not only to the East African ethnography but to studies of age set, grade, and generation worldwide. The Frazerian concern with the symbolic construction of age groups is revived, though not Frazer's emphasis on the violence—symbolic or enacted—of intergroup relations and thus his concern with the breakdown of signification.

Rey (92–94) raises the question of age groups as social classes in a structural Marxist framework, a point contested by Meillassoux in a well-known debate (73). Meillassoux's argument again centers on social reproduction: within the domestic mode of production, junior men become senior men and "recover the product of their productive agricultural labour" (p. 79), but the cycling of male bodies through systems of age stratification only intensifies sex stratification. Meillassoux develops the theme enunciated far earlier by Schurtz through a lineal rather than affinal interpretation of Levi-Strauss' celebrated figure of the circulation of women. Male intergenerational struggle becomes patriarchal *entente cordiale*.

Geroanthropological readings of these literatures misrepresent them as theoretically impoverished, maintaining the sense of mission. N. Foner's (34) anthropological interpretation of Riley's (95) and A. Foner's (33) age stratification theory begins with the requisite denial of a past: "there has been no systematic attempt in anthropology to build a model of age inequality—or for that matter, of age and aging" (34:xi). The French structural Marxists are begrudgingly mentioned but soon dismissed: "But the French…are so worried about whether or not elder-junior distinctions are class divisions that they overlook many critical features of inequalities between old and young"; thus, they ignore issues beyond male gerontocracy, such as the prevalence of disadvantaged and exploited elders and age inequalities between older and younger women.

Age stratification theory as adapted by N. Foner addresses these critical concerns. But the dismissal of an anthropological past is premature. Meillassoux does not closely examine age inequalities between women, but he does link the possibility of age inequalities between men to sexual stratification more generally, refusing to separate analyses of age from sexual inequality (73); the point is central to his critique of Rey. Foner ignores it, constructing a straw man in Meillassoux and offering in his stead a functionalist account (34:253–254), which neglects the economic questions he poses and articulates an adoptive lineage through American sociological theory. Foner's text is important in its consideration of gender-specific age inequalities, but it does not take up Maybury-Lewis' challenge to develop a symbolic anthropology of age (72). Nor is the work of Fortes (101), Goody (43), and Mandelbaum (69) on domestic cycles and the processual analysis of age stratification, offering another critical moment in the construction of a geroanthropological lineage, seen as relevant. Foner offers a neofunctionalist and highly tautological account of gerontocratic and gerontophobic roles of old women and old men, ultimately making few theoretical advances except for an iterated reminder that nonindustrial societies are often gerontophobic and not just gerontocratic: the invocation, again, of ambiguity.

Like other theorists of generation and the domestic cycle, Fortes (38) covers related terrain without the amnesia, noting that "the way [age and aging] are incorporated into tribal forms of social structure or invested with cultural value and significance is a topic of central relevance for anthropological theory." His review of a lifetime of his and others' work is read inversely by Kertzer & Keith as "an important first step." Fortes summarizes much work in West Africa and elsewhere on the processual relationship between biological, social, and cultural aging with a set of observations: 1. Intergenerational relations are characterized both by the continuity and the struggle inherent in generational reproduction. Fortes defines the latter in Oedipal terms. 2. Aging is an individual process positioned "between two poles of social structure," the domestic and juridical domains. Thus, the "recognition and consideration of chronological age as opposed to maturation and generation depend on the differentiation between the politicojural and the domestic domains of social life."

But the politicojural and the domestic—anthropological categories often rooted in colonial constructions of public and private domains—are not made objects of inquiry in themselves. Their respective logics are constructed through a universalizing sociological rationality. The symbolic, for Fortes, remains external to processual dynamics, as an "investment" of the interplay of biological (individual) and social (domestic and civic) structures with meaning. Radcliffe-Brown's legacy in Fortes is marked (35, 36); Frazer's legacy is limited to an acknowledgment of the struggle between generations, but here read solely in Oedipal terms. Age, generation, and time present social structural challenges rather than crises in meaning; intergenerational conflict is splayed between social and intrapsychic causes. The first step imagined by Kertzer & Keith, though demonstrating geroanthropology's rootedness in British structural functionalism, sidesteps most interpretive and symbolic disciplinary concerns, let alone the possibility of a poststructural inquiry.

AGING RELOCATED: PHENOMENOLOGIES, RATIONALITIES, AND HERMENEUTICS

A critical gerontology, of which this essay forms a part, is an inadequate response to geroanthropological amnesia if, like the Luborsky & Sankar review, it does little more than validate recent paradigms. I suggest three directions in which anthropologists have critically engaged the study of old age beyond current subdisciplinary isolation: a phenomenological focus on experience, embodiment, and identity; a critical focus on the rationalities and hegemonies through which aging is experienced and represented; and an interpretive focus on examining the relevance of the ethnographer's age to the forms of knowledge produced.

Phenomenologies

In *The Ageless Self*, Kaufman (51) challenges the professional search for the meaning of old age, suggesting that her old informants do not perceive being old as central to the experienced self. According to Kaufman, in looking for meaning in old age by assuming that old age is at the core of the meaningful, gerontologists often reify a political and bureaucratic identity as phenomenological universal. Against the moralism of the usual tropes of anger and ambiguity, Kaufman refuses to paint her subjects as *a priori* caricatures of wrenching pathos or gritty survivorship, and the result is a far subtler ethnographic texture. Kaufman's introduction is cited above as emblematic of the failure of geroanthropological authors to locate themselves generationally within a sustained hermeneutic; and yet against the language of mission inciting us to name Old Age, Kaufman problematizes the easy availability of the term as meaningful ethnographic construct.

The limits of Kaufman's project mark directions for further work building on her insights. The old persons in *The Ageless Self* experience the assaults of bodily aging as distinct from their sense of continuity in self; against an aging body and externally imposed labeling, individuals report experiencing an ageless self. In taking these reports of continuity as lived experience, Kaufman may neglect political and psychodynamic questions of denial and resistance in interpreting her subjects' construction of self against body. The text does not locate the specifics of cultural and more particularly class histories upon which the Cartesian embodiment of its subjects is predicated. The possibility that the experience of the body—and thus of the relationship between an aging body and an aging self—may be differentially constituted across class and cultural and other axes of social difference needs to be explored in the move toward a political phenomenology of age.

Rationalities

Work that links the study of old age to a critical focus on ideologies, nationalisms, modernities, and gender constructions, in various settings is emerging (16, 17, 61, 64, 65). In the Netherlands and in India, a group of South Asian scholars working under the auspices of the Indo-Dutch Programme for Alternatives in Development (IDPAD) have placed questions of modernity, postcoloniality, and the application of the social theory of Elias, Foucault, and Bakhtin at the center of a gerontological project (11, 12, 23, 87). The IDPAD is one of the few attempts to reverse the flow of anthropological knowledge production as well as to decenter international gerontology's Euro-American bias.

Much of this emergent work is characterized by attention to the complexities of symbolic structure and cultural politics. In *Encounters with Aging: Mythologies of Menopause in Japan and North America,* Lock (65) traces the replication of hegemonic constructions of the aging person within research and clinical practice, focusing on menopause and gendered aging. The text combines personal narrative, quantitative and comparative data, a critical but serious attention to biomedical discourse, and a historicized discussion of the politics of menopausal knowledge. Japanese scholarly literature on aging is engaged closely, against the usual Eurocentricism. Like Plath's (86) set of life histories of older Japanese, the cultural specificity of aging is closely examined, but here the invocation of cultural difference does not obscure the political dimensions of signification.

Lamb's (61) study of aging in a Bengali village engages multiple debates in the anthropology of South Asia on the nature of interpersonal transactions and the construction of persons and genders. Old age is central to the text, yet as in Kaufman's and Lock's work it resists becoming an end in itself. Processual attention to generation is central to Lamb's analysis, as in the work of Fortes, but the structural logics of practice are not presumed to be precultural but are rooted in local constructions of action and substance. Yet even as the experience of age is carefully located within the Bengali construction of the person, this construction is located within the phenomenology of aging. Lamb challenges static conceptions of personhood by tracing across the life cycle the meanings of and challenges to being a person in a Bengali village. The lesson of geroanthropology—that age is critical to the study of culture—is acknowledged without subdisciplinary impoverishment.

Modernity and the postcolony have become critical foci in some of this work in a different sense than in the aging and modernization literature of the 1970s. Questions of the constitution of the old person as subject are foregrounded through emphases on feminist theory, critical medical anthropology, and Gramsci. Cohen (17) situates Indian debates on senility within a universe of discourse in which the old body becomes a powerful sign both of the state and of imagined core values in Indian culture and their perceived disappearance. The politicization of the old body is juxtaposed with the experience of old persons across class and gender. Attention to local phenomenologies and hegemonies articulating the experience of the aging body is combined with a focus on the impact of shifting religious and state ideologies.

In Chatterji's work (11), the subjectivity of the older person is framed in terms of institutional practice in the context of the ongoing medicalization of old age. The old age home as a total institution is not just an impediment to personal integration as in Shield's work and the trope of anger literature but becomes the site of new forms of subjectivity. For example, Chatterji discusses the file self, the old person known through medical and professional records that increasingly determine the socially meaningful organization of his or her subjective experience. Like Lamb, Chatterji looks at the construction of the person in time, but here the construction of time itself is at stake. Like Ostör (85), who suggests that geroanthropology needs to locate not only age and generation but time in local practice and knowledge, Chatterji offers a subtle analysis of the construction of temporality within the intersecting forms of rationality of the multiply located institution. The file self of the medicalized old body presents the problem of a cyborg anthropology, after Haraway (45), the need to examine the constitution of aging within the implosion of ever more encompassing technologies, markets, and media representations.

Hermeneutics

Interpretive inquiries in which the age of the anthropologist is critical to the construction of gerontological knowledge are few. Myerhoff (77) was perhaps the first to explore the hermeneutics specific to generational difference, from arguably teaching herself to walk like an older woman to inserting herself centrally into her ethnography long before such a move became fashionable. Kaminsky (49) has pointed out the limits to Myerhoff's self-location, but his concern is less with the specific interpretive politics of generational difference than with more general questions of ethnographic representation.

The concerned younger gerontologist as angry spokesperson for the disenfranchised elderly is a stock character in gerontological writing, but such reflexivity—echoing Nascher's epiphany in the New York poorhouse—seldom extends to an interrogation of ethnographic practice. Two works that open up the interpretive politics of old age are by anthropologists writing not as old age professionals but as older persons. Colson (19) muses on the shifts in what anthropologists take as ethnographically relevant both as they age and as the persons with with whom they work and from whom they learn age. As Moore (76) and Lamb articulate in their work, a processual attention to individual and group practice over the course of a lifetime is critical to the analysis of social or symbolic structures at any moment in time. Colson applies a similar insight to the life of the anthropologist herself.

At age 78 the anthropologist Laird found herself ensconced in a Phoenix nursing home with no means, as she puts it, of escape. *Limbo* is her chronicle of the better part of a year at the pseudonymous Golden Mesa nursing home, written with often painful clarity and irony: "Recently a friend sent me a newspaper clipping telling of a senile patient in a Southern California nursing home who was found drowned in a therapy pool, still strapped in her wheelchair. Such an event would have been impossible at Golden Mesa; it had no therapy pool" (60:1). Anger here is powerful but nuanced. Laird's institutionalization is presented at the intersection of personal, kin, institutional, and state realities. The violence conveyed in the opening anecdote about the therapy pool is not, in her account of everyday life at Golden Mesa, the story of gross abandonment and abuse but rather of the ongoing banality, infantilization, and denial of personhood within the institution through the most minute, and damning, of gestures. Central to this denial, for Laird, is the grouping together of residents by physical functioning rather than social and cognitive awareness: the false mirror of demented roommates and hallmates. Ambiguity, the shifting meaning of old age, here as simultaneously wise and demented, is constructed, Laird suggests, through the social spaces mandating the institution. *Limbo* resists the easy romance of gerontological narratives of old age pathos and triumph. Laird had great difficulty finding a publisher; Buffington-Jennings (7) notes in an epilogue to the book that one prospective editor had written: "Maybe I'm a monster, but it doesn't move me."

The politics of catharsis in the construction of geroanthropological narratives are particularly critical. The unquestioned importance of the aging enterprise ("we must know") and more generally reified differences between generations as interpretive communities ("they can't understand") are at stake in geroanthropology's resistance to taking seriously the hermeneutics and politics of its appropriation of old persons' experience as a fundamental dimension of practice. The bulk of gerontological practice remains the transformation of critical agendas into routinized scientistic jargon abetting the biomedicalization of and control over old persons. Without a sustained effort at change, the concerns of the field will remain in subdisciplinary limbo.

ACKNOWLEDGMENTS

I am indebted to my mentors in gerontological activism and critique, Jerry Avorn, at Harvard Medical School, and Edith Stein, formerly of Action for Boston Community Development. Discussions with my students in a 1992 seminar on Old Age and Anthropological Theory at the University of California, Berkeley, were very helpful, particularly with Cheryl Theis. So were talks with Sarah Lamb, Robert LeVine, Elizabeth Colson, Sharon Kaufman, and Andrew Achenbaum. Veena Das started me thinking about the importance of Frazer to a theory of signification and time. It has been my good fortune to be affiliated with anthropologists at the University of California, San Francisco, where much work on geroanthropology is being pursued.

Literature Cited

1. Achenbaum WA. 1978. *Old Age in the New Land: The American Experience Since* *1790.* Baltimore: Johns Hopkins Univ. Press

2. Amoss PT, Harrell S. 1981. Introduction: an anthropological perspective on aging. In *Other Ways of Growing Old: Anthropological Perspectives*, ed. PT Amoss, S Harrell, pp. 1–24. Stanford, CA: Stanford Univ. Press

3. Baars J. 1991. The challenge of critical gerontology: the problem of social constitution. *J. Aging Stud.* 5:219–43

4. Baxter PTW, Almagor U, eds. 1978. *Age, Generation and Time: Some Features of East African Age Organisations.* London: Hurst

5. Bernardi B. 1984. *Age Class Systems: Social Institutions and Polities Based on Age.* Transl. DI Kertzer, 1985. Cambridge: Cambridge Univ. Press (From Italian)

6. Bohannan P. 1981. Food of old people in center-city hotels. See Ref. 42, pp. 185–200

7. Buffington-Jennings A. 1979. Epilogue: before and after limbo. See Ref. 60, pp. 171–78

8. Butler RN. 1975. *Why Survive? Being Old in America.* San Francisco: Harper & Row

9. Canguilhem G. 1978. *The Normal and the Pathological.* Transl. CR Fawcett, RS Cohen. Dordrecht: Reidel (From French)

10. Charcot JM. 1874. *Leçons Cliniques sur les Maladies des Vieillards et les Maladies Chroniques.* Paris: Delahaye. 2nd ed.

11. Chatterji R. 1989. *The organisation of the self under dementia.* Presented at Symp. Soc. Aging Comp. Perspect., New Delhi

12. Chattoo S. 1989. *The absence of geriatrics: the self that can be retrieved.* Presented at Symp. Soc. Aging Comp. Perspect., New Delhi

13. Clark M. 1967. The anthropology of aging, a new area for studies of culture and personality. *Gerontologist* 7(1):55–64

14. Climo J. 1992. The role of anthropology in gerontology—theory. *J. Aging Stud.* 6(1):41–55

15. Cohen CI, Sokolovsky J. 1989. *Old Men of the Bowery: Strategies for Survival Among the Homeless.* New York: Guilford

16. Cohen L. 1992. No aging in India: the uses of gerontology. *Cult. Med. Psychiatr.* 16:123–61

17. Cohen L. 1995. *No Aging in India: Alzheimer's, Bad Families, and Other Modern Things.* Berkeley: Univ. Calif. Press. In press

18. Cole TR. 1992. *The Journey of Life: A Cultural History of Aging in America.* Cambridge: Cambridge Univ. Press

19. Colson E. 1984. The reordering of experience: anthropological involvement with time. *J. Anthropol. Res.* 40(1):1–13

20. Cowgill DO. 1974. Aging and modernization: a revision of the theory. In *Late Life*, ed. J Gubrium, pp. 123–46. Springfield, IL: Thomas

21. Cowgill DO, Holmes LD, eds. 1972. *Aging*

and Modernization. New York: Appleton-Century-Crofts

22. Curtin SR. 1972. *Nobody Ever Died of Old Age: In Praise of Old People, In Outrage at their Loneliness.* Boston: Little, Brown

23. Dattachowdhury S. 1989. *The home in the city: privacy, space and the person in a home for the aged.* Presented at Symp. Soc. Aging Comp. Perspect., New Delhi

24. De Beauvoir S. 1970. *The Coming of Age.* Transl. P O'Brien, 1972. New York: Putnam (From French)

25. di Leonardo M. 1991. Acknowledgements. In *Gender at the Crossroads of Knowledge: Feminist Anthropology in the Postmodern Era*, ed. M di Leonardo, pp. xi–xii. Berkeley: Univ. Calif. Press

26. Eisenstadt SN. 1956. *From Generation to Generation: Age Groups and Social Structure.* Glencoe, IL: Free Press

27. Estes C. 1979. *The Aging Enterprise.* San Francisco: Jossey-Bass

28. Estes C. 1986. The politics of ageing in America. *Ageing Soc.* 6:121–34

29. Estes C. 1993. The aging enterprise revisited. *Gerontologist* 33:292–98

30. Estes C, Binney E. 1989. The biomedicalization of aging: dangers and dilemmas. *Gerontologist* 29:587–96

31. Evans-Pritchard EE. 1940. *The Nuer, A Description of the Modes of Livelihood and Political Institutions of a Nilotic People.* Oxford: Clarendon

32. Fischer DH. 1977. *Growing Old in America.* New York: Oxford Univ. Press

33. Foner A. 1974. Age stratification and age conflict in political life. *Am. Soc. Rev.* 39:187–96

34. Foner N. 1984. *Ages in Conflict: A Cross-Culural Perspective on Inequality Between Old and Young.* New York: Columbia Univ. Press

35. Fortes M. 1949. Time and social structure: an Ashanti case study. See Ref. 37, pp. 1–32

36. Fortes M. 1955. Radcliffe-Brown's contributions to the study of social organization. See Ref. 37, pp. 260–78

37. Fortes, M. 1970. *Time and Social Structure and Other Essays.* London: Athlone

38. Fortes M. 1984. Age, generation, and social structure. See Ref. 57, pp. 99–122

39. Frazer JG. 1935. *The Golden Bough: A Study in Magic and Religion.* London: Macmillan. 3rd ed.

40. Frisch CF, Setzer RG. 1982. *Bibliography/ Filmography: Ethnicity and Aging.* Salt Lake City: Univ. Utah Gerontol. Prog.

41. Fry CL. 1980. Toward an anthropology of aging. In *Aging in Culture and Society*, ed. CL Fry, pp. 1–20. South Hadley, MA: Bergin & Garvey

42. Fry CL, ed. 1981. *Dimensions: Aging, Culture, and Health.* New York: Bergin

43. Goody J. 1962. The fission of domestic

groups among the Lodagaba. In *The Developmental Cycle in Domestic Groups,* ed. J Goody, pp. 53–91. Cambridge: Cambridge Univ. Press

44. Gubrium JE. 1975. *Living and Dying at Murray Manor.* New York: St. Martin's

45. Haraway DJ. 1991. *Simians, Cyborgs, and Women: The Reinvention of Nature.* New York: Routledge

46. Hochschild AR. 1973. *The Unexpected Community: Portrait of an Old Age Subculture.* Englewood Cliffs, NJ: Prentice-Hall

47. Holmes L. 1976. From Simmons to the seventies: trends in anthropological gerontology. *Int. J. Aging Hum. Dev.* 7:211–20

48. Johnson SK. 1971. *Idle Haven: Community Building Among the Working-class Retired.* Berkeley: Univ. Calif. Press

49. Kaminsky M. 1992. Introduction. See Ref. 78, pp. 1–97

50. Katz S. 1992. Alarmist demography: power, knowledge, and the elderly population. *Int. J. Aging Stud.* 6:203–25

51. Kaufman SR. 1986. *The Ageless Self: Sources of Meaning in Late Life.* Madison: Univ. Wisc. Press

52. Kayser-Jones JS. 1981. *Old, Alone, and Neglected: Care of the Aged in the United States and Scotland.* Berkeley: Univ. Calif. Press

53. Keith J. 1980. "The best is yet to be": toward an anthropology of age. *Annu. Rev. Anthropol.* 9:339–64

54. Keith J. 1992. *An anthropological perspective on method and substance of gerontology in the 21st century.* Presented at Annu. Meet. Gerontol. Soc. Am., Washington, DC

55. Keith J, Kertzer DI. 1984. Introduction. See Ref. 57, pp. 19–61

56. Kertzer D. 1978. Theoretical developments in the study of age-group systems. *Am. Ethnol.* 5:368–74

57. Kertzer D, Keith J, eds. 1984. *Age & Anthropological Theory.* Ithaca, NY: Cornell Univ. Press

58. Kertzer D, Keith J. 1984. Preface. See Ref. 57, pp. 13–15

59. Kugelmass J. 1986. *The Miracle of Intervale Avenue: The Story of a Jewish Congregation in the South Bronx.* New York: Schocken

60. Laird C. 1979. *Limbo.* Novato, CA: Chandler & Sharp

61. Lamb S. 1993. *Growing in the net of Maya: persons, gender and life processes in a Bengali society.* PhD thesis. Univ. Chicago. 440 pp.

62. Laslett P. 1985. Societal development and aging. In *Handbook of Aging and the Social Sciences,* ed. RH Binstock, E Shanas, pp. 199–230. New York: Van Nostrand Reinhold. 2nd ed.

63. Legesse A. 1973. *Gada—Three Approaches to the Study of African Society.* New York: Free Press

64. Lock M. 1993. Ideology, female midlife, and the greying of Japan. *J. Jpn. Stud.* 19(1):43–78

65. Lock M. 1993. *Encounters with Aging: Mythologies of Menopause in Japan and North America.* Berkeley: Univ. Calif. Press

66. Lowie R. 1920. *Primitive Society.* New York: Liveright & Boni

67. Lowie R. 1930. Age societies. In *The Encyclopedia of the Social Sciences,* ed. ERA Seligman, 1:482–83. New York: Macmillan

68. Luborsky MR, Sankar A. 1993. Expanding the critical gerontology perspective: cultural dimensions—introduction. *Gerontologist* 33:440–44

69. Mandelbaum D. 1970. *Society in India.* Berkeley: Univ. Calif. Press

70. Marcus GE, Fischer MMJ. 1986. *Anthropology as Cultural Critique: An Experimental Moment in the Human Sciences.* Chicago: Univ. Chicago Press

71. Maybury-Lewis D. 1967. *Akwe-Shavante Society.* Oxford: Clarendon

72. Maybury-Lewis D. 1984. Age and kinship: a structural view. See Ref. 57, pp. 123–40

73. Meillassoux C. 1975. *Maidens, Meal, and Money: Capitalism and the Domestic Community.* Transl. Cambridge Univ. Press, 1981. Cambridge: Cambridge Univ. Press (From French)

74. Minois G. 1987. *History of Old Age: From Antiquity to the Renaissance.* Transl. SH Tenison, 1989. Chicago: Univ. Chicago Press (From French)

75. Moody HR. 1988. Toward a critical gerontology. In *Emergent Theories of Aging,* ed. JE Birren, VL Bengston, pp. 19–40. New York: Springer

76. Moore SF. 1978. Old age in a life-term social arena: some Chagga of Kilimanjaro in 1974. See Ref. 80, pp. 23–76

77. Myerhoff B. 1978. *Number Our Days.* New York: Simon & Schuster

78. Myerhoff B. 1992. *Remembered Lives: The Work of Ritual, Storytelling, and Growing Older,* ed. M Kaminsky. Ann Arbor: Univ. Mich. Press

79. Myerhoff B. 1970. Aging and the aged in other cultures: an anthropological perspective. See Ref. 78, pp. 101–26

80. Myerhoff BG, Simic A, eds. 1978. *Life's Career—Aging: Cultural Variations on Growing Old.* Beverly Hills, CA: Sage

81. Nascher IL. 1914. *Geriatrics: The Diseases of the Old Age and Their Treatment.* Philadelphia: Blakiston's

82. Nydegger CN. 1981. Gerontology and anthropology: challenge and opportunity. See Ref. 42, pp. 293–302

83. Nydegger CN. 1983. Family ties of the

aged in cross-cultural perspective. *Gerontologist* 23:26–32

84. Nydegger CN. 1983. Introduction. *Res. Aging* 5(4):451–53

85. Ostör A. 1984. Chronology, category, and ritual. See Ref. 57, pp. 281–304

86. Plath DW. 1980. *Long Engagements: Maturity in Modern Japan.* Stanford, CA: Stanford Univ. Press

87. Pradhan R. 1989. *Family, inheritance and the care of the aged: contractual relations and the axiom of kinship amity.* Presented at Symp. Soc. Aging Comp. Perspect., New Delhi

88. Quadagno J. 1982. *Aging in Early Industrial Society: Work, Family, and Social Policy in Nineteenth-Century England.* New York: Academic

89. Radcliffe-Brown AR. 1929. Age-organisation—terminology. *Man* 29:21

90. Radcliffe-Brown AR. 1940. On joking relationships. *Africa* 13:195–210

91. Radcliffe-Brown AR. 1949. A further note on joking relationships. *Africa* 19:133–40

92. Rey PP. 1971. *Colonialisme, Néo-Colonialisme et Transition au Capitalisme.* Paris: Maspero

93. Rey PP. 1975. L'esclavage lignager chez les Tsangui, Punu et les Kuni du Congo-Brazzaville. In *L'Esclavage en Afrique précoloniale,* ed. C Meillassoux, pp. 509–20. Paris: Maspero

94. Rey PP. 1979. Class contradiction in lineage societies. *Crit. Anthropol.* 4:41–60

95. Riley MW. 1971. Social gerontology and the age stratification of society. *Gerontologist* 11:79–87

96. Schurtz H. 1902. *Alterklasses und Männerbünde.* Berlin: Reimer

97. Schweitzer MM. 1991. *Anthropology of Aging: A Partially Annotated Bibliography.* New York: Greenwood Press

98. Shield RR. 1988. *Uneasy Endings: Daily Life in an American Nursing Home.* Ithaca, NY: Cornell Univ. Press

99. Simic A. 1978. Introduction: aging and the aged in cultural perspective. See Ref. 80, pp. 9–22

100. Simmons L. 1945. *The Role of the Aged in Primitive Society.* New Haven, CT: Yale Univ. Press

101. Smith WR. 1885. *Kinship and Marriage in Early Arabia.* Cambridge: Cambridge Univ. Press

102. Sokolovsky J. 1990. Introduction. In *The Cultural Context of Aging: Worldwide Perspectives,* ed. J Sokolovsky, pp. 1–11. New York: Bergin & Garvey

103. Sokolovsky J. 1993. Images of aging: a cross-cultural perspective. *In Generations* 17(2):51–54

104. Sokolovsky J, Cohen CI. 1978. The cultural meaning of personal networks for the inner-city elderly. *Urban Anthropol.* 7:323–43

105. Sokolovsky J, Cohen CI. 1981. Being old in the inner city: support systems of the SRO aged. See Ref. 42, pp. 163–84

106. Spencer P. 1965. *The Samburu: A Study of Gerontocracy in a Nomadic Tribe.* Berkeley: Univ. Calif. Press

107. Stewart FH. 1977. *Fundamentals of Age-Group Systems.* New York: Academic

108. Strathern M. 1981. Culture in a netbag: the manufacture of a subdiscipline in anthropology. *Man* 16:665–88

109. Thewlis MW. 1941. *The Care of the Aged (Geriatrics).* St. Louis: Mosby. 3rd ed.

110. United States Department of State. 1982. *U.S. National Report on Aging for the United Nations World Assembly on Aging.* Washington, DC: US Dept. State

111. Vesperi MD. 1985. *City of Green Benches: Growing Old in a New Downtown.* Ithaca, NY: Cornell Univ. Press

112. Webster H. 1908. *Primitive Secret Societies: A Study in Early Politics and Religion.* New York: Macmillan

113. Wilson M. 1951. *Good Company: A Study of Nyakyusa Age-Villages.* London: Oxford Univ. Press

Annu. Rev. Anthropol. 1994. 23:159–80

THE ARCHAEOLOGY OF EMPIRES

Carla M. Sinopoli

Museum of Anthropology, University of Michigan, Ann Arbor, Michigan 48109

KEY WORDS: complex societies, political economy, ideology

INTRODUCTION

Rome, Babylon, Mughal, Aztec, Inka...the names of these early empires evoke potent images of monumental ambition, grandeur, and decay. Empires are geographically and politically expansive polities, composed of a diversity of localized communities and ethnic groups, each contributing its unique history and social, economic, religious, and political traditions. This scale and variability pose considerable challenges to scholars who seek to study early empires. Attempts at comprehensive understandings benefit from and may be made more complex by the diversity of sources, including internal historic accounts and inscriptions, external accounts by conquerors or observers, and material remains, from monumental architecture to utilitarian artifacts. In this review, I focus primarily on recent studies of the material remains of empire, while also addressing works based on written records that have dominated our understandings of early empires (e.g. 60, 61, 86, 120, 125, 150, 152, 160, 184, 185, 221). I limit myself to what Schreiber (180) has called the "more archaic forms of empires," and do not discuss imperialism in the emergence of the modern world system (204, 205, 212).

I approach the archaeology of empire by drawing on sources from the New and Old World spanning from the third millennium B.C. to the eighteenth century A.D. Even in cases where archaeological research is limited (193), the relevant literature is vast and this review is necessarily selective. I examine those early empires whose status as empires is not in dispute (e.g. 220); thus, for the New World I focus primarily on the Aztec and Inka, with limited attention to earlier imperial polities (e.g. Chimu, Wari), while for the Old World, I draw on literature from the Middle East, South and Central Asia, Rome, and China. My emphasis is less on the historic sequences or artistic products of specific empires than on the development of comparative frameworks that allow for the recognition of similarities and differences in processes of imperial development.

FRAMEWORKS FOR THE STUDY OF ARCHAIC EMPIRES

Definitions and Classifications

Numerous definitions of empire can be found in the anthropological and historic literature (3, 51, 57, 64, 70, 71, 73, 77, 90, 96, 119, 127, 180, 199, 206). These definitions vary in emphasis, with geographic (199), economic (3, 57, 73, 214), political (64, 70), ideological (50, 51, 71, 83), or military (94–96, 126) dimensions of empire differentially stressed. They share in common a view of empire as a territorially expansive and incorporative kind of state, involving relationships in which one state exercises control over other sociopolitical entities (e.g. states, chiefdoms, non-stratified societies), and of imperialism as the process of creating and maintaining empires. The diverse polities and communities that constitute an empire typically retain some degree of autonomy—in self- and centrally-defined cultural identity (77), and in some dimensions of political and economic decision making. Most authors also share a conception of various kinds of empires distinguished by differing degrees of political and/or economic control, viewed either as discrete types or as variations along a continuum from weakly integrated to more highly centralized polities (see Table 1).

Each classification of empires shares a concern with the nature and intensity of control that imperial centers exert over imperial territories, and each acknowledges considerable variation both within and between empires. Internal variation has been attributed to a variety of factors, including 1. distance from the imperial center and logistical concerns (94–96, 126, 213), 2. preexisting political conditions in incorporated areas (100, 159, 178) and the nature

Table 1 Frameworks for Imperial Organization

Major author	Weakly integrated	Highly integrated	References
Eisenstadt	patrimonial	imperial-bureaucratic	70, 71, see also 22
Luttwak	hegemonic	territorial	126, see also 56, 57, 94–96
Mann	empire of domination	territorial	127, see also 90

and extent of resistance to imperial incorporation (95, 104), and 3. ecological factors and the distribution of important resources 68, 96). There is also an implicit temporal sequence embodied in these classifications, with weaker forms of organization preceding and potentially (though not inevitably) developing into more centralized imperial structures.

World Systems Perspectives

The extension of Wallerstein's world systems perspective (204) to pre-capitalist political and economic systems, including archaic empires, has been the focus of a number of historians and sociocultural anthropologists (1, 2, 13, 48, 73, 79–82, 89), and archaeologists (9–11, 24, 25, 46, 49, 69, 100, 112–114, 172, 173, 176, 177, 213). Although Wallerstein's original research was limited to the study of the development of the modern world economy, he has recently stressed the need for study of non- or pre-capitalist world systems (e.g. Abu-Lughod's work on the thirteenth century; 1, 2) as a major goal for the future of world systems research (205).

Applications of the world systems perspective to pre-modern periods have generated a wide range of approaches to the definition, scale, and structural interpretations of world systems (summarized in 48). These can be broadly grouped into two main perspectives. The first acknowledges qualitative discontinuities between the ancient and modern worlds but seeks to redefine or broaden the concept of world system to accommodate pre-capitalist systems (9, 10, 24, 25, 69, 213). Thus, Chase-Dunn & Hall have defined the world system as "intersocietal networks in which interaction…is an important condition of the reproduction of the internal structures of the composite units" (49:7). Such interaction may be political, military, or economic, and need not involve relations of inequality or exploitation between core and peripheries. Kohl has emphasized the existence of inequalities between more and less developed areas in third millennium B.C. West Asia but has stressed that the control exerted by more developed areas is limited by easily transferable technologies and by the ability of peripheral areas to interact with multiple cores, to their advantage (113, 114).

A second group of scholars has maintained Wallerstein's emphasis on capital accumulation, while critiquing the primitivist/substantivist distinction between pre-capitalist and capitalist societies (11, 73, 80, 81, 89, 113). Ekholm & Friedman have defined empires as political mechanisms that enable a center to accumulate capital from production in peripheral areas (73). For these scholars, capital need not be restricted to bulk goods, but may include a range of culturally defined forms of wealth (175).

Stages of Empire: Expansion, Consolidation, and Collapse

Ancient empires have varied considerably in duration (199). The Timurid empire of Central Asia (128) and the Ch'in empire of China (26) did not outlast the reign of their first ruler; the Inka (134, 140, 169), Aztec (19, 42, 61), and Mongol (12, 133, 194) empires endured less than a century; and the Akkadian (125, 209) and Neo-Assyrian (157, 159) empires of the Middle East (119), and the Mauryan (201, 202), Gupta (181), Mughal (22, 93, 168), and Vijayanagara (84, 145, 196) empires of South Asia ruled effectively for approximately two centuries. Others, including the Romans (16, 65, 86) and some of the dynasties of imperial China (74, 197, 218) spanned many centuries, though with considerable temporal variations in imperial extent and authority.

Even the shortest lived of these empires demonstrated dramatic success in the first stage of the creation of empire—territorial expansion. However, for empires to endure, expansion must be accompanied by processes of consolidation (70, 157, 178, 179, 182), through which conquered territories are incorporated into the empire's political, economic, and ideological domain.

EXPANSION   Territorial expansion, through conquest and incorporation, is the defining process in the creation of the geographic and demographic space of empire. The process of imperial expansion often begins opportunistically in a period of regional fragmentation or weakness, following the collapse of earlier centralized political systems, creating a vacant potential (96:166) for expansion (34, 39, 41, 44, 50, 70, 71, 138, 141).

The motives for imperial expansion are much more difficult to identify than is the end result, and participants in expansion undoubtedly have diverse motives (77). Expressed motivations may often result from post facto justification and legitimation processes. Doyle (64) has defined three loci of expansionist motivation—metrocentric, pericentric, and systemic—with expansion seen, respectively, as responses to conditions at a center, periphery, or in power differentials between the two. Motives include security concerns such as protection from perceived threats on the outskirts of a polity (87, 96); economic goals of security or acquisition of valued resources (68, 73, 102, 103, 168); ideological factors (50, 51, 122), or a result of the "natural consequences of power differences between polities" (96:3; 119). Most scholars acknowledge complex interrelations among varied goals.

The ability of an imperial center to lay claim to other territories and polities rests ultimately in military power (78, 95, 96, 126, 127; for a different perspective, see 9, 10). Military conquest is a costly route to imperial expansion, involving loss of lives and expenditures of resources and potentially resulting in massive disruption of subsistence and other production activities in defeated territories. Diplomatic activity, accompanied by a covert or overt threat of force, is a preferred path to territorial expansion in many contexts. An exception might occur in the case of an especially powerful or well-organized enemy, where destruction or disruption of local rulers is deemed necessary by empire builders to undermine any future threats they might pose (180).

The sequence of imperial expansion is affected by local political conditions and the distribution of resources and need not proceed in a straight line or continuous pattern (45, 95, 180). Empire builders may bypass areas of little strategic or economic value to focus on more distant areas with key resources or political significance. Further, conquest is rarely a single event; resistance, rebellions, and cycles of reconquest are common (94, 105, 141, 208).

Constraints on imperial expansion include distance-dependent logistical factors and communication costs, as well as ecological and political factors (96). However, logical constraints may not necessarily be heeded. The engine of imperial expansion, once started, may be difficult to turn off (96:179; 51) especially as systems of economic and social rewards and privileges become associated with expansion and with military success (142). Overexpansion may ultimately contribute to political collapse or reorganization (see below).

Imperial rulers   Perhaps more than any other ancient political formation, the history of imperial growth is closely associated with individual rulers, for example, Sargon (209), Chin Shih-huang (26), Asoka (201), Augustus (164, 183), Timur (128), Ghengis Khan (12, 167), Pachakuti (140), and Akbar (168). These founders or consolidators of empire were dynamic and brilliant leaders, who typically combined military skills with administrative abilities. The charisma of great leaders in empire formation is not incidental; the creation of personal loyalties and alliances between emperors and newly conquered elites may ameliorate costs of military domination, and the awesome or sacred name and reputation of the emperor may encourage conciliation and submission without the need for military activity or a permanent military presence.

CONSOLIDATION   For an empire to endure beyond the reigns of individual rulers, individual personal relations between rulers and the ruled must be transcended to create an imperial system of structural connections and dependencies among diverse regions and cultural traditions. This process involves a range of constructive and destructive strategies (EM Brumfiel, unpublished manuscript), including the creation of new institutions, administrative structures, and ideological systems, and the disruption of previously autonomous local institutions, as imperial elite seek to strengthen political and ideological allegiances to the center and regulate the flow of resources to imperial coffers (198). In different empires these ties can be effected in different ways, yielding considerable variation in the extent of imperial centralization, as well as varied organization within individual empires. Following Mann (127), I attempt to disassociate different dimensions of organization and imperial control, while at the same time acknowledging their interconnectedness (see also 78).

Politics and administration   Variation exists in the extent to which elites in conquered areas are incorporated into the imperial framework or displaced by imperial functionaries. The cooption of local elites may be a preferred strategy in the early stages of empire formation and in the less centralized empires described above, because existing organizational and revenue collecting structures can be exploited with relatively little central intervention. As long as obligations of tribute and loyalty are fulfilled, imperial administrators or military may not overtly intervene in many aspects of local affairs.

The extent to which local political relations are incorporated or disrupted is an outcome of several factors, including pre-existing political structures, the territory's strategic value and its resources, and resistance to imperial incorporation. For example, among the Aztecs, the status of local nobility and intensity of tribute demands were in large part determined by the degree of resistance to imperial authority; in those territories where surrender to Aztec rule preceded military intervention, tribute demands were much lighter and elites were less likely to be deposed than in areas where warfare had occurred (19, 42, 101, 104).

Connections between local elites and the imperial family may be solidified through the creation of kin relations; through royal marriages, adoptions, or fosterage, and required attendance at royal rituals and ceremonies (43, 170); as well as by the bestowal of elite goods and material symbols of empire, and other material and symbolic benefits that accrue to loyal retainers and followers (33, 182). Although ties between local elites and the center are encouraged, ties among local elites may be discouraged to limit potentials for alliance formation and organized resistance to imperial rule (57, 104).

The size and complexity of imperial bureaucracies and administrative institutions vary considerably, from the massive Chinese (108), Ur III, Old Babylonian, Assyrian, and Byzantine imperial bureaucracies (88, 160), to the much more limited bureaucracies of the Roman (86), Aztec (94, 101, 190), Inka (111, 140), and Vijayanagara (138, 188, 196) empires. Variations also exist in the extent to which administrative institutions are differentiated (70) and the degree to which they are autonomous of the imperial household (23).

Temporal changes in administrative strategies must also be considered and the direction of such changes (toward more or less control) may vary. Several scholars have suggested that just before Spanish conquest, the Inka were engaged in a series of reforms that would have led to increased centralized control of provincial territories and populations (57, 141). However, the opposite pattern seems to have occurred in the Neo-Assyrian empire, where central-ized administrative control may have become less direct over time (156, 157).

Economy   The acquisition of regularized revenues through tribute or taxes is both a major goal and a significant outcome of imperial expansion and consoli-dation. Rulers may engage directly and/or indirectly in production activities and in the collection of taxes and tributes. Indirect routes of revenue collection involve multiple levels of regional and community leaders, local elites, or organizations of producers (e.g. guilds), or may employ tax farmers who are awarded rights to collect and transfer resources from local regions to imperial centers or outposts (17, 157, 188). Such indirect routes allow for revenue collection in the absence of a developed bureaucracy, but also permit local elites to amass and, potentially, retain significant revenues beyond what is transported to the imperial center, creating the potential for independent bases of power and authority. The existence of multiple levels of extraction can also exacerbate economic stresses on tax-paying populations, and revolts are common, as are mass migrations of artisans and agriculturalists (105, 141, 152, 196).

The control of labor may contrast or complement the control of materials. Labor may be recruited for monumental constructions, the fulfillment of mili-tary obligations, or various productive tasks. The coordination of labor obliga-tions can be left in the hands of local elites, provincial administrators, or central institutions (e.g. the centralized Inka decimal hierarchy, 111). A dra-matic expression of the control of labor is seen in the practice of forced resettlement, documented from the Inka empire (118, 140, 171, 203) and also known from many other archaic empires, for example, Roman (7, 8), Aztec (45), Sassanian (208), Assyrian (144, 158), and Vijayanagara (196). Such resettlement probably serves a variety of purposes, shifting occupational com-munities to areas where resources are abundant and/or direct regulation of production activities is possible, and removing individuals and communities from their traditional territories and sources of authority to minimize the potential for resistance.

The nature and intensity of imperial involvement in production and acquisi-tion varies with administrative structure, distance to accumulation points (the imperial capital or other centers), the distribution of centralized institutions (centers, garrisons, or outposts), and the economic and symbolic significance of specific products. We should expect therefore the simultaneous existence of multiple levels of economic organization and control, varying with products, location, cultural meanings, and environmental conditions. The Aztec empire exhibited a well developed market system alongside elaborate tribute require-ments, international trade by private and state merchants, and local exchange relations among producers (20, 21, 94). D'Altroy & Earle (59, 66) have distinguished between empires that focus predominantly on the production and control of staples (staple finance) and those that emphasize the production and control of high status or valued goods (prestige finance), and they have suggested we should expect distinct organizational features and institutions in each of these contexts.

Transport conditions also affect the movement of goods. Vast quantities of foodstuffs, ceramics, and other goods were transported across the Roman empire and into the capital via maritime and riverine routes (85, 92, 107, 154, 163). The Inka capital in the rugged terrain of the central Andes received foodstuffs primarily from the Cuzco region, though precious metals and cloths were transported to the capital from much greater distances along the extensive Inka road system (109, 110).

The transformability of commodities, whether into currency or other categories of goods, also significantly affects patterns of revenue flow and transport of wealth. For example, the exchange of silver in the Neo-Assyrian empire (157) and the monetization of the Roman economy (92) allowed for some movement of wealth independent of the movement of bulk commodities (though this occurred as well). In the New World empires, we see marked differences in the transferability of commodities. Texts indicate that Aztec workers could exchange the products of their labor in markets for goods required to fulfill tribute obligations (20, 32, 36). In the Inka case there is little evidence for markets, and obligations were assessed as labor requirements (67, 140), although this may have been changing just prior to collapse (e.g. 141). Whether imperial involvement in production and acquisition of goods is indirect or direct, productive intensification is a common, though not inevitable (see 6), outcome of imperial incorporation. Along with increased revenue demands, intensification can result from improved conditions of transport, larger potential markets, and the needs of an expanding imperial elite (76). Productive intensification can lead to significant changes in the organization of labor and community structure (31, 37, 97). Near an imperial capital, intensification, especially in agriculture, may reflect security concerns and desires for a stable subsistence base (18, 136, 137), as well as the difficulties of transporting bulk goods (94). Intensification of craft production may contribute to increasing urbanization and the emergence of regional nodes of production and revenue collections (32, 33, 47, 195, 196).

Military   The ability to field large and effective military forces is essential to imperial success. These forces do not necessarily have significantly better technological resources than their opponents (95, 96, 113) but succeed on the basis of their numbers, organization, and ability to intimidate. For the empire, military success provides the basis for territories, revenues, and, often, slaves, employed as attached laborers or used as sacrifices. For the individual soldier, military success provides a route to social advancement; rewards of status, land, tribute, and other resources accrue to successful soldiers.

Military forces and strategies vary widely between empires and over time (141). In most cases, there is a core of professional fighting forces and an institutionalized military hierarchy. These forces are typically expanded as needed through recruitment from the population at large, including from recently conquered regions. Maintaining the allegiance of military leaders, whether local elites or centrally appointed officials, and of their troops is a high priority for imperial leaders, and requires substantial rewards for success (such as land grants, booty, and honors), as well as strict sanctions for disobedience. In Vijayanagara, mercenaries and landless populations constituted the heart of the military at the imperial capital, creating a community whose success lay primarily with the success of the imperial center; away from the core, military leaders who controlled substantial armies often posed a potent threat to imperial hegemony (138, 196).

Military confrontation is one extreme in a continuum of relations between dominant and subordinate polities. As noted above, coercive diplomacy (127), with the implied threat of force, is often the preferred alternative to conflict. The use of terror is also documented in a number of early empires, and includes the Roman destruction of Carthage and Corinth, which was later rebuilt as a Roman center (8), and the Inkan annihilation of the Cañari and Caranqui (151). Even in the absence of modern communication channels, word of such large scale destruction no doubt spread rapidly, and may have limited resistance in other areas that were the focus of imperial expansion. The practice of large-scale human sacrifices by the Aztecs is another example of the use of terror in imperial control (95).

Ideology   Recent studies on the importance of ideology in archaic empires have had two main emphases: 1. the role of ideology in motivating action, in particular, imperial expansion (50, 51, 122), and 2. the role of ideology in providing legitimation for and explanations of extant and emergent inequalities, especially in relations between superordinate and subject populations (5, 116, 117, 130, 161, 162). Both perspectives seek to situate ideology within a broader political and economic context, and both are concerned with what ideology does, beyond identifying specific beliefs (63). Research on imperial ideologies has tended to take a top-down approach, with an emphasis on centralized imposition of beliefs and practices, although more attention is now being paid to bottom-up ideological practices that result from local and potentially divergent responses to central institutions and current events (5, 39, 161).

Significant commonalities can be seen in top-down practices of early empires. Imperial leaders customarily seek to seize control of sources of legitimacy, through the cooption of local religious beliefs and/or the creation of new systems of belief that build on traditional elements. The appropriation of local beliefs and local deities is common. Davis (62) has viewed appropriations of sacred images as highly consequential political acts that express and establish relations of dominance and authority (see also 7, 19, 91, 104, 116, 139, 152). Such images often are transported to the imperial capital (e.g. the temple for the defeated gods at Tenochtitlán, 42). Appropriated images do not lose their sacred import but instead gain a new level of meaning associated with changing political realities (62).

The imposition or development of new imperial beliefs, gods, and practices among imperial populations in central and incorporated regions is also seen. This may involve the creation of new sets of beliefs that reposition the role of the emperor and/or empire within existent frameworks for understanding the world (50, 51, 116, 122, 123, 162, 168). Ideological, historical, and material (e.g. architectural or iconographic) connections may be drawn to earlier empires and emperors (52, 124). In other contexts, existing beliefs may be supplemented or reconfigured. In a controversial argument, Conrad & Demarest have stressed the conscious reconfiguration of traditional beliefs by Aztec and Inka elites into a set of beliefs that motivated, and demanded, continued imperial expansion (51; but see 95 for an emphasis on political and economic motivations for expansion). Ideological changes may also occur as subordinated peoples try to make sense of their new position in the world. Price (161) has examined the development of the Roman imperial cult in Asia Minor as the outcome of local elites' attempts to place the Roman emperor and their relations to him within a sacred framework.

COLLAPSE   As noted above, the duration of empires varies considerably. In many, if not all, areas where archaic empires emerged, specific imperial formations formed part of a cyclical pattern of political expansion and fragmentation (96). Fragmentation, or collapse, entails the dissolution of the centralized institutions that created and defined relations of control and dependency between political centers and subjugated territories (215). Tainter (200) has taken an economic perspective, arguing that imperial collapse is an outcome of inevitable declining marginal returns, as the immediate rewards of conquest are offset by the long-term costs of administering and regulating incorporated territories. When geographic expansion ends, the costs of maintaining empires soon exceed their material benefits. This may lead to a range of outcomes, including sacrifice of some territories in order to maintain a strongly ruled central core, emergence of new forms of organization, or political collapse. Contributors to a volume edited by Yoffee & Cowgill (217) examine collapse from a variety of perspectives and regions. Most focus on political collapse, instead of smaller scale dynastic transitions or larger scale civilizational collapse (4, 55). Both internal and external factors are considered. External factors include the impact of foreign intruders (30, 160), other states and empires, environmental changes (207), and collapse of long distance trade networks and mercantile systems (216). Internal factors include overcentralization (108, 216), communication problems (55), failure to integrate elites or establish legitimacy over diverse territories and long distances (4), and regional, ethnic, and factional dynamics and conflicts (38).

The web of complex relations between imperial centers and conquered territories is a delicate one (72). As the contributors to Yoffee & Cowgill emphasize, although individual political systems may last only a short time, this does not imply a total civilizational collapse. Institutions, social relations, and ways of perceiving the world may long outlast polities, and studies of collapse need to examine what persists in localized patterns, as well as to establish what has ended (72). Further, the idea of empire or impulse of expansion (44:147) seems to outlast specific polities or dynasties, and later empires often build on the cultural traditions and strategies and infrastructure of rule of earlier polities (96, 125, 139).

THE MATERIAL CONSEQUENCES OF EMPIRE

Empires are often characterized by dramatic material remains—large scale architecture, road systems, urban centers, temples, and elaborate prestige goods. But the absence of this set of imperial indicators does not demonstrate that specific areas were outside of an empire. Variations in the nature of imperial integration can be expected to lead to variations in its material indicators (193). Much recent archaeological research on archaic empires has focused on documenting economic and political transformations that occurred in formerly autonomous regions after their conquest or incorporation into imperial polities. Research on imperial centers or capitals has also been conducted (27, 28, 84, 149), although in many contexts it has been limited by post-imperial destruction and/or modern construction.

Imperial Geography

CORE AND PERIPHERY   An ideal graphic model of an empire might consist of multiple concentric rings depicting decreasing imperial authority with increasing distance from the imperial center (213), but the reality is often far more complex and inconstant. Territories are not necessarily continuous. Some regions may be bypassed while more distant, strategically and economically important areas are incorporated (45, 180). Core areas expand and contract and may be defined differently depending on variables considered (e.g. economic, political, or ideological). A weakly ruled periphery may contain dispersed areas with intense imperial presence in the form of garrisons or fortresses. A more realistic geographic model of specific empires would allow for a complex and changing mosaic of political, economic, and ideological interconnections.

IMPERIAL CAPITALS

> Who could conquer Tenochtitlan
> Who could shake the foundation of heaven
> (from an Aztec poem, 44:130)

> If there is paradise on earth
> It is here, it is here, it is here
> [inscription Shahjanabad (Delhi), Mughal capital, 15:197]

The imperial capital is typically the demographically, spatially, and symbolically highest order site in empire-wide settlement patterns (166). Like other capitals, imperial capitals are centers of administration, ritual, and economic activities. As royal residences and sacred centers, imperial capitals are characterized by monumental architecture and massive labor investment in the construction of defensive features, elite residences, administrative facilities, and sacred structures. Evidence for agricultural intensification may also be found in and around imperial capitals, to ensure stable food supplies during periods of conflict and to minimize transport costs (110, 115, 136, 137, 147). The extent to which a capital had a pre-imperial history and the potential for and range of elite participation in construction activities (e.g. Augustan Rome; 219) provide important sources of variation in the form and content of imperial centers.

As symbolic centers of empire, imperial capitals are characterized by a formal organization of space, often around a sacred place (28, 29, 44, 83, 84, 110, 129, 170). The construction of new capitals (189, 216) or additions to existing capitals (115, 219) can be an important political and ideological act differentiating a ruler from his predecessors and redefining the sacred center. New constructions may remove recalcitrant elites from traditional sources of power. Representations of the diverse territories claimed by imperial rulers are found within imperial capitals, including appropriated sacred objects and other goods associated with defeated peoples and polities, syncretic architectural styles (131, 139), and residences for elites of subject populations, who are often obliged to spend at least part of the year in the capital (42, 101, 110, 170). Imperial capitals are characterized by high artifact diversity, especially in elite goods, which reach the capital through tribute or trade from throughout the empire (33). These cities are also characterized by high ethnic and social diversity (40), as populations are drawn in through force or attracted to the capital's wealth and opportunities from regions within and beyond imperial boundaries.

REGIONAL SETTLEMENT   The impact of imperial incorporation on regional settlement varies with the nature of imperial control in specific parts of an empire (180). Where control is direct, significant impact is expected and regional centers may be constructed in formal imperial styles or with important imperial features (135, 155). In areas of weaker or indirect imperial control, impact on settlement distribution and content may be much less, although emulation of imperial styles and current material symbolism of political authority may occur (193). Features that facilitate movement such as roads, bridges, way-stations, and storehouses (92, 94, 109, 174) may be more widespread than formal imperial settlements or urban centers. Although the initial construction of transport features is often associated with military activities, such facilities may also enhance the movement of goods and people across imperial territories.

Shifts in regional settlement patterns may also occur. In many areas of the Andes we see population shifts from upland to lowland locations following Inka conquest. This has been seen as an outcome of deliberate Inka policy that removed populations from potentially defensible locations and into lowland maize-growing areas (97). This kind of movement may also be a response to declining levels of local conflict that permit settlement in more optimal environmental locales or along trade routes, for example. The forced resettlement of populations can lead to the creation of new kinds of sites, or the presence of distinct ethnic styles outside of their traditional territories. Land grants to imperial administrators, military elites, and successful, non-elite soldiers are a common imperial practice that can have significant impact on local settlement patterns and access to land and resources (6, 8). The distribution and form of sacred sites may also be affected dramatically by imperial incorporation (7, 8, 110). Imperial investment in new or existing temples and other religious facilities is often an important dimension of imperial legitimation (7, 8, 171, 187, 188). Other sites may fall out of use after removal of important images or the loss of their sacred power to changing political and ideological circumstances. Still other sacred sites may be foci for local activities or worship or for challenges to imperial rule.

Imperial Economy

Incorporation into an imperial system often has significant impact on local economies, as a result of top-down processes (i.e. tribute and labor demands) and bottom-up processes (i.e. local and individual responses to incorporation into larger political, economic, and prestige networks). The differentiation of these processes is difficult and requires the extremely fine resolution of participants, political boundaries, and the flow of goods. The much studied process of Romanization provides evidence for impositions of and local responses to the Roman imperial presence (132, 165).

Archaeological studies of production in imperial societies have ranged from the small-scale household level to larger scale studies of urban and regional economies. Some recent studies have focused on the impact of empire on patterns of production, the organization of labor, and community organization and differentiation at the local level. The Upper Mantaro Archaeological Project in highland Peru (53, 54, 57, 67, 68, 97–99) has examined changes in production and access to a range of subsistence and non-subsistence goods in elite and commoner households of the Wanka II (pre-Inka) and Wanka III (Inka) periods. Evans (75, 76) has examined community structure and relations in the Aztec period settlement of Cihuatecpan, and Brumfiel (31, 32, 35–37) has focused on the organization of labor and the impact of empire in a series of studies of pre-imperial and imperial Aztec materials from surface collections at the sites Xico, Huexotla, and Xaltocan in the Valley of Mexico (see also 190, 192, 193).

The organization of specialized production in rural and urban contexts has also been examined (33, 66). Studies on ceramics and other craft goods have focused on standardization, production scale and organization, and the identification of imperial styles and prestige goods (32, 33, 53, 54, 58, 66, 153, 154, 186, 210, 211). Agricultural sites such as raised field beds, canals, terraced fields, and reservoirs are common features in imperial landscapes, around the central and provincial capitals, imperial outposts, and in areas of high fertility or along major routes of transport (14, 41, 136, 137, 146–148). Storage features also provide important evidence of large-scale accumulation of goods (121, 135). Production demands and the movement of agricultural and other resources are linked to transport conditions and technologies.

The movement and structure of distribution mechanisms for raw materials and finished products is a research topic relevant to all ancient societies, and studies of imperial exchange and tribute relations are numerous. Patterns of tribute-flow (e.g. goods and obligations) to imperial centers vary with distance. Bulk goods typically are transported over shorter distances than are high-value low-bulk goods (21, 45, 59, 95, 97, 105, 138; but see 85). The coexistence of multiple mechanisms of material transfers (e.g. tribute, markets, and reciprocal trade relations) requires careful study of a range of material products, including their sources, quantities, and context of recovery (36, 47, 191). The exchange of high status goods among elites, as acknowledgments of subordination and acts of imperial beneficence, provides evidence for changing political relations (32, 66). With imperial expansion we might expect to see increased flows of elite goods of imperial status between local elites and imperial centers and declines in intraregional movement of regional status goods among local elites as their social connections and political prosperity are linked increasingly to the imperial center (97).

CHALLENGES OF THE ARCHAEOLOGY OF EMPIRE

The specific techniques of archaeology and approaches to analysis do not differ in the study of empires vs other kinds of early states, but the spatial scale, geographic and organizational variability, and the rapid rates of change in empires pose considerable challenges to archaeologists, whose focus of research is necessarily a small part of a large phenomenon.

Chronology

Empires are often characterized by extremely rapid growth and, in many cases, equally rapid dissolution. The major territorial expansion of the Inkas, for example, occurred over about 50 years under two dynamic rulers; imperial collapse followed soon thereafter, following the arrival of Pizarro in 1532. Few absolute dating techniques can yield the kind of chronological resolution necessary to document such rapid geopolitical changes. Specific elite goods or architectural styles may be affected dramatically by imperial developments, although imperial styles may be embedded in developments of broader regional styles and systems of material and political value. More common and archaeologically significant goods such as utilitarian ceramics and stone or metal tools may be relatively unaffected by large-scale political transformations, and patterns of technological and stylistic change cannot a priori be assumed to parallel or be directly related to political changes (6, 143, 180). For example, the broad ceramic chronology of the Aztec period (Early Aztec, 1150–1350, and Late Aztec, 1350–1520) only corresponds partly to the historical sequence of Aztec ascendancy (1428–1520; 106). The difficulty of chronological resolution creates a considerable challenge for documenting sequences of imperial growth and decline using material remains alone. In some contexts, this challenge can be partly met through the incorporation of inscriptions found on elite structures, mortuary goods, and other archaeological contexts as well as analyses of texts, but the association of written sources with material remains is often far from straightforward (190).

Sources of Data

In a recent discussion of Mesopotamia research, Adams (4) has lamented the traditional antipathy between scholars whose research focuses on texts and those who study material remains. For the majority of early empires, the methods of field archaeology examine only some of the potential sources of information, and anthropological archaeologists comprise a small portion of the scholarly community studying particular periods of regions. Productive studies from a variety of perspectives can only benefit from the judicious use of multiple lines of data. Anthropologists studying early empires must acquire the skills necessary to evaluate work from other academic traditions, and they must examine the range of sources of data relevant to their research questions. It is hoped that while drawing from other disciplines, we will contribute to them, through publishing in appropriate venues and, as much as possible, with non-exclusive terminologies.

Scale and Variability

Throughout this review, I have stressed issues of scale and variability in imperial histories and organization. I have discussed a general array of material signatures of empire, but I have also acknowledged that specific remains or kinds of remains will vary over space and time, and with the diverse ways in which particular regions were incorporated into particular empires. Individual archaeological or historic studies typically focus on only a small part of a much larger phenomenon. As such they contribute greatly to the understanding of empires, but the big picture requires syntheses of work in many areas by diverse scholars. The extent to which that can be accomplished depends on ongoing communication and cooperation in the development of archaeological classifications of materials, sites, and regional patterns, and in the development of comparable, or at least clearly stated, methodological and analytical approaches.

ACKNOWLEDGMENTS

Thanks to Rob Brubaker, Liz Brumfiel, Frank DeMita, Will Griffin, Sebastian Heath, Kate Keith, Dias Pradadimara, John Robb, and George Schwartz. Thanks also to Sue Alcock, Frances Hayashida, Joyce Marcus, Kathy Morrison, Gil Stein, Pati Wattenmaker, and Norman Yoffee for bibliographic recommendations and insightful comments.

Literature Cited

1. Abu-Lughod J. 1989. *Before European Hegemony: The World System A.D. 1250–1350*. New York: Oxford Univ. Press
2. Abu-Lughod J. 1990. Restructuring the premodern world-system. *Review* 13:273–86
3. Adams RMcC. 1979. Late prehispanic empires of the New World. See Ref. 120, pp. 59–74
4. Adams RMcC. 1988. Contexts of civilizational collapse: a Mesopotamian view. See Ref. 217, pp. 20–43

5. Adams RMcC. 1992. Ideologies: unity and diversity. See Ref. 63, pp. 205–22
6. Alcock S. 1989. Roman imperialism in the Greek landscape. *J. Roman Archaeol.* 2:5–34
7. Alcock S. 1993. Spaced-out sanctuaries: the ritual landscape of Roman Greece. In *Theoretical Roman Archaeology: First Conference Proceedings,* ed. E Scott, pp. 155–66. Avebury, UK: World Archaeol. Ser.
8. Alcock S. 1993. *Graecia Capta: The Land-*

scapes of Roman Greece. Cambridge: Cambridge Univ. Press

9. Algaze G. 1993. Expansionary dynamics of some early pristine states. *Am. Anthropol.* 95:304–33

10. Algaze G. 1993. *The Uruk World System.* Chicago: Univ. Chicago Press

11. Allen M. 1992. The mechanisms of underdevelopment: an ancient Mesopotamian example. *Review* 15:453–76

12. Allsen TT. 1987. *Mongol Imperialism.* Berkeley: Univ. Calif. Press

13. Amin S. 1991. The ancient world-systems versus the modern capitalist world-system. *Review* 14:349–85

14. Armillas P. 1971. Gardens in swamps. *Science* 174:653–61

15. Asher C. 1992. *Architecture of Mughal India.* Cambridge: Cambridge Univ. Press

16. Badian E. 1968. *Roman Imperialism.* Oxford: Blackwell

17. Badian E. 1972. *Publicans and Sinners: Private Enterprise in the Service of the Roman Republic.* Ithaca, NY: Cornell Univ. Press

18. Bauer BS. 1992. *The Development of the Inca State.* Austin: Univ. Texas Press

19. Berdan FF. 1982. *The Aztecs of Central Mexico: An Imperial Society.* New York: Holt, Rinehart, Winston

20. Berdan FF. 1986. Enterprise and empire in Aztec and early colonial Mexico. See Ref. 110a, pp. 281–302

21. Berdan FF. 1987. The economics of Aztec luxury trade and tribute. See Ref. 27, pp. 161–83

22. Blake SP. 1979. The patrimonial-bureaucratic empire of the Mughals. *J. Asian Stud.* 39:77–94

23. Blake SP. 1991. *Shahjahanabad: The Sovereign City in Mughal India.* Cambridge: Cambridge Univ. Press

24. Blanton RE, Feinman GM. 1984. The Mesoamerican world system: a comparative perspective. *Am. Anthropol.* 86:673–82

25. Blanton RE, Kowalewski SA, Feinman GM. 1992. The Mesoamerican world system. *Review* 15:419–26

26. Bodde D. 1967. *China's First Unifier.* Hong Kong: Hong Kong Univ. Press

27. Boone EH, ed. 1987. *The Aztec Templo Mayor.* Washington, DC: Dumbarton Oaks

28. Brand M, Lowry GD, eds. 1987. *Fatehpur Sikri.* Bombay: Marg

29. Broda J. 1987. Templo Mayor as ritual space. See Ref. 29a, pp. 61–123

29a. Broda J, Carrasco D, Matos Moctezuma E, eds. 1987. *The Great Temple at Tenochtitlán: Center and Periphery in the Aztec World.* Berkeley: Univ. Calif. Press

30. Bronson B. 1988. The role of barbarians in the fall of states. See Ref. 217, pp. 196–218

31. Brumfiel EM. 1986. The division of labor at Xico: the chipped stone industry. See Ref. 110a, pp. 245–80

32. Brumfiel EM. 1987. Consumption and politics at Aztec Huexotla. *Am. Anthropol.* 89:676–86

33. Brumfiel EM. 1987. Elite and utilitarian crafts in the Aztec state. In *Specialization, Exchange and Complex Societies,* ed. EM Brumfiel, TK Earle, pp. 102–18. Cambridge: Cambridge Univ. Press

34. Brumfiel EM. 1989. Factional competition in complex society. In *Domination and Resistance,* ed. D Miller, M Rowlands, C Tilley, pp. 127–39. London: Unwin Hyman

35. Brumfiel EM. 1991. Agricultural development and class stratification in the southern Valley of Mexico. See Ref. 93a, pp. 43–63

36. Brumfiel EM. 1991. Tribute and commerce in imperial cities: the case of Xaltocan, Mexico. In *Early State Economics,* ed. HJM Claessen, P van de Velde, pp. 177–98. New Brunswick, NJ: Transaction

37. Brumfiel EM. 1991. Weaving and cooking: women's production in Aztec Mexico. In *Engendering Archaeology: Women and Prehistory,* ed. JM Gero, MW Conkey, pp. 224–54. London: Blackwell

38. Brumfiel EM. 1992. Distinguished lecture in archaeology: breaking and entering the ecosystem—gender, class and faction steal the show. *Am. Anthropol.* 94:551–67

39. Brumfiel EM. 1994. Ethnic groups and political development in ancient Mexico. In *Factional Competition and Political Development in the New World,* ed. EM Brumfiel, JW Fox, pp. 89–102. Cambridge: Cambridge Univ. Press

40. Calnek EE. 1972. The internal structure of Tenochtitlán. In *The Valley of Mexico,* ed. ER Wolf, pp. 287–302. Albuquerque: Univ. N. Mex. Press

41. Calnek EE. 1972. Settlement patterns and chinampa agriculture at Tenochtitlán. *Am. Antiq.* 37:104–15

42. Calnek EE. 1982. Patterns of empire formation in the Valley of Mexico. Late Postclassic period, 1200–1521. See Ref. 49a, pp. 43–62

43. Carrasco P. 1984. Royal marriages in ancient Mexico. In *Explorations in Ethnohistory: Indians of Central Mexico in the Sixteenth Century,* ed. HR Harvey, H Prem, pp. 41–81. Albuquerque: Univ. N. Mex. Press

44. Carrasco P. 1987. Myth, cosmic terror and the Templo Mayor. See Ref. 29a, pp. 124–62

45. Carrasco P. 1991. The territorial structure of the Aztec empire. See Ref. 93a, pp. 93–112

46. Champion TC, ed. 1989. *Centre and Pe-*

riphery in the Ancient World. London: Unwin Hyman

47. Charlton CO, Charlton TH, Nichols DL. 1993. Aztec household-based craft production: archaeological evidence from the city-state of Otumba, Mexico. See Ref. 174a, pp. 147–72

48. Chase-Dunn C. 1992. The comparative study of world-systems. *Review* 15:313–33

49. Chase-Dunn C, Hall TD, eds. 1991. *Core-Periphery Relations in Precapitalist Worlds*. Boulder, CO: Westview

49a. Collier GA, Rosaldo RI, Wirth JD, eds. 1982. *The Inca and Aztec States 1400–1800*. New York: Academic

50. Conrad GW. 1992. Inca imperialism: the great simplification and the accident of empire. See Ref. 63, pp. 159–74

51. Conrad GW, Demarest AA. 1984. *Religion and Empire: The Dynamics of Aztec and Inca Expansionism*. Cambridge: Cambridge Univ. Press

52. Cooper JS. 1993. Paradigm and propaganda. The dynasty of Akkade in the 21st century. See Ref. 125, pp. 11–23

53. Costin CL. 1986. *From chiefdom to empire state: ceramic economy among the prehispanic Wanka of Highland Peru*. PhD thesis. Ann Arbor, MI: Univ. Microfilms

54. Costin CL, Earle TK, Owen B, Russell G. 1989. The impact of Inca conquest on local technology in the Upper Mantaro Valley, Peru. In *What's New? A Closer Look at the Process of Innovation*, ed. SE van der Leeuw, R Torrence, pp. 107–39. London: Unwin Hyman

55. Cowgill GL. 1988. Onward and upward with collapse. See Ref. 217, pp. 244–76

56. D'Altroy TN. 1987. Transition in power: centralization of Wanka political organization under Inka rule. *Ethnohistory* 34:78–102

57. D'Altroy TN. 1992. *Provincial Power in the Inka Empire*. Washington, DC: Smithsonian Inst. Press

58. D'Altroy TN, Bishop RA. 1990. The provincial organization of Inka ceramic production. *Am. Antiq.* 55:120–38

59. D'Altroy TN, Earle TK. 1985. Staple finance, wealth finance and storage in the Inka political economy. *Curr. Anthropol.* 26:187–206

60. Davies N. 1974. *The Aztecs: A History*. Norman: Univ. Okla. Press

61. Davies N. 1987. *The Aztec Empire: The Toltec Resurgence*. Norman: Univ. Okla. Press

62. Davis R. 1993. Art objects as loot. *J. Asian Stud.* 52:22–48

63. Demarest AA, Conrad GW, eds. 1992. *Ideology and Pre-Columbian Civilizations*. Santa Fe, NM: School Am. Res. Press

64. Doyle MW. 1986. *Empires*. Ithaca, NY: Cornell Univ. Press

65. Duncan-Jones RP. 1990. *Structure and Scale in the Roman Economy*. Cambridge: Cambridge Univ. Press

66. Earle TK. 1987. Specialization and the production of wealth: Hawaiian chiefdoms and the Inka empire. In *Specialization, Distribution and Exchange in Complex Societies*, ed. TK Earle, EM Brumfiel, pp. 64–75. Cambridge: Cambridge Univ. Press

67. Earle TK. 1992. Storage and the Inka imperial economy: archaeological research. See Ref. 121, pp. 287–342

68. Earle TK, D'Altroy TN. 1989. The political economy of the Inka empire: the archaeology of power and finance. In *Archaeological Thought in America*, ed. CC Lamberg-Karlovsky, pp. 183–204. Cambridge: Cambridge Univ. Press

69. Edens C. 1992. Dynamics of trade in the ancient Mesopotamia "world system." *Am. Anthropol.* 94:118–39

70. Eisenstadt SN. 1963. *The Political System of Empires*. Glencoe, IL: Free Press

71. Eisenstadt SN. 1979. Observations and queries about sociological aspects of imperialism in the ancient world. See Ref. 120, pp. 21–33

72. Eisenstadt SN. 1988. Beyond collapse. See Ref. 217, pp. 236–43

73. Ekholm K, Friedman J. 1979. "Capital" imperialism and exploitation in ancient world systems. See Ref. 120, pp. 41–58

74. Endicott-West E. 1986. Imperial governance in Yuan times. *Harvard J. Asiatic Stud.* 46:523–49

75. Evans ST. 1991. Architecture and authority in an Aztec village: form and function of the tecpan. See Ref. 93a, pp. 63–92

76. Evans ST. 1993. Aztec household organization and village administration. See Ref. 174a, pp. 173–89

77. Finley M. 1978. Empire in the Graeco-Roman world. *Review* 2:55–68

78. Foster BR. 1993. Management and administration in the Sargonic Period. See Ref. 125, pp. 25–39

79. Frank AG. 1990. A theoretical introduction to 5000 years of world system history. *Review* 13:155–248

80. Frank AG. 1991. A plea for world system history. *J. World Hist.* 2:1–28

81. Frank AG. 1993. Bronze Age world system cycles. *Curr. Anthropol.* 34:383–429

82. Friedman J. 1992. General historical and culturally specific properties of global systems. *Review* 15:335–72

83. Fritz JM. 1986. Vijayanagara: authority and meaning of a south Indian imperial capital. *Am. Anthropol.* 88:44–55

84. Fritz JM, Michell GA, Nagaraja Rao MS. 1985. *Where Kings and Gods Meet: The Royal Center at Vijayanagara*. Tucson: Univ. Ariz. Press

85. Garnsey P. 1983. *Famine and Food Supply*

in the Graeco-Roman World: Responses to Risks and Crises. Cambridge: Cambridge Univ. Press

86. Garnsey P, Saller RP. 1987. The Roman Empire: Economy, Society, and Culture. London: Duckworth

87. Garnsey P, Whittaker CR. 1978. Imperialism in the Ancient World. Cambridge: Cambridge Univ. Press

88. Gibson M, Biggs RD, ed. 1988. The Organization of Power: Aspects of Bureaucracy in the Ancient Near East. Chicago: Oriental Inst.

89. Gills BK, Frank AG. 1992. World system cycles, crises and hegemonial shifts, 1700 BC to 1700 AD. Review 15:621–87

90. Gledhill J. 1989. The imperial form and universal history: some reflections on relativism and generalization. In Domination and Resistance, ed. D Miller, M Rowlands, C Tilley, pp. 108–26. London: Unwin Hyman

91. Gordon RL. 1979. The real and the imaginary: production and religion in the Graeco-Roman world. Art Hist. 2:5–34

92. Greene K. 1986. The Archaeology of the Roman Economy. Berkeley: Univ. Calif. Press

93. Habib I. 1982. An Atlas of the Mughal Empire. Delhi: Oxford Univ. Press

93a. Harvey HR, ed. 1991. Land and Politics in the Valley of Mexico: A Two Thousand-Year Perspective. Albuquerque: Univ. N. Mex. Press

94. Hassig R. 1985. Trade, Tribute and Transportation: The Sixteenth Century Political Economy of the Valley of Mexico. Norman: Univ. Okla. Press

95. Hassig R. 1988. Aztec Warfare: Imperial Expansion and Political Control. Norman: Univ. Okla. Press

96. Hassig R. 1992. War and Society in Ancient Mesoamerica. Berkeley: Univ. Calif. Press

97. Hastorf C. 1990. The effect of the Inka state on Sausa agricultural production and crop consumption. Am. Antiq. 55:262–90

98. Hastorf CA, Earle TK. 1985. Intensive agriculture and the geography of political change in the Upper Mantaro Region of central Peru. In Prehistoric Intensive Agriculture in the Tropics, ed. I Farrington, pp. 569–95. Oxford: BAR Int. Ser., No. 232

99. Hastorf CA, Johannessen S. 1993. Pre-hispanic political change and the role of maize in the Central Andes of Peru. Am. Anthropol. 95:115–38

100. Hedeager L. 1987. Empire, frontier and the barbarian hinterland: Rome and northern Europe from AD 1–400. See Ref. 173, pp. 125–40

101. Hicks F. 1992. Subject states and tribute provinces: the Aztec empire in the northern Valley of Mexico. Ancient Mesoamerica 3:1–10

102. Hingley R. 1984. Roman Britain: the structure of Roman imperialism and the consequences of imperialism on the development of a peripheral province. In The Romano-British Countryside, ed. D Miles, pp. 17–52. Oxford: Br. Archaeol. Rep.

103. Hingley R. 1993. Attitudes to Roman imperialism. In Theoretical Roman Archaeology: First Conference Proceedings, ed. E Scott, pp. 23–28. Avebury, UK: World Archaeol. Ser.

104. Hodge M. 1984. Aztec City States. Mus. Anthropol., Memoir 18. Ann Arbor: Univ. Mich.

105. Hodge M. 1991. Land and lordship in the Valley of Mexico: the politics of Aztec provincial administration. See Ref. 93a, pp. 113–39

106. Hodge M, Minc L. 1990. The spatial patterning of Aztec ceramics: implications for prehistoric exchange systems in the Valley of Mexico. J. Field Archaeol. 17:415–37

107. Hopkins K. 1983. Models, ships and staples. In Trade and Famine in Classical Antiquity, ed. P Garnsey, CR Whittaker, pp. 84–109. Cambridge: Cambridge Univ. Press

108. Hsu Cho-yun. 1988. The role of literati and of regionalism in the fall of the Han Dynasty. See Ref. 217, pp. 176–95

109. Hyslop J. 1984. The Inka Road System. New York: Academic

110. Hyslop J. 1990. Inka Settlement Planning. Austin: Univ. Texas Press

110a.Isaac BL, ed. 1986. Research in Economic Anthropology: Economic Aspects of Prehispanic Highland Mesoamerica. Greenwich, CT: JAI

111. Julien CJ. 1988. How Inca decimal administration worked. Ethnohistory 35:257–79

112. Kohl P. 1978. The balance of trade in southwestern Asia in the mid-third millennium B.C. Curr. Anthropol. 19:463–92

113. Kohl P. 1987. The ancient economy, transferable technologies, and the bronze age world system: a view from the northeastern frontier of the ancient Near East. See Ref. 173, pp. 13–24

114. Kohl P. 1989. The use and abuse of world systems theory: the case of the pristine west Asian state. In Advances in Archaeological Method and Theory, ed. M Schiffer, 11:1–35. Orlando, FL: Academic

115. Kolata AL. 1990. The urban concept of Chan Chan. In The Northern Dynasties: Kingship and Statecraft in Chimor, ed. ME Moseley, A Cordy-Collins, pp. 107–44. Washington, DC: Dumbarton Oaks

116. Kolata AL. 1992. Economy, ideology and imperialism in the south-central Andes. See Ref. 63, pp. 65–86

117. Kurtz DV. 1978. The legitimation of the

Aztec state. In *The Early State,* ed. H Claessen, P Skalnik, pp. 169–89. The Hague: Mouton

118. LaLone MB, LaLone DE. 1987. The Inka state in the southern highlands: state administrative and production enclaves. *Ethnohistory* 34:47–62

119. Larsen MT. 1979. The tradition of empire in Mesopotamia. See Ref. 120, pp. 75–103

120. Larsen MT, ed. 1979. *Power and Propaganda: A Symposium on Ancient Empires.* Copenhagen: Akademisk Forlag

121. LeVine TY, ed. 1992. *Inka Storage Systems.* Norman: Univ. Okla. Press

122. Liverani M. 1993. Model and actualization. The Kings of Akkad in the historical tradition. See Ref. 125, pp. 41–67

123. Liverani M. 1979. The ideology of the Assyrian empire. See Ref. 120, pp. 297–318

124. Liverani M. 1990. *Prestige and Interest: International Relations in the Near East ca. 1600–100 BC.* Padua: Sargon

125. Liverani M, ed. 1993. *Akkad: The First World Empire.* Padua: Sargon

126. Luttwak EN. 1976. *The Grand Strategy of the Roman Empire.* Baltimore: Johns Hopkins Univ. Press

127. Mann M. 1986. *Sources of Social Power.* Cambridge: Cambridge Univ. Press

128. Manz BF. 1989. *The Rise and Rule of Tamerlane.* Cambridge: Cambridge Univ. Press

129. Matos Moctezuma E. 1987. The Templo Mayor of Tenochtitlán: history and interpretation. See Ref. 29a, pp. 15–60

130. McEwan C, Van de Guchte M. 1992. Ancestral time and sacred space in Inca state ritual. In *The Ancient Americas: Art From Sacred Landscapes,* ed. RF Townsend, pp. 359–71. Chicago: Art Inst. Chicago

131. Michell GA. 1992. *The Vijayanagara Courtly Style.* Delhi: Am. Inst. Indian Stud.

132. Millett M. 1990. *The Romanisation of Britain.* Cambridge: Cambridge Univ. Press

133. Morgan DO. 1986. *The Mongols.* Oxford: Oxford Univ. Press

134. Morris C. 1988. Progress and prospect in the archaeology of the Inca. In *Peruvian Prehistory,* ed. RW Keatinge, pp. 233–56. Cambridge: Cambridge Univ. Press

135. Morris C, Thompson DE. 1985. *Huánuco Pampa: An Inca City and its Hinterland.* London: Thames & Hudson

136. Morrison KD. 1992. *Transforming the Agricultural Landscape: Intensification of Production at Vijayanagara.* Ann Arbor, MI: Univ. Microfilms

137. Morrison KD. 1993. Supplying the city: the role of reservoirs in an Indian agricultural landscape. *Asian Perspect.* 32:133–52

138. Morrison KD, Sinopoli CM. 1992. Economic diversity and integration in a pre-colonial Indian empire. *World Archaeol.* 23:335–52

139. Moseley M. 1990. Structure and history in the dynastic lore of Chimor. In *The Northern Dynasties: Kingship and Statecraft in Chimor,* ed. ME Moseley, A Cordy-Collins, pp. 1–42. Washington, DC: Dumbarton Oaks

140. Murra JV. 1980. *The Economic Organization of the Inka State.* Greenwich, CT: JAI

141. Murra JV. 1986. The expansion of the Inka state: armies, war, and rebellions. In *Anthropological History of Andean Polities,* ed. JV Murra, N Wachtel, J Revel, pp. 49–58. Cambridge: Cambridge Univ. Press

142. Nash J. 1978. The Aztecs and the ideology of male dominance. *Signs* 4:349–62

143. Nissen HJ. 1993. Settlement patterns and material culture of the Akkadian period: continuity and discontinuity. See Ref. 125, pp. 91–105

144. Oded B. 1979. *Mass Deportations and Deportees in the Neo-Assyrian Empire.* Wiesbaden: Reichert

145. Palat R. 1987. The Vijayanagara empire: Re-integration of the agrarian order of Medieval South India, 1336–1569. In *Early State Dynamics,* ed. HJM Claessen, P Van de Velde, pp. 170–86. Leiden: Brill

146. Parsons JR. 1982. The role of chinampa agriculture in the food supply of Aztec Tenochtitlán. In *Cultural Change and Continuity: Essays in Honor of James B. Griffin,* ed. C Cleland, pp. 233–62. New York: Academic

147. Parsons JR. 1992. Political implications of prehispanic chinampa agriculture in the Valley of Mexico. See Ref. 93a, pp. 17–42

148. Parsons JR, Parsons M, Popper V, Taft M. 1985. Chinampa agriculture and Aztec urbanization in the Valley of Mexico. In *Prehistoric Intensive Agriculture in the Tropics,* ed. I Farrington, pp. 49–96. Oxford: BAR Int. Ser., No. 232

149. Patterson JR. 1992. Survey article. The city of Rome: from Republic to Empire. *J. Roman Stud.* 82:186–215

150. Patterson TC. 1986. Ideology, class formation and resistance in the Inca State. *Crit. Anthropol.* 6:75–85

151. Patterson TC. 1987. Tribes, chiefdoms, and kingdoms in the Inca empire. In *Power Relations and State Formation,* ed. TC Patterson, CW Gailey, pp. 117–27. Washington, DC: Am. Anthropol. Assoc.

152. Patterson TC. 1991. *The Inca Empire: The Formation and Disintegration of a Pre-Capitalist State.* New York: Berg

153. Peacock DPS. 1982. *Pottery in the Roman World: An Ethnoarchaeological Approach.* London: Longman

154. Peacock DPS, Williams DF. 1986. *Amphorae and the Roman Economy: An Introductory Guide.* London: Longman

155. Perring D. 1991. Spatial organization and social change in Roman towns. In *City and Country in the Ancient World*, ed. J Rich, A Wallace-Hadrill, pp. 273–93. London: Routledge

156. Postgate JN. 1974. *Taxation and Conscription in the Assyrian Empire*. Rome: Biblical Inst.

157. Postgate JN. 1979. The economic structure of the Assyrian Empire. See Ref. 120, pp. 193–222

158. Postgate JN. 1987. Employer, employee, and employment in the Neo-Assyrian empire. In *Labor in the Ancient Near East*, ed. M Powell, pp. 257–70. New Haven, CT: Am. Oriental Soc.

159. Postgate JN. 1992. The land of Assur and the yoke of Assur. *World Archaeol.* 23:247–63

160. Postgate JN. 1992. *Early Mesopotamia: Society and Economy at the Dawn of History*. London: Routledge

161. Price SRF. 1984. *Rituals and Power: The Roman Imperial Cult in Asia Minor*. Cambridge: Cambridge Univ. Press

162. Price SRF. 1987. From noble funerals to divine cult: the consecration of Roman Emperors. In *Rituals of Royalty: Power and Ceremonial in Traditional Societies*, ed. D Cannadine, SRF Price, pp. 56–105. Cambridge: Cambridge Univ. Press

163. Puuci G. 1983. Pottery and trade in the Roman period. In *Trade in the Ancient Economy*, ed. P Garnsey, K Hopkins, CR Whittaker, pp. 105–17. Berkeley: Univ. Calif. Press

164. Raaflaub KA, Tower M, eds. 1990. *Between Republic and Empire: Interpretations of Augustus and his Principate*. Berkeley: Univ. Calif. Press

165. Randsborg K. 1991. *The First Millennium A.D. in Europe and the Mediterranean*. Cambridge: Cambridge Univ. Press

166. Rapaport A. 1993. On the nature of capitals and their physical expression. In *Capital Cities: International Perspectives*, ed. J Taylor, J Lengellé, C Andrew, pp. 31–67. Ottawa: Carleton Univ. Press

167. Ratchenvsky P. 1991. *Genghis Khan: His Life and Legacy*. Oxford: Blackwell

168. Richards JF. 1993. *The Mughal Empire*. Cambridge: Cambridge Univ. Press

169. Rowe JH. 1963. Inca culture at the time of Spanish conquest. In *Handbook of South American Indians*, ed. JH Steward, 2:183–330. New York: Cooper Square

170. Rowe JH. 1967. What kind of settlement was Inca Cuzco? *Nawpa Pacha* 5:59–76

171. Rowe JH. 1982. Inca policies and institutions relating to the cultural unification of the empire. See Ref. 49a, pp. 93–118

172. Rowlands M. 1987. Centre and periphery: a review of a concept. See Ref. 173, pp. 1–12

173. Rowlands M, Larsen MT, Kristiansen K, eds. 1987. *Centre and Periphery in the Ancient World*. Cambridge: Cambridge Univ. Press

174. Santley R. 1986. Prehispanic roadways, transport network geometry, and Aztec politico-economic organization in the Basin of Mexico. See Ref. 110a, pp. 223–44

174a. Santley RS, Hirth KG, eds. 1993. *Prehispanic Domestic Units in Western Mesoamerica*. Boca Raton, FL: CRC

175. Schneider J. 1977. Was there a pre-capitalist world system? *Peasant Stud.* 6:20–29

176. Schortman EM, Urban PA. 1987. Modeling interregional interaction in prehistory. In *Advances in Archaeological Method and Theory*, ed. M Schiffer, 11:37–95. New York: Academic

177. Schortman EM, Urban PA, eds. 1992. *Resources, Power and Interregional Interaction*. New York: Plenum

178. Schreiber KM. 1987. Conquest and consolidation: A comparison of the Wari and Inka occupations of a highland Peruvian valley. *Am. Antiq.* 52:266–84

179. Schreiber KM. 1987. From state to empire: the expansion of Wari outside the Ayacucho Basin. In *The Origins and Development of the Andean State*, ed. J Haas, S Pozorski, T Pozorski, pp. 91–96. Cambridge: Cambridge Univ. Press

180. Schreiber KM. 1992. *Wari Imperialism in Middle Horizon Peru*. Anthropol. Pap. Mus. Anthropol., 87. Ann Arbor: Univ. Mich.

181. Sharma TJ. 1989. *A Political History of the Imperial Guptas*. New Delhi: Concept

182. Sherwin-White S, Kuhrt A. 1993. *From Samarkhand to Sardis: A New Approach to the Seleucid Empire*. Berkeley: Univ. Calif. Press

183. Shotter DCA. 1991. *Augustus Caesar*. London: Routledge

184. Silverblatt I. 1978. Andean women in the Inca empire. *Fem. Stud.* 4:37–61

185. Silverblatt I. 1987. *Moon, Sun, and Witches: Gender Ideologies and Class in Inca and Colonial Peru*. Princeton, NJ: Princeton Univ. Press

186. Sinopoli CM. 1988. The organization of craft production at Vijayanagara, South India. *Am. Anthropol.* 90:580–97

187. Sinopoli CM. 1993. Defining a sacred landscape: temple architecture and divine images in the Vijayanagara suburbs. In *South Asian Archaeology 1991*, ed. AJ Gail, GJR Mevissen, pp. 625–36. Stuttgart: Steiner

188. Sinopoli CM. 1994. Political choices and economic strategies in the Vijayanagara empire. In *The Economic Anthropology of the State*, ed. EM Brumfiel. *Monogr. Econ. Anthropol.* 11:223–43

189. Sinopoli CM. 1994. Monumentality and

mobility in Mughal imperial capitals. *Asian Perspect.* In press

190. Smith ME. 1987. The expansion of the Aztec empire: a case study in the correlation of diachronic archaeological and ethnohistorical data. *Am. Antiq.* 52:37–54

191. Smith ME. 1990. Long-distance trade under the Aztec empire: the archaeological evidence. *Ancient Mesoamerica* 1:153–69

192. Smith ME. 1993. Houses and the settlement hierarchy in late postclassic Morelos: a comparison of archaeology and ethnohistory. See Ref. 174a, pp. 191–206

193. Smith ME, Berdan FF. 1992. Archaeology and the Aztec empire. *World Archaeol.* 23: 352–67

194. Spuler B. 1967. *History of the Mongols.* New York: Dorset

195. Stein B. 1982. Vijayanagara, c. 1350–1564. In *The Cambridge Economic History of India.* Vol. I: *c. 1200–c. 1750,* ed. T Raychaudhuri, I Habib, pp. 102–24. Cambridge: Cambridge Univ. Press

196. Stein B. 1989. *Vijayanagara.* Cambridge: Cambridge Univ. Press

197. Steinhardt NS. 1990. *Chinese Imperial City Planning.* Honolulu: Univ. Hawaii Press

198. Streusand DE. 1989. *The Formation of the Mughal Empire.* Delhi: Oxford Univ. Press

199. Taagepera R. 1978. Size and duration of empires: growth-decline curves. *Soc. Sci. Res.* 7:180–96

200. Tainter JP. 1988. *The Collapse of Complex Societies.* Cambridge: Cambridge Univ. Press

201. Thapar R. 1981. The state as empire. In *The Study of the State,* ed. HJM Claessen, P Skalnik, pp. 409–26. The Hague: Mouton

202. Thapar R. 1984. *From Lineage to State.* Bombay: Oxford Univ. Press

203. Wachtel N. 1982. The mitimaes of the Cochabamba Valley: the colonization policy of Huayna Capac. See Ref. 49a, pp. 199–235

204. Wallerstein I. 1974. *The Modern World System I: Capitalist Agriculture and the Origins of the European World-Economy in the Sixteenth Century.* New York: Academic Press

205. Wallerstein I. 1990 World-systems analysis: the second phase. *Review* 13:287–93

206. Weber M. 1968. *Economy and Society,* Vol.

1–3, ed. G Roth, C Wittich. New York: Bedminster

207. Weiss H, Courtney M-A. 1993. The genesis and collapse of the Akkadian empire: the accidental refraction of historical law. See Ref. 125, pp. 131–55

208. Wenke RJ. 1987. Western Iran in the Partho-Sassanian period: the imperial transformation. In *The Archaeology of Western Iran,* ed. F Hole, pp. 251–82. Washington, DC: Smithsonian Inst. Press

209. Westenholz A. 1979. The Old Akkadian empire in contemporary opinion. See Ref. 120, pp. 107–24

210. Will EL. 1987. The Roman Amphoras. In *The Roman Port and Fishery of Cosa,* J Bourgeois, EK Gazda, JP Oleson, EL Will, pp. 171–220. Princeton, NJ: Princeton Univ. Press

211. Will EL. 1992. Production, distribution, and disposal of Roman amphoras. In *Ceramic Production and Distribution: An Integrated Approach,* ed. GJ Bey III, CA Pool, pp. 261–74. Boulder: Westview

212. Wolf ER. 1982. *Europe and the People Without History.* Berkeley: Univ. Calif. Press

213. Woolf G. 1990. World-systems analysis and the Roman Empire. *J. Roman Archaeol.* 3:44–58

214. Woolf G. 1992. Imperialism, empire, and the integration of the Roman economy. *World Archaeol.* 23:283–93

215. Yoffee N. 1988. Orienting collapse. See Ref. 217, pp. 1–19

216. Yoffee N. 1988. The collapse of ancient Mesopotamian states and civilizations. See Ref. 217, pp. 44–68

217. Yoffee N, Cowgill GL, eds. 1988. *The Collapse of Ancient States and Civilizations.* Tucson: Univ. Ariz. Press

218. Yü Y-s. 1967. *Trade and Expansion in Han China.* Berkeley: Univ. Calif. Press

219. Zanker P. 1988. *The Power of Images in the Age of Augustus.* Ann Arbor: Univ. Mich. Press

220. Zeitlin RN. 1990. The Isthmus and the Valley of Oaxaca: questions about Zapotec imperialism in formative period Mesoamerica. *Am. Antiq.* 55:250–61

221. Zuidema T. 1990. *Inca Civilization in Cuzco.* Transl. J-J Decoster. Austin: Univ. Texas Press

Annu. Rev. Anthropol. 1994. 23:181–208

CHANGING PERSPECTIVES ON MAYA CIVILIZATION

William L. Fash

Department of Anthropology, Northern Illinois University, DeKalb, Illinois 60115

KEY WORDS: Maya culture, archaeology, ethnology, epigraphy, sociopolitical evolution, demography, warfare

INTRODUCTION

The Maya world stands on a threshold between past and future scholarship, and more importantly, between an indigenous people hailed widely as the most advanced in the New World and other cultural traditions not necessarily interested in the survival or prosperity of Maya civilization. In this age of information explosion, electronic wizardry, and the sound bite, it is becoming harder for the complexities of the ancient and diverse Maya cultural tradition to be fathomed by the scholars who attempt to describe and understand it, let alone by the millions of people who set forth on pilgrimages to its holy sites, or who see it represented with varying degrees of inaccuracy on their television screens each day. Although the popularization of Maya civilization has made household words of Tikal, Lord Pacal, and sting-ray spines, it also has made for a great deal of misinformation in the mass media, undue politicization and occasional distortions of scholarship, and the commercialization of Maya culture and its homeland to an at times frightening degree. This review attempts to strike a balance between the often polarized views of Maya civilization held by various researchers in the past and present, and to highlight the need for scholars to think more carefully about the implications of their research and writings for living Maya peoples and the remarkable land they inhabit.

0084-6570/94/1015-0181$05.00

EARLIER VIEWS OF MAYA CIVILIZATION

No culture of the pre-Columbian Americas left a richer legacy of native history and world-view carved in stone than did the Maya, the name used by some natives of the Yucatán Peninsula to describe themselves to the sixteenth century Spanish explorers, conquistadores, and chroniclers (288:7). Occupying an area of roughly 325,000 sq km in southern Mexico and northern Central America that ranges from tropical lowlands to volcanic highlands, the Maya created a cultural tradition that is daunting in its diversity and intoxicating in its creativity. During the final centuries of the Formative or Preclassic period (2,000 B.C.–A.D. 250), throughout the Classic period (A.D. 250–900), and at the beginning of the Postclassic period (A.D. 900–1519), thousands of stone monuments and buildings were carved with hieroglyphic inscriptions, in addition to countless other texts and images painted or carved on more perishable media (e.g. cloth, wood, stucco, or bark-paper books).

Although the Classic period was the heyday of the Maya writing system and its creative scribes, the Maya of previous and subsequent periods were no less resourceful in their architectural achievements and their adornment of sacred objects with carved and painted decoration. Moreover, the passing on of oral history, religious lore, and prognostications both presaged and outlived the Classic period. The combination of pictorial imagery, hieroglyphic writing, and oral tradition allows for a truly remarkable understanding of Maya conceptions of themselves, the world, and their relationship to it. Indeed, recent efforts have shown that controlled historical analysis of imagery and writing from Classic Period stone monuments, Postclassic bark-paper books, and Colonial Spanish accounts can explain rituals and behaviors among the living Maya for which traditional ethnographic methods cannot account (34). Conversely, analogy with adaptations and lifeways of living Maya peoples provides the archaeologist with insights that no amount of digging or surveying could ever provide (14, 239, 266, 299, 311, 312).

In the early nineteenth century, a series of publications sparked interest in ancient Maya culture. Fray Diego de Landa's *Relación de las Cosas de Yucatán* (30), three Maya bark-paper books, and a series of superb photographs and drawings of inscriptions on stone monuments (198) spurred a great deal of interest in the decipherment of the Maya script (63, 275). What resulted was a flurry of readings of Maya calendric and astronomical hieroglyphs during the late nineteenth and early twentieth century, including the correlation of the Maya and Christian calendars (127). Scholars began to speculate about the nature of ancient Maya society, based on information available at that time: decipherable aspects of Maya writings, some preliminary surveys of the centers of a handful of archaeological sites, and some spotty knowledge of the peasant lifeways that characterized Maya villages at the turn of the century.

Eventually, the view became established that ancient Maya society was a theocracy, run by devoted calendar priests who resided in the temples at the heart of each "vacant ceremonial center," supported by maize-farming peasants, scattered in villages about the countryside, who came to the center only for important calendric and other religious rituals. Respected and important scholars like S. Morley and J.E.S. Thompson viewed the ancient Maya as so obsessed with marking the passage of time and the movements of the stars, that they never would have stooped so low as to go to war or record the doings of vainglorious kings. This myth of the Classic Maya became so pervasive that the civilization came to be thought of as unique in the annals of human history: flourishing in the jungle, with intelligentsia devoted to the arts and sciences (including fantastically accurate calculations of astronomical cycles and the passage of time), all the while removed from the plights of war, over-crowded cities, and despotic rulers, as the common people devoted themselves to the cult of their rain gods and peacefully tilled their fields (*milpa*) with corn, beans, and squash.

Revisionism and Realism in Recent Research

This misguided, albeit well-meaning, vision of the ancient Maya began to be dismantled in the middle of this century. When the Lacandón Maya of Chiapas took photographer G. Healy to see the painted murals, including an explicit battle scene, at the ruins of Bonampak in 1946, the view that the Classic Maya did not engage in warfare was shattered forever. Subsequent discoveries of defensive features associated with the major Classic period centers of Tikal (224), Becan (301, 302), Muralla de León (229), and in Yucatán (175, 303) provided independent evidence for Proskouriakoff's (218, 219) decipherments that rulers of Yaxchilán named the captives they had taken in war and even boasted of the number of captives secured.

One of the greatest contributions ever made to Maya studies was Proskouriakoff's discovery that the stone monuments were not devoid of historical information, as was previously thought. Quite the contrary, they recorded the important events in the lives of Maya rulers, such as their birth, inauguration, conquests, and death (216–220). Berlin's equally illuminating decipherments showed that each Classic Maya kingdom had its own name or emblem glyph, and that the royal houses were concerned with couching their achievements in mythological terms (25–27). It is now possible to decipher dynastic histories and royal genealogies from most of the major cities of the Classic Period.

Equally revolutionary developments in field archaeology produced data refuting many of the earlier ideas about ancient Maya culture. Inspired by Steward's (267a) and White's (308a) cultural ecological and evolutionary models, and by Willey's (313a) breakthrough in settlement pattern methodology, several generations of archaeologists engaged in important field research that also provided illuminating information about the structure of ancient Maya societies and their change through time and space. Beginning in the 1950s in the Belize River Valley (318), and continuing at Altar de Sacrificios (315), Seibal (321, 287), and the Copán Valley (319, 320), Willey opened new vistas onto the size, structure, and growth of ancient Maya rural and urban communities, through the application of the settlement analysis that he had pioneered in the Viruac Valley of Peru (313a). In this type of research, the archaeologist documents the size and distribution of human settlements and other landscape modifications as a springboard for inferring land-use, societal complexity and organization, defensive features and measures, and in larger terms the relations of people to their regional physical and cultural environment.

Settlement densities around the major Maya centers were demonstrated to be quite high—they were hardly vacant—and showed considerable evidence for social differentiation beyond the simple two tiers (priests and peasantry) previously envisioned (53, 111, 112, 145, 174, 223, 277, 285, 319). Excavations of the urban sectors of these centers confirmed the existence of social ranking if not stratification (11, 55, 111, 137, 144, 173, 246, 248, 320). Studies of drained marshes and swamps, and of agricultural relics such as raised fields, terraces, and other related features showed that the ancient Maya had practiced agricultural intensification on a significant scale (109, 142, 191, 195, 222, 264, 289–291). Ecological studies also showed there was more variability within the different environmental zones than was previously thought (244), and that the Maya exploited a variety of tree crops and other cultigens besides maize, beans, and squash (36, 221, 322).

Long-term excavation programs throughout the Maya area showed that the simplistic picture of sociopolitical development adumbrated by earlier researchers (humble Preclassic origins, Classic apogee, and Postclassic decline) needed drastic revision. Archaeologists proved that the Preclassic period was much more significant than was previously thought, with some of the largest construction projects ever undertaken in Mesoamerica carried out at such huge centers as El Mirador (193–196) and Nakbe (141) during the latter part of the Middle Preclassic and throughout the Late Preclassic. A fascinating development has been the demonstration of ancient and diverse occupations (138) in different parts of the Maya world, a subject so controversial and important that it merits a review of its own. Regarding the origins of Maya civilization and statehood, abundant evidence of religious, artistic, and architectural sophistication at El Mirador and Nakbe is bolstered by similar if less grandiose examples of the same at lowland sites such as Tikal (64, 65), Cerros (118, 120), Becán (20), Lamanai (210, 211), Komchen (233), Edzná (194), Uaxactun (293, 294), and in areas outside the lowlands, as well (61, 84:153, 130, 132, 143, 261, 262).

Studies of the origins of Maya civilization have also debated the importance of Olmec culture, and Teotihuacan, in the genesis and development of complex culture and the state. The presence of scattered finds of caches, jades, and ceramics with strong similarities to those of Gulf Coast Olmec sites originally was perceived as indicating a central role for the latter as a donor to incipient complex societies in the Maya area. This view has been revised, as archaeologists have become aware that such finds, nearly always in elite contexts, signal status-reinforcing strategies by local elites to enhance their prestige by showing their understanding of pan-Mesoamerican religious ideology and their participation in long-distance exchange networks (84, 133, 258; cf. 106). Comparative studies from the entire Maya area have shown that there is no direct evidence for Teotihuacan populations, or for direct political and economic control, in any of the Maya sites where such phenomena had previously been posited (84). Instead, these phenomena are now viewed as the result of local emulations of foreign elites (84, 253). Archaeological evidence demonstrating that the Maya developed large, complex polities that fit most criteria for statehood (194) long before Teotihuacan rose to prominence has disproven the idea that Maya civilization represented a secondary state formed as a result of political control or influence exerted from Central Mexico.

Likewise, the Postclassic period, far from being viewed as a time of universal decline or decadence, has emerged as a vigorous time of cultural change in which robust highland and lowland Maya societies responded to the failure of the Classic Maya sociopolitical order in the southern Maya lowlands (8, 9, 56, 116, 242).

The variability in timing of the development of the major Maya centers (316) led to the realization that the rise and fall of a particular kingdom was related to the fortunes of its neighbors, with the ascension of one polity often corresponding to the decline of one of its rivals (55, 76, 82, 253, 256). Thus, the records of captures of rival rulers and conquests of sites are of more than passing historical interest; they can be engaged in the anthropological analysis of the rise and fall of Maya kingdoms.

Other advances in archaeological method and theory allowed for the elucidation of stone age economics, Maya style. Theories about the origins and transformation of Maya civilization based on trade and sea-faring merchants, and the control of raw materials and finished products, were elaborated and tested (7, 8, 10, 29, 124, 125, 135, 136, 149, 199, 225, 232, 255, 286), resulting in useful data on resource acquisition, specialized production, and trade networks. A consensus is emerging that the control of exotic goods and their exchange was an important tool of power among the aristocratic elites of ancient Maya society, but that the majority of trade took the form of local exchange of utilitarian products and food resources among the commoners (82, 140).

Enormous strides have been made in ethnography and ethnohistory during the past 30 years. In addition to a number of classic ethnographies (45, 68, 97, 134, 205, 226, 297, 300), studies of a more specialized nature have been undertaken with great success. Bricker (31, 34) and Hunt (161) demonstrated the benefits of a historical approach to the analysis of living Maya ritual and belief systems. Invaluable analyses of social and economic change during the past century have been made in a number of Maya communities (13, 35, 46, 47, 70, 71, 152, 227). There has been an increasing interest in documenting the non-Maya context in which the Maya live (47). As in archaeology, there also has been a change from a characterization of communities/cultures as relatively homogeneous whole, to a focus on internal differences. Vogt (298) and Freidel (122, 123) contributed structuralist approaches to the understanding of Maya ritual, while Tedlock (282) and Colby & Colby (69) provided excellent studies of living Maya time-reckoning and concepts. A number of outstanding ethnohistoric studies have been made of the remarkable tenacity and resilience of Maya culture during the Colonial and post-Colonial periods (59, 98, 150, 151, 164, 165, 265).

Gossen provided compelling analyses of oral tradition and its use in shaping culture (128, 129), with important implications for the understanding of Maya texts in general. Such textual studies have been offered as an independent exercise (114), as part of historical and other analyses of Maya oral tradition (31, 34), and as part of the complex task of translating native Maya texts, of which a number of important new efforts have appeared (73, 92, 94, 95, 284). The publication of several outstanding dictionaries (22, 93, 177, 178) and grammars (96) also represents a tremendous advancement of knowledge. Linguistic studies have flourished, with important implications for historical studies (38, 39, 41, 42, 44, 170, 171, 323), for the decipherment of the Maya writing system (32, 43, 166, 167, 169; NA Hopkins, unpublished data), and for the decipherment of an even older script, now believed to have been developed by the neighboring Mixe-Zoque (168).

A remarkable development is the beginning of Maya anthropology, carried out and written by the Maya themselves (208, 283:168). As a result of recent confrontations in Guatemala, it is estimated that 50,000–70,000 Guatemalans were killed (most of them Maya), 500,000 became internal refugees, 150,000 escaped to Mexico, and over 200,000 fled to other nation-states (50, 185, 283). Insurgent takeovers of rural communities triggered massive attacks by the state, and both outside observers and Maya leaders have accused the Guatemalan government of those bleak days of using its counterinsurgency campaign as a pretext for genocide. Tedlock speculated that this violent uprooting and dispersion could lead to "a cultural and political regrouping into an ethnic nation that transcends the boundaries of established nation-states" (283:168). The Maya have developed their own alphabets for recording their languages

(6); they are encouraging the use of the Maya calendar, dress, art forms and lifeways; and they are writing down their biographies, thoughts, and folk tales (200, 204; see 283:168–169). Thus, the living Maya are now active players in the anthropological study of past and present aspects of their own culture. Equally important, they are taking Maya civilization into the future.

As a result of the efforts of both Western scholars and the Maya, many old notions have been discredited, and many productive new ones developed and criticized. One often problematic by-product of the revision of the older models of Maya civilization has been the effort by some North American scholars to compete for the attentions of the popular press (283:156). Earlier Western academics had put the Maya on a cultural pedestal; some publicity seekers seem to delight in knocking them from it. Sensationalist accounts of gory blood sacrifices, sexual mutilation, and the fall of the Maya based on their "bloodlust" and "penchant for warfare" have been common in the mass media. This reviewer had to vehemently insist that these very words be struck from a popular book he was sent for pre-publication review last year.

Granted, if an educator is presented with the chance to share the insights of years of thoughtful, hard work with millions of people rather than a few hundred, one would in a sense be untrue to his/her calling not to do so. A serious problem arises, however, when scholars are reduced to playing the game according to the needs of the media and the tastes of Western consumers. Sadly, the quest for public recognition on the part of some researchers has resulted in further polarization of entrenched positions, and considerable irritation about those publications where traditional standards of hypothesis testing, proof, and scholarship are conspicuously absent. Worse, some of the sensationalist popular treatments can provide certain sectors of the Ladino elite— who have been the dominant political force in the Maya world since the Spanish conquest—with the perfect excuse for further repression of the living Maya. After all, if the information comes from such a prestigious source, and is known around the world, it must be true that the Maya have a "bloodlust" and "penchant for warfare." Let us hope that the popularization of Maya culture does not continue to flourish at the expense of the living Maya, adding to a shameful legacy of Western exploitation that we as scholars should be working to redress, not contribute to.

CURRENT VIEWS ON THE NATURE OF MAYA CIVILIZATION

Settlement Patterns, Household Archaeology, and Ethnoarchaeology

Maya anthropology was forever changed for the better by the advent of settlement pattern research. Willey's lead was followed quickly by major research into settlement patterns throughout the Maya region. Over the years, studies have extended beyond Willey's original emphasis on rural settlement, to more holistic treatments of entire communities (e.g. 23, 55, 101, 243, 246, 248, 255), to even more inclusive regional settlement studies (85–88, 113, 180, 181, 296, 307), and to a single, amazing example of a macro-regional survey (126). Insights into many questions and problems have resulted. The critical use of ethnohistoric and ethnographic analogy (311) for the interpretation of these archaeological remains, and the recognition of the importance of analyzing variation in settlement patterns through time and space, have greatly strengthened the field.

Among the more important findings was the discovery that not all Maya settlements are archaeologically visible. Some did not endure the ravages of the tropics well after their abandonment, thus, leaving no surface traces in the jungle. Initial work on defining invisible structures (37) and the invisible universe (a term that elicited many jokes) was viewed with great skepticism, but further archaeological research confirmed that some remains of human settlements of varying densities are not visible on the modern landscape (16, 57, 101, 163, 309). Jones has shown that major Colonial period lowland Maya settlements—which are recent, in relative terms—are archaeologically invisible in the jungle (165). The important implication of Jones' findings for the so-called collapse at the end of the Classic period is that very large, relatively well-organized populations could have continued to thrive in the forest, and yet are not readily visible with present archaeological technology.

The most significant force in strengthening the study of settlement patterns and human adaptation has been the field of household archaeology, brought to the forefront in Mesoamerica by Flannery (108) and gaining increasing momentum in the Maya area (312, 313). This approach represents the opposite end of the spectrum from regional studies, and for a variety of reasons has become a growing concern throughout the Maya area. As Wilk has pointed out, "The household unit has become recognized as the most important and informative level of analysis for understanding how individual and group action does lead to structural transformation on a larger scale" (310:91). An exciting corollary development is ethnoarchaeology (147, 148, 266, 310, 312), with its unique potential for developing middle-range theory that can be applied to archaeological sites. Household archaeology may help resolve how to date residential sites, a key question in the ongoing debate about how to calculate pre-Columbian population size in the Maya area (78).

Demography and Agricultural Intensification

Population pressure is regarded by many anthropologists as a prime mover in the development of larger, more complex societies. The evidence for the growth of individual sites and human populations throughout the Maya area during the Preclassic period (1) was taken to mean that population growth, together with circumscription (whether ecological or social; 52, 302), was the driving force behind the nucleation of large numbers of peoples into urban organizational centers (316). The increasing evidence for agricultural intensification techniques was thought to represent either a response to increasing population, or even the impetus behind the development of large urban centers. This population curve was thought to have peaked at the end of the Classic period, with the resultant over-crowding creating huge problems for the lowland Maya, including the proliferation of communicable diseases (251, 263, 268), depletion of natural resources (particularly soil loss through erosion and insufficient fallow cycles), and other systemic stresses, resulting in the catastrophic demographic and ecological disaster referred to as the Classic Maya collapse (74, 75).

No one questions that human populations and social pressures did grow to unmanageable sizes by the end of the Classic period, but many researchers have reservations about just how overcrowded things really were, and whether the agricultural works by themselves could have supported some of the numbers that are being bandied about. In Santley's words, "it is difficult to have any confidence in theories of state development employing population pressure as a causal agent, because there is no theoretical calculus specifying the conditions that select for complexity given agricultural intensification, the dynamic linkages between variables assigned explanatory import, and the form emergent complex systems take" (250:339). The whole question of the Classic collapse is also being rethought (81, 236, 242, 257, 271, 306, 307), with most researchers seeing the process as much more protracted, complex, and full of regional variation than was previously believed. In the case of Lamanai, there apparently was no collapse (212).

The field of subsistence studies has seen enormous advances, both in theoretical formulations and in the quality and quantity of fieldwork (109, 142, 213, 214, 267, 291). Investigations have produced evidence for draining of swamps and raised fields (191, 214, 222, 264, 289, 291), hillside terracing (290), and other agricultural intensification strategies. Clearly, Maya kingdoms were directing the construction and maintenance of agricultural works, including hydraulic engineering projects, in some parts of the lowlands. Such direct control was often attributed to large polities in the heartland or core area of the Petén, based on initial reports of extensive raised fields and other agricultural works seen via satellite imagery (2, 3, 79). However, more recent on-the-ground checks have shown that most of these latter features were not cultural in origin (80, 215, 237), and the setting in which they were found was inappropriate for extensive raised field agriculture. Although there was a degree of capital investment in some areas that indicates short-fallow (rather than swidden) systems, most specialists now consider such artificial econiches as complementary to, rather than a substitution for, milpa farming. Most scholars agree that, in general, agricultural management was weakly developed among the indigenous city-states of the Maya. Comparative data corroborate the thesis that agricultural works began as local, small-scale operations that were only later, if at all, incorporated into larger, state-managed systems (4, 40, 54, 82).

The picture that is emerging is one of a series of localized adaptations and agricultural strategies, varying in scope and complexity based on the ecological setting and the degree of population pressure. This set of systems probably included an infield-outfield type (207), using garden plots near the houselot, including root crops as well as other cultigens, and arboriculture, in tandem with more distant plots dedicated to swidden agriculture, all (theoretically) in harmony with the potential of the local ecosystems into which they were implanted. Above all, an appreciation of the diversity of the rainforest, and of a conscious attempt by the Maya to mimic that bio-diversity under optimal conditions, is setting in (206, 237, 238, 322). This finding is of enormous importance for attempts to determine what is wrong with modern-day Mesoamerican agriculture and agronomy (230; NP Dunning, E Secaira, AA Demarest, & unpublished data), and how to correct those problems.

Sociopolitical Evolution

Archaeological excavations have shown that socioeconomic elites and elite interaction began before the start of the Classic period and continued into the Postclassic (139). Sabloff (240) proposed a radical departure from previous periodization schemes by defining the entire span from 300 B.C. to A.D. 1250 as a single, Middle Phase of pre-Columbian Maya civilization. Although significant variations in localized material culture and sociopolitical evolution are well appreciated, a strong degree of unity and interdependence by the elites who rose to power in each of the lowland Maya polities continues to be a fundamental tenet of studies of Maya culture change (139). As archaeologists have become broader in their anthropological perspectives, they have begun to see that the interaction (including intense competition) between elites and the centers they built up is a key to ancient Maya politics and is a fruitful basis for model-building and comparison with other societies at similar levels of sociopolitical complexity (81, 92, 120, 140, 228, 241).

Analogies are being made with patron-client systems in sub-Saharan Africa (89, 245, 247); theater states or "galactic polities" of Southeast Asia (60, 81, 82, 140, 263); and poleis (city-states) and nomes (departments) of ancient Greece and Egypt (140), third millenium Mesopotamia (325), and Zhou China (72, 140). The theater states of Southeast Asia seem particularly relevant, since Tambiah (279:86) posits that the resources to underwrite independent action on the part of a ruler came not from the pyramid of politico-economic relations within the polity, but from control of the supply of nonsubsistence goods from outside the system. Farriss reached such a conclusion in her compelling analysis of the Colonial Maya (98:178). The integration of communities into states depends on elite relations of trade as well as alliance and warfare, all made without reference to the mass of the population. These alliances, and the limits of the area that they could effectively control, created a highly fluid political landscape.

Thus, polities of numerous sizes and degrees of complexity, from large and powerful states such as Tikal and Calakmul, through smaller yet still powerful urban entities, down to minor centers and towns, existed side by side in complementary and often conflicting ways, from the Late Preclassic onward. Marcus has developed this view the most thoroughly (189, 190). Her dynamic model was inspired by analysis of ethnohistoric, archaeological, and epigraphic materials. Marcus follows Roys' (235) division of Maya sociopolitical entities into three types and encourages us to look at the kinds of interaction and degrees of inclusivity of the parties involved, through both time and space. Her insistence on the importance of secondary centers in Maya political evolution is a major contribution that will be pursued with vigor in ongoing and future studies.

Substantial progress has been achieved in discerning the degree of ranking or stratification in ancient Maya polities. The Chases have argued that there is evidence for a middle class in Caracol, (personal communication). Settlement pattern studies have shown rank-ordering in the size of site centers (292), of secondary and tertiary centers, and of the populations making up the urban wards of a single center (246, 248, 319, 320). In the hieroglyphic inscriptions, names of people and/or the offices they occupied or professions they held are being deciphered with increasing rapidity and specificity (157, 252, 253, 269, 270, 304), giving us clear indications of the level of complexity of the upper tier. Recent work at a Classic Maya council house (100) shows that it is possible to identify the buildings where ruling councils were held, and the names and locations of the lineage compounds or wards that were represented in those deliberations (12, 99). Farriss (98) has shown that in colonial Yucatán there were two tiers of elites and the offices they occupied, and that Colonial Maya society was an effective oligarchy.

As Marcus (189, 190) noted, a vital area for future research is to see if archaeological investigations can determine the shifting allegiances of the secondary elites and supporting populations that were pulled this way and that as the fortunes of individual kingdoms and their rulers rose and fell. Developing middle-range theory and methodologies to do so will be an exciting challenge for archaeologists and will give them much to discuss with their ethnologist colleagues. Such a conjoined approach has already been applied successfully to the analysis of the evolution of the Quiché capital (48, 49, 51,

115–117), with significant contributions to our understanding of the mechanics of segmentary lineage fission (cf. 89) and the on-the-ground architectural manifestations of successful unification strategies. Likewise, research at Ek Balam is also following an ethnohistorically enlightened approach to settlement dynamics, council houses, social structure, and political evolution (233).

Both the theater states and dynamic models of ancient Maya society enable researchers to focus on specific aspects of the archaeological and historical records that will illuminate the direction, duration, and results of elite interaction, and its impact, if any, on the supporting populations, through time and space. In the Petexbatún region of Guatemala, a multidisciplinary project is tackling the problem of the origins, development, and decline of a series of interrelated kingdoms during the closing centuries of the Classic period (82, 85–88, 296). Ecological investigations of carrying capacity and land use (179, 237) serve as the baseline for evaluating the density and distribution of settlement on a regional level (172), and at the larger centers (162, 209, 324). The political trajectories of the centers are measured by architectural energetics and complexity (209) and relevant historical records (157, 158), and their economic policies and trading patterns are traced through neutron activation studies of ceramics (110) and trace element analysis of other nonperishable trade goods. All of this work is being carried out within a comparative model of sociopolitical evolution that seeks to explain the Maya collapse through a critical manipulation of the role of warfare in the late eighth century A.D.

Causes and Consequences of Warfare in Ancient Maya Society

Opinions vary widely as to the origins and consequences of warfare in ancient times among the Maya, a nonissue for the old model of the Maya but literally a burning issue for modern investigators and the living Maya themselves. Webster's original path-breaking work led to the development of a robust materialist model (301, 302) that saw population pressure and elite competition driving the ancient Maya to warfare and to the evolution of still more complex forms of societal organization. Demarest (81) hypothesized two patterns of Maya warfare: 1. an open or unlimited type that is highly destructive and in which the participants do not hold to conventions and rules, and 2. a situational ethics type of warfare in which the participants agree on the conventions of ritual bellicose encounters designed primarily with political purposes in mind. This second, conventionalized type of warfare provided the opportunity for captive-taking by the ruler, who would then haul off the captive(s) to his own center for subsequent exploitation (in the case of sculptors or craftsmen), or humiliation and sacrifice (in the case of high-status captives, such as nobles or rival rulers). Similarly, Freidel (121:107) views Maya warfare as "a prerogative of the elite and fought primarily by the elite, (and) the bulk of the population was neither affected by, nor participated in, violent conflict."

Mathews (197) sees Classic Maya warfare as the raiding of marginal territory. But there are a few very well-publicized exceptions such as the purported
defeat of Tikal, twice, by Caracol (55, 58, 154; for other examples see 24, 102,
104, 146, 157, 186, 256, 269). The variation in cause and effect seen in these
cases means that we cannot presently say which one of the most recently
proposed models of Maya warfare is most generally applicable. Demarest
(83:101) posits that Rulers 2 and 3 of Dos Pilas changed the rules of Classic
Maya warfare (from ritualized wars to conquest warfare) in A.D. 771 in the
Petexbatuacn. Yet Schele & Freidel (253:145–149) make the same claim for
Tikal, which they believe conquered and absorbed Uaxactun in A.D. 326 (cf
196), emulating costumes and concepts of Tlaloc-Venus conquest war from
Teotihuacan. (For an alternative view on the Tikal-Uaxactun encounter, see
156, 220:7–9, 270). Obviously, much remains to be done before this important
issue is resolved, and the problem will surely be much more complex than we
realize currently. Webster's recent review (305) underscores the need to investigate and discriminate between ten separate issues in our attempts at understanding and building models about Maya warfare, and emphasizes the need to
examine multiple lines of evidence in doing so.

Literacy and Its Critics

The hieroglyphic decipherments and iconographic analyses that have rocked
Maya studies for the past 30 years have revolutionized our understanding of
elite history, political structure, royal symbolism, emic terminology (e.g. 160,
273), ritual behaviors, and worldview. The historical and phonetic approaches
to decipherment have combined to make it possible for epigraphers to understand in broad outline—and occasionally, in glyph-by-glyph decipherment—
virtually every Classic Maya text that has been discovered (63). Many archaeologists have aided and abetted the cause by discovering significant new texts,
and carefully documenting their archaeological contexts (12, 15, 55, 100, 105,
158, 211, 132, 261, 274, 276). Special recognition should go to Graham (131),
whose Corpus of Maya Hieroglyphic Writing Project is of fundamental importance to all epigraphers, and whose courageous efforts to that end often go
unheralded.

Sadly, the epigraphic revolution also has strengthened the divide between
the ideationists and the materialists, despite Flannery's (107) pleas that the two
camps see their perspectives and data as complementary rather than in conflict.
Many important critiques have been made by archaeologists of both the processualist and post-processualist persuasions. The processualists rightly point
out that the hieroglyphs can only tell the history of a tiny segment of the
population in Classic Maya times. Further, they contend (as do many other
social scientists) that social change came from below, not from above, and that

the emphasis on elite culture history is severely biased at best. It is also important to remember Hammond's observation that "we must not ignore the sobering reality that they [the epigraphers] have brought the Maya from the margins of prehistory into merely liminal history. A dozen royal marriages, a score of battles or royal visits, and the genealogies of a handful of dynasties do not give us a broad historical foundation on which to build, in the absence of economic information or any documentation of Maya society below the upper-most elite" (140:256). The post-processualists, meanwhile, believe that these texts are not objective sources of information, and that what is presently being published is as much an attempt at reinforcing the social position of the writer as it is a detached evaluation of events that purportedly took place in the past.

The lack of extant economic records is used by many scholars to minimize the achievements not only of the Maya scribes and their writing system, but of the civilization itself (249). However, Stuart recently (271) deciphered a glyph for *tribute* and showed that Late Classic inscriptions at Naranjo cite not only this glyph, but the goods given in tribute to that kingdom after its successful conquest of a neighboring polity. This decipherment means that booty was, in some cases, obtained from war (which Stuart notes is recorded as involving the burning of structures; 271, manuscript submitted for publication; cf. 12, 203), and that such accounts of tribute were sometimes important enough to be recorded on stone monuments. The latter datum is in striking contrast to the situation in Mesopotamia, for example, where economic transactions were always recorded on portable clay tablets and never displayed publicly. We should now reconsider why no economic codices have survived. Only four ancient Maya books remain of the hundreds that still existed in Postclassic times (versus the thousands that probably existed earlier). These four were devoted to religious and astronomical data, and are considered in more than one case to have been copies of earlier, Classic Period originals. Why would later Maya scribes and rulers want to recopy codices containing royal genealo-gies, or tribute records, of kingdoms that had long since perished? Such records may well have gone up in smoke with the fires that consumed the very cities they chronicled. Alas, unlike at Ebla, the Maya royal archives were made of paper, not clay.

Another major critique leveled at Maya inscriptions is that they were used as political propaganda and, therefore, are unreliable. Indeed, some scholars have taken an extreme postmodern/deconstructionist view that these texts are not only untrustworthy, but intrinsically deceptive, and unlikely to yield data that might be archaeologically demonstrable. Marcus has a more enlightened approach (188), noting that the Maya did not distinguish between history, myth, and propaganda. Indeed, Bricker (31) showed that there is no dividing line between history and myth in the oral traditions and rituals of the living Maya. However, Marcus does not go to the extreme of claiming "that Mesoamerican inscriptions are 'all lies' or 'pure propaganda,'" nor does she "embrace the deconstructionist view that history does not exist" (188:8). Instead, Marcus rightly cautions Mayanists not to take the claims of the Classic Maya kings and other Mesoamerican rulers at face value, given their intertwining of propaganda, myth, and history, particularly with respect to the lengths of their reigns and the conquests they claim to have made.

All good social scientists know that one needs more than one source for any text to be considered valid, in a historiographic sense. Many of the most important events in the lifetimes of rulers and in the history of their kingdoms were doubtless ephemeral affairs, difficult if not impossible to determine in the archaeological record alone. But others were of a nature and a magnitude that they can either be corroborated, or fail to be corroborated, by archaeological evidence and/or by other written records from independent sources. When texts at both Copán and Quiriguá refer to the death of the thirteenth Copán king in A.D. 738 (at the hands of his Quiriguá rival), we can take that as evidence that the historical veracity of this event and its perceived importance to the dynasties of both centers are corroborated. When the archaeological record shows that this event did not result in the absorption of the Copán kingdom into that of Quiriguá, we can adjudge the socioeconomic consequences of Copán's loss to have been less than devastating. The Petexbatuacn region has provided quite compelling, independent archaeological data verifying the presence and importance of fortification features and weaponry, in association with sites whose hieroglyphic records insist on the frequency and importance of bellicose encounters. Epigraphic data regarding rulers' ages and actions can be used to archaeologically cross-check the dates of construction of buildings, the placement and reentry of tombs, and the ages of their occupants (e.g. 5).

Such a "cross-cutting, self-corrective strategy," as Sharer calls it, for the evaluation of the evolution, degree, and forms of sociopolitical complexity—whether or not one cares to call it a conjunctive approach—has been applied productively throughout the Maya lowlands (12, 15, 55, 77, 83, 99, 100, 103, 105, 155, 176, 182, 210, 212, 253, 256, 259, 260, 269, 295). Obviously, when independent archaeological lines of evidence fail to corroborate a particular text or set of texts, we are faced with a challenge both to the official history of their commissioner and to our own interpretive abilities and limitations. To cavalierly dismiss the records as completely untrustworthy, or worse, unworthy of attention or unusable in the interpretation of the archaeological record, is to bury one's head in the sand. Rather, the richness and complementarity of the data sets available to the Maya archaeologist (187) is an inviting challenge that we most certainly can and should live up to.

Ideology as a Causal Force in Maya Civilization

At the same time that Proskouriakoff and Berlin were opening the road to historiography for the ancient Maya, Willey (314) was trying to convince New World archaeologists to address ideology in their attempts at explaining the past. Given the rising tide of evolutionism in American archaeology, processualists preferred to follow Willey's lead on the utility of settlement pattern work and Steward's call for ecological research; some even dismissed historical studies outright (28). The lead in studying ideology and its political uses was instead taken up by epigraphers, linguists, art historians, ethnologists, and a handful of archaeologists who risked the wrath of their more doctrinaire processualist colleagues by daring to suggest that ideas had a primary role in the evolution of Maya civilization. Today, this is one of the most dynamic and productive areas of research in the field.

One of the more interesting pendulum swings in the study of the ancient Maya is that the original model of the star-gazing calendar-priests is making a strong comeback, although it is still challenged and belittled by materialists to this day. But there is now a broader anthropological perspective on the role and significance of ideology (62, 82, 119, 122), a better grasp of the underlying cosmology (21, 67, 123, 201, 202, 253, 254, 280, 281), phonetic and other irrefutable translations of critical glyphs and concepts (32, 33, 123, 183), meticulous documentation of living Maya concepts of time and astrology (69, 282), and active participation by professional astronomers in the study of calendric and astronomical phenomena recorded in Maya codices, inscriptions, and buildings (17–19, 123, 183, 184).

A finding of tremendous anthropological significance is the discovery that the Classic Maya had a glyph for, and an all-pervasive concept of, spiritual co-essences (159; see also 63:256). Houston & Stuart (159) note that the concept of animal spirit companions had been documented for the Mexica at the time of the Spanish conquest and among modern-day cultures of Mesoamerica, but that among the Maya, a co-essence could assume virtually any form and was an integral part of the person in whose honor the text was written. This key decipherment shows an underlying role for shamanism in Maya culture, and Classic Maya kingship, which is now being explored in depth (122, 123).

Another significant contribution to anthropology is Demarest's model for ideology and statecraft, based on analogy with the galactic polities or theater states of Southeast Asia. Demarest sees religious ideology as the main focus of power for the Maya kings of the Classic period. Given Sabloff's (240) view that the apogee of Maya civilization lasted from 300 B.C. to A.D. 1250, Demarest's model could apply to earlier and later periods as well. The Petexbatuacn Project has provided archaeological data in support of the thesis that control over land, labor, and produce was weakly developed among the lowland Maya kingdoms, and that the ruler's chief source of power was his control over nonsubsistence elite goods and, especially, ritual, public displays of his charismatic leadership and religious authority. These data support Farriss' findings (98) for the Colonial Maya, as well as studies of trade in the Maya area. Besides being firmly grounded in comparative anthropology, this elegant model accounts for the interrelated rises and falls of rival kingdoms. It also shows the value of documenting and analyzing historical records (which clarify who was in alliance against whom, when), and why the study of religious and political ideology is vitally important for model-building and analysis of the cultural evolution of civilization in the Maya world.

Many archaeologists worry that with the growing emphasis on segmentary lineages and theater states, the pendulum is swinging too far back in the direction of the old model of Maya civilization: theocratic elites with no economic or coercive powers drawing corn-farming peasants to their centers for ceremonies that highlighted astrological knowledge and the dispatching of captives taken in occasional raids. Indeed, even the term ceremonial center is making a comeback. But a shift to a theater states or dynamic model does not imply that we are merely reverting to the schema used decades ago. The truly amazing advances seen during the last three decades in the realms reviewed here are not going to be dispensed with. The greatest strength of current studies of Maya civilization rests precisely in the fact that all of these realms and many more are under intense scrutiny and subject to lively debate by dedicated scholars, and that the lifeways and concerns of all segments of the ancient, colonial, and modern Maya people are being illuminated as a result.

PROSPECTS FOR THE FUTURE

Obviously, Maya studies are stronger than ever, with a greater time depth and anthropological breadth than even an optimist like Willey (317) could have hoped for, only a decade and a half ago. The prospects for multidisciplinary studies of Maya civilization are better than ever, given our increasing theoretical, methodological, and technological sophistication, and our burgeoning data base. In Willey's words, "there is a progression in this coordination of data that is almost geometric" (personal communication). Particularly encouraging is the manner in which the ethnohistoric, ethnographic, and ethnoarchaeological materials are enlightening our vistas of modern, colonial, and ancient Maya cultural ecology, economic structures, household organization, settlement and land-use patterns, power relations, religion, myth, and ritual. Indeed, the need is ever greater for archaeologists and ethnologists to engage in active exchange, so that both can proceed on a stronger footing.

I think the greatest need for change in the anthropological study of Maya civilization is in the ethical, rather than the theoretical realm. At this point, Maya studies should be pursued from an enlightened anthropological perspective, dedicated above all to the conservation of the human, cultural, and biotic resources of the Maya world. Rather than just talking to each other, Maya archaeologists should emulate the participant observer example provided by our ethnographer colleagues. All of us should be talking with, and listening to, the people in the Maya world: fellow researchers, educators, students, conservation specialists, leaders, and just plain folk (278, 310:92). Researchers interested in making a contribution to fieldwork in the Maya area should cease to think of what they do as merely an intellectual exercise and start to regard it as a way of contributing to the preservation of a priceless cultural and biological legacy. Archaeologists interested in stopping the wanton destruction caused by the looting of archaeological sites should view this not simply as a way of saving the archaeological remains for scientific purposes, but more importantly as a way of securing the cultural heritage of the Maya people for the future.

With the signing of the Declaration of Copán in May 1993, the governments of the five countries with Maya archaeological sites have committed themselves to ecological conservation and cultural resource management in their plans for the economic development of the Mundo Maya. This is a significant, positive step in the right direction, but scholars need to be sure that the terms of this historic accord are respected in all five nations, and they must engage themselves, and the governments of those countries, in an active dialogue with the Maya people who will take their civilization into the future.

After the Crusades, Western civilization flowered during the Rennaissance, aided by archaeological, historical, and religious studies. Could it be that with the end of the Colonial, Independent, and Cold War periods—together forming the Dark Ages of the Maya world—Maya civilization will now undergo a similar rebirth, aided by the same kinds of studies? Or do recent events in the highlands of Chiapas presage continuing cycles of ethnic conflict, with significant roles played by foreign peoples and ideologies, as so often chronicled/prophesied in Maya history, myth, and ritual? The ancient Maya prophesied that at the time of the completion of the 13th *baktun* or "Great Cycle" of their Long Count calendar (falling in our year A.D. 2012), this world would come to an end, and another would presumably take its place. Perhaps by then we will have an answer to these questions.

Literature Cited

1. Adams REW, ed. 1977. *The Origins of Maya Civilization.* Albuquerque: Univ. N. Mex. Press
2. Adams REW. 1983. Ancient land use and culture history in the Pasión River region. See Ref. 299a, pp. 319–36
3. Adams REW, Brown WE Jr, Culbert TP. 1981. Radar mapping, archaeology, and ancient Maya land use. *Science* 213:1457–63
4. Adams RM, Nissen HJ. 1972. *The Uruk Countryside.* Chicago: Univ. Chicago Press
5. Agurcia R, Fash WL. 1989. A royal Maya tomb discovered. *Natl. Geogr.* 176(4):480–87
6. ALMG (Academia de las Lenguas Mayas de Guatemala). *Lenguas mayas de Guatemala: documento de referencia para la pronunicación de los nuevos alfabetos oficiales.* Guatemala City: Inst. Indigenista Nacional
7. Andrews AP. 1983. *Ancient Maya Salt Production and Trade.* Tucson: Univ. Ariz. Press
8. Andrews AP. 1990. The fall of Chichen Itza: a preliminary hypothesis. *Latin Am. Antiq.* 1(3):258–67
9. Andrews AP. 1993. Late Postclassic lowland Maya archaeology. *J. World Prehist.* 7(1):35–69
10. Andrews AP, Gallareta Negrón T, Robles Castellanos F, Cobos Palma R, Cervera Rivero P. 1988. Isla Cerritos: an Itzá trading port on the north coast of Yucatán, Mexico. *Natl. Geogr. Res* 4:196–207
11. Andrews EW IV, Andrews EW V. 1980. *Excavations at Dzibilchaltucan, Yucatán, Mexico.* Publ. No. 48. New Orleans: Middle Am. Res. Inst., Tulane Univ.
12. Andrews EW V, Fash BW. 1992. Continuity and change in a royal Maya residential complex at Copan. *Ancient Mesoamerica* 3(1):63–88
13. Annis S. 1987. *God and Production in a Guatemalan Town.* Austin: Univ. Texas Press
14. Ashmore W, ed. 1981. *Lowland Maya Settlement Patterns.* Albuquerque: Univ. N. Mex. Press
15. Ashmore W. 1984. Quiriguá archaeology and history revisited. *J. Field Arch.* 11:365–86
16. Ashmore W. 1990. Ode to a dragline: demographic reconstructions at Quiriguá, Guatemala. See Ref. 79, pp. 63–82
17. Aveni AF. 1980. *Skywatchers of Ancient Mexico.* Austin: Univ. Texas Press
18. Aveni AF. 1991. *World Archaeoastronomy.* Cambridge: Cambridge Univ. Press
19. Aveni AF. 1992. *The Sky in Maya Literature.* New York: Oxford Univ. Press
20. Ball JW, Andrews EW V. 1978. *Preclassic Architecture at Becan, Campeche, Mexico.* Occas. Pap. No. 3. New Orleans: Middle Am. Res. Inst., Tulane Univ.
21. Barrera Vásquez A. 1980. *Diccionario Cordemex: Maya-Español, Español-Maya.* Mérida, Yucatán, Mexico: Cordemex
22. Bassie-Sweet K. 1991. *From the Mouth of the Dark Cave.* Norman: Univ. Okla. Press
23. Baudez CF, ed. 1983. *Introducción a la arqueología de Copán,* Vols. 1–3. Tegucigalpa: Secr. Estado Despacho Cultura Turismo
24. Baudez CF, Mathews P. 1979. Capture and sacrifice at Palenque. In *Tercera Mesa Redonda de Palenque,* ed. MG Robertson, DC Jeffers, pp. 31–40. Palenque/Monterey, CA: Precolumbian Art Res./Herald Printers
25. Berlin HB. 1958. El glifo "emblema" en las inscripciones Mayas. *J. Soc. Américanistes* (NS) 47:111–19
26. Berlin HB. 1959. Glifos nominales in el scarcófago de Palenque. *Humanidades* 2(10):1–8. Guatemala: Univ. San Carlos
27. Berlin HB. 1963. The Palenque Triad. *J. Soc. Américanistes* 53:91–99
28. Binford LR. 1968. Some comments on historical versus processual archaeology. *Southwest. J. Anthropol.* 24(3):267–75
29. Bishop RL, Rands RL. 1982. Maya fine paste ceramics: a compositional perspective. In *Excavations at Seibal: Analyses of Fine Past Ceramics,* ed. JA Sabloff. Mem-oirs Peabody Mus. Archaeol. Ethnol., Vol. 15(2)
30. Brasseur de Bourbourg CE. 1864. *Relation des choses de Yucatán.* Paris
31. Bricker VR. 1981. *The Indian Christ, the Indian King: The Historical Substrate of Maya Myth and Ritual.* Austin: Univ. Texas Press
32. Bricker VR. 1986. *A Grammar of Mayan Hieroglyphs.* New Orleans: Middle Am. Res. Inst., Tulane Univ.
33. Bricker VR. 1988. A phonetic glyph for zenith: reply to Closs. *Am. Antiq.* 53:394–400
34. Bricker VR. 1989. The calendric meaning of ritual among the Maya. In *Ethnographic Encounters in Southern Mesoamerica,* ed. VR Bricker, GH Gossen, pp. 231–50. Albany, NY: Inst. Mesoamerican Stud.
35. Brintnall DE. 1979. *Revolt Against the Dead: The Modernization of a Maya Community in the Highlands of Guatemala.* New York: Gordon & Breach
36. Bronson B. 1966. Roots and the subsistence of the ancient Maya. *Southwest. J. Anthropol.* 22:251–79
37. Bronson B. 1968. *Vacant Terrain.* Philadelphia: Univ. Mus., Univ. Penn.

200   FASH

38. Brown CH. 1991. Hieroglyphic literacy in ancient Mayaland: inferences from linguistic data. *Curr. Anthropol.* 32(4): 489–96

39. Brown CH, Witkowski SR. 1979. Aspects of the phonological history of Mayan-Zoquean. *Int. J. Am. Ling.* 45:34–47

40. Butzer K. 1982. *Hydraulic Agriculture and the Origins of Egyptian Civilization.* Chicago: Univ. Chicago Press

41. Campbell LR. 1976. The linguistic prehistory of the southern Mesoamerican periphery. *XIV Mesa Redonda, Soc. Mexicana Antropol.* 1:157–83

42. Campbell LR. 1977. *Quichean Linguistic Prehistory.* Univ. Calif. Publs. Linguistics, No. 8. Berkeley: Univ. Calif.

43. Campbell LR. 1984. The implications of Mayan historical linguistics for glyphic research. See Ref. 167, pp. 1–16

44. Campbell LR, Kaufman T. 1985. Mayan linguistics: where are we now. *Annu. Rev. Anthropol.* 14:187–98

45. Cancian F. 1965. *Economics and Prestige in a Maya Community.* Stanford, CA: Stanford Univ. Press

46. Cancian F. 1972. *Change and Uncertainty in a Peasant Economy: The Maya Corn Farmers of Zinacatán.* Stanford, CA: Stanford Univ. Press

47. Cancian F. 1992. *The Decline of Community in Zinacantán.* Stanford, CA: Stanford Univ. Press

48. Carmack RM. 1973. *Quichean Civilization: The Ethnohistoric, Ethnographic, and Archaeological Sources.* Berkeley/Los Angeles: Univ. Calif. Press

49. Carmack RM. 1981. *The Quiché Mayas of Utatlán.* Norman: Univ. Okla. Press

50. Carmack RM. 1988. *Harvest of Violence: The Maya Indians and the Guatemalan Crisis.* Norman: Univ. Okla. Press

51. Carmack RM, Fox J, Stewart R. 1975. *La formación del reino quiché: Seguacn la arqueología y etnología.* Inst. Nacl. Antropol. Hist. Guatemala, Publ. Espec. 7

52. Carneiro RL. 1970. A theory of the origin of the state. *Science* 169:733–38

53. Carr RE, Hazard JE. 1961. *Map of the Ruins of Tikal, El Petén, Guatemala.* Tikal Rep. 11. Philadelphia: Univ. Mus., Univ. Penn

54. Chang KC. 1976. *Early Chinese Civilization: Anthropological Perspectives.* Cambridge, MA: Harvard Univ. Press

55. Chase AF, Chase DZ. 1987. Investigations at the Classic Maya City of Caracol, Belize: 1985–1987. Monogr. No. 3. San Francisco: Pre-Columbian Art Res. Inst.

56. Chase AF, Rice PM. 1985. *The Lowland Maya Postclassic.* Austin: Univ. Texas Press

57. Chase DZ. 1990. The invisible Maya: population history and archaeology at Santa Rita Corozal, Belize. See Ref. 79, pp. 199–214

58. Chase DZ, Chase AZ. 1991. *Warfare and the classic Maya collapse: the perspective from Caracol, Belize.* Presented at Int. Congr. Americanists, 47th, New Orleans

59. Clendinnen I. 1987. *Ambivalent Conquests: Maya and Spaniard in Yucatán, 1517–1570.* Cambridge: Cambridge Univ. Press

60. Coe MD. 1957. The Kmer settlement pattern: a possible analogy with that of the Maya. *Am. Antiq.* 22:409–10

61. Coe MD. 1957. Cycle 7 monuments in Middle America: a reconsideration. *Am. Anthropol.* 59(4):597–611

62. Coe MD. 1981. Religion and the rise of Mesoamerican states. In *The Transition to Statehood in the New World,* ed. GD Jones, RR Kautz, pp. 155–79. Cambridge: Cambridge Univ. Press

63. Coe MD. 1992. *Breaking the Maya Code.* London: Thames & Hudson

64. Coe WR. 1965. Tikal, Guatemala, and emergent Maya civilization. *Science* 147:1401–19

65. Coe WR. 1990. *Excavations in the Great Plaza, North Terrace and North Acropolis of Tikal.* Tikal Report 14. Philadelphia: Univ. Mus., Univ. Penn.

66. Coggins CC. 1975. *Painting and drawing styles at Tikal: an historical and iconographic reconstruction.* PhD thesis. Harvard Univ.

67. Coggins CC. 1983. *The Stucco Decoration and Architectural Assemblage of Structure 1-sub, Dzibilchaltun, Yucatan, Mexico.* Publ. No. 49. New Orleans: Middle Am. Res. Inst., Tulane Univ.

68. Colby BJ, vandenBurghe PL. 1969. *Ixil Country: A Plural Society in Highland Guatemala.* Berkeley/Los Angeles: Univ. Calif. Press

69. Colby BN, Colby LM. 1981. *The Daykeeper: The Life and Discourse of an Ixil Diviner.* Cambridge: Harvard Univ. Press

70. Collier GA. 1975. *Fields of the Tzotzil: The Ecological Bases for Tradition in Highland Chiapas.* Austin: Univ. Texas Press

71. Collier J. 1973. *Law and Social Change in Zinacantan.* Stanford, CA: Stanford Univ. Press

72. Cowgill GL. 1979. Teotihuacan, internal militaristic competition, and the fall of the Classic Maya. In *Maya Archaeology and Ethnohistory,* ed. N Hammond, pp. 51–62. Austin: Univ. Texas Press

73. Craine ER, Reindorp RC. 1979. *The Codex Perez and the Book of Chilam Balam of Mani.* Norman: Univ. Okla. Press

74. Culbert TP. 1973. *The Classic Maya Collapse.* Albuquerque: Univ. N. Mex. Press

75. Culbert TP. 1977. Maya development and collapse: an economic perspective. In *So-*

cial Process in Maya Prehistory, ed. N Hammond, pp. 510–31. London: Academic
76. Culbert TP. 1990. Maya political history and elite interaction: a summary view. See Ref. 79, pp. 311–46
77. Culbert TP. 1991. Classic Maya Political History. Albuquerque: Univ. N. Mex. Press
78. Culbert TP, Magers P, Spencer M. 1978. Regional variability in Maya lowland agriculture. See Ref. 142, pp. 157–67
79. Culbert TP, Rice DS, eds. 1990. Precolumbian Population History in the Maya Lowlands. Albuquerque: Univ. N. Mex. Press
80. Dahlin BH, Foss JE, Chambers ME. 1980. Project Alcaches. See Ref. 192, pp. 138–69
81. Demarest AA. 1978. Interegional conflict and "situational ethics" in Classic Maya warfare. In Codex Wauchope, ed. M Giardino, M Edmonson, W Crearmer, pp. 101–11. New Orleans: Tulane Univ. Press
82. Demarest AA. 1992. Ideology in ancient Maya cultural evolution: the dynamics of galactic polities. In Ideology and Pre-Columbian Civilizations, ed. AA Demarest, GW Conrad, pp. 135–58. Santa Fe, NM: School Am. Res.
83. Demarest AA. 1993. The violent saga of a Maya kingdom. Natl. Geogr. 183(2):95–111
84. Demarest AA, Foias AE. 1993. Mesoamerican horizons and the cultural transformations of Maya civilization. In Latin American Horizons, ed. DS Rice, pp. 147–91. Washington, DC: Dumbarton Oaks
85. Demarest AA, Houston SD, eds. 1989. El Proyecto Arqueológico Regional Petexbatun, Informe Preliminar 1, Primera Temporada 1989. Nashville, TN: Dept. Anthropol., Vanderbilt Univ.
86. Demarest AA, Houston SD, eds. 1990. Proyecto Arqueológico Regional Petexbatun, Informe Preliminar 2, Segunda Temporada 1990. Nashville, TN: Dept. Anthropol., Vanderbilt Univ.
87. Demarest AA, Inomata T, Escobedo H, Palka J. 1991. Proyecto Arqueologico Regional Petexbatun, Informe Preliminar 3, Tercera Temporada 1991, Vols. 1–2. Nashville, TN: Dept. Anthropol., Vanderbilt Univ.
88. Demarest AA, Inomata T, Escobedo H. 1992. Proyecto Arqueológico Regional Petexbatun, Informe Preliminar 4, Cuarta Temporada 1992.
89. deMontmollin O. 1989. The Archaeology of Political Structure. Cambridge: Cambridge Univ. Press
90. Deleted in proof
91. Deleted in proof
92. Edmonson MS. 1971. The Book of Counsel: The Popol Vuh of the Quiché Maya of Guatemala. Publ. No. 35. New Orleans: Middle Am. Res. Inst., Tulane Univ.
93. Edmonson MS. 1976. Quiché-English Dic-

tionary. Publ. No. 30. New Orleans: Middle Am. Res. Inst., Tulane Univ.
94. Edmonson MS. 1982. The Ancient Future of the Itza: The Book of Chilam Balam of Tizimin. Austin: Univ. Texas Press
95. Edmonson MS. 1986. Heaven Born Mérida and its Destiny: The Book of Chilam Balam of Chumayel. Austin: Univ. Texas Press
96. England NC. 1983. A Grammar of Mam, A Mayan Language. Austin: Univ. Texas Press
97. Fabrega H, Silver DB. 1973. Illness and Shamanistic Curing in Zinacantan. Stanford, CA: Stanford Univ. Press
98. Farriss N. 1984. Maya Society under Colonial Rule: The Collective Enterprise of Survival. Princeton, NJ: Princeton Univ. Press
99. Fash BW. 1992. Late Classic architectural sculpture themes in Copan. Ancient Mesoamerica 3(1):89–104
100. Fash BW, Fash WL, Lane S, Larios R, Schele L, et al. 1992. Investigations of a Classic Maya council house at Copán, Honduras. J. Field Archaeol. 19(4):419–42
101. Fash WL. 1986. History and characteristics of settlement in the Copán Valley, and some comparisons with Quiriguá. In The Southeast Maya Periphery, ed. PA Urban, EM Schortman, pp. 72–93. Austin: Univ. Texas Press
102. Fash WL. 1991. Scribes, Warriors and Kings. London: Thames & Hudson
103. Fash WL, Sharer RJ. 1991. Sociopolitical developments and methodological issues at Copán, Honduras: a conjunctive perspective. Latin Am. Antiq. 2(2):166–87
104. Fash WL, Stuart DS. 1991. Dynastic history and cultural evolution at Copán, Honduras. See Ref. 76, pp. 147–79
105. Fash WL, Williamson RV, Larios CR, Palka J. 1992. The hieroglyphic stairway and its ancestors. Ancient Mesoamerica 3(1):105–16
106. Flannery KV. 1968. The Olmec and the Valley of Oaxaca: a model for inter-regional interaction in formative times. In Dumbarton Oaks Conference on the Olmec, ed. B Benson, pp. 79–110. Washington, DC: Dumbarton Oaks
107. Flannery KV. 1972. The cultural evolution of civilizations. Annu. Rev. Ecol. Syst. 3:339–46
108. Flannery KV. 1976. The Early Mesoamerican Village. New York: Academic
109. Flannery KV. 1982. Maya Subsistence. New York: Academic
110. Foias A, Bishop R, Hagstrum M, Verhagen I. 1991. Artifacts, chronolgy and exchange systems in the Petexbatun: a preliminary laboratory analysis. Presented at Int. Congr. Americanists, 47th, New Orleans
111. Folan WJ, Kintz ER, Fletcher LA. 1983.

Cobá, a Classic Maya Metropolis. New York: Academic

112. Folan WJ, May Hau J. 1984. Proyecto Calakmul, 1982–1984: El Mapa. *Información* 8:1–14. Campeche: Cent. Estud. Hist. Soc., Univ. Autónoma Sudeste

113. Ford A. 1986. *Population Growth and Social Complexity.* Anthropol. Res. Pap. No. 35. Tempe: Ariz. State Univ

114. Fought JG. 1972. *Chorti (Mayan) Texts.* Philadelphia: Univ. Penn. Press

115. Fox JW. 1978. *Quiché Conquest.* Albuquerque: Univ. N. Mex. Press

116. Fox JW. 1987. *Maya Postclassic State Formation.* Cambridge: Cambridge Univ. Press

117. Fox JW. 1989. On the rise and fall of Tuláns and Maya segmentary states. *Am. Anthropol.* 91:656–81

118. Freidel DA. 1979. Culture areas and interaction spheres: contrasting approaches to the emergence of civilization in the Maya lowlands. *Am. Antiq.* 44:36–54

119. Freidel DA. 1981. Civilization as a state of mind: the cultural evolution of the lowland Maya. In *The Transition to Statehood in the New World,* ed. GD Jones, RR Kautz, pp. 188–227. Cambridge: Cambridge Univ. Press

120. Freidel DA. 1986. The monumental architecture. In *Archaeology at Cerros, Belize, Central America.* Vol. 1: *An Interim Report,* ed. RA Robertson, DA Freidel, pp. 1–22. Dallas: S. Methodist Univ. Press

121. Freidel DA. 1986. Maya warfare: an example of peer polity interaction. See Ref. 228, pp. 93–108

122. Freidel DA. 1992. The trees of life: *Ahau* as idea and artifact in lowland Classic Maya civilization. In *Ideology and Pre-Columbian Civilizations,* ed. AA Demarest, GW Conrad, pp. 115–34. Santa Fe, NM: School Am. Res.

123. Freidel DA, Schele L, Parker J. 1993. *Maya Cosmos.* New York: Morrow

124. Fry RE. 1979. The economics of pottery at Tikal, Guatemala: Models of Exchange for Serving Vessels. *Am. Antiq.* 44:494–512

125. Fry RE. 1980. *Models and Methods in Regional Exchange.* Pap. Soc. Am. Archaeol. No. 1. Washington, DC: Soc. Am. Archaeol.

126. Garza S, Kurjack EB. 1980. *Atlas arqueológico del estado de Yucatán,* Vol. 1–2. México, D.F.: Inst. Nacl. Antropol. Hist.

127. Goodman JT. 1905. Maya dates. *Am. Anthropol.* 7:642–47

128. Gossen GH. 1974. *Chamulas in the World of the Sun.* Cambridge, MA: Harvard Univ. Press

129. Gossen GH, ed. 1986. *Symbol and Meaning Beyond the Closed Corporate Community.* Albany, NY: Inst. Mesoamerican Stud.

130. Graham I. 1967. *Archaeological Researches in El Petén, Guatemala.* Publ. No. 33. New Orleans: Middle Am. Res. Inst., Tulane Univ.

131. Graham I. 1975. Introduction to the Corpus. In *Corpus of Maya Hieroglyphic Inscriptions,* Vol. 1. Cambridge, MA: Peabody Mus. Press

132. Graham JA. 1977. Discoveries at Abaj Takalik, Guatemala. *Archaeology* 30:196–97

133. Grove DC. 1989. Olmec: what's in a name? In *Regional Perspectives on the Olmec,* ed. DC Grove, RJ Sharer, pp. 8–16. Cambridge: Cambridge Univ. Press

134. Guiteras-Holmes C. 1961. *Perils of the Soul: The World View of a Tzotzil Indian.* New York: Free Press

135. Hammond N. 1972. Obsidian trade routes in the Mayan area. *Science* 178:1092–93

136. Hammond N. 1973. Models for Maya trade. In *The Explanation of Culture Change,* ed. C Renfrew, pp. 601–7. Pittsburgh: Pittsburgh Univ. Press

137. Hammond N. 1975. *Lubaantun: A Classic Maya Realm.* Monogr. No. 2. Cambridge, MA: Peabody Mus. Archaeol. Ethnol.

138. Hammond N. 1991. *Cuello, An Early Maya Community in Belize.* Cambridge: Cambridge Univ. Press

139. Hammond N. 1991. Introduction. See Ref. 76, pp. 1–18

140. Hammond N. 1991. Inside the black box: defining Maya polity. See Ref. 76, pp. 253–84

141. Hansen R. 1991. On the road to Nakbe. *Nat. Hist.* May:9–14

142. Harrison PD, Turner BL II. 1978. *Pre-Hispanic Maya Agriculture.* Albuquerque: Univ. N. Mex. Press

143. Hatch MP. 1987. La importancia de la cerámica utilitaria en la arqueología, con observaciones sobre la prehistoria de Guatemala. *Anal. Acad. Geogr. Hist. Guatemala* 61:151–84

144. Haviland WA. 1968. Ancient lowland Maya social organization. In *Archaeological Studies in Middle America.* Publ. No. 26. New Orleans: Middle Am. Res. Inst., Tulane Univ.

145. Haviland WA. 1970. Tikal, Guatemala, and Mesoamerican urbanism. *World Archaeol.* 2:186–98

146. Haviland W. 1991. *Star Wars at Tikal, or did Caracol do what the glyphs say they did?* Presented at Annu. Meet. Am. Anthropol. Assoc., 90th, Chicago

147. Hayden B. 1987. *Lithic Studies Among the Contemporary Highland Maya.* Tucson: Univ. Ariz. Press

148. Hayden B, Cannon A. 1984. *The Structure of Material Systems: Ethnoarchaeology in the Maya Highlands.* Pap. No. 3. Washington, DC: Soc. Am. Archaeol.

149. Hester TR, Shafer HJ. 1994. The ancient

PERSPECTIVES ON MAYA CIVILIZATION   203

Maya craft community at Colha, Belize, and its external relationships. In *Village Communities in Early Complex Societies,* ed. S Falconer, G Falconer. Washington, DC: Smithsonian Inst. Press. In press
150. Hill RM II. 1992. *Colonial Cakchiquels: Highland Maya Adaptation to Spanish Rule, 1600–1700.* Fort Worth, TX: Harcourt Brace Jovanovitch
151. Hill RM II, Monaghan J. 1987. *Continuities in Highland Maya Social Organization: Ethnohistory in Sacapulas, Guatemala.* Philadelphia: Univ. Penn. Press
152. Hinshaw RE. 1975. *Panajachel: A Guatemalan Town in Thirty Year Perspective.* Pittsburgh: Pittsburgh Univ. Press
153. Deleted in proof
154. Houston SD. 1987. Notes on Caracol epigraphy and its significance. See Ref. 55, Appendix II, pp. 85–100
155. Houston SD. 1989. Archaeology and Maya writing. *J. World Prehist.* 3(1):1–32
156. Houston SD. 1992. Telling about the Maya. *Science* 256:1062–63
157. Houston SD. 1993. *Hieroglyphs and History at Dos Pilas.* Austin: Univ. Texas Press
158. Houston SD, Mathews P. 1985. *The Dynastic Sequence of Dos Pilas, Guatemala.* Monogr. No. 1. San Francisco: Pre-Columbian Art Res. Inst.
159. Houston SD, Stuart DS. 1989. *The Way Glyph: Evidence for "Co-essences" among the Classic Maya.* Res. Rep. on Maya Writing, No. 30. Washington, DC: Cent. Maya Res.
160. Houston SD, Stuart DS, Taube KA. 1989. Folk classification of Maya pottery. *Am. Anthropol.* 91:720–26
161. Hunt E. 1977. *The Transformation of the Hummingbird: Cultural Roots of a Zinacatecan Mythical Poem.* Ithaca, NY: Cornell Univ. Press
162. Inomata T. 1991. *Excavations and survey of the Petexbatun fortress capital of Aguateca.* Presented at Int. Congr. Americanists, 47th, New Orleans
163. Johnston K. 1990. *Invisible structures in the Petexbatun.* Paper presented at Annu. Meet. Soc. Am. Arch.
164. Jones GD. 1987. *Anthropology and History in Yucatán.* Austin: Univ. Texas Press
165. Jones GD. 1989. *Maya Resistance to Spanish Rule: Time and History on a Colonial Frontier.* Albuquerque: Univ. N. Mex. Press
166. Josserand K. 1990. The narrative structure of hieroglyphic texts at Palenque. In *Sixth Palenque Round Table, 1986,* ed. MG Robertson. Norman: Univ. Okla. Press
167. Justeson JS, Campbell L, eds. 1984. *Phoneticism in Mayan Hieroglyphic Writing.* Publ. No. 9. Albany, NY: Inst. Mesoamerican Stud.

168. Justeson JS, Kaufman T. 1993. A decipherment of Epi-Olmec hieroglyphic writing. *Science* 259:1703–10
169. Justeson JS, Norman WM, Campbell L, Kaufman TS. 1985. *The Foreign Impact on Lowland Mayan Language and Script.* Publ. No. 53. New Orleans: Middle Am. Res. Inst., Tulane Univ.
170. Kaufman TS. 1976. Archaeological and linguistic correlations in Mayaland and associated areas of Mesoamerica. *World Archaeol.* 8:101–18
171. Kaufman TS, Norman WN. 1984. An outline of Proto-Cholan phonology and morphology. See Ref. 167, 77–166
172. Killion T, Triadan D, Van Tuerenhout, Chatham R. 1991. *Broken heartland of cities: intersite settlement survey in the Petexbatun region.* Presented at Int. Congr. Americanists, 47th, New Orleans
173. Kurjack EB. 1974. *Prehistoric Lowland Maya Community and Social Organization: A Case Study at Dzibilchaltuacn, Yucatán, Mexico.* Publ. No. 38. New Orleans: Middle Am. Res. Inst., Tulane Univ.
174. Kurjack EB. 1979. *Introduction to the Map of the Ruins of Dzibilchaltuacn, Yucatán, Mexico.* Publ. No. 47. New Orleans: Middle Am. Res. Inst., Tulane Univ.
175. Kurjack EB, Andrews EW V. 1976. Early boundary maintenance in northwest Yucatán, Mexico. *Am. Antiq.* 41:318–25
176. LaPorte JP, Fialko V. 1990. New perspectives on old problems: dynastic references for the Early Classic at Tikal. In *Vision and Revision in Maya Studies,* ed. F Clancy, P Harrison, pp. 33–66. Albuquerque: Univ. N. Mex. Press
177. Laughlin RB. 1975. *The Great Tzotzil Dictionary of San Lorenzo Zinacantan.* Smithsonian Contributions to Anthropol. 19
178. Laughlin RB (with JB Haviland). 1988. *The Great Tzotzil Dictionary of Santo Domingo Zinacantán, with Grammatical Analysis and Historical Commentary.* Smithsonian Contributions to Anthropol. 31
179. Lentz D, Emery K. 1991. *Prehistoric subsistence systems in the Petexbatun region: palaeobotanical and zooarchaeological data.* Presented at Int. Congr. Americanists, 47th, New Orleans
180. Leventhal RM. 1990. Southern Belize: an ancient Maya region. In *Vision and Revision in Maya Studies,* ed. F Clancy, P Harrison, pp. 125–42. Albuquerque: Univ. N. Mex. Press
181. Leventhal RM, Ashmore W, LeCount L, Hetrick V, Jamison T. 1992. *Xunantunich archaeological project.* Research paper presented at Annu. Meet. Am. Anthropol. Assoc., 91st, San Francisco
182. Lincoln CE. 1986. The chronology of

Chichen Itzá: a review of the literature. See Ref. 242, pp. 141–96

183. Lounsbury FG. 1978. Maya numeration, computation, and calendric astronomy. In *Dictionary of Scientific Biography*, ed. CC Gillispie, 15(Suppl. 1):759–818

184. Lounsbury FG. 1991. A Palenque king and the planet Jupiter. See Ref. 18, pp. 246–59

185. Manz B. 1988. *Refugees of a Hidden War: The Aftermath of Counterinsurgency in Guatemala*. Albany: State Univ. NY Press

186. Marcus J. 1976. *Emblem and State in the Classic Maya Lowlands*. Washington, DC: Dumbarton Oaks

187. Marcus J. 1983. Lowland Maya archaeology at the crossroads. *Am. Antiq.* 48:454–88

188. Marcus J. 1992. *Mesoamerican Writing Systems*. Princeton, NJ: Princeton Univ. Press

189. Marcus J. 1992. Dynamic cycles of Mesoamerican states. *Natl. Geogr. Res.* 8(4): 392–411

190. Marcus J. 1993. Ancient Maya political organization. In *Lowland Maya Civilization in the Eighth Century A.D.*, ed. JA Sabloff, JS Henderson, pp. 111–83. Washington, DC: Dumbarton Oaks

191. Matheny RT. 1976. Maya lowland hydraulic systems. *Science* 193:639–46

192. Matheny RT. 1980. *El Mirador, Peten, Guatemala: An Interim Report*. Pap. New World Archaeol. Found. No. 45. Provo, UT: New World Archaeol. Found.

193. Matheny RT. 1986. Investigations at El Mirador, Petén, Guatemala. *Natl. Geogr. Res.* 2:332–53

194. Matheny RT. 1987. Early states in the Maya lowlands during the late Preclassic period: Edzna and El Mirador. In *The Maya State*, ed. B Benson, pp. 1–44. Denver, CO: Rocky Mtn. Inst. Precolumbian Stud.

195. Matheny RT, Gurr DL, Forsyth DW, Hauck FR. 1983. *Investigations at Edzná, Campeche, Mexico*. Vol. 1, Part 1: *The Hydraulic System*. Pap. New World Archaeol. Found. No. 46

196. Mathews P. 1985. Maya early classic monuments and inscriptions. In *A Consideration of the Early Classic Period in the Maya Lowlands*, ed. GR Willey, P Mathews, pp. 5–54. Albany, NY: Inst. Mesoamerican Stud.

197. Mathews P. 1991. Classic Maya emblem glyphs. See Ref. 76, pp. 19–29

198. Maudslay AP. 1889–1902. *Biologia Centrali-Americana: Archaeology*. London: Porter & Dulau

199. McAnany PP. 1989. Economic foundations of prehistoric Maya society: paradigms and concepts. In *Res. Econ. Anthropol.* Suppl. 4: *Prehistoric Maya Economies of Belize*, ed. PA McAnany, BL Isaac, pp. 347–72. Greenwich: JAI

200. Menchuac R. 1984. *I, Rigoberta Menchuac, an Indian Woman in Guatemala*, ed. E Burgos-Debray. London: British Library

201. Miller AG. 1986. *Maya Rulers of Time*. Philadelphia: Univ. Mus., Univ. Penn.

202. Miller ME, Taube K. 1993. *Gods and Symbols of Ancient Mexico and the Maya*. London: Thames & Hudson

203. Millon R. 1981. Teotihuacan: City, State, and Civilization. In *Supplement to the Handbook of Middle American Indians*. Vol. 1: *Archaeology*, ed. JA Sabloff, pp. 198–243. Austin: Univ. Texas Press

204. Montejo V. 1991. *The Bird Who Cleans the World and Other Maya Fables*. Willimantic, CT: Curbstone

205. Morris WF Jr. 1987. *Living Maya*. New York: Abrams

206. Nations JD, Nigh RB. 1980. The evolutionary potential of Lacandon Maya sustained-yield tropical forest agriculture. *J. Anthropol. Res.* 83:28–56

207. Netting RM. 1977. Maya subsistence: mythologies, analogies, possibilities. See Ref. 1, pp. 299–333

208. Otzoy I, Sam Colop LE. 1988. *Mayan ethnicity and modernization*. Presented at Annu. Meet. Am. Anthropol. Assoc., 67th, Phoenix

209. Palka J, Escobedo H, Chinchilla O. 1991. *Settlement and architecture at the Petexbatun capital center of Dos Pilas*. Presented at Int. Congr. Americanists, 47th, New Orleans

210. Pendergast DM. 1981. Lamanai, Belize: summary of excavation results 1974–1980. *J. Field Archaeol.* 8:29–53

211. Pendergast DM. 1988. *Lamanai Stela 9: The Archaeological Context*. Res. Rep. Ancient Maya Writing, No. 20. Washington, DC: Cent. Maya Res.

212. Pendergast DM. 1986. Stability through change: Lamanai, Belize, from the ninth to the seventeenth century. See Ref. 242, pp. 223–49

213. Pohl M. 1985. *The Economic Basis for Maya Civilization*. Pap. Peabody Mus. Archaeol. Ethnol., No. 77. Cambridge, MA

214. Pohl MD, ed. 1990. *Ancient Maya Wetland Agriculture: Excavations on Albion Island, Northern Belize*. Boulder, CO: Westview

215. Pope KA, Dahlin B. 1989. Ancient Maya wetland agriculture: new insights from ecological and remote sensing research. *J. Field Archaeol.* 16:87–106

216. Proskouriakoff T. 1960. Historical implications of a pattern of dates at Piedras Negras. *Am. Antiq.* 25:454–75

217. Proskouriakoff T. 1961. The lords of the Maya realm. *Expedition* 4(1):14–21

218. Proskouriakoff T. 1963. Historical data in the inscriptions of Yaxchilan, part I. *Estud. Cult. Maya* 3:169–67

219. Proskouriakoff T. 1964. Historical data in

the inscriptions of Yaxchilan, part II. *Estud. Cult. Maya* 4:177–201
220. Proskouriakoff T. 1993. *Maya History.* Austin: Univ. Texas Press
221. Puleston DE. 1968. *Brosimum alicastrum as a subsistence alternative for the classic Maya of the central south lowlands.* MA thesis. Univ. Penn.
222. Puleston DE. 1977. The art and archaeology of hydraulic agriculture in the Maya lowlands. In *Social Process in Maya Prehistory,* ed. N Hammond, pp. 449–69. London: Academic
223. Puleston DE. 1983. *The Settlement Survey of Tikal.* Tikal Rep. No. 13. Philadelphia: Univ. Mus., Univ. Penn.
224. Puleston DE, Callender DW. 1967. Defensive earthworks at Tikal. *Expedition* 9:40–48
225. Rathje WL. 1971. The origin and development of Classic Maya civilization. *Am. Antiq.* 36:275–85
226. Reina RE. 1966. *The Law of the Saints: A Pokomam Pueblo and its Community Culture.* New York: Bobbs-Merrill
227. Reina RE, Hill R. 1973. *The Traditional Pottery of Highland Guatemala.* Austin: Univ. Texas Press
228. Renfrew C, Cherry JF. 1986. *Peer Polity Interaction and the Development of Sociopolitical Change.* Cambridge: Cambridge Univ. Press
229. Rice DS, Rice PM. 1981. Muralla de Leon: a lowland Maya fortification. *J. Field Archaeol.* 8:271–88
230. Rice DS, Rice PM. 1984. Lessons from the Maya. *Latin Am. Res. Rev.* 19:7–34
231. Rice PM. 1987. Economic change in the lowland Maya Late Classic period. In *Specialisation, Exchange, and Complex Societies,* ed. E Brumfiel, T Earle, pp. 128–45. Cambridge: Cambridge Univ. Press
232. Rice PM, Michel HV, Asaro F, Stross F. 1985. Provenience analysis of obsidians from the central Peten lakes region, Guatemala. *Am. Antiq.* 50(3):591–604
233. Ringle WM, Andrews EW V. 1988. Formative residences at Komchen, Yucatán, Mexico. See Ref. 313, pp. 171–97
234. Ringle WM, Bey GJ, Hanson CA. 1991. *Ek Balam and the Dilemma of Kingship.* Presented at Annu. Meet. Soc. Am. Archaeol., 90th, Chicago
235. Roys RL. 1957. *The Political Geography of the Yucatán Maya.* Publ. No. 548. Washington, DC: Carnegie Inst. Washington
236. Rue DJ. 1987. Early agriculture and Early Postclassic Maya occupation in western Honduras. *Nature* 326:6110
237. Rue DJ, Dunning N, Beach T, Secaira E, Beekman J. 1991. *Ecology and settlement in the Petexbatun: a preliminary assessment.* Presented at Int. Congr. Americanists, 47th, New Orleans

238. Ruthernberg H. 1981. *Farming Systems in the Tropics.* Oxford: Oxford Univ. Press
239. Sabloff JA. 1983. Classic Maya settlement studies: past problems, future prospects. See Ref. 299a, pp. 413–22
240. Sabloff JA. 1985. Ancient Maya civilization: an overview. In *Maya, Treasures of an Ancient Civilization,* ed. C Gallenkamp, RE Johnson, pp. 34–46. New York/Albuquerque: Abrams/Albuquerque Mus.
241. Sabloff JA. 1986. Interaction among Classic Maya polities: a preliminary examination. See Ref. 228, pp. 109–16
242. Sabloff JA, Andrews EW V. 1986. *Late Lowland Maya Civilization: Classic to Postclassic.* Albuquerque: Univ. N. Mex. Press
243. Sabloff JA, Tourtellot G, Fahmel Beyer B, McAnany PA, Christensen D, et al. 1985. *Settlement and Community Patterns at Sayil, Yucatan, Mexico: The 1984 Season.* Latin Am. Inst. Res. Pap. Ser., No. 17. Albuquerque: Univ. New Mexico
244. Sanders WT. 1977. Environmental heterogeneity and the evolution of lowland Maya civilization. See Ref. 1, pp. 287–97
245. Sanders WT. 1981. Classic Maya settlement patterns and ethnographic analogy. See Ref. 14, pp. 351–69
246. Sanders WT. 1986. Introducción. In *Excavaciones en el área urbana de Copán,* Vol. 1, ed. WT Sanders, pp. 11–25. Tegucigalpa: Inst. Hondurenaco Antropol. Hist.
247. Sanders WT. 1989. Household, lineage, and state in eighth-century Copan, Honduras. See Ref. 79, pp. 89–105
248. Sanders WT, Webster DL. 1988. The Mesoamerican urban tradition. *Am. Anthropol.* 90:521–46
249. Sanders WT, Webster DL, Evans S. 1992. *Out of the Past.* New York: Holt Rinehart
250. Santley RS. 1990. Demographic archaeology in the Maya lowlands. See Ref. 79, pp. 325–44
251. Saul FP. 1973. Disease in the Maya area: the pre-Columbian evidence. See Ref. 74, pp. 301–24
252. Schele L. 1990. The demotion of Chac-Zutz': lineage compounds and subsidiary lords at Palenque. In *Sixth Palenque Round Table, 1986,* ed. MG Robertson, pp. 48–67. Norman: Univ. Okla. Press
253. Schele L, Freidel DA. 1991. *A Forest of Kings.* New York: Morrow
254. Schele L, Miller ME. *The Blood of Kings.* Fort Worth, TX: Kimbell Art Mus.
255. Shafer HJ, Hester TR. 1983. Ancient Maya Chert workshops in Northern Belize, Central America. *Am. Antiq.* 48:519–43
256. Sharer RJ. 1978. Archaeology and history at Quiriguá. *J. Field Archaeol.* 5:51–70
257. Sharer RJ. 1982. Did the Maya collapse? A New World perspective on the demise of Harappan civilization. In *Harappan Civili-*

zation: A Contemporary Perspective, ed. GA Possehl, pp. 327–54. Oxford/IBH: Am. Inst. Indian Stud.

258. Sharer RJ. 1989. The Olmec and the southeast periphery of Mesoamerica. In *Regional Perspectives on the Olmec*, ed. RJ Sharer, DC Grove, pp. 247–74. Cambridge: Cambridge Univ. Press

259. Sharer RJ. 1990. *Quiriguá: A Classic Maya Center and its Sculptures*. Durham, NC: Carolina Acad. Press

260. Sharer RJ, Miller JC, Traxler LP. 1992. Evolution of Classic period architecture in the eastern acropolis, Copán. *Ancient Mesoamerica* 3(1):145–60

261. Sharer RJ, Sedat DW. 1973. Monument 1, El Portón, Guatemala, and the development of Maya calendrical and writing systems. In *Contributions of the University of California Archaeological Research Facility*, No. 18, pp. 177–94. Berkeley: Univ. Calif. Press

262. Sharer RJ, Sedat DW. 1987. *Archaeological Investigations in the Northern Maya Highlands, Guatemala*. Philadelphia: Univ. Mus., Univ. Penn.

263. Shimkin DB. 1973. Models for the collapse: some ecological and cultural-historical considerations. See Ref. 74, pp. 269–99

264. Siemens AH, Puleston DE. 1972. Ridged fields and associated features in southern Campeche: new perspectives on the lowland Maya. *Am. Antiq.* 37:228–39

265. Smith CA. 1990. *Guatemalan Indians and the State, 1540–1988*. Austin: Univ. Texas Press

266. Smyth MP. 1991. *Modern Maya Storage Behavior*. Mem. Latin Am. Archaeol., No. 3. Pittsburgh: Univ. Pitt.

267. Stark BL, Voorhies B. 1978. *Prehistoric Coastal Adaptations: The Economy and Ecology of Maritime Middle America*. New York: Academic

267a. Steward JH. 1955. *Theory of Culture Change*. Urbana: Univ. Ill. Press

268. Storey R. 1992. The children of Copan: issues in paleopathology and paleodemography. *Ancient Mesoamerica* 3(1):161–68

269. Stuart DS. 1992. Hieroglyphs and archaeology at Copan. *Ancient Mesoamerica* 3(1):169–84

270. Stuart DS. 1993. Historical inscriptions and the Maya collapse. In *Lowland Maya Civilization in the Eighth Century A.D.*, ed. JA Sabloff, JS Henderson, pp. 321–54. Washington, DC: Dumbarton Oaks

271. Stuart DS. 1993. *Deciphering Maya Hieroglyphs*. Am. Inst. Archaeol. Lecture, Cambridge, MA

272. Deleted in proof

273. Stuart DS, Houston SD. 1994. *Classic Maya Place Names*. Washington, DC: Dumbarton Oaks

274. Stuart GE. 1981. Maya art treasures discovered in cave. *Natl. Geogr.* 160(2):220–35

275. Stuart GE. 1992. Quest for decipherment: a historical and biographical survey of Maya hieroglyphic investigation. In *New Theories on the Ancient Maya*, ed. EC Danien, RJ Sharer, pp. 1–63. Philadelphia: Univ. Mus., Univ. Penn.

277. Stuart GE, Scheffler JC, Kurjack EB, Cottier W. 1979. *Map of the Ruins of Dzibilchaltuacn, Yucatán, Mexico*. Publ. No. 47. New Orleans: Middle Am. Res. Inst., Tulane Univ.

276. Stuart GE. 1993. The carved stela from La Mojarra, Veracruz, Mexico. *Science* 259: 1700–1

278. Sullivan P. 1989. *Unfinished Conversations: Mayas and Foreigners Between Two Wars*. New York: Knopf

279. Tambiah SJ. 1977. The galactic polity: the structure of traditional kingdoms in southeast Asia. *Ann. NY Acad. Sci.* 293:69–97

280. Taube K. 1985. The Classic Maya maize god: a reappraisal. In *Fifth Palenque Round Table*, ed. MG Robertson, 7:171–81. San Francisco: Pre-Columbian Art Res. Inst.

281. Taube K. 1993. *Aztec and Maya Myths*. London/Austin: Br. Mus Press/Univ. Texas Press

282. Tedlock B. 1992. *Time and the Highland Maya*. Albuquerque: Univ. N. Mex. Press

283. Tedlock B. 1993. Mayans and Mayan studies from 2,000 B.C. to A.D. 1992. *Latin Am. Res. Rev.* Fall:153–73

284. Tedlock D. 1985. *Popol Vuh, the Mayan Book of the Dawn of Life*. New York: Simon & Schuster

285. Thomas PM. 1981. *Prehistoric Maya Settlement Patterns at Becán, Campeche, Mexico*. Publ. No. 45. New Orleans: Middle Am. Res. Inst., Tulane Univ.

286. Thompson JES. 1970. *Maya History and Religion*. Norman: Univ. Okla. Press

287. Tourtellot G III. 1988. *Excavations at Seibal: Peripheral Survey and Excavations*. Mem. Peabody Mus. Archaeol. Ethnol, No. 16. Cambridge, MA: Harvard Univ. Press

288. Tozzer AM. 1941. *Landa's Relación de las Cosas de Yucatán*. Pap. Peabody Mus. Am. Archaeol. Ethnol., Vol. 18. Cambridge, MA: Harvard Univ. Press

289. Turner BL II. 1974. Prehistoric intensive agriculture in the Mayan lowlands. *Science* 185:118–24

290. Turner BL II. 1978. Ancient agricultural land use in the central Maya lowlands. See Ref. 142, pp. 163–83

291. Turner BL II, Harrison PD. 1983. *Pulltrouser Swamp: Ancient Maya Habitat, Agriculture, and Settlement in Northern Belize*. Austin: Univ. Texas Press

292. Turner ES, Turner NI, Adams REW. 1981. Volumetric assessment, rank ordering,

and Maya civic centers. See Ref. 14, pp. 71–88

293. Valdez JA. 1990. Observaciones iconográficas sobre las figuras Preclásicas de cuerpo completo en el Area Maya. *Estudios* 2:23–49

294. Valdez JA. 1992. The beginnings of Preclassic Maya art and architecture. In *The Ancient Americas*, ed. RF Townsend, pp. 147–58. Chicago: Art Inst.

295. Valdez JA, Fahsen F. 1993. Gobernantes y gobernados: la secuencia dinástica de Uaxactuacn para el clásico Temprano. In *Sexto Simposio de Investigaciones Arqueológicas en Guatemala*, pp. 25–55. Guatemala: Ministerio de Cultura y Deportes

296. Valdez JA, Foias A, Inomata T, Escobedo H, Demarest AA. 1993. *Proyecto Arqueológico Regional Petexbatuacn, Informe Preliminar 5, Quinta Temporada 1993.*

297. Vogt EZ. 1969. *Zinacantan: A Maya Community in the Highlands of Chiapas.* Cambridge, MA: Harvard Univ. Press

298. Vogt EZ. 1976. *Tortillas for the Gods: A Symbolic Analysis of Zinacanteco Rituals.* Cambridge, MA: Harvard Univ. Press

299. Vogt EZ. 1983. Ancient and contemporary Maya settlement patterns: a new look from the Chiapas highlands. See Ref. 299a, pp. 89–114

299a. Vogt EZ, Leventhal RM, eds. 1983. *Prehistoric Settlement Pattern: Essays in Honor of Gordon R. Willey.* Albuquerque: Univ. N. Mex. Press

300. Watanabe JM. 1992. *Maya Saints and Souls in a Changing World.* Austin: Univ. Texas Press

301. Webster DL. 1976. *Defensive Earthworks at Becan, Campeche, Mexico.* Publ. No. 41. New Orleans: Middle Am. Res. Inst., Tulane Univ.

302. Webster DL. 1977. Warfare and the evolution of Maya civilization. See Ref. 1, pp. 335–72

303. Webster DL. 1978. Three walled sites of the northern Maya lowlands. *J. Field Archaeol.* 5(4):375–90

304. Webster DL. 1989. *The House of the Bacabs.* Washington, DC: Dumbarton Oaks Res. Libr. Coll.

305. Webster DL. 1993. The study of Maya warfare: what it tells us about the Maya and what it tells us about Maya archaeology. In *Lowland Maya Civilization in the Eighth Century A.D.*, ed. JA Sabloff, J. Henderson, pp. 415–44. Washington, DC: Dumbarton Oaks

306. Webster DL, Freter A. 1990. Settlement history and the Classic collapse at Copan: a redefined chrological perspective. *Latin Am. Antiq.* 1:66–85

307. Webster DL, Freter A. 1990. The demogra-

phy of Late Classic Copán. See Ref. 79, pp. 37–62

308. Wesson RG. 1978. *State Systems.* New York: Free Press

308a. White LA. 1959. *The Evolution of Culture.* New York: McGraw-Hill

309. Wilk RR. 1983. *The missing Maya.* Presented at Annu. Meet. Am. Anthropol. Assoc., 80th, Washington, DC

310. Wilk RR. 1987. The search for tradition in southern Belize. *América Indígena* 47:1: 77–95

311. Wilk RR. 1988. Maya household organization: evidence and analogies. See Ref. 313, pp. 135–51

312. Wilk RR. 1991. *Household Ecology: Economic Change and Domestic Life Among the Kekchi Maya in Belize.* Tucson: Univ. Ariz. Press

313. Wilk RR, Ashmore W, eds. 1988. *Household and Community in the Mesoamerican Past.* Albuquerque: Univ. N. Mex. Press

313a. Willey GR. 1953. *Prehistoric Settlement Patterns in the Viruac Valley, Peru.* Bull. No. 155. Washington, DC: Bureau Am. Ethnol.

314. Willey GR. 1962. The early great art styles and the rise of the pre-Columbian civilizations. *Am. Anthropol.* 64:1–14

315. Willey GR. 1973. *The Altar de Sacrificios Excavations: General Summary and Conclusions.* Pap. Peabody Mus. Am Archaeol. Ethnol. 64(3)

316. Willey GR. 1977. The rise of Maya civilization: a summary view. See Ref. 1, pp. 383–423

317. Willey GR. 1980. Towards an holistic view of ancient Maya civilization. *Man* (NS) 15:249–66

318. Willey GR, Bullard WR, Glass J, Gifford J. 1965. *Prehistoric Settlements in the Belize Valley.* Pap. Peabody Mus. Am. Archaeol. Ethnol., Vol. 54

319. Willey GR, Leventhal RM. 1979. Prehistoric settlements at Copán. In *Maya Archaeology and Ethnohistory*, ed. N Hammond, G Willey, pp. 75–102. Austin: Univ. Texas Press

320. Willey GR, Leventhal RM, Fash WL. 1978. Maya settlement in the Copán Valley. *Archaeology* 31(4):32–43

321. Willey GR, Smith AL, Tourtellot G, Graham I. 1975. *Excavations at Seibal. Introduction: The Site and its Setting.* Mem. Peabody Mus. Am. Archaeol. Ethnol. 13(1)

322. Wiseman FM. 1978. Agricultural and historical ecology of the Maya lowlands. In *Pre-Hispanic Maya Agriculture*, ed. PD Harrison, BL Turner II, pp. 63–116. Albuquerque: Univ. N. Mex. Press

323. Witkowski SR, Brown CH. 1978. Mesoamerican: a proposed language phylum. *Am. Anthropol.* 80:942–44

324. Wooley C, Inomata T, Demarest A. 1991.

Excavaciones en Punta de Chimino: un centro fortificado del Clásico Tardío y Terminal. Presented at Int. Congr. Americanists, 47th, New Orleans

325. Yoffee N. 1991. Maya elite interaction: through a glass, sideways. See Ref. 76, pp. 285–310

Annu. Rev. Anthropol. 1994. 23:209–29

THE NORTHWEST COAST: Complex Hunter-Gatherers, Ecology, and Social Evolution

Kenneth M. Ames

Department of Anthropology, Portland State University, Portland, Oregon 97207

KEY WORDS: Northwest Coast, foragers, hunter-gatherers, affluence, complexity, subsistence, social organization, art, ritual

INTRODUCTION

Northwest Coast cultures have long held a central place in anthropology. Recently, the coast has become important in two major topics of theoretical interest: 1. the existence and socioeconomic evolution of complex hunter-gatherers (74) and 2. the origins and evolution of permanent forms of social inequality (3). The coast's culture history also has intrinsic value to its native and non-native peoples. This review focuses on recent developments in the coast's archaeology relevant to theories and questions about its culture history and the evolution of social complexity among hunter-gatherers.

THE NORTHWEST COAST

The Northwest Coast extends some 2000 linear km from Icy Bay, Alaska, to Cape Mendocino, California. It is divisible into three subareas: the northern coast (the northern British Columbia mainland, the Queen Charlotte Islands, and southeast Alaska), the central coast (most of Vancouver Island and the adjacent mainland), and the southern coast (southern British Columbia mainland, southern Vancouver Island, western Washington and Oregon, and the northern California coast). Archaeological coverage of the coast is spatially and temporally spotty. The Gulf of Georgia on the southern coast is the best known archaeological region (see 116). Some portions of the coast remain archaeologically unknown. The earliest sites tend to date ca 9000–10,000 B.P., but few excavated sites pre-date 5000 B.P. (dates in this paper are based on uncorrected ^{14}C dates). Almost all excavated sites post-dating 5000 B.P. are highly visible shell middens.

SOCIAL COMPLEXITY ON THE NORTHWEST COAST

Ethnographically described Northwest Coast societies varied among themselves, but shared basic traits: the extended household was the long-term unit of production and consumption; crucial resource localities were owned, but variation existed in what social entity owned them; and households were partially to fully sedentary, reliant on winter stores, and resided together in villages and towns ranging from only a few score to over a thousand people. Household members were ranked by ascribed statuses; the highest ranking household members formed an elite dependent on slave labor (49, 92). Subsistence emphasized a wide range of pelagic/littoral/riverine/terrestrial resources, but focused on salmon. Specialists were economically important and the sexual division of labor was relatively strong (but see 99). Seasonal mobility patterns could be complex, requiring water-borne cartage. Key issues in the evolution of these societies include the importance and strength of variance in the coast's environment; the role of salmon, including salmon ecology and intensification of salmon fishing, in social and economic evolution on the coast; the mode of production; and the tempo and mode of cultural evolution.

Suttles (114) was the first to examine the importance of variability in the coast's environment. His major insight was that although the coast is a rich environment for humans, it is also a variable one. He criticized earlier workers for emphasizing the coast's average production, ignoring its variance. Recent workers, rejecting functionalist or adaptationist models, sometimes miss this point, basing models on mean environmental conditions or simply ignoring the issue. Temporal and spatial variations in salmon runs are a major source of the variance stressed by Suttles.

Salmon are anadromous, spawn in fresh water, achieve maturity in saltwater, and return to their natal streams to spawn and die. Salmon have advantages for foragers (72, 111); they occur at predictable times, in predictable places, and in once prodigious numbers. But they also have disadvantages. For storage, they must be processed promptly (105). Runs are sensitive to environmental insults (72, 111), particularly on small streams and upper tributaries. Runs on large rivers, such as the Columbia and Fraser, are buffered by the sheer volume of fish in them. Salmon runs, rich in the aggregate, are highly variable species to species, stream to stream, and year to year. They are subject to patterned variation (72), with large runs only every second, third, or fourth years. Absolute fish abundance may be less important for labor organization and settlement patterns than is the temporal clumping of runs (104). In a good year on the Klukshu River in the Southwest Yukon, for example, half the sockeye salmon run passes in 7.5 days; in a bad year (in terms of clumping, not numbers) half go by in only 2.5 days (104). Such variation in clumping is not predictable.

Several issues surround the intensification of salmon harvesting (measured as increased production per capita): 1. What resources in what quantities and variety were required to sustain historic Northwest Coast societies? 2. Virtually all workers accept the crucial role of salmon intensification in socioeconomic evolution on the coast. But differences exist over whether salmon intensification alone was sufficient to produce major socioeconomic changes, or whether it should be understood as part of a diverse set of subsistence strategies initiated to achieve higher levels of food production. 3. When did the coast's historic storage-based economy evolve? 4. Salmon occupy a central position in Northwest Coast ritual, world view, and cultural identity. Documenting the history of salmon's non-subsistence roles is a major cultural-historical problem. The focus on salmon production has tended to inhibit consideration of other elements of the mode of production in the coast's social and economic history.

Large households were the elemental units in production during the early nineteenth century (95). These households featured complex divisions of labor along lines of gender, age, free/slave, specialist/non-specialist, and elite/non-elite. Such households were parts of a mode of production requiring multiple simultaneous tasks and management of spatially clustered, temporally varying, and clumped resources (120). These households were integrated into larger social and economic spheres (e.g. villages, regions) through exchange and kin ties. Archaeologists interested in Northwest Coast production typically stress linkages between household production of salmon and elite formation, usually without exploring other aspects of household production. The relationships among households, production, regional interaction, and elite formation are more complex than previously thought.

The final issue raised above stems from disagreement among archaeologists over the mode and tempo of cultural evolution on the coast. Some are inclined to see all aspects of ethnographic culture as developing together at the same time, while others see cultural evolution on the coast as a mosaic, in which different aspects of the ethnographic pattern developed at different times and at different rates. This is essentially a disagreement over whether the ethnographic pattern appeared fully developed and integrated at a certain time, and then persisted, unchanged over long periods (31), or whether that pattern is the result of either cumulative gradual changes, or swift, saltative changes (or both) during a long and complex history (6).

Fladmark (54) proposed the first recent model of the evolution of complexity on the coast. In his model, social complexity resulted from the exploitation of regular, large salmon runs when they developed. The key questions were when and why intensification occurred. He argued that it happened ca 5000 B.P., when post-glacial sea levels and river drainages achieved their modern positions, permitting the growth of salmon runs. People inevitably began taking advantage of the rich, predictable resource. Increased salmon production led to semi- to full-sedentism, evidenced by the appearance at ca 5000 B.P. of large shell middens along the coast. Aspects of Fladmark's model, most importantly the proposed temporal relationship between sea-level stabilization and the appearance of large middens, was later refuted (e.g. 8). But his work, coupled with Suttles' earlier papers, sparked the current interest in social evolution on the coast.

A second model, by Burley (21), saw specialized salmon production developing along the region's major salmon streams, where the fish are more accessible than in coastal waters. In British Columbia this would have happened first in the Fraser River canyon before spreading downstream to the coast. Burley dates the arrival of specialized salmon production at the mouth of the Fraser to ca 2400 B.P. But this model is too limited geographically to account for social complexity along the entire coast.

Schalk (111) focuses on the spatial and temporal variations in salmon productivity, arguing that salmon intensification was not an automatic result of salmon abundance. Intensification occurred as a result of human population growth and greater reliance on storage. There were population size thresholds below which salmon intensification would not occur. Expanding storage resulted from innovations in storage technology. Elite leadership roles evolved from the needs of households to coordinate complex subsistence tasks. Groups intensifying fish production experienced increasing scheduling conflicts, requiring increased coordination. Schalk argues that storage, as delayed consumption, was the systemic cause of Northwest Coast complexity (112). Fladmark saw the cause as regular large bursts of energy, whereas Schalk sees it as the delayed consumption of those bursts.

For Ames (3), inequality resulted from the interplay among 1. circumscription caused by the temporal and spatial distribution of resources, resource ownership, and sedentism; 2. a specialization in salmon fishing (amending that now to a focus on salmon fishing and an array of other aquatic and terrestrial resources) requiring specialized tackle, knowledge, and coordination of complex tasks; 3. population growth; 4. sedentism; and 5. ritual promotion (a process by which certain individuals or families in a group gain control over ritual or central social symbols, and manipulate these to turn themselves into an elite). In the original model, societies with elites had a competitive edge because of their greater efficiencies in information processing capabilities, relative to non-hierarchical societies. These advantages existed in variable environments where, because of circumscription, groups were unable to move or fission as a response to environmental problems (3). The initial steps toward permanent leadership were consequences of organizational stresses (4) caused by a complex domestic economy, logistical mobility patterns, and circumscription. The evolution of the Northwest Coast subsistence and political economies was rooted in the evolution of the Northwest Coast's version of a domestic mode of production (DMP) (4). Besides household subsistence (9, 10), the Northwest Coast DMP involved household participation in exchange networks of varying scale, including some quite large interaction spheres (5). The evolution of an elite on the Northwest Coast, then, must be seen in two contexts: the DMP and regional interaction and exchange.

Kelly (71) stresses the interplay among sedentism, storage, and particular environmental stresses. Sedentism or storage are insufficient by themselves to account for inequality. Critical dimensions in his model are the amplitude of resource fluctuations and the degree of spatial heterogeneity of those fluctuations. If resource fluctuations are strong and heterogenous, storage alone will not dampen their effects, and groups will need access to other groups' resources, while restricting access to their own. Kelly suggests that as a result of restricting such access, access in both directions will be funneled through a few individuals who control the "social activities of individuals in his or her group" (71:145). It is from this circumstance that inequality evolves.

Matson's model emphasizes resource productivity and predictability (84–87). Although intensification of salmon production was the ultimate cause of status differentiation on the coast, the proximate cause was ownership and control of resource patches. Among Northwest Coast cultures, social entities owned the rights to exploit resource patches. Variation existed among them as to what social entity owned these rights (ranging from individuals to villages) and the way patches were owned (106). In some instances, the entire patch was owned, including the ground and all the organisms therein; in other cases, only a certain resource in the patch was owned, and everything else was free for harvesting (106). Matson reasons that intensification, sedentism, and ownership of resource patches evolved among hunter-gatherers when the resources were sufficiently abundant, reliable, predictable, and limited geographically and temporally. Groups came to depend on resources with these qualities, increasing production levels if possible, and settling near such resources, becoming sedentary, and trying to control the resources. Because resource patches inevitably varied in relative productivity, groups owning them eventually differed in relative wealth, leading to ranking. This argument rests upon Donald & Mitchell's demonstration that relative group rank and size among the Northern Kwakiutl is predicted by the productivity of the group's salmon stream (50). Matson holds that intensification, inequality, and sedentism each flow as inevitable consequences of the structure of the resource base, but only intensification and status differentials are causally linked. Sedentism is not a cause of inequality. Intensification results from resource abundance as people become increasingly knowledgeable about their environment and develop means to more efficiently exploit it.

Suttles, Ames, Schalk, and Kelly stress that the Northwest Coast's environment was rich but subject to important variation and that Northwest Coast social forms were in part responses to these twin circumstances. Matson's view is that Northwest Coast societies would only develop in an environment that was reliably rich and predictable. O'Leary's work undercuts aspects of both perspectives. She shows that abundant salmon coupled with storage led neither to specialized use of salmon nor to storage-based sedentism (104).

Coupland (37, 39–41) adopts Matson's premise in a Marxist form, contending that Northwest Coast elites developed when individuals or families gained control over crucial resource patches directly through violence. For Matson, differences in social rank were the inevitable result of differences in the resource base. But for Coupland, rank itself arose from individuals' efforts to control that base. Coupland also stresses the need to understand the evolution of social hierarchies on the coast within the context of the household as the basic unit of production, but emphasizing salmon production, rather than the overall DMP (39).

Maschner (81, 82) rejects adaptationist models, particularly those resting on population pressure, arguing for an approach based on evolutionary psychology and methodological individualism. Elites were neither a response to nor a consequence of qualities of the resource base, but rather the consequence of individuals striving for prestige (and ultimately reproductive advantage) in a rich environment. His arguments are similar to those advanced recently by Hayden (61), but Maschner places heavier explanatory emphases on warfare.

In contrast to the foregoing, Croes & Hackenberger (44, 45) tackle these issues with a simulation model of subsistence changes at the Hoko River locality on the northern Olympic Peninsula. For them, population growth is the prime mover of social evolution and their model uses Malthusian population assumptions. The simulation was developed to predict the optimum resource mix for the locality's subsistence economy. Some of their results are provocative and discussed where appropriate below. The simulation's predictions are difficult to test elsewhere on the coast because its empirical base is closely tied to the Hoko locality, and the simulation is so complex that it is difficult to know why predictions are met or not met. The authors adopt Matson's approach to the development of social inequality.

Carlson is developing a complex model for the development of Northwest Coast culture, of which social inequality is only one part (28–31). Carlson sees salmon intensification as the major causal factor in the evolution of Northwest Coast culture, but he emphasizes ritual and Northwest Coast art (52) and their origins in shamanism, a view shared by MacDonald (78). Carlson is the primary proponent of the view that the major traits of ethnographic Northwest Coast culture developed as a single, integrated complex and then persisted with little change.

DEMOGRAPHY

Boyd (19) reconstructs late eighteenth and early nineteenth century population levels for Northwest North America and the region's disease history from contact to the end of the nineteenth century. His study is now the base line for all work on Northwest Coast demography. He conservatively estimates the coast's immediate pre-contact population at 188,000, based on a estimated 33% loss from what he considers the region's first smallpox epidemic at ca 1775. Cybulksi reviews the coast's ancient demography, drawing on the region's extensive sample of excavated human skeletons spanning the last 5000 years (47).

There are only three limited studies of Northwest Coast population trends spanning a significant portion of the entire prehistoric period. Fladmark built a curve for the entire coast using radiocarbon dates. Ames (6) and Maschner (81) present similar ^{14}C date–based curves for the southern and northern Northwest Coasts, respectively, based on much larger samples than Fladmark's. These latter curves suggest somewhat differing patterns of population growth for the two regions and that peak populations may have occurred several hundred years before contact (ca 900 B.P.). Croes & Hackenberger (45) predict that population growth in the region entered a log phase between 4000 and 3000 B.P., a prediction paralleled by Ames' southern coast curve. Archaeologists have estimated general patterns of population growth from increasing rates of shell midden accumulation (79) and site numbers. As will be seen below, many crucial socioeconomic developments on the coast occurred during times of apparent population growth and/or high densities.

SUBSISTENCE AND SEDENTISM

Aquatic vs Terrestrial Resources

Researchers often stress the importance of aquatic resources in the evolution of complex hunter-gatherers (e.g. 15, 63). On the Northwest Coast, the relative importance through time of terrestrial and maritime resources is an old research question (e.g. 17, 76). The evidence for the period between 10,000 and 5500 B.P. indicates broad spectrum foraging with hunting, fishing, and gathering by the end of that period. This assessment must be based on a small sample of sites: Five Mile Rapids (42), Glenrose Cannery (83), Chuck Lake (2), Namu (26), and Bear Cove (27). These sites show that large and medium land mammals, marine mammals (seals and sea lions), and an array of fish, including salmon, smelt, sturgeon, and large minnows were taken. Mollusks and probably plant foods also were collected.

Analyses of human bone chemistry of a male skeleton dating 8200 B.P. from interior British Columbia (48) indicates 9% to 18% of his diet was from marine resources, presumably salmon given the site's upstream position in the Fraser River drainage (33). Similar analyses (34, 35) of a small sample of skeletons recovered from burials along the British Columbia coast spanning the last 5000 years concluded that marine resources contributed as much 90% of the diet during that period.

Salmon Intensification

Research on intensification on the coast emphasizes the timing of increases in salmon production and the development of a storage-based economy. There is no consensus as to when these occurred. This uncertainty results from several factors: the small sample of sites pre-dating 5000 B.P.; differing assumptions about the causal connections among salmon production, storage, sedentism, and evolving social hierarchies; and a lack of consensus as to what constitutes direct evidence for salmon intensification and storage. Some researchers have concluded on good evidence that heavy reliance on salmon coupled with storage began along the coast ca 3500–3000 B.P. These data are summarized in a series of recent papers (40, 87, 99a).

A few sites on or near the coast show evidence of local heavy use of salmon much earlier than 3500 B.P. Two of these are Namu on the central Northwest Coast and Five Mile Rapids on the Columbia River in Oregon. Salmon dominate archaeofaunas from Namu dating 4000–5000 B.P., leading Carlson (29) and Cannon (26) to argue that coast-wide reliance on salmon dates from that time, if not earlier. Deposits at Five Mile Rapids at the upstream end of the Columbia River Gorge dating ca 7600–9800 B.P., produced 150,000–200,000 salmon vertebrae (42), convincing Cressman that the ethnographic salmon focus existed by that early date. Recent work (23, 24) tested the possibility that the presence of these bones was the result of natural formation processes but showed that the fish were deposited through human agency. Other sites predating 3500 B.P. contain salmon bones and, occasionally, fishing gear. These and other data (52) do not seem to indicate a coast-wide intensification of salmon before 3500 B.P. They do show that subsistence intensification proceeded at different tempos in different places and that the resources intensified were determined by local ecology rather than by regional levels of productivity.

Whenever it began, salmon intensification did not end at 3500 B.P. Several subsequent technological changes (55, 72, 91) and innovations (51) indicate continuing efforts to raise productivity. A significant aspect of intensification was probably expansion of the number of habitats from which fish could be taken (72). There is also evidence of resource depletion (45).

Storage

Although it is widely accepted that storage played an important role in the evolution of complexity, the nature of that role is controversial. The relative shelf life of stores (105) is as important in these dynamics as is the simple act of putting up stores. Several lines of evidence suggest the appearance of a storage-based economy by ca 3500–3000 B.P. (much of this evidence also suggests salmon intensification): 1. Rectangular surface dwellings and villages appeared by 3000 B.P. These dwellings were the major food processing and storage facilities during the last millennium (9, 10, 12, 67, 69, 114, 118), and their presence suggests the potential for that role at 3000 B.P. The houses and villages indicate some degree of sedentism, which is quite implausible without storage on the coast (38, 111). 2. The use of wooden boxes as coffins indicates that the technology and skill needed to make storage boxes was present by 3500 B.P. (46). 3. Evidence for expanded use of mass-harvesting techniques, including nets and weirs, points to larger harvests and, indirectly, to increased demand for and capacity to process more fish for storage (100). 4. Large numbers of smelt and salmon remains have been recovered as far away as 100 km from where they were caught. Transportation of such large volumes of fish and the likely presence of freight canoes both imply processing and storage (8). 5. Tools have been found that may have been part of gear for processing fish for storage (91). 6. Head element/vertebrae ratios are currently viewed as the definitive indicator of salmon storage on the coast. It is reasoned, based on ethnographic data (25), that where salmon are stored, cranial skeletal elements will be rare or absent relative to post-cranial elements. However, this ratio has taphonomic problems, because salmon head bones have lower structural densities than do vertebrae. If both cranial and vertebral elements undergo similar destructive processes, cranial elements will be rarer than would be predicted based only on their relative frequency in the fish's skeleton (24).

The development of a storage-based economy may have required innovations in technology or technique (87, 111), but the basic simplicity of the key storage techniques (air drying [via sun and wind], smoking, and freezing) impose no special technological barriers to storage having great antiquity (15). The Northwest Coast's recent climate, which has persisted perhaps 5000–6000 years, makes sun and air drying chancy. The major technological innovation required for large-scale and long-term food storage would have been large smoke houses. Arguments for storage before 4000 B.P. rest ultimately on the presence of large numbers of salmon remains in a few particular sites (29), or evidence for the capacity to harvest large numbers of fish (52).

Secondary Resources

Some workers feel that the anthropological focus on salmon obscures the importance of other resources. This issue results in part from increasingly sophisticated analyses of vertebrate and invertebrate archaeofaunas with results that do not fit expectations based on salmon as the single most important resource on the coast (e.g. 57, 59, 60, 97, 105, 107). In some cases, salmon are rather minor members of the assemblages (e.g. 60). These studies also show considerable inter-locality variation in subsistence. Ethnographically a variety of organisms were exploited, some certainly for purposes other than food, but the diet was diverse. Secondary resources were necessary for nutritional and physiological reasons (e.g 105). Dietary sources of oil, fats, and carbohydrates were particularly prized. In an ingenious argument, Monks (96) attempts to show that some Northwest Coast hunting/fishing practices were designed to exploit as wide an array of resources as possible from a single, well-placed facility. Establishment of the relative dietary roles for these resources and the techniques used for getting them raises some important methodological issues that have yet to be resolved, including recovery techniques and quantification methods (e.g. 64, 75, 76, 119).

The most obvious evidence for subsistence intensification anywhere along the coast is the widespread appearance of large numbers of shell middens at ca 5500–4500 B.P. Much earlier shell deposits exist (2) but are thin and discontinuous, in marked contrast to the sometimes massive later middens. Croes & Hackenberger's simulation suggests that shellfish along with elk and deer, rather than salmon, limited human populations on the Straits of Juan de Fuca (45).

Sedentism and Mobility Patterns

Sedentism is widely seen as a significant factor in the development of social complexity among hunter-gatherers; however, alone it cannot explain that development. In fact, sedentism, as well as mobility and settlement patterns, have received little separate attention on the coast. The appearance of large shell middens is usually thought to signal the beginnings of semi- to full sedentism on the coast. Although seasonality studies have also been used (e.g. 107), direct or indirect evidence of substantial houses (similar to the nineteenth century houses [115] on the coast) and villages is the best primary evidence for some degree of sedentism. Substantial rectangular surface houses appear around 3000 B.P., although these are not the earliest structures on or near the coast. There is at least one pit-dwelling above the mouth of the Fraser River that dates to ca 4000 B.P. (73). It has long been supposed that pit houses preceded plank houses on the coast. Pit houses appear east of the Cascades by 5500–5000 B.P., becoming common after 3500 B.P. (7). In the absence of contrary evidence, it is reasonable to conclude that shell middens on the coast were associated with residence in pit houses. The associated (and preceding) mobility patterns are unknown. Pit houses by themselves are poor predictors of mobility patterns (7).

The oldest firmly dated village on the coast, the Paul Mason site near the northern coast, contains depressions of twelve small, rectangular houses, ten of which are in two rows (37). It dates to ca 3200–2800 B.P. (37). The Boardwalk site, on the northern British Columbia coast, is a two-row village that may be contemporary with Paul Mason (8). The Palmrose site in Seaside, Oregon, has a large rectangular house as old as 2600 B.P. (36). Given the presence of these dwellings at both ends of the coast, they probably were also present along the intervening coast. The apparent absence of such dwellings in between probably reflects methodological problems. Dwellings are hard to recognize in shell middens (e.g. 16); most of those excavated are either on shell midden surfaces, or are not associated with middens at all. Historic Northwest Coast houses were large, and excavations were not always of sufficient scope to find or identify them (76). Many excavations have not been designed to find houses. The appearance of rectangular structures may indicate the formation of closed corporate groups (62), but it may also point to the evolution of an economy heavily reliant on extensive food processing and storage. By all evidence, houses were the primary food processing and storage facilities in Northwest Coast material culture (9, 12, 32, 69, 109, 114, 118).

The appearance of villages is accompanied by evidence for logistical mobility patterns, at least in the Gulf of Georgia and Prince Rupert Harbor on the northern coast. Gulf of Georgia settlement patterns grew increasingly complex through time, particularly after 1500 B.P. (117). In Prince Rupert Harbor there is evidence for increased use of inshore and offshore islands near rich, shallow saltwater habitats and for long-distance bulk transport of resources, suggesting movements requiring large canoes (8). There also appear to have been major shifts in regional settlement patterns, including episodes when some regions were abandoned or the residents displaced by others (93, 122).

SOCIAL, ECONOMIC, AND POLITICAL ORGANIZATION

Household Archaeology

The study of households provides perhaps the best entry point into questions about power (80), specialization (32), control of production (10), gender (103), and trade (68) on the coast. A growing sample of excavated plank houses spanning the last 3000 years on the southern coast (e.g. 12, 32, 37, 53) includes the famous Ozette houses, which date to the early eighteenth century (see 110). Despite the methodological difficulties sketched above, these excavations show that it is possible to archaeologically investigate aspects of Northwest Coast households, including their modes of production and how those modes evolved.

Production

Matson argues that ownership of scattered resource patches by households was the crucial socioeconomic development in the evolution of stratification (84, 85). Work at Ozette and other excavated houses (32) shows that such ownership patterns can be demonstrated empirically for the period immediately before contact. Different Ozette households exploited different resource patches and the higher status house had access to more culturally preferred foods (69, 118). Matson argues that the practice of resource ownership was a result of exploiting predictable, clustered resources. Research elsewhere on peasant agriculturalists suggests (a) that owning several, scattered patches is a predictable outcome of strategies to minimize the risk of crop failure in a variable environment (121) and (b) that ownership of such plots does not inevitably lead to elite formation (102). The latter work also shows that a complex division of labor does not necessarily require leadership for coordination, undermining Ames' and Schalks' arguments that elites developed from the need to manage the Northwest Coast's complex subsistence economy. Indeed, Ames' own recent work suggests that management may have been more apparent then real (10).

There is evidence for elite control of some elements of production on the southern coast immediately before European contact (12, 69, 109). Dwellings were the objects of considerable labor and resources (89) and control of the house as an instrument of production may have been a crucial base for the authority of the coast's elite (9, 10, 114). There is also evidence for complex production patterns before ca 1000 B.P., including the existence of intrahouse specialists in food procurement by ca 1600 B.P. (32). The presence of well-made copper artifacts in burials along the coast (9, 22) indicates that specialized production of copper prestige goods occurred by ca 2500 B.P. Some specialization in carving and woodworking could be considerably earlier (31). There may have been village-level specialization in the production of prestige and wealth goods (2a), and regional specialization in the production of red cedar and whale bone products (68). Interestingly, although North America's major dentalium sources lie off Vancouver Island's west coast, there is no evidence for its production.

Gender (98) and the division of labor have played little role in discussions of the evolution of production on the coast. Recent work, including Norton's (103) and Moss' (98, 99) studies, clearly show that such inquiry is necessary. Their research demonstrates the significant roles played by women in economic production both at the household and regional level. In addition, as the archaeological evidence summarized below indicates, gender was one of the major dimensions structuring the evolution of Northwest Coast systems of status, including both elite status and slavery.

Rank, Stratification, and Social Organization

Our knowledge of the development of stratification comes from analyses of burials, including burial patterns, grave goods, labrets (lip plugs), and patterns of cranial deformation. People were buried in shell midden sites between ca 5000 and 1500 B.P., after which inhumations virtually ceased. Only a minority of all deceased individuals were buried in these places; mortuary treatment for the majority of the population during that lengthy period is unknown (47). Stone labrets leave facets on the wearer's teeth (46), which indicate a labret-wearer even in the absence of the labret, although postmortem tooth loss can obscure these patterns (46). In the nineteenth century, free women on the northern coast wore labrets (70). Labret wear occurs on the teeth of very few individuals dating between ca 5000 and 3500 B.P. It is more common between 3500 and 2500 B.P. On the south coast, cranial deformation appears to have replaced labrets as a visual, permanent status marker (5) after 2500 B.P., although the practice persisted on the northern coast until the nineteenth century. The reasons for that change are unknown. The social significance of labrets in early periods is an important problem. Matson speculates that the presence of both labret wear and a labret in a burial indicates achieved high status, and the presence of labret wear without a labret indicates ascribed status (in this case, the labret is an heirloom) (86). Moss critiques the idea that labret wear alone equals high status, showing that all free north coast women wore labrets (99). High status women wore large labrets.

Mortuary patterns of at least two of the earliest burial populations on the coast (Pender Island in the south and Blue Jackets Creek in the north) were complex, including both prone and seated individuals, red ochre and grave goods. The grave goods at Blue Jackets Creek appear to be utilitarian items (113), but those at Pender Island include ten antler spoons with zoomorphic effigy handles (31). Richly furnished graves (with costly or exotic grave goods other than labrets) occurred before 2500 B.P., but they became common along the entire coast after that date (22). To some (22), including me, the coast-wide advent of elaborate burials at 2500 B.P. signals the appearance of an elite. Others place that development at ca 3500 or earlier, based on the presence of labrets or labret wear (see 99) and complex burial rituals (31).

Gender and region-of-origin play crucial roles in structuring these patterns. On the northern coast between 3500 and 1500 B.P., labret wear is restricted primarily to males, but in contemporary samples in the Gulf of Georgia both labret wear and cranial deformation are more evenly distributed among males and females. After 1500 in the north, labret wear occurs only on females. Gender also plays subtle roles in the distribution of grave goods in the northern burials between 3500 and 1500 B.P. (8). Contrasting regional patterns of cranial deformation and labret wear would clearly mark the region-of-origin of high status individuals after 2500 B.P. (5). Cybulksi speculates that the balanced sex ratios in the south for both labret wear and cranial deformation reflect bilateral kinship organization, while the shifting sex ratios in the north point to a change from a patrilineal to a matrilineal system (47).

The distinctive status of labret-wearer predates both the subsistence and settlement changes at 3500–3000 B.P. and the widespread appearance of rich burials. This suggests a complex and theoretically important interplay among a preexisting special status, household and cooperate group formation, intensification, storage and sedentism—more complex, I believe, than current models accommodate. There is tantalizing evidence for that interplay. Acheson (1), Coupland (41), and Maschner (81, 82) independently conclude from limited evidence that large high status households and large multi-kin group villages only formed on the northern coast after 1500 B.P., at the same time as the shift in labret wear patterns in the north.

Establishing the development of slavery on the coast is exceedingly difficult. Buried remains show that individuals (usually female) were sometimes bound and decapitated in the north (see 8, 46) and scalped in the south (13), perhaps indicating slave raiding between ca 3500 and 2200 B.P. (46). Cybulski (46) suggests that the biased sex ratio among the Prince Rupert Harbor burial population (1.89 males:1 female) indicates slavery. Historically, slaves were seldom buried, and hence would rarely be recovered. If a significant portion of a population were female slaves, then such a biased ratio would result. However, any relationship between biased sex ratios and slavery needs further exploration. Similarly biased sex ratios occur in such diverse burial samples as Yangshao China (58) and the Natufian (14). Sex ratios in burial populations on the south Northwest coast approach 1:1, which would mean, in Cybulski's logic, that slavery did not exist there prehistorically. The Tsawwassen data cited above (13) suggests otherwise.

Some researchers have uncovered evidence of potlatching and associated feasting. Huelsbeck (69) infers feasting by high status individuals from the spatial distribution of food remains in the late prehistoric Ozette houses. Carlson (31) speculates that the funerary ritual at Pender Island before 3500 B.C. included feasting and potlatching. Cybulski (46) wonders whether plant and animal remains associated with later burials (ca 1600–1000 B.P.) at Greenville may also be the results of funerary feasting, and by implication, potlatching. Generally, however, workers on the coast are reluctant to speculate on the history of the potlatch.

REGIONAL DYNAMICS: INTERACTION, TRADE, AND WARFARE

Although there is little doubt of strong regional interaction through time (5, 115), available archaeological evidence is limited. The spatial patterning of a number of traits (labret wear, cranial deformation, art styles) indicates that the Northwest Coast had one or more large overlapping interaction spheres (5, 115) during the last several millennia (5, 77). Obsidian sourcing indicates relatively far flung trade networks extending well back into prehistory (28a). The copper present in graves by 2500 B.P. suggests long-distance movement of the metal by that time (8, 22). The distributions of particular art motifs also suggests long-distance contact along the coast between 4000 and 3300 B.P. (5, 66). Some researchers are beginning to investigate the history of ethnicity on the coast using material culture (43, 94).

There is evidence for continual warfare on the coast during the past 5000 years. Evidence of violence-caused trauma is found on adult skeletons from the period between 5000 B.P. and contact, peaking in frequency after 1500 B.P. (47). Such trauma is more common in the north, at least for the period between 3500 and 1500 B.P. In Prince Rupert Harbor these skeletons were buried with trophy skulls and weapons. Other evidence for increased levels of warfare after 1500 B.P. includes the construction of fortifications throughout southeast Alaska (100) and perhaps in the Gulf of Georgia as well (55). This trend is contemporary with possible evidence for peak population densities and changes in organization. Maschner (82) suggests that the post-1500 B.P. increase in warfare resulted at least partially from the diffusion of the bow and arrow into the region. Given the wealth of warfare accounts in the north coast's oral traditions, this period of warfare probably extended into the nineteenth century (8, 122).

ART AND RITUAL

Archaeological studies of Northwest Coast art have focused on dating the emergence and evolution of the nineteenth century style (e.g. 30). Ironically, given the modern emphasis on the style's northern variant (e.g. 65), the richest and longest archaeological record is from southern British Columbia (18, 30, 66). Basic motifs of the nineteenth century style are at least 4000 years old (66). The style (in a comprehensive sense) existed by 2500–2000 B.P. with some of its most subtle compositional rules in play by then (56, 90). Some aspects of the northern style may not have been fully established until after ca 1000 B.P. (78). Theories on the origins of the art style seek its roots in shamanism (28, 29, 52) and diffusion from Northeast Asia (see 52a). The history of regional and temporal variation of motifs is little known. Archaeological artifacts displaying zoomorphic or anthropomorphic motifs are rare (66). Motifs and their execution are quite variable. Holm suggests this variability reflects the social functions of particular carving techniques and the visibility of the motifs (66).

Studies of context and disposal patterns may give insights into the style's evolution. For example, in the Gulf of Georgia, zoomorphic effigies are commonly recovered either as grave goods or in association with graves. In Prince Rupert Harbor, zoomorphic effigies are rarely grave goods (only one has been found) and are seldom recovered in cemetery areas. The condition of these objects when discarded may also be important. Labrets were frequently broken before they were discarded.

Burials are the only obvious archaeological record for ritual on the coast. When that record began, the dead were already being handled in complex and varying ways (31, 113). Carlson argues there is evidence at Pender Island for mortuary feasts, and therefore, funerary potlatches, before 3000 B.P. (31). There is no similar evidence in Prince Rupert Harbor (8). The coast-wide shift away from inhumation began before 1000 B.P. and indicates a significant change in ritual. Although this change probably marks the development of ethnographically documented funerary practices, its causes and ramifications are little understood and are a major research problem. Interestingly, this shift appears to have occurred all along the coast at about the same time. Finally, recent excavations (G Coupland, personal communication) in southern British Columbia suggest that we do not have a representative sample of the range of funerary practices prior to the shift away from inhumations.

CONCLUSIONS

Cultural evolution on the Northwest Coast was a mosaic of local and regional events and dynamics at differing temporal and spatial scales (6). The theories and models reviewed here, including my own, do not yet adequately address that fundamental fact, but after many years of work, Northwest Coast archaeologists have begun to achieve a critical mass of evidence with which to address these and other issues.

ACKNOWLEDGMENTS

Many people assisted in the preparation of this paper by providing access to unpublished data, by clarifying their own ideas or some of the basic issues for me, and by being sounding boards for some of my thoughts. I thank Virginia

Butler, Roy Carlson, Gary Coupland, Jerome Cybulski, David Huelsbeck, R. Lee Lyman, R.G. Matson, Herb Maschner, Al McMillan, Madonna Moss, and Bruce Winterhalter. R. Lee Lyman spent part of a sabbatical leave at Portland State University in the fall of 1993, and many of my notions for this paper were thrashed out over coffee and a table of faunal remains. I thank George MacDonald for continued access to the Prince Rupert Harbor materials. My research on the Prince Rupert artifacts was supported by the National Museums of Canada and by the National Science Foundation (grants BNS 8311299 and 8406343). On a personal note, I thank my immediate family, and my brother-in-law Robert Melville, for helping me achieve a balance between family and work during the period when this paper was finished.

Any *Annual Review* chapter, as well as any article cited in an *Annual Review* chapter, may be purchased from the Annual Reviews Preprints and Reprints service. 1-800-347-8007; 415-259-5017; email: arpr@class.org

Literature Cited

1. Acheson SR. 1991. *In the wake of the ya'åats' xaatgáay ['Iron People']: a study of changing settlement strategies among the Kunghit Haida.* PhD thesis. Oxford Univ.
2. Ackerman RE, Hamilton DT, Stuckenrath R. 1985. *Archaeology of Hecata Island, a survey of 16 timber harvest units in the Tongass National Forest.* Cent. Northwest Anthropol. Proj. Rep. No. 3. Pullman: Washington State Univ.
2a. Allaire L. 1984. A native mental map of Coast Tsimshian villages. In *The Tsimshian: Images of the Past, Views of the Present,* ed. M Seguin, pp. 82–98. Vancouver: Univ. B.C. Press
3. Ames KM. 1981. The evolution of social ranking on the Northwest Coast of North America. *Am. Antiq.* 46:789–805
4. Ames KM. 1985. Hierarchies, stress and logistical strategies among hunter-gatherers in northwestern North America. In *Prehistoric Hunter-Gatherers: the Emergence of Cultural Complexity,* ed. TD Price, JA Brown, pp. 155–80. Orlando, FL: Academic
5. Ames KM. 1989. Art and regional interaction among affluent foragers on the North Pacific Rim. In *Reprint Proc. Circumpacific Prehist. Conf., Seattle,* Vol. III, Part 2
6. Ames KM. 1991. The archaeology of the *longue durée:* temporal and spatial scale in the evolution of social complexity on the southern Northwest Coast. *Antiquity* 65:935–45
7. Ames KM. 1991. Sedentism, a temporal shift or a transitional change in hunter-gath-

erer mobility strategies. In *Between Bands and States: Sedentism, Subsistence and Interaction in Small Scale Societies,* ed. S Gregg, pp. 103–33. Carbondale: S. Ill. Univ. Press
8. Ames KM. 1993. *The archaeology of the northern Northwest Coast: the North Coast Prehistory Project excavations in Prince Rupert Harbour, British Columbia.* Report on file with the Archaeological Survey of Canada, Ottawa
9. Ames KM. 1994. Life in the big house, household labor and dwelling size on the Northwest Coast. In *People Who Live in Large Houses,* ed. G. Coupland, T Banning. Tucson: Univ. Ariz. Press. In press
10. Ames KM. 1994. Chiefly power and household production on the Northwest Coast. In *The Origins of Inequality,* ed. TD Price, GM Feinman. New York: Plenum. In press
11. Deleted in proof
12. Ames KM, Raetz DF, Hamilton SH, McAfee C. 1992. Household archaeology of a southern Northwest Coast plank house. *J. Field Archaeol.* 19:275–90
13. ARCAS (ARCAS Consulting Archaeologists Ltd). 1991. *Archaeological Investigations at Tsawwassen, B.C.* Report on file B.C. Heritage Branch, Victoria
14. Belfer-Cohen A, Schepartz LA, Arensburg B. 1991 New biological data for the Natufian populations in Israel. In *The Natufian Culture in the Levant,* ed. O Bar-Yosef, FR Valla, pp. 411–24. Int. Monogr. Prehist., Archaeol. Ser. 1. Ann Arbor: Univ. Mich. Press
15. Binford LR. 1990. Mobility, housing and

environment: a comparative study. *J. Anthropol. Res.* 46:119–52

16. Blukis Onat AR. 1985. The multifunctional use of shellfish remains: from garbage to community engineering. *Northwest Anthropol. Res. Notes* 19:201–7

17. Borden CC. 1975. Origins and development of early Northwest Coast culture to about 3000 B.C.. *Archaeol. Surv. Can. Mercury Ser.* 45

18. Borden CC. 1983. Prehistoric art in the lower Fraser region. See Ref. 27a, pp. 131–65

19. Boyd RT. 1985. *The introduction of infectious diseases among the Indians of the Pacific Northwest, 1774–1874.* PhD thesis. Univ. Wash., Seattle

20. Deleted in proof

21. Burley DV. 1980. *Marpole: anthropological reconstructions of a prehistoric culture type.* Dept. Archaeol. Publ. No. 8. Burnaby, BC: Simon Fraser Univ.

22. Burley DV, Knusel C. 1989. Burial patterns and archaeological interpretation: problems in the recognition of ranked society in the Coast Salish region. In *Reprint Proc. Circumpacific Prehist. Conf., Seattle,* Vol. III, Part 2

23. Butler VL. 1993. Natural vs. cultural salmonid remains: origin of the Dalles Roadcut bones, Columbia River, Oregon. *J. Archaeol. Sci.* 20:1–24

24. Butler VL, Chatters JC. 1994. The role of bone density in structuring prehistoric salmon bone assemblages. *J. Archaeol. Sci.* In press

25. Calvert SG. 1973. *Cultural and non-cultural variation in the artifact and faunal samples from the St. Mungo Cannery site, B.C. (DgRr2).* MA thesis. Univ. Victoria, British Columbia

26. Cannon A. 1991. *The Economic Prehistory of Namu.* Burnaby, BC: Archaeology Press, Simon Fraser Univ.

27. Carlson C. 1979. The early component at Bear Cove. *Can. J. Archaeol.* 3:177–94

27a. Carlson RL, ed. 1983. *Indian Art Traditions of the Northwest Coast.* Burnaby, BC: Simon Fraser Univ. Press

28. Carlson RL. 1983. Change and continuity in Northwest Coast art. See Ref. 27a, pp. 197–205

28a. Carlson RL. 1983. Prehistory of the Northwest Coast. See Ref. 27a, pp. 13–32

29. Carlson RL. 1990. Cultural and ethnic continuity on the Pacific Coast of British Columbia. In *Traditional Cultures of the Pacific Societies,* ed. S-B Han, K-O Kim, pp. 79–88. Seoul: Seoul Univ. Press

30. Carlson RL. 1993. Content and chronology of Northwest coast (North America) rock art. In *Time and Space, Dating and Spatial Considerations in Rock Art Research,* ed. J Steinbring, A Watchman, pp. 7–12. Occas.

AURA Publ. No. 8. Melbourne: Aust. Rock Art Res. Assoc.

31. Carlson RL, Hobler PM. 1993. The Pender Island excavations and the development of Coast Salish culture. *B. C. Stud.* 99 (Autumn):25–50

32. Chatters JC. 1989. The antiquity of economic differentiation within households in the Puget Sound region, Northwest Coast. See Ref. 79a, pp. 168–78

33. Chisholm BS, Nelson DE. 1983. An early human skeleton from south central British Columbia: dietary inference from carbon isotope evidence. *Can. J. Archaeol.* 7:85–87

34. Chisholm BS, Nelson DE, Scharcz HP. 1982. Stable carbon isotope ratios as a measure of marine vs. terristrial protein in ancient diets. *Science* 216:1131–32

35. Chisholm BS, Nelson DE, Scharcz HP. 1983. Marine and terristrial protein in prehistoric diets on the British Columbia coast. *Curr. Anthropol.* 24:396–98

36. Connelly TJ. 1992. *Human responses to change in coastal geomorphology and fauna on the southern Northwest Coast. Archaeological investigations at Seaside, Oregon.* Univ. Oregon Anthropol. Pap. No. 45. Eugene: Oregon State Mus. Anthropol.

37. Coupland G. 1985. Household variability and status differentiation at Kitselas Canyon. *Can. J. Archaeol.* 9:39–56

38. Coupland G. 1985. Restricted access, resource control and the evolution of status inequality among hunter-gatherers. In *Status, Structure and Stratification: Current Archaeological Reconstructions,* ed. M Thompson, MT Garcia, FJ Kense, pp. 217–26. Calgary, Alberta: Archaeol. Assoc., Univ. Calgary

39. Coupland G. 1988. Prehistoric economic and social change in the Tsimshian area. *Res. Econ. Anthropol. Suppl.* 3:211–45

40. Coupland G. 1993. *Maritime adaptation and evolution of the developed Northwest West Coast pattern on the central Northwest Coast.* Presented Int. Sem. Orig., Dev. Spread Prehist. Pacific-Bering Sea Maritime Cult., Honolulu, HI

41. Coupland G. 1994. The evolution of multifamily households on the Northwest Coast of North America. In *People Who Live in Large Houses,* ed. G. Coupland, T Banning. Tucson: Univ. Ariz. Press. In press

42. Cressman LS, Cole DL, Davis WA, Newman TJ, Scheans DJ. 1960. Cultural sequences at The Dalles, Oregon: a contribution to Pacific Northwest prehistory. *Trans. Am. Philos. Soc. New Ser.* 50(10)

43. Croes DR. 1989. Prehistoric ethnicity on the Northwest Coast of North America: an evaluation of style in basketry and lithics. *J. Anthropol. Archaeol.* 8:101–30

44. Croes DR. 1991. Exploring prehistoric subsistence change on the Northwest Coast. *Res. Econ. Anthropol. Suppl.* 6:337–66

45. Croes DR, Hackenberger S. 1988. Hoko River archaeological complex: modeling prehistoric Northwest Coast economic evolution. *Res. Econ. Anthropol. Suppl.* 3:19–86

46. Cybulski JS. 1993. *A Greenville burial ground: human remains in British Columbia coast prehistory.* Ottawa: Archaeol. Surv. Can., Can. Mus. Civiliz.

47. Cybulski JS. 1994. Culture change, demographic history, and health and disease on the Northwest coast. In *In the Wake of Contact, Biological Responses to Conquest,* ed. CS Larsen, GR Milner, pp. 75–85. New York: Wiley-Liss

48. Cybulski JS, Howes DE, Haggarty JC, Eldridge M. 1981. An early human skeleton from south-central British Columbia: dating and bioarchaeological inference. *Can J. Archaeol.* 5:49–60

49. Donald L. 1983 Was Nuu-chah-nulth-aht (Nootka) society based on slave labor? In *The Development of Political Organization in Native North America,* ed. E Tooker, pp. 108–19. Washington, DC: Proc. Am. Ethnol. Soc.

50. Donald L, Mitchell DH. 1975. Some correlates of local group rank among the Southern Kwakiutl. *Ethnology* 14:325–46

51. Easton NA. 1985. *The underwater archaeology of Straits Salish reef-netting.* MA thesis. Univ. Victoria, B.C.

52. Eldridge M, Acheson S. 1992. The antiquity of fish weirs on the southern Coast: a response to Moss, Erlandson and Stuckenrath. *Can. J. Archaeol.* 16:112–15

52a. Fitzhugh WW. 1988. Comparative art of the North Pacific Rim. In *Crossroads of Continents: Cultures of Siberia and Alaska,* ed. WW Fitzhugh, A. Crowell, pp. 294–313. Washington, DC: Smithsonian Inst. Press

53. Fladmark KR. 1973. The Richardson Ranch site: a 19th century Haida house. In *Historical Archaeology in Northwestern North America,* ed. RM Getty, KR Fladmark, pp. 53–95. Calgary, Alberta: Archaeol. Assoc. Univ. Calgary

54. Fladmark KR. 1975. A paleoecological model for Northwest Coast prehistory. *Archaeol. Surv. Can. Mercury Ser.* 43

55. Fladmark KR. 1982. An introduction to the prehistory of British Columbia. *Can. J. Archaeol.* 3:131–44

56. Fladmark KR, Nelson DE, Brown TA, Vogel JS, Southen JA. 1987. AMS dating of two wooden artifacts from the Northwest Coast. *Can. J. Archaeol.* 11:1–12

57. Ford PJ. 1989. Archaeological and ethnographic correlates of seasonality: problems and solutions on the Northwest Coast. *Can. J. Archaeol.* 13:133–50

58. Gao Q, Lee YK. 1993. A biological perspective on Yangshao kinship. *J. Anthropol. Archaeol.* 13:266–98

59. Ham LC. 1982. *Seasonality, shell midden layers, and Coast Salish subsistence activities at the Crescent Beach site, DgRr 1.* PhD thesis. Univ. B.C., Vancouver

60. Hanson DK. 1991. *Late prehistoric subsistence in the Strait of Georgia region of the Northwest Coast.* PhD thesis. Simon Fraser Univ., Burnaby, B.C.

61. Hayden B. 1992. Conclusions: ecology and complex hunter-gatherers. In *A Complex Culture of the British Columbia Plateau: Traditional Stl'átl'imx Resource Use,* ed. B Hayden, pp. 525–63. Vancouver: Univ. B.C. Press

62. Hayden B, Cannon A. 1982. The corporate group as an archaeological unit. *J. Anthropol. Archaeol.* 1:132–58

63. Henry DO. 1991. Foraging, sedentism, and adaptive vigor in the Natufian: rethinking the linkages. In *Perspectives on the Past, Theoretical Biases in Mediterranean Hunter-Gatherer Research,* ed. GA Clark, pp. 353–70. Philadelphia: Univ. Penn. Press

64. Hildebrandt WR, Jones TL. 1992. Evolution of marine mammal hunting: a view from the California and Oregon Coasts. *J. Anthropol. Archaeol.* 11:360–401

65. Holm B. 1965. *Northwest Coast Indian art: an analysis of form.* Thomas Burke Mem. Mus. Monogr. 1. Seattle: Univ. Wash. Press

66. Holm MA. 1990. *Prehistoric Northwest Coast art: a stylistic analysis of the archaeological record.* MA thesis. Univ. B.C., Vancouver

67. Huelsbeck DR. 1983. Mammals and fish in the subsistence economy of Ozette. PhD thesis. Wash. State Univ., Pullman

68. Huelsbeck DR. 1988. The surplus economy of the Northwest Coast. *Res. Econ. Anthropol. Suppl.* 3:149–77

69. Huelsbeck DR. 1989. Food consumption, resource exploitation and relationships with and between households at Ozette. See Ref. 79a, pp. 157–66

70. Keddie GR. 1981. The use and distribution of labrets on the North Pacific Rim. *Syesis* 14:60–80

71. Kelly RL. 1991. Sedentism, sociopolitical inequality, and resource fluctuations. In *Between Bands and States: Sedentism, Subsistence and Interaction in Small Scale Societies,* ed. S Gregg, pp. 135–60. Carbondale: S. Ill. Univ. Press

72. Kew M. 1992. Salmon availability, technology, and cultural adaptation in the Fraser River watershed. In *A Complex Culture of the British Columbia Plateau: Traditional Stl'átl'imx Resource Use,* ed. B

Hayden, pp. 177–221. Vancouver: Univ. B.C. Press

73. LeClair R. 1976. Investigations at the Mauer site near Agassiz. In *Current Research Reports*, ed. RL Carlson, pp. 33–42. Dept. Archaeol. Publ. No. 3. Burnaby, B.C.: Simon Fraser Univ.

74. Lightfoot KG. 1993. Long-term developments in complex hunter-gatherer societies: recent perspectives from the Pacific Coast of North America. *J. Archaeol. Res.* 1:167–200

75. Lyman RL. 1989. Seal and sea lion hunting: a zooarchaeological study from the southern Northwest Coast of North America. *J. Anthropol. Archaeol.* 8:68–99

76. Lyman RL. 1991. *Prehistory of the Oregon Coast: the Effects of Excavation Strategies and Assemblage Size on Archaeological Inquiry.* Orlando, FL: Academic

77. MacDonald GF. 1969. Preliminary culture sequence from the Coast Tsimshian area, British Columbia. *Northwest Anthropol. Res. Notes* 3:240–54

78. MacDonald GF. 1983. Prehistoric art of the northern Northwest Coast. See Ref. 27a, pp. 99–120

79. MacDonald GF, Inglis RI. 1981. An overview of the North Coast prehistory project (1966–1980). *B.C. Stud.* 48:37–63

79a. MacEachern S, Archer DJW, Garvin RD, eds. 1989. *Households and Communities.* Calgary, Alberta: Archaeol. Assoc., Univ. Calgary

80. Marshall Y. 1989. The house in Northwest Coast, Nuu-Chal-Nulth, society: the material structure of political action. See Ref. 79a, pp. 15–21

81. Maschner HDG. 1991. The emergence of cultural complexity on the northern Northwest Coast. *Antiquity* 65:924–34

82. Maschner HDG. 1992. *The origins of hunter-gatherer sedentism and political complexity: a case study from the northern Northwest Coast.* PhD thesis. Univ. Calif., Santa Barbara

83. Matson RG. 1976. The Glenrose Cannery site. *Archaeol. Surv. Can. Mercury Ser.* 52

84. Matson RG. 1983. Intensification and the development of cultural complexity: Northwest versus the Northeast Coast. In *The Evolution of Maritime cultures on the Northeast and Northwest Coasts of North America*, ed. RJ Nash, pp. 124–48. Dept. Archaeol. Occas. Pap. No. 11. Burnaby, BC: Simon Fraser Univ.

85. Matson RG. 1985. The relationship between sedentism and status inequalities among hunter-gatherers. In *Status, Structure and Stratification: Current Archaeological Reconstructions*, ed. M Thompson, MT Garcia, FJ Kense, pp. 245–52.

86. Matson RG. 1989. The Locarno Beach Phase and the origins of the Northwest Coast ethnographic pattern. *Reprint Proc. Circumpacific Prehist. Conf., Seattle*, Vol. III, Part 2

87. Matson RG. 1992. The evolution of Northwest Coast subsistence. *Res. Econ. Anthropol. Suppl.* 6:367–430

88. Deleted in proof

89. Mauger JE. 1978. *Shed roof houses at the Ozette archaeological site: a protohistoric architectural system.* Wash. Archaeol. Res. Cent. Proj. Rep. No. 73. Pullman: Wash. State Univ.

90. McMillan AD, Nelson DE. 1989. Visual punning and the whale's tail: AMS dating of a Marpole-age art object. *Can. J. Archaeol.* 13:212–18

91. Mitchell D. 1971. Archaeology of the Gulf of Georgia area, a natural region and its culture types. *Syesis* 4(Suppl. 1)

92. Mitchell D. 1984. Predatory warfare, social status and the North Pacific slave trade. *Ethnology* 23:39–48

93. Mitchell D. 1988. Changing patterns of resource use in the prehistory of Queen Charlotte Strait, British Columbia. *Res. Econ. Anthropol. Suppl.* 3:245–92

94. Mitchell D, Donald L. 1985. Some economic aspects of Tlingit, Haida and Tsimshian slavery. *Res. Econ. Anthropol.* 7:19–35

95. Mitchell D, Donald L. 1988. Archaeology and the study of Northwest Coast economies. In *Res. Econ. Anthropol. Suppl.* 3: 293–351

96. Monks GG. 1987. Prey as bait: the Deep Bay example. *Can. J. Archaeol.* 11:119–42

97. Moss ML. 1989. *Archaeology and cultural ecology of the prehistoric Angoon Tlingit.* PhD thesis. Univ. Calif., Santa Barbara

98. Moss ML. 1993. Shellfish, gender and status on the Northwest Coast: reconciling archeological, ethnographic, and ethnohistoric records of the Tlingit. *Am. Anthropol.* 95:631–52

99. Moss ML. 1993. *Gender, social inequality, and cultural complexity: Northwest Coast women in prehistory.* Presented Chacmool Conf., 26th, Univ. Calgary, Alberta

99a. Moss ML. 1993. *Northern Northwest Coast regional overview.* Presented Int. Sem. Orig., Dev. Spread Prehist. Pacific-Bering Sea Maritime Cult., Honolulu, HI

100. Moss ML, Erlandson JM. 1992. Forts, refuge rocks, and defensive sites: the antiquity of warfare along the North Pacific Coast of North America. *Arctic Anthropol.* 29:73–90

101. Moss ML, Erlandson JM, Stuckenrath R. 1990. Wood stake fish weirs and salmon fishing on the Northwest Coast: evidence

from Southeast Alaska. *Can. J. Archaeol.* 14:143–58

102. Netting RM. 1990. Links and boundaries: reconsidering the alpine village as ecosystem. In *The Ecosystem Approach in Anthropology,* ed. EF Moran, pp. 229–46. Ann Arbor: Univ. Mich. Press

103. Norton HH. 1985. *Women and resources on the Northwest Coast: documentation from the eighteenth and nineteenth centuries.* PhD thesis. Univ. Wash., Seattle

104. O'Leary BL. 1985. *Salmon and storage: Southern Tutchone use of an "abundant" resource.* PhD thesis. Univ. N. Mex.

105. Panowski EJT. 1985. *Analyzing hunter-gatherers: population pressure, subsistence, social organization, Northwest Coast societies, and slavery.* PhD thesis. Univ. N. Mex.

106. Richardson A. 1981. The control of productive resources on the Northwest Coast of North America. In *Resource Managers: North American and Australian Hunter-Gatherers,* AAAS Selected Symp. No. 67, ed. NN Williams, ES Hunn, pp. 93–112

107. Saleeby B. 1983. *Prehistoric settlement patterns in the Portland Basin on the Lower Columbia River: ethnohistoric, archaeological and biogeographic perspectives.* PhD thesis. Univ. Oregon, Eugene

108. Deleted in proof

109. Samuels SR. 1989. Spatial patterns in Ozette longhouse middens. See Ref. 79a, pp. 143–56

110. Samuels SR, ed. 1991. *House Structure and Floor Midden. Ozette Archaeological Project Research Reports,* Vol. I. Pullman: Wash. State Univ.

111. Schalk RF. 1977. The structure of an anadromous fish resource. In *For Theory Building in Archaeology,* ed. LR Binford, pp. 207–49. Orlando, FL: Academic

112. Schalk RF. 1981. Land use and organizational complexity among foragers of northwestern North America. In *Affluent Foragers, Pacific Coasts East and West,* ed. S Koyama, DH Thomas, pp. 53–76. Senri Ethnol. Ser. 9. Osaka, Jpn: Natl. Mus. Ethnol.

113. Severs P. 1973. A view of island prehistory: archaeological investigations at Blue Jackets Creek 1972–73. *The Charlottes, J. Queen Charlotte Islands* 3:2–12

114. Suttles W. 1968. Coping with abundance: subsistence on the Northwest Coast. In *Man the Hunter,* ed. RB Lee, I DeVore, pp. 56–68. Chicago: Aldine

115. Suttles W. 1990. Introduction. See Ref. 116, pp. 1–15

116. Suttles W, ed. 1990. *Handbook of North American Indians.* Vol. 7: *Northwest Coast.* Washington, DC: Smithsonian Inst. Press

117. Thompson G. 1978. *Prehistoric settlement changes in the southern Northwest Coast. A functional approach.* Rep. Archaeol. 5. Seattle: Univ. Wash., Dept. Anthropol.

118. Wessen G. 1982. *Shell middens as cultural deposits: a case study from Ozette.* PhD thesis. Wash. State Univ., Pullman

119. Wessen G. 1988. The use of shellfish resources on the Northwest Coast: the view from Ozette. *Res. Econ. Anthropol. Suppl.* 3:179–210

120. Wilk RR, Rathje WL. 1982. Household archaeology. *Am. Behav. Sci.* 25:631–40

121. Winterhalter B, Goland C. 1992. *Food sharing to field scattering: risk and the origins of agriculture.* Presented Annu. Meet. Soc. Am. Archaeol., 57th, Pittsburgh

122. Wooley CB, Haggarty JC. 1989. *Tlingit-Tsimshian interaction in the southern Alexander Archipelago.* Presented Annu. Meet. Alaska Anthropol. Assoc., 17th, Anchorage

Annu. Rev. Anthropol. 1994. 23:231–53

BIOLOGICAL ASPECTS OF MENOPAUSE: Across the Lifespan

L. E. Leidy

Department of Anthropology, University of Massachusetts, Amherst, Massachusetts 01003-4805

KEY WORDS: lifespan approach, age, symptoms, ovary, atresia

INTRODUCTION

Menopause is defined biomedically as the last menstrual period, identified in retrospect after 12 months of amenorrhea (178). Menopause is a biological universal among human females who live through their middle age (32). It is an event that transects the biological and psychosocial trajectories threading through a woman's life. As an event, menopause is a parameter closing the reproductive phase of life (52, 167), a marker in the linear progression of bone loss with advancing age (123, 129, 156), and an indicator of changing serum lipid profiles (150, 164).

Menopause occurs within what is called the climacteric, the transition from the reproductive to post-reproductive phase of life. Although defined biomedically as an event, menopause is experienced as a process by individual women (68). For example, the physiological transition from reproductive to post-reproductive life is associated with a decline in estrogen levels (77, 92). Over time, this decline may be experienced as a change in skin elasticity (17), altered cognitive abilities (143), lengthened or shortened menstrual patterns (160, 161), or discomforts such as vaginal dryness, night sweats, and hot flashes (35). The decline in serum estrogen levels is just one of a patchwork of hormonal changes associated with menopause. Similarly, menopause—or the

0084-6570/94/1015-0231$05.00

231

entire climacteric—is just one piece of the dynamic, ongoing physiological and sociocultural process of aging (26a).

Menopause is both a biological aging event (8) and a maturational process in the context of aging (125) that coincides with age-related changes in, for instance, bone density and immune response (148). One challenge of menopause research is to identify physiological changes that are specific to menopause, separate from the other progressive, irreversible, universal processes of aging (75). Another challenge is to differentiate between biological and cultural effects. For instance, hot flashes are measurable, physiological occurrences (73, 79, 80); however, the frequency and severity of hot flashes differ between cultures (3, 10).

In the discussion presented here, menopause will be conceived of as both a process and an event. Menopause will also be envisioned as both a dependent and an independent variable. As an event, the timing of menopause is best modeled as a single outcome from multivariate input. For example, the timing of menopause varies between populations (49, 52, 55, 86, 167, 178) and within populations (for the United States, see 95, 159). Dependent variables related to intrapopulation variation in age at menopause include smoking habits, parity, education, and body mass index (106). As an independent variable, the process of menopause is just one factor contributing to menopausal symptoms such as hot flashes or bone loss. For example, the recent medical emphasis on osteoporosis as a symptom of menopause (96, 177) downplays a myriad of risk factors including white or Asian ethnicity, family history of osteoporosis, lifelong low calcium intake, lack of physical activity in childhood and adulthood, alcohol abuse, cigarette smoking, and high caffeine intake (28, 90).

Cross-species studies identify aspects of menopause that are unique to humans. The macaque (60) and the chimpanzee (50, 51) provide lifespan stage, hormonal, and anatomical points of comparison for the study of menopause. Cross-cultural studies tease apart the human universal (biological) aspects of menopausal symptoms from culture-specific variation. For example, cross-cultural studies have pointed to lifestyle changes (83), parity (11), and nutrition (8) as explanations for iation differences in bone loss and fracture rates in pre- and postmenopausal women.

An understanding of the biological aspects of menopause is relevant for evolutionary comparative work; for biocultural investigations of intra- and interpopulation variation; for informing and framing theoretical discussions in medical anthropology; and for examining menopause in relation to nutritional status, genetics, fertility, and mortality. It is also an appropriate adjunct to the comparative study of menstruation (18a, 129a).

Menopause is a "distinct window" (181) into a long process of ovarian aging. Menopause follows years of exposure to infectious disease, childbearing, changes in marital status, smoking and drinking habits, and fluctuations in nutritional status. The event of menopause cannot be separated from ongoing life. Nonetheless, except for the window of menopause, the long process of ovarian aging is hidden from noninvasive observation. It is not known when, or even whether, there are critical moments in ovarian development and/or aging that determine age at menopause or particular symptom experience. All that can be observed is the cessation of menses at the individual or population level, coupled with hormonal changes.

This review outlines the biological basics of menopause and then places menopause within the context of a dynamic lifespan. The basic tenets of the lifespan approach maintain that, for each individual, aging and development are lifelong processes from birth to death; biological, psychological, and sociocultural trajectories interweave across the life course; the entire lifespan serves as a frame of reference for understanding particular events or transitions; and the life course can be affected by environmental change (16, 134, 144, 147).

This review also points to the gap between population-level studies of menopause and studies carried out at the biochemical, cellular, or organ systems level. Filling this gap between the "students of the whole" and "students of the fragments" (153) offers the most interesting directions for future anthropological research.

BIOLOGICAL BASICS

Science presently wields technology capable of extending the female reproductive lifespan beyond intrinsic limits, as evidenced by widely publicized success in postmenopausal pregnancies (8a). For most women, however, menopause signals the end of childbearing. Female reproductive aging may relate to uterine aging (110) or to a decline in oocyte quality with age (44, 118); however, once the egg supply is exhausted, natural fertility is terminated (133). Evidence of ovulation and primordial follicles have been found in the ovaries of women older than 50 (24, 122); nonetheless, exhaustion of oocyte stores is central to the onset of menopause. The event of menopause clearly demonstrates that ovarian aging is lifelong, progressive, and irreversible: the incessant loss of oocytes leads to menopause.

Aging changes also occur in the neuroendocrine system. Although menopause fundamentally is an ovarian phenomenon, the ovarian changes cannot be considered out of the context of larger neuroendocrine and immunological systems. Both "pelvic clocks" and "neural clocks" (9) are involved in the onset of menstrual cessation.

Ovarian Follicles

In simple terms, the timing of menopause and onset of menopausal symptoms is determined by the number of eggs present in the ovaries at birth and by the rate of egg loss through ovulation and degenerative processes. More technically, within the human fetus, primordial germ cells exist prior to the differentiation of the gonad. These ovoid, ameboid-like cells migrate to the ovary by the fifth or sixth week of gestation. From the eleventh or twelfth week onward the germ cells (called oogonia at this stage) form oocytes by mitosis (7, 27, 116). Oocytes are undeveloped eggs stored in the ovary. Oocyte formation ceases by the fifth month in utero (7). Although fish, amphibians, and reptiles continue oogenesis throughout adult life (137), most mammals do not (7, 57).

The size of the fetal follicular endowment is species-specific (41, 119, 127, 168) and is probably under genetic control (49). In humans, there are an estimated two million oocytes present at birth (7). This extraordinary number of oocytes may be an evolutionary carryover from ancestors (e.g. fish) that relied on external fertilization (97).

Within the ovaries, at about 16 weeks in utero, oocytes are surrounded by a layer of flattened granulosa cells (116). These are the primordial follicles. Oocytes that remain naked, without a layer of granulosa cells, degenerate (168). Primordial follicles act as a pool from which all developing follicles emerge (20, 127). Primordial follicles can develop further into preantral follicles, then antral follicles (see Figure 1). These more developed follicles contain oocytes encircled by granulosa and theca cellular envelopes (97, 127). Estrogen is produced in the granulosa cells; the rate of hormone secretion increases in proportion to follicle size. Maximum rates of estrogen production are attained just before ovulation in mature (preovulatory) follicles. Following ovulation the follicle becomes a corpus luteum, which secretes large amounts of progesterone (97).

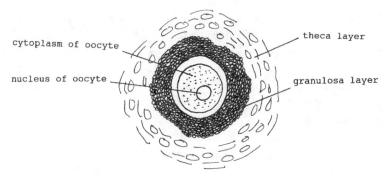

cytoplasm of oocyte

theca layer

nucleus of oocyte

granulosa layer

Figure 1   Preantral follicle (based on 97:62).

Follicles at all stages of development are present in the ovaries during the reproductive years. Although follicular development can lead to ovulation, ovulation accounts for very few of the follicles lost across a woman's lifespan. Instead, 99.9% of all oocytes disappear from the ovary by the process of atresia (degeneration), not ovulation (40, 127). In the human ovaries there are 6.8 million germ cells at the fifth month post-conception. This number declines to 2 million oocytes in the ovaries at birth (7) and to some 390,000 at menarche (19). The greatest loss of oocytes occurs during the fetal and prepubertal periods (27, 59).

The causes and rates of atresia differ by follicular developmental stage (20, 57, 127). Atresia of small follicles originates in the oocyte, which undergoes lysis or phagocytosis (20, 57). Atresia of preantral and antral follicles originates in the granulosa cells, which shrink as cells of the theca layer increase in size (20, 57, 168). Atresia occurs more frequently in the late preantral and antral stages even though there are more follicles in the early stages of development in the ovary at any one time (127).

Cells going through, or about to enter, atresia can be identified microscopically, chemically, and molecularly (27, 61, 158). The process of atresia begins prenatally and continues throughout the lifespan (7, 57). Mathematical models have attempted to determine whether number of follicles at birth or rate of atresia is more important in determining age at menopause (102, 155), whether there is a limiting threshold number of follicles needed to maintain menstrual cycles (119, 133), and whether there is an acceleration of follicle loss as menopause approaches (37). With respect to the latter model, Faddy et al (37) mistakenly argue for an accelerated rate of follicular atresia in women older than 37 based on log transformed data (LR Godfrey, LE Leidy, manuscript in preparation). The actual decline in number slows with age (40, 155).

There are various arguments for a genetic component to age at menopause. Women experiencing premature ovarian failure—before the age of 40—have exhibited Mendelian inheritance patterns (101). X-chromosome monosomy in both mice and women (Turner's syndrome) is associated with an early age at reproductive failure (49), as is partial deletion of the long arm of the X chromosome (78). Trisomies of chromosome 18 (Edward's syndrome) and chromosome 21 (Down's syndrome) are associated with reduced numbers of both non-growing and growing follicles (49). In addition, early age at menopause is related to a genetic deficiency of galactose-1-phosphate uridyl transferase, an enzyme used in the conversion of galactose to glucose (25). In this case the genetic control of the timing of menopause alters the rate of follicular atresia, first in utero, then during the first decades of life, through the accumulation of galactose metabolites, which damage the ovary (72).

Atresia may be an evolved mechanism that facilitates reproduction by means of relatively small numbers of live offspring. Alternatively, atresia may be a mechanism whereby products of many follicles are produced to serve a chosen few (27). In some mammals (e.g. the Canadian porcupine) accessory corpora lutea are formed from follicles that do not ovulate. The extra corpora lutea produce progesterone, which maintains pregnancies (126). Similarly in other mammals, ovarian inhibin is produced by all antral follicles in the ovary, rather than only the dominant follicle (as with estradiol) (5). Inhibin is an ovarian hormone that has a negative feedback effect on pituitary follicle stimulating hormone (FSH). Extra inhibin could function to maintain the low levels of FSH required during the early stages of pregnancy.

Some researchers argue that atresia represents an example of apoptosis (61, 157, 158), which is "an active, genetically governed process whereby cells die by following what appears to be a controlled, intrinsic program designed for their demise" (61:2416). Hughes & Gorospe (61), for example, hypothesize that apoptosis is responsible for the demise of the granulosa cells, which causes follicular atresia. If cell death is preprogrammed, however, the trigger for cell death still needs to be explained. Something induces apoptosis. The trigger may be an imbalance between pituitary and ovarian hormones or it may have an immunological component.

Neuroendocrine Aspects of Menopause

To better grasp the process of atresia, which leads to the cessation of menses and to symptoms such as vaginal dryness, hot flashes, increasing levels of low density lipoprotein (LDL) cholesterol, and bone thinning, it is important to understand the hormonal aspects of menopause.

The hypothalamus, pituitary, and ovaries integrate neural and hormonal signals into a physiological rhythm that continues for almost 40 years. Beginning with the brain (an arbitrary starting point), the hypothalamus transmits gonadotrophin releasing hormone (GnRH) in episodic pulses directly to the anterior pituitary (153). In the anterior pituitary, plasma membrane receptors for GnRH sense the pulse frequency and amplitude of GnRH (39) and respond by producing two gonadotrophins, follicle stimulating hormone (FSH) and luteinizing hormone (LH). FSH and LH are also characterized by episodic secretion, which continues after menopause (39, 173). Catecholamines (dopamine and norepinephrine), serotonin, endogenous opioid peptides (enkephalins and β-endorphin), and hypothalamic peptides (such as neurotensin and gastrin) influence the secretion of GnRH, thereby influencing the secretion of LH and FSH (9, 39, 56, 109, 139, 174). Although FSH and LH are both stimulated by GnRH, they appear to be under separate regulatory control as evidenced by higher levels of FSH during the follicular phase of menstrual cycles (4), an earlier rise in FSH levels prior to menopause (22, 113), and different effects of endogenous opioid peptides on LH and FSH secretion (39).

Within the ovaries, FSH receptors are present only on follicular granulosa cells, while LH receptors are found on granulosa, thecal, interstitial, and luteal cells. FSH and LH stimulate oogenesis, follicular growth, and the production of estrogen and progesterone (57, 97, 153). Granulosa cells also produce the peptide inhibin (22). Estrogen, progesterone, and inhibin send feedback to the brain, which generally decreases the secretion of FSH and LH (39, 153).

In an ovulatory cycle, FSH levels begin to rise prior to menstruation and continue to rise through the early follicular phase. LH pulses increase in frequency throughout the follicular phase (days 1–14 of the cycle; see Figure 2). Levels of estradiol (the major premenopausal estrogen) and estrone (the predominant postmenopausal estrogen) increase from the mid-follicular to the late follicular phase of the cycle, eventually causing the decline in FSH levels (4, 142). Inhibin levels remain low (5). During the luteal phase (days 15–28), inhibin levels increase (5) while LH and FSH pulse amplitude and frequency decline. Estradiol levels decline from the mid-follicular phase to the end of the luteal phase while progesterone levels increase (4). In reality, it is misleading to speak of days 1–14 and 15–28 because menstrual cycle length varies quite a bit at different points in a woman's lifespan (77, 161).

Across the lifespan, the sequence of hormonal rhythms stays the same, but hormonal levels are modified with age. Specifically, estrogen levels increase with age during the late follicular phase and decline with age during the luteal phase. An age-related decline of corpora lutea causes progesterone levels to fall during the luteal phase (77). The follicular phase of the cycle shortens

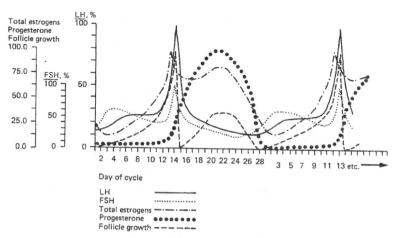

Figure 2 Summary of hormonal events—normal ovulation cycle (138a). Hormone levels are presented as percent maximum secretion.

(141). FSH levels increase throughout the cycle, particularly during the early follicular phase, despite levels of ovarian estrogen that would be expected to suppress pituitary FSH secretion (141, 142). The increase in FSH, which occurs when women are in their thirties (163), is the result of follicular oocyte depletion, which results in lower inhibin secretion (5, 77). As with menstrual cycle length, hormonal changes also vary greatly with age, ranging from ovulatory cycles with low premenopausal levels of FSH to transient episodes of high levels of FSH and LH (112).

Menopause is characterized by elevated serum levels of LH and FSH, and a reduced level of circulating estrogen (92). In one longitudinal study (132), menopause was characterized by a marked drop in the levels of all steroids except those of adrenal origin. Estradiol declines markedly. Postmenopausal estrone is converted from adrenal and ovarian androstenedione in peripheral tissues such as muscle and adipose (21, 77, 93, 128).

Because it is difficult to separate the changes of aging from those specific to menopause, the trigger for menopause is still debated. The etiology of menopause may lie in age-related changes at the level of the hypothalamus. For example, there are age-related changes in dopamine, norepinephrine, serotonin, and β-endorphin levels (41, 114, 151), and a loss of hypothalamic neurotransmitter receptors may occur with age (109). A reduction in GnRH pulse frequency is associated with a decline in follicular maturation (39). The rise in FSH levels prior to the decline in ovarian steroid levels could be the result of an age-related decrease in sensitivity of the hypothalamic-pituitary axis to ovarian steroids (112, 113). In rats the loss of estrous cycles lies in the failure of the hypothalamo-pituitary system (41, 109). The National Research Council points out, however, that anestrous female rats are different from postmenopausal women:

> In the rat, the ovaries appear to be capable of normal or near normal function throughout the lifespan, whereas the ovaries of women cease to function around midlife. ...In addition, the hypothalamo-pituitary system of the rat shows a reduced capacity to secrete gonadotropins, whereas gonadotropin levels in postmenopausal women are increased (117:413).

The primate is a much better model for the human menopause (13, 50, 51, 60, 125).

Based on human and non-human primate observations, many researchers argue that menopause is initiated by the ovary as oocytes are depleted through atresia (54, 77, 92, 97, 127, 133, 141, 142). The loss of oocytes results in a decline in ovarian estrogen and inhibin. Lack of negative feedback increases FSH and, later, LH production (22). As with all aspects of menopause, there are also age-related changes that are independent of oocyte loss. For example, with increasing age the numbers of theca and granulosa cells decrease, so estrogen and progestogen levels also decline (171).

Immunological Aspects of Menopause

At the 1993 meetings of the North American Menopause Society, Anderson (2) pointed out that the immunological changes in T cell immunity and humoral immunity occuring in association with menopause are "only beginning to be appreciated." Various linkages between neuroendocrine aging and immune system changes with age have been hypothesized (41).

Clues to the etiology of menopause may be found in an examination of premature ovarian failure because, as Cramer et al point out (25:610), the line dividing cases of early menopause from the clinical norm is arbitrary. Biomedical anthropologists, well acquainted with the arbitrary cutoffs that identify clinical diseases, could examine the relevance and meaning of the boundary. For example, Ginsburg's (46) summary of premature ovarian failure applies equally well to menopause at the age of 50:

> In women with premature ovarian failure it is not clear whether fewer primordial germ cells migrate to the germinal ridge in fetal life, whether the rate of multiplication up to the fifth month of intrauterine life is reduced, whether the rate of follicular loss thereafter is greater than normal, or whether there is a combination of all three factors (p.1289).

Another interesting observation concerns the relationship between autoimmune disorders and early menopause. Autoimmune disorders are more common among women (12), and higher rates of early menopause have been observed among women with autoimmune disorders involving the thyroid and adrenal glands, as well as women diagnosed with diabetes, pernicious anemia, myasthenia gravis (36), alopecia, vitiligo, Crohn's disease (87), and systemic lupus erythematosus (12, 18, 94). In addition, anti-ovarian antibodies have been identified in the serum from women with the diagnosis of Addison's disease (108) and premature menopause (130, 135). Because of documented relationships between handedness (a measure of cerebral lateralization) and various autoimmune disorders, one study examined age at menopause in relation to handedness (85). Left-handed women reported a significantly earlier age at menopause. Other studies have not demonstrated such a relationship (1, 86).

BIOBEHAVIORAL FACTORS ASSOCIATED WITH MENOPAUSE

The entire female lifespan—fetal, prepubertal, and reproductive—ultimately determines the cessation of menses by influencing the environment of the ovary. The range in variation in age at menopause and onset of symptoms is familial in two ways. Genetically, parents pass to their daughter the parameters for number of oocytes and/or rate of atresia. Behaviorally, a mother's activity while pregnant affects the ovarian store her daughter possesses at birth (49). From birth until menopause the environment and behavior of the individual affects her own ovarian stores. "Extensive epigenetic influences" (41:569) result in variation in age at menopause and symptom experience between and within populations.

Age at Menopause

Age at menopause is defined as age at last menstrual period after at least 12 months of amenorrhea (70, 165, 178). Cross-sectional, retrospective, and longitudinal studies have consistently placed the median age of menopause at 49–51.5 years among women in relatively well-nourished populations of industrialized societies (49, 52, 53, 55, 86, 167, 178). In contrast, average age at menopause is 43–47 years among women in New Guinea (175), India (138), Pakistan (166) and the Philippines (47). Age at menopause is of interest in relation to fertility (176), mortality (145, 146), and morbidity. Late age at menopause is associated with increased risk of endometrial and breast cancers (31, 81).

Problems in menopause research and cross-study comparison have been reviewed elsewhere (14, 52, 55, 69, 107). For example, comparisons of mean age at menopause between populations are confounded by error in recalled age at menopause (23). A cross-sectional status quo approach, such as probit analysis (42), avoids error in recall. Probit analysis computes the proportions of women who are or are not menstruating at each age to construct the median age at menopause—the age at which 50% of the population ceased menstruating. From a lifespan perspective, a major limitation in cross-sectional or retrospective studies is the measure of cause and effect at the same point in time, which may result in an erroneous association between variables.

The patterns of constancy or change in variables such as smoking habits, body weight, or marital status may be important in relation to the process of atresia. Smoking is associated with a significantly earlier age at menopause (65, 71, 86, 88, 106, 120, 124, 172). Body size is less clearly associated with age at menopause. In many studies lean women appear to experience a natural menopause slightly earlier than heavier women (15, 67, 89, 95, 120). Marital status, for unexplained reasons, is related to the onset of menopause. Married women report a later age at menopause than do single women (15, 120). Women of higher income status have also demonstrated a later age at menopause than do women with lower incomes (131, 149).

Menopause is later among women who use estrogen replacement therapy during the 12 months preceding the last menstrual period (160). Most studies have found no demonstrable relationship between age at menarche and age at menopause (120, 159, 170), although an inverse relationship has been found in poorly nourished populations (52, 53) and among women with a history of mumps (26).

Menstrual cycle length and regularity has a significant relationship to age at natural menopause (149, 170). Several studies have shown a later age at menopause with increasing numbers of pregnancies (64, 86, 120, 170), although other studies have shown no significant association between age at menopause and parity (15, 48, 131). Mothers of multiple births (i.e. twins) have a significantly earlier natural menopause than do women who have given birth to a single offspring (179).

Other variables associated with menopause include blindness (84) and living at high altitudes (7a, 66, 131). There is no difference in age at menopause between urban and rural women (76, 131). Nor is there an association between age at menopause and the use of oral contraception (15), months spent breastfeeding (48), miscarriages (120, 170), or abortions (120).

The influence of biobehavioral and reproductive factors on the timing of menopause may be the result of an altered rate of atresia. This places menopause within the context of a dynamic lifespan. For all of the above variables, the questions to be asked go beyond cross-sectional vs longitudinal study design. Specifically, when is diet, a marriage, or a two-pack-a-day smoking habit important? What are the threshold numbers of years? Do biobehavioral factors have more of an effect when there are many oocytes present in the ovary, or when there are few?

Symptom Experience

The same process of follicular decline responsible for the timing of menopause is also responsible for what have been called the symptoms of menopause.[1] As was pointed out above, the follicle, which nourishes the oocyte, is also the major site of estrogen production in the body. The decline in follicle number across the lifespan eventually results in lowered levels of circulating estrogen. As estrogen is withdrawn from estrogen-responsive tissues, symptoms may be acute (e.g. hot flashes or night sweats), or they may develop slowly (e.g. urogenital atrophy) (171). The symptoms of menopause include changes in the vagina, cervix, uterine ligaments, and skin. There is decreased pubic hair, loss

---

[1]

Symptoms are defined as "any perceptible change in the body or its functions that indicate disease or the kind or phases of disease" (154). To use the word symptom thus implies that menopause is a disease or, more precisely, an endocrinopathy (104, 163). It may be more accurate to refer to hot flashes, vaginal dryness, and night sweats as discomforts; to point out that increasing LDL levels are symptomatic of future cardiovascular disease; and to argue that bone thinning is a risk factor for osteoporosis. However, in literature, research funding, and clinical treatment, the biology of menopause remains tightly bound to the medicine of menopause.

of subcutaneous fat, bone loss, and increased risk of cardiovascular disease (58, 115, 171). There is some evidence of altered cognitive ability (143). Although related to lower levels of estrogen, hot flashes, night sweats, and vaginal dryness (35) are far from universal (3).

Hot flashes and night sweats occur during the perimenopause, which is a time of hormonal flux that is defined as the interval from just before the last menstrual period until a full year after it (178). The perimenopause is more difficult to define than is menopause. Irregular menses begin on average at age 45.5 (160), but the range is 41–59. Hot flashes may begin several years before the cessation of menses; osteoporosis may not be visible for decades after. Also, symptoms such as vaginal dryness and dyspareunia (pain with intercourse) increase with advancing age, although hot flashes lessen in frequency and intensity (73). For all symptoms of menopause, the effects of aging and lifestyle need to be taken into account before menopause is identified as causal.

Especially with regard to psychological symptoms, endocrine changes need to be disentangled from lifespan stage to assess whether symptoms such as anxiety or depression (105) are associated with menopause. The rise and fall of the diagnostic category involutional melancholia (169) is a good example of a culture-bound syndrome. This is a depressive psychosis once thought to occur among women ages 40–60 because of the hormonal changes of menopause. It was removed from the psychiatric nosology in 1979 when studies failed to show that rates of depression were any higher, or of a distinct pattern, among menopausal women compared to nonmenopausal women (169).

The most obvious place for anthropologists in the study of menopausal symptoms is in the realm of cross-cultural comparisons to identify the biological vs cultural components. For example, studies carried out in Greece and Mexico (10), Newfoundland (30), Israel (29), Indonesia (43), Japan (91), Ghana (82), South Africa (33), Pakistan (166), Nigeria (6), Canada, and the United States (3) demonstrate different frequency rates for hot flashes among women in these populations.

Avis et al (3) suggest that the academic and clinical community should accept the normality of the menopause transition and explain the deviance of symptoms. In doing so, however, it is important not to abandon a biocultural approach in the pursuit of menopause as a normal or biologically uneventful life transition.

Consider the pathophysiology of hot flashes. Hot flashes are related to pituitary LH pulses, increases of plasma epinephrine, and decreases of norepinephrine (73, 79, 80). Symptomatic women have lower levels of serum estrogens than do asymptomatic women (73). Visible signs of hot flashes are reddening of the skin accompanied by profuse sweating (171). Peripheral temperature rises 4–5°C in fingers and toes (73, 79). For cross-cultural research and studies of intrapopulation variation, it is extremely interesting that women can demonstrate the peripheral temperature changes without feeling the flush. Clinicians conclude that asymptomatic women are evidence that the objective parameters are more reliable indicators of vasomotor instability than are the subjective sensation of hot flushes (73:55). Anthropologists should go even further to question why the threshold of sensitivity to universal physiologic change differs so dramatically between women and between populations.

Just as there is a need for a lifespan approach in considering the timing of menopause, there is also a call for the lifespan approach in considering bone loss leading to osteoporosis (28, 129, 180). Consider the similarity between ovarian aging and the following description of bone loss: "The risk of a woman experiencing an osteoporotic fracture within her lifetime depends upon 2 factors: the peak bone mass achieved and the rate of bone loss after the menopause" (171:16). Taking a lifespan approach involves considering childhood activity levels, participation in college sports, lifelong calcium intake, and exposure to sunshine, in addition to the endocrine changes of menopause.

Menopause is also associated with increases in total cholesterol, triglycerides, and LDL cholesterol, and with reductions in high density lipoprotein cholesterol. These changes are seen in longitudinal study (164) and are independent of age and body mass index (150).

THE GAP BETWEEN LEVELS OF BIOLOGICAL ORGANIZATION

Follicular atresia eventually results in both the cessation of menstruation and the low estrogen environment associated with various menopausal symptoms. Because ovarian decline through atresia is hidden from view, the best we can do at the level of whole individuals or populations is to make observations through the window of menopause; assay hormone levels in blood, urine, and saliva; and identify attributes that may have altered the rate of atresia across the lifespan. The rate of follicular atresia is fastest during the fetal and prepubertal stage (27, 59). Of interest, then, are fetal impacts, such as history of a malnourished or smoking mother, and effects of prepubertal nutrition or infectious disease. Body weight at age 18, for example, is more strongly associated with age at menopause than is body weight at the cessation of menses (140). Cramer et al (26) hypothesize that age at menopause is earlier among women with a history of mumps because the infection may damage the ovaries, causing premature depletion of oocytes.

During the reproductive years, attention should be directed toward physiological changes (e.g. pregnancy, weight gain) and behaviors (e.g. smoking) to assess impact on rate of atresia. For example, smoking may result in an earlier menopause because of effects on the central nervous system or liver metabolism (65, 88, 100, 120), through hypoxic effects on the ovaries (49), or through the destruction of primordial oocytes (103).

While looking across the lifespan for health-related behaviors and patterns of physiological change associated with the timing of menopause or symptom experience, investigations should be informed by a biological understanding of what turns menstrual cyclicity off. The process of atresia is still not well understood. Some hypotheses involve apoptosis (61, 157, 158); others point to ovarian toxicants (27, 155). Farookhi (38) suggests that atresia is an inflammatory response. Most other hypotheses target specific hormonal triggers (141). Factors that appear to influence the rate of follicular atresia include genetics, age, stage of reproductive cycle, pregnancy, lactation, hypophysectomy (removal of the pituitary), unilateral ovariectomy, exogenous hormones, chemical messengers, nutrition, and ischemia (local obstruction of blood flow) (57). Guraya (57) concludes that even though the basic biochemical or endocrinological aspects of follicular atresia are still unknown, it is apparent that the process of atresia is regulated by the interaction of gonadotrophins and steroids. In particular, the process of atresia appears to be affected by the imperfect balance or lack of these hormones, at least in the mammalian ovary. Elevated estrogen levels (63, 168), intra- and extra-ovarian androgen, prolactin (57), and altered FSH and LH levels (57, 59, 136) all have been implicated in increased rates of follicular atresia. Epidermal growth factor has been implicated recently in oocyte atresia (99).

Observations made at the level of whole individuals suggest underlying biological mechanisms for atresia (74). Similarly, hypotheses developed from an understanding of physiological systems can be tested in survey populations. Atresia begins in the fifth month in utero and continues for 40 or 50 years; therefore, one might expect that longitudinal studies are the best method for studying menopause (69).

Longitudinal Studies

The changes of menopause have been approached longitudinally by endocrinologists, epidemiologists, and anthropologists. Sherman & Korenman (142) conducted one of the first studies on hormonal correlations of the menstrual cycle. Fifty complete menstrual cycles in 37 women were examined. Women with regular menstrual cycles were grouped by age: 18–30 (n = 10), 40–41 (n = 5), and 46–51 (n = 6). Endocrine profiles were collected for cycles lasting 20–54 days. The authors demonstrated that FSH levels were increased dramatically throughout the cycle among the women ages 46–51, while LH levels remained indistinguishable from levels in younger women. During the early follicular phase, estradiol levels were the same in women ages 46–51 as among younger women, but the mid-cycle peak and luteal phase concentration were significantly lower among the older women. Endocrine profiles, menstrual history, and reproductive history were reported for the women studied.

Metcalf et al (112) measured FSH, LH, and estrogens in weekly urine samples from 31 women, ages 36–55, who had recently experienced a change in menstrual cyclicity. Samples were obtained from each woman for 14 to 87 weeks. The hormone patterns observed varied widely. For example, in 14 women, both FSH and LH concentrations rose temporarily to postmenopausal levels in association with high estrogen levels; in 18 women, there was a temporary elevation of LH, but not FSH, into the postmenopausal range. Ovulatory cycles were observed to within 16 weeks of the last menstrual period. Medical, reproductive, and contraceptive information was provided, along with body weight.

Trevoux et al (162) also carried out a longitudinal study that demonstrated wide inter- and intraindividual variation. Their longitudinal study covered 13 years, from 6 years before to 7 years after the last menstrual period (n = 483). From 2 to 7 endometrial biopsies were obtained (n = 388) for comparison and correlation with progesterone, estradiol levels, and menopause status. Information on medical history and HRT use was provided.

In another study, Rannevik et al (132) conducted a prospective 7-year analysis of serum hormone levels in 30 women, ages 48 and 49. Data collection included clinical and biochemical indices of health, height, weight, and use of hormonal supplementation. Also prospectively, Longcope et al (92) followed 88 women, ages 45–58, for 2.5 years. As with the above studies, menstrual characteristics, mean age and weight, general health, and use of hormone replacement were reported.

One of the problems encountered in attempting to bridge physiological and population levels of biological organization is that each level brings its own methodological baggage. For example, hormonal sampling problems include diurnal and menstrual variation in hormone levels, laboratory expense, and the particular disadvantages of sample source, whether it be urine, blood, or saliva. Even so, the inter- and intraindividual variation reported in the above longitudinal endocrine studies raises questions about the impact of biobehavioral variables beyond height, weight, and general health. Biobehavioral variables (e.g. smoking or alcohol intake) have been shown to have hormonal impact (45). Endocrinological investigations should cross boundaries between levels of organization; gather more biobehavioral data when carrying out hormonal assays in large study populations; and compare assay results among women who vary in symptom experience, body shape, body size, and behavior. For example, do smokers have higher levels of FSH at an earlier age in relation to declining inhibin levels caused by oocyte damage?

An example of a population-level longitudinal study is Treloar's Menstruation and Reproductive History Study, which was initiated in Minnesota in

1934 (140, 159–161, 170). This study was the first to show the variability in cycle length experienced by women immediately prior to menopause (161). Data collected included menstrual, contraceptive, reproductive, and medical history (140). Data on exogenous factors (e.g. smoking), which may have influenced age at menopause, were not included (170). In 1975, questionnaires were mailed to current and previous study participants to collect data on weight at current age and recalled weight at age 18. Analyses demonstrated that women who were heavier at age 18 had a later menopause than did leaner women (140). Sherman et al concluded that "the nutritional factors that influence menopausal age are exerted early in life" (p. 317). However, the investigators did not examine the effect of weight *change* across the lifespan. Instead of exploiting the dynamic potential of a longitudinal data set, the authors used the data as if they were cross-sectional. Weight change affects the hormonal milieu of the ovary (128) and may thus affect age at menopause and symptom experience.

The dynamic nature of biological change is better illustrated by the New England Research Institute's longitudinal study (3, 14, 106), which collected demographic data on age, marital status, number of children, smoking habits, medical and menstrual history, symptoms, and use of hormone replacement therapy. Data were collected premenopausally (baseline) and at the first 9-month follow up. Menstrual status was monitored through five years of follow-up of 2570 women (106). Change in variables such as weight or marital status was not monitored (14). The study showed the central role of smoking in influencing age at menopause, and that smokers have not only an earlier menopause, but also an earlier and shorter perimenopause (106). Other longitudinal population surveys include the Manitoba Project on Women and Their Health in the Middle Years (70) and the South-East England Longitudinal Study (62).

To consider only one level of biological organization is to forfeit valuable insight. For example, a negative aspect of focusing on only endocrine relationships is that menopause is construed as pathological, a disruption rather than a natural lifespan change. At the other extreme, considering the symptoms of menopause strictly from the level of the individual or population does not help explain why the symptoms of menopause vary. Bridging these levels of organization may yield meaningful answers to questions raised at all levels.

Symptoms can be studied in association with neuroendocrine changes (80) or clinically through changes in core temperature (i.e. esophageal, rectal, or tympanic membrane) or peripheral temperature (i.e. forehead or fingers and toes) (111, 152). Symptoms can also be examined at the level of populations by checklist (3). For example, Beyene (10) found that among the Mayan Indians of Yucatan, Mexico, menopause occurs at a relatively early age, 41–45, and is not accompanied by hot flashes. In addition, elderly Mayan women

do not typically experience osteoporotic fractures (98). Because of these findings, Martin et al (98) examined Mayan women for endocrinological and
bone-density differences. They found that endocrine changes were not significantly different from those reported in the United States. In fact, estrogen
levels were at or below levels expected for United States populations. Also,
bone demineralization was shown to occur despite the lack of fractures. They
conclude that the same endocrine events, menopause and bone loss, can result
in different clinical manifestations.

CONCLUSIONS

Getting at the how and why of human variation calls for an understanding of
biology at more than one level of organization. For this reason, across different
levels of organization, a lifespan approach is ideal for gaining a clearer understanding of the timing of menopause and symptoms of menopause, including
bone loss and changing serum lipid levels. The study of menopause, osteoporosis, and heart disease can be used to illustrate how events early in life have
later effects, how sociocultural and biological components interact, and how
patterns of change may be as important as cross-sectional measures.

The lifespan approach is enhanced by longitudinal research, but it is important to point out that lifespan and longitudinal are not synonymous. The
lifespan approach can also inform cross-sectional studies. Questions can be
designed to allow for the interweaving of biological and sociocultural trajectories, to encourage an understanding of the effect of change in body size,
smoking habits, or activity levels.

In a discussion of demographic and physiologic studies of reproduction,
Ellison pointed out that "it is valuable to push both forms of inquiry forward
without ceding ascendancy to either, in the expectation of benefiting from the
dialectic that emerges" (34:934). This integration of different levels of biological organization has been demonstrated in studies of reproduction (34b; see
also 34a). For example, Wood et al combined demographic and endocrinological data to examine low rates of fertility among the Gainj of highland Papua
New Guinea (175).

The process of follicular atresia leading to menopause is hidden within
layers of physical body. Less tangibly, the consequences of follicular atresia
are confounded by cultural expectations with regard to menopause and lifestyle practices. For example, women may not experience symptoms such as
hot flashes despite measurable, physiological change (73, 98). Similarly,
women may not evidence osteoporotic fractures despite postmenopausal bone
loss (98). The biological aspects of menopause have been investigated by
teams of researchers who have approached the perimenopausal transition from
endocrinological and epidemiological angles. Broader insight may be gained

by integrating the two approaches to consider how follicular atresia is influenced across the lifespan by endocrinological and lifestyle variables. The menopausal transition provides a rich opportunity for researchers to bridge levels of biological organization in holistic and comparative study.

Literature Cited

1. Allaway S, Last P, Hale A. 1991. What determines the age at the menopause? *Br. Med. J.* 303:250
2. Anderson DJ. 1993. *Immunology of menopause and aging.* Presented at 4th Annu. North Am. Menopause Soc. Meet., San Diego
3. Avis NE, Kaufert PA, Lock M, McKinlay SM, Vass K. 1993. The evolution of menopausal symptoms. *Bailliere's Clin. Endocrinol. Metabol.* 7:17–32
4. Backstrom CT, McNeilly A, Leask RM, Baird DT. 1982. Pulsatile secretion of LH, FSH, prolactin, estradiol, and progesterone during the human menstrual cycle. *Clin. Endocrinol.* 17:29–42
5. Baird DT, Smith KB. 1993. Inhibin and related peptides in the regulation of reproduction. *Oxford Rev. Reprod. Biol.* 15:191–232
6. Bajulaiye O, Sarrel PM. 1986. A survey of perimenopausal symptoms in Nigeria. In *The Climacteric in Perspective,* ed. M Notelovitz, P van Keep, pp. 161–75. Boston: MTP Press
7. Baker TG. 1986. Gametogenesis. In *Comparative Primate Biology,* ed. WR Dukelow, J Erwin, 3:165–213. New York: Liss
7a. Beall CM. 1982. Ages at menopause and menarche in a high-altitude Himalayan population. *Ann. Hum. Biol.* 10:365–70
8. Beall CM. 1987. Nutrition and variation in biological aging. In *Nutritional Anthropology,* ed. FE Johnston, pp. 197–221. New York: Liss
8a. Beck M, Hager M, Wingert P, King P, Gordon J, et al. 1994. How far should we push mother nature? *Newsweek* Jan. 17:54–57
9. Bennett GW, Whitehead SA. 1983. *Mammalian Neuroendocrinology.* New York: Oxford Univ. Press
10. Beyene Y. 1989. *From Menarche to Menopause: Reproductive Lives of Peasant Women in Two Cultures.* Albany: State Univ. NY Press
11. Biberoglu KO, Yildiz A, Kandemir O. 1993. Bone mineral density in Turkish postmenopausal women. *Int. J. Gynecol. Obstet.* 41:153–57
12. Bottazzo GF, Doniach D. 1985. Polyendocrine autoimmunity: an extended concept. In *Autoimmunity and Endocrine Disease,* ed. R Volpe, pp. 375–403. New York: Dekker
13. Bowden D. 1979. *Aging in Nonhuman Primates.* New York: Van Nostrand Reinhold
14. Brambilla D, McKinlay SM. 1990. A prospective study of factors affecting age at menopause. *J. Clin. Epidemiol.* 42:1031–39
15. Brand PC, Lehert PH. 1978. A new way of looking at environmental variables that may affect the age at menopause. *Maturitas* 1:121–32
16. Brim OG, Kagan J. 1980. *Constancy and Change in Human Development.* Cambridge, MA: Harvard Univ. Press
17. Brincat M, Studd J. 1987. Skin and the menopause. See Ref. 115, pp. 103–14
18. Bronson R. 1993. *Immunology and hypergonadotropic ovarian dysfunction.* Presented at 4th Annu. North Am. Menopause Soc. Meet., San Diego
18a. Buckley T, Gottlieb A. 1988. *Blood Magic: The Anthropology of Menstruation.* Los Angeles: Univ. Calif. Press
19. Byskov AG. 1978. Follicular atresia. In *The Vertebrate Ovary,* ed. RE Jones, pp. 533–62. New York: Plenum
20. Byskov AG. 1979. Atresia. In *Ovarian Follicular Development and Function,* ed. MA Rees, WA Sadler, pp. 41–57. New York: Raven
21. Casey ML, MacDonald PC. 1983. Origin of estrogen and regulation of its formation in postmenopausal women. In *The Menopause,* ed. HJ Buchsbaum, pp. 1–12. New York: Springer-Verlag
22. Channing CP, Gordon WL, Liu WK, Ward DN. 1985. Physiology and biochemistry of ovarian inhibin. *Proc. Soc. Exp. Biol. Med.* 178:339–61
23. Colditz GA, Stampfer MJ, Willett WC, Stason WB, Rosner B, et al. 1987. Reproducibility and validity of self-reported meno-

pausal status in a prospective cohort study. *Am. J. Epidemiol.* 126:319–25

24. Costoff A, Mahesh VB. 1975. Primordial follicles with normal oocytes in the ovaries of postmenopausal women. *J. Am. Geriatr. Soc.* 23:193–96

25. Cramer DW, Harlow BL, Barbieri R, Ng WG. 1989. Galactose-1-phosphate uridyl transferase activity associated with age at menopause and reproductive history. *Fertil. Steril.* 51:609–15

26. Cramer DW, Welch WR, Cassells S, Scully RE. 1983. Mumps, menarche, menopause, and ovarian cancer. *Am. J. Obstet. Gynecol.* 147:1–6

26a. Crews DE. 1993. Biological anthropology and human aging: some current directions in aging research. *Annu. Rev. Anthropol.* 22:395–423

27. Crisp TM. 1992. Organization of the ovarian follicle and events in its biology: oogenesis, ovulation or atresia. *Mutat. Res.* 296:89–106

28. Dargent P, Breart G. 1993. Epidemiology and risk factors of osteoporosis. *Curr. Opin. Rheumatol.* 5:339–45

29. Datan N, Antonovsky A, Maoz B. 1981. *A Time to Reap: The Middle Age of Women in Five Israeli Subcultures.* Baltimore: Johns Hopkins Univ. Press

30. Davis DL. 1983. *Blood and Nerves: An Ethnographic Focus on Menopause.* St. John's: Memorial Univ. Newfoundland Inst. Soc. Econ. Res.

31. de Graaff J, Stolte LAM. 1978. Age at menarche and menopause of uterine cancer patients. *Eur. J. Obstet. Gynecol. Reprod. Biol.* 8:187–93

32. Diczfalusy E. 1986. Menopause, developing countries and the 21st century. *Acta Obstet. Gynecol. Scand.* Suppl. 134:45–57

33. du Toit BM. 1990. *Aging and Menopause Among Indian South African Women.* Albany: State Univ. NY Press

34. Ellison PT. 1990. Human ovarian function and reproductive ecology: new hypotheses. *Am. Anthropol.* 92:933–52

34a. Ellison PT. 1994. Human reproductive ecology. *Annu. Rev. Anthropol.* 23:255–75

34b. Ellison PT, Panter-Brick C, Lipson SF, O'Rourke MT. 1993. The ecological context of human ovarian function. *Hum. Reprod.* 8:2242–58

35. Erlik Y, Meldrum DR, Judd HL. 1982. Estrogen levels in postmenopausal women with hot flashes. *Obstet. Gynecol.* 59:403–7

36. Escobar ME, Cigorrage SB, Chiauzzi VA, Charreau EH, Rivarola MA. 1982. Development of the gonadotrophin resistant ovary syndrome in myasthenia gravis: suggestions of similar autoimmune mechanisms. *Acta Endocrinol.* 99:431–36

37. Faddy MJ, Gosden RG, Gougeon A,

Richardson SJ, Nelson JF. 1992. Accelerated disappearance of ovarian follicles in mid-life: implications for forecasting menopause. *Hum. Reprod.* 7:1342–46

38. Farookhi R. 1981. Atresia: a hypothesis. In *Dynamics of Ovarian Function,* ed. NB Schwartz, M Hunzicker-Dunn, pp. 13–23. New York: Raven

39. Ferin M, Van Vugt D, Wardlaw S. 1984. The hypothalamic control of the menstrual cycle and the role of the endogenous opioid peptides. *Recent Progr. Horm. Res.* 40: 441–85

40. Finch CE, Gosden R. 1986. Animal models for the human menopause. In *Aging Reproduction, and the Climacteric,* ed. L Mastroianni, CA Paulsen, pp. 3–34. New York: Plenum

41. Finch CE, Landfield PW. 1985. Neuroendocrine and autonomic functions in aging mammals. See Ref. 41a, pp. 567–94

41a. Finch CE, Schneider EL, eds. 1985. *Handbook of the Biology of Aging.* New York: Van Nostrand Reinhold

42. Finney DJ. 1962. *Probit Analysis: Statistical Treatment of the Sigmoid Response Curve.* Cambridge: Cambridge Univ. Press

43. Flint M, Samil RS. 1990. Cultural and subcultural meanings of the menopause. *Ann. NY Acad. Sci.* 592:134–48

44. Gaulden ME. 1992. Maternal age effect: the enigma of Down syndrome and other trisomic conditions. *Mutat. Res.* 296:69–88

45. Gavaler JS. 1985. Effects of alcohol on endocrine function in postmenopausal women: a review. *J. Stud. Alcohol* 46:495–516

46. Ginsburg J. 1991. What determines the age at the menopause? *Br. Med. J.* 302:1288–89

47. Goodman MJ, Estioko-Griffin A, Griffin PB, Grove JS. 1985. Menarche, pregnancy, birth spacing and menopause among the Agta women foragers of Cagayan Province, Luzon, the Philippines. *Ann. Hum. Biol.* 12: 169–77

48. Goodman MJ, Grove JS, Gilbert F. 1978. Age at menopause in relation to reproductive history in Japanese, Caucasian, Chinese and Hawaiian women living in Hawaii. *J. Gerontol.* 33:688–94

49. Gosden RG. 1985. *Biology of Menopause: The Causes and Consequences of Ovarian Ageing.* New York: Academic

50. Gould K, Flint M, Graham C. 1981. Chimpanzee reproductive senescence: a possible model for evolution of the menopause. *Maturitas* 3:157–66

51. Graham CE. 1986. Endocrinology of reproductive senescence. *Comp. Primate Biol.* 3:93–99

52. Gray RH. 1976. The menopause—epidemiological and demographic considerations. In *The Menopause,* ed. RJ Beard, pp. 25–40. Baltimore: Univ. Park Press

53. Gray RH. 1977. Biological factors other than nutrition and lactation which may influence natural fertility: a review. In *Natural Fertility,* ed. H Leridon, J Menken, pp. 217–51. Belgium: Ordina Editions

54. Gray RH. 1979. Biologial and social interactions in the determination of late fertility. *J. Biosoc. Sci.* (Suppl.) 6:97–115

55. Greene JG. 1984. *The Social and Psychological Origins of the Climacteric Syndrome.* Brookfield, VT: Gower

56. Grossman A. 1989. Opioid peptides, prolactin, and gonadotrophin regulation in the human. In *Brain Opioid Systems in Reproduction,* ed. RG Dyer, RJ Bicknell, pp. 325–39. New York: Oxford Univ. Press

57. Guraya SS. 1985. *Biology of Ovarian Follicles in Mammals.* New York: Springer-Verlag

58. Hammond CB, Haseltine FP, Schiff I. 1989. *Menopause: Evaluation, Treatment, and Health Concerns.* New York: Liss

59. Harman SM, Talbert GB. 1985. Reproductive aging. See Ref. 41a, pp. 457–510

60. Hodgen GD, Goodman AL, O'Connor A, Johnson DK. 1977. Menopause in rhesus monkeys: model for study of disorders in the human climacteric. *Am. J. Obstet. Gynecol.* 127:581–84

61. Hughes FM, Gorospe WC. 1991. Biochemical identification of apoptosis (programmed cell death) in granulosa cells: evidence for a potential mechanism underlying follicular atresia. *Endocrinology* 12:2415–22

62. Hunter M. 1992. The south-east England longitudinal study of the climacteric and postmenopause. *Maturitas* 14:117–26

63. Hutz RJ, Dierschke DJ, Wolf RC. 1990. Role of estradiol in regulating ovarian follicular atresia in rhesus monkeys: a review. *J. Med. Primatol.* 19:553–71

64. Jeune B. 1986. Parity and age at menopause in a Danish sample. *Maturitas* 8:359–65

65. Jick H, Porter J, Morrison AS. 1977. Relation between smoking and age of natural menopause. *Lancet* 1(8026):1354–55

66. Kapoor AK, Kapoor S. 1986. The effects of high altitude on age at menarche and menopause. *Int. J. Biometeorol.* 30(1):21–26

67. Karim A, Chowdhury AKMA, Kabir M. 1985. Nutritional status and age at secondary sterility in rural Bangladesh. *J. Biosoc. Sci.* 17:497–502

68. Kaufert P. 1988. Menopause as process or event: the creation of definitions in biomedicine. In *Biomedicine Examined,* ed. M Lock, DR Gordon, pp. 331–49. Dordrecht: Kluwer Academic

69. Kaufert P, Lock M, McKinlay SM, Beyene Y, Coope J, et al. 1986. Menopause research: the Korpilampi workshop. *Soc. Sci. Med.* 22(11):1285–89

70. Kaufert P, Gilbert P, Tate R. 1987. Defining menopausal status: the impact of longitudinal data. *Maturitas* 9:217–26

71. Kaufman DW, Slone D, Rosenberg L, Miettinen OS, Shapiro S. 1980. Cigarette smoking and age at natural menopause. *Am. J. Public Health* 70:420–22

72. Kaufman FR, Xu YK, Ng WG, Silva PD, Lobo RA, Donnell GN. 1989. Gonadal function and ovarian galactose metabolism in classic galactosemia. *Acta Endocrinol.* 120:129–33

73. Kletzky OA, Borenstein R. 1987. Vasomotor instability of the menopause. See Ref. 115, pp. 53–65

74. Kline J, Levin B. 1992. Trisomy and age at menopause: predicted associations given a link with rate of oocyte atresia. *Paediatr. Perinat. Epidemiol.* 6:225–39

75. Kohn RR. 1971. *Principles of Mammalian Aging.* Englewood Cliffs, NJ: Prentice-Hall

76. Kono S, Sunagawa Y, Higa H, Sunagawa H. 1990. Age of menopause in Japanese women: trends and recent changes. *Maturitas* 12:43–49

77. Korenman SG, Sherman BM, Korenman JC. 1978. Reproductive hormone function: the perimenopausal period and beyond. *Clin. Endocrinol. Metab.* 7(3):625–43

78. Krauss CM, Turksoy RN, Atkins L, McLaughlin C, Brown LG, Page DC. 1987. Familial premature ovarian failure due to an interstitial deletion of the long arm of the X chromosome. *N. Engl. J. Med.* 317(3):125–31

79. Kronenberg FL. 1990. Hot flashes: epidemiology and physiology. *Ann. NY Acad. Sci.* 592:52–86

80. Kronenberg FL, Cote J, Linkie DM, Dyrenfurth I, Downey JA. 1984. Menopausal hot flashes: thermoregulatory, cardiovascular, and circulating catecholamine and LH changes. *Maturitas* 6:31–43

81. Kvale G, Heuch I. 1988. Menstrual factors and breast cancer risk. *Cancer* 62:1625–31

82. Kwawukume EY, Ghosh TS, Wilson JB. 1993. Menopausal age of Ghanian women. *Int. J. Gynecol. Obstet.* 40:151–55

83. Lau EMC, Cooper C. 1993. Epidemiology and prevention of osteoporosis in urbanized Asian populations. *Osteoporosis Int.* Suppl. 1:S23–26

84. Lehrer S. 1981. Fertility and menopause in blind women. *Fertil. Steril.* 36(3):396–98

85. Leidy L. 1990. Early age at menopause among left-handed women. *Obstet. Gynecol.* 76(6):1111–14

86. Leidy L. 1991. *The timing of menopause in biological and sociocultural context: a lifespan approach.* PhD thesis. State Univ. NY, Albany

87. Lichtarowicz A, Norman C, Calcraft B, Morris JS, Rhodes J, Mayberry J. 1989. A

study of the menopause, smoking, and contraception in women with Crohn's disease. *Q. J. Med.* 72:623–31
88. Lindquist O, Bengtsson C. 1979. Menopausal age in relation to smoking. *Acta Med. Scand.* 205:73–77
89. Lindquist O, Bengtsson C. 1980. Serum lipids, arterial blood pressure and body weight in relation to the menopause: results from a population study of women in Göteborg, Sweden. *Scand. J. Clin. Lab. Invest.* 40:629–36
90. Lindsay R. 1987. Prevention of postmenopausal osteoporosis. *Obstet. Gynecol. Clin. N. Am.* 14:63–76
91. Lock M. 1986. Ambiguities of aging: Japanese experience and perceptions of menopause. *Cult. Med. Psychiatry* 10:23–46
92. Longcope C, Franz C, Morello C, Baker R, Johnston CC. 1986. Steroid and gonadotropin levels in women during the perimenopausal years. *Maturitas* 8:189–96
93. Longcope C, Pratt JH, Schneider S, Fineberg SE. 1978. Aromatization of androgens by muscle and adipose tissue in vivo. *J. Clin. Endocrinol. Metab.* 46:146–52
94. Maclaren NK, Blizzard RM. 1985. Adrenal autoimmunity and autoimmune polyglandular syndromes. In *The Autoimmune Diseases,* ed. NR Rose, IR Mackay, pp. 201–25. New York: Academic
95. MacMahon B, Worcester J. 1966. *Age at Menopause: United States 1960–1962.* DHEW Publ. Natl. Cent. Health Stat. Ser. 11(19)
96. MacPherson KI. 1985. Osteoporosis and menopause: a feminist analysis of the social construction of a syndrome. *Adv. Nurs. Sci.* 7:11–22
97. Martin CR. 1985. *Endocrine Physiology.* New York: Oxford Univ. Press
98. Martin MC, Block JE, Sanchez SD, Arnaud CD, Beyene Y. 1993. Menopause without symptoms: the endocrinology of menopause among rural Mayan Indians. *Am. J. Obstet. Gynecol.* 168:1839–45
99. Maruo T, Ladines-Llave CA, Samoto T, Matsuo H, Manalo AS, et al. 1993. Expression of epidermal growth factor and its receptor in the human ovary during follicular growth and regression. *Endocrinology* 132:924–31
100. Mattison DR. 1982. The effects of smoking on fertility from gametogenesis to implantation. *Environ. Res.* 28:410–33
101. Mattison DR, Evans MI, Schwimmer W, White B. 1984. Familial premature ovarian failure. *Am. J. Hum. Genet.* 36:1341–48
102. Mattison DR, Thomford PJ, Jelovsek FR. 1988. Disposition of oocytes and age at menopause. *N. Engl. J. Med.* 318:644
103. Mattison DR, Thorgeirsson SS. 1978. Smoking and industrial pollution and their

effects on menopause and ovarian cancer. *Lancet* 1:187–88
104. McCrea FB. 1983. The politics of menopause: the "discovery" of a deficiency disease. *Soc. Probl.* 31:111–23
105. McKinlay JB, McKinlay SM, Brambilla D. 1987. The relative contributions of endocrine changes and social circumstances to depression in mid-aged women. *J. Health Soc. Behav.* 28:345–63
106. McKinlay SM, Brambilla DJ, Posner JG. 1992. The normal menopause transition. *Am. J. Hum. Biol.* 4:37–46
107. McKinlay SM, McKinlay JB. 1973. Selected studies of the menopause: a methodological critique. *J. Biosoc. Sci.* 5:533–55
108. McNatty KP, Short RV, Barnes EW, Irvine WJ. 1975. The cytotoxic effect of serum from patients with Addison's disease and autoimmune ovarian failure on human granulosa cells in culture. *Clin. Exp. Immunol.* 22:378–84
109. Meites J, Huang H, Simpkins J, Steger R. 1982. Central nervous system neurotransmitters during the decline of reproductive activity. In *The Menopause: Clinical, Endocrinological and Pathophysiological Aspects,* ed. P Fiorette, L Martini, G Melis, S Yen, pp. 3–13. New York: Academic
110. Meldrum DR. 1993. Female reproductive aging—ovarian and uterine factors. *Fertil. Steril.* 59:1–5
111. Meldrum DR, Shamonki IM, Frumar AM, Tataryn IV, Chang RJ, Judd HL. 1979. Elevations in skin temperature of the finger as an objective index of postmenopausal hot flushes: standardization of the technique. *Am. J. Obstet. Gynecol.* 135:713–17
112. Metcalf MG, Donald RA, Livesey JH. 1981. Pituitary-ovarian function in normal women during the menopausal transition. *Clin. Endocrinol.* 14:245–55
113. Metcalf MG, Livesey JH. 1985. Gonadotrophin excretion in fertile women: effect of age and the onset of the menopausal transition. *J. Endocrinol.* 105:357–62
114. Minaker KL, Meneilly GS, Rowe J. 1985. Endocrine systems. See Ref. 41a, pp. 433–56
115. Mishell DR. 1987. *Menopause: Physiology and Pharmacology.* Chicago: Year Book Medical
116. Moore KL. 1988. *Essentials of Human Embryology.* Philadelphia: Decker
117. National Research Council. 1981. *Mammalian Models for Research on Aging.* Washington, DC: Natl. Acad. Press
118. Navot D, Bergh PA, Williams MA, Garrisa GJ, Guzman I, et al. 1991. Poor oocyte quality rather than implantation failure as a cause of age-related decline in female fertility. *Lancet* 337:1375–77

119. Nelson JF, Felicio LS. 1985. Reproductive aging in the female: an etiological perspective. *Rev. Biol. Res. Aging* 2:251–314
120. Neri A, Bider D, Lidor U, Ovadia J. 1982. Menopausal age in various ethnic groups in Israel. *Maturitas* 4:341–48
121. Deleted in proof
122. Novak ER. 1970. Ovulation after fifty. *Obstet. Gynecol.* 36:903–10
123. Nuti R, Martini G. 1993. Effects of age and menopause on bone density of entire skeleton in healthy and osteoporotic women. *Osteoporosis Int.* 3:59–65
124. Parazzini F, Negri E, La Vecchia C. 1992. Reproductive and general lifestyle determinants of age at menopause. *Maturitas* 15:141–49
125. Pavelka MS, Fedigan LM. 1991. Menopause: a comparative life history perspective. *Yearb. Phys. Anthropol.* 34:13–38
126. Perry JS. 1971. *The Ovarian Cycle of Mammals.* Edinburgh: Oliver & Boyd
127. Peters H, McNatty KP. 1980. *The Ovary: A Correlation of Structure and Function in Mammals.* New York: Granada
128. Poortman J, Thijssen JHH, De Waard F. 1981. Plasma oestrone, oestradiol and androstenedione levels in postmenopausal women: relation to body weight and height. *Maturitas* 3:65–71
129. Pouilles JM, Tremollieres F, Ribot C. 1993. The effects of menopause on longitudinal bone loss from the spine. *Calcif. Tissue Int.* 52:340–43
129a. Profet M. 1993. Menstruation as a defense against pathogens transported by sperm. *Q. Rev. Biol.* 68(3):335–86
130. Rabinowe SL, Ravnikar VA, Dib SA, George KL, Dluhy RG. 1989. Premature menopause: monoclonal antibody defined T lymphocyte abnormalities and antiovarian antibodies. *Fertil. Steril.* 51:450–54
131. Randhawa I, Premi HK, Gupta T. 1987. The age at menopause in women of Himachai Pradesh and the factors affecting the menopause. *Indian J. Public Health* 31(1):40–44
132. Rannevik G, Carlstrom K, Jeppsson S, Bjerre B, Svanberg L. 1986. A prospective long-term study in women from premenopause to postmenopause: changing profiles of gonadotrophins, oestrogens, and androgens. *Maturitas* 8:297–307
133. Richardson SJ, Senikas V, Nelson JF. 1987. Follicular depletion during the menopausal transition: evidence for accelerated loss and ultimate exhaustion. *J. Clin. Endocrinol. Metab.* 65:1231–37
134. Riley MW. 1979. *Aging from Birth to Death: Interdisciplinary Perspectives.* Boulder, CO: Westview
135. Ruehsen MDM, Blizzard RM, Garcia-Bunuel R, Jones GS. 1972. Autoimmunity

and ovarian failure. *Am. J. Obstet. Gynecol.* 112(5):693–703
136. Ryan RJ. 1981. Follicular atresia: some speculations of biochemical markers and mechanisms. In *Dynamics of Ovarian Function,* ed. NB Schwartz, M. Hunzicker-Dunn, pp. 1–11. New York: Raven
137. Sadleir RM. 1973. *The Reproduction of Vertebrates.* New York: Academic
138. Sarin AR, Singla P, Sudershan KG. 1985. A 5-year clinicopathological study of 2000 postmenopausal women from northern India. *Asia-Oceania J. Obstet. Gynaecol.* 11(4):539–44
138a. Schnatz PT. 1985. Neuroendocrinology and the ovulation cycle—advances and review. *Adv. Psychosom. Med.* 12:4–24
139. Seckl J, Lightman SL. 1989. Opioid peptides, oxytocin, and human reproduction. In *Brain Opioid Systems in Reproduction,* ed. RG Dyer, RJ Bicknell, pp. 309–24. New York: Oxford Univ. Press
140. Sherman B, Wallace R, Bean J, Schlabaugh L, Treloar A. 1981. Menopause: relationship to body weight. In *Dynamics of Ovarian Function,* ed. NB Schwartz, M Hunzicker-Dunn, pp. 315–18. New York: Raven
141. Sherman BM. 1987. Endocrinologic and menstrual alterations. See Ref. 115, pp. 41–51
142. Sherman BM, Korenman SG. 1975. Hormonal characteristics of the human menstrual cycle throughout reproductive life. *J. Clin. Invest.* 55:699–706
143. Sherwin BB. 1988. Estrogen and/or androgen replacement therapy and cognitive functioning in surgically menopausal women. *Psychoneuroendocrinology* 13:345–57
144. Silverman P. 1987. Introduction: the life course perspective. In *The Elderly as Modern Pioneers,* ed. P Silverman, pp. 1–16, Indianapolis: Ind. Univ. Press
145. Snowdon DA. 1990. Early natural menopause and the duration of postmenopausal life. *J. Am. Geriatr. Soc.* 38:402–8
146. Snowdon DA, Kane RL, Beeson WL, Burke GL, Sprafka JM, et al. 1989. Is early natural menopause a biologic marker of health and aging? *Am. J. Public Health* 79:709–14
147. Sorensen A, Weinert F, Sherrod L. 1986. *Human Development and the Life Course: Multidisciplinary Perspectives.* Hillsdale, NJ: Erlbaum Assoc.
148. Spence A. 1989. *Biology of Human Aging.* Englewood Cliffs, NJ: Prentice Hall
149. Stanford JL, Hartge P, Brinton LA, Hoover RN, Brookmeyer R. 1987. Factors influencing the age at natural menopause. *J. Chron. Dis.* 40:995–1002
150. Stevenson JC, Crook D, Godsland IF. 1993. Influence of age and menopause on serum

lipids and lipoproteins in healthy women. *Atherosclerosis* 98:83–90

151. Strong R. 1985. Neurochemistry of aging: 1982–1984. *Rev. Biol. Res. Aging* 2:181–96

152. Tataryn IV, Lomax P, Meldrum DR, Bajorek JG, Chesarek W, Judd HL. 1981. Objective techniques for the assessment of postmenopausal hot flushes. *Obstet. Gynecol.* 57:340–44

153. Tepperman J, Tepperman HM. 1987. *Metabolic and Endocrine Physiology.* Chicago: Year Book Medical

154. Thomas CL, ed. 1981. *Taber's Cyclopedic Medical Dictionary.* Philadelphia: Davis. 14th ed.

155. Thomford PJ, Jelovsek FR, Mattison DR. 1987. Effect of oocyte number and rate of atresia on the age of menopause. *Reprod. Toxicol.* 1:41–51

156. Thomsen K, Gotfredsen A, Christiansen C. 1986. Is postmenopausal bone loss an age-related phenomenon? *Calcif. Tissue Int.* 39: 123–27

157. Tilly JL, Kowalski KI, Johnson AL, Hsueh AJW. 1991. Involvement of apoptosis in ovarian follicular atresia and postovulatory regression. *Endocrinology* 129(5):2799–2801

158. Tilly JL, Kowalski KI, Schomberg DW, Hsueh AJW. 1992. Apoptosis in atretic ovarian follicles is associated with selective decreases in messenger ribonucleic acid transcripts for gonadotropin receptors and cytochrome P450 aromatase. *Endocrinology* 131(4):1670–76

159. Treloar AE. 1974. Menarche, menopause, and intervening fecundability. *Hum. Biol.* 46(1):89–107

160. Treloar AE. 1981. Menstrual cyclicity and the premenopause. *Maturitas* 3:249–64

161. Treloar AE, Boynton RE, Behn BG, Brown BW. 1967. Variation of the human menstrual cycle through reproductive life. *Int. J. Fertil.* 12(1,pt.2):77–126

162. Trevoux R, De Brux J, Castanier M, Nahoul K, Soule J-P, Scholler R. 1986. Endometrium and plasma hormone profile in the peri-menopause and postmenopause. *Maturitas* 8:309–26

163. Utian WH. 1987. Overview on menopause. *Am. J. Obstet. Gynecol.* 156:1280–83

164. van Beresteijn ECH, Korevaar JC, Huijbregts PCW, Schouten EG, Burema J, Kok FJ. 1993. Perimenopausal increase in serum cholesterol: a 10-year longitudinal study. *Am. J. Epidemiol.* 137:383–92

165. Wallace RB, Sherman BM, Bean JA, Treloar AE, Schlabaugh L. 1979. Probability of menopause with increasing duration of amenorrhea in middle aged women. *Am. J. Obstet. Gynecol.* 135:1021–24

166. Wasti S, Robinson SC, Akhtar Y, Khan S, Badaruddin N. 1993. Characteristics of menopause in three socioeconomic urban groups in Karachi, Pakistan. *Maturitas* 16: 61–69

167. Weg RB. 1987. Demography. See Ref. 115, pp. 23–40

168. Weir BJ, Rowlands IW. 1977. Ovulation and atresia. In *The Ovary,* ed. L Zuckerman, BJ Weir, pp. 265–301. New York: Academic

169. Weissman MM. 1979. The myth of involutional melancholia. *J. Am. Med. Assoc.* 242:742–44

170. Whelan E, Sandler D, McConnaughey D, Weinberg C. 1990. Menstrual and reproductive characteristics and age at natural menopause. *Am. J. Epidemiol.* 131(4): 625–32

171. Whitehead MI, Whitcroft SIJ, Hillard TC. 1993. *An Atlas of The Menopause.* New York: Parthenon

172. Willett W, Stampfer MJ, Bain C, Lipnick R, Speizer FE. 1983. Cigarette smoking, relative weight and menopause. *Am. J. Epidemiol.* 117:651–58

173. Wise AJ, Gross MA, Schalch DS. 1973. Quantitative relationships of the pituitary-gonadal axis in postmenopausal women. *J. Lab. Clin. Med.* 81(1):28–36

174. Wise PM. 1989. Influence of estrogen on aging of the central nervous system: its role in declining female reproductive function. In *Menopause: Evaluation, Treatment, and Health Concerns,* ed. CB Hammond, FP Haseltine, I Schiff, pp. 53–70. New York: Liss

175. Wood JW, Johnson PL, Campbell KL. 1985. Demographic and endocrinological aspects of low natural fertility in highland New Guinea. *J. Biosoc. Sci.* 17:57–79

176. Wood JW, Weinstein M. 1988. A model of age-specific fecundability. *Popul. Stud.* 42: 85–113

177. Worcester N, Whatley MH. 1992. The selling of HRT: playing on the fear factor. *Fem. Rev.* 41:1–26

178. World Health Organization. 1981. *Research on the Menopause.* World Health Organization: Tech. Rep. Ser. No. 670. Geneva: WHO

179. Wyshak G. 1985. Menopause in mothers of multiple births and mothers of singletons only. *Soc. Biol.* 25(1):52–61

180. Wyshak G, Frisch RE, Albright TE, Albright NL, Schiff I. 1987. Bone fractures among former college athletes compared with nonathletes in the menopausal and postmenopausal years. *Obstet. Gynecol.* 69:121–26

181. Yen SSC. 1993. *Neuroendocrine-metabolic changes during menopause and aging.* Presented at 4th Annu. North Am. Menopause Soc. Meet., San Diego

Annu. Rev. Anthropol. 1994. 23:255–75

ADVANCES IN HUMAN REPRODUCTIVE ECOLOGY

P. T. Ellison

Department of Anthropology, Harvard University, Cambridge, Massachusetts 02138

KEY WORDS: fertility, fecundity, age, energetics, ovarian function

WHAT IS HUMAN REPRODUCTIVE ECOLOGY?

Human reproductive ecology is the study of reproduction as an aspect of human biology that is responsive to ecological context. This includes the interpretation of many features of reproductive biology, even some now unresponsive to environmental influences, as the product of adaptation to formative environments, as well as the effort to document and understand the sensitivity of other features to current environmental influences. Human reproductive ecology as a field is located in the larger domain of evolutionary ecology, distinct in its motivation and goals from cognate clinical, epidemiological, and demographic approaches to the study of human reproduction and fertility. Unlike most clinical and epidemiological studies, human reproductive ecology is not built on a dichotomous model of biological variation between alternative states of health and disease (48). Unlike most demographic approaches, the focus of inquiry in human reproductive ecology is not limited to the determination of vital rates (156). Responses to ecological conditions that buffer variation in human fertility and features of reproductive biology that are invariant are as central to the study of human reproductive ecology as are responses that generate variation in fertility.

Despite the differences in motivation and ultimate goals, there is considerable overlap in data and methods among these distinct approaches to the study of human reproduction. Human reproductive ecologists make liberal use of the results generated by clinical, epidemiological, and demographic research and borrow heavily from their methodologies of data collection and analysis. The emphasis of the ecological approach, however, has placed a premium on the collection and analysis of data representing normal, non-pathological states and a broad range of ecological conditions. To date, the notable contribution of human reproductive ecology to the empirical study of human reproduction has been through the development and application of methods to investigate reproductive physiology in field, rather than clinical, settings. This has included methods for monitoring gonadal, adrenal, and placental steroids, and pituitary and trophoblastic protein hormones in saliva, urine, or small amounts of serum or plasma (21, 22, 38, 41, 42, 84, 115, 163). As a result of these methods, new information is accumulating on variation in human reproductive physiology that is challenging the conventional paradigms generated by clinical and epidemiological research (43, 47, 48, 86, 163).

This review focuses on a few recent advances in our understanding of human female reproductive ecology, particularly the importance of age and energetics in modulating female fecundity (the biological capacity to bear live offspring). Important advances in quantitative methods and analytical models have been the subjects of recent reviews elsewhere (151, 154, 155, 158). Wood (157) provides a comprehensive overview of the field with particular emphasis on the integration of physiological and demographic perspectives. Two recent conferences on this topic have produced excellent edited volumes (23a, 35a). Human male reproductive ecology is as yet underdeveloped, both empirically and theoretically, although new efforts in this area are promising (16, 20a, 22).

AGE AND FEMALE FECUNDITY

Age and Natural Fertility

Henry (64) defined natural fertility as the absence of parity-specific fertility limitation to permit the categorization of populations as displaying natural or controlled fertility behavior on the basis of empirical observations of parity progression ratios. Although debate continues to surround this definition (18, 153), it has a distinct advantage over other possible definitions, such as the absence of any conscious manipulation of fertility, which might have intuitive appeal but are difficult to apply empirically. Using this definition and restricting his analysis to female marital fertility, Henry made two striking observations regarding natural human fertility that have become foci of subsequent research: (a) there is considerable variation in the level of fertility among natural fertility populations, and (b) there is a remarkably consistent age pattern of fertility across different natural fertility populations. Henry suggested that the first observation might result from the variable effect of lactation in delaying the resumption of ovulation postpartum. He had less to say about the second observation, except that the declining fertility of women over 30 years of age was a consequence both of increasing numbers of infertile women with age and of increasing birth intervals among those who remain fertile.

Accumulating data on natural fertility populations in succeeding years has confirmed Henry's observations (19, 20, 23, 65, 81, 99, 153–155). The consistency of the age pattern of female natural fertility is usually demonstrated by standardizing fertility rates on the rate for the 20–24 year old age class and comparing the trajectory of declining fertility after that age between populations (65, 81, 154). The rise in marital fertility between menarche and the early twenties is less often displayed but is also a characteristic feature of the age pattern of natural female fertility (15). Fertility levels in the 20–24 and 25–29 year age classes are usually nearly equal, with the highest levels occurring in the latter age class in many populations (81, 154). In general, the pattern is roughly parabolic, with rising fertility until the mid-twenties and falling fertility after the mid-thirties (Figure 1). It should be noted, however, that this trajectory characterizes cross-sectional data. The longitudinal trajectories implied by the reproductive histories of individual women may be much more rectangular, beginning and ending more abruptly.

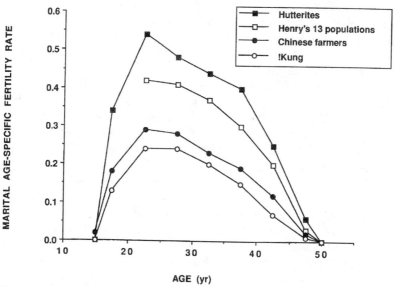

Figure 1   Age-specific marital fertility rates in a range of natural fertility populations. Redrawn from Henry (64) and Howell (65).

Traditional explanations for the characteristic age pattern of natural fertility have stressed the role of behavioral changes, particularly declining coital frequency (71–73, 125, 141), as well as the onset of permanent sterility (64, 99, 153), in mediating the declining fertility of later reproductive life. Recent quantitative models that incorporate available data indicate, however, that changing rates of sexual intercourse probably make only minor contributions to age-specific declines in natural fertility (151, 161). Nor do increasing rates of permanent sterility with age account for increasingly long waiting times to conception among those still fertile (64, 99). Rather, demographic evidence (59, 81, 99) points to age-specific changes in female reproductive physiology that reduce, but do not eliminate, female fecundity in later life (84a). As noted previously, little attention has been given to the separate question of increasing marital natural fertility in the first decade after menarche, although this is usually also assumed to be a function of female reproductive physiology (15, 65, 99, 154).

Clinical and Epidemiological Evidence for Age Variation in Female Reproductive Physiology

Until recently, specific information on age variation in female reproductive physiology has been sparse and often indirect. Treloar et al (140) presented over 25,000 person-years of data on menstrual cycle variability gathered from over 2000 women indicating longer and more irregular cycle lengths in the years immediately after menarche and immediately before menopause, but with very little variability over the majority of the reproductive span from 20 to 40 years of age. Döring (35) analyzed basal body temperature recordings, an indirect reflection of progesterone secretion and the presence of a corpus luteum, representing 3264 person-months of observation on 481 women. He concluded that ovulatory frequency and rates of luteal sufficiency increase with age after menarche until the mid-twenties and begin to decline as early as the mid-thirties. More direct endocrinological investigations have confirmed the high frequency of anovulatory and luteally insufficient cycles in the peri-menarcheal and perimenopausal periods (4, 5, 85, 101, 102, 133, 134, 145), but the notion persists that ovarian function levels are rather constant between these extremes of the reproductive span (151, 154, 161).

Cumulative data from infertility treatment programs, however, consistently depict a pattern of declining success rates with age in women past the mid-thirties. Different studies control for different potential confounding effects, but most control for coital frequency and male fecundity, either by relying on timed artificial insemination by donor (AID), or on in vitro fertilization (IVF). *Fédération des Centres d'Etude et de Conservation du Sperme Humain* (Fédération CECOS) reported on success rates in AID for 2193 women in

France, noting that success rates in establishing a pregnancy begin to decline significantly in women over age 30 and increasingly in women over age 35 (130a). Subsequent studies of women undergoing AID elsewhere have confirmed this finding (37, 146). Similarly, success rates in establishing ongoing pregnancies have been found to vary inversely with age in women undergoing IVF (1, 52, 106, 138), ovulation induction (33, 96, 114, 137), and ovum donation (53, 88, 98, 103, 124, 127). The single largest study is the report of cumulative results from more than 77,000 IVF procedures carried out in France between 1986 and 1990 (52). Like the Fédération CECOS data, the study by French In Vitro National (FIVNAT) showed a progressive decline in success rates with female age, detectable as early as age 30 and accelerating after age 35.

Several attempts have been made to use the data from infertility treatment programs to localize the anatomical source of declining female fecundity with age. Ovum donation provides particularly useful data (89, 103, 124), because the age of the ovary and oöcyte and of the uterus can vary independently. The data must be interpreted with caution, because the hormonal milieu of both the donor and the recipient is manipulated exogenously. Some aspects of age-related variation in female fecundity may nevertheless be revealed by analyzing success rates in this procedure. That successful pregnancies can be established through ovum donation even in postmenopausal women indicates that uterine age is not ultimately limiting on female fecundity. Given appropriate hormonal stimulation and a viable embryo, the reproductive system of a postmenopausal woman is capable of successful implantation and gestation (127–129). Success rates in ovum donation decline with recipient age, however, indicating some reduction in the capability of the endometrium to implant and sustain an embryo (53, 88, 98). Meldrum (98) reported that the lower success rate in recipients over 40 years of age compared to those under 40 can be corrected by doubling the dose of exogenous progesterone administered. Postmenopausal pregnancies are in fact established and maintained with supraphysiological levels of progesterone administration (127, 128).

Navot et al (103) and Abdalla et al (1) reported that pregnancy success rates for ovum donation in women over 40 years of age are higher than success rates for IVF in similarly aged women using their own ova. They interpreted the data to indicate a significant effect of age on oöcyte quality. Flamigni et al (53) compared the pregnancy success rates in women undergoing ovum donation to the success rates in their specific donors undergoing IVF with eggs from the same harvested cohort. They found a significant decline in success rates with the age of the ovum donation recipients and interpreted the results as an effect of uterine age. In a design in which both the age of the recipients (over and under 33 years) and the age of the donors (over and under 32 years) in an ovum donation program were analyzed, Levran et al (88) found that recipient age affects the probability of a pregnancy being established initially, while donor age affects the probability of successful continuance of those established pregnancies. Taken together, the results from ovum donation programs seem to indicate that both the age of the recipient (uterine age) and the age of the donor (ovarian and oöcyte age) have a negative effect on the probability of a successful pregnancy. It should be noted that, although donor age is often interpreted as equivalent to oöcyte age, it cannot be distinguished in these designs from the age of the ovary and its effect on the development and maturation of the oöcyte. In particular, it should be remembered that the granulosa cells of primordial follicles are themselves as old as the oöcyte they contain (9, 150).

Basal follicle-stimulating hormone (FSH) levels have been used as an index of ovarian age inversely reflecting the remaining follicular supply of the ovary (114, 138). A smaller follicular reserve is assumed to result in less negative feedback, by estradiol and/or inhibin, on FSH release by the pituitary (see 84a). Both chronological age and basal FSH have been found to contribute independently to success rates in IVF (138) and ovulation induction (114). McClure et al (96) reported that both chronological age and basal, unstimulated estradiol levels are predictive of success in ovulation induction (higher estradiol levels correlate positively with success rate). The predictive value of follicular estradiol may be related to its positive correlation with endometrial thickness (135), and to the independently demonstrated importance of endometrial thickness in predicting success in ovulation induction (33, 34). From these data it appears that the functional capacity of the ovary in its endocrine role, in addition to the quality of the oöcytes themselves, may be compromised by increasing age and contribute to declining female fecundity.

Declining female fecundity at older ages has received considerable attention because it is linked to a tremendous demand for clinical infertility services. The increase in female fecundity with age in women in their teens and early twenties has been a subject of clinical research for different reasons, because of the link between early gynecological history and the later risk of breast and reproductive tract cancers (4, 62, 63, 79, 80). Apter and Vihko (4, 145) have found that the frequency of anovulatory cycles declines slowly in the years following menarche, confirming Döring's earlier observations (35). The androgen/estrogen ratios in the cycles of teenage women are also higher than in women in their twenties and thirties (95, 144), and ovulation occurs from smaller preovulatory follicles at lower levels of peak follicular estradiol (3). Ellison et al (46) reported that indices of luteal function are lower in women aged 18–22 years than in women aged 23–35 of similar weight for height.

Age and Ovarian Function in Non-clinical Populations

Other than the results of AID, normally undertaken to treat male factor infertility, many of the clinical data on age and female fecundity are derived from women with impaired reproductive physiology. In a study of healthy women, Lenton et al found a progressive shortening of follicular phase length, from a geometric mean of 12.9 days in women 20–24 years old to 10.4 days in women 40–44 years old (85). Few other studies of age variation in the reproductive physiology of normal women have been conducted, partly because it is difficult to monitor ovarian function longitudinally with traditional methods.

Lipson & Ellison (90, 91) collected daily saliva samples from 124 healthy, regularly menstruating women from the Boston area between the ages of 18 and 44, all of whom were of stable weight, within normal ranges of weight for height, and none of whom exercised regularly or used oral contraception. Measurements of progesterone levels in these samples indicate significant age variation in luteal activity; levels increase with age between age 18 and 24, and decline with age after age 35. Average values for several indices of luteal function (ovulatory frequency, average luteal progesterone, average midluteal progesterone, and the number of luteal days with values $\geq$ 300 pmol/L) all show parabolic trajectories across the age groups studied, and are well fit by second-order polynomial regressions (an example is shown below) (43, 90). Based on these results, Lipson & Ellison generated age-stratified reference values for assessing luteal function (91).

O'Rourke & Ellison reported on estradiol profiles in 53 healthy, regularly menstruating women between the ages of 24 and 48, meeting the same subject criteria as in the Lipson & Ellison study (45 of the women were subjects in both studies) (104). Average follicular and average luteal estradiol values decline with increasing subject age, with significant differences apparent after age 30. Low follicular estradiol is correlated with smaller follicular size (3), low oöcyte fertilizability (164), reduced endometrial thickness (135), and low pregnancy rates in ovulation induction (96). Luteal phase estradiol is important in inducing progesterone receptors in the endometrium (12, 58) and in regulating pituitary gonadotropin secretion (32). Declining estradiol profiles with increasing age may thus contribute to lower female fecundity in several ways. Conversely, the high estradiol profiles of women under 30 may contribute to the poorer prognosis for survival and recurrence of breast cancer diagnosed in women in this age range (30, 105).

The existence of significant age variation in ovarian function makes it important to control for age in studies of other variables that might also affect female reproductive physiology, such as nutrition or disease (90, 91), and in making comparisons between populations (39, 41–43, 48–50, 110). It also raises the question of the comparability of age variation in ovarian function across populations. At least two studies, one in Papua New Guinea (159), and one in Africa (115), seemed to indicate that female fecundity in those populations may not decline with age, or may even increase.

Using the same laboratory and field protocols, researchers have now collected salivary progesterone data from three populations—middle class women in Boston, the Lese of Zaïre, and the Tamang of Nepal—on sufficient numbers of subjects to allow a direct comparison of age variation in luteal function (43, 48). The Boston data described above (90, 91) were extended to include 12 cycles from women between the ages of 45 and 49 (43, 48). Data from Zaïre covered 144 cycles collected in 1984 and 1989 (7, 17, 50). Some women were represented in the data for both seasons at ages 5 years apart. The Nepal data included one cycle collected in 1990 from each of 45 women (110). A two-way analysis of variance of the data by population and age across seven five-year age groups from 15 to 49 indicates highly significant differences between age groups in all three populations ($p < 0.001$), and between populations at each age ($p < 0.001$), but no significant interaction effect ($F = 0.35$, $p = 0.98$). The near perfect parallelism of the age trends is also apparent in the best fitting second-order polynomial regressions obtained for each population (Figure 2) (42, 43, 48). The consistency of the age pattern of luteal function across such genetically, ecologically, and culturally distinct populations suggests strongly that age variation in luteal function represents a general feature of human female reproductive physiology largely unaffected by environmental circumstances. The overall level of luteal function, however, varies markedly between populations (47). In fact, as reflected in salivary progesterone levels, ovarian function displays the same two features, variance in level between populations and consistency in age pattern across populations, that Henry originally observed in natural fertility.

Understanding Age Variation in Ovarian Function

As was true of the age pattern of natural fertility itself, the age patterns of female reproductive physiology and fecundity described above are cross-sectional. The trajectory of ovarian function by age, for example, in an individual woman may rise and fall more abruptly at the extremes of her reproductive career than the curves in Figure 2 suggest. On the other hand, the restriction of observations to women with regular menses (90, 91, 104) removes the effect of the peri-menarcheal and perimenopausal transitions, reducing the discrepancy between cross-sectional and longitudinal trajectories. These trajectories are only central tendencies about which considerable variation in individual levels remains, and energetic factors can produce acute variability in ovarian function within individuals. The age trajectory of ovarian function can be thought of as the baseline about which such acute variation occurs.

Given that the age pattern of ovarian function appears so robust, it is reasonable to ask whether it is of functional significance. It may reflect some unavoidable constraint of development and aging. For example, the sustained rise in levels of luteal function into the twenties could be a reflection of a prolonged process of reproductive maturation that does not end until nearly a decade after menarche. The sustained decline in follicular and luteal function that begins in the thirties could be a manifestation of unavoidable senescence of aging primordial follicles. It is also possible that the age trajectory of ovarian function represents an evolved mechanism to modulate reproductive effort with age by modulating the length of the interbirth interval. It is a standard prediction of life history theory that the reproductive effort of a female should increase with age after maturity as her own reproductive value declines (136, 152). To this extent, the continued rise in ovarian function in the decade after menarche is consistent with theoretical expectations. Declining ovarian function over the decade preceding menopause may represent a shift in the optimal distribution of effort in favor of offspring already born over those not yet conceived, a shift that could be accelerated by the declining average

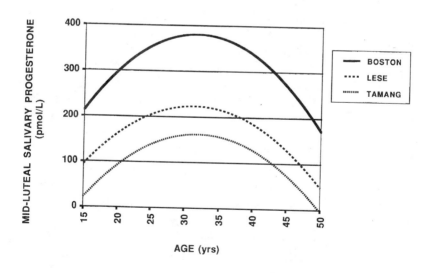

Figure 2   Best fit second-order polynomial regressions of mid-luteal progesterone levels on age for three populations (43, 48).

quality of ova in later life. Comparative studies of other species may help to test these interpretations. One would predict, for example, that ovarian function should not decline with age in species, such as mice and rats, where the duration of maternal investment is short and where follicular exhaustion of the ovary is rarely approached in nature. This prediction holds: terminal permanent acylicity occurs in laboratory rodents not because estrogen levels decline to inadequate levels, but because estrogen production increases with age to such levels that the reproductive system becomes fixed in constant proestrus or pseudopregnancy (77, 148).

A second question relates to variation in the level of age trajectories of ovarian function in different populations. These chronic differences in baseline levels are distinct from the additional variation that stems from acute environmental and physiological conditions. I have suggested elsewhere (39–43) that differences in baseline ovarian function in adulthood may be determined by chronic conditions experienced during prepubertal growth and development. Chronic conditions that result in slow growth and delayed reproductive maturation may lead to lower levels of ovarian function throughout adult life. Such a mechanism would allow adult baselines for fecundity and reproductive effort to be adjusted to chronic conditions governing the energy available for growth or reproduction. Longitudinal data on the relationship between menarcheal age and subsequent ovarian function substantiates this relationship within populations (4, 143, 144). Charnov & Berrigan (25) have described a general theory of primate life histories in which the correlation between rate of prepubertal growth and rate of adult reproduction plays a pivotal role. The margin of energy over and above maintenance requirements available to invest in growth, they argue, should be correlated strongly with the margin of energy available to invest in reproduction. Hence, rate of juvenile growth should be positively associated with adult rate of reproduction. Adequate tests of this hypothesis will require additional comparative data on age patterns of ovarian function in different populations in relation to childhood growth and adolescent maturation.

In summary, recent evidence suggests that age variation in female reproductive physiology contributes significantly to age variation in female fecundity. The age pattern of ovarian function appears consistent across different populations and may contribute to the consistent age pattern of natural fertility. The age pattern of female fecundity itself may represent adaptive modulation of reproductive effort with age and not simply unavoidable constraint. Finally, developmental adjustment of baseline trajectories of ovarian function may represent a mechanism to modulate adult fecundity and reproductive effort with respect to chronic conditions.

ENERGETICS AND FEMALE FECUNDITY

The relationship of female fecundity to energetic stress has been a matter of interest since Frisch & Revelle first postulated a critical weight for the attainment of menarche (57). Numerous studies have now documented interruptions of menstrual function in association with low weight for height or intense aerobic exercise (see reviews in 28, 39, 40, 56, 123, 149). In addition, quantitative variations in ovarian function have been documented in association with milder levels of exercise and with simple weight loss, even in women of normal weight for height (39, 45, 83, 116, 131, 132). I have argued elsewhere that ovarian function responds to energetic stress along a continuum, ranging from fully competent cycles through intermediate stages of follicular and luteal suppression and irregular ovulation to oligomenorrhea and amenorrhea, depending on the intensity and duration of the stress (39, 40). Such a model fits the available data better than a dichotomous, clinical model of discrete states of function and dysfunction (48). The relationship between moderate levels of energetic stress and female fecundity has also been documented, clinically (10, 11) and epidemiologically (60, 61). It remains a question, however, whether energetic stress deriving from ecological conditions (as opposed to self-imposed regimes of dieting or exercise) effectively modulates ovarian function or female fecundity in non-clinical human populations.

Energetics and Ovarian Function in Human Populations

Variation in ovarian function associated with variation in energy balance or workload as a consequence of subsistence ecology has now been documented in three populations—the Lese of Zaïre's Ituri Forest (7, 50), the Tamang of highland Nepal (109, 110), and rural Polish farm women outside Crakow (75). The Lese are subsistence horticulturalists who annually clear and burn small patches of primary or secondary rain forest in order to plant peanuts, cassava, maize, and dry rice (6, 8). Because of the periodicity of the harvests and generally poor conditions for long-term food storage, the nutritional status of the entire population varies annually with a typical period of nutritional stress in the months preceding the June peanut harvest (7, 8, 49). Relative indices of luteal function and ovulatory frequency derived from salivary progesterone measurements are lower when women have been losing weight (50). During the preharvest hunger season, progesterone levels, ovulatory frequency, and the duration of menstrual bleeding (a reflection of endometrial thickness) decline in parallel with average body weight while cycle length increases; after the harvest, the trends are reversed (7, 17).

The Tamang are agro-pastoralists of Tibetan origin living in the Himalayan foothills between 1350 and 3800 meters, where they plant crops of wet rice, millet, wheat, barley, and maize, and herd mixed flocks of sheep, goats, oxen, and cattle. Female workloads vary in intensity and duration seasonally, with particularly heavy work occurring during the summer monsoon associated with transplanting rice seedlings (107, 108). Indices of luteal function and ovulatory frequency are lower for the population as a whole during the monsoon than during the winter dry season. The seasonal difference in ovarian function is entirely confined, however, to individuals who lose weight between the seasons. Individuals of stable or increasing weight show no differences in their steroid profiles (109, 110).

Farm women of the Polish countryside around Crakow are healthy and well-nourished, but are also faced with demanding workloads that vary seasonally. Much of the agricultural work is still done manually and, especially in the summer, involves both long hours of labor and considerable distances of daily travel on foot (75). Preliminary results based on salivary progesterone profiles from 20 women indicate that women who work longer hours have, as a group, lower indices of ovarian function during the agricultural season than those who work shorter hours (75). Research currently underway will elucidate the degree to which such variation is associated with energy balance and whether it is structured seasonally.

Energetics and Birth Seasonality

Some degree of birth seasonality is a common, though not universal, feature of human populations (36, 74, 111). There is no reason to suppose that birth seasonality as a whole is a monocausal phenomenon. There may be different causes of seasonality in different populations, and more than one cause within a given population. Patterns of social behavior affecting the probability of sexual intercourse are often invoked to explain observations of birth seasonality (74, 142). In some populations, for example, birth seasonality can be explained by seasonal spousal separations caused by labor migration (69), or in other populations, by festivals, holidays, or vacation seasons (27, 76, 130). Given the evidence that energetic stress modulates ovarian function, however, it is also possible that birth seasonality may be affected in some populations, at least in part, by seasonal patterns of energy balance.

Bailey et al (7) found a significant pattern of birth seasonality among the Lese, with a dearth of conceptions occurring during hunger season when negative energy balance predominates and ovarian function among the women is generally suppressed. They noted that the severity of the hunger season varies between years, and that conceptions are significantly fewer in severe hunger seasons than in mild hunger seasons. They also documented a lack of birth seasonality among the Efe pygmies who cohabit the Lese section of the Ituri Forest, but whose mobile lifestyle and ability to forage forest resources protects them to a significant degree from the seasonal alteration of energy balance to which the Lese are subject.

Leslie & Fry (87) documented pronounced birth seasonality among Turkana pastoralists of northern Kenya. There is a significant dearth of conceptions during the long dry season followed by a conception peak after the onset of the rainy season. As Leslie & Fry noted, there are numerous mechanisms that might be involved in this birth seasonality. However, the pattern of conceptions parallels the milk yield of the herds, which is the primary source of dietary energy for the Turkana.

Birth seasonality has been found among rural Bangladeshis in Matlab Thana (13, 14, 26). Data on the frequency of intercourse in the same population also show seasonality, but out of phase with the pattern of conceptions (13). The pattern of conceptions corresponds to annual weight cycles, however, with a low point preceding the harvest.

Seasonality of energy balance is probably a common feature of many human populations, especially those based on subsistence agriculture (24, 29, 70, 100, 126). There should be ample opportunity to test the hypothesis that such seasonality of energy balance affects female fecundity and hence the seasonality of births in natural fertility populations. It should be emphasized, however, that this hypothesis is not based on the optimal timing of births, nor is that envisioned as a result. Rather, the hypothesis is built on evidence of the sensitivity of female reproductive physiology to energetic stress, and assumes that this sensitivity functions to balance the distribution of resources between maintenance and reproduction. Birth seasonality, then, becomes a result of seasonal energetic stress, not an end in itself.

Energetics and Lactation

There is abundant evidence that variation in the duration of postpartum amenorrhea is the most important single component of variation in the length of interbirth intervals in natural fertility populations (19, 59), and considerable evidence links the duration of postpartum amenorrhea to the duration and intensity of lactation (31, 44, 66, 78, 82, 160). Early studies linked the suppressive effect of lactation on ovarian function to the frequency and patterning of suckling (31, 66, 82, 160).

Recent evidence, however, suggests that lactation itself is best understood as an energetic stress upon the mother, and the intensity of the suckling stimulus a direct reflection of the intensity of that stress (92, 93, 97). Women in poorer nutritional status may require more intense nipple stimulation in order to drive their metabolisms to produce sufficient milk for their offspring, while women in better nutritional status may require less intense stimulation to produce comparable amounts of milk. This would explain the fact that nutritional status does not affect the quantity or quality of milk produced by Gambian mothers (118–120, 122), but does affect prolactin profiles and the time to resumption of menses (94, 95). Moreover, Worthman et al (162) have reported that the suppression of ovarian function by lactation appears to be attenuated by nutritional status among Amele women in Papua New Guinea. In Bangladesh, interbirth intervals have been inversely correlated with maternal nutritional status independently of the duration of lactation, while maternal weight has been inversely correlated with the duration of lactation and postpartum amenorrhea (13, 54, 55, 68).

Understanding Energetics and Female Fecundity

There are several hypotheses regarding the functional significance of the relationship between energetics and female fecundity. Frisch has suggested that female body fat represents a necessary caloric reserve for successful gestation and lactation, and that when reserves fall below some minimum threshold ovarian function is interrupted to prevent a pregnancy with little chance of success (56). This hypothesis is difficult to reconcile with many observations, including the fact that body fat is accumulated, not depleted, during gestation (121), and that postpartum resumption of menses normally occurs when body fat is being depleted, not accumulated (67). In less rigid formulations, Vitzthum (147) and Peacock (112, 113) have argued that female reproductive physiology should be designed to respond to variable reproductive opportunities, foregoing reproduction when the chances of success are poor but likely to improve. Chronically poor conditions, however, should not produce the same result according to this argument. There is no advantage to be gained from postponing reproduction if the prospects for success are unlikely to change.

I have suggested a different model in which fecundity is modulated to optimize lifetime reproductive effort by balancing the distribution of maternal resources between maintenance and reproduction (including gestation, lactation, and parenting effort) (39, 40, 42, 43). Human female reproductive physiology appears to be geared to the problem of maintaining long-term energy balance despite the quantum energy demands of pregnancy and lactation (2, 117, 121). Reproduction can succeed when energy reserves and availability are poor, but only at significant cost to the mother's ability to invest in her own maintenance (121, 139). Slowing the rate of reproduction in an environment of low but stable energy availability can thus be an advantageous strategy in terms of lifetime reproductive success. Even if the probability of successful reproduction is not altered by a longer interbirth interval, the probability of maternal survival may be increased. As noted above, the rate of childhood growth and adolescent maturation should provide a reliable bioassay and empirical index of chronic energy availability with which adult fecundity would be expected to show a positive correlation. Responses to chronically poor energy availability may thus distinguish between current functional hypotheses regarding the relationship of female fecundity to energetic stress.

In summary, evidence is accumulating that energetic stress deriving from aspects of subsistence ecology is associated with lower indices of ovarian function in human populations of distinct genetic, ecological, and social backgrounds. Seasonality of energy balance, particularly in subsistence agricultural communities, may be related to seasonality of female fecundity and conceptions. The variable effect of lactation in suppressing the reproductive function of females may depend on the degree of energetic stress that lactation represents. Competing hypotheses regarding the functional significance of the sensitivity of female reproductive physiology to energetic stress may be discriminated on the basis of the expected effects of chronically poor energy availability.

CONCLUSION

Our understanding of human reproduction has profited greatly from our ability to place it in an ecological context, as an evolved aspect of our physiology manifesting variability that is functional and not merely pathological (48). Our ability to expand our perspective in this way has depended on our ability to expand the research venue for studies of female reproductive physiology beyond the clinic and beyond non-representative subsets of our own population (e.g. athletes, anorexics) into field settings where we encounter a broader sampling of the actual contexts of women's lives. As continued efforts and new techniques increase the quantity and quality of such information, we can expect to further deepen our understanding of this important aspect of the biology of our species.

ACKNOWLEDGMENTS

I thank all the members of the Reproductive Ecology Laboratory at Harvard University, past and present, especially Richard Bribiescas, Ben Campbell, Drew Colfax, Marion Eakin, Diana Graham, Grazyna Jasienska, Cheryl Knott, Catherine Lager, Susan Lipson, Deborah Lotstein, Mary O'Rourke, Diana Sherry, Sara Sukalich, and my collaborators in the field, especially Robert Bailey, Gillian Bentley, Alisa Harrigan, Mark Jenike, Catherine Panter-Brick, Nadine Peacock, and Virginia Vitzthum for their many substantive contributions to the work reviewed here. I also thank those women of Boston, Zaïre, Nepal, Poland, and Bolivia who have graciously aided us in our studies. This work has been supported by the National Science Foundation, Washington, DC.

Literature Cited

1. Abdalla HI, Burton G, Kirkland A, Johnson MR, Leonard T, et al. 1993. Age, pregnancy, and miscarriage: uterine versus ovarian factors. *Hum. Reprod.* 8:1512–17
2. Adair LS. 1984. Marginal intake and maternal adaptation: the case of rural Taiwan. *Curr. Top. Nutr. Dis.* 11:33–55
3. Apter D, Raisanen I, Ylostalo P, Vihko R. 1987. Follicular growth in relation to serum hormonal patterns in adolescents compared with adult menstrual cycles. *Fertil. Steril.* 47:82–88
4. Apter D, Vihko R. 1983. Early menarche, a risk factor for breast cancer, indicates early onset of ovulatory cycles. *J. Clin. Endocrinol. Metab.* 57:82–88
5. Apter D, Viinkka L, Vihko R. 1978. Hormonal pattern of adolescent menstrual cycles. *J. Clin. Endocrinol. Metab.* 47:944–54
6. Bailey RC, DeVore I. 1989. Research on the Efe and Lese populations of the Ituri Forest, Zaire. *Am. J. Phys. Anthropol.* 78:459–72
7. Bailey RC, Jenike MR, Bentley GR, Harrigan AM, Ellison PT. 1992. The ecology of birth seasonality among agriculturalists in central Africa. *J. Biosoc. Sci.* 24:393–412
8. Bailey RC, Peacock NR. 1988. Efe pygmies of northeastern Zaire: subsistence strategies in the Ituri Forest. In *Uncertainty in Food Supply,* ed. I de Garine, GA Harrison, pp. 88–117. Cambridge: Cambridge Univ. Press
9. Baker TG. 1972. Oogenesis and ovulation. In *Reproduction in Mammals.* Vol. I: *Germ Cells and Fertilization,* ed. CR Austin, RV Short, pp. 14–45. Cambridge: Cambridge Univ. Press
10. Bates GW. 1985. Body weight control practice as a cause of infertility. *Clin. Obstet. Gynecol.* 28:632–44
11. Bates GW, Bates SR, Whitworth NS. 1982. Reproductive failure in women who practice weight control. *Fertil. Steril.* 37:373–78
12. Baulieu E-E. 1990. Hormones, a complex communication network. In *Hormones,* ed. E-E Baulieu, PA Kelly, pp. 3–169. New York: Chapman & Hall
13. Becker S, Chowdhury A, Leridon H. 1986. Seasonal patterns of reproduction in Matlab, Bangladesh. *Popul. Stud.* 40:457–72
14. Becker S, Sardar MA. 1981. Seasonal patterns of vital events in Matlab Thana, Bangladesh. In *Seasonal Dimensions to Rural Poverty,* ed. R Chambers, R Longhurst, A Pacey, pp. 149–56. London: Pinter
15. Bendel JP, Hua C. 1978. An estimate of the natural fecundability ratio curve. *Soc. Biol.* 25:210–27
16. Bentley GR, Harrigan AM, Campbell B, Ellison PT. 1993. Seasonal effects on salivary testosterone levels among Lese males of the Ituri Forest, Zaire. *Am. J. Hum. Biol.* 5:711–17
17. Bentley GR, Harrigan AM, Ellison PT. 1990. Ovarian cycle length and days of menstruation of Lese horticulturalists. *J. Phys. Anthropol.* 81:193–94 (Abstr.)
18. Blake J. 1985. The fertility transition: continuity or discontinuity with the past? In *International Population Conf., Florence,* Vol. 4, pp. 393–405. Liege, Belgium: IUSSP
19. Bongaarts J, Potter RG. 1983. *Fertility, Biology, and Behavior: An Analysis of the Proximate Determinants.* New York: Academic
20. Breckenridge MB. 1983. *Age, Time, and Fertility.* New York: Academic
20a. Campbell BC, Leslie PW. 1994. Reproductive ecology of human males. *Yearb. Phys. Anthropol.* 37:In press
21. Campbell KL. 1985. Methods of monitoring ovarian function and predicting ovulation. *Res. Front. Fertil. Regul.* 3:1–16
22. Campbell KL. 1994. Blood, urine, saliva and dip-sticks: experiences in Africa, New Guinea and Boston. See Ref. 23a, pp. 312–30
23. Campbell KL, Wood JW. 1988. Fertility in traditional societies. In *Natural Human Fertility and Biological Determinants,* ed. P Diggory, M Potts, S Teper, pp. 39–69. London: Macmillan
23a. Campbell KL, Wood JW, eds. 1994. Human Reproductive Ecology: Interactions of Environment, Fertility, and Behavior. *Ann. NY Acad. Sci.* 709
24. Chambers R, Longhurst R, Pacey A. 1981. *Seasonal Dimensions to Rural Poverty.* London: Pinter
25. Charnov EL, Berrigan D. 1993. Why do female primates have such long lifespans and so few babies? or Life in the slow lane. *Evol. Anthropol.* 1:191–94
26. Chen LC, Ahmed S, Gesche M, Mosley WH. 1974. A prospective study of birth interval dynamics in rural Bangladesh. *Popul. Stud.* 28:277–97
27. Condon RG, Scaglion R. 1982. The ecology of human birth seasonality. *Hum. Ecol.* 10:495–510
28. Cumming DC. 1990. Physical activity and control of the hypothalamic-pituary-gonadal axis. *Semin. Reprod. Endocrinol.* 8:15–23
29. de Garine I, Harrison GA. 1988. *Coping*

HUMAN REPRODUCTIVE ECOLOGY 271

with Uncertainty in Food Supply. Oxford: Oxford Univ. Press
30. de la Rochefordiere A, Asselain B, Campana F, Scholl SM, Fenton J, et al. 1993. Age as a prognostic factor in premenopausal breast carcinoma. Lancet 341: 1039–43
31. Delvoye P, Demaegd M, Delogne-Desnoeck J, Robyn C. 1977. The influence of the frequency of nursing and of previous lactation experience on serum prolactin in lactating mothers. J. Biosoc. Sci. 9:447–51
32. de Ziegler D, Bergeron C, Cornel C, Medalie DA, Massai MR, et al. 1992. Effects of luteal estradiol on the secretory transformation of human endometrium and plasma gonadotropins. J. Endocrinol. Clin. Metab. 74:322–31
33. Dickey RP, Olar TT, Taylor SN, Curole DN, Harrigill K. 1993. Relationship of biochemical pregnancy to pre-ovulatory endometrial thickness and pattern in patients undergoing ovulation induction. Hum. Reprod. 8:327–30
34. Dickey RP, Olar TT, Taylor SN, Curole DN, Matulich EM. 1993. Relationship of endometrial thickness and pattern to fecundity in ovulation induction cycles: effect of clomiphene citrate alone and with human menopausal gonadotropin. Fertil. Steril. 59:756–60
35. Döring GK. 1969. The incidence of anovular cycles in women. J. Reprod. Fertil. Suppl. 6:77–81
35a. Dunbar RIM, ed. 1994. Human Reproductive Decisions: Biological and Social Perspectives. London: Macmillan
36. Dyson T, Crook N. 1981. Seasonal patterns in births and deaths. In Seasonal Dimensions to Rural Poverty, ed. R Chambers, R Longhurst, A Pacey, pp. 135–62. London: Pinter
37. Edvinsson A, Forssman L, Milson I, Nordfors G. 1990. Factors in the infertile couple influencing the success of artificial insemination with donor semen. Fertil. Steril. 53: 81–87
38. Ellison PT. 1988. Human salivary steroids: methodological considerations and applications in physical anthropology. Yearb. Phys. Anthropol. 31:115–32
39. Ellison PT. 1990. Human ovarian function and reproductive ecology: new hypotheses. Am. Anthropol. 92:933–52
40. Ellison PT. 1991. Reproductive ecology and human fertility. In Biological Anthropology and Human Affairs, ed. GW Lasker, N Mascie-Taylor, pp. 14–54. Cambridge: Cambridge Univ. Press
41. Ellison PT. 1993. Measurements of salivary progesterone. Ann. NY Acad. Sci. 694: 161–76
42. Ellison PT. 1994. Salivary steroids and

natural variation in human ovarian function. See Ref. 23a, pp. 285–98
43. Ellison PT. 1994. Understanding natural variation in human ovarian function. In Human Reproductive Decisions: Biological and Social Perspectives, ed. RIM Dunbar. London: Macmillan. In press
44. Ellison PT. 1994. Breastfeeding and fertility. In Breastfeeding: A Biocultural Perspective, ed. KA Dettwyler, P Stuart-Macadam. Hawthorne, NY: Aldine de Gruyter. In press
45. Ellison PT, Lager C. 1986. Moderate recreational running is associated with lowered salivary progesterone profiles in women. Am. J. Obstet. Gynecol. 154: 1000–3
46. Ellison PT, Lager C, Calfee J. 1987. Low profiles of salivary progesterone among college undergraduate women. J. Adolesc. Health Care 8:204–7
47. Ellison PT, Lipson SF, O'Rourke MT, Bentley GR, Harrigan AM, et al. 1993. Population variation in ovarian function. Lancet 342:433–43
48. Ellison PT, Panter-Brick C, Lipson SF, O'Rourke MT. 1993. The ecological context of human reproduction. Hum. Reprod. 8:2248–58
49. Ellison PT, Peacock NR, Lager C. 1986. Salivary progesterone and luteal function in two low-fertility populations of northeast Zaire. Hum. Biol. 58:473–83
50. Ellison PT, Peacock NR, Lager C. 1989. Ecology and ovarian function among Lese women of the Ituri Forest, Zaire. Am. J. Phys. Anthropol. 78:519–26
51. Deleted in proof
52. FIVNAT. 1993. French national IVF registry: analysis of 1986 to 1990 data. Fertil. Steril. 59:587–95
53. Flamigni C, Borini A, Violini F, Bianchi L, Serrao L. 1993. Oocyte donation: comparison between recipients from different age groups. Hum. Reprod. 8:2088–92
54. Ford K, Huffman S. 1988. Nutrition, infant feeding and post-partum amenorrhea in rural Bangladesh. J. Biosoc. Sci. 20:461–69
55. Ford K, Huffman SL, Chowdhury AKMA, Becker S, Allen H, Menken J. 1989. Birthinterval dynamics in rural Bangladesh and maternal weight. Demography 26:425–37
56. Frisch RE. 1990. Body fat, menarche, fitness and fertility. Prog. Reprod. Biol. Med. 14:1–26
57. Frisch RE, Revelle R. 1970. Height and weight at menarche and a hypothesis of critical body weights and adolescent events. Science 169:397–99
58. Fritz MA, Westfahl PK, Graham RL. 1987. The effect of luteal phase estrogen antagonism on endometrial development and luteal function in women. J. Clin. Endocrinol. Metab. 65:1006–13

59. Goldman N, Westhoff CF, Paul LE. 1987. Variations in natural fertility: the effect of lactation and other determinants. *Popul. Stud.* 41:127–46
60. Green BB, Daling JR, Weiss NS, Liff JM, Koepsell T. 1986. Exercise as a risk factor for infertility with ovulatory dysfunction. *Am. J. Public Health* 76:1432–36
61. Green BB, Weiss NS, Daling JR. 1988. Risk of ovulatory infertility in relation to body weight. *Fertil. Steril.* 50:721–26
62. Henderson BE, Ross RK, Bernstein L. 1988. Estrogens as a cause of human cancer: the Richard and Hilda Rosenthal Foundation Award Lecture. *Cancer Res.* 48:246–53
63. Henderson BE, Ross RK, Judd HL. 1985. Do regular ovulatory cycles increase breast cancer risk? *Cancer* 56:1206–8
64. Henry L. 1961. Some data on natural fertility. *Eugen. Q.* 8:81–91
65. Howell N. 1979. *Demography of the Dobe !Kung.* New York: Academic
66. Howie PW, McNeilly AS. 1982. Effect of breast feeding patterns on human birth intervals. *J. Reprod. Fertil.* 65:545–57
67. Huffman SL, Chowdhury AKMA, Mosley WH. 1978. Difference between postpartum and nutritional amenorrhea. *Science* 203:921–22
68. Huffman SL, Ford K, Allen HA, Streble P. 1987. Nutrition and fertility in Bangladesh: breastfeeding and post partum amenorrhea. *Popul. Stud.* 41:447–62
69. Huss-Ashmore R. 1988. Seasonal patterns of birth and conception in rural highland Lesotho. *Hum. Biol.* 60:494–506
70. Huss-Ashmore R, Curry JJ, Hitchcock RK. 1988. *Coping with Seasonal Constraints.* Philadelphia: Univ. Museum, Univ. Penn.
71. James WH. 1979. The causes of the decline in fecundability with age. *Soc. Biol.* 26:330–34
72. James WH. 1981. Distributions of coital rates and of fecundability. *Soc. Biol.* 28:334–41
73. James WH. 1983. Decline in coital rates with spouses' ages and duration of marriage. *J. Biosoc. Sci.* 15:83–87
74. James WH. 1990. Seasonal variation in human births. *J. Biosoc. Sci.* 22:113-19
75. Jasienska G, Ellison PT. 1993. Heavy workload impairs ovarian function in Polish peasant women. *Am. J. Phys. Anthropol. Suppl.* 16:117–18 (Abstr.)
76. Johnson JT, Ann TB, Palan VT. 1975. Seasonality of births for West Malaysia's two main racial groups. *Hum. Biol.* 47:295–307
77. Jones EE, Seifer DB, Naftolin F. 1991. Effects of hypothalamic-pituitary aging on reproduction. *Semin. Reprod. Endocrinol.* 9:221–30
78. Jones RE. 1988. A hazards model analysis of breastfeeding variables and maternal age

on return to menses postpartum in rural Indonesian women. *Hum. Biol.* 60:853–71
79. Kelsey JL, Gammon MD. 1991. The epidemiology of breast cancer. *CA-Cancer J. Clin.* 41:146–65
80. Key TJA, Pike MC. 1988. The role of oestrogens and progestagens in the epidemiology and prevention of breast cancer. *Eur. J. Clin. Oncol.* 24:29–43
81. Knodel J. 1983. Natural fertility: age patterns, levels, and trends. In *Determinants of Fertility in Developing Countries,* ed. RA Bulatao, RD Lee, 1:61–102. New York: Academic
82. Konner M, Worthman C. 1980. Nursing frequency, gonadal function, and birth spacing among !Kung hunter-gatherers. *Science* 207:788–91
83. Lager C, Ellison PT. 1990. Effect of moderate weight loss on ovarian function assessed by salivary progesterone measurements. *Am. J. Hum. Biol.* 2:303–12
84. Lasley BL. 1994. The use of urinary assays to monitor human reproduction. See Ref. 23a, pp. 299–311
84a. Leidy L. 1994. Biological aspects of menopause: across the lifespan. *Annu. Rev. Anthropol.* 23:231–53
85. Lenton EA, Landgren B-M, Sexton L. 1984. Normal variation in the length of the luteal phase of the menstrual cycle: identification of the short luteal phase. *Br. J. Obstet. Gynaecol.* 91:685–89
86. Leslie PW, Campbell KL, Little MA. 1993. Pregnancy loss in nomadic and settled women in Turkana, Kenya: a prospective study. *Hum. Biol.* 65:237–54
87. Leslie PW, Fry PH. 1989. Extreme seasonality of births among nomadic Turkana pastoralists. *Am. J. Phys. Anthropol.* 79:103–15
88. Levran D, Ben-Shlomo I, Dor J, Ben-Rafael Z, Nebel L, Mashiach S. 1991. Age of endometrium and oocytes: observations on conception and abortion rates in an egg donation model. *Fertil. Steril.* 56:1091–94
89. Levran D, Dor J, Rudak E, Nebel L, Ben-Shlomo I, Mashiach S. 1990. Pregnancy potential of human oöcytes—the effect of cryopreservation. *N. Engl. J. Med.* 323:1153–56
90. Lipson SF, Ellison PT. 1992. Normative study of age variation in salivary progesterone profiles. *J. Biosoc. Sci.* 24:233–44
91. Lipson SF, Ellison PT. 1994. Reference values for luteal progesterone measured by salivary radioimmunoassay. *Fertil. Steril.* 61:448–54
92. Lunn PG. 1992. Breast-feeding patterns, maternal milk output and lactational infecundity. *J. Biosoc. Sci.* 24:317–24
93. Lunn PG. 1994. Lactation and other metabolic loads affecting human reproduction. See Ref. 23a, pp. 77–85

94. Lunn PG, Austin S, Prentice AM, White-head RG. 1984. The effect of improved nutrition on plasma prolactin concentrations and postpartum infertility in lactating Gambian women. *Am. J. Clin. Nutr.* 39: 227–35

95. Lunn PG, Prentice AM, Austin S, Whitehead RG. 1980. Influence of maternal diet on plasma-prolactin levels during lactation. *Lancet* 1(8169):623–25

96. McClure N, McDonald J, Kovacs GT, Healy DL, McCloud PI, McQuinn B. 1993. Age and follicular phase estradiol are better predictors of pregnancy outcome than luteinizing hormone in menotropin ovulation induction for anovulatory polycycstic ovarian syndrome. *Fertil. Steril.* 59:729–33

97. McNeilly A. 1994. Breastfeeding and the baby: natural contraception. In *Reproductive Decisions: Biological and Social Perspectives,* ed. RIM Dunbar. London: Macmillan. In press

98. Meldrum DR. 1993. Female reproductive aging—ovarian and uterine factors. *Fertil. Steril.* 59:1–5

99. Menken J, Trussell J, Larsen U. 1986. Age and infertility. *Science* 233:1389–94

100. Messer E. 1989. Seasonality in food systems: anthropological perspective on household food security. In *Seasonal Variability in Third World Agriculture,* ed. DE Sahn, pp. 151–75. Baltimore: Johns Hopkins Univ. Press

101. Metcalf MG, Donald RA, Livesey JH. 1981. Classification of menstrual cycles in pre- and perimenopausal women. *J. Endocrinol.* 91:1–10

102. Metcalf MG, Skidmore DS, Lowry GF, Mackenzie JA. 1983. Incidence of ovulation in the years after menarche. *J. Endocrinol.* 97:213–19

103. Navot D, Bergh PA, Williams M, Garrisi GJ, Guzman I, et al. 1991. An insight into early reproductive processes through the in-vivo model of ovum donation. *J. Clin. Endocrinol. Metab.* 72:408–14

104. O'Rourke MT, Ellison PT. 1993. Salivary estradiol levels decrease with age in healthy, regularly-cycling women. *Endocrinol. J.* 1:487–94

105. O'Rourke MT, Ellison PT. 1993. Age and prognosis in premenopausal breast cancer. *Lancet* 342:60

106. Padilla SL, Garcia JE. 1989. Effect of maternal age and number of in vitro fertilization procedures on pregnancy outcome. *Fertil. Steril.* 52:270–73

107. Panter-Brick C. 1992. The energy cost of common tasks in rural Nepal: levels of energy expenditure compatible with sustained physical activity. *Eur. J. Appl. Physiol.* 64:477–84

108. Panter-Brick C. 1993. Seasonality and levels of energy expenditure during pregnancy and lactation for rural Nepali women. *Am. J. Clin. Nutr.* 57:620–28

109. Panter-Brick C, Ellison PT. 1994. Seasonality of workloads and ovarian function in Nepali women. See Ref. 23a, pp. 234–35

110. Panter-Brick C, Lotstein DS, Ellison PT. 1993. Seasonality of reproductive function and weight loss in rural Nepali women. *Hum. Reprod.* 8:684–90

111. Pasamanick BS, Dinitz S, Knobloch H. 1960. Socio-economic and seasonal variations in birth rates. *Milbank Mem. Fund Q. Bull.* 38:249-63

112. Peacock NR. 1990. Comparative and cross-cultural approaches to the study of human female reproductive failure. In *Primate Life History and Evolution,* ed. CJ DeRousseau, pp. 195–220. New York: Wiley-Liss

113. Peacock NR. 1991. An evolutionary perspective on the patterning of maternal investment in pregnancy. *Hum. Nat.* 2:351–85

114. Pearlstone AC, Oei ML, Wu T-CJ. 1992. The predictive value of a single, early human chorionic gonadotropin measurement and the influence of maternal age on pregnancy outcome in an infertile population. *Fertil. Steril.* 57:302–4

115. Phillips J, Worthman CM, Stallings JF. 1991. New field techniques for detection of female reproductive status. *Am. J. Phys. Anthropol. Suppl.* 12:143 (Abstr.)

116. Pirke M, Schweiger U, Lemmel W, Krieg JC, Berger M. 1985. The influence of dieting on the menstrual cycle of healthy young women. *J. Clin. Endocrinol. Metab.* 60: 1174–79

117. Prentice AM. 1984. Adaptations to long-term low energy intake. In *Energy Intake and Activity,* pp. 3–31. New York: Liss

118. Prentice AM, Lunn PG, Watkinson M, Whitehead RG. 1983. Dietary supplementation of lactating Gambian women. II. Effect on maternal health, nutritional status and biochemistry. *Hum. Nutr. Clin. Nutr.* 37:65–74

119. Prentice AM, Paul AA, Prentice A, Black AE, Cole TJ, Whitehead RG. 1986. Cross-cultural differences in lactational performance. In *Human Lactation.* Vol. 2: *Maternal and Environmental Factors,* ed. M Hamosh, AS Goldman, pp. 13–44. New York: Plenum

120. Prentice AM, Roberts SB, Prentice A, Paul AA, Watkinson M, et al. 1983. Dietary supplementation of lactating Gambian women. I. Effect on breast-milk volume and quality. *Hum. Nutr. Clin. Nutr.* 37:53–64

121. Prentice AM, Whitehead RG. 1987. The energetics of human reproduction. *Symp. Zool. Soc. London* 57:275–304

122. Prentice AM, Whitehead RG, Roberts SB, Paul AA, Watkinson M, et al. 1980. Dietary supplementation of Gambian nursing mothers and lactational performance. *Lancet* 2(8200):886–88
123. Rosetta L. 1993. Female reproductive dysfunction and intense physical training. *Oxford Rev. Reprod. Biol.* 15:113–41
124. Rotsztejn DA, Asch RH. 1991. Effect of aging on assisted reproductive technologies (ART): experience from egg donation. *Semin. Reprod. Endocrinol.* 9:272–79
125. Ruzicka LT, Bhatia S. 1982. Coital frequency and sexual abstinence in rural Bangladesh. *J. Biosoc. Sci.* 14:397–420
126. Sahn DE. 1989. *Seasonal Variability in Third World Agriculture.* Baltimore: Johns Hopkins Univ. Press
127. Sauer MV, Paulson RJ, Lobo RA. 1990. A preliminary report on oocyte donation extending reproductive potential to women over 40. *N. Engl. J. Med.* 323:1157–60
128. Sauer MV, Paulson RJ, Lobo RA. 1992. Reversing the natural decline in human fertility: an extended clinical trial of oocyte donation to women of advanced reproductive age. *J. Am. Med. Assoc.* 268:1275–79
129. Sauer MV, Paulson RJ, Lobo RA. 1993. Pregnancy after 50: application of oocyte donation to women after natural menopause. *Lancet* 341:321–23
130. Scaglion R. 1978. Seasonal births in a western Abelam village, Papua New Guinea. *Hum. Biol.* 50:313–23
130a. Schwartz D, Mayaux MJ. 1982. Female fecundity as a function of age. *N. Engl. J. Med.* 306:404–6
131. Schweiger U, Laessle R, Pfister H, Hoehl C, Schwingenschloegel M, et al. 1987. Diet-induced menstrual irregularities: effects of age and weight loss. *Fertil. Steril.* 48:746–51
132. Shangold M, Freeman R, Thyssen B, Gatz M. 1979. The relationship between long-distance running, plasma progesterone, and luteal phase length. *Fertil. Steril.* 31:699–702
133. Sherman BM, Korenman SG. 1975. Hormonal characteristics of the human menstrual cycle throughout reproductive life. *J. Clin. Invest.* 55:699–706
134. Sherman BM, West JH, Korenman SG. 1976. The menopausal transition: analysis of LH, FSH, estradiol, and progesterone concentrations during menstrual cycles of older women. *J. Clin. Endocrinol. Metab.* 42:629–36
135. Shoham Z, DiCarlo C, Patel A, Conway GS, Jacobs HS. 1991. Is it possible to run a successful ovulation induction program based solely on ultrasound monitoring? The importance of endometrial measurements. *Fertil. Steril.* 56:836–41
136. Stearns SC. 1992. *The Evolution of Life Histories.* Oxford: Oxford Univ. Press
137. Steinkampf MP. 1991. Effect of aging on ovulation induction. *Semin. Reprod. Endocrinol.* 9:266–71
138. Toner JP, Philiput CB, Jones GS, Muasher SJ. 1991. Basal follicle-stimulating hormone level is a better predictor of in vitro fertilization performance than age. *Fertil. Steril.* 55:784–91
139. Tracer DP. 1991. Fertility-related changes in maternal body composition among the Au of Papua New Guinea. *Am. J. Phys. Anthropol.* 85:393–405
140. Treloar AE, Boynton RE, Behn BG, Brown BW. 1967. Variation of the human menstrual cycle through reproductive life. *Int. J. Fertil.* 12:77–126
141. Udry JR, Deven FR, Coleman SJ. 1982. A cross-national comparison of the relative influence of male and female age on the frequency of intercourse. *J. Biosoc. Sci.* 14:1–6
142. Udry JR, Morris NM. 1967. Seasonality of coitus and seasonality of birth. *Demography* 4:673–90
143. Venturoli S, Porcu E, Gammi L, Magrini O, Fabbri R, et al. 1987. Different gonadotropin pulsatile fashions in anovulatory cycles of young girls indicate different maturational pathways in adolescence. *J. Clin. Endocrinol. Metab.* 65:785–91
144. Vihko R, Apter D. 1980. Hormones in the menstrual cycle and prediction and detection of ovulation by hormonal measurement: the role of androgens in adolescent cycles. *J. Steroid Biochem.* 12:369–73
145. Vihko R, Apter D. 1984. Endocrine characteristics of adolescent menstrual cycles: impacts of early menarche. *J. Steroid Biochem.* 20:231–36
146. Virro MR, Shewchuk AB. 1984. Pregnancy outcome in 242 conceptions after artificial insemination with donor sperm and effects of maternal age on the prognosis for successful pregnancy. *Am. J. Obstet. Gynecol.* 148:518–24
147. Vitzthum VJ. 1990. *An adaptational model of ovarian function.* Res. Rep. No. 90–200. Ann Arbor: Popul. Stud. Cent., Univ. Mich.
148. vom Saal FS, Finch CE. 1988. Reproductive senescence: phenomena and mechanisms in mammals and selected vertebrates. In *The Physiology of Reproduction,* ed. E Knobil, JD Neill, 2:2351–2413. New York: Raven
149. Warren MP. 1990. Weight control. *Semin. Reprod. Endocrinol.* 8:25–31
150. Wassarman PM. 1988. The mammalian ovum. In *The Physiology of Reproduction,* ed. E Knobil, JD Neill, 1:69–102. New York: Raven
151. Weinstein M, Wood J, Stoto MA, Green-

dield DD. 1990. Components of age-specific fecundability. *Popul. Stud.* 44:447–67
152. Williams GC. 1966. Natural selection, the costs of reproduction, and a refinement of Lack's principle. *Am. Nat.* 100:687–90
153. Wilson C, Oeppen J, Pardoe M. 1988. What is natural fertility? The modeling of a concept. *Popul. Index* 54:4–20
154. Wood JW. 1989. Fecundity and natural fertility in humans. *Oxford Rev. Reprod. Biol.* 11:61–109
155. Wood JW. 1990. Fertility in anthropological populations. *Annu. Rev. Anthropol.* 19:211–42
156. Wood JW. 1994. Nutrition and reproduction: why demographers and physiologists disagree about a fundamental relationship. See Ref. 23a, pp. 101–16
157. Wood JW. 1994. *Dynamics of Human Reproduction: Biology, Biometry, Demography.* Hawthorne, NY: Aldine de Gruyter. In press
158. Wood JW, Holman DJ, Weiss KM, Buchanan AV, LeFor B. 1992. Hazards models for human population biology. *Yearb. Phys. Anthropol.* 35:43–88

159. Wood JW, Johnson PL, Campbell K. 1985. Demographic and endocrinological aspects of low natural fertility in highland New Guinea. *J. Biosoc. Sci.* 17:57–79
160. Wood JW, Lai D, Johnson PL, Campbell KL, Maslar IA. 1985. Lactation and birth spacing in Highland New Guinea. *J. Biosoc. Sci. Suppl.* 9:159–73
161. Wood JW, Weinstein M. 1988. A model of age-specific fecundability. *Popul. Stud.* 42:85–113
162. Worthman CM, Jenkins CL, Stallings JF, Lai D. 1993. Attenuation of nursing-related ovarian suppression and high fertility in well-nourished, intensively breastfeeding Amele women of lowland Papua New Guinea. *J. Biosoc. Sci.* 25:425–43
163. Worthman CM, Stallings JF, Gubernick D. 1991. Measurement of hormones in blood spots: a non-isotopic assay for prolactin. *Am. J. Phys. Anthropol. Suppl.* 12:186–87 (Abstr.)
164. Yoshimura Y, Wallach EE. 1987. Studies of the mechanism(s) of mammalian ovulation. *Fertil. Steril.* 47:22–34

Annu. Rev. Anthropol. 1994. 23:277–302

HONORIFICATION

Asif Agha

Department of Applied Linguistics, University of California, Los Angeles, California
90024

KEY WORDS: honorifics, pragmatics, politeness, registers, language in society

INTRODUCTION

The role of linguistic categories in establishing and maintaining social
relationships and, thus, in maintaining and renewing patterns of culture and
society is of fundamental interest to anthropologically oriented studies of
language. Within this broad area of concern, the last two or three decades have
seen especially detailed studies of the linguistic means of marking relationships of honorification—relationships involving social status, respect, or deference between communicative interactants. The subject matter has been
approached from a number of different perspectives. It is generally agreed, for
example, that a logical precondition on the occurrence of honorific phenomena
is the existence of intersubjectively shared codes of behavior available to
interactants as such. Yet the way in which such codes are best described, the
way in which they are invoked or appealed to by interactants, the extent to
which they are susceptible to strategic manipulation, and their place within the
larger nexus of preconditions on discursive interaction—as an order of meaningful activity—are matters of some dispute and debate. Indeed, the literature
here reviewed is characterized not only by a substantial variability in research
goals and agendas but also by a range of methods used to formulate and test
empirical generalizations.

This review covers studies of honorific phenomena of several types, including honorific pronouns and terms of address, politeness in language use, and
honorific registers. From the point of view of their capacity to mark honorific

relationships, honorific registers are considerably more elaborate than the others, since they consist of rich repertoires of honorific items that may be used concurrently in utterances to mark deference to a variety of individuals, and sometimes to a number of individuals at the same time. For a discussion of issues related to the ones discussed here, the reader may find it useful to consult two other reviews that have appeared previously (109, 154) and one that appears in this volume (220).

PRONOUNS AND ADDRESS FORMS

All human languages contain a repertoire of relatively localizable devices— pronouns, nouns, or noun phrases—the very use of which in designating, addressing, or referring to individuals has immediate consequences for the social evaluation of respect or deference to the individual thus picked out. A large literature on honorification by the use of pronouns and address forms is now available, including a number of studies of particular languages (5, 9, 14, 15, 17, 18, 22, 26, 30–32, 42, 43, 46, 59, 60, 94, 114–116, 119, 122, 133, 134, 138, 146, 158–160, 175, 176, 188, 190, 194, 198–200, 204, 205), as well as fairly comprehensive bibliographies of other related work (23, 164, 170, 171, 179).

The most influential single framework for the study of pronominal honorification in the literature is Brown & Gilman's (27) power-and-solidarity model of pronominal usage. Brown & Gilman's theory evaluates the historical developments in usage of the familiar two-way pronominal contrast in European languages—i.e. the T form (e.g. French *tu,* Russian *ty,* German *du*) and the V form (e.g. French *vous,* Russian *vy,* German *Sie*)—in terms of two universal and logically linked functional (or "semantic") dimensions termed power and solidarity, applicable to all interactional dyads. Power is an inherently asymmetric relation, the ability of one individual "to control the behavior of the other" (p. 255), signaled by nonreciprocal usage of pronoun forms; solidarity is an inherently symmetric relation, based on the likeness of both individuals by membership in the same social group, such as family, religion, school, or profession (p. 258), resulting in reciprocal usage. Brown & Gilman argue that although the solidarity semantic was once applied in European societies only when the power semantic was undecidable or irrelevant, it has prevailed over the power semantic in modern societies due to changes in "social attitude"— such as the spread of egalitarianism.

Subsequent research has called into question at least three critical assumptions underlying Brown & Gilman's theory: 1. that pronoun choice primarily reflects macrosociological relationships; 2. that social ideologies influence usage uniformly across society, independently of differences in the positional identity of speakers; and 3. that linguistic change is a dependent order of phenomena caused by independent changes in social mind.

Wales (208), for example, questions the validity of any direct, unmediated linkage between social ideology and linguistic patterns (see also 3, 136, 157), arguing that many mutually opposed ideologies about interpersonal relations have continued to exist in England but are simply not reflected in pronouns of address. The argument from recent changes in social ideologies leaves unexplained the fact that in English texts of the thirteenth and fourteenth centuries, pronoun choice exhibits considerable variability, sometimes within the same sentence. Wales argues that such pronominal shifts reflect interactional stances of individual interlocutors as well as macrosociological relationships between social dyads, thus arguing against the exclusive appeal to macrosociological factors as explanatory variables in historical change. Moreover, the generic notion of power, for example, leaves undifferentiated social variables such as rank, economic class, and social status (see also 84, 85, 189, 203, 217). Wales suggests that the spread of *you* over *thou* in English was not the result of any generalized victory of egalitarianism over a power semantic in the crucial period between 1540 and 1640. Social stratification had, if anything, intensified because of the seismic growth of London's population. The change was due partly, she suggests, to a heightened social awareness in the English middle class at the end of the sixteenth century; the middle class aspired "towards the habits of polite society" (208:119) whose speech they sought to emulate. Wales argues, moreover, that the spread of *you* over *thou* in English also involves a language-structural dynamic. By the late sixteenth and early seventeenth centuries, *thou* appears to be the marked form; it also takes the overt verbal ending *-est*, while *you* does not; the disappearance of English verb endings in all but the third person singular may have constituted a language-structural force toward change, leading to the disfavoring of the *thou* V-*est* construction, and eventually of *thou*.

The argument that actual usage cannot be explained by macrosociological variables alone has been made most insightfully, perhaps, by Friedrich, in a detailed study of pronominal usage in nineteenth century Russian literary texts (63). Friedrich shows that the choice of pronoun forms in Russian is sensitive not only to macrosociological variables (e.g. age, generation, sex, kinship status, group membership, and relative authority), but also to speech event variables (e.g. topic, context, and affective relation between speaker and addressee). This suggests that the functional interpretation of honorific usage requires a more fine-grained analysis of social and interactional variables than Brown & Gilman's early study would suggest.

Ervin-Tripp (56) has shown that configurations of co-factors which determine pronominal choice in Friedrich's data (and in other, similar studies) cluster in certain patterned ways, describable as paths in a flowchart representation. Building on these results, Silverstein (186) has argued that since there exist multiple such paths (or configurations of situational factors) leading to each of the two outputs, T and V, a token of either T or V is interpretable in any of several distinct ways. For example, the use of T can index that the addressee is a child, a kin of descending generation, a member of the same household, or some combination of these. The use of V can index that the interaction occurs in a status-marked setting (e.g. in a court), that the addressee is a kin of ascending generation, or older in age, etc, or some combination of these. Thus, no two tokens of T or V can necessarily be interpreted as alike. Consequently, even if an individual consistently uses T forms over an entire stretch of discourse, different tokens of T may reflect distinct configurations of situational variables at different points in the same discourse. Silverstein suggests that the data of honorific usage does not permit any kind of "social semantic" calculus at all. Rather, the norms of usage in some particular community indexically associate linguistic categories with multiple, alternative configurations of contextual factors that become apparent only in the T or V usage responding to the one at issue, confirming, as it were, or disconfirming its invoked social dimensions "in play." Any account of the contextual dimension of usage appears, then, to require a functional evaluation sensitive to: 1. the fact of the occurrence of T vs V; 2. the indexical values conventionally associated with these forms in particular speech communities; and 3. the real-time variation of symmetric vs asymmetric usage as it changes back and forth across interactional turns.

Other criticisms of Brown & Gilman's model have come from more detailed surveys of pronominal honorification in a number of languages (79, 117). In discussing a sample of some 80 Indo-European (IE) languages and dialects, Joseph (117) argues that explanations from notional-sociological and mentalist variables which treat linguistic change as a secondary, derivative phenomenon both simplify the historical facts of linguistic change and assume a greater cross-cultural provenance for the explanatory variables than the historical record suggests. Brown & Gilman argued, for example, that the use of plural V forms for a singular addressee in several IE languages can be traced back to the change in rulers from a single emperor to rule by joint emperors in the late Roman empire of the fourth century, thus leading to a change in the mental representation of grammatical person in many European societies. Joseph argues, however, that the languages in which such change has been noted were not united by any shared political contact of the sort required by the hypothesis. Joseph attributes the change to several factors, including the tendency or "slant" (a notion based on the Sapirean account of drift) across the IE family for languages to move from a synthetic to an analytic stage. As a result, the use of an independent subject pronoun becomes obligatory, rather than optional, leading to a greater prominence for number and person categories in utterances. Joseph argues that, in the context of this historical change, referentially less specific categories such as second person dual and plural forms (nonspecific because they additionally include nonaddressees within their referential domain) were extended in usage to mark deference to singular addressee by a figurative extension, the synecdoche of whole for part. Once such a form (whose literal meaning includes nonaddressee) is used deferentially for a single addressee, an analogous figurative extension occurs in many languages whereby third person pronouns (nonspecific because they refer to non–speech act participant) are used for deferential address to a speech-act participant (i.e. the addressee). Joseph argues that in every IE language where the latter extension occurs, the former extension co-exists with it, or has occurred in an earlier stage of the language.

Malsch (142) lists a number of shifts involving several noun phrase categories found in languages both within and outside the IE family, including 1. plural → singular and 2. third person → second, the latter having at least the following varieties: (a) deictic → second, (b) last name → second, (c) title and last name → second, and (d) kinterm → second (where → should be interpreted as "may be used isoreferentially in place of"). Malsch argues that models accounting for such shifts in terms of independently motivated metaphoric extensions fail to explain why such shifts sometimes occur conjointly in languages (142:412). Malsch prefers to interpret these shifts in terms of face-redressive strategies of impersonalization (cf 25), which mark "the unwillingness of the speaker to bind the addressee to the behavioral obligations of the interaction" (142:417). Although this explanation is appealing because of its greater simplicity, it is too powerful in another respect. As Joseph points out in great detail, such shifts operate conjointly only in some languages, and not in others. Explanations of such changes in terms of universal speaker strategies do not explain why speakers of all languages are not free to express such unwillingness by using all of these shifts in every historical period. It appears, therefore, that a modular account such as Joseph's, which is based on several independent, interacting principles—markedness, semantic content, indexical focus, and historical drift—is necessary to account for the character of sociohistorical variability. Scherl (175) has proposed a similar account for the development of honorific pronouns in the Dravidian language, Tamil: "innovative forms initially arise as contextualizations of relatively unmarked forms in relatively marked positions, and then over time, enter into unmarked positions through processes of 'analogy'" (175:2). Finally, Bogusławski's insightful study of honorific address (22) is one of the few explicit discussions of the semantic and pragmatic criteria necessary to isolate the terms involved in such pronominal shifts.

POLITENESS

A second type of approach to honorific behavior formulates the study of politeness in language use, in terms of culturally universal models of rational speaker strategy (see 21, 98, 99, 209, 213). Most work within this paradigm has held to an individualistic, speaker-centric perspective on discursive inter-action, relative to which the existence of culturally *differing* norms—norms of behavior that are only differentially and asymmetrically locatable across socio-historical groups of speakers—is viewed either as a dependent social fact, explicable in terms of rational individual strategy, or as an independent vari-able exogenous to the model-theoretic explanation of behavioral regularities. Most theories of this type build on the Gricean notions of conversational maxims/principles (see 62, 76 for exceptions). Eschewing the phenomenal variability of actually observable cultural norms, these approaches appeal to abstract normative principles held to be universal logical preconditions on interaction as such. The rules and principles of politeness proposed in these terms are rational reconstructions of behavioral propensities that are consistent with the originally Kantian notion of "maxim" proposed by Grice himself, but differ in that they treat the Gricean maxims of conversation as a set of baseline regularities (observed by a homuncular rational agent) against which polite-ness behavior can be scaled as a kind of systematic deviation.

Lakoff (132), for example, proposed three rules of politeness of this type: (R1) "Don't impose," (R2) "Give options," and (R3) "Make addressee feel good, be friendly." Each of these rules, she argued, selects the use of distinc-tive types of politeness devices; inversely, insofar as speakers use such de-vices, they observe certain rules. Thus, in using passives and impersonal expressions, speakers observe R1 by marking a certain distance from the utterance or the addressee. Insofar as speakers use hedges and euphemisms they observe R2 (and sometimes, simultaneously, R1), giving the addressee more latitude in construal and response. And insofar as speakers give compli-ments, use T pronouns and affective particles, they are observing R3, building a greater sense of camaraderie with addressee. Gricean rules of conversation are a special sub-case of R1 in that efficient communication is viewed as involving inherent nonimposition on addressee. However, this analysis leaves unclear how R1-based politeness is differentiable from ordinary conversation in the Gricean sense, also belonging to the same R1 domain. Lakoff does propose two other overarching "rules of pragmatic competence"—"Be clear" and "Be polite"—perhaps for this purpose: the Gricean rules of conversation apply to the first meta-rule just as the rules of politeness apply to the second. Yet since "sometimes...clarity is politeness" (132:297), the argument provides no clear criteria for isolating "politeness" as an empirical phenomenon even in model-internal terms (cf 61).

A more elaborate theory involving "rule interaction" of this type is offered by Leech (135): Six interpersonal maxims for speakers to observe, at least five scales of tact (a special type of politeness, but only one such type, according to Leech), and four illocutionary functions are associated with politeness according to this account. But, as Fraser (61) notes, despite the elaborate architecture of rules, the theory remains "difficult to evaluate, since there is no way of knowing which maxims are to be applied, what scales are available, how they are formulated, what their dimensions are, when and to what degree they are relevant, and so forth" (61:227). Moreover, when the theory is applied to other languages, it appears to be inadequate unless a number of culture-specific norms are incorporated into the repertoire of maxims, as Gu demonstrates in his study of politeness in Chinese (71). For the case of Chinese, Gu adduces the self-denigration maxim (denigrate self and elevate others), the address maxim (address interlocutor with an appropriate address term), and the Balance Principle (if S is polite to H, H must be polite to S). But the necessity of these innovations suggests that "maxims" in Leech's sense merge with socio-historically distributed cultural norms, and are perhaps just as variegated and diverse.

Other work has pointed to additional problems with Lakoff's and Leech's notion of politeness. In a study of politeness in Hindi, Srivastava & Pandit (195) demonstrate the impossibility of directly identifying "politeness hierarchies" with grammatical constructional facts by appeal to conventional implicatures from grammatical categories alone, as Lakoff attempts to do. Whether or not a grammatical construction is considered "polite" by native speakers appears to depend on other factors as well, including 1. the particular social categories of the individuals recruited to the roles of speaker and addressee in the instance; 2. context- and co-text-dependent indexical entailments of particular words and expressions in situated utterances; and 3. conventional social meanings of construction, as distinct from their conventional pragmatic implicatures.

Perhaps the most influential theory in this tradition is that of Brown & Levinson (25). Although this theory is far more attentive to sociocultural differences than were those of Lakoff and Leech, it programmatically rejects explanations of behavior in terms of cultural norms and conventions, attempting instead to motivate explanations in terms of certain rational capacities attributed to an idealized "model person." All competent members of society are said to be concerned universally with "face," a notion derived from the work of Goffman, though considerably simplified in the borrowing, as Werkhofer (215:174–182) notes. The notion of face is bifurcated into negative face (the want to be unimpeded by others) and positive face (the want to have one's wants desired by others). Rather than assuming the inherent politeness/impoliteness of certain acts and stipulating a politeness principle, Brown &

Levinson assume instead that certain utterances are inherently face-threatening acts (FTAs), and they propose a taxonomy of possible strategies for performing such FTAs relative to a speaker's computation of the risk (to speaker, to hearer, or to both) of face-loss (surprisingly, they claim that *whose* face is at risk is not important). For a given FTA, x, any speaker, S, in addressing a hearer, H, can compute the weightiness, W_x, of the risk of face-loss, in terms of three variables [social distance (D) and relative power (P) of speaker/hearer (cf Brown & Gilman's solidarity and power), and the ranking of the impositions of FTA x, R_x, in the culture] as the following linear sum: $W_x = D(S, H) + P(H,S) + R_x$. Relative to such a computation, the speaker can choose one of five strategies: 1. proceed with the FTA as "bald on record" (essentially, choosing to speak in accordance with Gricean maxims); or avoid such an inherently threatening posture by giving redress to H in terms of 2. positive politeness, or 3. negative politeness, or 4. by speaking "off record," or 5. by avoiding the FTA altogether. Relative to such a calculus of rational choice and available strategy, Brown & Levinson propose an analysis of a much wider range of utterance types than is offered by any other theorist working on politeness.

Several writers have found difficulties with this theory after evaluating it on internal grounds and subjecting it to empirical tests with different types of data (19, 20, 24, 33, 34, 57, 58, 61, 67, 71, 80, 86, 97, 100, 102, 103, 113, 120, 130, 144, 145, 172, 181, 191, 211, 212, 215, 218). There appear to be three major types of purely internal difficulties with the theory. One difficulty lies with Brown & Levinson's polemical stance regarding the exclusion of cultural norms from theoretical consideration. As Hymes (97) notes, the ranking of impositions (R) in particular cultures is clearly a cultural-norm variable. Once introduced, however, the term disappears from actual explanations of politeness phenomena in Brown & Levinson's account, suggesting an awkward lack of fit between terminological apparatus, explicit polemic, and underlying explanatory power within the theory (97:76, 86; see also 19, 67). Some doubts have also been raised about the independence of R from P and D (61, 212), pointing to a deeper underlying problem.

The other two conceptual difficulties involve the term *strategy*. As Hymes points out, Brown & Levinson consider only individual utterances as data, largely ignoring the role of connected discourse structure as constitutive of interactant awareness of what is going on, and of the kinds of acts which might count as strategically relevant to the moment of action. Thus, the theory is really a theory of the politeness force of linguistic devices rather than a theory of strategies in any useful sense (97:78). The use of *strategy* is also problematic in psychological terms. To speak of strategic choice suggests a concern with real-time cognitive processes. But Brown & Levinson define the term as including both conscious and unconscious strategies (25:85) without being troubled by the fact that the psychological commitments of the latter notion have never, in fact, been clarified. In their actual usage, moreover, the term is used only to describe a rational reconstruction of overt behavior; but here it is divorced from any attempt to model real-time process, a fact that has led to some confusion in the literature.

Several objections have emerged on empirical grounds as well. Some studies suggest that the foundational notions of the theory (e.g. face, nonimposition) are implicitly culture-bound notions lacking the kind of cross-cultural validity necessary for constructing a universal theory of politeness (71, 86, 100, 113, 144, 145, 181, 211, 212, 218). Matsumoto (144) has argued forcefully that the definition of face in Brown & Levinson's account tacitly incorporates certain modern European and American cultural notions that are simply inapplicable to Japanese culture. The notion of "negative face wants," in particular, defined as the desire of the individual to be unimpeded in his/her actions, does not appear to be central to Japanese politeness behavior. More important than this individualistic concern with the self's own territorial claims is the establishment of the self's position in relation to others, and the self's desire to be accepted by others by virtue of such appropriate positioning. Thus, it is not uncommon for direct, unmitigated requests (which inherently constitute an imposition on others, according to Brown & Levinson) to be construed not as impolite (as one would expect if "face" is foundational for politeness) but as polite and deferential. In Japanese society, it is interdependence, not independence, that is socially valued. Gu (71) has raised a similar objection in his discussion of Chinese notions of politeness. Under ordinary circumstances, offering, inviting, and promising are not viewed as threatening H's negative face or impeding H's freedom in Chinese society. Rather, such acts by S are considered inherently polite. Matsumoto and Gu both argue that politeness behavior cannot be reduced to instrumental considerations issuing from individualistic face wants alone. Politeness as a behavioral regularity in these cultures appears to derive its character from cultural norms that impose constraints on individuals according to their place in society (71:242). Others have attempted to formulate the role of such norms and conventions in polite discourse in terms of the notion of discernment (86, 100).

Another type of objection has come from Blum-Kulka's work on politeness and indirectness in Hebrew (19). Many politeness theories, including Brown & Levinson's, claim a direct relationship between the indirectness and the politeness of an utterance: the more indirect an utterance, the more polite it is assumed to be (e.g. 135:108). However, Blum-Kulka finds that although both Hebrew and English speakers rank hints as more indirect than explicit performatives, only English speakers judge hints to be more polite. Hebrew speakers judge hints to be less polite than performatives, even though they are judged to be more indirect. Blum-Kulka accounts for these differences in terms of variations in cultural norms.

The relationship of variables such as power and distance to levels of politeness is not as straightforward as Brown & Levinson's theory suggests. To investigate the role of power in determining levels of politeness, Cherry (33) examines a written discourse corpus consisting of 22 letters written to the president of a university to protest the denial of tenure to a professor who is highly regarded by colleagues and students. The ranking of imposition and social distance are constant across the sample. Brown & Levinson's theory predicts higher levels of politeness with growing power differential. Cherry finds that whereas the associate professors in the sample do exhibit greater politeness than full professors do, assistant professors are actually less polite than associate professors, and graduate students even less so. Thus, increasing differences in power do not yield the monotonic increase in levels of politeness which the theory predicts.

HONORIFIC REGISTER

Several studies have explored honorific registers in different languages in considerable empirical detail. The language-specific studies may be grouped as follows: Japanese (35, 38, 39, 41, 75, 81, 86, 90, 92, 100, 104, 105, 128, 129, 139, 141, 144, 145, 150–152, 155, 156, 168, 174, 177, 201, 206, 214, 217), Korean (93, 95, 161, 192, 193, 210), Japanese and Korean (84, 85, 143), Javanese (51–55, 66, 69, 166, 189, 202, 207, 219), African languages (106–108, 110, 111, 149, 169), Nahuatl (28, 87, 88, 118, 165), Persian (10–13, 89, 91, 123), Samoan (47–49, 148), Australian languages (8, 45, 74, 77, 78, 83), Lhasa Tibetan (1:95–98, 2, 44, 73), Ladakhi (125), Sundanese (4, 216), Madurese (197), Urdu-Hindi (112), Tongan (162), Mongolian (167), Thai (40, 127), Zuñi (153), Uyghur (205), and Ponapean (65).

Early Studies

Early studies led to two kinds of simplifications. First, a number of studies attempted "syntactic" analyses of the pragmatic phenomena at issue. Some studies sought to explain co-occurrence restrictions on honorific items in terms of selectional restrictions on lexemes (141, 168). But, as Loveday (139:50, 51) has argued, this approach fails to account for the flexibility of co-occurrence phenomena in honorific usage. An abstract performative-verb hypothesis (e.g. 173:42–43; 90:103–138) is similarly inadequate in generating the range of observed utterances (75:559, 560; 139:53–56). These frameworks correctly recognize that grammatical patterning is crucial in honorific speech but prove to be inadequate in motivating purely syntactic-semantic explanations for the radically context-dependent aspects of honorific discourse. Curious inconsistencies between theory and practice occur. Although Harada (75) argues that honorific syntax is independent of politeness, his transformational analysis of honorification involves "syntactic" rules based on speech-event conditions on utterances, such as whether or not the referent of the subject noun phrase is "socially superior to speaker" (75:517, 518), thus confounding the methodological distinction between grammatical sentence and contextualized utterance in the transformational framework which he employs. Nor do such semantico-syntactic formulations of pragmatic phenomena as logical presupposition (cf 131) and conventional implicature adequately account for honorific phenomena: sentence presuppositions are defeasible in embedded clauses, but honorific presuppositions are not (139:52); the appeal to conventional implicature (25, 137) fails to account for the ubiquitous violation of conventional relationships in honorific discourse (139:59).

A second type of approach in early work described honorific registers as strictly status-based systems (66, 112, 148, 197, 216). Geertz (66), for example, attempted to link speech style narrowly to facts of social status in Javanese society. The proposal proved to be problematic in three important respects. First, Geertz incorrectly proposed that different arrays of respect forms are used exclusively by different social categories of speaker. Second, as Uhlenbeck points out, Geertz's tabular representations of speech styles inaccurately suggest that "once the social relation between the speech partners is established and the choice of one of the five styles is made, one keeps to that speech style in further speech contact" (207:448). Third, Geertz relied too exclusively on elicited forms and native speaker reports about usage, and too little on the observed data of use itself, thus narrowly mirroring aspects of native speaker ideology about usage in his model of honorific use and function (183).

Brown & Levinson's theory of honorifics (25) consists of four central claims: 1. The functional basis of honorific systems lies in the strategic use of honorifics "to soften FTAs" (p. 182), thus constituting the rational underpinnings of most, if not all, honorific systems. 2. Honorifics derive from frozen outputs of face-oriented politeness strategies (pp. 23, 179, 279). 3. These outputs are analyzable in terms of Gricean principles of conventional implicature (p. 23). 4. Interactionally, honorifics are "direct grammatical encodings of relative social status" between participants, or between participants and referents (p. 179). Note that the last claim unites the assumptions of the grammar-based and status-based theories discussed above.

Some authors have questioned the validity of the first two claims. The calculus of face does not appear to adequately explain honorific phenomena with sufficient generality, partly because the universality of Brown & Levinson's conception of face has been questioned on the basis of cross-cultural data, and partly because honorific forms also occur in linguistic acts which do not involve face threats in any obvious way (145). Moreover, many of the most interesting pragmatic effects in honorific discourse cannot be explained in terms of conventional implicatures—contra Brown & Levinson's third claim—especially the commonly observed creativity of honorific usage, both in violating conventional status differentials and in constituting new, sometimes fictive relationships (139:59–61, 145:213–215). Some studies have challenged the fourth central claim of the theory as well—the claim that honorific forms grammatically encode relative social status. These studies have uncovered a substantial amount of cross-linguistic data that suggest the absence of any direct, contextually and interactionally unmediated relationship between grammaticalized honorific form and pre-existing social status (2, 4, 11, 38, 49, 85).

Honorific usage appears to be independent of the notional rubric of politeness in a number of important respects. First, measures of politeness and measures of honorification appear to cross-cut each other. In comparing honorific phenomena in English, Japanese, and Korean, Hijirada & Sohn note that the same honorific expression may be polite in certain contexts, but impolite in others (85:367). Similarly, Hwang lists four Korean utterances that are, respectively, deferential and polite, deferential but impolite, nondeferential but polite, and nondeferential and impolite (95:48). Second, honorific forms belong to delimited repertoires in any language and are not open-ended in number and variety in the way Brown & Levinson's politeness strategies appear to be (100:227). Third, whereas politeness is understood inherently to be an aspect of speaker-addressee relationships, honorific systems mark deference to a number of role categories [e.g. addressee, referent, bystander (37)], and not always from the speaker's point of view (2, 4, 54). Finally, whereas politeness theories have attempted to conceptualize the pragmatic force of politeness in terms of the notion of degrees of deviation from a Gricean baseline of "ordinary" conversation, it seems clear that in languages which have elaborate honorific registers, there are no utterances which may be regarded as pragmatically neutral from a culture-internal perspective. Matsumoto (145) shows that even in the case of an innocuously information-bearing sentence like "Today is Saturday," all of the variant forms, when communicated, have a direct and unavoidable social consequentiality, so that none of the variants may be regarded as socially neutral. It appears that in languages containing elaborate register systems, virtually any act of speaking is evaluable for social consequentiality in a manner much more transparent to native speakers than in languages which lack such formations.

Social Indexicality

A different approach to honorific phenomena may be found in Silverstein's broadly semiotic approach to the study of language structure and function (182–187). Building on earlier work by Peirce and Jakobson, Silverstein (182) argues that an understanding of pragmatic phenomena—such as the use of honorifics—requires consideration of several interacting principles: 1. the classifiability of indexical properties of honorific devices in terms of their capacity to point to different aspects of the conditions of their production; 2. the lamination of such indexical properties with semantico-referential properties in the same stretch of utterance; 3. the degree of speaker awareness of different types of linguistic devices; and 4. the types of metapragmatic frameworks which regiment the pragmatics of speech use. I turn now to a discussion of each of these points and their implications for the study of honorifics.

First, indexical signs may be classified with respect to the relationships they contract with the very contextual variables which they index: if the sign at issue indexes some contextual variable which is independently known at the moment of semiosis, the index itself is relatively presupposing of (that aspect of) its context; on the other hand, if the indexical sign itself serves "to make explicit and overt the parameters of the structure of ongoing events" (182:34), the sign phenomenon may be said to be relatively entailing or creative or transformative of its context. The place of some honorific phenomenon on the continuum of indexical presupposition/entailment constitutes a measure of its rigidity/flexibility relative to its contextual surround.

Second, since indexical and semantico-referential properties may be laminated simultaneously in the same stretch of signal form, we would expect that certain types of differentiation along the dimension of social indexicality would be interpretable independently of any variation of semantico-referential content. This property of the total semiotic phenomenon constitutes the basis of the existence of the isoreferential speech levels—indexically differentiated ways of "saying the same thing"—that have been noted in many languages.

Third, Silverstein (185) argues that not all aspects of the semiotic phenomena at issue are equally accessible to native speakers' awareness. In thinking about the consequences of their own speech practices, native speakers tend to be most acutely aware of referentially valued, continuously segmentable, and relatively localizable items in honorific repertoires. Thus, the cross-culturally robust notion that it is words and expressions which achieve the social effects of marking deference indicates only a partial grasp of the total semiotic fact.

The fourth point concerns the way in which indexical phenomena may be regularized (rendered rule-like, imbued with an indexical force which is constant across diverse interactional events). Silverstein argues that such constant capacity for indexical semiosis in pragmatic phenomena may be created by different types of frameworks of metapragmatic regimentation—frameworks which are metapragmatic to the extent that they regiment the very pragmatics of speech use. Such frameworks may be implicit in speech practices (e.g. the grammatical code, norms of usage in interaction), or explicitly articulated as systems of conscious belief—matters of verbalizable ideology—about usage itself.

Since the same social-indexical phenomenon may be the object of more than one regimenting framework, we should expect—and do indeed find—interesting kinds of variance among these multiple modes of regimentation of interactional events within society (183, 185, 187). Such variance has critical implications for an understanding of the social character of honorific phenomena, particularly when the distribution of these metapragmatic frameworks is mapped onto characteristics of social aggregation or group formation within society. Both implicit norms of usage and explicitly articulated ideologies, for example, tend to be asymmetrically distributed across social divisions (e.g. clan, tribe, caste, class, lineage). The modes of dispersion of social ideologies, in particular, are influenced not only by the socially distributed character of loci of institutional legitimation, but also by the principles of recruitment of individuals to those social groups for which the ideologies in question have a constitutive role in defining group identity. There is, then, an agonistic character to the interplay of metapragmatic norms within society, leading sometimes to contest and sometimes to coercion (64, 87, 124, 126, 162, 163, 187).

The most detailed set of studies of honorific phenomena in a single language within this (or, indeed, any other unified) framework are Errington's studies of Javanese (51–54; see also 29 for a review of 54). Errington shows that speech-level differentiation in Javanese is organized around two different axes of honorification: a speaker-addressee axis, leading to a three-way differentiation of speech repertoires, termed *krama, madya,* and *ngoko* by natives (and listed here in descending order of deference); and a speaker-referent axis, leading to a two-way differentiation, termed *krama inggil* and *krama andhap.* Errington argues that a sign-based approach, sensitive to speaker's awareness of sign-value (in a cultural scheme of stratified value from *ngoko* to *krama andhap*), explains strategic choice as a dependent variable. Given that speakers differ with respect to their command of these repertoires, native ideology conceptualizes the speaker's ability to use higher speech levels toward a valued addressee in terms of an ethic of speaker refinement (*alus*) vs coarseness (*kasar*). Consequently, different social categories of speakers resort to different strategies: lower-class commoners attempt to speak in as high a speech-level as possible, thus attempting to "raise themselves up" by a relatively creative use of *alus* speech; however, this strategy often fails because their imperfect command of the *krama* variety yields many incorrect forms, somewhat scornfully termed *krama désa* by traditional nobles or *priyayi.* The *priyayi,* who consensually occupy the highest echelons of the Javanese social hierarchy, regard the highest level variety, *krama,* as their speech, regarding *madya* and below as out-group speech. Only for modern speakers does *madya,* though still interstitial, become part of the single continuum of *ngoko-madya-krama*.

Thus, although all speakers vary the choice of repertoires by context, different social categories of speakers are neither capable of the same strategic choices, nor regard style shifting by others in the same way. Errington argues that notions of strategy—such as Brown & Levinson's—which are insensitive to the differential distribution and provenance of metapragmatic norms in a culture, and which neglect the point of view of socially positioned individuals in favor of claims about an abstract model person, fail to account for these critical aspects of the socially meaningful character of strategic choice (54:237–246).

Beeman's work on Modern Persian (10–13) confirms the outlines of the general picture that is here emerging. First, linguistic items may be said to possess a first-order capacity to index speaker's deferential relation to other social beings (e.g. as topic or addressee of an utterance). Second, such indexical categories are assimilated into an order of cultural normativity which unites speech behaviors across social groups, applying differently by speaker type (in the Iranian case, the norm of deference for high status individuals is one of *noblesse oblige*; for low-status individuals, a norm of duty; compare the Javanese example above). Third, the strategic use of honorifics by individuals involves the manipulation of such cultural schemes of stratified value through a manipulation of associated norms in what is now perceived as a second-order system of indexical valorizations—a scheme of *speaker stereotypes.*

Particularly interesting are the avoidance registers in Australian languages (8, 45, 77, 78, 83, 182). Silverstein (182) described the Dyirbal mother-in-law register as a relatively presupposing, nonreferential indexical formation: relatively presupposing because the use of this register is a fairly rigidly automatized consequence of the presence within earshot of a classificatory mother-in-law; nonreferential because the relevant social category of affine is a bystander-to rather than a referent-of the utterance at issue. Haviland (77, 78) shows that Guugu-Yimidhirr brother-in-law register is an indexical formation of a similar semiotic type. In traditional Guugu-Yimidhirr society, a man may never address his classificatory mother-in-law. When the mother-in-law is within earshot as bystander, a man may either remain silent or use brother-in-law language, which is used to address the wife's brothers (and sometimes the wife's father, with wife as intermediary). Although social norms rigidly prescribe such usage in the presence of a criterial affine, an individual may use the brother-in-law vocabulary in a creative or performative way in the presence of noncriterial affines: for example, in constituting a distant classificatory kinsman as closer and more worthy of deference by the use of brother-in-law speech alone.

REGISTERS, SPEECH LEVELS, AND SOCIAL STEREOTYPES

Honorific devices may be classified into several distinct types which recur in a number of genetically unrelated languages. Pronouns and titles have already been discussed above. Within nominal repertoires, a number of languages also differentiate distinct honorific vs nonhonorific forms for inanimate nouns denoting parts of the human body, or objects which are possessions or appurtenances of honored persons (2, 49, 68, 148). Two types of referent-honorific verbs have been distinguished in the literature. The first type mark speaker's deference to the utterance topic—here used as a convenient label for "the referent of the verb's subject argument." The second type marks the speaker's evaluation of a relationship of deference between the actor (or referent of agent noun phrase) and receiver of the action [or referent of dative or (promoted animate) accusative noun phrase], where the direction of the evaluated deference relationship is from actor to receiver. Addressee and bystander honorifics tend to be realized across a diverse range of grammatical devices as well. Moreover, many languages which employ such devices also employ a number of paralinguistic and kinesic devices, often used conjointly with them, and which are of critical importance in understanding the interactional use and functions of these forms.

The way in which such socially meaningful varieties of "saying the same thing" are united into some type of cohesive register formation seems to involve a number of factors (but see 82 for a discussion of certain inconsistencies in traditional usages of the term *register*). In the case of honorific registers, five aspects of honorific structure and use appear to be involved: 1. the types of honorific devices available; 2. the elaborateness of honorific repertoires; 3. the existence of systems of lexical conjugates which organize utterances by words and expressions into distinct speech levels; 4. differences, by social category of speaker, in the command of such repertoires and speech levels across society; and 5. the existence of native ideologies about honorific speech and of social stereotypes about types of speakers.

The simplest kinds of speech levels are defined by patterns of pronoun-verb agreement. Thus, crossed paradigms of honorific pronouns and honorific verb endings yield four degrees of respect in Uyghur (205) and five degrees in Maithili (188).

For languages with more elaborate honorific registers, speech level stratification is based on repertoire differentiation within a much wider range of grammatical classes, including noun and verb stems, adjectives and adverbs, and in some instances, case markers and adpositions. For these languages, pure speech levels are defined by cross-repertoire consistency in the use of items both within and across sentence boundaries. Sentence-internal grammatical agreement in the simplest cases is but a pale echo of these considerably more elaborate restrictions on discourse organization through textual cohesion.

For such languages, native speakers tend to show the highest degrees of metapragmatic awareness of the linguistic structure and pragmatic function of honorific speech. In some languages—particularly where the organization of speech levels is based on extensive differentiation of lexical items—native terminologies for describing these speech levels are commonly found, and these are sometimes quite elaborate, as in the case of Javanese and Japanese (54, 105). In languages such as Korean, where relatively few noun and verb lexemes show honorific lexical alternants, and where speech level differentiation is based to a greater degree on the productive use of suffixes and adpositions, the descriptive terminology tends to be more restricted to the tradition of native grammatology, and even here there are some differences in traditional descriptions (210).

Philips (162) argues that the usual tripartite description of Tongan speech levels—commoner vs noble vs kingly speech—is a native metapragmatic construction which does not accord perfectly with native speech use, and that it tends to focus on localizable segmentable morphology in the manner predicted by Silverstein (185). The tripartite scheme is a government-sponsored idealization or simplification to which native speakers have direct access, for example, through school textbooks. But actual speech use is subject to considerable manipulation, not only in highly genred speech types (e.g. oratory, legal discourse, poetry, and prayer) but also in ordinary conversation, sometimes varying discourse internally even for the same referent. There are plenty of words (not mentioned in school textbooks) for which there are neutralizations across several levels. For some items, there are neutralizations of the commoner-noble distinction or of the noble-kingly distinction; and for others, identical words occur in commoner and kingly speech but with different referential meaning. Interesting extensions of usage also occur. Kingly speech is extended in usage to God and Jesus; noble speech is used not only for non-nobles of high social status but also for commoners, thus raising the level of formality and politeness in public discourse. Studies of changes in address forms resulting from mass ideological transformations (e.g. 60, 123) complement Philips' work by showing that government-sponsored ideologies of language use tend to focus on relatively localizable segmental morphology, such as pronouns and address forms, leaving other more pervasive structural-functional dimensions of honorific usage relatively untouched (see also 54:55 ff, 239 ff; 29:157 ff; 94).

Status, Deference, and Demeanor

Three distinct aspects of social meaning—status, deference, and demeanor—appear to be involved in honorific phenomena. Shils (178) first distinguished social status as the objective status role of an individual (defined in terms of macrosociological variables such as birth, breeding, profession, and wealth) from deference-entitlement (namely the event-specific evaluation of one individual by another with respect to worthiness of deference). Goffman (68) attempted to build on Shils' work (cf 68:note 4) by distinguishing deference (the comportment of an actor toward the recipient of an action) from demeanor (the comportment of an actor serving to express his or her own characteristics, independently of anyone else). Although Goffman's conceptions of deference and demeanor were cast in a rather individualistic framework (appealing to notions such as "a particular image of self" held by individuals, and social sanctions by society against the individual), subsequent research has shown that even individual conceptions of deference and demeanor are not *sui generis* phenomena, that they are themselves subject to the interplay of social semiotic processes that construct and valorize systems of local beliefs relative to collective ideologies (2, 124, 186, 187, 220).

The use of honorifics in all societies is constrained by the social status of individuals to whom deference is paid, but it is also sensitive to interactional variables. With regard to status, the general norm seems to be: the higher the status, the greater the degree of deference. Some studies have also shown that different macrosociological measures of social status can be ranked relative to each other in determining levels of deference. Singh (188) describes the following ranking for honorific usage in Maithili: kinship > socioeconomic status > sex > age. Nonetheless, as Singh notes, violations of these sociocultural norms also occur, based on interactional variables not interpretable in macrosociological terms (e.g. speaker's mood, social setting, a particular speaker's attitude toward a particular addressee).

Anderson (4) has offered a more detailed discussion of types of norm violation in a study of speech levels in Sundanese. Anderson concludes that speech-level differentiation has a number of interactional stance-marking functions in addition to its well-known social status sensitivity. Individuals switch to the honorific *Lemes* styles in expressing thanks and in discussing sensitive topics. When male conversants are joined by an attractive female, they switch to *Lemes* even when the woman is not of high social status. *Kesar,* or nonhonorific speech, is used to express anger, *Lemes* to deflect it (see also 38, 57, 166). Similarly, Agha (2) argues that in Lhasa Tibetan, honorific speech violations of interactionally presupposable cultural norms frequently are interpreted as various types of voicing phenomena whereby individuals take on the interested perspective of other interactants in order to achieve interaction-specific strategic goals (see also 35:443, 54:160–162).

Moreover, in all languages containing honorific registers, both social prescriptions of etiquette and the differentiation of speech levels (including impure or mixed levels) tend to be sociolinguistically distributed by social categories of speaker across several dimensions (e.g. social class, region, gender, age), yielding extremely important culture-internal measures of positional identity, interpreted as indices of demeanor. In the Korean spoken in rural Yanbian, for example, the differentiation of speech levels is higher than in the standard language. As a result, the innovative second formal grade sounds rustic to speakers of the standard language (161). Thus, in some languages, differential patterns of usage of addressee- and referent-honorifics are evaluated secondarily in terms of social stereotypes about different kinds of speakers, often asserted by natives in the form of explicit metapragmatic claims. But when such claims—for example, the claim that Japanese women are more polite than men—are studied in empirical terms, what is actually discovered about women differs, again, from what the ideology would stipulate as true of them (101, 104). Ideology provides an orientation only from the point of view of practical action, an orientation which is often "false" when articulated into claims about empirical phenomena. Yet questions of truth or falsity are not the most basic questions in matters of ideology, since, very often, such orientations may not be describable in the form of explicit claims which are falsifiable at all (e.g. beliefs about God). The more basic questions about ideologies are questions concerning their mode of emergence as social fact, their modes of dispersion through society, and their modes of institutional legitimation.

A growing body of research suggests that the relationship between lexico-grammatical honorific forms and macrosociological facts about social status is mediated by socially distributed metapragmatic norms, including beliefs about usage (24, 77, 111, 183). If such metapragmatic norms do indeed constitute an irreducible, third component of the total sociocultural phenomenon at issue, we would expect that correlations between honorific forms and status variables would tend to show up in a more robust fashion in studies which explicitly control the data of metapragmatic norms of honorification, rather than in those which do not incorporate such data into their research design. A number of such studies have been made of Japanese honorifics in particular (86, 92, 104, 155, 156, 174). These studies investigate the data of conscious beliefs about usage, not the data of usage itself.

Ogino et al (156) asked a large sample of Tokyo residents (1009 individuals, all above the junior high school age level) for their judgments about the usage of addressee honorifics for eight imagined categories of addressee. The study shows that whereas younger students admit to using few or no honorific forms, college students lay claim to a much more extensive use of honorifics, and in a wider variety of settings. This suggests the existence of social stereotypes about honorific usage which identify individuals who use more honorifics as educated and more adult and, therefore, of higher social status (see also 81, 161, 174).

In discussing the way social stereotypes about women are expressed in Javanese, Smith-Hefner (189) argues that the social domain of language use is a critical dimension of the process by which first-order facts of honorifics use may be reinterpreted in terms of second-order stereotypes of speaker refinement. In the household, women use highly deferential speech in addressing their husbands. Moreover, as caregivers who teach children the proper use of honorific forms, women frequently use their husband—the children's father—as referential target. In contrast, men in the household use honorifics to a lesser degree in addressing their wives, and tend to abstain from the role of caregiver to children. In the public realm, on the other hand, men tend to cultivate the most elaborate type of honorific speech that they can attain, whereas women, who tend to stay out of political affairs, use honorific speech to a much smaller extent. Smith-Hefner argues that social stereotypes about men and women are sensitive to the different social domains in which honorific speech is used (see also 92). The study shows that status is not simply an independent variable that drives honorific usage. To an extent, it is a dependent, ideologically informed characteristic attributed to individuals on the basis of selected aspects of their speech use. As such, it is "judged differently from different perspectives and by different individuals within the same speech community" (189:552). Citing Keenan's early study (121), Smith-Hefner suggests that politeness and status—like many macrosociological characteristics—are not fixed properties of expressions and individuals, respectively. Rather, they are attributes whose projectability to such loci involves appeals to (potentially several) independent ideological norms whose differential provenance across types of social setting is, itself, a constitutive element of the socially meaningful character of honorific speech.

Literature Cited

1. Agha A. 1993. *Structural Form and Utterance Context in Lhasa Tibetan: Grammar and Indexicality in a Non-configurational Language.* Monogr. Linguist. Philos. Lang., ed. S Belasco, Vol. 2. New York: Lang
2. Agha A. 1993. Grammatical and indexical convention in honorific discourse. *J. Linguist. Anthropol.* 3(2):131–63
3. Alrabaa S. 1985. The use of address pronouns by Egyptian adults. *J. Pragmat.* 9: 645–57
4. Anderson EA. 1993. Speech levels: the

case of Sundanese. *Pragmatics* 3(2):107–36
5. Annamalai E. 1986. Caste and variation in language form and language use. *Int. J. Dravidian Linguist.* 15(1):35–41
6. Basso KH, Selby HA, eds. 1976. *Meaning in Anthropology.* Albuquerque: Univ. N. Mex. Press
7. Bauman R, Sherzer J, eds. 1974. *Explorations in the Ethnography of Speaking.* Cambridge: Cambridge Univ. Press
8. Bavin EL. 1990. The acquisition of Walpiri kin terms. *Pragmatics* 1(3):319–44

9. Bean SS. 1978. *A Kannada System of Address*. Chicago: Univ. Chicago Press
10. Beeman WO. 1974. *The meaning of stylistic variation in Iranian variation*. PhD thesis. Univ. Chicago
11. Beeman WO. 1976. Status, style and strategy in Iranian interaction. *Anthropol. Linguist.* 18:305–22
12. Beeman WO. 1977. The hows and whys of Persian style: a pragmatic approach. In *Studies in Language Variation*, ed. RW Fasold, RW Shuy, pp. 269–82. Washington, DC: Georgetown Univ. Press
13. Beeman WO. 1986. *Language, Status and Power in Iran*. Bloomington: Ind. Univ. Press
14. Benveniste E. 1971. Relationships of person in the verb. See Ref. 16, pp. 195–204
15. Benveniste E. 1971. The nature of pronouns. See Ref. 16, pp. 217–22
16. Benveniste E. 1971. *Problems in General Linguistics*. Coral Gables, FL: Univ. Miami Press
17. Bhat DNS. 1968. The secret code of South Kanara devil dancers. *Anthropol. Linguist.* 10(4):15–18
18. Biq Y-O. 1991. The multiple uses of the second person singular pronoun *ni* in conversational Mandarin. *J. Pragmat.* 16:307–21
19. Blum-Kulka S. 1987. Indirectness and politeness in requests: same or different? *J. Pragmat.* 11(2):131–46
20. Blum-Kulka S. 1992. The metapragmatics of politeness in Israeli society. See Ref. 213, pp. 255–80
21. Blum-Kulka S, Kasper G, eds. 1990. Politeness. *J. Pragmat.* 14 (Special issue)
22. Bogusławski A. 1987. On honorific forms of address in German and Polish. In *Sprach- und Kulturkontakte im Polnischen*, ed. G Hentschel, G Ineichen, A Pohl, pp. 17–24. Munich: Sagner
23. Braun F. 1988. *Terms of Address: Problems of Patterns and Usage in Various Languages and Cultures*. Contrib. Sociol. Lang., ed. JA Fishman, Vol. 50. Berlin: Mouton de Gruyter
24. Brown P. 1990. Gender, politeness, and confrontation in Tenejapa. *Disc. Proc.* 13: 123–41
25. Brown P, Levinson SC. 1987. *Politeness: Some Universals in Language Usage*. Cambridge: Cambridge Univ. Press
26. Brown R, Ford M. 1964. Address in American English. See Ref. 96, pp. 234–44
27. Brown R, Gilman A. 1960. The pronouns of power and solidarity. In *Style in Language*, ed. TA Sebeok, pp. 253–76. Cambridge, MA: MIT Press
28. Buchler IR. 1967. The analysis of pronominal systems: Nahuatl and Spanish. *Anthropol. Linguist.* 9(5):37–43
29. Caton SC. 1990. Speech styles, status, and speaker awareness. *Semiotica* 80(1/2): 153–60
30. Chandrasekhar A. 1970. Personal pronouns and pronominal forms in Malayalam. *Anthropol. Linguist.* 12(7):246–55
31. Chandrasekhar A. 1977. Degrees of politeness in Malayalam. *Int. J. Dravidian Linguist.* 6(1):85–96
32. Chao YR. 1956. Chinese terms of address. *Language* 32(1):217–41
33. Cherry RD. 1988. Politeness in written persuasion. *J. Pragmat.* 12:63–81
34. Chilton D. 1990. Politeness, politics, and diplomacy. *Disc. Soc.* 1(2):201–24
35. Clancy P. 1985. The acquisition of Japanese. In *The Cross-linguistic Study of Language Acquisition*, ed. DI Slobin, pp. 373–524. Hillsdale, NJ: Erlbaum
36. Comrie B. 1975. Polite plurals and predicate agreement. *Language* 51(2): 406–18
37. Comrie B. 1976. *Linguistic politeness axes: speaker-addressee, speaker-referent, speaker-bystander.* Pragmat. Microfiche. 1.7:A3. Cambridge: Linguist. Dept., Cambridge Univ.
38. Cook HM. 1988. *The Japanese -masu suffix as an indexical of affective distance.* Presented at Reed/PSU Honorifics Conf., April 8–10
39. Cook HM. 1988. *Sentential particles in Japanese conversation: a study of indexicality.* PhD thesis. Univ. S. Calif.
40. Cooke JR. 1968. *Pronominal Reference in Thai, Burmese, and Vietnamese.* Berkeley: Univ. Calif. Press
41. Coulmas F. 1992. Linguistic etiquette in Japanese Society. See Ref. 213, pp. 299–323
42. Danesi M, Lettieri M. 1983. The pronouns of address in Italian: sociolinguistic and pedagogical considerations. *Stud. Italiani Linguist. Teorica Appl.* 12:323–33
43. Das SK. 1968. Forms of address and terms of reference in Bengali. *Anthropol. Linguist.* 10(4):19–31
44. DeLancey S. 1988. *Semantic categorization in Tibetan honorific nouns.* Presented at Reed/PSU Honorifics Conf., April 8–10
45. Dixon RMW. 1971. A method of semantic description. See Ref. 196, pp. 436–71
46. Drown NK. 1979. Racine's use of 'tutoiement' and 'vouvoiement.' *Mod. Lang.* 60(3):142–56
47. Duranti A. 1990. Politics and grammar: agency in Samoan political discourse. *Am. Ethnol.* 17(4):646–66
48. Duranti A. 1992. Language and bodies in social space: Samoan ceremonial greetings. *Am. Anthropol.* 94:657–91
49. Duranti A. 1992. Language in context and language as context: the Samoan respect vocabulary. See Ref. 50, pp. 77–99
50. Duranti A, Goodwin C, eds. 1992. *Rethinking Context: Language as an Interactive*

Phenomenon. Cambridge: Cambridge Univ. Press

51. Errington JJ. 1981. *Changing speech levels among a traditional Javanese elite group.* PhD thesis. Univ. Chicago

52. Errington JJ. 1985. *Language and Social Change in Java: Linguistic Reflexes of Modernization in a Traditional Royal Polity.* Monogr. Int. Stud., SE Asia Ser., No. 65. Athens, OH: Ohio Univ. Cent. Int. Stud.

53. Errington JJ. 1985. On the nature of the sociolinguistic sign: describing the Javanese speech levels. See Ref. 147, pp. 287–310

54. Errington JJ. 1988. *Structure and Style in Javanese: A Semiotic View of Linguistic Etiquette.* Philadelphia: Univ. Penn. Press

55. Errington JJ. 1992. On the ideology of Indonesian language development: the state of a language of state. *Pragmatics* 2(3): 417–26

56. Ervin-Tripp SM. 1986. On sociolinguistic rules: alternation and co-occurrence. See Ref. 72, pp. 213–50

57. Ervin-Tripp SM. 1988. *The learning of social style marking and of honorifics.* Presented at Reed/PSU Honorifics Conf., April 8–10

58. Ervin-Tripp SM, Guo J, Lampert M. 1990. Politeness and persuasion in children's control acts. *J. Pragmat.* 14:307–31

59. Evans-Pritchard EE. 1964. Nuer modes of address. See Ref. 96, pp. 221–27

60. Fang H, Heng JH. 1983. Social changes and changing address norms in China. *Lang. Soc.* 12:495–507

61. Fraser B. 1990. Perspectives on politeness. *J. Pragmat.* 14:219–36

62. Fraser B, Nolen W. 1981. The association of deference with linguistic form. *Int. J. Soc. Lang.* 27:93–109

63. Friedrich P. 1986. Social context and semantic feature: the Russian pronominal usage. See Ref. 72, pp. 270–300

64. Gal S. 1992. Multiplicity and contention among ideologies: a commentary. *Pragmatics* 2(3):445–49

65. Garvin PL, Riesenberg SH. 1952. Respect behavior on Ponape: an ethnolinguistic study. *Am. Anthropol.* 54(1):201–20

66. Geertz CH. 1960. *The Religion of Java.* New York: Free Press

67. Glick DJ. 1994. A reappraisal of Brown and Levinson's 'Politeness: Some Universals of Language Use.' *Semiotica* In press

68. Goffman E. 1956. The nature of deference and demeanor. *Am. Anthropol.* 58:473–502

69. Gonda J. 1948. The Javanese vocabulary of courtesy. *Lingua* 1(3):333–76

70. Goody EN, ed. 1978. *Questions and Politeness: Strategies in Social Interaction.* Cambridge: Cambridge Univ. Press

71. Gu Y. 1990. Politeness phenomena in Modern Chinese. *J. Pragmat.* 14:237–57

72. Gumperz JJ, Hymes DH, eds. 1986. *Directions in Sociolinguistics: The Ethnography of Communication.* New York: Blackwell

73. Hajime K. 1975. The honorifics in Tibetan. *Acta Asiatica* 29:56–74

74. Hale K. 1971. A note on a Walbiri tradition of antonymy. See Ref. 196, pp. 472–82

75. Harada SI. 1976. Honorifics. In *Syntax and Semantics.* Vol. 5: *Japanese Generative Grammar,* ed. M Shibatani, pp. 499–561. New York: Academic

76. Haverkate H. 1988. Toward a typology of politeness strategies in communicative interaction. See Ref. 98, pp. 385–409

77. Haviland JB. 1979. Guugu-Yimidhirr brother-in-law language. *Lang. Soc.* 8: 365–93

78. Haviland JB. 1979. How to talk to your brother-in-law in Guugu Yimidhirr. See Ref. 180, pp. 161–239

79. Head B. 1978. Respect degrees in pronominal reference. In *Universals of Human Language.* Vol. 3: *Word Structure,* ed. JH Greenberg, pp. 151–212. Stanford, CA: Stanford Univ. Press

80. Held G. 1992. Politeness in linguistic research. See Ref. 213, pp. 131–54

81. Hendry J. 1992. Honorifics as dialect: the expression and manipulation of boundaries in Japanese. *Multilingua* 11(4):341–54

82. Hervey S. 1992. Registering registers. *Lingua* 86:189–206

83. Hiatt LR. 1984. Your mother-in-law is poison. *Man* (NS) 19(2):183–98

84. Hijirada K, Sohn H. 1983. Communality and relativity in address-reference term usages. *Lang. Res.* 19(2):139–68

85. Hijirada K, Sohn H-M. 1986. Cross-cultural patterns of honorifics and sociolinguistic sensitivity to honorific variables: evidence from English, Japanese, and Korean. *Pap. Linguist.* 19(3):365–401

86. Hill B, Ide S, Ikuta S, Kawasaki A, Ogino T. 1986. Universals of linguistic politeness: quantitative evidence from Japanese and American English. *J. Pragmat.* 10:347–71

87. Hill JH. 1992. 'Today there is no respect': nostalgia, 'respect' and oppositional discourse in Mexicano (Nahuatl) language ideology. *Pragmatics* 2(3):263–80

88. Hill JH, Hill KC. 1978. Honorific usage in Modern Nahuatl. *Language* 54(1):123–55

89. Hillmann MC. 1981. Language and social distinctions in Iran. In *Modern Iran: The Dialectics of Continuity and Change,* ed. ME Bonine, NR Keddie, pp. 327–40. Albany: State Univ. NY Press

90. Hinds J. 1976. *Aspects of Japanese Discourse Structure.* Tokyo: Kaitakusha

91. Hodge CT. 1957. Some aspects of Persian style. *Language* 33(3):355–69

92. Hori M. 1986. A sociolinguistic analysis of the Japanese honorifics. *J. Pragmat.* 10: 373–86

93. Howell RW. 1965. Linguistic status markers in Korean. *Kroeber Anthropol. Soc. Pap.* 33:91–97
94. Hucker CO. 1985. *A Dictionary of Official Titles in Imperial China.* Stanford, CA: Stanford Univ. Press
95. Hwang J-R. 1990. 'Deference' versus 'politeness' in Korean speech. *Int. J. Soc. Lang.* 82:41–55
96. Hymes DH, ed. 1964. *Language in Culture and Society: A Reader in Linguistics and Anthropology.* New York: Harper & Row
97. Hymes DH. 1986. Discourse: scope without depth. *Int. J. Soc. Lang.* 57:49–89
98. Ide S, ed. 1988. Linguistic Politeness I *Multilingua* 7(4) (Special issue)
99. Ide S, ed. 1989. Linguistic Politeness II *Multilingua* 8(2/3) (Special issue)
100. Ide S. 1989. Formal forms and discernment: neglected aspects of universals of linguistic politeness. See Ref. 99, pp. 223–48
101. Ide S. 1990. How and why do women speak more politely in Japanese? In *Aspects of Women's Language,* ed. S Ide, N McGloin, pp. 63–79. Tokyo: Kurosio
102. Ide S. 1993. Preface: The search for integrated universals of linguistic politeness. *Multilingua* 12(1):7–11
103. Ide S, Hill B, Carnes YM, Ogino T, Kawasaki A. 1992. The concept of politeness: an empirical study of American English and Japanese. See Ref. 213, pp. 281–97
104. Ide S, Hori M, Kawasaki A, Ikuta S, Haga H. 1986. Sex difference and politeness in Japanese. *Int. J. Soc. Lang.* 58:25–36
105. Inoue K. 1979. Japanese: a story of language and people. See Ref. 180, pp. 241–300
106. Irvine JT. 1974. Strategies of status manipulation in the Wolof greeting. See Ref. 7, pp. 167–91
107. Irvine JT. 1978. Wolof noun classification: the social setting of divergent change. *Lang. Soc.* 7:37–64
108. Irvine JT. 1983. Wolof speech styles and social status. In *Case Studies in the Ethnography of Speaking,* ed. J Sherzer, R Bauman, pp. 1–12. Austin, TX: SW Educ. Dev. Lab.
109. Irvine JT. 1985. Status and style in language. *Annu. Rev. Anthropol.* 14:557–81
110. Irvine JT. 1988. *Honorific devices in Africa.* Presented at Reed/PSU Honorifics Conf., April 8–10
111. Irvine JT. 1992. Ideologies of honorific language. *Pragmatics* 2(3):251–62
112. Jain DK. 1969. Verbalization of respect in Hindi. *Anthropol. Linguist.* 11(3):79–97
113. Janney RW, Arndt H. 1993. Universality and relativity in cross-cultural politeness research: a historical perspective. *Multilingua* 12(1):13–50
114. Jayapal S. 1986/1987. Address terms in Tamil. *Indian Linguist.* 47(1–4):7–15
115. Jensen JB. 1981. Forms of address in Brazilian Portuguese: standard European or Oriental honorifics? In *From Linguistics to Literature: Romance Studies Offered to Francis M. Rogers,* ed. BH Bichakjian, pp. 45–66. Amsterdam: Benjamins
116. Jenson KM. 1988. Forms of address in Indonesian. *I.T.L.* 81–82:113–38
117. Joseph JE. 1987. Subject relevance and deferential address in the Indo-European languages. *Lingua* 73:259–77
118. Karttunen F. 1988. *Conventions of polite speech in Nahuatl.* Presented at Reed/PSU Honorifics Conf., April 8–10
119. Karunatillake WS, Suseendirarajah S. 1975. Pronouns of address in Tamil and Sinhalese: a sociolinguistic study. *Int. J. Dravidian Linguist.* 4(1):83–96
120. Kasper G. 1990. Linguistic politeness: current research issues. *J. Pragmat.* 14:193–218
121. Keenan EO. 1974. Norm-makers, norm-breakers: uses of speech by men and women in a Malagasy community. See Ref. 7, pp. 125–43
122. Kempf R. 1985. Pronouns and terms of address in Neues Deutschland. *Lang. Soc.* 14:359–86
123. Keshavarz MH. 1988. Forms of address in post-revolutionary Iranian Persian: a sociolinguistic analysis. *Lang. Soc.* 17:565–75
124. Kochman T. 1984. The politics of politeness. In *Meaning, Form and Use in Context: Linguistic Applications,* ed. D Schiffrin, pp. 200–9. Washington, DC: Georgetown Univ. Press
125. Koshal S. 1987. Honorific systems of the Ladakh language. *Multilingua* 6(2):149–68
126. Kroch A, Small C. 1978. Grammatical ideology and its effect on speech. In *Linguistic Variation: Models and Methods,* ed. D Sankoff, pp. 45–55. New York: Academic
127. Kummer M. 1992. Politeness in Thai. See Ref. 213, pp. 325–36
128. Kuno S. 1973. *The Structure of the Japanese Language. Current Studies in Linguistics,* Ser. 3. Cambridge, MA: MIT Press
129. Kuno S. 1987. *Functional Syntax: Anaphora, Discourse and Empathy.* Chicago: Univ. Chicago Press
130. Kwarciak BJ. 1993. The acquisition of linguistic politeness and Brown and Levinson's theory. *Multilingua* 12(1):51–68
131. Lakoff G. 1971. Presupposition and relative well-formedness. See Ref. 196, pp. 329–40
132. Lakoff R. 1973. The logic of politeness, or minding your P's and Q's. In *Pap. Ninth Regional Meet., Chicago Linguist. Soc.,* ed.

C Corum, TC Smith-Stark, A Weiser, pp. 292–305. Chicago: Chicago Linguist. Soc.

133. Lambert WE. 1967. The use of *tu* and *vous* as forms of address in French Canada: a pilot study. *J. Verbal Learn. Verbal Behav.* 6:614–17

134. Larsen TW. 1988. *The morphosyntax of polite pronouns in Aguacatec and Quiché.* Presented at Reed/PSU Honorifics Conf., April 8–10

135. Leech G. 1983. *Principles of Pragmatics.* London: Longman

136. Leith D. 1982. *Tudor London: sociolinguistic stratification and linguistic change.* Presented at Sociolinguist. Symp., Univ. Sheffield

137. Levinson SC. 1977. *Social deixis in a Tamil village.* PhD thesis. Univ. Calif., Berkeley

138. Levinson SC. 1982. Caste rank and verbal interaction in western Tamilnadu. In *Caste Ideology and Interaction,* ed. DB McGilvray, pp. 98–203. Cambridge: Cambridge Univ. Press

139. Loveday L. 1982. Japanese donatory forms: their implications for linguistic theory. *Stud. Linguist.* 36(1):39–63

140. Loveday L. 1986. *Japanese Sociolinguistics.* Amsterdam: Benjamins

141. Makino S. 1970. Two proposals about Japanese polite expressions. In *Studies Presented to Robert B. Lees by His Students,* ed. JM Sadock, AL Vanck, pp. 163–87. Edmonton, Canada: Linguist. Res.

142. Malsch DL. 1987. The grammaticalization of social relationship: the origin of number to encode deference. In *Pap. Seventh Int. Conf. Hist. Linguist.,* ed. AG Ramat, O Carruba, G Bernini, pp. 407–18. Amsterdam: Benjamins

143. Martin SE. 1964. Speech levels in Japan and Korea. See Ref. 96, pp. 407–15

144. Matsumoto Y. 1988. Reexamination of the universality of face: politeness phenomena in Japanese. *J. Pragmat.* 12:403–26

145. Matsumoto Y. 1989. Politeness and conversational universals—observations from Japanese. See Ref. 99, pp. 207–21

146. Mehrotra RR. 1981. Non-kin forms of address in Hindi. *Int. J. Soc. Lang.* 32:121–37

147. Mertz E, Parmentier R, eds. 1985. *Semiotic Mediation.* New York: Academic

148. Milner GB. 1961. The Samoan vocabulary of respect. *J. R. Anthropol. Inst.* 91(2):296–317

149. Mufwene SS. 1986. Kinship terms (and related honorifics): an issue in bilingual lexicography. *Pap. Linguist. (Edmonton, Alb.)* 19(1):19–35

150. Neustupny JV. 1968. Politeness patterns in the system of communication. In *Proc. 8th Int. Congr. Anthropol. Ethnol. Sci.,* pp. 412–18. Tokyo: Sci. Counc. Jpn.

151. Neustupny JV. 1978. *Post-Structural Approaches to Language: Language Theory in a Japanese Context.* Tokyo: Univ. Tokyo Press

152. Neustupny JV. 1986. Language and society: the case of Japanese politeness. In *The Fergusonian Impact: In Honor of Charles A. Ferguson on the Occasion of his 65th Birthday,* ed. JA Fishman, A Tabouret-Keller, M Clyne, et al, pp. 59–71. Berlin: Mouton de Gruyter

153. Newman S. 1964. Vocabulary levels: Zuñi sacred and slang usage. See Ref. 96, pp. 397–406

154. Nichols J. 1984. Functional theories of grammar. *Annu. Rev. Anthropol.* 13:97–117

155. Ogino T. 1986. Quantification of politeness based on the usage patterns of honorific expressions. *Int. J. Soc. Lang.* 58:37–58

156. Ogino T, Misono Y, Fukushima C. 1985. Diversity of honorific usage in Tokyo: a sociolinguistic approach based on a field survey. *Int. J. Soc. Lang.* 55:23–39

157. Partridge AC. 1969. *Tudor to Augustan English.* London: Deutsch

158. Pattanayak DP. 1975. Caste and language. *Int. J. Dravidian Linguist.* 4(1):97–104

159. Pattanayak DP. 1976. Reply to comments on 'Caste and language.' *Int. J. Dravidian Linguist.* 5(1):82–85

160. Paulston CB. 1976. Pronouns of address in Swedish: social class semantics and a changing system. *Lang. Soc.* 5:359–86

161. Pei JC. 1992. Honorific usage in spoken Korean in Yanbian. *Int. J. Soc. Lang.* 97: 87–95

162. Philips SU. 1991. Tongan speech levels: practice and talk about practice in the cultural construction of social hierarchy. In *Currents in Pacific Linguistics: Papers on Austronesian Languages and Ethnolinguistics in Honor of George Grace,* ed. R Blust, pp. 369–82. Pacific Linguist., Ser. C-117. Canberra: Res. Sch. Pacific Stud., Aust. Natl. Univ.

163. Philips SU. 1992. A Marx-influenced approach to ideology and language: comments. *Pragmatics* 2(3):377–85

164. Philipsen G, Huspek M. 1985. A bibiliography of sociolinguistic studies of personal address. *Anthropol. Linguist.* 27(1):94–101

165. Pittman RS. 1948. Nahuatl honorifics. *Int. J. Am. Linguist.* 14(3):236–39

166. Poedjosoedarmo S. 1968. Javanese speech levels. *Indonesia* 6:54–81

167. Poppe N. 1970. On some honorific expressions in Mongolian. In *Studies in General and Oriental Linguistics,* ed. R Jakobson, S Kawamoto, pp. 484–99. Tokyo: T.E.C

168. Prideaux GD. 1970. *The Syntax of Japanese Honorifics.* The Hague: Mouton

169. Pumphrey M. 1937. Shilluk 'royal' language conventions. *Sudan Notes Rec.* 20(2):319–21

170. Qinsheng Z. 1992. Aspects of Chinese eth-

nosociolinguistic studies: a report on the literature. *Int. J. Soc. Lang.* 97:59–73

171. Qinsheng Z. 1992. A selected bibliography of Chinese ethnosociolinguistics, 1890–1990. *Int. J. Soc. Lang.* 97:97–118

172. Rhodes R. 1989. We are going to go there: positive politeness in Ojibwa. See Ref. 99, pp. 249–58

173. Sadock JM. 1974. *Towards a Linguistic Theory of Speech Acts.* New York: Academic

174. Sanada S. 1993. The dynamics of honorific behavior in a rural community in Japan. *Multilingua* 12(1):81–94

175. Scherl R. 1988. *Mariyaatai and language: a look at honorification and markers of plurality in Tamil.* Presented at Reed/PSU Honorifics Conf., April 8–10

176. Shanmugan Pillai M. 1965. Caste Isoglosses in kinship terms. *Anthropol. Linguist.* 7(3):59–66

177. Shibamoto JS. 1987. The womanly woman: manipulation of stereotypical and non-stereotypical features of Japanese female speech. In *Language, Gender and Sex in a Comparative Perspective,* ed. SU Phillips, S Steele, C Tanz, pp. 26–49. Cambridge: Cambridge Univ. Press

178. Shils E. 1982. Deference. In *The Constitution of Society,* pp. 143–75. Chicago: Univ. Chicago Press

179. Shinn HK. 1990. A survey of sociolinguistic studies in Korea. *Int. J. Soc. Lang.* 82:7–23

180. Shopen T, ed. 1979. *Languages and Their Speakers.* Cambridge, MA: Winthrop

181. Sifianou M. 1992. The use of diminutives in expressing politeness: Modern Greek versus English. *J. Pragmat.* 17:155–73

182. Silverstein M. 1976. Shifters, linguistic categories, and cultural description. See Ref. 6, pp. 11–56

183. Silverstein M. 1979. Language structure and linguistic ideology. In *The Elements: A Parasession on Linguistic Units and Levels,* ed. PR Clyne, WF Hanks, CL Hofbauer, pp. 193–247. Chicago: Chicago Linguist. Soc.

184. Silverstein M. 1981. *The limits of awareness.* Sociolinguist. Work. Pap., No. 84. Austin, TX: SW Educ. Dev. Lab.

185. Silverstein M. 1985. Language and the culture of gender: at the intersection of structure, usage, and ideology. See Ref. 147, pp. 219–59

186. Silverstein M. 1988. *Demeanor indexicals and honorific registers.* Presented at Reed/PSU Honorifics Conf., April 8–10

187. Silverstein M. 1992. The uses and utility of ideology: some reflections. *Pragmatics* 2(3):311–23

188. Singh UN. 1989. How to honor someone in Maithili. *Int. J. Soc. Lang.* 75:87–107

189. Smith-Hefner NJ. 1988. Women and politeness: the Javanese example. *Lang. Soc.* 17:535–54

190. Snell-Hornby M. 1984. The linguistic structure of public directives in German and English. *Multilingua* 3(4):203–11

191. Snow CE, Perlmann RY, Gleason JB, Hooshyar N. 1990. Developmental perspectives on politeness: sources of children's knowledge. *J. Pragmat.* 14:289–305

192. Sohn H-M. 1983. Power and solidarity in the Korean language. *Korean Linguist.* 3:97–122

193. Sohn H-M. 1988. *Typological characteristics of Korean honorifics.* Presented at Reed/PSU Honorifics Conf., April 8–10

194. Southerland RH. 1988. *Third person in direct and indirect address: honorific or dishonorific?* Presented at Reed/PSU Honorifics Conf., April 8–10

195. Srivastava RN, Pandit I. 1988. The pragmatic basis of syntactic structures and the politeness hierarchy in Hindi. *J. Pragmat.* 12:185–205

196. Steinberg DD, Jakobovits LA, eds. 1971. *Semantics: An Interdisciplinary Reader in Philosophy, Linguistics and Psychology.* Cambridge: Cambridge Univ. Press

197. Stevens A. 1965. Language levels in Madurese. *Language* 41(2):294–302

198. Sullivan WJ. 1987. Sociolinguistic rules and dynamiticity: insights from Polish modes of address. *LACUS Forum* 14:446–51

199. Suryakumari S. 1986. A sociolinguistic study of names and address system in Telugu. *Int. J. Dravidian Linguist.* 15(2):311–24

200. Suseendirarajah S. 1970. Reflections of certain social differences in Jaffna Tamil. *Anthropol. Linguist.* 12(2):239–45

201. Tagashira Y. 1973. Polite forms in Japanese. In *You Take the High Node and I'll Take the Low Node,* ed. C Corum, TC Smith-Stark, A Weiser, pp. 121–34. Chicago: Chicago Linguist. Soc.

202. Tanner N. 1967. Speech and society among the Indonesian elite: a case study of a multilingual community. *Anthropol. Linguist.* 9(3):15–40

203. The Second Foundation. 1980. Frogs into princes: conflict between organizational structures as revealed by forms of address. *LACUS Forum* 7:573–80

204. Tiugan M. 1984. Aspects of the verbal behavior in an urban community: the usage of the personal pronouns of direct address. *Rev. Roumaine Linguist.* 24(3):203–19

205. Tohti L, Lindblad VM. 1988. *Honorifics in Uyghur.* Presented at Reed/PSU Honorifics Conf., April 8–10

206. Tokunaga M. 1992. Dichotomy in the struc-

tures of honorifics of Japanese. *Pragmatics* 2(2):127–40
207. Uhlenbeck EM. 1970. The use of respect forms in Javanese. In *Pacific Linguistic Studies in Honour of Arthur Capell*, ed. SA Wurm, DC Laycock, pp. 441–66. Pacific Linguist., Ser. C-13. Canberra: Aust. Natl. Univ.
208. Wales KM. 1983. *Thou* and *You* in early Modern English: Brown and Gilman re-appraised. *Stud. Linguist.* 37(2):107–25
209. Walters J, ed. 1981. The sociolinguistics of deference and politeness. *Int. J. Soc. Lang.* 27 (Special issue)
210. Wang H-S. 1990. Toward a description of the organization of Korean speech levels. *Int. J. Soc. Lang.* 82:25–39
211. Watts RJ. 1989. Relevance and relational work: linguistic politeness as politic behavior. See Ref. 99, pp. 131–66
212. Watts RJ, Ide S, Ehlich K. 1992. Introduction. See Ref. 213, pp. 1–17
213. Watts RJ, Ide S, Ehlich K, eds. 1992. *Politeness in Language: Studies in its History, Theory and Practice*. Trends Linguist.

Stud. Monogr., Vol. 59. Berlin: Mouton de Gruyter
214. Wenger JR. 1982. *Some universals of honorific language with special reference to Japanese*. PhD thesis. Univ. Ariz., Tucson
215. Werkhofer KT. 1992. Traditional and modern views: the social constitution and the powers of politeness. See Ref. 213, pp. 155–99
216. Wessing R. 1974. Language levels in Sundanese. *Man* (NS) 9(1):5–22
217. Wetzel PJ. 1988. Are 'powerless' communication strategies the Japanese norm. *Lang. Soc.* 17:555–64
218. Wierzbicka A. 1985. Different cultures, different languages, different speech acts. *J. Pragmat.* 9:145–61
219. Wolff JU, Poedjosoedarmo S. 1982. *Communicative codes in Central Java*. SE Asia Progr., Data Pap. 116. Ithaca, NY: Dept. Asian Stud., Cornell Univ.
220. Woolard KA, Schieffelin BB. 1994. Language ideology. *Annu. Rev. Anthropol.* 23: 55–82

Annu. Rev. Anthropol. 1994. 23:303–23

HUNTERS AND FARMERS: Then and Now

Katherine A. Spielmann and James F. Eder

Department of Anthropology, Arizona State University, Tempe, Arizona 85287-2402

KEY WORDS: hunter-gatherers, farmers, exchange, Africa, Southeast Asia

INTRODUCTION

This review provides a critical examination of the voluminous literature on present and past relations between hunter-gatherers and farming peoples. Pastoralist populations also have been included, given that many issues pertain to hunter-gatherer relations with food-producing populations in general. We first consider relations in the twentieth century, particularly those documented for sub-Saharan Africa, South Asia, and Southeast Asia, and focus on the kinds of materials that are exchanged, the social relations of exchange, and issues of class and power. We then address the historic and prehistoric antecedents of interaction as well as prehistoric hunter-farmer relations in Europe and North America. Finally, we consider how a focus on hunter-farmer interaction has led to new perspectives on the ethnic identity of hunters themselves.

The sources of data on hunter-farmer relations include ethnographic, archaeological, linguistic, genetic, oral history, and historic documents. Not surprisingly, there are diverse and often contradictory interpretations of these data (e.g. 17 vs 21), best epitomized by the current revisionist debate in the San literature (e.g. 91, 106, 107). These debates are also addressed.

HUNTERS AND FARMERS IN THE TWENTIETH CENTURY

Our discussion below reflects the nature of recent ethnographic research on relations between hunter-gatherers and food-producing peoples. This research has focused in particular on populations in Africa (e.g. the San of the Kalahari Desert, the Efe of northeastern Zaire, the Okiek of Kenya), Southeast Asia (e.g. the Agta of the Philippines), and South Asia (e.g. the Hill Pandaram).

Materials Exchanged

Reflecting the ecological orientation of much of the earlier research on foraging peoples, and a continuing preoccupation with how such peoples earn their living, much of the literature on foragers emphasizes the quantitative or qualitative importance of material exchange with surrounding food-producing peoples. The particular goods and services that foragers supply to their farming neighbors vary widely, but the need or desire of foragers to obtain, in exchange, grain or other domestic carbohydrates is commonly emphasized. For convenience we distinguish between exchanges of food, products, and labor, recognizing that any particular case may include exchanges of several sorts.

Understanding the implications of these exchanges hinges upon adequate study of a variety of ancillary issues including the proportional volume of exchanges between foragers and farmers, the degree to which the goods or services exchanged are indispensable to one or both sides, and whether or not the exchanges are balanced (110). These issues are examined below.

FOOD   One commonly reported transaction involves the exchange of forager-obtained wild protein foods for farmer-produced carbohydrate foods (3, 6, 7, 63, 68, 78, 79, 86, 93, 94, 110), although the degree to which farmers depend on meat supplied by hunter-gatherers varies considerably. Traded meat helps alleviate shortfalls of locally procured protein in some cases (e.g. 68), while in others, close to half the meat eaten by villagers may be obtained through trade (e.g. 7). Because pastoralists may consider the consumption of wild game repugnant, they generally do not exchange for meat (40, 63).

In contrast, current hunter-gatherer dependency on domestic carbohydrates is consistently high, with the Efe of Zaire and Okiek of Kenya consuming over half their calories in garden produce (6, 17). Among the Maku of Bolivia (68) and the Batua of Zaire (86), who cultivate small gardens of their own, manioc (cassava) is part of every meal.

In tropical forest settings, the frequency and apparent importance of such food exchanges to foraging peoples has prompted some scholars to propose that the functional interdependence or apparent symbiosis of tropical forest foragers and their agricultural neighbors is mutually beneficial (34, 79), or even represents a longstanding adaptive strategy for the exploitation of such forests (52, 54). A more extreme form of this functional interdependence view suggests that, from the standpoint of potential human habitation, tropical forests are such food-poor environments that pure foraging is not possible there. Any full-time forest dwellers would have required access to neighboring peoples from whom they could obtain carbohydrate foods (8, 53). The response to this hypothesis has been mostly skeptical (20, 35; see also 22), and the issue remains unresolved.

COMMODITIES   In South and Southeast Asia, exchanges involving forager-obtained forest products (e.g. honey, beeswax, resins, rattan, ivory, medicinal herbs) go back hundreds and perhaps thousands of years (13, 27, 39, 41, 57, 59, 71, 87, 90, 103). In fact, forest products rather than food appear to be the primary commodities provided to farmers by Asian hunter-gatherers. Demand for forest products appears to be the result of long-term participation in regional and overseas trading networks into which these products move, rather than being the result of local farming population needs.

African foragers also trade gathered products, especially honey (7, 63, 78, 86, 110). The Okiek, in particular, trade large quantities of honey to Maasai pastoralists who use it in ritual activities (63, 110), and they appear to be unique in their construction of beehives to increase honey production for exchange.

In Africa, products of the hunt, especially hides, are sought by both farmers and pastoralists (63, 89, 91, 94, 110). Additional byproducts of the hunt that are exchanged to farmers include ornaments made of zebra, giraffe, and wildebeest tails, buffalo hide shields, and buffalo horn (110). Hunting technology, however, appears rarely as an exchange item in the ethnographic literature. This contrasts with prehistoric situations in the Kalahari and Neolithic Europe, in which indigenous hunting technology is found on the sites of in-migrating pastoralists and farmers.

After carbohydrates, technological items constitute the second most prevalent type of exchanged good that hunter-gatherers receive from farmers. Metal or items made from metal such as arrowheads, axes, knives, and machetes (3, 7, 68, 110) are the most eagerly sought.

Tobacco (7, 68, 91, 110) and commodities that facilitate hunting are often obtained in exchange [e.g. dogs (17, 63, 104) and traps (89, 104)]. Cloth, clothing, and cooking pots are also obtained from farmers through exchange (7, 110), although pottery may move in the other direction as well (e.g. 63).

LABOR   Although products of the hunt and of the forest have been the traditional focus of hunter-farmer exchange discussions (e.g. 79, 93, 94), many foraging peoples also appear to have long histories of labor relationships with surrounding farming peoples. Hunter-gatherers may act as guides for hunting expeditions or other excursions into the forest (42, 56, 71, 90:388, 110), they may serve as porters for neighboring traders (80), or today, they may even seek wage employment (15). On occasion hunter-gatherers may provide ritual services to food-producing populations (e.g. 101). More often, however, they labor in agricultural fields and herd domestic stock, to the point that they become incorporated into the economic structure of the food-producing economies, thereby obscuring the economic complementarity entailed in the exchange of commodities.

Where labor is exchanged, some authors simply report that hunter-gatherer groups or families provide labor to their farming neighbors, without discussing gender (34, 80). Others report that women tend to work in farmers' gardens or in the household (e.g. 7, 78, 89) while men may help clear vegetation prior to planting gardens, work in the household, or herd animals (e.g. 5). An emphasis on hunter-gatherer labor rather than products has been linked to the labor demands of certain types of crops (104), to the expansion of agricultural (3) and pastoral (e.g. 56) populations into hunter-gatherer lands, as well as to a decline in the availability of forest products for exchange (86). Waehle (104) has proposed that the success of swidden farming in the Ituri Forest of Zaire is predicated upon the availability of hunter-gatherer labor.

Social Relations

Reflecting wider paradigmatic shifts in anthropology, there has been increased emphasis on the historical trajectories, rather than the evolutionary status, of foraging peoples, and on internal dynamics rather than external conditions as the cause of change (12). These changes in emphasis have in turn been reflected in greater concern with the broadly social dimensions of forager-farmer interaction. This concern is often accompanied by a rejection of simple materialist explanations for such interaction. For example, Bird-David contends that although much of the contact between Naiken and non-Naiken involves economic transactions, "this is not to the exclusion of social contact; indeed, in some cases economic interactions take place because of pre-existing social ties" (16:23).

The study of South Asian foraging peoples, with their long histories of embeddedness in wider and extraordinarily complex social systems, has been particularly fertile ground for developing these new emphases. Morris's work (71, 72) among the Hill Pandaram is illustrative. Morris distinguishes several levels of forager social organization and argues that the fragmentary nature of the Hill Pandaram's own social forms is not explained satisfactorily either by their status as foragers or as a response to cultural encapsulation by oppressive neighbors. Rather, such group structuring reflects the dual nature of an economy long geared both to subsistence production and to external trade (72).

Such insights helped open the door to much productive inquiry. Taking this general line of reasoning further, Bird-David (16) examines the degree to which the social organization of foraging groups may not merely be affected by contact with neighboring peoples, but may somehow integrate or include these peoples (see also 10, 60). She proposes that foraging peoples, such as the Naiken, who interact frequently with nonforaging neighbors consider their neighbors to stand within their own social structure, albeit while remaining culturally distinct. Non-Naiken are included in the Naiken world as occupants of roles that materialize in interactional settings and hence articulate with Naiken social structure (16).

Finally, Gardner (43), drawing on observations of Paliyan-Tamil interactions, takes this approach even further and asks, in effect, if Paliyan social structure does somehow include or take heed of Tamil individuals or Tamil social structure, in what specific ways is this manifest? He finds that it is in kinship and marriage, "the heart of the elegant Tamil social system," that organizational changes in Paliyan social life are most visible.

The African cases we examined provided valuable insights into how, precisely, these sorts of organizational and behavioral convergences between interacting groups of hunters and farmers are associated with exchanges of commodities and labor. A key aspect of such convergence, noted by Kratz (63) among the Okiek and widely reported elsewhere, is that the hunter-gatherers conform to the organizational and behavioral expectations of villagers, rather than the reverse (see also 16) and, further, hunter-gatherer cultures appear to have changed in the direction of conformity to facilitate interaction.

In hunter-farmer interactions, the hunter-gatherers often speak the same language or a language related to that of the food producers, suggesting a long period of extensive interaction between the two populations (3, 4, 17, 75, 78, 104). When they do not speak the same language as their agricultural or pastoral neighbors, hunter-gatherers typically acquire that language (4, 17, 63, 89, 102, 110), a circumstance also common among Southeast Asian hunter-gatherers (e.g. 29). The reverse, however, is not the case; agriculturalists rarely learn a hunter-gatherer language (e.g. 63).

Although language acquisition facilitates communication in general, hunter-gatherer conformity to the social structure of neighboring agriculturalists and pastoralists enhances the development of individual trade partnerships through which much exchange takes place. Pederson & Waehle (78) argue that organization of pygmy local groups depends on their relationships with farmers, which influence their resource base, opportunities, and constraints. Winter (108) notes that data from sub-Saharan Africa show that hunter-gatherer kinship systems are often structurally similar to those of their food-producing neighbors. These parallel systems define fictive kinship ties that are important in inter-ethnic exchange. For example, the Okiek share the age set and clan system of the Maasai, and most Okiek males have at least one trade partner-ship with a Maasai male of their same age set and clan (17). Among the Baka (78), a hunter-gatherer patriline is linked with a clan or with an entire agricul-tural village. Ritual activities establish fictive kinship ties between the two groups.

Hereditary trade partnerships maintain predictable economic ties (38) and characterize relations between many hunter-gatherer and food-producing peo-ples (e.g. 38, 78, 99). Participation in ritual events (63, 78, 101; see also 18), or at least attendance at ritual activities, probably also enhances inter-ethnic relations (38, 63). Because hunter-gatherers may share aspects of culture as diverse as language and ritual with their farming neighbors, Bird-David's (16) proposition that hunters may integrate their neighbors into a single social order while remaining culturally distinct may be over-simplified. Gardner's (43) analysis of Tamil-induced change among the Paliyan illustrates this point. His explicit focus is on change in Paliyan social organizational principles, but there is also cultural convergence in the realm of gender and in notions of propriety.

Affinal kinship ties, established by intermarriage, may provide yet another dimension to hunter-farmer social interaction. In some areas such intermar-riage is proscribed (68, 97), in other areas hypergyny is common (5, 92), and men from farming villages marry hunter-gatherer women. This pattern has been noted among the Hadza (110), the Efe (6), and the Okiek (17, 63). In contrast, it is rare for farming women to marry hunter-gatherer men.

Hunter-gatherer settlement patterns often reflect interactions with neighbor-ing food-producing populations. In one common pattern, groups of hunter-gatherers occupy fairly permanent camps near farming villages or pastoral camps for much of the year, typically coinciding with periods when villagers or pastoralists need hunter-gatherer labor. During the remainder of the year, most or all such hunter-gatherers disperse to hunt and collect in the forest (7, 11, 17, 68, 78, 89). In some cases, this dispersal also reflects seasonalities in forest resource availability (e.g. honey, 17). At times, hunter-gatherer camps are close enough to the villages to allow women to continue working in the fields while men hunt in the forest (7, 9).

Systematic attention to the social dimensions of hunter-gatherer/farmer interaction has helped anthropologists move beyond the simple equation of foraging as a lifeway with an alleged forager form of social organization. Ironically, eschewal of a narrow focus on environmental and technological factors, in favor of greater attention to the historical and cultural circumstances attending hunter-gatherer interactions with others, has helped render hunter-gatherers' own social lives more understandable (72, 110).

Class Relations

Hunter-gatherer populations appear to have transformed linguistically, socially, and economically to facilitate interaction with food-producing populations, but there is a concomitant lack of similar efforts on the part of the food producers. This suggests that hunter-gatherers are far more dependent on food producers than food producers are on hunter-gatherers. Although in the past, hunter-farmer relations have been characterized as mutualistic (93) or symbiotic (4, 62, 68, 91), some current hunter-gatherer/food producer systems belie this view. Differing degrees of economic dependency suggest that food producers may exercise enough power over hunter-gatherer populations that foraging peoples have been shaped for the worse by interaction with neighboring farming peoples (29, 106). In this perspective, most contemporary foragers are not merely embedded in some wider social system. They are embedded in a wider class system, typically on marginal terms, and as a result, they suffer the political subordination and economic exploitation that such systems characteristically engender.

It is not a novel observation that foragers have suffered at the hands of outsiders. As Woodburn (110) says, it seems that most of the world's foragers are a stigmatized minority, insecure in their landholdings and vulnerable to ridicule, persecution, and encroachment (see also 3, 68, 89). Fear of physical abuse by their pastoral patrons, for example, compels some San to remain with them rather than seasonally hunting and gathering (56), and the Okiek prefer to camp well-hidden in the forest (17). Several ethnographers have noted the difficulty of finding appropriate terminology to adequately describe hunter-farmer relations (91). Others have observed that hunters and farmers may express the same relationship differently (60), but the persistent use of such terms of control as slavery, serfdom, and clientage to characterize hunter-gatherer/food producer relations suggests that hunter-gatherers may not control their own labor (and the rest of their lives) as freely as some have assumed.

Pederson & Waehle (78) have noted that Lese farmers may consider neighboring Efe hunters to be their property, but it may be difficult to control them, and the farmers cannot always rely on hunter-gatherer labor when it is needed. But how do you theorize such circumstances of apparent domination/subordination and how much explanatory import should be ascribed to them? Ironically, Woodburn (110) continues to maintain that the Hazda are not significantly dominated by their neighbors, echoing similar claims in the past about the Mbuti (101). For students of contemporary foraging peoples, however, these are emotional issues, and the possibility of exploitation by outsiders is not dismissed readily. The personal involvement of many anthropologists who work with foragers in advocating native rights also imparts a political stridency or moral indignation to analyses of the class circumstances of foragers that is generally absent from the research considered above. In these circumstances, it is not surprising that the issues are not readily decided by the data.

An instructive example is Peterson's (79) earlier-mentioned analysis of Agta-Palanan food exchange. Although Peterson acknowledges the existence of conflict between Agta and Palanan over land, usually to the disadvantage of the Agta, her overwhelming emphasis is on the mutually beneficial nature of the exchange relationships in question. Thus, Palanan-Agta exchange "represents a labor specialization that coordinates the two populations in a higher order economic system" (p. 343) and allows "particularly effective utilization of land and labor resources" (p. 344). Peterson's ahistorical analysis, by reifying cultural boundaries and subsistence economic types, and by emphasizing complementarity and voluntarism, obscures a vital, broader historical process of political and economic changes involving Agta and Palanan—and tribal Filipinos and lowland Filipinos generally. Trade between these two groups has not merely served each group's respective economic interests. It has helped to make tribal Filipino resources available to outside peoples and has brought tribal Filipinos—particularly Negritos, such as the Agta—under wider orbits of political control. Further, population growth in the lowland Philippines and the continuing expansion of lowland peoples into the uplands, with attendant encroachment on tribal domains, has ensured that exchange is eventually accompanied everywhere by less complementary relations such as exploitative labor relations and land appropriation.

Consideration of these broader processes suggests that what appear, in Peterson's analysis, to be symmetrical, complementary exchange relationships between two otherwise independent populations have at least the potential to become class-like relations of exploitation and attendant marginalization within a single wider social system (30). Such is the emphasis in Wilmsen's (106) revisionist study of the San, which locates them together with other tribal peoples at the margins of the Capitalist World System.

Wilmsen argues that the San form part of a dispossessed underclass in southern Africa, best understood as a degraded cultural residual created by marginality to a wider African social formation. Central to Wilmsen's argument, and to the resulting debate surrounding his work (e.g. 91), is his contention that the San's current (twentieth century) status as subsistence foragers is a recent historical development and not some sort of survival from an isolated past. Indeed, with respect to alleged San isolation, Wilmsen claims that there is in fact considerable congruence between San and Bantu institutional forms, reflecting a long period of economic and social interaction—albeit, again, on ultimately disadvantageous terms.

Attention to the manner in which many hunter-gatherers historically have been subordinated to or exploited by more powerful neighbors is a critical tool for the analysis of their present-day economic and social attributes. Considerations of power may even help account for some of the more narrowly cultural attributes of contemporary hunter-gatherers, such as their often-noted peacefulness and emphasis on nonaggression (26, 33).

HUNTERS AND FARMERS: PRESENT TO PAST

Given the long-standing incorporation of hunter-gatherers into larger agricultural and pastoral societies, it is reasonable to question how hunter-gatherers persisted for so long in a world dominated by food producers (102, 106). The key to their persistence appears to be the availability of land that was both adequate to sustain a hunter-gatherer lifeway and unattractive to pastoralists and farmers (2, 17, 64, 74, 91). Some hunter-gatherers may have cultivated a fear of their sorcery to enhance their hold over their territory (3, 64). Military prowess capable of keeping food producers at bay may also have been significant (e.g. 106). Interestingly, none of the authors noting the importance of various hunted and gathered resources to food-producing economies have suggested a need for these products as a reason for the persistence of hunting and gathering populations.

Since the nineteenth century, technological developments have increased the settlement of many hunter-gatherer–occupied territories by pastoralists and farmers, thereby bringing hunters and food producers into more intensive interaction. In some regions, the appropriation of land for stock-raising has resulted in overgrazing and a loss of adequate wild food supplies to sustain a hunter-gatherer lifeway (23, 55, 91, 102, 110). In other regions, deforestation attending land clearance by advancing agriculturalists has had comparable effects. Everywhere, however, the outcome has been the increasing dependence of hunter-gatherers on pastoralists and farmers for a secure food supply.

But hunter-farmer relations did not spring to life, full-blown, in the nineteenth and twentieth centuries. There is considerable time depth to hunter-gatherer/food producer relations, and considerable variability over time and space in the nature of those relations.

Prehistoric Origins of Hunter-Farmer Interaction

Archaeological research in those areas of Africa where hunter-gatherers persisted into the twentieth century has demonstrated that contact between hunters and food producers occurred from several hundred to two thousand years ago, with the expansion of pastoral populations into areas occupied by hunter-gatherers. Comparable time depths are today attributed to the participation of Southeast Asian hunter-gatherers in regional and international trading networks (49, 59). Unfortunately, the archaeological record from the tropical forests of Africa and insular Southeast Asia is poorly known, so much of the following discussion focuses on the more arid parts of eastern and southern Africa.

Among the most clearly documented cases of hunter-gatherer/pastoral contact is that for the southwestern Cape (76, 77). Pastoral populations appear to have moved into the area 1800 to 2000 years ago and to have displaced indigenous hunter-gatherer populations, leading to marked changes in hunter-gatherer subsistence, settlement, and ritual behaviors. Following the immigration of pastoral populations, hunter-gatherer camps shifted from riverine locations on the sandveld to the uplands, where they were often located in rock-shelters and caves. These upland sites are smaller than those on the sandveld, and the upland lithic assemblage contains more wood-working tools, which suggests greater production of plant-extracting technology like digging sticks. Remains of a few domestic animals on these sites indicate some contact with the pastoral groups. Focusing on the stress that a pastoral intrusion would have produced for indigenous hunter-gatherers, Parkington et al (77) argue that the increase in rock art, and association of rock art with upland domestic sites, reflect an increase in the use of ritual, specifically trance dances, to deal with their dislocation.

The model that Parkington provides for this initial encounter between hunter-gatherers and pastoralists is one of competitive exclusion, with pastoralists out-competing hunter-gatherers for the better watered sandveld area. Avoidance rather than interaction appears to characterize inter-ethnic relations, although ceramics and sheep remains have been found in many of the hunter-gatherer sites. Similarly, Ambrose (2) has proposed that advancing pastoralists on the savannas of East Africa caused hunter-gatherers to restrict their hunting to the forest.

A different scenario has been presented for interaction between Early Iron Age pastoralists and Late Stone Age hunter-gatherers in the Kalahari. Archaeological data document sparse, pre–Iron Age evidence of ceramic-making sheep herders on the fringes of the Kalahari between around 200 B.C. and A.D. 200 (25). Pastoralist presence increased between around A.D. 700 and A.D. 1000 in both the western and eastern Kalahari. Several pastoral sites have been found, ranging in type from those dominated by large animal enclosures (kraals), with over 80% of the fauna from domestic animals, and by sorghum, millet, and cow peas, large quantities of metal, some Late Stone Age lithics, and trade goods, to sites dominated by Late Stone Age lithic assemblages with less metal, few trade goods, and very few domestic animals (23, 106, 107). Denbow (23, 24) interprets these sites as pastoralist and hunter-gatherer, respectively, suggesting that the two groups had entered into an exchange relationship. Wilmsen (105) suggests that Bantu herders were involved in some hunting and gathering, while San hunter-gatherers had taken up pastoralism, at least to some degree. This kind of mixed economy is also envisioned for East

Africa following the initial expansion of pastoralism in the Turkana basin (64, 75). In keeping with his more political approach to San ethnography, Wilmsen (106, 107) has suggested that the smaller sites document the pattern of San subordination that he argues exists in the twentieth century. Yellen notes, however, the lack of published archaeological data with which to evaluate Wilmsen's and Denbow's interpretations (112).

European Contact and the Historic Period

A wealth of data from historic documents has been used to study changes in hunter-gatherer societies that resulted from contact with European populations. South and Southeast Asian hunter-gatherer groups, with their long histories of involvement in external trading systems, had evolved in the context of a relatively persistent and long-term external demand for forest products. These hunter-gatherers were, however, relatively isolated geographically from the activities and interests of outsiders and moved only gradually into the orbits of European colonial powers. In contrast, dramatic and sweeping changes appear to have occurred in Africa during the nineteenth century, when a constellation of factors combined to change radically and permanently the conditions under which hunter-gatherers lived. These factors include technological changes that allowed the expansion of agropastoralists into the remaining hunter-gatherer territories, participation in merchant capitalism, and inter-tribal warfare. Marked changes, finally, in the demand for products supplied by African hunter-gatherers may have led to a boom-bust cycle in late nineteenth century hunter-gatherer economies (56).

The plethora of historic factors influencing African hunter-gatherer populations has been most thoroughly discussed for the San, as part of the revisionist debate that has dominated San literature in the past decade. Although the historic documents are fairly mute on actual hunter-gatherer activities (106), there are enough data about European and agropastoral activities in the Kalahari to identify various agents of change. Primary among these is the fact that the Kalahari supplied large quantities of trade items, particularly ivory, ostrich feathers, and hides, to meet the demands of a European market. It is inferred that San populations were responsible for providing the bulk of these goods (56, 91, 106). Both Wilmsen (106) and Solway & Lee (91) note that this time period was one of economic prosperity for the San. Wilmsen uses historical documents to establish that at least some San owned relatively large herds of domestic animals. Through oral history, Solway & Lee note that the nineteenth century was viewed by the San as a time of plenty. Other sources of disruption in the nineteenth century include the digging of wells and expansion of permanent pastoralist settlements (55), and the introduction of firearms, which changed the military balance of power between hunter-gatherer and agropastoralist populations (44). The increasing power of incipient Bantu states on the fringes of the Kalahari, and their demands for trade goods and tribute, also affected hunter-gatherer populations of the Kalahari (23, 56, 91, 106).

Researchers with long ties to the Kalahari have begun to marshall a wealth of historic data concerning non–hunter-gatherer activities in the Kalahari. But there has yet to be an in-depth evaluation of the long-term impact of these various factors, or of the degree of variability in hunter-gatherer experience during the nineteenth century. Solway & Lee (91) view the period as a mere perturbation in San history. They argue that production for the hide trade changed neither the internal organization of the San nor their economic production. But San hunters were taking elephant, a species not generally hunted, to the point that elephant-hunting specialists developed (56). San were also apparently accumulating stock or other trappings of prosperity that certainly would have affected internal relations. Moreover, Solway & Lee do not consider the long-term effects of over-hunting large game for hides.

Wilmsen, on the other hand, paints the Kalahari situation with too broad a brush. Although he acknowledges that the documents contain little specific data on the San, he assumes that all San across the Kalahari experienced and were affected by the events of the nineteenth century in the same way, becoming subservient to more powerful societies. The situation probably was much more variable, as Solway & Lee (91, see also 47) attempt to demonstrate with their two case studies. More careful consideration of variation in the degree of economic penetration of the Kalahari and some solid archaeological data would help provide a more accurate picture of this critical period.

The experience of other African hunter-gatherer societies was similar to that of the Kalahari San. All appear, to one degree or another, to have been drawn into the ivory, feather, and hide trade (3, 21, 67, 104), as well as the slave trade (104). Inter-tribal warfare is also cited as having a marked effect on hunter-gatherer activities and their relationships with agriculturalists (104).

By the early twentieth century those hunter-gatherers who remained had become increasingly dominated by their agropastoral neighbors. Like that of the nineteenth century, however, the literature on the twentieth century tends to be descriptive rather than analytical. Pastoralist demands for San labor are said to have increased (e.g. 23, 91, 106,), yet only the revisionists provide an explanation for this trend: the San had become the underclass in expanding Bantu states and had no choice in the matter. One is left to conclude that the combined factors of over-hunting in the nineteenth century and continued agropastoralist expansion simply made hunting and gathering too risky an occupation in much of the Kalahari (56). Patron-client relationships (23, 91, 106) appear to have increased in intensity in the early twentieth century.

Thus far no one seems to have taken into account the impact of the relatively prosperous hunting existence supported by the ivory and hide trade of the nineteenth century. Such prosperity must have profoundly affected hunter-gatherer societies in Africa. This boom period collapsed in the 1890s, and was followed by drought, disease, and the increasing encroachment of farming and pastoral populations (56). Close study of how African hunter-gatherers dealt with the transition from hunting for a world market to farming and herding for local food producers would be extremely useful in evaluating the ethnographic record of twentieth-century hunter-gatherer populations.

Elsewhere in Africa, twentieth-century forced relocations of agricultural populations and their hunter-gatherer partners (e.g. the Efe, 104), and expansion of agricultural populations into hunter-gatherer areas (e.g. the Aka, 3; the Okiek, 63) have equally affected the remaining African hunter-gatherers. That most of these people have not become full members of the dominant societies is usually attributed to their inability to obtain the necessary capital (e.g. land, flocks) to become herders or farmers, and to the lack of time to engage in economic activities that would otherwise enhance their position (3, 21, 73, 77, 102).

Implications for the Past

In hindsight, it was rather naive to believe that studies of extant hunter-gatherer groups in the 1960s and 1970s would readily provide us with a very clear picture of what hunting and gathering had been like in prehistory (see critiques in 12, 16, 49, 85, 105, 106). Even if they did not all become the abject serfs of Wilmsen's view, their ability, and perhaps their desire to maintain a hunting and gathering lifeway were greatly undermined. It is noteworthy that even for those hunter-gatherers that some consider the least dependent on external trade, the Okiek (17, 110), the fact that women today do not participate in forest-related subsistence activities (17) suggests that profound changes have nevertheless occurred in the Okiek economy in response to interaction with pastoralists.

Questioning whether twentieth-century hunter-gatherers are appropriate analogs for the past should be remarkably liberating to archaeologists. Over a decade ago Wobst (109) argued that archaeologists *should not* rely on ethnographic data as the primary source of their interpretations of past behavior, but the current literature suggests that they *cannot* do so; the ethnographic record is not simply incomplete, it may be largely unrelated to the experiences of many prehistoric hunter-gatherers. Thus, the forager way of life defined in *Man the Hunter* (e.g. 66), and extended to archaeological analyses, in many cases may be a function of interaction with food-producing populations in prehistory (76) and historically. Prior to the decimation of large game for the nineteenth century hide trade and the dispossession of hunter-gatherer populations of prime hunting land (e.g. 2, 76), large mammal hunting may have been far more important to hunter-gatherer subsistence than is usually inferred for populations in this latitude (37, 50). Although patterns of sharing, exchange, camp organization, and group membership have been shown to be adaptive for twentieth-century hunter-gatherers (66, 71, 72, 104a), it must be demonstrated, rather than assumed, that these patterns have any great time depth. Moreover, we should not assume that the co-occurrence of a series of behaviors observed among modern hunter-gatherers also existed in the past. Parkington (76), for example, has argued that hunter-gatherer economies became more forager-like with the advent of pastoralism in the Cape area prehistorically. He notes, however, the marked differences in forager camp (and presumably social) arrangements between his prehistoric forager sites and those of the San camps mapped by Yellen (111) in the 1960s.

The intense historic period of hunter-gatherer/food producer interaction was preceded by a long period of prehistoric contact between hunter-gatherers and agropastoralists. The nature and impact of this interaction are only beginning to be understood. Conflicting models and broad generalizations have been offered for prehistoric interaction. In particular, opinions differ as to the ability of hunter-gatherers to cycle between hunting and gathering and pastoral economies. On one side are researchers such as Parkington (77, see also 102) who argue that the reciprocal sharing ethic of hunter-gatherers makes it difficult to accumulate enough stock for a viable herd. They also contrast the hierarchical nature of pastoralist societies with the relative egalitarianism of modern-day hunter-gatherers. The vulnerability of small herds to raiding is cited as another source of difficulty (76, 98). On the other side are those such as Schrire (83) and Elphick (32) who use historic data to document that at European contact in the seventeenth century some San populations were noted to have cattle on one encounter, but to have lost them by another. Guenther (47) has made the argument that a flexible, persistent band mode of social organization facilitated transitions between hunting and food production for San populations.

In contrast to pastoralism, gardening of variable intensity by otherwise mobile hunter-gatherers has been noted in a number of ethnographic cases (2, 51, 63, 68, 78, 86, 89). Part-time agriculture appears particularly common among Southeast Asian hunter-gatherers (29, 46, 80). In some cases, farming provides a significant component of the diet (68, 86), while in others the casual nature and limited production of gardens are emphasized. Although successful pastoralism requires a fairly sizeable investment to create a sustainable herd, one may reap useful returns from fairly small-scale farming. Thus, casual gardening on the part of hunter-gatherers who trade with farmers is likely to be a stable strategy with some time depth, as in Southeast Asia where many hunter-gatherers have histories of gardening that go back hundreds of years. The strategy probably has more to do with ensuring that hunter-gatherers can fall back on cultivation, should their source of traded carbohydrates become unreliable, than with supplementing the hunter-gatherer diet (94). Thus, the degree of cultivation practiced by hunter-gatherers is expected to relate directly to the stability and productivity of the trading system in which they are engaged. This may be particularly true when domestic carbohydrate consumption by hunter-gatherers takes on cultural as well as economic significance, as where the eating of rice or corn instead of wild yams, for example, symbolically represents hegemonic notions of so-called civilized behavior.

Observations from the archaeological record of extant hunter-gatherers provide insights into prehistoric hunter-farmer relations elsewhere in the world. For example, prehistoric patterns of interaction were probably structured by the degree to which food-producing and hunter-gatherer populations were in competition for land. To illustrate this point we briefly contrast prehistoric North American Plains-Pueblo and European Mesolithic-Neolithic relations. In the Plains-Pueblo case, the land base that sustained the hunter-gatherers, the southern High Plains, was not amenable to agriculture with prehistoric technologies. Only the historic introduction of the plow allowed the Plains sod to be cut. Thus, there was little competition for access to hunter-gatherer land, and long-term, interdependent relations developed between Pueblo farmers and Plains hunter-gatherers (94, 95). In contrast, in-migrating Neolithic populations probably required a great deal of the European Mesolithic land base not only for their fields, but also for grazing their stock. Livestock grazing could have put farmer and hunter in competition for land, and also depleted resources for local game animals, thereby threatening the Mesolithic subsistence base. Moreover, simulation of the Neolithic economy (45) suggests that trade with Mesolithic hunter-gatherers did not provide more efficient access to subsistence resources, and thus was probably not sought after by Neolithic farmers (96).

There are several approaches to documenting and assessing prehistoric hunter-gatherer responses to the arrival of food producers and to interaction with them. First, settlement pattern studies (e.g. 28, 76) are useful for assessing the degree to which hunter-gatherer systems were altered. This presupposes an ability to distinguish hunter-gatherer from food producer signatures on the landscape, which may be difficult.

Second, patterns of technological transfer may assist in evaluating the importance of exchanged foods. For example, although pottery has been noted on hunter-gatherer sites, particularly after contact with Early Iron Age pastoralists, the significance of the use of this pottery is rarely addressed. Nor is the source of it always clear. Habicht Mauche's (48) approach to southern Plains hunter-gatherer production of pottery could be enlightening in this case. Through petrographic analysis she documented a shift from trade for pottery to production of pottery by southern Plains hunters, and she argues that this shift reflects the increasing importance of corn, and thus the importance of corn processing technology, to the adaptation of these hunter-gatherers.

Third, if hunter-gatherers are intensifying hunting to participate in an exchange system, the organization of the hunt and/or species targeted for the hunt will probably change from the pre-trade situation. The ethnographic record contains numerous references to differences in hunter-gatherer hunting techniques and technology that are attributed to demands of exchange (1, 3, 6, 31, 51, 56, 69, 107, but see 81). Following this line of reasoning, for example, the increasing emphasis on large-scale bison kills on the Plains in the late prehistoric period, and the butchering of these animals for transport of the meat (100), may be the result of the appearance of aggregated farming populations on the eastern and western edges of the Plains, as well as along major Plains river valleys during this period. Such populations would have been reliable sources of carbohydrates for Plains hunters (94).

Relations of dominance and subordination are difficult to infer from the prehistoric record. However, one indicator may be the degree to which hunters and farmers intermarried. An interesting case study from South Africa has documented a pattern that conforms with the expectations of hypergyny. Based on an analysis of a series of prehistoric burials from the Reit River valley and published data on contemporaneous Bantu populations, Morris (70) argues that there is a unidirectional gene flow from the San populations to the Bantu in this area.

DISCUSSION

Several debates fundamental to anthropology as a whole emerge from the literature on hunter-gatherer/food producer interactions. The most important is the debate over the concept of ethnicity. In the African literature, for example, contrasting points of view abound. One anthropologist claims that the Okiek maintain a distinctive series of noneconomic, cultural characteristics (17). Another quotes an Okiek as saying that once they cease being hunter-gatherers, they cease being Okiek (63, see also the discussion in 40). Likewise, while Wilmsen (106:250) denies that the San have any ethnic distinctiveness, Barnard (11) argues strongly for the existence of multiple levels of ethnic identity, from a pan-Khoisan constellation of economic, social, and religious institutions that cross-cuts the hunter/herder dichotomy (see 36 for genetic data that parallel this argument) to self-identified (usually linguistically) subgroups of San within the Kalahari. Barnard denies the importance of economic activities as the structuring elements in ethnic identity, while others (4, 40, 63, 75) suggest that it is the economic complementarity that maintains ethnic differentiation.

Such differences of interpretation remind us that culture remains a central problem in anthropology, visible in the case at hand in differing perspectives on how the construction and maintenance of cultural identities is best conceptualized. Although a focus on forager-farmer interaction is a powerful analytical tool for increasing our understanding of both foraging and farming societies, it can also mislead. Interaction is easy to assert, and evidence is frequently available, but the significant issue is what explanatory import to ascribe to it. To merely assume, for example, that this or that cultural attribute of a particular foraging group is the consequence of a long history of interaction with outside peoples is no more legitimate than assuming that such attributes are the product of evolutionary stages preserved in isolation. Such consequences need to be demonstrated, not just assumed or asserted (see 110), and such demonstrations will still require good data as well as appeals to currently popular theoretical or methodological perspectives.

An instructive case-in-point concerns Hoffman's (57, 58) work on the Punan of Borneo. Hoffman argues that the various peoples known collectively as Punan are not autochthonous foraging groups. Rather, they derive from sedentary agricultural peoples, principally the Kayan. Punan foraging, in Hoffman's view, is essentially a trade-based adaptation to the presence of the Kayan, the Kenyah, and other Dayak groups—i.e. Dayak demand for various jungle products essentially called the Punan into being. In making such a claim Hoffman was in good company at the time; in general form his argument resembled numerous others offered during the 1980s to better locate foragers vis a vis their neighbors, and his own version of the argument is quite compelling.

Most other experienced observers of the Punan (19, 82, 88), however, reject Hoffman's interpretation. Their challenge is largely on empirical grounds: the available data (much of which Hoffman is said to misrepresent or ignore) simply do not support his argument, and the historical evidence suggests a long history of once-isolated hunter-gatherers gradually settling down to become agriculturalists. No one is denying the importance of trade in forest products to some or most Punan groups; the issue is that the fact of trade does not itself justify using a vogue functional interdependence model of forager-farmer interaction to imply that Punan are mere "Kayan on the hoof," when Punan are in fact authentic, culturally distinctive foraging folk, quite capable of independent living (19).

The critical reaction to Wilmsen's (106) formulation of San identity similarly focuses in part on the apparent denigration of that identity. As Solway & Lee (91) ask, is it really the most insightful conclusion we can draw about the San, that they are the product of a history of oppression by outside peoples? We risk trivializing the San (or the Punan, or any hunter-gatherer people) if we ignore their internal social dynamics and portray their cultural identity only in reactive terms, thereby failing to represent those aspects of identity that matter most to the people, as well as their own historical agency in maintaining or changing these aspects (11). Hunter-gatherer/farmer interaction, after all, may have been around a long time, but hunter-gatherers, it seems, are still with us—in all their cultural diversity. How such diversity is best understood continues to merit the attention of all anthropologists.

Any *Annual Review* chapter, as well as any article cited in an *Annual Review* chapter, may be purchased from the Annual Reviews Preprints and Reprints service. 1-800-347-8007; 415-259-5017; email: arpr@class.org

Literature Cited

1. Abruzzi WS. 1979. Population pressure and subsistence strategies among the Mbuti Pygmies. *Hum. Ecol.* 7:183–89
2. Ambrose SH. 1986. Hunter-gatherer adaptations to non-marginal environments: an ecological and archaeological assessment of the Dorobo model. *Sprache Gesch. Afr.* 7(2):11–42
3. Bahuchet S, Guillaume H. 1982. Aka-farmer relations in the northwest Congo Basin. See Ref. 65, pp. 189–211
4. Bahuchet S, Thomas JMC. 1986. Linquistique et histoire des Pygmees de l'Ouest du Bassin Congolais. *Sprache Gesch. Afr.* 7(2):73–103
5. Bailey RC. 1991. *The Behavioral Ecology of Efe Pygmy Men in the Ituri Forest, Zaire.* Anthropol. Pap. No. 86. Ann Arbor: Univ. Mich., Mus. Anthropol.
6. Bailey RC, Aunger R. 1989. Net hunters vs. archers: variation in women's subsistence strategies in the Ituri forest. *Hum. Ecol.* 17:273–97
7. Bailey RC, DeVore I. 1989. Research on the Efe and Lese populations of the Ituri forest, Zaire. *Am. J. Phys. Anthropol.* 78: 459–71
8. Bailey RC, Head G, Jenike M, Owen B, Rechtman R, Zechenter E. 1989. Hunting and gathering in a tropical rain forest: Is it possible? *Am. Anthropol.* 91:59–82
9. Bailey RC, Peacock N. 1988. Efe Pygmies of northeast Zaire: subsistence strategies in the Ituri forest. In *Coping with Uncertainty in Food Supply,* ed. I de Garine, GA Harrison, pp. 88–117. Oxford: Clarendon
10. Barnard A. 1988. Kinship, language, and production: a conjectural history of Khoisan social structure. *Africa* 58:29–50
11. Barnard A. 1992. *Hunters and Herders of Southern Africa: A Comparative Ethnography of the Khoisan Peoples.* Cambridge: Cambridge Univ. Press
12. Bender B, Morris B. 1988. Twenty years of history, evolution, and social change in gatherer-hunter studies. See Ref. 61, pp. 4–14
13. Benjamin G. 1973. Introduction. In *Among the Forest Dwarfs of Malaya,* ed. P Schebesta, pp. v-xii. Kuala Lumpur: Oxford Univ. Press
14. Bicchieri MG, ed. 1972. *Hunters and Gatherers Today.* New York: Holt, Rinehart & Winston
15. Bird-David NH. 1983. Wage-gathering: socio-economic change and the case of the Naiken of south India. In *Rural South Asia: Linkages, Changes, and Development,* ed. P Robb, pp. 57–88. London: Curzon
16. Bird-David NH. 1988. Hunters and gatherers and other people—a re-examination. See Ref. 61, pp. 17–30
17. Blackburn RH. 1982. In the land of milk and honey: Okiek adaptations to their forests and neighbors. See Ref. 65, pp. 283–305
18. Blakeslee DJ. 1976. *The Plains interband trade system: an ethnohistoric and archaeological investigation.* PhD thesis. Univ. Wisc., Milwaukee. 358 pp.
19. Brosius JP. 1988. A separate reality: comments on Hoffman's *The Punan: Hunters and Gatherers of Borneo. Borneo Res. Bull.* 20:81–106
20. Brosius JP. 1991. Foraging in tropical rain forests: the case of the Penan of Sarawak, East Malaysia (Borneo). *Hum. Ecol.* 19: 123–50
21. Chang C. 1982. Nomads without cattle: East African foragers in historical perspective. See Ref. 65, pp. 269–82
22. Colinvaux PA, Bush MB. 1991. The rain forest ecosystem as a resource for hunting and gathering. *Am. Anthropol.* 93:153–60
23. Denbow JR. 1984. Prehistoric herders and foragers of the Kalahari: the evidence of 1500 years of interaction. See Ref. 84, pp. 175–93
24. Denbow JR. 1990. Comment on Solway and Lee. *Curr. Anthropol.* 31:124–26
25. Denbow JR, Campbell A. 1986. The early stages of food production in southern Africa and some potential linguistic correlations. *Sprache Gesch. Afr.* 7(1):83–103

26. Dentan RK. 1992. The rise, maintenance, and destruction of peaceable polity: a preliminary essay on political ecology. In *Aggression and Peacefulness in Humans and other Primates*, ed. J Silverberg, JP Gray, pp. 214–70. New York: Oxford
27. Dunn FL. 1975. *Rain-forest Collectors and Traders: A Study of Resource Utilization in Modern and Ancient Malaya.* Kuala Lumpur: Malaysian Branch R. Asiatic Soc.
28. Eder JF. 1984. The impact of subsistence change on mobility and settlement patterns in a tropical forest foraging economy: some implications for archaeology. *Am. Anthropol.* 86:837–53
29. Eder JF. 1987. *On the Road to Tribal Extinction: Depopulation, Deculturation, and Adaptive Well-being among the Batak of the Philippines.* Berkeley: Univ. Calif. Press
30. Eder JF. 1988. Hunter-gatherer/farmer exchange in the Philippines: some implications for ethnic identity and adaptive well-being. In *Ethnic Diversity and the Control of Natural Resources in Southeast Asia*, ed. AT Rambo, K Gillogly, KL Hutterer, pp. 37–57. Mich. Pap. South and Southeast Asia. Ann Arbor: Univ. Mich.
31. Eder JF. 1988. Batak foraging camps today: a window to the history of a hunting-gathering economy. *Hum. Ecol.* 16:35–55
32. Elphick R. 1977. *Kraal and Castle: Khoikhoi and the Founding of White South Africa.* New Haven, CT: Yale Univ. Press
33. Endicott KM. 1983. The effects of slave raiding on the aborigines of the Malay Peninsula. In *Slavery, Bondage, and Dependency in Southeast Asia*, ed. A Reid, J Brewster, pp. 216–45. Brisbane: Univ. Queensland Press
34. Endicott KM. 1984. The economy of the Batek of Malaysia: annual and historical perspectives. *Res. Econ. Anthropol.* 6:26–52
35. Endicott KM. Bellwood P. 1991. The possibility of independent foraging in the rain forest of Peninsular Malaysia. *Hum. Ecol.* 19:151–85
36. Fleming HC. 1986. Hadza and Sandawe genetic relationships. *Sprache Gesch. Afr.* 7(2):157–87
37. Foley R. 1982. A reconsideration of the role of predation on large mammals in tropical hunter-gatherer adaptations. *Man* 17:393–402
38. Ford RI. 1972. Barter, gift, or violence: an analysis of Tewa intertribal exchange. In *Social Exchange and Interaction*, ed. E Wilmsen, pp. 21–45. Anthropol. Pap. No. 46. Ann Arbor: Univ. Mich., Mus. Anthropol.
39. Fox RG. 1969. "Professional primitives": hunters and gatherers of nuclear South Asia. *Man India* 49:139–60

40. Galaty JG. 1986. East African hunters and pastoralists in a regional perspective: an "ethnoanthropological" approach. *Sprache Gesch. Afr.* 7(1):105–31
41. Gardner PM. 1972. The Paliyans. See Ref. 14, pp. 404–7
42. Gardner PM. 1982. Ascribed austerity: a tribal path to purity. *Man* 17:462–69
43. Gardner PM. 1988. Pressures for Tamil propriety in Paliyan social organization. See Ref. 60, pp. 91–106
44. Gordon RJ. 1984. The !Kung in the Kalahari exchange: an ethnohistorical perspective. In *Past and Present in Hunter Gatherer Studies*, ed. C Schrire, pp. 195–224. Orlando, FL: Academic
45. Gregg SA. 1988. *Foragers and Farmers.* Chicago: Univ. Chicago Press
46. Griffin PB. 1984. Forager land and resource use in the humid tropics: the Agta of northeastern Luzon. See Ref. 84, pp. 95–121
47. Guenther MG. 1986. From foragers to miners and bands to bandits: on the flexibility and adaptability of Bushman band societies. *Sprache Gesch. Afr.* 7(1): 133–59
48. Habicht Mauche JA. 1988. *An analysis of Southwestern-style utility ware ceramics from the Southern Plains in the context of protohistoric Plains-Pueblo interaction.* PhD thesis. Harvard Univ.
49. Hall KR. 1985. *Maritime Trade and State Development in Early Southeast Asia.* Honolulu: Univ. Hawaii Press
50. Harris M. 1977. *Cannibals and Kings: the Origins of Cultures.* New York: Random House
51. Hart JA. 1978. From subsistence to market: a case study of the Mbuti net hunters. *Hum. Ecol.* 6:325–53
52. Hart TB, Hart JA. 1986. The ecological basis of hunter-gatherer subsistence in African rain forests: the Mbuti of eastern Zaire. *Hum. Ecol.* 14:29–55
53. Headland TN. 1987. The wild yam question: how well could independent hunter-gatherers live in a tropical rain forest ecosystem? *Hum. Ecol.* 15:463–91
54. Headland TN, Reid LA. 1989. Hunter-gatherers and their neighbors from prehistory to the present. *Curr. Anthropol.* 30:43–66
55. Hitchcock RK. 1982. Patterns of sedentism among the Basarwa of eastern Botswana. See Ref. 65, pp. 223–67
56. Hitchcock RK. 1987. Socio-economic change among the Basarwa in Botswana: An ethnohistorical analysis. *Ethnohistory* 34:219–55
57. Hoffman CL. 1984. Punan foragers in the trading networks of Southeast Asia. See Ref. 84, pp. 123–49
58. Hoffman CL. 1986. *The Punan: Hunter-*

Gatherers of Borneo. Ann Arbor: UMI Res. Press

59. Hutterer KL. 1977. Prehistoric trade and the evolution of Philippine societies: a reconsideration. In *Economic Exchange and Social Interaction in Southeast Asia: Perspectives from Prehistory, History, and Ethnography,* ed. KL Hutterer, pp. 177–96. Mich. Pap. South and Southeast Asia 13. Ann Arbor: Univ. Mich.

60. Ingold T. 1990. Comment on Solway and Lee. *Curr. Anthropol.* 31:130–31

61. Ingold T, Riches D, Woodburn J, eds. 1988. *Hunters and Gatherers,* Vol. 1, *History, Evolution, and Social Change.* Oxford: Berg

62. Ichikawa M. 1986. Ecological basis of symbiosis, territoriality, and intra-band cooperation of the Mbuti Pygmies. *Sprache Gesch. Afr.* 7(1):161–88

63. Kratz CA. 1986. Ethnic interaction, economic diversification, and language use: a report on research with Kaplelach and Kipchornwonek Okiek. *Sprache Gesch. Afr.* 7(2):189–226

64. Lamphear J. 1986. The persistence of hunting and gathering in a "pastoral" world. *Sprache Gesch. Afr.* 7(2):227–65

65. Leacock E, Lee R, eds. 1982. *Politics and History in Band Societies.* Cambridge: Cambridge Univ. Press

66. Lee RB. 1968. What hunters do for a living, or, how to make out on scarce resources. In *Man the Hunter,* ed. RB Lee, I DeVore, pp. 30–43. Chicago: Aldine

67. Marks S. 1972. Khoisan resistance to the Dutch in the seventeenth and eighteenth centuries. *J. Afr. Hist.* 13:55–80

68. Milton K. 1984. Protein and carbohydrate resources of the Maku Indians of northwestern Amazonia. *Am. Anthropol.* 86:7–27

69. Milton K. 1985. Ecological foundations for subsistence strategies among the Mbuti Pygmies. *Hum. Ecol.* 13:71–78

70. Morris AG. 1992. *The Skeletons of Contact.* Johannesburg: Witwatersrand Univ. Press

71. Morris B. 1982. *Forest Traders: A Socio-Economic Study of the Hill Pandaram.* London: Athelone

72. Morris B. 1982. The family, group structuring, and trade among south Indian hunter-gatherers. See Ref. 65, pp. 171–88

73. Motzafi P. 1986. Whither the "true Bushmen": the dynamics of perpetual marginality. *Sprache Gesch. Afr.* 7(1):295–328

74. Ndagala DK. 1988. Free or doomed? Images of Hadzabe hunters and gatherers of Tanzania. See Ref. 60, pp. 65–72

75. Odner K. 1986. Economic differentiation and origin of Dorobo (Okiek) ethnicity. *Sprache Gesch. Afr.* 7(2):307–22

76. Parkington JK. 1984. Soaqua and Bush-

men: hunters and robbers. See Ref. 84, pp. 151–74

77. Parkington JK, Yates R, Manhire A, Halkett D. 1986. The social impact of pastoralism in the southwestern Cape. *J. Anthropol. Archaeol.* 5:313–29

78. Pederson J, Waehle E. 1988. The complexities of residential organization among the Efe (Mbuti) and the Bagombi (Baka): a critical view of the notion of flux in hunter-gatherer societies. See Ref. 60, pp. 75–90

79. Peterson JT. 1978. Hunter-gatherer/farmer exchange. *Am. Anthropol.* 80:335–51

80. Rai NK. 1990. *Living in a Lean-to: Philippine Negrito Foragers in Transition.* Anthropol. Pap. No. 80. Ann Arbor: Univ. Mich., Mus. Anthropol.

81. Roscoe PR. 1990. The bow and spreadnet: ecological origins of hunting technology. *Am. Anthropol.* 92:691–701

82. Rousseau J. 1984. Review article: four theses on the nomads of central Borneo. *Borneo Res. Bull.* 16:35–95

83. Schrire C. 1980. An inquiry into the evolutionary status and apparent identity of San hunter-gatherers. *Hum. Ecol.* 8:9–32

84. Schrire C, ed. 1984. *Past and Present in Hunter Gatherer Studies.* Orlando, FL: Academic

85. Schrire C. 1984. Wild surmises on savage thoughts. See Ref. 84, pp. 1–25

86. Schultz M. 1986. Economic relations between the Batua and Baoto of Bibelo village, Bikoro Zone, Republic of Zaire: a preliminary report on new fieldwork. *Sprache Gesch. Afr.* 7(2):339–59

87. Scott WH. 1984. *Prehispanic Source Materials for the Study of Philippine History.* Quezon City, Philippines: New Day

88. Sellato BJL. 1988. The nomads of Borneo: Hoffman and "devolution." *Borneo Res. Bull.* 20:106–20

89. Silberbauer GB, Kuper AJ. 1966. Kgalagari masters and Bushman serfs: some observations. *Afr. Stud.* 25:171–79

90. Sinha DP. 1972. The Birhors. See Ref. 14, pp. 371–403

91. Solway JS, Lee RB. 1990. Foragers, genuine or spurious? *Curr. Anthropol.* 31:109–46

92. Speth JD. 1991. Some unexplored aspects of mutualistic Plains-Pueblo food exchange. See Ref. 96, pp. 18–35

93. Spielmann KA. 1986. Interdependence among egalitarian societies. *J. Anthropol. Archaeol.* 5:279–312

94. Spielmann KA. 1991. *Interdependence in the Protohistoric Southwest: An Ecological Analysis of Plains-Pueblo Interaction.* New York: Garland

95. Spielmann KA, ed. 1991. *Farmers, Hunters, and Colonists.* Tucson: Univ. Ariz. Press

96. Spielmann KA. 1992. Review of *Foragers*

and Farmers by Susan A. Gregg. *Hum. Ecol.* 20:254–57

97. Sulzmann E. 1986. Batwa und Baoto—die symbiose von wildbeutern und pflanzern bei den Ekonda und Bolia. *Sprache Gesch. Afr.* 7(1):369–89

98. Ten Raa E. 1986. The acquisition of cattle by hunter-gatherers: a traumatic experience in cultural change. *Sprache Gesch. Afr.* 7(2):361–74

99. Terashima H. 1986. Economic exchange and the symbiotic relationship between the Mbuti (Efe) Pygmies and the neighboring farmers. *Sprache Gesch. Afr.* 7(1):391–405

100. Todd L. 1987. Analysis of kill-butchery bonebeds and interpretation of paleoIndian hunting. In *The Evolution of Human Hunting,* ed. MH Nitecki, DV Nitecki, pp. 225–66. New York/London: Plenum

101. Turnbull C. 1965. *Wayward Servants: The Two Worlds of the African Pygmies.* Garden City, NY: Nat. Hist. Press

102. Vierich HID. 1982. Adaptive flexibility in a multi-ethnic setting: the Basarwa of the southern Kalahari. In *Politics and History in Band Societies,* ed. E Leacock, R Lee, pp. 213–22. Cambridge: Cambridge Univ. Press

103. Waehle E. 1986. Efe (Mbuti Pygmy) relations to Lese Dese villagers in the Ituri forest, Zaire: historical changes during the last 150 years. *Sprache Gesch. Afr.* 7(2):375–411

104. Warren JF. 1981. *The Sulu Zone, 1768–1898.* Singapore: Singapore Univ. Press

104a. Wiessner P. 1982. Risk, reciprocity and social influences on !Kung San economics. See Ref. 65, pp. 61–84

105. Wilmsen EN. 1983. The ecology of illusion: anthropological foraging in the Kalahari. *Rev. Anthropol.* 10:9–20

106. Wilmsen EN. 1989. *Land Filled with Flies.* Chicago: Univ. Chicago Press

107. Wilmsen EN, Denbow JR. 1990. Paradigmatic history of San-speaking peoples and current attempts at revisionism. *Curr. Anthropol.* 31:489–524

108. Winter JC. 1986. Structural specifics of hunter-gatherer kinship terminologies. *Sprache Gesch. Afr.* 7(2):433–52

109. Wobst HM. 1978. The archaeo-ethnology of hunter-gatherers, or the tyranny of the ethnographic record in archaeology. *Am. Antiq.* 43:303–9

110. Woodburn J. 1988. African hunter-gatherer social organization: Is it best understood as a product of encapsulation? See Ref. 60, pp. 31–64

111. Yellen JE. 1977. *Archaeological Approaches to the Present.* New York: Academic

112. Yellen JE. 1990. Comment on Wilmsen and Denbow. *Curr. Anthropol.* 31:137–38

Annu. Rev. Anthropol. 1994. 23:325–45

THEORIES AND POLITICS IN AFRICAN AMERICAN ENGLISH

Marcyliena Morgan

Department of Anthropology, University of California, Los Angeles, California 90024

KEY WORDS: Black English vernacular, language and gender, language and identity, language ideology

INTRODUCTION

Scholarly research and public attitudes concerning the language behavior of African Americans have evolved throughout the twentieth century, from early theories that described it in relation to various types of US speech spoken by those of British descent (121, 122, 123, 183) to increasing efforts to describe its features, use, and function within or among members of the African American speech community (42, 163, 177) irrespective of other varieties of American English. To explore and critique this evolution, I situate much of this review within the theoretical and political arguments that have portended each analytical shift. These arguments, while centered around language, concern the larger question of how to address the multicultural contact first experienced by Africans and their descendants, who were both sold and born into slavery in the United States, as well as how to interpret the role and constitutive elements of African American culture and language in American society today.

In the United States, comments about the language of African Americans are consistently linked to comments about African Americans' cognitive ability and culture (eg. 26, 64, 87, 183), so it is not surprising that some linguists lament the shroud of controversy often accompanying research on African American varieties (12, 20, 21, 160). This controversy reflects the multilayered political and ideological issues embodying scholarly work with any marginalized group that is characterized or marked by language use. It also introduces the problematic of both researchers and/or members as social actors in this process. This review addresses many of the fundamental questions concerning linguistic analysis and linguistic ideology (92, 138), language ideology (101, 130, 134, 193), language and identity (22, 23, 48, 49, 57a, 73, 76, 114, 130, 132–134, 150, 181), and the politics of linguistic representation (92, 144). These issues have been embodied in scholarly work on African American language behavior and culture since the publication in the early 1900s of poetry by Paul Laurence Dunbar (46), one of the first American authors of "pure" African ancestry.

Dunbar's achievements were plagued by debate within and between both black and white America over the communicative and linguistic norms and values of Americans of African descent. Dunbar was treated as a novelty of his time because few African Americans had advanced literacy skills, and it was routinely argued that only African Americans with discernable European ancestry possessed such skills (146). Additional irony accompanied Dunbar's work because, though well educated, he wrote many of his poems in plantation dialect—the early twentieth century literary version of the vernacular—because, according to Johnson (88), Dunbar believed that plantation dialect was the only variety that a white readership would find acceptable.

Although Dunbar's writings are often cited as the first example of a culturally rich and insightful portrayal of typical black life of the time, they were also vilified by African American writers and critics (88, 117, 146) as generally sentimental, humorous, childlike, optimistic, and agonizingly uncritical of slavery. This rather harsh assessment occurred because Dunbar's cultural portrayals were constructed with categorically stereotypical language that, according to the above writers, confirmed and reconstituted racist stereotypes of African Americans. The ideological and political conflict surrounding Dunbar's writing is reflected in the research of some linguists who considered the phenomenon of educated African Americans using non-educated varieties of language subversive (eg. 121, 182) and others (eg. 172) who considered criticism of such varieties by educated African Americans as pathological and reflective of self-hate.

The polemics surrounding Dunbar's work embody nearly every issue that has emerged concerning African American language over the last thirty years: Is African American English a language or a dialect? Who speaks it? What are its linguistic origins? From which social, cultural, and political conditions did it emerge? What are its identifying features? In what context is information about it gathered? Why does it exist? What are the social and political implications of its continued existence? What is its orthographic representation? And what is the role of African American activism in the scholarly representation of culture and language?

AFRICAN AMERICAN CULTURE AND LANGUAGE: IDEOLOGIES AND POLITICS

The political and scholarly debate over what to call African American English (AAE)[1] reflects the debate over the role of African Americans in the history and culture of America (cf 161, 175). Simply put, the conflict concerns whether African Americans are culturally distinct, when compared to other Americans who have also experienced multicultural contact. American anthropological theories on race and culture, while effectively arguing against racial determination of culture, have also argued that differences between African Americans and other Americans are not cultural (27, 28). Instead, as Szwed (175) and others (124, 184) report, the theory that persisted in both anthropology and sociology was that slavery deprived African Americans of any cultural roots (eg. 25). Ironically, anthropologists interpreted African American acceptance of their scholarly theories as self-hate (or low self-esteem) and as proof that African Americans are ashamed of their African and slave heritage (184). Some sociologists (eg. 136a, 142) interpreted the anthropological view to mean that African American behavior that did not mirror white behavior was pathological or deviant, while others (eg. 56, 57) considered attempts to mimic white behavior pathological. The assumption of deprivation and deviance certainly affected scholarly views of the language of African Americans (26, 72, 145, 178, 182): AAE was viewed variously as an ineffective attempt to speak AE and/or an indication of cognitive and/or environmental deficiency.

Although the situation described above represents the dominant view of anthropology and linguistics until the late 1960s, there were, in fact, competing views concerning African American culture and language. Herskovits (79–81) and others (e.g. 85, 115, 173, 174) introduced the notion of African continuity. Herskovits greatly influenced Turner (179), who presented, through the use of word lists, the first conclusive evidence of Africanisms in Gullah. Dalby (36, 37), Dillard (42), and Stewart (169) later identified features of AAE [e.g. absence of the copula ("Sinbad funny.") and use of a marker *be*

---

[1] I use African American English (AAE) to refer to the language varieties used by people in the United States whose major socialization has been with US residents of African descent. AAE is both a cultural and historical term in that it acknowledges that speakers are of African descent and connects US speakers with those in the African diaspora in general and the English-speaking diaspora in the Americas in particular. I use American English (AE) to refer to the general discussion of US varieties of English when it does not focus on social or cultural language markedness and in cases where class, region, gender, and age are not the focus of discussion. These AE varieties include those known as standard, network, and mainstream as well as working class, southern, Brooklyn, etc. As Mufwene (140) reports, there have been several other terms used for AAE over the years, the most widespread being Negro speech (123), Negro Nonstandard (170), Black English (42), Black English Vernacular or Black Vernacular English (105), Ebonics (84), and Bilalian language (162).

for habitual aspect ("Whoopi be tellin' jokes on T.V.")]. But it was not until Labov and his team of researchers (112) applied to the study of AAE the methodological innovations he had introduced to dialectology (103) that linguists and social scientists began to consider that the language use of African Americans did not represent impaired cognitive development.

VERNACULAR SPEECH AND CULTURE

Labov (105, 113) refuted the attempts of some sociologists to consider African American behavior that is different from white middle class as deviant and socially pathological (e.g. 34, 142, 61). He also countered psychological theories linking African American language behavior to deficits in culture, intelligence, and personal character (26, 72, 178). Labov (104, 105, 112) examined the grammatical and phonological features of AAE in various linguistic environments and contexts, and he discussed the relationship of these features to American English (AE). He argued that rather than reflecting deprivation and deviance, AAE grammatical and phonological features are related to AE in logical and systemic ways (104, 105).

Labov and many others (e.g. 16, 17, 41, 42, 171) were instrumental in limiting the influence of the deficit theory on the education of African American children and in reopening the debate about the nature of AAE. His research introduced quantitative methods to analyze what he called linguistic variables: structural items that occur frequently in natural conversation and whose frequency of occurrence is highly stratified according to age, class, etc (107:8). Labov's strategy was effective against the racist theories mentioned earlier and introduced new and more accurate measures for identifying and analyzing variation and language use. Yet, one aspect of his arguments inadvertently mirrored the depiction of the African American community by some anthropologists and sociologists (56, 136a, 142, 184) as ashamed of its historical origins and cultural practices.

Labov's description of AAE or vernacular speakers as "black youth from 8 to 19 years old who participate in the street culture of inner cities" (105:xiii) exists in contrast to "lames," the term his young participants used for those outside their peer group, who, coincidentally, did not use AAE features with the same frequency of variation as did the street youths. Labov's use of the term vernacular is problematic for three reasons. First, Labov considered the language variety spoken by the participants in his study to be the authentic or core AAE. Second, he invoked cultural and social descriptions to contrast his core group with the lames (105:259). This description of vernacular or core black culture (compare 74) constructs authentic African American membership and language as male, adolescent, insular, and trifling. By default, everyone else in the black community, regardless of age, is a lame. Because lames do not participate in core culture, having "suffered a loss of some magnitude" (p. 287) in terms of verbal skills, do not use AAE features in ways significantly related to vernacular members, and speak some version of AE (compare 167), they are not culturally African American.

Finally, in contrast to the way the African American community was defined, the white community was referred to as a Standard English–speaking community except on the rare occasions when white vernacular varieties were mentioned. In these cases, the AE vernacular referred either to the working class or to informal varieties irrespective of age, gender, or whether speakers were found in the home or on the street.

The African American community's consistent resistance to the above formulation of the speech community has befuddled many linguists who view their work as thwarting rather than perpetuating racist stereotypes. Oddly enough, it was precisely because Labov's arguments were powerful and persuasive that his work became the focus of the conflict over how to define the African American community. It also challenged the already intense debate among and between linguists and members of the African American community on the origins of AAE, its linguistic and pragmatic features, and how the frequent use of these features contributes to definitions of the speech community.

THEORIES OF THE ORIGIN(S) OF AFRICAN AMERICAN ENGLISH

Discussions about the constitutive phonological, morphological, syntactic, semantic, and pragmatic features of AAE are characterized by discussions of whether it is best to describe their historical ancestry primarily in terms of AE varieties, other languages and varieties in the African diaspora, African languages, or a combination of the three (cf 139). In linguistic terms, the first view is considered to be the dialectologist or sociolinguistic position (11, 51, 52, 53, 82, 99, 102, 105, 121, 160, 183, 192); the second and third approaches reflect the creolist or substratist position (9, 36, 37, 39, 42, 169, 179, 188, 189, 190); and the fourth view, the multiple influence position, has been held at various times by both sociolinguists and creolists, depending on the linguistic level of analysis and whether the research was a synchronic or diachronic study (6, 19, 138–140, 149, 152). Although many linguists analyze and collect data using more than one perspective, each approach is based on specific notions of representative speaker and linguistic features and suggests different ideologies concerning the conditions and contexts under which AAE emerged.

Sociolinguists and creolists consider the features of AAE to be variable (105), but they disagree over the reason for and significance of the variation. Often embedded in this discussion is recognition that these theories have political implications for educational psychology and language arts and planning programs. Consequently, and perhaps unfairly, members of the African American community view proponents of various theories as holding specific political beliefs because of the way policy makers have adapted their theories or because linguists have not appreciated the political terrain their work encompasses. For example, although many African American writers (e.g. 13, 77, 91) and some language arts scholars and linguists (31, 40, 162, 177) widely support the creolist/substratist view, they severely criticize what they perceive to be the tendency of sociolinguists to reinscribe racist stereotypes about African American language and culture by comparing AAE features to AE without considering African language influences.

Linguists are divided over whether AAE should be described as it functions and appears across a wide range of everyday interactions, cultural contexts, and social variables within the African American community, or whether it should be defined in relation to other languages. This theoretical issue has led to widespread disagreement over how to describe its features and how to determine the significance of their occurrence across contexts.

THE FEATURES OF AFRICAN AMERICAN ENGLISH

There are many excellent reviews of the features of AAE (e.g. 20, 21, 33, 140, 149, 150, 152, 160). Most of the variable phonological and syntactic features and lexical principles associated with AAE have been reported from as early as 1865 (40). With few exceptions (20, 166), the features identified were marked in relation to AE and were thought to operate differently. Linguists often acknowledge that a full description of AAE does not exist (e.g. 110, 150), but only a few studies (125, 129, 131, 154, 163) have considered African American language use across a variety of cultural and social contexts within a network of speakers. Although linguists discuss the importance of representative numbers of core participants (20, 107, 150, 151), the number of tokens across speakers, rather than the number of speakers who use tokens, is the significant unit of measure (e.g. 113). Essentially, linguistic features have not been gathered according to anthropological notions of "naturally occurring speech" (i.e. recorded in and across cultural events and/or social contexts). Instead, the focus has been on the effect of the interviewer/recorder on the type of speech (e.g. casual, monitored) (107, 113, 150, 154) or formal versus informal conversational topics (107). As a result, features have been identified and counted in relation to linguistic contexts or the type of discourse undertaken (33, 138, 140).

One phonological feature that was stereotyped earlier (140) as AAE but is widespread in many AE dialects is the variable absence of interdental fricatives such as *th*ink, *th*en, substituted by /t/ or /d/ in word initial position. In intervocalic and word final position these interdentals are pronounced /f/ and /v/, producing /wIf/ or /wIv/ for *with,* and sometimes /t/ producing mʌnt for *month* (15, 32, 53, 140). AAE is often characterized as /r/-less (15, 32, 105, 119) or non-rhotic (140) in word final position, thus producing /mo:/ for *more* or, before a consonant, producing /hɔd/ for *hard.* There is also the general phenomenon of consonant simplification or absence, usually in word final position. Thus, *must* is often pronounced /mʌs/. For the alveolar stops /t,d/, Labov (105) suggests an AAE rule where deletion applies in AE monomorphemic words such as *past* and less often in polymorphemic words such as *passed.* Some creolists argue that unmarked verbs in AAE are typical of Caribbean Creoles where the tense system is not verbally marked (15, 42, 140, 169, 170) so that, for example, *walk* and *walked* are both produced as *walk.*

There has been renewed discussion of the phonological feature, /r/, because of its contrasting use and function in AE and AAE. Bailey & Maynor (11) argue that the use of postvocalic /r/ in the South suggests that black and white varieties are diverging (7, 158). They believe that white use of postvocalic /r/ is increasing, while AAE is not participating in the change. Butters (33) questions Bailey & Maynor's claim of an enormous decrease in /r/-lessness for whites as well as blacks because the researchers did not account for regional variation among whites (33:40), and other studies (e.g. 141, 180) suggest a decrease in /r/-lessness within the lifetime of older African American speakers. Categorical claims like Bailey & Maynor's are further challenged by findings (20) that in formal contexts, AAE speakers actually self-monitor their use of /r/.

AAE methods of pluralization, possessive marking, and verbal agreement also differ significantly when contrasted with AE. Labov (109) argues that unlike white varieties, AAE does not use verbal -*s* in subject-verb agreement. As a result, AAE speakers do not have underlying third singular -*s.* When it does appear, Labov considers it is a case of hypercorrection, a stylistic feature used when speakers shift their speech to Standard English. Mufwene (140) suggests that AAE third person singular -*s* further supports the theory that it is related to Caribbean varieties, which exhibit similar characteristics. Myhill & Harris (141) claim that verbal -*s* marks the historical present in AAE, although Rickford (154) considers the absence of third singular -*s* nearly categorical among his young speakers. The occurrence of /s/ where the form can represent pluralization, possession, and subject-verb agreement can also depend on the speech event (20). Baugh (20:96) reports that third person singular -*s* is the least likely form to occur, followed by possessive and plural, respectively. In contrast, Butters (33) argues that the form's only importance is that it can occasionally lead to misunderstandings between AAE and AE speakers (cf 113).

For creolists and sociolinguists, the most significant grammatical feature of AAE, especially in terms of its historical development and genetic and/or typological relationships, involves the occurrence and function of the copula *be*. For example, the AE sentence "She is the president" can also be "She the president" in AAE. Fasold (52) argued that AAE *be* represents a substantial difference in tense usage compared to AE, and Baugh (19) called it one of the best examples of dialect distinction. Early accounts of the occurrence and usage of *be* were reported widely (9, 51, 112, 169, 170, 191). These discussions centered on whether or not the copula exists as a grammatical category in AAE. Current research has considered various arguments on how the AE copula is deleted in AAE and how it is grammatically inserted (19, 84, 105, 138, 140, 152, 153, 189, 190).

AAE's habitual marker *be* has also been the focus of theories regarding black and white speech differences. Rickford (151a) offers persuasive evidence that *be* emerged as part of a decreolization process involving *does*, rather than from other varieties of English. Mufwene (140) describes it as *be* + nonverbal predicate, as in "I be tired by the end of the day," meaning "I am [usually] tired by the end of the day." When a verb heads the predicate phrase, the verb must be in the progressive, as in "She be talkin' every time I come." Although these constructions are usually non-stative, they also occur with stative constructions (133, 148). In addition to arguments that AAE and AE are less similar than in the past, Bailey et al (10, 11) suggest that younger speakers are introducing a grammatical change that is not occurring with older speakers. They believe that younger speakers use *be* as a verbal auxiliary in AAE and that they are in the process of revising the meaning and syntactic distribution of *be* to a verbal auxiliary. Some linguists (e.g. 33, 152) disagree with this claim and argue that constructions like "I be kickin'" may be common among adolescents and teenagers because they are age-graded forms rather than a sign that AAE is changing.

Much of the theoretical debate surrounding the features of AAE has centered around whether or not AAE is participating in a change that is occurring in AE. The debate has little to do with what occurs in AAE (compare 38) or whether AE affects AAE. Fortunately, the discussion of these issues has encouraged some sociolinguists to review weaknesses in sociolinguistic methodology (e.g. 33, 152, 180, 189) to try to clarify some of the arguments and suggest new approaches for study.

DISCOURSE AND VERBAL GENRES

Descriptions of men's discourse styles and verbal genres have dominated the scholarly literature on African American communication and folklore (1, 5, 58, 93, 94, 105, 106). Most of the attention has focused on signifying in the form of "sounding" or "playing the dozens," which is a form of verbal play performed mainly by adolescent boys (1, 5, 54, 58, 94, 96, 105, 106, 115). Although playing the dozens may be an important part of adolescent male activity, members also recognize it as a language socialization activity (cf 68, 69, 159), especially for conversational signifying. Mitchell-Kernan describes signifying as "the recognition and attribution of some implicit content or function which is obscured by the surface content or function" (126:317–318). Gates (59:48) considers signifying to be "the trope of tropes" of African American discourse and believes that it functions as a stylish critique of African American rhetorical and cultural styles. Gates' definition is a far cry from earlier assessments that signifying functioned as a way for adolescent males to cope with overbearing mothers and as an outlet for racial oppression (44). In fact, scholarly descriptions of verbal play probably suffered most from anthropology's reluctance to describe US African American experience as a cultural one (described above). Some folklorists and anthropologists (especially 5, 93, 94) successfully placed signifying within verbal performance genres, but they focused on the place where they saw these performances—the street—as the locus of men's cultural and social activity. Everyday life stories generally are not the focus of discussion in the street, where fantastic, fantasized, and improbable tales of heroism, strength, wit, and virility function as semiotic or symbolic capital (29, 155). Renewed interest in the characteristics of signifying and the dozens is largely the result of the recognition of its centrality in African American discourse (59, 128, 135, 163, 168) and its use among popular stand-up comedians in the United States.

The notion of play involved in the dozens differentiates the real from the serious (cf 5, 18, 63, 97, 98) by placing that which is culturally significant (e.g. mothers, identity, political figures, economic independence) in implausible contexts. Whether a context is plausible or implausible is culturally determined. For example, a signifying episode that includes a police officer who "serves and protects" would be considered an implausible context in signifying episodes. Once the implausible or unreal state is established, these cultural signs interact with the context through irony, sarcasm, wit, and humor in order to play with the serious signifier. If it is plausible that the sign fits the context, the interaction is considered to be an insult rather than play.

The dozens are often characterized by "your mother" (or "yo mama") statements, which both highlight and subvert the notion that mothers are sacred (163). These statements should not be misunderstood to relate specifically to someone's particular mother since that is not a requirement for participation (compare 105, 106). "Your mother" statements are a device used to practice and perform verbal skill. This practice often occurs in the presence of family members, including mothers, who help judge their effectiveness and comment on the wit or irony in the statements, often offering other examples they deem more impressive.

Once a "your mother" sequence is launched, it is usually acknowledged as being in play within an interactive episode when another person responds with a statement and is therefore in competition with the initiator (1, 97, 105, 106). The episode continues until someone delivers enough witty, acerbic, and indirect statements that the audience or interactors determine the winner. As Hutcherson (86) explains, the true essence of the dozens is the relationship between choice of signs and the logic of the implausibility. For Hutcherson, this logic is culturally loaded and refers to African American local theories (cf 60, 116) that include knowledge of cultural celebrations as well as US racism, bigotry, and injustice. One of Hutcherson's "logical" examples is "Your mother is so fat they won't let her have an X jacket because helicopters keep trying to land on her back" (86:52). The local information necessary to understand the irony in the signification is that the X jacket is in reference to an emblem associated with Malcolm X, an African American leader and activist known for his criticism of US racism and anti-capitalist leanings. Malcolm X was assassinated in 1965 and a movie depicting his life was released in 1991. The X appeared on clothing of urban youth in the early 1990s as part of the massive commodification of Malcolm X. The helicopter reference is related to both a knowledge of landing markings and a first-hand knowledge of how helicopters (called ghetto birds) patrol, constantly scan, descend, and land in urban areas.

Morgan (129, 132, 135) considers all forms of signifying to be part of the system of African American indirectness (see also 59). She identifies two dominant types: pointed and baited. Pointed indirectness involves mock targets, while baited indirectness focuses on attributes that suggest a particular target. In this sense, either a mock target or attribute can serve as the intermediary of the message (194) in that the success of the communication is determined through the social collaboration of the African American audience or hearers (cf 47, 98).

LANGUAGE AND GENDER

A cursory glance at the body of work on AAE elicits the question, "Where are the women!?" Although reviews of language and gender studies have noted that African American women have either been excluded or marginalized (48, 57a, 78, 168), they were mentioned. For example, Abrahams (2:9–10) reports that the women refused to participate in his Philadelphia folklore project with no explanation and later describes them as not participating in verbal play, and "restrained in their talk, less loud, less public, and much less abandoned" (3:242), when compared to men. In his later examination of the representation of women's speech styles in literature, he suggests that women may have the same expressive acuity as men (4:77).

Early reports, although rare, characterized African American women's language and role in communicative practices as (a) linguistically conservative when compared to men (107, 191), (b) targets of male discourse and interaction (1, 2, 96, 105), (c) collaborators in male street remarks (96), and (d) controllers and censors of men's interactions (2, 44, 96). Mitchell-Kernan's (125) was one of the few works of the 1970s that did not describe urban African American women as aggressive, controlling, domineering, and emasculating. In contrast to the other community research studies of the 1960s and 1970s (112, 191), Mitchell-Kernan's (125) ethnography discussed a range of social contexts and cultural perceptions of members. Her study mainly of women in West Oakland, demonstrated that women participated in conversational signifying (125:65–106) and used linguistic practices similar to those used by men (105, 191). Although Mitchell-Kernan (125) did not report on a large number of speakers, she discussed the importance of both topic and social context (e.g. formal vs informal) for the type of and distribution of features produced (pp. 107–109). Her findings seemed to have little influence on research in the African American community. This may be because she was, I think, personally attacked in a major review of her work (95). The review was filled with innuendo and criticism regarding Mitchell-Kernan's methodology, class, gender, and knowledge of the black community. Before discussing her work, the reviewer described Mitchell-Kernan as "a young attractive Black woman (p. 969)" as part of an explanation for why she was accepted in the community and why men were willing to talk to her. The reviewer also referred to her middle-class image (p. 970) in arguing that her analysis of verbal performance and member assessments and attitudes of language misrepresented and distorted community attitudes (p. 917). When these comments are related to earlier discussions about lames and authenticity, it seems that the only African American working on language in the community at the time was not qualified because of gender and class categories (along with race), for which the other researchers were not criticized. In many respects, it is a vindication of Mitchell-Kernan's work that 15 years later Gates (59) relied heavily on her description of signifying as a foundation for his theory on African American discourse.

Fortunately, the body of work on both women's language use and community views of their own language practices is growing. Current research examines and critiques the prevailing literature on African American women and girls' interaction (14, 65–69, 78, 129, 130, 131, 135, 168), and narratives (50, 55, 130, 131). Goodwin's (65, 66, 69) analysis of he-said-she-said disputes among African American girls reveals the elaborate lengths to which they are willing to go in order to determine who said what behind someone's back and whether the person reporting is, in reality, an instigator attempting to start trouble. Morgan (135) explores how signifying is conversationally constructed through the systematic use of particular grammatical, prosodic, and discursive structures to convey indirect messages. Stanback (168) provides one of the few discussions of discursive features of middle-class black women's interactions and notes that they use both AAE and AE linguistic and discourse features. Women's interactions also form the bases for Morgan's analysis of pointed and baited indirectness in African American discourse and interaction (129, 135) and for her discussion of counterlanguage (129, 132). Similarly, much of Rickford's (152–154) work on variation and style-shifting in AAE is the result of long-term interviews with a young woman community participant.

AFRICAN AMERICAN ATTITUDES TOWARD AAE

Between the late 1970s and 1980s, two major events highlighted disagreements about AAE between linguists and the African American community. The first event involved the legal decision of the Martin Luther King Junior Elementary School vs Ann Arbor School District Board (120). The case charged that school officials had placed African American children in learning disabled and speech pathology classes and held them at low grade levels because of AAE (164, 165). The King case was won largely because linguists (e.g. 110) argued successfully that AAE has systemic features that are not all related to English. The second event occurred in the late 1980s during a special symposium to discuss the findings and social implications of Labov's research project on "The Increasing Divergence of Black and White Vernaculars" (111). Labov, along with Bailey (11), argued that AAE and AE varieties, which they believed were previously on a course of convergence, were beginning to diverge, largely because of the social and historical factors of migration and continued segregation of races (7, 33, 70). Labov suggested that the only reasonable response to this situation was integration. Neither the King case's argument for representations of AAE in the schools nor Labov's suggestion that AAE speakers use more AE to enhance educational and economic success were supported by the wider African American community. Members of the black middle class (134, 164, 165) argued in the King Case that AAE and AE were not sufficiently different to impede comprehension of teachers or students and that the language of instruction should be AE. In contrast, once race, rather than class, was specifically identified in relation to using AE (113), community spokespersons argued that AE-speaking models were plentiful in the community (89, 167).

As the introduction to this review suggests, the most dissident and serious obstacle to representing AAE outside of the African American community has been its members (15, 21, 83, 134, 164, 165, 172). In some cases, linguists have criticized members for not accepting their educational plans or theories about African American language and communication styles (e.g. 172). Yet the reasons for resistance to programs are only superficially class based.

It is impossible to provide a simple definition of the African American speech community or, for that matter, any urban speech community. This is true because of its complex history, and because the community expands and contracts across class and geographic lines. Considering its complexity, it is not surprising that one source of criticism of linguistic plans and proposals can be traced to early descriptions of the African American speech community and what constitutes membership. Confusion regarding who speaks AAE began in the late 1960s with the pronouncement from creolists and dialectologists that "80% of all Black people speak Black English" (42:229). In rendering his legal decision in the King case (see above), the judge referred to 80% of African American speakers of AAE. The "80% theory" emerged during the deficit/difference debates in an attempt to identify African Americans as a working-class people who have their own culture, history, and language and whose rights, therefore, must be protected. However, the theory that 80% of all African Americans speak AAE competes with the definition of vernacular speakers and culture (described above), which excludes those who are not male, adolescent, jobless, or underemployed and irresponsible.

How the African American community assigns class and status remains open to question, because the community historically has been denied access to traditional indicators of the dominant social class: housing, employment, and occupation. In his analysis of the basis of social prestige found in studies on the African American community between 1899 and 1960, Glenn (62) found that in all but one case, African Americans considered education more important than income and occupation in determining class and status. These findings corroborated Drake & Cayton's (45) earlier study of Chicago's African American community, where they found that during the 1940s, advanced education virtually secured membership at the top of the black social hierarchy of Chicago. Wilson (186, 187) argued that middle class African Americans are increasing in numbers and changing in terms of occupational choices, neighborhoods, etc. One consequence of the change is that African American middle and working classes are becoming more stratified. However, Dillingham (43) argued that in an ethnically stratified society, subjective feelings of ethnic group or racial identification become a more powerful determinant of behavior than do objective assessments of socioeconomic status (43). In a study of three hundred African Americans, Dillingham (43) found that the higher the class of the respondent, the higher the racial consciousness. Other studies (e.g. 100, 156) also reported that middle class African Americans may attach greater importance to racial identities than class identities (40a, 84a, 86a, 100, 156). African American newspaper columnists (35, 143) have corroborated the notion that the middle class have either a strong African American and racial identity or a sense that as members of the middle class, cultural identity is continually examined. In light of the persistence of racial consciousness, it is not surprising that AAE marks cultural and racial identity across classes.

The importance of AAE among those middle class African Americans who were not socialized in the speech community is apparent, especially among youth, with the variety of AAE favored by rap and hip-hop artists (133). Baugh (22, 24) identified a developing tendency among upper middle class African American students attending elite college campuses to use lexical, phonological, and grammatical features of AAE in both formal and informal contexts. Research on language use among working and middle class African American adults (38, 167, 168) found that both AAE and AE are used in informal mixed class conversations irrespective of the class of the speaker. Morgan (135) also reported that working class speakers use both AAE and AE for conversational signifying. In addition, she (133) reported that hip-hop artists, who are self-described as using real street language, rely on AE grammar while using AAE phonological, lexical, and morphological style.

AFRICAN AMERICAN ENGLISH AND IDENTITY

African American scholars and community activists in popular, theoretical, and research journals have written extensively about AAE and the politics of language use in the United States. Poets, writers, and musicians contributed to the developing positions that were often framed within a particular understanding of Africans before US slavery. AAE has been discussed from three related perspectives: 1. in terms of its expressive African character (13, 31, 77, 89, 136, 163), 2. as a symbol of resistance to slavery and oppression (31, 77, 91, 134, 162, 163), and, the opposite view, and 3. as an indicator of a slave mentality or consciousness (157).

In the first conception of AAE, the indigenous languages of Africa were considered to be symbolic of African culture, identity, and power. Some scholars attached metaphysical significance to African continuity (31:14). This attention to African identity and AAE has been addressed by language scholars (e.g. 162, 163, 176) as well as by writers of the African American experience (13, 90, 136). Rather than focus on the details or particulars of the historical origins of AAE, they have concentrated on how African language practices were used to adjust to the conditions of slavery and Jim Crow laws. The resistance theory of AAE is based on the function, nature, and importance of indirect speech and ambiguity in African American speech.

Perhaps the force in the African American community most resistant to the African influence interpretation of AAE is the Nation of Islam. According to Samuel 17X (156), speakers of AAE invoke a slave mentality because AAE developed during slavery and is emblematic of the subservient relationship between master and slave. Although this position has been critiqued (162), the perspective still echoes in current popular debates about AAE (90, 190).

The tension that emerges from AAE as a complex sign of both resistance and oppression problematizes any attempt to present plans or policies of AAE. Questions concerning the language legitimacy of African Americans who seek citizenship rights have been a recurring issue in American society (57, 126, 127, 190). Yet, as Mitchell-Kernan (126, 127) observed, the interplay between "good" English and AAE is extremely complex because both are considered crucial to improving life chances (cf 30, 89, 91, 165). Those who choose to accommodate the demands of non-African American society and use AE exclusively risk losing membership status and, as Mitchell-Kernan (126, 127) warned, risk being labeled as cultural misfits (cf 8, 90).

CONCLUSION

Many scholars who research African American language have done so in a climate of social injustice, intense political debate, and social scrutiny. This atmosphere, although complex in terms of competing ideologies among members and from the dominant culture, does not represent chaos. The language experience of the African diaspora is enmeshed with issues of culture, identity, memory, and citizenship. To advance the language study of African Americans, future theories, descriptions, and methods must reflect how language and communication styles constitute and construct African American identity. The result will be rich linguistic descriptions and theories that aim to describe the African American speech community across contexts, classes, age, and gender. These data can be a resource for linguistic analyses that explore the relationship between these thick descriptions of AAE and aspects of Creole and African languages and English. The study of interactions and verbal genres should also be considered within the larger cultural framework. As the fields of linguistics and anthropology continue to expand in order to address the increasing complexity of the African American experience, they will also continue to expand our knowledge and understanding of how speakers use language to construct politics, identity, and culture. In this respect, the study of African American language and culture is also the study of US culture and scholarship.

ACKNOWLEDGMENTS
I thank Bambi Schieffelin and Valerie Smith for their encouragement throughout the writing of this essay. I also thank Sepa Sete for her bibliographic
assistance and Devery Rodgers for her fantastic detective work in search of
African American publications. I also appreciate the assistance and comments
from Salikoko Mufwene, John Rickford, Lawrence Bobo, and John Singler.
This essay is dedicated to my students in my African American English
courses at the University of California, Los Angeles.

Any *Annual Review* chapter, as well as any article cited in an *Annual Review* chapter,
may be purchased from the Annual Reviews Preprints and Reprints service.
1-800-347-8007; 415-259-5017; email: arpr@class.org

Literature Cited

1. Abrahams RD. 1962. Playing the dozens. *J. Am. Folk.* 75:209–18
2. Abrahams RD. 1970. *Deep Down in the Jungle.* Chicago: Aldine
3. Abrahams RD. 1974. Black talking on the streets. In *Explorations in the Ethnography of Speaking,* ed. R Bauman, J Sherzer, pp. 240–62. London: Cambridge Univ. Press
4. Abrahams RD. 1975. Negotiating respect: patterns of presentation among black women. *J. Am. Folk.* 88:58–80
5. Abrahams RD. 1976. *Talking Black.* Rowley, MA: Newburg
6. Alleyne M. 1980. *Comparative Afro-American—An Historical Comparative Study of English Based Afro-American Dialects.* Ann Arbor, MI: Karoma
7. *American Speech.* 1987. Are black and white vernaculars diverging? *Pap. NWAVE XIV Panel Disc.* 62
8. Aponte WL. 1989. 'Talkin' White.' *Essence* 1:11
9. Bailey B. 1965. Toward a new perspective in Negro English dialectology. *Am. Speech* 40:171–77
10. Bailey G, Bassett M. 1986. Invariant *be* in the lower South. In *Language Variety in the South,* ed. M Montgomery, G Bailey, pp. 158–79. University, AL: Univ. Ala. Press
11. Bailey G, Maynor N. 1987. Decreolization? *Lang. Soc.* 16:449–73
12. Bailey G, Maynor N. 1989. The divergence controversy. *Am. Speech* 64(1):12–39
13. Baldwin J. 1979. If Black English isn't a language, then tell me, what is? *New York Times* July 29
14. Ball AF. 1992. The discourse of power and solidarity: language features of African-American females and a male program leader in a neighborhood based youth

dance program. In *Locating Power: Proceedings of the 1992 Berkeley Women and Language Group,* ed. K Hall, M Bucholtz, B Moonwoman, pp. 23–35. Berkeley, CA: Berkeley Women & Lang. Group, Linguist. Dept.
15. Baratz J. 1973. Language abilities of black Americans. In *Comparative Studies of Blacks and Whites in the United States,* ed. KS Miller, R Mason Dreger, pp. 125–83. New York: Seminar
16. Baratz J, Baratz C. 1972. Black culture on black terms: a rejection of the social pathology model. See Ref. 96, pp. 3–16
17. Baratz S, Baratz J. 1970. Early childhood intervention: the social science base of institutional fascism. *Harvard Educ. Rev.* 40: 29–50
18. Bateson G. 1972. *Steps to an Ecology of Mind.* New York: Harper & Row
19. Baugh J. 1980. A re-examination of the Black English copula. In *Locating Language in Time and Space,* ed. W Labov, pp. 83–106. Philadelphia: Univ. Penn. Press
20. Baugh J. 1983. *Black Street Speech: Its History, Structure, and Survival.* Austin, TX: Univ. Texas Press
21. Baugh J. 1983. A survey of Afro-American English. *Annu. Rev. Anthropol.* 12:335–54
22. Baugh J. 1987. The situational dimension of linguistic power. *Lang. Arts* 64:234–40
23. Baugh J. 1991. The politicalization of changing times of self-reference among American slave descendants. *Am. Speech* 66:133–46
24. Baugh J. 1992. Hypocorrection: mistakes in production of vernacular African American English as a second dialect. *Lang. Commun.* 12(3/4):317–26

25. Benedict R. 1959. *Race: Science and Politics.* New York: Viking
26. Bereiter C, Engelman S. 1966. *Teaching Disadvantaged Children in the Preschool.* Englewood Cliffs, NJ: Prentice-Hall
27. Boas F. 1945. Commencement address at Atlanta University. In *Race and Democratic Society,* ed. EP Boas, pp. 61–69. New York: Augustin
28. Boas F. 1963. *The Mind of Primitive Man.* New York: Macmillan
29. Bourdieu P. 1991. *Language & Symbolic Power.* Cambridge, MA: Harvard Univ. Press
30. Brown D. 1991. Communications skills: Is black dialect keeping us out of corporate America? *Upscale* Oct/Nov:34–35
31. Burgest D. 1973. The racist use of the English language. *Black Sch.* 9:37–45
32. Burling R. 1973. *English in Black and White.* New York: Holt, Rinehart & Winston
33. Butters R. 1989. *The Death of Black English: Divergence and Convergence in Black and White Vernaculars.* Frankfurt: Lang
34. Clark K. 1965. *The Dark Ghetto.* New York: Harper & Row
35. Cose E. 1993. *The Rage of A Privileged Class.* New York: Harper Collins
36. Dalby D. 1969. *Black Through White: Patterns of Communication in Africa and the New World.* Bloomington: Ind. Univ. Press
37. Dalby D. 1972. The African element in Black American English. See Ref. 93, pp. 170–86
38. DeBose C. 1992. Codeswitching: Black English and standard English in the African-American linguistic repertoire. *J. Multiling. Multicult. Dev.* 131(1–2):157–67
39. DeBose C, Faraclas N. 1993. An Africanist approach to the linguistic study of Black English: getting to the roots of the tense-aspect-modality and copula systems in Afro-American. In *Africanisms in Afro-American Language Varieties,* ed. S Mufwene, pp. 364–87. Athens, GA: Univ. Georgia Press
40. DeFrantz A. 1979. A critique of the literature on Ebonics. *J. Black Stud.* 9(4):383–96
40a. Demo D, Hughes M. 1990. Socialization and racial identity among black Americans. *Soc. Psychol. Q.* 53:364–74
41. Dillard JL. 1968. Nonstandard Negro dialects: convergence or divergence? *Fla. FL Report.* 6.2:9–12
42. Dillard JL. 1972. *Black English: Its History and Usage in the United States.* New York: Random House
43. Dillingham G. 1981. The emerging black middle class: class conscious or race conscious? *Ethnic Racial Stud.* 4(4):432–51
44. Dollard J. 1973. The dozens: dialectic of insult. In *Motherwit from the Laughing Barrel,* ed. A Dundes, pp. 277–94. Jackson, MS: Univ. Miss. Press
45. Drake S, Cayton H. 1945. *Black Metropolis.* New York: Harcourt, Brace
46. Dunbar PL. 1893. *Oak and Ivy.* Dayton, OH: Brethren
47. Duranti A. 1993. Truth and intentionality: an ethnographic critique. *Cult. Anthropol.* 8(2):214–45
48. Eckert P, McConnell-Ginet S. 1992. Thinking practically and looking locally: language and gender as community-based practice. *Annu. Rev. Anthropol.* 21:461–90
49. Edwards J. 1985. *Language, Society and Identity.* Oxford: Oxford Univ. Press
50. Etter-Lewis G. 1991. Standing up and speaking out: African American women's narrative legacy. *Disc. Soc.* 2:425–37
51. Fasold R. 1969. Tense and the form *Be* in Black English. *Language* 45:763–76
52. Fasold R. 1972. *Tense Marking in Black English: A Linguistic and Social Analysis.* Arlington, VA: Cent. Appl. Linguist.
53. Fasold R, Shuy R. 1970. Some linguistic features of Negro dialect. In *Teaching Standard English in the Inner City,* ed. R Fasold, R Shuy, pp. 41–86. Washington, DC: Cent. Appl. Linguist.
54. Folb E. 1980. *Runnin' Down Some Lines: The Language and Culture of Black Teenagers.* Cambridge, MA: Harvard Univ. Press
55. Foster M. 1994. Are you with me? Power, solidarity and community in the discourse of African American women. In *Locating Power: Proceedings of the Second Berkeley Women and Language Conference,* ed. K Hall, M Bucholtz, B Moonwoman, pp. 132–43. Berkeley, CA: Berkeley Women Lang. Group
56. Frazier EF. 1934. Traditions and patterns of Negro family life in the United States. In *Race and Culture Contacts,* ed. EB Reuter, pp. 191–201. New York: McGraw-Hill
57. Frazier EF. 1939. *The Negro Family in the United States.* Chicago: Univ. Chicago Press
57a. Gal S. 1991. Between speech and silence: the problematics of research on language and gender. In *Gender at the Crossroads of Knowledge: Feminist Anthropology in the Postmodern Era,* ed. M Di Leonardo, pp. 175–203. Berkeley: Univ. Calif. Press
58. Garner T. 1983. Playing the dozens: folklore as strategies for living. *Q. J. Speech* 69:47–57
59. Gates HL. 1988. *The Signifying Monkey: A Theory of African-American Literary Criticism.* Oxford: Oxford Univ. Press
60. Geertz C. 1973. *The Interpretation of Cultures.* New York: Basic Books
61. Glazer N, Moynihan DP. 1963. *Beyond the*

Melting Pot. Cambridge, MA: MIT Press/ Harvard Univ. Press
62. Glenn N. 1963. Negro prestige criteria: a case study in the base of prestige. *Am. J. Sociol.* 68(6):645–57
63. Goffman I. 1974. *Frame Analysis.* New York: Harper & Row
64. Gonzales A. 1922. *The Black Border: Gullah Stories of the Carolina Coast.* Columbia, SC: State
65. Goodwin MH. 1980. He-said-she-said: formal cultural procedures for the construction of a gossip dispute activity. *Am. Ethnolog.* 7:674–95
66. Goodwin MH. 1982. 'Instigating': storytelling as a social process. *Am. Ethnol.* 9:76–96
67. Goodwin MH. 1985. The serious side of jump rope: conversational practices and social organization in the frame of play. *J. Am. Folk.* 98:315–30
68. Goodwin MH. 1988. Cooperation and competition across girl's play activities. In *Gender and Discourse: The Power of Talk,* ed. S Fisher, A Todd, pp. 55–94. Norwood, NJ: Ablex
69. Goodwin MH. 1990. *He-Said-She-Said: Talk as Social Organization Among Black Children.* Bloomington: Ind. Univ. Press
70. Graff D, Labov W, Harris W. 1986. Testing listener's reactions to markers of ethnic identity. In *A New Method for Sociolinguistic Research,* ed. D Sankoff, pp. 45–58. Amsterdam: Benjamins
71. Deleted in proof
72. Grier W, Cobbs P. 1968. *Black Rage.* New York: Basic Books
73. Gumperz J. 1982. *Language and Social Identity.* Cambridge: Cambridge Univ. Press
74. Gwaltney J. 1981. *Drylongso.* New York: Vintage
75. Deleted in proof
76. Hanchard M. 1990. Identity, meaning and the African-American. *Soc. Text* 24(8.2): 31–42
77. Harrison PC. 1972. *The Drama of Nommo.* New York: Grove
78. Henley NM. 1994. Ethnicity and gender issues in language. In *Handbook of Cultural Diversity in Feminist Psychology,* ed. H Landrine. Washington, DC: Am. Psychol. Assoc. In press
79. Herskovits M. 1925. The Negro's Americanism. See Ref. 117, pp. 353–60
80. Herskovits M. 1935. What has Africa given America? *New Repub.* 84(1083):92–96
81. Herskovits M. 1941. *The Myth of the Negro Past.* Boston: Beacon
82. Holm J. 1984. Variability of the copula in Black English and its creole kin. *Am. Speech* 59:291–309
83. Hoover MR. 1978. Community attitudes toward Black English. *Lang. Soc.* 7(1):65–87
84. Hoover MR. 1990. A vindicationist perspective on the role of Ebonics (Black language) and other aspects of ethnic studies in the university. *Am. Behav. Sci.* 34.2:251–62
84a. Hughes M, Demo D. 1989. Self-perceptions of black Americans: self-esteem and personal efficacy. *Am. J. Soc.* 95:132–59
85. Hurston ZN. 1935. *Mules and Men.* Philadelphia: Lippincott
86. Hutcherson W. 1993. Dr. Hutcherson's guide to mother jokes. *Source* 4:52
86a. Jackman MR, Jackman R. 1983. *Class Awareness in the United States.* Berkeley, CA: Univ. Calif. Press
87. Jensen A. 1969. How much can we boost IQ and scholastic achievement? *Harvard Educ. Rev.* 39:1–123
88. Johnson JW. 1922. *The Book of American Negro Poetry.* New York: Harcourt, Brace
89. Jones K. 1986. Blacktalk: the controversy and color of Black speech. *Ebony Man* 9:68–69
90. Jones R. 1982. What's wrong with Black English. *Newsweek* Dec. 27:7
91. Jordan J. 1973. White English: the politics of language. *Black World* 22(10):4–10
92. Joseph JE, Taylor TJ. 1990. *Ideologies of Language.* London: Routledge
93. Kochman T. 1972. *Rappin' and Stylin' Out: Communication in Urban Black America.* Urbana: Univ. Ill. Press
94. Kochman T. 1972. Toward an ethnography of Black American speech behavior. See Ref. 93, pp. 241–64
95. Kochman T. 1973. Review of language behavior in a black urban community by Claudia Mitchell-Kernan. *Language* 49(4): 967–83
96. Kochman T. 1981. *Black and White Styles in Conflict.* Chicago: Univ. Chicago Press
97. Kochman T. 1983. The boundary between play and nonplay in Black verbal dueling. *Lang. Soc.* 12(3):329–37
98. Kochman T. 1986. Strategic ambiguity in Black speech genres: cross-cultural interference in participant-observation research. *Text* 6(2):153–70
99. Krapp G. 1924. The English of the Negro. *Am. Mercury* 2:190–95
100. Kronus S. 1970. Some neglected aspects of Negro class comparison. *Phylon* 31(4): 359–71
101. Kroskrity P, Schieffelin B, Woolard K. 1992. Language ideologies. *Pragmatics* 2(3):235–453 (Special Issue)
102. Kurath H. 1928. The origin of dialectal differences in spoken American English. *Mod. Philol.* 25:285–95
103. Labov W. 1966. *The Social Stratification of*

English in New York City. Washington, DC: Cent. Appl. Linguist.

104. Labov W. 1969. Contraction and deletion and inherent variability of the English copula. *Language* 45:715–62

105. Labov W. 1972. *Language in the Inner City. Studies in the Black English Vernacular.* Philadelphia: Univ. Penn. Press

106. Labov W. 1972. Rules for ritual insult. See Ref. 93, pp. 265–314

107. Labov W. 1977. *Sociolinguistic Patterns.* Philadelphia: Univ. Penn. Press

108. Deleted in proof

109. Labov W. 1980. Is there a creole speech community? Theoretical orientations in creole studies. In *Theoretical Orientations in Creole Study,* ed. A Valdman, A Highfield, pp. 369–88. New York: Academic

110. Labov W. 1982. Objectivity and commitment in linguistic science: the case of the Black English trial in Ann Arbor. *Lang. Soc.* 11:165–201

111. Labov W. 1987. Are black and white vernaculars diverging? See Ref. 7, pp. 5–12, 62–74

112. Labov W, Cohen P, Robins C, Lewis J. 1968. *A Study of the Non Standard English of Negro and Puerto Rican Speakers in New York City.* USOE Final Rep., No. 3288. Philadelphia: US Regional Surv.

113. Labov W, Harris W. 1986. De facto segregation of black and white vernaculars. See Ref. 158, pp. 1–24

114. LePage RB, Tabouret-Keller A. 1985. *Acts of Identity: Creole Based Approaches to Language and Ethnicity.* Cambridge: Cambridge Univ. Press

115. Levine L. 1977. *Black Culture and Black Consciousness.* Oxford: Oxford Univ. Press

116. Lindstrom L. 1992. Context contests: debatable truth statements on Tanna (Vanuata). In *Rethinking Context,* ed. A Duranti, pp. 101–24. Cambridge: Cambridge Univ. Press

117. Locke A, ed. 1974. *The New Negro.* New York: Atheneum

118. Luelsdorff P, ed. 1975. *Linguistic Perspectives on Black English.* Regensburg, Germany: Verlag Hans Carl

119. Luelsdorff P. 1975. *A Segmental Phonology of Black English.* The Hague: Mouton

120. Martin Luther King Junior Elementary School Children et al vs Ann Arbor School District Board. 1979. US Dist. Court East. Dist. Mich., South. Div. No. 77186

121. McDavid R, ed. 1963. *The American Language by H.L. Mencken (with the assistance of DW Maurer).* New York: Knopf

122. McDavid RI, McDavid VG. 1951. The relationship of the speech of American Negroes to the speech of whites. *Am. Speech* 26:3–17

123. Mencken HL. 1977. *The American Language: An Inquiry Into the Development of English in the United States.* New York: Knopf. 4th ed.

124. Mintz S. 1970. Foreword. In *Afro-American Anthropology: Contemporary Perspectives,* ed. N Whitten, J Szwed, pp. 1–15. New York: Free Press

125. Mitchell-Kernan C. 1971. *Language Behavior in a Black Urban Community.* Monogr. Lang. Behav. Lab., No. 2. Univ. Calif., Berkeley

126. Mitchell-Kernan C. 1972. Signifying, loud-talking, and marking. See Ref. 93, pp. 315–35

127. Mitchell-Kernan C. 1972. On the status of Black English for native speakers: an assessment of attitudes and values. In *Functions of Language in the Classroom,* ed. C Cazden, V John, D Hymes, pp. 195–210. New York: Teachers College Press

128. Mitchell-Kernan C. 1973. Signifying. In *Mother Wit From The Laughing Barrel,* ed. A Dundes, pp. 310–28. New York: Garland

129. Morgan M. 1989. *From down south to up south: the language behavior of three generations of black women residing in Chicago.* PhD Diss. Univ. Penn

130. Morgan M. 1991. Indirectness and interpretation in African American women's discourse. *Pragmatics* 1(4):421–52

131. Morgan M. 1991. Language and communication style among African American women. *UCLA Cent. Stud. Women Newsl.* 7(Spring):13

132. Morgan M. 1993. The Africanness of counterlanguage among Afro-Americans. In *Africanisms in Afro-American Language Varieties,* ed. S Mufwene, pp. 423–35. Athens: Univ. Georgia Press

133. Morgan M. 1993. *Hip Hop Hooray!: The linguistic production of identity.* Presented at Annu. Meet. Am. Anthropol. Assoc., 92nd, Washington, DC

134. Morgan M. 1994. The African American speech community: reality and sociolinguistics. In *The Social Construction of Reality in Creole Situations,* ed. M Morgan, pp. 121–50. Los Angeles: Cent. Afr. Am. Stud.

135. Morgan M. 1993. *Conversational signifying: grammar and indirectness among African American women.* Presented at Interaction and Grammar Workshop, Univ. Calif., Los Angeles, March 5–6

136. Morrison T. 1994. *Nobel Lecture in Literature 1993.* New York: Knopf

136a. Moynihan DP. 1965. *The Negro Family: The Case for National Action.* Washington, DC: US Govt. Print. Office

137. Mufwene S. 1983. *Some observations on the verb in Black English vernacular.* Afr.

Afro-Am. Stud. Res. Cent. Pap. Ser. 2. Austin: Univ. Texas

138. Mufwene S. 1992. Ideology and facts on African American English. *Pragmatics* 2(2):141–66

139. Mufwene S. 1992. Why grammars are not monolithic. In *The Joy of Grammar: A Festschrift in Honor of James D. McCawley,* ed. D Brentari, GN Larson, LA Macleod, pp. 225–50. Amsterdam: Benjamins

140. Mufwene S. 1994. African-American English. In *The Cambridge History of the English Language,* Vol. 6, ed. J Algeo. Cambridge: Cambridge Univ. Press. In press

141. Myhill J, Harris W. 1986. The use of verbal -s inflection in BEV. See Ref. 158, pp. 25–32

142. Myrdal G. 1944. *An American Dilemma: The Negro Problem and Modern Democracy.* New York: Harper & Row

143. Nelson J. 1993. *Volunteer Slavery: My Authentic Negro Experience.* Chicago: Noble

144. Ochs E. 1979. Transcription as theory. In *Developmental Pragmatics,* ed. E Ochs, B Scheiffelin, pp. 43–72. New York: Academic

145. Pfaff C. 1971. *Historical and Structural Aspects of Sociolinguistic variation: The Copula in Black English.* Inglewood, CA: SW Reg. Lab.

146. Rauch EN. 1991. Paul Lawrence Dunbar 1872–1906. In *African American Writers,* ed. V Smith, pp. 87–102. New York: Scribner

147. Deleted in proof

148. Richardson C. 1991. Habitual structure among blacks and whites in the 1990s. *Am. Speech* 66:92–302

149. Rickford J. 1977. The question of prior creolization of Black English. In *Pidgin and Creole Linguistics,* ed. A Valdman, pp. 190–221. Bloomington: Ind. Univ. Press

150. Rickford J. 1985. Ethnicity as a sociolinguistic boundary. *Am. Speech* 60(2):99–124

151. Rickford J. 1986. The need for new approaches to social class analysis in sociolinguistics. *Lang. Commun.* 6(3):215–21

151a. Rickford J. 1986. Social contact and linguistic diffusion: Hiberno English and New World Black English. *Language* 62(2): 245–89

152. Rickford J. 1992. Grammatical variation and divergence in vernacular Black English. In *Internal and External Factors in Syntactic Change,* ed. M Gerristen, D Stein, *Stud. Monogr.* 61:175–200. The Hague: Mouton

153. Rickford J, Ball A, Blake R, Jackson R, Martin N. 1991. Rappin on the copula coffin: theoretical and methodological issues in the analysis of copula variation in African American vernacular. *Lang. Var. Change* 3(1):103–32

154. Rickford J, McNair-Knox F. 1993. Addressee and topic-influenced-style shift: a quantitative sociolinguistic study. In *Perspectives on Register: Situating Register Variation Within Sociolinguistics,* ed. D Biber, E Finegan, pp. 235–76. Oxford: Oxford Univ. Press

155. Rossi-Landi F. 1983. *Language as Work & Trade: A Semiotic Homology for Linguistics and Economics.* South Hadley, MA: Bergin & Garvey

156. Sampson W, Milam V. 1975. The interracial attitudes of the Black middle-class: Have they changed? *Soc. Probl.* 23(2):151–65

157. Samuel 17X. 1975. Analysts warn about pitfalls of "Black" English. *Bilalian News* 10:22

158. Sankoff D, ed. 1986. *Diversity and Diachrony.* Amsterdam: Benjamins

159. Schieffelin B, Ochs E. 1986. *Language Socialization Across Cultures.* Cambridge: Cambridge univ. Press

160. Schneider E. 1989. *American Earlier Black English.* Tuscaloosa: Univ. Ala. Press

161. Scott D. 1991. That event, this memory: notes on the anthropology of African diasporas in the new world. *Diaspora* 1(3): 261–84

162. Smith E. 1976. *Correspondence to Brother Lawrence X.* 11 pp.

163. Smitherman G. 1977. *Talkin' and Testifyin': The Language of Black America.* Boston: Houghton Miflin

164. Smitherman G. 1981. "What go round come round": King in perspective. *Harvard Educ. Rev.* 1:40–56

165. Smitherman G. 1981. *Black English and the Education of Black Children and Youth—Proceedings of the National Invitational Symposium on the King Decision.* Detroit: Harpo

166. Spears A. 1982. The semi-auxiliary come in Black English vernacular. *Language* 58: 850–72

167. Spears A. 1988. Black American English. In *Anthropology for the Nineties: Introductory Readings,* ed. J Cole, pp. 96–113. New York: Free Press

168. Stanback MH. 1986. Language and black woman's place: evidence from the black middle class. In *For Alma Mater: Theory and Practice in Feminist Scholarship,* ed. PA Treichlet, C Kramare, B Stafford, pp. 177–96. Urbana: Univ. Ill. Press

169. Stewart W. 1967. Sociolinguistic factors in the history of American Negro dialects. *Fla. FL Report.* 5:11

170. Stewart W. 1968. Continuity and change in American Negro dialects. *Fla. FL Report.* 6:3–4, 14–16, 18

171. Stewart W. 1969. Historical and structural

bases for the recognition of Negro dialect. In *School of Languages and Linguistics Monogr. Ser. No. 22,* ed. J Alatis, pp. 215–25. Washington, DC: Georgetown Univ. Press

172. Stewart W. 1975. Teaching blacks to read against their will. See Ref. 118, pp. 107–32

173. Stuckey S. 1971. Twilights of our past: reflections on the origins of Black history. In *Amistad 2,* ed. JA Williams, CF Harris, pp. 261–95. New York: Vintage

174. Stuckey S. 1987. *Slave Culture: Nationalist Theory and the Foundation of Black America.* Oxford: Oxford Univ. Press

175. Szwed J. 1974. An American anthropological dilemma: the politics of African-American culture. In *Reinventing Anthropology,* ed. D Hymes, pp. 153–81. New York: Vintage

176. Taylor O. 1975. Black language and what to do about it. In *Ebonics: The True Language of Black Folks,* ed. R Williams, pp. 28–39. St Louis: Robert Williams

177. Tolliver-Weddington G. 1979. Introduction: Ebonics (Black English): implications for education. *J. Black Stud.* 9(4):364–66

178. Triandis HC, ed. 1976. *Variations in Black and White Perceptions of the Social Environment.* Urbana: Univ. Ill. Press

179. Turner L. 1949. *Africanism in the Gullah Dialect.* Chicago: Univ. Chicago Press

180. Vaughn-Cooke F. 1987. Contribution to NWAV-14 Panel Discussion "Are Black and White Vernaculars Diverging." *J. Am. Speech* 62(1) (Special Issue)

181. Volosinov VN. 1986/1929. *Marxism and the Philosophy of Language.* Cambridge, MA: Harvard Univ. Press

182. Williamson J. 1970. Selected features of speech: black and white. *Coll. Lang. Assoc. J.* 13(4):420–23

183. Williamson J. 1971. A look at Black English. *Crisis* 78:169–73

184. Willis W. 1970. Anthropology and Negroes on the southern colonial frontier. In *The Black Experience in America,* ed. JC Curtis, LL Gould, pp. 33–50. Austin: Univ. Texas Press

185. Willis W. 1973. Franz Boas and the study of Black folklore. In *The New Ethnicity: Perspectives from Ethnography,* ed. JW Bennett, pp. 307–34. St. Paul: West

186. Wilson WJ. 1978. *The Declining Significance of Race.* Chicago: Univ. Chicago Press

187. Wilson WJ. 1987. *The Truly Disadvantaged.* Chicago: Univ. Chicago Press

188. Winford D. 1990. Copula variability, accountability and the concept of "polylectal" grammars. *J. Pidgin Creole Lang.* 5(2):223–52

189. Winford D. 1992. Another look at the copula in Black English and Caribbean Creoles. *Am. Speech* 67(1):21–60

190. Winfrey O. 1987. *Standard and Black English. The Oprah Winfrey Show.* Transcr. No. W309. Nov. 19, WLS-TV

191. Wolfram W. 1969. *A Sociolinguistic Description of Detroit Negro Speech.* Washington, DC: Cent. Appl. Linguist.

192. Wolfram W. 1971. Black-White speech differences revisited. *Viewpoints* 47:27–50

193. Woolard K, Schieffelin B. 1994. Language ideology. *Annu. Rev. Anthropol.* 23:55–82

194. Yankah K. 1991. Power and the circuit of formal talk. *J. Folk. Res.* 28(1):1–22

Annu. Rev. Anthropol. 1994. 23:347–77

LAND AND CULTURE IN TROPICAL AFRICA: Soils, Symbols, and the Metaphysics of the Mundane

Parker Shipton

Harvard Institute for International Development, and Department of Anthropology, Harvard University, Cambridge, Massachusetts 02138

KEY WORDS: land tenure, agriculture, pastoralism, kinship, sexuality, religion

A NEW PROMISCUITY

A wall is coming down in the anthropology of Africa. Symbolic and ecological concerns, for decades treated as the separate provinces of different kinds of scholars, have lately been coursing into each other, exciting a sense of discovery mixed with trepidation. Although the new work revisits some old themes, it makes it clearer than ever that religion, ritual, and cognition, on the one hand, and adaptation, sustenance, and production, on the other, cannot be kept pure of each other. Landholding is at the center of the confluence. Nothing evokes more varied symbolic connotations or more intricate legal philosophies. Nothing excites deeper passions or gives rise to more bloodshed than do disagreements about territory, boundaries, or access to land resources. Nor is anything more likely to prevent misunderstandings across cultures, harmful to both humans and their habitat, than are thoughtful definitions of landholding in the first place.

Anthropologists' interest in land issues sharpened in the late 1980s, for the first time since most African countries' colonial periods ended in the early 1960s, and many more authors have written on these issues than this brief review cites. The anthropology of the 1980s and early 1990s, captivated by

0084-6570/94/1015-0347$05.00

political economy, local-supralocal relations, and cultural complexity, among other things, looked hard into struggles for resource control and processes of expropriation and resistance. An aspect of these contests and of landholding more broadly is interpretive, concerning unannounced meanings and contested identities of persons, places, and things. Many of these meanings revolve around links between human and terrestrial fertility. In this review I outline and comment on just a few trends in culturally informed writings on rural landholding in the vast area roughly bounded by the Tropics of Cancer and Capricorn. Although the region's ecosystems range from desert to rainforest, my emphasis is on more heavily settled farming and herding zones between.

Three triangles frame the topic. First, land produces nothing without water, labor, capital, or all three. Second, people seek in land not just material satisfaction but also power, wealth, and meaning—their aims, that is, can be political, economic, and cultural. Finally, people relate to land not just as individuals, but also as members of groups, networks, and categories. In just about any inhabited part of Africa, one finds multiple ways of getting access to land and justifying claims to it. Some of these are birthright, first settlement, conquest, residence, cultivation, habitual grazing visitation, manuring, tree planting, spiritual sanction, bureaucratic allocation, loan, rental, and cash purchase. Several of these principles are usually at play, but the ones involving markets and states have lately received the most attention. Although distribution of landholdings in Africa has so far been more equitable than in any other continent in the tropics, most contemporary observers have perceived bureaucratic, commercial, or other processes increasingly concentrating land into fewer hands. And these processes always have social and cultural dimensions.

The literature on landholding includes a number of broad reviews with different emphases (e.g. 10, 22, 26, 126, 206, 234, 265). Also noteworthy are several classic general surveys (7, 10, 30, 87, 120, 190) and broad contemporary collections in English (15, 27, 72, 76, 78, 236) and in French (64, 66, 162–164, 286, 287). Strictly urban issues (see 17, 133, 178, 218, 222, 287) must await another review, though I discuss some country-city connections involved in rural land tenure.

CLASSIC AND RECURRING THEMES

How one defines and translates land in posing a question always affects the answer. Land can mean soil and sand, a piece of a map, a political power base, an aspect of divinity, or a resource to be exploited. How many dimensions (37, 65; see also 2) and what minerals, plants, animals, buildings, and people it includes varies from culture to culture, and from language to language. Who gets to control the language, the translations, the mapping, the demarcations? These controls legitimize or delegitimize units of aggregation, kinds of rights, or ways of land use, or they justify appropriations and expropriations (15, 109, 164, 211, 226).

If land can be hard to define in tropical Africa, landholding or tenure is harder still. The continent is infinitely diverse and dynamic, and as Herskovitz wrote in 1940, "the variety of forms of land tenure that can exist at a given time among a people is seldom recognized" (131:343). During the 1940s and 1950s numerous well-known anthropologists (including I. Schapera, C.K. Meek, P.C. Lloyd, and P.H. Gulliver) helped codify what were deemed the customary laws of particular ethnic groups for colonial administrators variously trying to preserve or, more often, to Europeanize them. By the late 1960s, these anthropologists and diverse others like A. Richards (233), Colson (57), P. Bohannan (37), Beattie (18), Gluckman (106, 107), and Mair (182)— and the Africans informing them—had established several points that keep reappearing in African landholding studies. African tenures (the plural indicates different understandings of human attachments to land) are neither communalistic nor individualistic in essence. Overlapping and interlocking rights in land are part of whatever a people deem their social fabric, whether woven around kinship, bureaucratic hierarchy, age grading, or other principles (57)— this fact has long been considered the essence of African tenures. The relevant group depends on the use: individual or family farming commonly yields to others' grazing or thatch or firewood collection between cropping seasons. "Bundles of rights" and nested "hierarchies of estates" (106) are familiar themes, and access to land for one purpose may not imply access to it for another. And whether rosy-spectacled or not, anthropologists' interlocutors in countless tropical African settings have long insisted that the living hold the land in trust—in some cultures, a sacred trust—for the dead and the yet unborn.

Ever since Bohannan pulled apart the concept of land tenure in 1963 (37), and Gluckman described Rotse property law as defining "not so much the rights of persons over things as the duties between persons in respect of things" (106:136), anthropologists have perceived in African land tenure not ownership per se, but instead, rights and duties of use, transfer, and administration; of access, occupation, and reversionary control. These combine in ways that tend to differ from property or ownership (180) as conventionally understood in Europe or North America (27, 41, 169, 198, 199, 211–213, 287). Words like tenancy, possession, feudalism, secure title, and even rights and duties, if translatable at all, can impose alien assumptions or emotional charges on African tenures. Legal language implying human mastery over land misfits some peoples who speak of it more often the other way around.

Meek's Lockean aphorism that "labour creates rights" (190:24) applies better, I find, to men than to women. In tropical Africa most farm labor remains family labor in one way or another, and on the whole, female hands do more of it than do male—a rule with local exceptions (27, 28; see also 104, 274). Most of the continent's female farmers work on land under rights deemed dependent on or ancillary to those of males, though many recent writings depict women as investing much energy and creativity to gain more control over land (e.g. 15, 43, 72, 108, 129, 172, 216, 240).

Whether land is a commodity is an old and thorny problem (11, 15, 78, 109). Here historically debarred from sale, here redeemable if sold, here pledgeable but not rentable, mortgageable, or saleable; land is nearly everywhere the subject of special protective strictures in local if not also imported custom. Despite what economic development planners may think and hope, land is seldom if ever just a commodity. In fact, some tenure reforms aimed at making land marketable have made it explosive.

Egalitarianism has been a stock theme in African anthropology. But true equality is ever elusive in Africa, and egalitarian ideals often evaporate under a spotlight. What Macquet, writing on Rwanda, called a "premise of inequality" (181; cf 103) seems to take even more forms than he noted. Inequalities between ages, genders, castes, classes, religious statuses, and military ranks all tie into land inequalities in their different ways in different settings, often combining. The leveling liminal phases of some peoples' rites of passage, familiar to anthropologists since Van Gennep (77, 279, 280, 284), are the exceptions that prove the rule. They remind us, among other things, of the inequitable nature of ordinary worldly attachments.

In almost any part of agrarian tropical Africa, those who arrive first think themselves superior to latecomers. What matters is who, among the living, can persuade others to think their ancestors pioneered a place. This gives one ascendancy by what might be called a principle of pioneer primacy. Diverse tropical African class (18, 277), caste (275), and other stratification systems (83, 89, 261, 277) and their mythological charters (18, 86, 89, 186, 294) typically revolve around this principle, dichotomizing and opposing autochthons ("sons of the soil") and aliens, hosts and guests, permanents and temporaries. Host-stranger distinctions are variously political, economic, and symbolic in nature; these qualities often are perceived and manipulated differently by the parties involved. Arrangements that level status in one way can stratify it in another (109, 266).

Still, an ideal often perceived to underlie indigenous tropical tenure systems across the continent might be called fairness in flexibility. According to this principle, access to land should go to those who need and can use it, and no one should starve for special want of it, at least not within a group whose members consider themselves the same people, which usually has meant a kin group or ethnic group.

SOME BASIC RETHINKING

Structure and Process

Land rights are always political. Tributes, taxes, or reversionary rights based on landholding can prop up different kinds of leaders' political authority, but land is also an idiom for establishing or challenging power relations among almost any broader public. The literature since the 1970s treats custom and tradition about land and other things not just as incorporating conflict in their own process (106), but also as being inventable, manipulable, renegotiable, and selectively invoked to serve personal ends (15, 28, 46, 78, 105, 164, 199, 220, 249). Structure (as static sets of social rules, roles, and relationships) has seemed to many less real than has process (how these elements are handled as they change or repeat over time). Custom can differ by age, gender, or class, and it can spring from cosmopolitan capitals as well as bush hamlets. Reflecting the new emphasis on agency and manipulation, the literature on land disputes and their settlement has burgeoned, particularly it seems in eastern (e.g. 115, 123, 198, 199) and southern (48, 62, 224, 240) Africa, and comparatively (109, 122, 123). Disputes appear to multiply as rural populations grow denser, although changes in court structures and jurisdictions challenge diachronic study. Some of the most careful cultural accounts of landholding since the early 1980s have treated the evolving nature of land contests within small areas over periods of a century or more (105, 172, 199, 202, 226, 240). Time has been everything; and history, like politics, has been "in."

But this too is changing. Over the past decade anthropology has paid increasing attention to space and place along with time. In Africa, space and design have looked, to some postmodernists and others, like texts where culture and power relations could be read deconstructively (149, 160, 197; see also 159). Some authors have projected ideas like landscape or spatiality onto nongeographic things (52, 207). In another vein, ecological concerns like population densities and carrying capacities have been focused upon and tied to kinship by cultural anthropologists, archaeologists, and others. Much of this last research, like geographers' earlier work, comes unsurprisingly from the almost uniquely dense Igbo, Yoruba, and Hausa regions in Nigeria, Africa's most populous nation (203, 204, 271, 278; see also 241) and one with the full gradient from rainforest to arid land (59, 278). Much also comes from Kenya, with its dense central and western highlands, and its own broad ecological gradient. Methods rather new to cultural anthropology, like the use of systematic aerial and satellite photos, have been combined with old fashioned ethnography to study adaptive land use (118; cf 162). Detailed, interethnic regional comparisons on African landholding, seemingly almost a lost art since Pélissier's tome on agrarian peoples of Senegal (223), have reappeared in vanguard anthropological and historical literature on the African tropics (e.g. 28, 50, 172). Anthropology and geography have been flirting again.

Borders, Boundaries, and Units of Aggregation Reconsidered

Questions about the legitimacy of borders and boundaries, and about the sanctity or naturalness of the units of aggregation these delineate, have profoundly altered scholarship on land and society in tropical Africa. This rethinking has partaken of both political economy and a critical deconstructionism of the postmodern period, though the ideas need not be pitched in either's terms.

At a macro-level, African and other anthropologists have scrutinized the nation-states that Victorian Europeans etched so arbitrarily onto the continent. These "imagined communities" (8) now look more artificial or dangerous, more brittle or hopeless, than ever. Border people (13), labor migrants (50, 201, 239, 270, 273, 274), voluntary and involuntary resettlers (50, 58, 227, 260, 294), refugees (51, 124), and other crossers and in-betweeners (85, 228) have received increasing attention. The trend shall surely continue. Indeed, Africa's own boundaries as a continent and a concept have come under question.

At a meso-level, ethnolinguistic groups ("tribes" to some) and their homes and territories have been portrayed increasingly as interconnected, shifting, manipulable, or redefinable (14, 52, 252, 281, 294). New attention is being paid to heterogeneous peoples colonially cemented into blocs, like *the* Yoruba in Nigeria or *the* Luhya in Kenya, and to contested paramount and subordinate chieftaincies (78). In many of these nested polities, struggles over land custom and jurisdiction are also ethnic identity struggles. Communities are now defined not just by territorial or administrative units but also, or even instead, by social affiliations and migration linkages, as in diasporas of home townmates. Villages tend to mean different things in West Africa, where nucleated settlements are more common, than in eastern and southern Africa, where scattered homesteads are more the rule.

Clans, Lineages, and their Nine Lives

Lineages and their lands are battlegrounds in gender wars, and sometimes in age wars. Some authors overgeneralize unilineal descent groups to the whole continent. More than a few authorities (e.g. 52, 158) have deemed clans and lineages an outworn anthropological model, an opinion with which some hopeful feminists who feel trapped in patrilineal, virilocal cultures would concur (72). Someone is always blasting at the concept of lineages, but the idea keeps appearing, in both insiders' and outsiders' minds—and in places, with striking clarity, on land maps superimposed with genealogies. What to think of it?

First, lineages are not important everywhere in tropical Africa. Nor is the continent sharply divided into unilineal and nonunilineal peoples (141, 230). Land can pass down the generations along different lines from names, offices, group ascriptions, or movable property; lineages can refer to some of these without others. Second, lineages are facts and fictions (15, 199; see also 105, 220), though not everywhere in the same measures. In some settings, lineages and clans exist more as ideological constructs than as settlement patterns, as in the Nuer case (81; see also 154, 244, 269). But they are facts both in local ideology and in settlement patterns in some areas of land scarcity and competition in eastern (105, 121, 155, 199, 262, 266, 269) and western Africa (36, 88, 248, 249; cf 171, 253). Not even in these areas, though, are lineages fully localized or wholly discrete in their territories: people move in and out as borrowers, land clients, or quasi-members. Although many anthropologists perceive technical distinctions between clans and lineages (for instance, in whether living members can trace all the genealogical links connecting them to a founder at the apex, or whether the group is spatially cohesive), the anglophone African public frequently prefers to use the term clan more generally to include what foreign-trained anthropologists call lineages. Maximal, major, minor, and minimal lineages (88) are a purely heuristic gradation not readily suited to comparison across cultures, since different societies' descent groups vary not just in size but also in kind and in meaning. This is particularly true in land matters.

Agnatic lineages may serve men's interests more than women's, and there is a kind of cultural fit (for better or worse) between lineage organization and bridewealth in some contexts south of the Sahara (see 112, 121, 220). But these are not just men's ideas. Landholding lineages, where found, also have their ironies. In systems deemed patrilineal, farmland commonly passes from mothers-in-law to daughters-in-law in its real usage. Virilocal patterns, on close inspection, sometimes conceal uxorilocal land clientage. In matrilineal areas including the variegated "matrilineal belt" crossing central and southern Africa from Congo to Mozambique, and also including the Akan region of southern Ghana, allocative rights or jural authority commonly devolve from mother's brother to sister's son (230). In unilineal systems as well as ambilineal (139) and bilineal ones (103), tropical Africans tend to keep male and female sorts of property (which may or may not include land) sharply discrete in inheritance or devolution *inter vivos* (110, 112). And like others everywhere, they sometimes contravene their own land inheritance norms (253). But these norms aren't timeless—a point to which we return.

Continuing down to the most micro-levels, households and farms also have been radically reconceived. These units are lately understood to be porous, interlinked, or shifting social nexuses, or as foreign notions that never really applied well to African multi-house extended family homesteads or quasi-family compounds (109, 116, 117, 119, 195, 205, 239). Female-headed hearth-holds, or domestic groups that can be independent or within polygynous groups, and that may hold their own lands, have become foci of analysis in their own right (72, 119).

Space within homes or domestic compounds is typically differentiated by gender and age. This too becomes political. A wave of cultural-architectural studies (see 160) inspired by Foucault (92), Bourdieu (39), S. Ardener (12), and others (e.g. 65, 197; see also 85a, 159, 218) analyzes the dominant inter-pretations imposed by power, showing, for example, how the placement of houses, graves, and refuse can symbolically denigrate women. That many women play along with these spatial orders, as they play along with patriliny, some analysts put down to mystification or male hegemony. This last point is debatable by nature. Although women may take part in their own subordina-tion by having to communicate in a biased idiom, an accumulation of practical actions that instantiate or dramatize new spatial symbolics might gradually subvert a repressive cultural order (60, 65, 72, 172, 197).

Contemporary scholarship should not be content merely to torch all con-ventional units of aggregation, like nation, lineage, or household, as terms and concepts. Some are still needed, and they keep arising from the ashes anyway. Once a critical perspective is gained, the aim instead should be to remain pluralistically open-minded about self-defined spaces and memberships—of groups, networks, or categories.

ADAPTING TO DENSITY AND LAND SHORTAGE

Evolutionary Theories Revised

Land tenure relates persons to other persons or to things. Whereas most British structural-functionalists of the late colonial and early independent periods played up the social dimension of tenure relations, and played down the ecological or technological ones, other anthropologists have treated land ten-ure both ways more equally, as person-person and person-thing relations. Research in the past two decades has challenged many older conceptions of evolution and adaptation in land use.

To begin with some of the most sparsely settled areas, Kalahari peoples including the San groups, once lumped as hunter-gatherers ("Bushmen"), have been portrayed recently as socio-politically complex and heterogeneous people deliberately marginalized to inferior lands and livelihoods, rather than as rem-nants of an earlier stage of human evolution—a hotly debated question that may have more than one right answer (296; cf 113, 165, 297). Here as else-where (e.g. Efe in Zaire, Twa in Rwanda, Hadza in Tanzania), hunter-gatherers have tended to become servant, laborer, or outcast underclasses—altogether less romantic. Pastoralism and the different kinds of territoriality it can involve (79) are no longer assumed to be primeval hangovers either. Mixed livelihoods (e.g. farming, herding, trading, wage labor migration) and multiple income streams for families have become more standard suppositions (195, 196).

Denser settlements mean altered livelihoods. Updating earlier geographical studies on concomitants of densities (157, 229), and economists' debates about the relative factor efficiencies of production (38, 183), anthropologists have shown that individual and collective strategies of settlement and agricultural technique tend to change predictably with demographic growth. These strategies do so as causes or effects of growth, or as parallel effects of other factors. According to the Malthusian view, high human fertility reduces the land's fertility, thus threatening human population. But this logic is not accepted universally. Demographic growth can also stimulate agricultural labor and production. Large farms are not necessarily more efficient than small ones. What counts as efficiency depends on the factor of production (e.g. land, labor, capital) used as the gauge, and on what kinds of mechanization the topography and climate permit (204). The question also depends on family labor availability, and this means it ties tightly into kinship, neighborly exchange, and contract labor.

For any level of settlement density, the most efficient agricultural techniques and the best-adapted social systems depend partly on where soil fertility comes from. Swidden, sedentary rainfed, irrigated, and flood recession farming all require different modes of field rotation and support different population densities, and thus fit best with particular kinds of family or compound labor organization, though every rule has its exceptions (204, 205, 235, 243, 278). Shifting or swidden cultivation, which is often found in low agrarian densities, can be more efficient than sedentary farming in terms of labor use and weed and pest control. As land becomes short, movements up mountainsides (199), into swamps (125a, 172), or into lands cleared of diseases (189) may precede, follow, or forestall efforts to intensify production on land already in use.

Intensification need not always entail hybrid seed and chemical packages, but it usually means more use of scarce labor or capital. Switching from grains toward bulky root and tuber crops can help denser populations sustain themselves, though not necessarily at high levels of nutrition. Intercropping, shortened fallows, crop rotation, terracing, manuring, mulching, irrigation, herd restructuring (within or across species), and foddering are among the techniques used to conserve land or intensify its use as agrarian densities rise—whether such practices allow higher densities to begin with or arise in response to them (31, 65, 204, 234, 235, 243, 278, 291). The animal-drawn plow was known to tropical Africa only in Ethiopia until this century but is now widespread. Animal or mechanical plowing can release human labor, but it also can sharpen competition for arable land (291). It may alter the relative values of male and female labor and thus is likely to affect marriage payments and inheritance (112). But densities, competition for land, and the value of labor are always conditioned by off-farm incomes. A concept like carrying capacity or demographic pressure on land makes little sense, on the small scale or large, unless migrations and remittances are taken into account.

Settlement densities and social organization have much to do with each other. Old assumptions (200) about lineages and clans as a primordial social order of sparse populations that yield to chiefdoms and states under rising population densities have been seriously challenged in much of Africa. Hierarchical, statelike forms of political organization turn out, at least in much of agrarian eastern and southern Africa, to have corresponded historically with shifting agriculture and easier rural mobility. In many places where lineages or clans are discernible on the landscape, bureaucratic polities preceded these; in others, lineages or clans have long coexisted with these polities. Rising densities seem to have corresponded with changes in kinship systems, from non-unilineal to patrilineal (262; see also 204), from matrilineal to patrilineal, and much less commonly it seems, from unilineal to nonunilineal. A tendency to cluster in lineage-based settlements, however old the idea may be, seems now to be a quite contemporary adaptation to competition for land (244, 262; see also 271). Mbeere of Kenya and others are reported to have broadened lineages to protect and extend members' claims under colonially and nationally defined concepts of what is customary (105; see also 21, 27, 28).

Rising population pressure, labor-saving technology like the plow, and high-value cash cropping intervene in the relation between demographic densities and kinship. These factors can militate for stronger individual rights over land, and countless indeed are the observers who have reported this happening. But such a process does not occur necessarily, inexorably, or irreversibly (28, 78). In some densely settled areas, for instance in western Kenya, where rural homes mean social identities as well as production bases, rural people who sell off other lands still cling to their houses and the land on which these stand.

As densities rise, farming with shade trees or alley crops can help intensify production. But it can also intensify some kinds of disputes (e.g. between male tree farmers and female ground farmers; 257). Tropical African understandings of tree rights differ broadly from Anglo-American legal ones in that land, trees, and even fruits on the trees are more frequently claimed by different people (90, 91, 231; see also 191, on Zanzibar; 220, on palms on the Kenya coast; 1, 94, on Nigeria; 28, 209, on cocoa in Ghana; 24, 96, 97, 223, 268, on Senegal; 28, 239, comparative). Planting trees means planting land rights too; hence, in many places, there are stiff rules and bitter disputes about tree planting as claim-staking by land borrowers or clients. Tree rights may not amount to individual property. They can proliferate to different people over time through inheritance, migration, share contracting, or contrary interpretations of history by witnesses (21, 28).

Detailed studies of sharecropping and other share contracting in tropical African settings (71, 239, 273, 274; see also 134) have shown that whatever exploitation these terms may connote, they can help even out imbalances between land, labor, and capital endowments of domestic and larger groups, at least temporarily. The flexibility of year-by-year contracts allows important adjustments as family and farm circumstances change. This does not imply social egalitarianism, of course, because sharecropping can perpetuate micro-level dependencies and can involve rigid status distinctions. Sharecroppers' rights over the land they farm may or may not gradually solidify into more permanent rights (28, 239).

Demographic growth often seems to spur crop innovation (38, 204, 243, 278), but not always, since it can squeeze farmers out of farming. Land shortage and related capital investment may widen class inequalities (162–164, 285), but richer farmers who buy out smaller ones are often using capital from urban and other off-farm sources and aiming to reinvest profits in town (28, 128, 211). Still poorly understood is how African farming peoples adapt their own modes of land tenure and share contracting to new corporate contract farming, which combines the farmer's land and labor with an agribusiness' or state enterprise's capital or material inputs. This kind of arrangement is replacing the large plantation system for many crops and in many countries, with mixed results (42, 43, 74, 175).

At the densely settled end of the spectrum, substantial amounts of small-scale farming and even foraging go on in and around some African cities. Rural land poverty and landlessness helps force migrations into the same or other predicaments in cities. Circular town-country migrations complicate the picture further. Much of the new research is humbling to evolutionists who assume everyone is or should be moving toward states, markets, contracts, individualism, or impersonal rule of law. Emerging, I venture to hope, is a lateral kind of evolutionism that does not presume upward or downward progress. It should also be an a-teleological evolutionism, a nonracial kind without presumptions about progress toward statehood, or toward socialism or capitalism.

Farmers, Herders, and Farmer-herders

Recent scholarship complicates distinctions among hunter-gatherers, herders, farmers, and others. Most of Africa's herders also farm or do other things, simultaneously or intermittently, and people who do either may also hunt or gather in famines. The categories blur, even in the arid, scarcely farmed, peri-Saharan areas; or in the humid tsetse zones of central, and coastal western Africa where large livestock cannot survive.

Small-scale farmers in Africa guard against risks by diversifying their lands and what they grow—up to a point. They may keep fragmented landholdings (23), farm thin strips stretching from dry uplands to wet valleys, keep multiple crops and animal species with different maturation cycles (65, 147, 196), or live on much else besides farming and herding in the first place. Land consolidation and development programs that have not respected these patterns have usually failed, as countless studies suggest.

If diversity is the essence of small-scale farming, mobility is the essence of herding. Whether in the Sahel, the Serengeti, or the Kalahari, herders need to move their animals to survive as herders (16, 99, 100, 137, 143, 156, 166). Few can predict where it will rain on these landscapes, but herds, unlike crops, can move to where it has rained. Different ethnic or sub-ethnic groups who pass their animals temporarily through the same transition zones often coordinate their movements subtly and delicately. Transhumant herders know an iron rule: to prevent overgrazing and overbrowsing, they must be able to disperse herds away from concentrated dry-season grazing grounds when the wet season comes. Those who purport to help plan those peoples' futures, and to impose regulations about "vacant" or "ownerless" lands, must learn this rule.

Pastoralists are not necessarily at fault for overgrazing (173, 174). Herding strategies that appear to threaten grazing grounds have often proved on closer examination to be sensible and conservationist in some ways (on western Africa, 101, 156, 272; on eastern Africa, 95, 150; on southern Africa, 136, 137; on Africa generally, 9, 16, 32, 33, 143, 147, 151). Some of the research even suggests that heavier grazing can sometimes boost growth of particular plant species. Farming and grazing strategies that are individually sensible can be collectively destructive, and vice versa. Commons or group-based land management are not the same as open access and do not always lead to a free-for-all "tragedy of the commons" (40, 161, 187, 192, 214, 225; cf 125). Where herders do appear to overgraze, they have usually been driven into it by land encroachments, structural poverty, and unfair policies.

State and international developers' attempts to sedentarize herding peoples (described in 16, 22), fence them into "managed rangeland" projects (98, 247, 293), or focus them around deep new borehole wells (109, 224–226) usually have been based on mistaken presumptions about what pastoralists want to maximize or optimize. Often at root are urban bureaucrats' desires to strengthen control over these people—to count, police, or tax them. In country after country, such programs have nearly always failed and caused misery or perversely sped up ecological degradation (16, 22, 95, 143, 147, 166, 210, 247, 272).

Why Farmers and Herders Clash So Much

In Africa's main agropastoral zones, people who depend on herding for their main livelihoods and identities have clashed frequently, often violently, with those who depend on farming—no matter that many herders farm and farmers herd. Such strife has been analyzed in the Sahel (e.g. 15, 63, 101, 143, 256, 267), in eastern Africa (173), and in southern Africa (293; cf 250). These farmer-herder conflicts, paralleled in other continents, are in many African cases ethnic (e.g. between Gusii farmers and Maasai herders in Kenya or between Tswana farmers and Herero herders in Botswana) and, sometimes, religious (e.g. between Wolof farmers and Fulani herders in eastern Senegal). Typically, in these contested areas, farmers delimiting spaces for cropping have neglected to leave access routes for herders to pass through; and herders, assuming such routes to be natural rights, have, willingly or not, allowed their animals to trample or eat those crops. What the farmers see as turf disputes, the herders see as trail disputes.

There are more subtle reasons for the clashes as well. The farming populations tend to be far more densely settled than transhumant or nomadic herding ones, and geometric population growth widens the gap, giving both incentives and advantages to encroaching farmers. Another reason is migratory drift. Sahelian land desiccation and drought force pastoralists and semi-pastoralists south for water (6, 15, 101; see also 217, 272). Although cattle, camels, sheep, and goats can thrive on land too poor to farm, rising densities force farmers to reclassify poorer and poorer land as arable. What tilts farmers into conflict with herders, then, are often both demographic and conceptual shifts.

State intervention tips the balance itself. When graziers, monitoring milk yields, reclass desiccating grazing land as useless, official classifications like "rangeland" remain unchanged. It is people of farming rather than herding societies that make up, and feed, most African governments. Herders, for their part, are more likely than cultivators to need to cross national borders, if only to pasture or trade animals. Not coincidentally, African governments have usually sided with farmers, further fueling herder-state antagonism (16, 66, 143, 156, 163, 164). Enlightened, pluralistic land administration can help prevent herder-farmer clashes (and herder-tourist ones as well) by ensuring that potential tracks are left open for migration routes that shift as circumstances change. Centralized governmental attempts to gazette and police forest or wildlife land have seldom kept graziers, woodcutters, farmers, or poachers out.

How people make their livelihood has much to do with how they perceive and interpret space from the outset. Hunter-gatherers and nomadic or transhumant pastoralists appear less apt to interpret land as bounded or boundable territory than are, say, densely settled farmers or bureaucrats from farming societies. Gabbra camel nomads of the Ethiopian-Kenyan borderlands, for instance, imbue landscape with meanings of ritual topography linking holy sites, pilgrimage routes, myths, times of year, identities within initiation cycles, and concepts of community (16, 65, 252). Most important for mobile pastoralists are access routes—one-dimensional paths or tracks—and water points that to a foreigner are mere dots on a map (65; see also 2). Two- or three-dimensional territories, like nations, can lack such richly layered meanings for them.

HUMANIZED LANDS

Spatial Symbolics: Male and Female, Natural and Cultural

Perceiving human attributes in land, or projecting these onto it, is a common feature of symbolic culture (65, 85a, 149, 172, 237, 253). In tropical Africa, a familiar theme in origin stories is a tragic human, and most often female, misdeed or failing that prompted a divine act separating earth from sky, rendering humans mortal (186). Sacred kings, where found, have sometimes been perceived as embodiments of human and natural fertility (86, 186, 299). Humans often perceive earthly substance as the stuff of their own bodily creation and disintegration (e.g. ashes to ashes, or often in Africa, clay to clay). Conversely, they perceive their bodies in parts of houses, settlements, or territories (76a, 85a, 114, 149, 282), as African variants of English terms like river mouth, foothill, and heartland imply. Land grabbing is widely spoken of in terms that translate as eating someone—the person as well as the possession.

Soil and seed are bound up symbolically with sex and gender, and similes between women and virgin or sown fields are widely adduced to bolster male claims or lineage claims over children. In some societies, women's farming during menstruation is deemed as dangerously polluting (72, 77; cf 12) or associated with uncontrolled flooding. Blood and other bodily fluids, just like soil or silt, are dirt only when out of place (76a, 77). These are by no means exclusively African ideas. Along another line, implied or explicit analogies like "male is to female as town is to bush" have been recorded almost continent-wide. Civilization and wilderness variously connote sterility and fertility, restriction and freedom (237); structure and anti-structure (278); controlled and uncontrollable fecundity (60, 149). Or they can mean safety and danger, weakness and power, order and chaos, temporality and spirituality, day and night. Polyvalent symbols link up different oppositions, though seldom can we tell just where the informants' narratives end and the analysts' interpretations begin.

These Levi-Straussian metaphors are not cognitively arranged just in simple or consistent ways (60, 65, 85a, 149a, 170; cf 177). Real people think not just in binarisms, but also in continua; they associate different aspects of bush or civilization with different genders (or vice versa; 65), and they make inversions or reversals. It remains debatable whether the cognitive gendering of lands depends on actual division of labor, or comprises a purer and more independent symbolic order (65, 90, 114). Heated gender politics color both men's and women's writings on land's symbolism, and not without some projection or wishful thinking.

Where bodies are buried—as they now are in nearly all parts of the continent—the burial sites variously identify citizenship, ethnicity, clan or lineage, or religion, just as they can identify gender. These placements can thus be argued or fought over, at the time of burial or afterward (34, 37, 52, 53, 110, 146, 219, 266). In the Gambia, for example, Muslims and Christians living intermixed bury their dead in separate graveyards, as if to underline or reaffirm their differences. Among Luo in Kenya, grave, house, and field placements symbolically connect oppositions between male and female, old and young, married and unmarried, named and unnamed, right and left, and central and peripheral, though not all Luo agree among themselves on the norms and metaphors involved. Also charged with meaning, in different tropical African agrarian settings, are the places where placentas, umbilical cords, or foreskins are buried, or where initiation blood is spilled on soil. These are signs of personal attachment to a place and, in some contexts, to a spot in the social order.

Religion and Ideologies of Attachment

Control over land in much of tropical Africa is, and will surely remain, as much tied up with the major religions as with kinship or politics. Some religions are place-bound, with pilgrimage sites, for example; others place more emphasis on movable objects of veneration like talismans or temporary spirit shrines. But tropical Africa's rich syncretisms and pluralisms, its partial and shifting conversions, and its recombinations of images or practices defy generalization in this as in other respects (33a, 188, 255, 259, 283, 294). Land itself is an object of reverence among some African peoples but not others; many sparsely settled shifting cultivators and herders seem to treat it matter-of-factly. Some peoples identify with what they deem sacred, "pure" ethnic heartlands (84a, 219) or look to local shrines (281a, 287, 294, 299; cf 34, 68, 85a) without actually frequenting them, suggesting sacredness in voids (219). Female earth deities and earth spirits, while often associated with matrilineal peoples, are by no means exclusive to them (65, 86, 88, 294). Ritual prescriptions and proscriptions (taboos), for instance about sexual separation, age sequencing, ancestor propitiation, or prayer, are widely assumed to influence land's fertility (65, 77, 86, 186, 249). Breaches of such rules help to explain agrarian crises or secularly worsening conditions when other causes seem harder to pinpoint. In Africa as elsewhere, contemporary secular education often challenges, alters, and supplements, but does not just expunge, such knowledge or beliefs.

Christianity's uneven mixture with indigenous religions over the southern half of the continent, and Islam's over the northern half and some coastal areas and enclaves inland farther south, bring myriad ideological charges to tenure issues. Biblical passages like the injunction to fructify and to replenish and subdue the earth (Genesis 1:28) have been invoked to rationalize invasions, colonial settlement, and many agricultural programs. Catholic brotherhoods have served in places as instruments of land acquisition, as in Portuguese São Tomé, where they organized royal land grants for their members (82). In Côte d' Ivoire and certainly elsewhere, at other times, Christian missionaries have abetted plantation labor recruitment (172, 290), while in Kenya and other countries, sensitive missionaries have championed the public cause against draconian tenure reforms. In parts of eastern and southern Africa, Christianity tempers local decisions about growing morally debated crops like tobacco; and farmers have changed churches, and churches changed their strictures, as a result. Christianity ties into land tenure not just philosophically but also politically and economically.

African Islam also ties into land tenure, sometimes more directly than does Christianity, since Islamic scripture and exegesis specifically prescribe and proscribe more kinds of behavior. Islam's shari'a, or sacred law, condones sales, regulates financial transactions, and governs inheritance, prescribing, for instance, the relative shares passing to male and female heirs (102). Some African Muslim peoples apply the shari'a to land, but others do not; and it is ever subject to local inflection and debate. Shifts toward Islam have played a part in movements toward cash cropping in West (65, 172) and East Africa (220). Islam may provide land or tree accumulators a kind of escape from local redistributive customs (220; see also 219), encourage movement from matrilineal to patrilineal inheritance, or combine with other economic and religious forces to influence conservation (65).

Religion can also structure accumulation. In the western Sahel, the centuries-old Maraboutic tradition of organizing Malian grazing lands (6) is in part an outgrowth of holy wars that sometimes pitted herders against farmers and centralized against decentralized polities. The more recent expansion of groundnut farming, Wolof-speaking Murids (Mourides) in Senegal (6, 63, 69, 70, 256) illustrates how politico-religious power can translate into expanded hectarage, or losses for those (here notably western Fulani agropastoralists) without it. In this case, many Qur'anic masters use student disciples to help them and their families do clearing and farm work, and how many hands they control in this way influences field allocation within and between communities. Religion can be, among all else, a territorial instrument.

A spate of new research on rice-growing areas of coastal West Africa, where crops as well as lands are gendered, reveals many interesting symbolic contests over land and its meanings, both ideological and practical (65, 172, 253). Among Jola (or Diola) in the Casamance, these contests tie into complex debates about cash cropping and about locally specific influences, from Mandinka-speaking people nearby, toward Islam and multifaceted social hierarchy (172). Among nearby Ehing (253), a hatchet spirit or blood spirit seems to mediate gender tensions over both terrestrial and human fertility—for they commingle—in males' favor. A common theme in recent scholarship is men's perceived attempts to co-opt women's fertility in both production and reproduction (compare Kenyan cases in 121, 197; see also 149, 149a).

Gender politics and symbolism can bear directly upon the outcomes of rice development programs, and vice versa. Among Gambian Mandinko who have moved into the perimeters of new rice irrigation schemes, semantic distinctions between family fields and personal fields mark the rice, and cash from it, as men's or women's to control. National and international developers have taken sides on the issue, not always in concert (42, 43, 289; see also 72, 75, 292). Ideologies of attachment do not always translate into official terms.

Ethnicity, Race, and Space

Race and ethnicity, like land tenure, are about arbitrary cognitive classification and exaggerated differences. Something's usually wrong with the basic idea of race, and where race means class in practice, something's wrong indeed. South Africa's tragic and violent history of land expropriations south of the tropics would require a separate review, but the cultural dimensions of formal and informal apartheid and the syndrome of "Bantustan" land poverty in southern Africa are discussed in many works by anthropologists (61, 80, 113, 135, 136, 201), historians (19, 20, 281; see also 207), and geographers (15, 50). The "varieties of dispossession" (202:85ff) (e.g. legal, military, economic) are numerous, and some of these have been paralleled in the invaded and colonized lands of Zimbabwe (47, 48), Kenya (152), and other countries (15, 50, 78).

What matters is not just the land's quantity, but its quality too. The nineteenth and early twentieth century processes that tended to put the lighter skins in control of the darker soils, and vice versa, have been only partly reversed by spontaneous squatting and voluntary, state-run resettlement programs in Kenya, where an African bureaucratic elite has tended to replace large-scale colonial farmers (50, 167). Still less have these processes been alleviated in Zimbabwe. Undoing semantic classifications for land and people—e.g. reserves, communal lands, and homelands for the former, and at the starkest, white, black, and colored for the latter—sooner or later becomes the task of scholars and land reformers alike, not just in a changed South Africa, but elsewhere in the region too. Farming or herding skills, once lost, can be hard to relearn. Other aspects of land restitution are ideological. Many of the region's exogenous and independent local churches and cults are concerned fundamentally with, among other things, territorial inclusion and exclusion, and their paradoxes and ironies (60, 61, 255, 281a, 294).

Linked to race in some cases but not others, violent ethnic cleansing pogroms focus frequently on intersettled land. Often, as lately among Moors and Fulani or Toucouleur in Mauritania, or between Kalenjin and Kikuyu (and others) in Kenya, these disputes involve land long ago lent or granted—the oral histories usually clash on this point—and now, under changed conditions, wanted back. Very high population densities and competition for land have contributed to civil wars ostensibly about much else besides land, as in the cases of Hutu and Tutsi in both Rwanda and Burundi, or Igbo and their neighbors in Nigeria. Sometimes attributed to divide-and-rule colonial policies, tribalism in tropical Africa acquires new life (e.g. the self-styled "Nandi Warriors" in 1990s Kenya) without ever being everyone's, or even anyone's, ideal.

TENURE REFORMS AND CULTURE

The Limits of Individualism: Land Titling and its Outcomes

Land reform can mean either redistributing holdings or changing the nature of the rights and duties underlying tenure. Since the turn of the twentieth century, tropical Africa has seen a series of rural land tenure reforms, many rooted in simplistic economic ideologies and political dogmas under colonial and independent governments. The most ambitious and famous example among the individual land titling or privatization programs has been Kenya's, based on a British colonial 1954 blueprint, carried on through Independence, and continuing to this day. The concept of secure tenure in individual titles is treacherously misleading. Untitled lands are by no means necessarily insecure, and such titling more often than not seems to heighten insecurity of tenure (263). The new system of titles does not expunge customary tenure or what is so deemed, but only adds another legal framework alongside it with its own room to maneuver. Legal uncertainties multiply, and disputants turn selectively to the written cadastre or to local witnesses who will satisfy their interests. The rural public resists registering its continuing transactions and subdivisions with the government. The real and the recorded diverge, and savvy players, including urban-based speculators, capitalize on the discrepancies at the expense of less advantaged rural people (15, 56, 105, 127, 128, 211, 263).

Individual titling threatens several previously disadvantaged categories. It can legally disenfranchise women, *de facto* if not *de jure,* as many women (15, 72, 78, 104, 179, 215, 216, 288; see also 151) and some men (211, 263; cf 105) have observed. It can give the rich, clever, or well-connected new ways to consume the land of less-privileged neighbors (105, 127, 128, 193), and it discriminates against herders (16, 98, 263). Titling has profound effects on local land lending and entrustment, often benefiting existing borrowers but sometimes stifling new lending and kindling disputes between land borrowers and lenders, or land patrons and clients, in the meantime. A market in title deeds, divorced from actual land use, may make absentee landlordism easier and more tempting. If holdings become concentrated into fewer hands after titling, as most expect, some of them still get split up or claims to them multiply (28, 78). Many economic promises of titling have failed to materialize and others have backfired, while some remain unknown or unmeasured (128, 192; see also 176).

The freehold-mortgage system, a main strategic aim of many foreign development planners, remains a foreign fantasy in areas settled by lineages. Among Luo, Gusii, southern Luhya, and neighboring western Kenyans, the presence of sacred graves on, and living kin around, the land of loan defaulters inhibits creditors' attempts at seizure—these attempts are perceived as something like acts of war. Disputes over mortgaged land frequently have turned violent and torn families apart (266; cf 287). Among these peoples and others (264), even after titling, norms proscribe individuals' selling family or lineage land, and the cash from selling out is expected to bring grievous harm to them and their kin or descendants, by divine or spiritual agency, unless they undergo expensive, and possibly dangerous, ritual purification. In land titling programs, market logic never simply shuts out political or cultural reason.

Private titling has produced unimpressive though mixed results in Uganda (295), Somalia (29, 140), Zimbabwe's "black freehold" areas (47, 48) and South Africa's "reserves" (19), and in other countries and settings (15, 41, 76, 192, 208). In special circumstances, such as interethnic settlement schemes, individual titling may make some sense for keeping peace. Where state titling is welcome locally, it is often as a defense against dispossession by other arms of the state, or by persons acting for themselves under the state's aegis.

Other Kinds of Tenure Reform

Socialist tenure reforms have tended to work no better, and often worse, than capitalist ones in African settings. In Ethiopia (51, 54, 55, 73, 138, 221), Tanzania (3, 50, 148), Mozambique (15, 72, 130), and elsewhere (49) in the 1970s and 1980s, some kinds of large landholders were swept away. But new collective state farms performed poorly because of inefficient and dirigistic bureaucracy, elite co-optation, and lack of material incentives for farmers to cooperate in the collective parts of their agrarian pursuits. In Ethiopia and Tanzania, "villagization" programs, never popular, have largely been dropped, and new nucleated settlements abandoned. Among other problems, soil exhaustion around big new villages forced farmers to travel farther and farther, centrifugally, as they sought new fields. Unfortunately, under capitalist or socialist regimes, ostensibly redistributive land reforms have backfired in the past, worsening class inequalities.

In another kind of tenure reform, exemplified by Nigeria in 1978 (84, 93) and numerous francophone countries before and since (66, 132, 163, 164, 287), the government declares the state the owner of all the land, in effect demoting most everyone's rights within. In a number of these cases, laws declaring "vacant and ownerless" lands to be national property appropriable for development (*mise en valeur*) have been seriously abused. Such terms ignore needs for long- or medium-term fallow rotations or for occasional grazing, browsing, and passage. They also give license to land grabs by civil servants and their informal clients (15, 78, 232, 254). Where compensations are promised, they usually come as lump-sum cash to individual men: too little, unreliable, slow, and volatile to compensate for the loss of socially meaningful or indefinitely productive land. Land nationalization, like individual titling, appears to open new doors for rural speculation by urban-based elites, as the opportunities to learn about and take advantage of abrupt change are never fairly spread.

Experimentation proceeds in several countries with group land titling (based on lineage, village, or other local units) and with decentralized control of forests (76, 97, 153). Findings are still too few and mixed to generalize, though pilot projects always seem more successful than are attempts to replicate them. Anthropologists have tended to argue for flexible approaches that give official recognition, under national legal codes, to diverse local patterns of access and control of land, water, trees, and other resources.

River Basins and Resettlement

Little of Africa's agriculture takes place under large-scale irrigation, but in many areas where this occurs it is the main source of livelihood. Big state-run and other irrigation boards, most studies find, have overregulated land rights (and life generally) in their scheme perimeters, exceeding their own mandates, being surprised by active and passive resistance (238, 258), and remaining too insensitive to their own mistakes (25, 245, on Sudan; 42, 43, 75, 228, on the Gambia; 4, 15, 67, 78, 217, 246, on the Senegal River; 126, 145, 185, on wider West Africa; 242, on Kenya and Zimbabwe; 5, 22, 35, 50, 194, comparative).

Resettlement studies reveal many similarities between histories, suggesting lessons about culture more generally. Classic longitudinal studies of relocated Gwembe Tonga of the Zambezi Basin in Zambia (58, 59, 124) have influenced many other resettlement studies (25, 145, 189, 242, 245, 246). No kind of development intervention has more consistently caused major cultural and psychological disruption than has forced or involuntary resettlement (e.g. 45, 51, 59, 194; see also 50), whether associated with damming or not. It seems the same people turn more and then less cautious or traditional in broadly predictable ways (124, 260) in the course of resettlement—suggesting that technical and social innovations must be sequenced carefully. Desiccation downstream from a dam (like flooding upstream) can wreak havoc on livelihoods, health, and ecosystems, unless it is redressed with carefully controlled artificial flooding at seasonal intervals (144, 246; see also 67).

Land resettlement has a symbolic side. Uprooting a people from culturally and psychologically significant markers (e.g. shrines, graves, sacred grottoes, trees, watercourses) makes it hard for them to navigate through time, space, and society. Resettlement shakes confidence in local religious and political leaders because, *ipso facto,* they have failed to prevent the cataclysm itself (58, 124, 260). Anthropologically informed policy guidelines formulated for the World Bank recommend avoiding resettlement programs where possible, and suggest caution, predictability, and gradualness where not. These directives say that self-defined communities should be allowed to resettle intact and that they should be given more diverse means for economic recovery than in the past (44, 45, 298; see also 124). Whether the Bank and other development agencies follow their own officers' policy guidelines is another matter.

A generation of scholars critical of state bureaucracy has scrutinized impositions of codified law, fixed nucleated settlements, straight boundaries and rows, written cadastres, and so on—devices to centralize control and information. Tropical Africa does not divide neatly into dominators and resistors. But rural Africans, like people elsewhere, sometimes publicly resist bureaucratic regulation in passive, foot-dragging ways, or in songs, myths, epithets, or religious imagery that no one can regulate (60, 61, 258, 283, 286). Whether such expressive and symbolic responses galvanize political and economic action, divert attention from it, or just make control easier to give up, is usually easier to explain than to predict.

CONCLUSION

Research on African landholding, while concentrating mainly on power and wealth, and on changing strategies of access and denial, also has elicited deeper meanings about more than land and livelihoods. Linking religion and economy, ritual and subsistence, sacred and profane, the most interesting new research challenges assumptions about who is who, who belongs where, and why. Debates about whether ecological practices and adaptations govern symbolic thought or vice versa will never end, for the links between any such causes and effects, where they exist, are variable, elastic, and recursive. But these spheres are inextricable, and it is the links between human and terrestrial fertility—both practical and figurative—that seem so often to make property, however defined, into what Morgan called "a passion over all other passions" (200:6).

In a cognitive and comparative vein, few studies yet broadly relate land-holding to symbolic, ritual, or religious life, though there are area-specific models (see 65, 172, 218, 220, 253, 255, 283, 294). How do people perceive the dimensions and classify spaces and lands? Why do they draw, interlink, and exaggerate binary oppositions? Whether different kinds of territoriality are innate, learned, or invented, those who seek to erase boundaries may end up drawing others. Will axioms of inequality only flourish in new forms if ritually or rhetorically denied? What are the roles of age and stage of family cycle (111) and, beyond kinship, of friendship, patronage, and clienthood (see 52, 115), in human-land attachments? Few studies have seriously compared forest with savannah (142, 276), or West African–style nucleated and East African–style scattered settlements and their many exceptions.

In a more political and economic vein, rural-urban linkages, peri-urban tenure, rental markets, new rural land speculation by urbanites, and struggles over invasive shanty demolition are critical topics in a continent with burgeoning cities (17, 66, 133, 178, 222, 236, 287). Tenure changes in civil wars and ethnic purges are scantly studied, for to do so requires outmigrants or a lapse of time. Research on borders and boundaries leads inexorably into the hot topic of barriers to international and intercontinental migration.

In yet another vein, how a radical land redistribution may be carried out without causing violence or actually worsening distribution remains a mystery. The effects of titling on the distribution of holdings still need reliable measurement over time, and controlled comparison based on culturally sensitive categories and translations. Group titling, community forestry, contract farming, and land mortgaging can mesh or collide with existing connections between persons and land; and the voices of the newly experienced, particularly women, elders, and youth, need recording. More collaborative studies between African and other scholars (for models, see 52, 53, 169), and more two-way translations, will be welcome.

Indigenous and exogenous anthropology have helped interpret, but they have also complicated the picture and made action harder to plan or justify. To serious scholars it is no longer a secret that, as Herskovitz noted in 1940, many forms of tenure can exist among the same people at the same time. In land matters as in other things, "*Afrique diverse, Afrique complexe*" (168:53) has been anthropology's orthodox conclusion for a generation. The next step requires broader comparisons—without losing the local nuance and texture—to reach a broader readership and to help reverse expropriations, minimize farmer-herder violence, dismantle race barriers, or otherwise make a difference. If any single aim should be kept in mind, it is fairness. More realistic than equality, less uncaring than efficiency, this ideal rings true to a tropical African spirit.

ACKNOWLEDGMENTS

For intelligent research assistance, thanks go to Ann Lewinson, Julie Miller, and Katherine Yost, the last of whom also provided much editorial help. Other colleagues, Jean Comaroff, William Durham, Vukani Magubane, Sally Falk Moore, Pauline Peters, and Jesse Ribot, commented helpfully on drafts. Ray Abrahams, the late John Beattie, and H.W.O. Okoth-Ogendo long ago welcomed me into topics on their turf.

Any *Annual Review* chapter, as well as any article cited in an *Annual Review* chapter, may be purchased from the Annual Reviews Preprints and Reprints service.
1-800-347-8007; 415-259-5017; email: arpr@class.org

Literature Cited

1. Abasiekong EM. 1981. Pledging oil palms. *Afr. Stud. Rev.* 24(1):73–82
2. Abbott E. 1952. *Flatland.* New York: Dover. Reprint
3. Abrahams RG, ed. 1985. *Villagers, Villages and the State in Tanzania.* Cambridge: Cambridge Univ. Afr. Stud. Cent.
4. Adams A. 1985. *La Terre et les Gens du Fleuve.* Paris: Harmattan
5. Adams WM, Grove AT. 1983. *Irrigation in Tropical Africa: Problems and Problem Solving.* Cambridge: Cambridge Univ. Afr. Stud. Cent.
6. Adamu M, Kirk-Greene AHM, eds. 1986. *Pastoralists of the West African Savannah.* Manchester: Manchester Univ. Press
7. Allan W. 1965. *The African Husbandman.* London: Oliver & Boyd
8. Anderson B. 1983. *Imagined Communities: Reflections on the Origin and Spread of Nationalism.* London: Verso
9. Anderson D, Grove R, eds. 1987. *Conservation in Africa: People, Policies and Practice.* Cambridge: Cambridge Univ. Press
10. Anderson TJ, Land Tenure Center Library Staff. 1976. *Land Tenure and Agrarian Reform in Africa and the Near East: An Annotated Bibliography.* Boston: Hall
11. Appadurai A, ed. 1986. *The Social Life of Things: Commodities in Cultural Perspective.* Cambridge: Cambridge Univ. Press
12. Ardener S, ed. 1981. *Women and Space: Ground Rules and Social Maps.* London: Croom Helm
13. Asiwaju AI, Adeniyi PO, eds. 1989. *Borderlands in Africa: A Multidisciplinary and Comparative Focus on Nigeria and West Africa.* Lagos: Univ. Lagos Press
14. Barth F. 1969. *Ethnic Groups and Boundaries: The Social Organization of Culture Difference.* Boston: Little Brown
15. Bassett TJ, Crummey DE, eds. 1993. *Land in African Agrarian Systems.* Madison: Univ. Wisc. Press
16. Baxter PTW, Hogg R, eds. 1990. *Property, Poverty and People: Changing Rights in Property and Problems of Pastoral Development.* Manchester: Univ. Manchester, Dept. Soc. Anthropol., Int. Dev. Cent.
17. Baydas M, Cochrane J, Dickerman C, Graffy E, Hardman A, et al. 1990. *Peri-urban studies in Africa: Annotated and general bibliographies.* Working Pap. 88. Binghamton, NY: Inst. Dev. Anthropol.
18. Beattie JHM. 1971. *The Nyoro State.* Oxford: Clarendon
19. Beinart W, ed. 1989. The politics of conservation in Southern Africa. *J. South. Afr. Stud.* 15(2) (Special issue)
20. Beinart W, Ranger T, Turrell R, eds. 1992. Political violence in Southern Africa. *J. South. Afr. Stud.* 18(3) (Special issue)
21. Bennett JW, Bowen JR, eds. 1988. *Production and Autonomy: Anthropological Studies and Critiques of Development.* Monogr. Econ. Anthropol. No. 5. Lanham, MD: Univ. Press Am.
22. Bennett JW, Lawry SW, Riddell JC. 1986. *Land Tenure and Livestock Development in*

370   SHIPTON

Sub-Saharan Africa. AID Evaluation Special Study 39. Washington, DC: Agency Int. Dev.

23. Bentley JW. 1987. Economic and ecological approaches to land fragmentation. *Annu. Rev. Anthropol.* 16:31–67

24. Bergeret A, Ribot JC. 1990. *L'Arbre Nourricier en Pays Sahélien.* Paris: Edit. Maison Sci. Homme

25. Bernal V. 1991. *Cultivating Workers: Peasants and Capitalism in a Sudanese Village.* New York: Columbia Univ. Press

26. Berry SS. 1984. The food crisis and agrarian change in Africa. *Afr. Stud. Rev.* 27(2): 59–112

27. Berry SS, ed. 1989. Access, control and use of resources in African agriculture. *Africa* 59(1) (Special issue)

28. Berry SS. 1993. *No Condition is Permanent: The Social Dynamics of Agrarian Change in Sub-Saharan Africa.* Madison: Univ. Wisc. Press

29. Besteman C. 1989. *Land tenure in the Middle Jubba Valley: customary tenure and the effect of land registration.* LTC Res. Pap. 104. Madison: Univ. Wisc. Land Tenure Cent.

30. Biebuyck D, ed. 1963. *African Agrarian Systems.* Oxford: Oxford Univ. Press, Int. Afr. Inst.

31. Biswas AK, Odero-Ogwel LA, eds. 1986. Land use in Africa. *Land Use Policy* 3(4) (Special issue)

32. Blaikie P. 1985. *The Political Economy of Soil Erosion.* London: Longman

33. Blaikie P, Brookfield H, eds. 1987. *Land Degradation and Society.* London: Methuen

33a. Blakely TD, van Beek WEA, Thomson DL, eds. 1994. *Religion in Africa.* Portsmouth, NH: Heinemann

34. Bloch M. 1994. *Placing the Dead: Tombs, Ancestral Villages, and Kinship Organization in Madagascar.* Prospect Heights, IL: Waveland. 2nd ed.

35. Bloch PC, Phillips LC, Riddell JC, Stanning JL, Park TK. 1986. *Land tenure issues in river basin development in sub-Saharan Africa.* LTC Res. Pap. 90. Madison: Univ. Wisc. Land Tenure Cent.

36. Bohannan P. 1954. *Tiv Farm and Settlement.* London: HMSO

37. Bohannan P. 1963. "Land", "tenure" and land-tenure. See Ref. 30, pp. 101–15

38. Boserup E. 1965. *The Conditions of Agricultural Growth: The Economics of Agrarian Change Under Population Pressure.* Chicago: Aldine

39. Bourdieu P. 1977. *Outline of a Theory of Practice.* Cambridge: Cambridge Univ. Press

40. Bromley DW, Feeney D, McKean MA, Peters PE, Gilles JL, eds. 1992. *Making the Commons Work: Theory, Practice and Policy.* San Francisco: ICS

41. Bruce JW. 1986. *Land tenure issues in project design and strategies for agricultural development in sub-Saharan Africa.* LTC Pap. 128. Madison: Univ. Wisc. Land Tenure Cent.

42. Carney J. 1988. Struggles over crop rights and labor with contract farming households in a Gambian irrigated rice project. *J. Peasant Stud.* 15:334–49

43. Carney J, Watts M. 1990. Manufacturing dissent. *Africa* 60(2):207–41

44. Cernea MM. 1988. *Involuntary resettlement in development projects: policy guidelines in World Bank–financed projects.* World Bank Tech. Pap. 80. Washington, DC: World Bank

45. Cernea MM, ed. 1991. *Putting People First.* New York: Oxford Univ. Press. 2nd ed.

46. Chanock M. 1985. *Law, Custom and Social Order: The Colonial Experience in Malawi and Zambia.* Cambridge: Cambridge Univ. Press

47. Cheater AP. 1981. Women and their participation in commercial agricultural production: the case of medium-scale freehold in Zimbabwe. *Dev. Change* 12(3):349–78

48. Cheater AP. 1987. Fighting over property: the articulation of dominant and subordinate legal systems governing the inheritance of immovable property among blacks in Zimbabwe. *Africa* 57(2):173–95

49. Clarence-Smith WG. 1980. Review article: Class structure and class struggles in Angola in the 1970s. *J. South. Afr. Stud.* 7(1): 109–26

50. Clarke JI, Khogali M, Kosinski LA, eds. 1985. *Population and Development Projects in Africa.* Cambridge: Cambridge Univ. Press

51. Clay JI, Holcomb B. 1985. *Politics and the Ethiopian Famine.* Cambridge, MA: Cult. Surv.

52. Cohen DW, Atieno-Odhiambo ES. 1989. *Siaya: The Historical Anthropology of an African Landscape.* London/Nairobi/Athens, OH: Currey/Heinemann Kenya/Ohio Univ. Press

53. Cohen DW, Atieno-Odhiambo ES. 1992. *Burying SM: The Politics of Knowledge and the Sociology of Power in Africa.* London/Portsmouth, NH: Currey/Heinemann

54. Cohen JM. 1980. Land tenure and rural development in Africa. In *Agricultural Development in Africa: Issues of Public Policy,* ed. RH Bates, MJ Lofchie, pp. 349–400. New York: Praeger

55. Cohen JM. 1984. Foreign involvement in tenure reform: the case of Ethiopia. In *International Dimensions of Tenure Reform,* ed. JD Montgomery, pp. 169–219. Boulder, CO: Westview

56. Coldham SFR. 1978. The effect of registration of title upon customary land rights in Kenya. *J. Afr. Law* 22(2):91–111
57. Colson E. 1971. The impact of the colonial period on the definition of land rights. In *Colonialism in Africa: 1870–1960*. Vol. 3: *Profiles of Change: African Society and Colonial Rule*, ed. V Turner, pp. 193–215. Cambridge: Cambridge Univ. Press
58. Colson E. 1971. *The Social Consequences of Resettlement*. Manchester: Manchester Univ. Press
59. Colson E. 1989. Overview. *Annu. Rev. Anthropol.* 18:1–16
60. Comaroff J. 1985. *Body of Power, Spirit of Resistance: The Culture and History of a South African People*. Chicago: Univ. Chicago Press
61. Comaroff J, Comaroff J. 1991. *Of Revelation and Revolution: Christianity, Colonialism and Consciousness in South Africa*. Chicago: Univ. Chicago Press
62. Comaroff J, Roberts S. 1981. *Rules and Processes: The Cultural Logic of Dispute in an African Context*. Chicago: Univ. Chicago Press
63. Copans J. 1980. *Les Marabouts de l'Arachide: La Confrérie Mouride et les Paysans du Senegal*. Paris: Edit. Sycomore
64. Couty P, Marchal J-Y, Pélissier P, Poussi M, Savonnet G, Schwartz A, eds. 1979. *Maîtrise de l'Espace Agraire et Développement en Afrique Tropicale: Logique Paysanne et Rationnalité Technique*. Paris: ORSTOM
65. Croll E, Parkin D, eds. 1992. *Bush Base: Forest Farm—Culture, Environment, and Development*. London: Routledge
66. Crousse B, Le Bris E, Le Roy E, eds. 1986. *Espaces Disputés en Afrique Noire: Pratiques Foncières Locales*. Paris: Karthala
67. Crousse B, Mathieu P, Seck SM. 1991. *La Vallée du Fleuve Sénégal: Evaluations et Perspectives d'une Décennie d'Aménagements 1980–1990*. Paris: Karthala
68. Crowley E. 1990. *Contracts with spirits: religion, asylum and ethnic identity in the Cacheu region of Guinea-Bissau*. PhD diss. Yale Univ.
69. Cruise O'Brien DB. 1971. *The Mourides of Senegal: The Political Organization of an Islamic Brotherhood*. Oxford: Clarendon
70. Cruise O'Brien DB. 1975. *Saints and Politicians: Essays in the Organisation of a Senegalese Peasant Society*. Cambridge: Cambridge Univ. Press
71. David P. 1980. *Les Navetanes: Histoire des Migrants Saisonniers de l'Arachide en Sénégambie dès Origines à nos Jours*. Dakar: Nouvelles Edit. Afr.
72. Davison J, ed. 1988. *Agriculture, Women, and Land: The African Experience*. Boulder, CO: Westview
73. Dejene A. 1987. *Peasants, Agrarian Socialism and Rural Development in Ethiopia*. Boulder, CO: Westview
74. de Treville D. 1986. *Contract farming, the private sector, and the state: an annotated and comprehensive bibliography with particular reference to Africa*. Work. Pap. 62. Binghamton, NY: Inst. Dev. Anthropol.
75. Dey J. 1981. Gambian Women: unequal partners in rice development projects? *J. Dev. Stud.* 17(3):109–22
76. Dickerman C. 1987. *Security of tenure and land registration in Africa: literature review and synthesis*. LTC Pap. 137. Madison: Univ. Wisc. Land Tenure Cent.
76a. Douglas M. 1973. *Natural Symbols: Exploration in Cosmology*. New York: Vintage. 2nd ed.
77. Douglas M. 1984. *Purity and Danger: An Analysis of Concepts of Pollution and Taboo*. Boston: Ark. 2nd ed.
78. Downs RE, Reyna SP, eds. 1988. *Land and Society in Contemporary Africa*. Hanover, NH: Univ. Press N. Engl.
79. Dyson-Hudson R, Smith EA. 1978. Human territoriality: an ecological reassessment. *Am. Anthropol.* 80:21–41
80. Eckert J. 1980. *Lesotho's land tenure: an analysis and annotated bibliography. Special bibliography 2. Lesotho Agricultural Sector Analysis Project*. Madison: Univ. Wisc. Land Tenure Cent.
81. Evans-Pritchard EE. 1940. *The Nuer*. Oxford: Clarendon
82. Eyzaguirre P. 1988. Competing systems of land tenure in an African plantation society. See Ref. 78, pp. 340–61
83. Fallers LA. 1973. *Inequality: Social Stratification Reconsidered*. Chicago: Univ. Chicago Press
84. Famoriyo S. 1979. *Land Tenure and Agricultural Development in Nigeria*. Ibadan: Ibadan Univ. Press
84a. Fardon R. 1991. *Between God, The Dead and the Wild*. Edinburgh/Washington, DC: Edinburgh Univ. Press/Smithsonian Inst. Press
85. Ferguson J, Gupta A, eds. 1992. Space, place, and the politics of difference. *Cult. Anthropol.* 7(1) (Special issue)
85a. Fernandez J. 1977. *Fang Architectonics*. Philadelphia: Inst. Stud. Hum. Issues
86. Forde D, ed. 1954. *African Worlds: Studies in the Cosmological Ideas and Social Values of African Peoples*. London: Oxford Univ. Press
87. Forde D, ed. (Serial). *Ethnographic Survey of Africa*. London: Int. Afr. Inst.
88. Fortes M. 1945. *The Dynamics of Clanship Among the Tallensi*. London: Oxford Univ. Press
89. Fortes M, Evans-Pritchard EE, eds. 1958. *African Political Systems*. London: Oxford Univ. Press. 2nd ed.

90. Fortmann L, Bruce J. 1988. *Whose Trees? Proprietary Dimensions of Forestry.* Boulder, CO: Westview

91. Fortmann L, Riddell JC. 1985. *Trees and Tenure: An Annotated Bibliography for Agroforesters and Others.* Madison: Univ. Wisc. Land Tenure Cent.

92. Foucault M. 1970. *The Order of Things: An Archaeology of the Human Sciences.* New York: Random House

93. Francis P. 1984. For the use and common benefit of all Nigerians: consequences of the 1978 land nationalization. *Africa* 54(3): 5–27

94. Francis P. 1987. Land tenure systems and agricultural innovation: the case of alley farming in Nigeria. *Land Use Policy* 4(3): 305–19

95. Fratkin E, Galvin KA, Roth EA, eds. 1994. *African Pastoralist Systems: The Frontiers of Theory and Method.* Boulder, CO: Rienner. In press

96. Freudenberger MS. 1993. Regenerating the Gum Arabic Economy: local-level resource management in northern Senegal. In *In Defense of Livelihood,* ed. J Friedman, H Rangan, pp. 52–78. West Hartford, CT: Kumarian

97. Freudenberger MS. 1993. *Land Tenure, Local Institutions and Natural Resources in Senegal.* Rep. to USAID. Madison: Univ. Wisc. Land Tenure Cent.

98. Galaty J. 1992. The land is yours: social and economic factors in the privatization, subdivision and sale of Maasai ranches. *Nomadic Peoples* 30:26–40

99. Galaty J, Bonte P, eds. 1991. *Herders, Warriors and Traders: Pastoralism in Africa.* Boulder, CO: Westview

100. Galaty J, Johnson D, eds. 1990. *The World of Pastoralism: Herding Systems in Comparative Perspective.* New York/London: Guilford/Behaven

101. Gallais J, ed. 1977. *Stratégies Pastorales et Agricoles des Saheliens durant la Sécheresse 1969–1974.* Travaux et documents de géographie tropicale, 30. Paris: Cent. Etud. Geogr. Tropicale

102. Gast M, ed. 1987. *Hériter en Pays Musulman: Ḥabus, Lait Vivant, Manyahuli.* Paris: Cent. Nat. Rech. Sci.

103. Gastellu J-M. 1981. *L'Egalitarisme Economique des Serer du Sénégal.* Paris: ORSTOM

104. Gladwin C. 1990. *African Women Farmers and Structural Adjustment.* Gainesville: Univ. Fla. Press

105. Glazier J. 1985. *Land and the Uses of Tradition Among the Mbeere of Kenya.* Lanham, MD: Univ. Press Am.

106. Gluckman M. 1965. *The Ideas in Barotse Jurisprudence.* New Haven, CT: Yale Univ. Press

107. Gluckman M, ed. 1969. *Ideas and Procedures in African Customary Law.* London: Oxford Univ. Press

108. Goheen M. 1994. *Men Own the Fields, Women Own the Crops: Gender and Power in the Cameroon Highlands.* Madison: Univ. Wisc. Press

109. Goheen M, Shipton P, eds. 1992. Rights over land: categories and controversies. *Africa* 62(3) (Special issue)

110. Goody JR, ed. 1962. *Death, Property and the Ancestors.* Stanford, CA: Stanford Univ. Press

111. Goody JR, ed. 1971. *The Developmental Cycle in Domestic Groups.* Cambridge: Cambridge Univ. Press. 2nd ed.

112. Goody JR. 1976. *Production and Reproduction: A Comparative Study of the Domestic Domain.* Cambridge: Cambridge Univ. Press

113. Gordon RJ. 1992. *The Bushman Myth: The Making of a Namibian Underclass.* Boulder, CO: Westview

114. Griaule M. 1970. *Conversations with Ogotemmêli: An Introduction to Dogon Religious Ideas.* London: Oxford Univ. Press. 2nd ed.

115. Gulliver PH. 1971. *Neighbours and Networks: The Idiom of Kinship in Social Action Among the Ndendeuli of Tanzania.* Berkeley: Univ. Calif. Press

116. Guyer JI. 1981. Household and community in African studies. *Afr. Stud. Rev.* 24(2/3): 87–137

117. Guyer JI. 1984. *Family and Farm in Southern Cameroon.* Boston: Boston Univ. Afr. Stud. Cent.

118. Guyer JI, Lambin EF. 1993. Land use in an urban hinterland: ethnography and remote sensing in the study of African intensification. *Am. Anthropol.* 95(4):839–59

119. Guyer JI, Peters PE, eds. 1987. Conceptualizing the household: issues of theory and policy in Africa. *Dev. Change* 18(2) (Special issue)

120. Hailey W. 1957. *An African Survey.* London: Oxford Univ. Press

121. Hakansson NT. 1988. *Bridewealth, Women and Land: Social Change Among the Gusii of Kenya.* Stockholm: Almqvist & Wiksell

122. Hamnett I. 1975. *Chieftainship and Legitimacy.* London/Boston: Routledge & Kegan Paul

123. Hamnett I, ed. 1977. *Social Anthropology and Law.* New York: Academic

124. Hansen A, Oliver-Smith A, eds. 1982. *Involuntary Migration and Resettlement: The Problems and Responses of Dislocated People.* Boulder, CO: Westview

125. Hardin G, Baden J. 1977. *Managing the Commons.* San Francisco: Freeman

125a. Harms R. 1987. *Games Against Nature: An Eco-cultural history of the Nunu of Equatorial Africa.* Cambridge: Cambridge Univ. Press

LAND AND CULTURE IN TROPICAL AFRICA 373

126. Hart K. 1982. *The Political Economy of West African Agriculture*. Cambridge: Cambridge Univ. Press
127. Haugerud A. 1983. The consequences of land tenure reform among smallholders in the Kenya highlands. *Rural Afr.* 15/16:65–89
128. Haugerud A. 1989. Land tenure and agrarian change in Kenya. *Africa* 59(1): 61–90
129. Hay MJ, Wright M, eds. 1982. *African women and the law: historical perspectives*. Pap. on Africa VII. Boston: Boston Univ. Afr. Stud. Cent.
130. Hermele K. 1988. *Land Struggles and Social Differentiation in Southern Mozambique: A Case Study of Chokwe, Limpopo, 1950–1987*. Uppsala: Scand. Inst. Afr. Stud.
131. Herskovitz M. 1965. *Economic Anthropology*. New York: Norton
132. Hesseling G. 1982. *Le Droit Foncier au Sénégal: L'Impact de la Réforme Foncière en Basse Casamance*. Leiden, Netherlands: Afr. Stud. Cent.
133. Hesseling G. 1992. *Pratiques Foncières à l'Ombre du Droit: l'Application du Droit Foncier Urbain à Ziguinchor, Sénégal*. Leiden, Netherlands: Afr. Stud. Cent.
134. Hill P. 1972. *Rural Hausa: A Village and a Setting*. Cambridge: Cambridge Univ. Press
135. Hitchcock R. 1982. Tradition, social justice and land reform. In *Land Reform in the Making*, ed. RP Werbner, pp. 1–34. London: Collings
136. Hitchcock R, Smith M, eds. 1982. *Proceedings on the Symposium on Settlement in Botswana*. Marshalltown, S. Africa: Heinemann Educ.
137. Hjort A, ed. 1985. *Land Management and Survival*. Uppsala, Sweden: Scand. Inst. Afr. Stud.
138. Hoben A. 1972. Social anthropology and development planning—a case study in Ethiopian land reform policies. *J. Mod. Afr. Stud.* 10(4):561–82
139. Hoben A. 1973. *Land Tenure Among the Amhara of Ethiopia*. Chicago: Univ. Chicago Press
140. Hoben A. 1988. The political economy of land tenure in Somalia. See Ref. 78, pp. 192–220
141. Holy L, ed. 1979. *Segmentary Lineage Systems Reconsidered*. Belfast, N. Ireland: Dept. Soc. Anthropol., Queens Univ. Belfast
142. Hopkins B. 1977. *Forest and Savanna*. London: Heinemann
143. Horowitz MM. 1979. *The sociology of pastoralism and African livestock projects*. AID Prog. Eval. Discuss. Pap. No. 6. Washington, DC: Off. Eval., Bur. Prog. Policy Coord., Agency Int. Dev.
144. Horowitz MM. 1991. Victims upstream and down. *J. Refugee Stud.* 4(2):164–81
145. Horowitz MM, Painter TM, eds. 1986. *Anthropology and Rural Development in West Africa*. Boulder, CO: Westview
146. Humphreys SC. 1981. *Mortality and Immortality: The Anthropology and Archaeology of Death*. London: Academic
147. Huss-Ashmore R, Katz S. 1990. *African Food Systems in Crisis*. Part II: *Contending with Change*. New York/London: Gordon & Breach
148. Hyden G. 1980. *Beyond Ujamaa in Tanzania: Underdevelopment and an Uncaptured Peasantry*. Berkeley: Univ. Calif. Press
149. Jacobson-Widding A, ed. 1991. *Body and Space: Symbolic Models of Unity and Division in African Cosmology and Experience*. Uppsala Stud. Cult. Anthropol. 16. Uppsala, Sweden: Acta Univ. Upsaliensis. Distr. Stockholm: Almqvist & Wiksell
149a. Jacobson-Widding A, Van Beek W, eds. 1990. *The Creative Communion: African Folk Models of Fertility and the Regeneration of Life*. Uppsala, Sweden: Acta Univ. Upsaliensis. Distr. Stockholm: Almqvist & Wiksell
150. Johnson D, Anderson D. 1988. *The Ecology of Survival: Case Studies from Northeast African History*. London/Boulder, CO: Crook/Westview
151. Jowkar F. 1991. *Gender relations of pastoral and agropastoral production: a bibliography with annotations*. Working Pap. 79. Binghamton, NY: Inst. Dev. Anthropol.
152. Kanogo T. 1987. *Squatters and the Roots of Mau Mau*. London: Currey
153. Kariro A, Juma C, eds. 1991. *Gaining Ground: Institutional Innovations in Land-use Management in Kenya*. Nairobi: Afr. Cent. Technol. Stud.
154. Kelly R. 1985. *The Nuer Conquest: The Structure and Development of an Expansionist System*. Ann Arbor: Univ. Mich. Press
155. Kerner DO. 1988. Land scarcity and rights of control in the development of commercial farming in Northeastern Tanzania. See Ref. 78, pp. 159–91
155a. Khasiani SA, ed. 1992. *Groundwork: African Women as Environmental Managers*. Nairobi: Afr. Cent. Technol. Stud.
156. Kintz D. 1991. Le foncier dans la pensée et dans la pratique des éleveurs et des agropasteurs. See Ref. 164, pp. 37–48
157. Kjekshus H. 1977. *Ecology Control and Economic Development in East African History: The Case of Tanganyika 1850–1950*. Nairobi: Heinemann
158. Kuper A. 1982. Lineage theory: a critical retrospect. *Annu. Rev. Anthropol.* 11:71–95

159. Kuper H. 1972. The language of sites in the politics of space. *Am. Anthropol.* 74:411–25

160. Lawrence DL, Low SM. 1990. The built environment and spatial form. *Annu. Rev. Anthropol.* 19:453–505

161. Lawry SW. 1989. *Tenure policy toward common property natural resources.* LTC Pap. 134. Madison: Univ. Wisc. Land Tenure Cent.

162. Le Bris E, Le Roy E. 1986. Politiques foncières et territoriales. *Politique Afr.* 21 (Special isssue)

163. Le Bris E, Le Roy E, Leimdorfer F, eds. 1982. *Enjeux Fonciers en Afrique Noire.* Paris: Karthala

164. Le Bris E, Le Roy E, Mathieu P, eds. 1991. *L'Appropriation de la Terre en Afrique Noire: Manuel d'Analyse, de Décision et de Gestion.* Paris: Karthala

165. Lee RB. 1979. *The !Kung San: Men, Women, and Work in a Foraging Society.* Cambridge: Cambridge Univ. Press

166. Lefébure C, ed. 1979. *Pastoral Production and Society/Production Pastorale et Société.* Cambridge: Cambridge Univ. Press

167. Leo C. 1984. *Land and Class in Kenya.* Toronto: Univ. Toronto Press

168. Le Roy E. 1991. De "l'hortus à l'ager". See Ref. 164, pp. 49–53

169. Le Roy E, Niang M. 1970. *Régime Juridique des Terres chez les Wolof Ruraux du Sénégal.* Paris: Lab. Anthropol. Juridique, Univ. Paris. Distr. L'Harmattan

170. Levi-Strauss C. 1963. *Structural Anthropology.* Transl. C Jacobson, BG Schoepf. Garden City, NJ: Doubleday Anchor

171. Lewis J Van D. 1981. Domestic labor intensity and the incorporation of Malian peasant farmers into localized descent groups. *Am. Ethnol.* 8(2):53–73

172. Linares O. 1992. *Power, Prayer, and Production: The Jola of Casamance, Senegal.* Cambridge: Cambridge Univ. Press

173. Little PD. 1992. *The Elusive Granary: Herder, Farmer, and State in Northern Kenya.* Cambridge: Cambridge Univ. Press

174. Little PD, Horowitz MM, with Nyerges AE, eds. 1987. *Lands at Risk in the Third World: Local-Level Perspectives.* Boulder, CO: Westview

175. Little PD, Watts M, eds. 1994. *Living Under Contract: Contract Farming and Agrarian Transformation in Sub-Saharan Africa.* Madison: Univ. Wisc. Press

176. Lott CE. 1979. *Land concentration in the Third World: statistics on number and area of farms classified by size of farms.* Training & Methods Ser. 28. Madison: Univ. Wisc. Land Tenure Cent.

177. MacCormack C, Strathern M, eds. 1980. *Nature, Culture and Gender.* Cambridge: Cambridge Univ. Press

178. Macharia K. 1992. Slum clearance and the informal economy in Nairobi. *J. Mod. Afr. Stud.* 30(2):221–36

179. Mackenzie F. 1986. Local initiatives and national policy: gender and agricultural change in Murang'a District, Kenya. *Can. J. Afr. Stud.* 20(3):377–401

180. MacPherson CB, ed. 1978. *Property: Mainstream and Critical Positions.* Toronto: Univ. Toronto Press

181. Macquet J. 1961. *The Premise of Inequality in Ruanda.* London: Oxford Univ. Press

182. Mair LP, ed. 1957. *Studies in Applied Anthropology.* London: Athlone

183. Malthus T. 1959. *Population: The First Essay.* Ann Arbor: Univ. Mich. Press

184. Martin F. 1991. Natural resource systems in the Sahel (annotated bibliography). Prepared for Workshop Polit. Theory Policy Anal. for OECD & ARD, Indiana Univ.

185. Mathieu P. 1991. De la maîtrise de l'eau au contrôle de la terre. See Ref. 164, pp. 62–76

186. Mbiti JS. 1969. *African Religions and Philosophy.* New York: Praeger

187. McKay B, Acheson JM, eds. 1987. *The Question of the Commons: The Culture and Ecology of Communal Resources.* Tucson: Univ. Ariz. Press

188. McLaughlin PFM, ed. 1970. *African Food Production Systems.* Baltimore, MD: Johns Hopkins Univ. Press

189. McMillan D, Painter T, Scudder T. 1990. *Settlement experiences and development strategies in the onchocerciasis controlled area of West Africa.* IDA Work. Pap. 68. Binghamton, NY: Inst. Dev. Anthropol.

190. Meek CK. 1946. *Land Law and Custom in the Colonies.* Oxford: Oxford Univ. Press

191. Middleton J. 1961. *Land Tenure in Zanzibar.* Colonial Res. Stud. 33. London: HMSO

192. Migot-Adholla ES, Hazell P, Blarel B, Place F. 1991. Indigenous land rights systems in sub-Saharan Africa: a constraint on productivity? *World Bank Econ. Rev.* 5(1):155–75

193. Mkangi GC. 1983. *The Social Cost of Small Families and Land Reform: A Case Study of the Wataita of Kenya.* New York: Pergamon

194. Montgomery E, Bennett JW, Scudder T. 1973. The impact of human activities on the physical and social environments: new directions in anthropological ecology. *Annu. Rev. Anthropol.* 2:27–61

195. Moock JL, ed. 1986. *Understanding Africa's Rural Households and Farming Systems.* Boulder, CO: Westview

196. Moock JL, Rhoades RE, eds. 1992. *Diversity, Farmer Knowledge, and Sustainability.* Ithaca, NY: Cornell Univ. Press

197. Moore H. 1986. *Space, Text and Gender: An Anthropological Study on the Marakwet*

of Kenya. Cambridge: Cambridge Univ. Press
198. Moore SF. 1978. *Law as Process: An Anthropological Approach.* London: Routledge & Kegan Paul
199. Moore SF. 1986. *Social Facts and Fabrications: 'Customary' Law on Kilimanjaro, 1880–1980.* Cambridge: Cambridge Univ. Press
200. Morgan LH. 1877. *Ancient Society.* New York: Holt
201. Murray C. 1981. *Families Divided: The Impact of Migrant Labour in Lesotho.* Johannesburg: Ravan
202. Murray C. 1992. *Black Mountain: Land, Class and Power in the Eastern Orange Free State, 1880s to 1980s.* Edinburgh: Edinburgh Univ. Press
203. Netting RMcC. 1968. *Hill Farmers of Nigeria: Cultural Ecology of the Kofyar of the Jos Plateau.* Seattle: Univ. Wash. Press
204. Netting RMcC. 1993. *Smallholders, Householders: Farm Families and the Ecology of Intensive, Sustainable Agriculture.* Stanford, CA: Stanford Univ. Press
205. Netting RMcC, Wilk R, Arnould E, eds. 1984. *Households: Comparative and Historical Studies of the Domestic Group.* Berkeley: Univ. Calif. Press
206. Noronha R. 1985. *A review of the literature on land tenure systems in Sub-Saharan Africa.* Rep. to Agricult. Dev. Dept., World Bank. Washington, DC: World Bank
207. Noyes JK. 1992. *Colonial Space: Spatiality, Subjectity and Society in the Colonial Discourse of German South West Africa.* Philadelphia: Harwood
208. Obol-Ochola J, ed. 1969. *Land Law Reform in East Africa.* Kampala: Milton Obote Found.
209. Okali C. 1983. *Cocoa and Kinship in Ghana: The Matrilineal Akan of Ghana.* London: Kegan Paul
210. O'Keefe P, ed. 1977. *Land and Development in Africa.* London: Int. Afr. Inst.
211. Okoth-Ogendo HWO. 1976. African land tenure reform. In *Agricultural Development in Kenya,* ed. J Heyer, JK Maitha, WM Senga, pp. 152–85. Nairobi: Oxford Univ. Press
212. Okoth-Ogendo HWO. 1989. Some issues of theory in the study of tenure relations in African agriculture. *Africa* 59(1):6–17
213. Okoth-Ogendo HWO. 1991. *Tenants of the Crown: Evolution of Agrarian Law and Institutions in Kenya.* Nairobi: Afr. Cent. Technol. Stud.
214. Ostrom E. 1990. *Governing the Commons: The Evolution of Institutions for Collective Action.* Cambridge: Cambridge Univ. Press
215. Pala AO. 1980. Daughters of the lakes and rivers: colonization and the land rights of Luo women. In *Women and Colonization:*

Anthropological Perspectives, ed. M Etienne, E Leacock, pp. 186–213. New York: Praeger
216. Pala AO. 1983. Women's access to land and their role in agriculture and decision-making on the farm: experiences of the Joluo of Kenya. *J. East. Afr. Res. Dev.* 13:69–85
217. Park TK, ed. 1993. *Risk and Tenure in Arid Lands: The Political Ecology of Development in the Senegal River Basin.* Tucson: Univ. Arizona Press
218. Parkin DJ. 1975. *Town and Country in Central and Eastern Africa.* Oxford: Oxford Univ. Press
219. Parkin DJ. 1991. *Sacred Void: Spatial Images of Work and Ritual Among the Giriama of Kenya.* Cambridge: Cambridge Univ. Press
220. Parkin DJ. 1994. *Palms, Wine and Witnesses: Public Spirit and Private Gain in an African Farming Community.* Prospect Heights, IL: Waveland. 2nd ed.
221. Pausewang S. 1983. *Peasants, Land and Society: A Social History of Land Reform in Ethiopia.* Afrika-Studien 110. Munich: Weltforum Verlag
222. Peil M. 1981. *Cities and Suburbs: Urban Life in West Africa.* New York/London: Africana
223. Pélissier P. 1966. *Les Paysans du Senegal: Les civilisations agraires du Cayor à la Casamance.* St.-Yrieix, France: Imprimerie Fabrègue, Cent. Natl. Rech. Sci.
224. Peters PE. 1984. Struggles over water, struggles over meaning: cattle, water and the state in Botswana. *Africa* 54(3):29–49
225. Peters PE. 1987. Embedded systems and rooted models: the grazing lands of Botswana and the commons debate. See Ref. 187, pp. 171–94
226. Peters PE. 1994. *Dividing the Commons: Politics, Policy, and Culture in Botswana.* Charlottesville: Univ. Press Va. In press
227. Pottier J. 1988. *Migrants No More: Settlement and Survival in Mambwe Villages, Zambia.* Edinburgh: Edinburgh Univ. Press
228. Pred A, Watts MJ. 1992. *Reworking Modernity: Capitalisms and Symbolic Discontent.* New Brunswick, NJ: Rutgers
229. Prothero RM, ed. 1972. *People and Land in Africa South of the Sahara.* New York: Oxford Univ. Press
230. Radcliffe-Brown AR, Forde D, eds. 1964. *African Systems of Kinship and Marriage.* London: Oxford Univ. Press
231. Raintree J, ed. 1987. *Land, Trees and Tenure.* Nairobi/Madison: Int. Counc. Res. Agroforestry/Univ. Wisc. Land Tenure Cent.
232. Reyna SP. 1987. The emergence of land concentration in the west African savannah. *Am. Anthropol.* 14(3):523–42
233. Richards A. 1939. *Land, Labour and Diet*

in Northern Rhodesia. Oxford: Oxford Univ. Press

234. Richards P. 1983. Ecological change and the politics of African land use. *Afr. Stud. Rev.* 26(2):1–71

235. Richards P. 1985. *Indigenous Agricultural Revolution: Ecology and Food Production in West Africa.* Boulder, CO: Westview

236. Riddell JC, Dickerman C. 1986. *Country Profiles of Land Tenure: Africa 1986.* Madison: Univ. Wisc. Land Tenure Cent.

237. Riesman P. 1977. *Freedom in Fulani Social Life.* Chicago: Univ. Chicago Press

238. Robertson AF. 1984. *People and the State: An Anthropology of Planned Development.* Cambridge: Cambridge Univ. Press

239. Robertson AF. 1987. *The Dynamics of Productive Relationships: African Share Contracts in Comparative Perspective.* Cambridge: Cambridge Univ. Press

240. Rose LL. 1992. *The Politics of Harmony: Land Dispute Strategies in Swaziland.* Cambridge: Cambridge Univ. Press

241. Ross PJ. 1987. Land as a right to membership: land tenure dynamics in a peripheral area of the Kano Close-Settled Zone. In *State, Oil and Agriculture in Nigeria,* ed. M Watts, pp. 223–47. Berkeley: Univ. Calif. Inst. Int. Stud.

242. Ruigu GM, Rukuni M, eds. 1990. *Irrigation Policy in Kenya and Zimbabwe.* Nairobi: Univ. Nairobi Inst. Devel. Stud.

243. Ruthenberg H. 1980. *Farming Systems in the Tropics.* Oxford: Clarendon. 3rd ed.

244. Sahlins MD. 1961. The segmentary lineage: an organization of predatory expansion. *Am. Anthropol.* 63:322–45

245. Salem-Murdock M. 1989. *Arabs and Nubians in New Halfa: A Study of Settlement and Irrigation.* Salt Lake City: Univ. Utah Press

246. Salem-Murdock M, Niasse M. 1993. *Senegal River Basin Monitoring Activity. II: Final Report.* Binghamton, NY: Inst. Dev. Anthropol.

247. Salzman P, ed. 1980. *When Nomads Settle.* New York: Praeger

248. Saul M. 1988. Money and land tenure as factors in farm size differentiation in Burkina Faso. See Ref. 78, pp. 243–79

249. Saul M. 1993. Land custom in Bare: agnatic corporation and rural capitalism in Western Burkina. See Ref. 15, pp. 75–100

250. Schapera I. 1943. *Native Land Tenure in the Bechuanaland Protectorate.* Lovedale, S. Africa: Lovedale

251. Schilder K. 1988. *State formation, religion and land tenure in Cameroon: a bibliographical survey.* Res. Rep. 32. Leiden, Netherlands: Afr. Stud. Cent., Dept. Polit. Hist. Stud.

252. Schlee G. 1989. *Identities on the Move: Clanship and Pastoralism in Northern Kenya.* Manchester: Manchester Univ. Press

253. Schloss M. 1988. *The Hatchet's Blood: Separation, Power, and Gender in Ehing Social Life.* Tucson: Univ. Ariz. Press

254. Schoepf BG, Schoepf C. 1988. Land, gender, and food security in eastern Kivu, Zaire. See Ref. 72, pp. 106–30

255. Schoffeleers JM, ed. 1978. *Guardians of the Land: Essays on Central African Territorial Cults.* Gwelo, Zimbabwe: Mambo

256. Schoonmaker Freudenberger K. 1991. Mbegué: l'habile destruction d'une forêt sahélienne. Dossier 29. London: Int. Inst. Environ. Dev.

257. Schroeder R. 1993. Shady practice: gender and the political ecology of resource stablilization in Gambian garden orchards. *Econ. Geogr.* 69(4):349–65

258. Scott JC. 1985. *Weapons of the Weak.* New Haven, CT: Yale Univ. Press

259. Scott J, Simpson-Housley P, eds. 1991. *Sacred Places and Profane Spaces: Essays in the Geographics of Judaism, Christianity, and Islam.* New York: Greenwood

260. Scudder T. 1991. A sociological framework for the analysis of new land settlements. In *Putting People First: Sociological Variables in Rural Development,* ed. MM Cernea, pp. 148–87. New York: Oxford Univ. Press

261. Shack WA, Skinner EP, eds. 1979. *Strangers in African Societies.* Berkeley: Univ. Calif. Press

262. Shipton PM. 1984. Strips and patches: a demographic dimension in some African landholding and political systems. *Man* 19: 617–34

263. Shipton PM. 1988. The Kenyan land tenure reform: misunderstandings in the public creation of private property. See Ref. 78, pp. 91–135

264. Shipton PM. 1989. *Bitter Money: Cultural Economy and Some African Meanings of Forbidden Commodities.* Am. Ethnol. Soc. Monogr. 1. Washington, DC: Am. Anthropol. Assoc.

265. Shipton PM. 1990. African famines and food security: anthropological perspectives. *Annu. Rev. Anthropol.* 19:353–94

266. Shipton PM. 1992. Debts and trespasses: land, mortgages, and the ancestors in western Kenya. *Africa* 62(3):357–88

267. Shipton PM. 1993. *The control of land on the upper Gambia River.* Rep. to USAID and OECD. Cambridge, MA: Harvard Inst. Int. Dev.

267a. Shipton PM, Goheen M. 1992. Understanding African land-holding: power, wealth, and meaning. *Africa* 62(3):307–26

267b. Simpson SR. 1978. *Land Law and Registration.* Cambridge: Cambridge Univ. Press

268. Snyder F. 1981. *Capitalism and Legal*

Change: An African Transformation. New York: Academic

269. Southall A. 1986. The illusion of Nath agnation. *Ethnology* 25(1):1–20

270. Stichter S. 1985. *Migrant Laborers.* Cambridge: Cambridge Univ. Press

271. Stone GD, Stone MP, Netting RM. 1990. Seasonality, labor scheduling, and agricultural intensification in the Nigerian Savanna. *Am. Anthropol.* 92(1):7–23

272. Swift J. 1977. Sahelian pastoralists: underdevelopment, desertification, and famine. *Annu. Rev. Anthropol.* 6:457–78

273. Swindell K. 1981. *The Strange Farmers of The Gambia.* Norwich: Geo

274. Swindell K. 1985. *Farm Labour.* Cambridge: Cambridge Univ. Press

275. Tamari T. 1991. The development of caste systems in West Africa. *J. Afr. Hist.* 32: 221–50

276. Tosh J. 1980. The cash crop revolution in tropical Africa. *Afr. Aff.* 79:79–94

277. Tuden A, Plotnicov L. 1970. *Social Stratification in Africa.* New York: Free

278. Turner BL II, Hyden G, Kates R, eds. 1993. *Population Growth and Agricultural Change in Africa.* Gainesville: Univ. Fla. Press

279. Turner VW. 1967. *The Forest of Symbols: Aspects of Ndembu Ritual.* Ithaca, NY: Cornell Univ. Press

280. Turner VW. 1969. *The Ritual Process: Structure and Anti-Structure.* Chicago: Aldine

281. Vail L, ed. 1989. *The Creation of Tribalism in Southern Africa.* London/Berkeley: Currey/Univ. Calif. Press

281a. van Binsbergen W. 1981. *Religious Change in Zambia: Exploratory Studies.* London/Boston: Kegan Paul

282. van Binsbergen W. 1988. The land as body: an essay on the interpretation of ritual among the Manjaks of Guinea-Bissau. *Med. Anthropol. Q.* 2(4):386–401

283. van Binsbergen W, Schoffeleers M. 1985. *Theoretical Explorations in African Religion.* London: KPI

284. Van Gennep A. 1960. *The Rites of Passage.* Chicago: Univ. Chicago Press. Reprint

285. Van Hekken N, Van Velzen H. 1972. *Land Scarcity and Rural Inequality in Tanzania: Some Case Studies of Rungwe District.* The Hague: Mouton

286. Van Rouveroy van Niewaal EAB, ed. 1979. La réforme agro-foncière dans les pays du conseil de l'entente en Afrique de l'Ouest. *Afr. Perspect.* 1979/1. Leiden: Afrika-Studiecentrum. (Special issue)

287. Verdier R, Rochegude A. 1986. *Systèmes Fonciers à la Ville et au Village: Afrique Noire Francophone.* Paris: L'Harmattan

288. Wangari E. 1990. *Effects of land registration on small-scale farming in Kenya: the case of Mbeere in Embu District.* PhD thesis. New Sch. Soc. Res.

289. Watts M. 1993. Idioms of land and labor: producing politics and rice in Senegambia. See Ref. 15, pp. 157–93

290. Webster JB. 1968. The bible and the plough. *J. Hist. Soc. Nigeria* 2:418–34

291. Weil P. 1970. The introduction of the ox plough in Central Gambia. See Ref. 188, pp. 231–63

292. Weil P. 1973. Wet rice, women, and adaptation in the Gambia. *Rural Afr.* 19:20–29

293. Werbner RP, ed. 1982. *Land Reform in the Making: Tradition, Public Policy and Ideology in Botswana.* London: Collings

294. Werbner RP. 1989. *Ritual Passage, Sacred Journey.* Washington, DC: Smithsonian Inst. Press

295. West HW. 1972. *Land Policy in Buganda.* London: Cambridge Univ. Press

296. Wilmsen EN. 1989. *Land Filled with Flies.* Chicago: Univ. Chicago Press

297. Wilmsen EN, ed. 1989. *We Are Here: Politics of Aboriginal Land Tenure.* Berkeley: Univ. Calif. Press

298. World Bank. 1990. *Involuntary Resettlement.* Operational Directive 4.30. Washington, DC: World Bank

299. Zahan D. 1979. *The Religion, Spirituality, and Thought of Traditional Africa.* Chicago: Univ. Chicago Press

Annu. Rev. Anthropol. 1994. 23:379–405

THE POLITICS OF SPACE, TIME AND SUBSTANCE: State Formation, Nationalism, and Ethnicity

Ana María Alonso

Department of Anthropology, University of Arizona, Tucson, Arizona 85721

KEY WORDS: state formation, nationalism, ethnicity, hegemony, space-time

We have come to take the state for granted as an object of political practice and political analysis while remaining quite spectacularly unclear as to what the state is.

P Abrams (2:59)

Nation, nationality, nationalism—all have proved notoriously difficult to define, let alone to analyse.

B Anderson (7:3)

Ethnicity is like family or marriage: everybody knows what it means but nobody can define it.

RT Smith (118:1)

What is the relationship between common sense categories of experience and analytical concepts developed in order to understand the processes that produce such categories and effect their taken-for-grantedness? This question is crucial for those working on nationalism, ethnicity, and state formation. Much of the misplaced concreteness that bedevils this scholarship results from an uncritical reproduction of common sense that poses intellectual as well as political problems.

MISPLACED CONCRETENESS AND THE STATE

Abrams long ago pointed out that by positing a mystifying separation of the political and the social, scholars have objectified and personified the state (2). A product of practices of politically organized subjection in capitalist societies, this misplaced concreteness resonates with and is reinforced by everyday experience and becomes "commonsensical" (56). As an alternative, Abrams proposes that we study the state-system, which is "a palpable nexus of practice and institutional structure centred in government and more or less extensive, unified and dominant in any given society" (2:82), as well as the state-idea, which is a "message of domination—an ideological artefact attributing unity, morality and independence to the disunited, amoral and dependent workings of the practice of government" (2:81). Understanding the state as a mask entails grasping its importance as a historically constructed and contested "exercise in legitimation, in moral regulation" (2:77).

Corrigan & Sayer's work (35) on English state formation demonstrates that modern relations of rule and forms of discipline construct and are constructed in everyday practices. Corrigan & Sayer argue that state formation is cultural revolution, highlighting in their analysis the ways in which everyday state routines, rituals, activities, and policies, which are themselves material cultural forms, constitute and regulate the social making of meaning and of subjects. Anchored in relations of inequality, cultural revolution is not "merely an ideational matter, and cannot be considered independently of the materiality of state formation—what state agencies are, how they act, and on whom" (p. 191). Their work "draws attention to the totalizing dimension of state formation,...to its constructions of 'national character' and 'national identity'...and the individualizing dimension of state formation, which is organized through impositional claims embodied in distinctive categories...that are structured along the axes of class, occupation, gender, age, ethnicity and locality" (75:20; see 35:4–5). These totalizing and individualizing processes generate "a common discursive framework" (102:361), articulated by nonlinguistic as well as linguistic signifiers, which forms and is formed by the lived experience of state subjects (75:20). "Making this conscience genuinely collective is always an accomplishment, a struggle against other ways of seeing, other moralities, which express the historical experiences of the dominated" (35:6). Thus, an anthropology of state formation needs to consider what states are formed against: "Neither the shape of the state, nor oppositional cultures, can be properly understood outwith the context of the mutually formative (and continuing) struggle between them: in other words, historically" (p. 7; see also 75:21–22).

There are some obvious parallels between Corrigan & Sayer's theorizing of state formation on the one hand, and Gramsci's (56) on the other, but there are also key differences. Gramsci's double definition of the state has both a narrow and an expanded sense (56). In the narrow sense, the state, equated with government, functions by command and coercion (see also 23). In the expanded sense, the state, equated with political society and civil society, is defined as "hegemony protected by the armour of coercion" (p. 263). Both formulations privilege civil society as the site of production of hegemony; hence, there is no way to theorize either "the process of penetration of civil society by agencies of government" or "what is special about non-governmental forms of control" (23:101, 40:112–113). For Corrigan & Sayer, the power of the state "rests not so much on the consent of its subjects but with the state's regulative and coercive forms and agencies, which define and create certain kinds of subjects and identities while denying" others through everyday routines and rituals of ruling (102:357).[1]

Having said all this, I still find much of value in Gramsci's notion of hegemony, provided the role of the state in hegemonic processes is recognized. In addition, it is worth recalling that hegemony "was a more material and political concept in Gramsci's usage than it has since become" (102:358; cf 56, 79) and that for Gramsci, hegemony was not "a finished and monolithic ideological formation" (cf 6) but "a problematic, contested political process of domination and struggle" (102:358). Precisely because hegemony is fragile, it must be constantly "renewed, recreated, defended and modified" (141:112) as the "relations of forces" (56:180–185) in society shift. Cultural inscription is key for transforming the fragile into the monumental, limiting polysemy by removing hegemonic meanings from the immediate circumstances of their creation and endowing them with a misplaced concreteness. At the same time, cultural inscription connects hegemonic meanings with the experience and understanding of social actors (101).

The cultural inscription of the idea of the state has in part been secured through the spatialization of time, the transformation of becoming into Being (65:273), and through the symbolic and material organization of social space (65, 80, 147). The widely held notion of the state as the representative of the public will, a neutral arbiter above the conflicts and interests of society, is an effect of a topography of hierarchized binaries whose terms are constructed as autonomous spaces (85). This topography conceals the workings of relations of rule and forms of discipline in day to day life. Although binaries such as state/civil society and public/private have been critiqued frequently in recent scholarship, analysis of how they are constructed through representations of space and place has been less common (but see 49, 60, 61, 65, 80, 147). And if this topography of modern state formation has been linked by feminists to the

---

[1]
   Because Gramsci does not theorize the coercion implicit in state forms of moral regulation, his vision of the state in a communist, regulated society is naive.

consolidation of gender inequalities, it has less frequently been seen as crucial to the imagining of national and sub-national communities and identities and, hence, to the production of status hierarchies of ethnic inequality.

Anderson's argument that nations are "imagined political communities" (7:6) has done much to expose the misplaced concreteness in nationalist common sense and scholarly literature (cf 52, 71, 112). But Anderson does not go far enough in identifying the strategies through which "the imagined" becomes "second nature," a "structure of feeling" (141:132) embodied in material practice and lived experience. For example, tropes of space and place are integral to Mexican nationalist discourses; the nation is rendered real through a "vast iconic structuring of 'public' social space" that "transforms what was once the terrain of local and regional autonomies into a homogenized and nationalized domain, where an objectified official history makes the presence of the state palpable in everyday life" (4:41). Hegemonic strategies, at once material and symbolic, produce the idea of the state while concretizing the imagined community of the nation by articulating spatial, bodily and temporal matrixes through the everyday routines, rituals, and policies of the state system.

Spatialization and Territorialization

Modern forms of state surveillance and control of populations as well as of capitalist organization and work discipline have depended on the homogenizing, rationalizing, and partitioning of space (65:213, 49, 95:99–107). Moreover, the transformation of space into territory that has been central to nationalism has relied on the conceptualization of people as living within a single, shared spatial frame (7, 65). Harvey argues that "time-space compression" (65:240–241) has enabled nationalism's tendency to universality, while simultaneously undermining its tendency to particularism, creating a tension between space and place (p. 257). Nationalism attempts to reconcile the absolute "perspective of place with the shifting perspectives of relative space" engendered by the globalization of capitalism (65:262, 270). The role of the state in the organization and representation of space is key for this reconciliation.

How does the identity of place and people get reaffirmed in the midst of the growing homogeneity and fragmentation of space? How is the misplaced concreteness of states and nations secured through tropes given material form in ordinary language and everyday life as well as in scholarship? Malkki shows how an identity between people and territory (and, I would add, the state) is created and naturalized through the visual device of the map, which represents the world of nations "as a discrete spatial partitioning of territory" with no "bleeding boundaries": Each nation is sovereign and limited in its membership (83:26; cf 7, 52, 71). The enclosure, measurement, and commodification of space have been key for the production of the modern notion of a national territory bounded by frontiers that sharply distinguish inside from outside: Baptized with a proper name, space becomes national property, a sovereign patrimony fusing place, property, and heritage, whose perpetuation is secured by the state (cf 95:104).

This identity between people, heritage, territory, and state is also brought about by the use of botanical metaphors that "suggest that each nation is a grand genealogical tree, rooted in the soil that nourishes it" (83:28). Like the map, these metaphors configure the nation as limited in its membership, sovereign, and continuous in time. And they are critical for conceptualizing the state as "a compulsory organization with a territorial basis" (135:56), as "'the stable centre...of [national] societies and spaces'" (65:273).

Malkki's examples are drawn from English, Quebecois, and Basque nationalisms. United States nationalism privileges the symbol of the Sierra redwood, named *Sequoia gigantea* after the Indian chief Sequoyah. This symbol roots the distinctiveness of the United States in a "New World wonder" while identifying indigenous people with nature (104:27; D Nugent reminds me that the symbol of the National Park Service is an Indian arrowhead). Yet arborescent metaphors are not confined to the West. They occur in discourse about Maori ethnicity and the New Zealand nation (137) and about Sinhala ethnicity and the Sri Lankan nation (21, 77a, 119a). A state-organized exhibit about difference and unity in the Mexican nation, which I viewed in Tijuana in 1988, represented the Constitution through the medium of a tree of life, a popular craft item that usually draws on Catholic symbols. I can attest to the importance of arborescent imagery in Cuban nationalism: As a child living outside of my homeland, I would wonderingly contemplate a photograph of the Cuban royal palm tree, while struggling for rootedness in my displacement (M Alvarez reminds me that the royal palm tree is one of the signifiers displayed on the Cuban national shield).

Other images from nature are also used widely. Comparative investigations of how nationalisms construe nature and make it available for public consumption, and studies of the register of nature tropes drawn on by particular forms of imagining peoplehood, are needed. United States nationalism's pathetic fallacy, according to Runte, is confined to wild nature: The natural wonders of the West became construed as national "earth monuments," key signifiers of the grandeur and distinctiveness of the United States and its contribution to world culture (104:22). But examples of nationalist pastorals also abound. Sweedenburg documents the centrality of the signifier of the peasant in contemporary Palestinian nationalism (123) as does Verdery for Romanian nationalism (133). Brow points out that the Sinhalese nation is "most typically represented as a nation of villages" (21:13; see 77a, 119a). Boyarin notes the agriculturalist emphasis of early Zionism and the importance of the pastoral in French nationalism (19:2). Manthei argues that Brazil's military regime fostered a nationalism that promoted capitalist development and urbanization as progress and modernity while mitigating the effects of time-space compression through a nostalgia for the rural (84).

Does the prevalence of arborescent and other nature imagery suggest the existence of a transnational culture of nationalism (83; cf 7:135, 27:5–6)? Such a culture could be viewed as a "common material and meaningful framework...that sets out the central terms" (102:361), deployed and, hence, transformed in historically and socially specific, contested processes of nation making and state formation, a repetoire of signifiers with multiple and heterogeneous significations, rather than a unified system of beliefs. Can the genealogy of such a transnational culture of nationalism be traced to a transcolonial culture of colonialism, which shaped nationalism and state formation in the metropole as well as provided the terms against which anti-colonial nationalism in the periphery was formed (32, 109; cf 7, 26)? To what extent are particular nationalisms not simply the product of such a transnational culture but also of local cultures (77a)? Are arborescent tropes rooted in religious symbolism? If so, is this another instance in which "pastoral power" (48) laid the foundations for technologies of ruling in at least some modern nation-states?

Substantialization

The spatial matrix materialized in the operation of the state system shapes the imagining of personhood as well as place. The bounding of the nation as a collective subject, as a superorganism with a unique biological-cultural essence (63), replicates the enclosure of national territory. Tropes of territorialized space are articulated with tropes of substance in the imagining of collective and individual national bodies (cf 95).

As Malkki points out, tropes of arborescent roots configure a genealogical form of imagining nations. Botanical metaphors and tropes of shared bodily substance (e.g. blood, genes) are combined in the "family tree" (83:38, note 7). The Constitutional tree of life I mentioned earlier is also an icon of the relations among the founding fathers of the Mexican "Revolutionary Family" as configured in official discourse. Widespread use of terms such as motherland or fatherland indicates the articulation of these two registers of tropes in national imaginings. Yet the substantialization of nations and states through tropes of blood and kinship, although noted frequently, is rarely analyzed fully (e.g. 7:143–144).

The idiom of kinship, Brow comments, has a "special potency as a basis of community" because "it can draw upon the past not simply to posit a common origin but also to claim substantial identity in the present" (20:3). More than twenty years ago, Schneider pointed to the links between the symbolism of kinship and nationality: "In American culture, one is 'An American' either by birth or through a process which is called...'naturalization.' In precisely the same terms as kinship, there are the same two 'kinds of citizens,' those by birth and those by law" (105:120). The solidarity that is supposed to exist among nationals rests on tropes of kinship, reproduction, "shared substance" (biogenetic and psychic), and "codes for conduct" (105). So too does the substantialization of the state as a supersubject, as *paterfamilias,* an effect of power that Trouillot argues is key for moral regulation (128:20). He notes that not only is this the dominant model of the state in Haiti, but it "is preferred by elites the world over because it gives them a choice role" (p. 20). Representation of states and nations that draw on kinship tropes are polysemous. For example, in Mexico, government officials are simultaneously the sons of the nation, conceived as the place that is the mother of all Mexicans, and the fathers of the nation, conceived as the collective patrimony or as the political community (90:235).

Kinship tropes substantialize hierarchical social relations and imbue them with sentiment and morality. Kinship tropes can also sacralize the state and the imagined relations among state, nation, and people: The father-son-mother relations in Mexican nationalist discourse recall the relations among God, Jesus, and Mary; or priests, the Church, and the religious community, in Catholic discourse. P Corrigan notes that "recent historiography accents the continuity between forms of Christian surveillance and state forms that are ostensibly rational and secular" (personal communication).

Significantly, the symbol selected by *Time* magazine to represent "the future, multiethnic face of America" is a "beguiling if mysterious" woman, "our new Eve," the "offspring" of "morphing," a computer process that images the products of "racial and ethnic miscegenation" (127:2). The substantialization of sociocultural forms of peoplehood enables their embodiment and rests on the naturalization and objectification of constructions and relations of gender and sexuality.

Though scant, some of the best literature on nationalism, ethnicity, and the state has been produced by scholars for whom gender and sexuality are central analytical concerns: The denaturalizing of gender and sexuality leads to the dismantling of ethnicity and nationalism as primordial essences (e.g. 27, 36c, 37, 42, 78, 86, 87, 92, 93, 146). Yuval-Davis & Anthias summarize the themes in this literature by identifying five major ways in which women have been viewed in relation to ethnic and national processes and practices of state formation: 1. as biological reproducers of members of ethnic collectivities; 2. as reproducers of the boundaries of ethnic/national groups; 3. as participating centrally in the ideological reproduction of the collectivity and as transmitters of its culture; 4. as signifiers of ethnic/national differences—as a focus and symbol in ideological discourses used in the construction, reproduction, and transformation of ethnic/national categories; and 5. as participants in national, economic, political and military struggles (8:7).

Because constructions of gender and sexuality have been key for the formation of ethnic and national subjectivities and collectivities, the technologies of bio-power wielded by the state have had differential consequences for men and women, for heterosexuals and homosexuals, for ethnic minorities and majorities. Likewise, men and women have been positioned in different ways by discourses of inter-ethnic and inter-national conflict: The rape and murder of women become key signifiers of victory and defeat in conflicts that are imagined to be agons of heroic masculinity; or conversely, the rescue of "other men's women" has been used to legitimate state deployments of force (36c, 42). Similarly, at least in Latin America, the state's torture of its subjects, including members of ethnically subordinated groups, has been gendered and sexualized (5). My only criticism of this literature is that it focuses, almost exclusively, on femininities and women. More research is needed on the reciprocal relations between the construction of masculinities and of collective subjectivity and community.

The persuasiveness of nationalism as a structure of feeling (141; see 60) that transforms space into homeplace and interpolates individual and collective subjects as embodiers of national character (viewed as shared bio-genetic and psychic substance) hinges on tropes of kinship, gender, and sexuality. Not surprisingly, gendered alimentary tropes (e.g. cooking, food, digestion) are also salient in nationalist discourses. Feminist critiques of the rhetoric, sentiments, and practice of kinship provide valuable points of entry into a critique of nationalism.

Although tropes of nationalism exhibit the properties that Turner identified as characterizing ritual symbols—condensation, unification of disparate significata, and polarization of meaning (130:27–30)—this point is rarely explored in the literature and deserves more attention. Many scholars of nationalism ask, "Why have so many people been willing to kill and die in the name of the nation?" A partial answer is found in the fusion of the ideological and the sensory, the bodily and the normative, the emotional and the instrumental, the organic and the social, accomplished by these tropes and particularly evident in strategies of substantialization by which the obligatory is converted into the desirable. As Daniel argues, Peircean semeiotics can illuminate how this is accomplished, enabling an analysis of how nationalism becomes a structure of feeling through the articulation of different modes of signification (36a).

As Anderson notes, nations inspire a self-sacrificing love, which is thought to be primordial rather than socially created (p. 143). For Anderson, this love is a product of the "deep horizontal comradeship" of nationalist fraternity (p. 7). Not only does he ignore the filial dimension of nationalist love, but he does not explore the "commerce between eros and nation" and the gender and sexual politics entailed in love of country (94:1–2). Feminist scholarship has long questioned the common sense notion that power and hierarchy are exiled from the realm of kinship and love (see 29). Many nationalisms use tropes of kinship that naturalize age and gender hierarchies. Moreover, through metaphor and metonymy, the meanings of kinship terms are extended and are used to construct vertical relations of class and ethnicity, of state and people, of heterosexuals and homosexuals. Nationalist forms of community may possess both horizontal and vertical dimensions (20:2). Even when the idiom of kinship is used to express a sense of equality as sameness, as in Guyana, the notion of nationals as belonging to one family is not incompatible with hierarchy. Rather, egalitarianism and hierarchy are complexly concatenated in this notion of "moral equality among all socially unequal persons" (140:99). Looking at nationalism as a structure of feeling is key for the denaturalizing of hierarchy as well as to an understanding of how effects of power are simultaneously effects of pleasure, and of how love, sexuality, and dominance are interconnected in lived experience.

Temporalization and Memory

Temporalizing and memory-making mediate the identity of people and heritage in space just as the representation and organization of space mediates the identity of people and heritage through time. Indeed, as Boyarin points out, memory is associated with both time and space, and in France and Israel, for example, this link is "connected to the reinforcement of national identity, a process in which the ideological constructions of uniquely shared land, language, and memory become props for the threatened integrity of the nation-state" (19:1). In a similar vein, Harvey comments on the importance of time and space to remembering: "Immemorial spatial memory" is so critical to the stable realization of myths of community that the "spatial image...asserts an important power over history" (65:218). The spatial, temporal, and bodily matrices are conjoined in nationalism. As the state marks out frontiers, "it constitutes what is within (the people-nation) by homogenizing the before and after of the content of this enclosure" (95:114).

Anderson argues that a conception of "'homogeneous, empty time' in which simultaneity is...traverse, cross-time, marked not by prefiguring and fulfillment but by temporal coincidence, and measured by clock and calendar" (7:24) is critical for the birth of the nation since it is conceived as a "solid community moving steadily down (or up) history" (p. 26). The novel, in this account, is a key genre for the presentation of this notion of time (p. 25 ff). Yet Anderson's dismissal of the importance of prefiguring and fulfillment in nationalist temporalizing seems hasty (and overly dependent on an opposition between religion and nationalism). Nations, after all, are commonly imagined as having a destiny and a heritage rooted in an immemorial past (7, 52, 71, 112). Moreover, the "selective tradition" (141:115) through which this past is constructed frequently is sacralized (13:3–40, 20:3, 135:215). Pace Anderson, not only Christian imaginings but also nationalist ones—whether overtly secular (and implicitly sacralized) or openly religious—are omnitemporal. Societies, as Harvey points out, are characterized by multiple and heterogenous senses of time (65).

The rationalization of time has been integral to nationalism's universalist tendency, enabling the location of the members of a nation in the same temporal frame, one marked by progress (15:283), as well as to capitalist development and modern state formation. But nationalism also has a tendency to particularism: "It cultivates the symbols, the fetishes of an autochthonous national character, which must be preserved against dissipation" (p. 283). Particularism, what makes a nation distinct, is undermined by the time-space compression produced by modernization, which relativizes and accelerates time, fragments continuity, and generates a global temporal frame in which simultaneity is universalized and decentered, no longer confined to fellow nationals (65:201–307). This is the time of many modernist novels (13, 65:260–283), a time centered on a present moving into a future, a time of incompleteness and inconclusiveness "where there is no first word...and the final word has not yet been spoken" (13:30), a time of diversity of speech and voice. According to Harvey, the aestheticization of politics is one nationalist response to the dissipation of essence produced by a decentered temporality (65:207–209). But particularism is secured not just through the spatialization of time, as Harvey argues, but also through the deployment of another temporal modality, epic time, an absolute time of Being, of first and last words, of prefiguring and fulfillment, of tradition and destiny.

Bakhtin characterizes the epic as a nationalist genre that has three constitutive features: 1. a national epic past, as the subject, 2. national tradition, as the source, and 3. an absolute epic distance, separating the epic world from contemporary reality (13:13). Temporal categories are valorized creating a hierarchy among past, present, and future in which the past becomes "the single source and beginning of everything good for all later times" (p. 13); the distance between past and present is mediated by national tradition (p. 14). Bakhtin's reflections provide a suggestive point of departure for analyses of nationalist constructions of memory and time and the effects of power they produce—even when the genre of the epic, narrowly construed, is not their vehicle. For it is through epic discourses, broadly conceived, that the nation is particularized and centered, imagined as eternal and primordial, and that nationalist love becomes a sacralized and sublime sentiment, indeed, a form of piety (p. 16). And the sacralization of the nation is simultaneously the sacralization of the state.

Postcolonial Sinhalese nationalism provides a good example of epic nationalist discourse (21, 77a, 119a, 142, 143; cf 76, 106). A valorized, epic past is configured by idealized images of a harmonious, precolonial social order of beneficent kings and flourishing village communities. The distance of this absolute past from the present is marked by the rupture of colonialism; but simultaneously, this past is represented as a latent presence (and promise) in contemporary reality, one that can be made manifest "if political leaders follow the example of the ancient kings by governing righteously and pursuing policies of development that promote both the moral and material welfare of the people" (21:9). By configuring the past-present relationship as entailing both rupture and continuity, distance and proximity, nostalgia and plenitude, official Sinhalese nationalism modernizes the traditional and traditionalizes the modern (21:9), turning continuity into fatality (cf 7:11).

The authority of Sinhalese nationalist rhetoric is partly secured by the temporal hierarchy that renders absolute an official version of the past produced by a number of agents and institutions of the state system, a version whose selectivity demonstrates that remembering is also forgetting (19:1–8; 113). The absoluteness of this past and, hence, the primordial character of Sinhalese community are constructed through the articulation of tropes of space, substance and time.

The rhetorical strategies used in the construction of authoritative memories merit more attention than they have received. In my own investigation of the re-presentation of the past in scholarly texts and Mexican popular and official discourses, I argue for the importance of analyzing manipulations of framing, voice, and narrative structure for understanding how histories produce effects of power/knowledge (4). I examine how nationalist re-presentations of the past, produced by those in control of the state system, appropriate and transform local and regional histories and the memories of subordinated groups through the strategies of naturalization, idealization, and de-particularization. Pasts that cannot be incorporated are privatized and particularized, consigned to the margins of the national and denied a fully public voice (4; see 17:266–267). Through these strategies, a selective tradition of nationalism, which is key for the consolidation of the idea of the state, is produced by the institutions and personnel of the state system. This tradition is critical to the construction of hegemony by agents and institutions of the state system.

The production of a selective tradition by the state system is a powerful and vulnerable hegemonic process (141:116–117). A hegemonic selective tradition is always challenged by alternative and oppositional traditions that dispute dominant articulations of space, time, and substance and can even question the identity between nation and state (4, 17, 20–22, 36, 39, 68, 82, 90, 96, 117, 123, 133, 133a, 142).

The degree of persuasiveness of the selective traditions of official nationalisms hinges on state systems' control over the means of distribution of social meanings (4; see 64) and on the relations of forces in society (56:180–185).

Sinhalese nationalism once again provides an example. To gain the support of subordinated groups, rulers make rhetorical concessions that place the peasantry at "the moral core of the nation" (21:9). This rhetoric of inclusion is disseminated by "virtually all the apparatuses of the state" (p. 13) and is accompanied by the distribution of material benefits. However, these concessions and benefits never jeopardize the reproduction of the hegemonic bloc or undermine the fundamental exclusions on which Sinhalese nationalism is predicated. If the use of tropes from a pastoral register celebrates peasants' contributions to the nation, it also creates an identification between state, nation, and territory that empowers state personnel to oversee rural development and, hence, to create new relations of ruling in the countryside (21, 119a, 142, 143). Moreover, rulers' definition of the nation as Sinhalese relies on the epic past to exclude Tamils from the imagined community, as well as to represent the struggles between Sinhalese and Tamils as the result of primordial animosities (36b, 77a, 119a, 125). The genealogy of this form of exclusion lies in the colonial conflation of cultural and biological differences (21:11).

Pace Anderson (7:141–154), nationalism and ethnicity are constructed reciprocally. Patriotism is not simply about loving one's fellow nationals. It is also about hating or, at best, condescending to tolerate others without and within national space. In contrast to Anderson, Balibar argues that nationalisms have been imagined as communities of shared blood and heritage as well as language, and that fraternity has been predicated on "an excess of 'purism'" (15:284). The self-identity of nations has been secured partly through the construction of internal Others, whose markedness assures the existence of a national identity that, remaining invisible or unmarked, is successfully inscribed as the norm (15:284-286, 140:20). In numerous nationalisms, the ethnic identity of the dominant group is privileged as the core of imagined community (18, 27, 36, 36b, 50, 53, 77a, 88, 119a, 144). Not surprisingly, European nationalisms formed in relation to colonialism and colonial technologies of rule (15:286–287; 109; 140:xvi). More research is needed on this point. Likewise, the ethnic hierarchies of the colonial past have had significant impact on the formation of nationalisms in postcolonial states (18, 26, 27, 36, 50, 88, 122, 140, 144, 145).

NATIONALISM AND ETHNICITY

Defining Ethnicity

Because of the fuzziness of the term ethnicity, the frequent conflation of nationality, ethnicity, and race in the literature and in common sense, and the problematic politics of ethnicity as evinced in its intellectual genealogies, some scholars have suggested replacing the term as an analytical category with peoplehood (39:11), race (118), or nationalist ideology (47:3). Although I agree with these critiques of ethnicity, I remain convinced that drawing analytical distinctions between different forms of imagining peoplehood is methodologically useful.

Nationalism is partly an effect of the totalizing and homogenizing projects of state formation (35). These projects produce an imagined sense of political community that conflates peoplehood, territory, and state. But state formation also generates categories of Self and Other within a polity. In contrast to nationalism, ethnicity is partly an effect of the particularizing projects of state formation, projects that produce hierarchized forms of imagining peoplehood that are assigned varying degrees of social esteem and differential privileges and prerogatives within a political community (38, 89, 118, 124, 135, 140; see also 3, 16, 25, 31, 97). Anthropologists rarely have examined the reciprocal relations between processes of state formation and ethnogenesis (but see 38, 88, 118, 140; S Rivera Cusicanqui, unpublished observations); more research is needed along these lines.

Along with class, gender, age, and sexual orientation, ethnicity is one of the dimensions of identity key for the construction and negotiation of status (135:305) and, hence, of power in state societies (34, 89:427, 118, 139:70–71). More specifically, ethnicity entails "a subjective belief in...common descent because of [subjectively perceived] similarities of physical type or of customs or both, or because of memories of colonization and migration" (135:389). Ethnic affiliation is calculated contextually, through the concatenation of ethnic boundary markers (16)—culturally constructed indexes of categorical identities endowed with differential worth and purpose.

What is called race in much of the literature is the variant of ethnicity that privileges somatic indexes of status distinctions such as skin color, hair quality, shape of features, or height. What is called ethnicity is the variant that privileges style-of-life indexes of status distinctions such as dress, language, religion, food, music, or occupation. As Szwed points out, somatic and style-of-life indexes are used simultaneously as signifiers of hierarchized categorical identities (124:20–21); hence, there is no sharp distinction between these two variants of ethnicity.

Despite its lack of scientific validity and the widespread rumors of its demise, the belief in biological races, what Appiah calls racialism (10:5), is widespread in media discourse (e.g. 127) and is by no means dead in scholarship (110:16ff). Cohen claims that the "notorious aggressiveness and drive for localized political autonomy of celtic fringe groups" may be either "a form of learning passed from one generation to the next" or "a genetic proclivity based on favoured breeding for these traits" (28:257, note 3). Even more disturbing is Guidieri & Pellizzi's representation of *métissage*, which they see as a form of genetic and cultural mixing, as a pathological process (58:33).

The false precept that underlies such observations is that ethnic groups are genetically pure breeding populations with distinct, homogeneous, and bounded cultures. Ethnicity is thus rendered primordial and ethnic groups become viewed as superorganisms characterized by unique repetoires of cultural traits that can be transmitted, borrowed, or lost (for critiques of primordialism see 41a, 63, 108, 109, 118, 119, 137, 140). As Barth argued more than twenty years ago, this notion of ethnicity "begs all the critical questions" (16:11).

Weber, sometimes cited as one of the ancestors of primordialism (e.g. 31), recognized that "ethnic fictions" were the product of the diverse economic and political conditions of social groups and that phenotypic or cultural differences did not lead to the production of these fictions or to group formation (135:389–395; see 118). Indeed, as RT Smith's reading of Weber stresses, even when categorical identities become one of the bases for status group formation, group boundaries are not fixed but shift in relation to struggles for power, prestige, and privilege (118). Moreover, group boundaries do not enclose unique cultural essences. Instead, differences in style of life are the historical product of groups' distinct social and economic locations, everyday practices, and differential interpretations of a shared idiom of distinction (118).

Ethnic constructionists are the most visible critics of primordialists. Yet, some of their work is overly focused on discourse and fails to recognize fully that ethnicity is invented in the course of cultural, political, and economic struggles (e.g. 119, 120). The point "is not to declare ethnicity invented and stop there, but to show in historical perspective how it was invented and with what consequences" (100:27). The repeated insistence in the constructionist literature on the fluidity of ethnicity illustrates the limitations of a narrow, discursive focus. Ethnicity is constructed; hence, it follows in principle that ethnicity is fluid, but this fluidity is limited by hegemonic processes of inscription and by the relations of forces in society. That this obvious point is widely ignored only attests to the relative privilege of many of those writing on ethnicity. Fanon illustrates that from a position of ethnic subordination, the possibility of counter-inventing ethnicity is not always already there and the struggle against the weight of a history that produces "a definitive structuring of the self and of the world" is one in which even laughter becomes impossible (43, 45:109–110). Likewise, Anzaldúa (9) and Gómez-Peña (55) question the dominant topography of discrete and homogeneous nations, cultures, and identities, while highlighting the difficulties faced by those whom the state categorizes as Hispanic in negotiating alternative senses of individual and collective personhood.

Nationalism, Ethnicity and Hegemony: Exclusions and Inclusions

Some of the best approaches in the field are based on Gramsci's work or on Marxist cultural studies. These approaches examine the role of the state in the dialectic of nationalism and ethnicism, while recognizing the mutually formative struggles between the state and subordinated ethnic subjects (e.g. 36, 53, 62, 88, 91, 140). Hall identifies some of the features of a Gramscian perspective that are useful for an analysis of ethnicity, including (*a*) the emphasis on historical specificity; (*b*) the nonreductive approach to class and ethnicity; (*c*) the lack of assumed correspondence between the economic, political, and ideological dimensions of society; (*d*) the notion of hegemony; and (*e*) the importance accorded to the state (62:5–27). West's neo-Gramscian methodology for analyzing African-American oppression relies on the articulation of three "moments": modes of domination, forms of subjugation, and types of exploitation (136:21–25). West's methodology is applicable to other cases, though the role of the state in ethnic domination, subjugation, and exploitation needs to be integrated into his scheme.

B Williams's reformulation of hegemony is particularly useful for an analysis of how paradoxes of homogeneity and heterogenity are negotiated by the state through "different modes of political incorporation" of ethnicized subjects (139:408) and diverse forms of representation and appropriation of their cultural products and practices (140:31). She uses Gramsci's concept of transformism to analyze how official nationalism and state routines simultaneously homogenize community while creating heterogeneity (140). Indeed, union is shaped through an "incorporation of difference [along lines of ethnicity, class, gender, locality, age, and sexual orientation, which] hierarchically organizes subject positions for diverse groups of citizens" (60:72). State strategies of spatialization, substantialization, aestheticization, commodification, and temporalization are key for the construction of transformist forms of hegemony.

Spatialization

As Corrigan demonstrates (33), ethnicity is "used to name and mark off culturally and racially varied 'places'" that are space and time locations (111:35). Despite Barth's proposal that anthropologists examine ethnic formation by focusing on the creation of social boundaries, which may have territorial counterparts, rather than on the unique "cultural stuff" that these boundaries are alleged to enclose, anthropological research on the role of space and place in boundary creation is scarce (16:15). I think anthropologists must examine how the organization and representation of space is implicated in ethnic formation and inequality, in state strategies of asymmetric incorporation and appropriation, and in the complex dialectic between hierarchy and egalitarianism, heterogeneity and homogeneity, in the imagining of nations. How is the partitioning of space connected to ethnic inequality? How are dominant and subordinated ethnic subjects differentially situated in relation to spaces of production, distribution, and consumption, and what state policies and practices are implicated in the politics of ethnic location? How are categorical identities unequally positioned in relation to public and private spaces, sacred spaces, work spaces, carceral spaces, and home spaces? How does the contemporary, international, and national politics of space and place result in environmental racism both globally and locally? How do spatial practices become a focus of intense social struggles?

The centrality of space to the hegemonic strategy of transformism is well illustrated by "the model village program" in Guatemala, linchpin of the military's counter-insurgency campaign (98). According to Richards, the ideology of ethnicity deployed by the Guatemalan state and the military is predicated on a hierarchized urban and rural dichotomy that equates the urban with the "civilized" Ladino Self, the Subject of nationalism, and the rural with the "backwards" Indian Other, defined as the source of national distinctiveness and the obstacle to national development. Indian "backwardness," attributed to a historical legacy of Indian regional autonomy, is held to explain resistance to the state. Hence, the model villages, "urban microcosms" that are simultaneously spaces of discipline and of civilization, have become the "nucleii into which the dispersed population of a war-torn region can be gathered and controlled" as well as "developed" in the name of the nation (p. 8). Mayas' establishment of Communities of Population in Resistance is one response to current social struggles over ethnic formation and spatial location.

The equation of the dominant ethnic identity with the core of the nation, and the location of subordinated ethnic identities at its peripheries, is secured partly through differential power over private and public spaces. For example, Eidheim demonstrates how the identification of Norway with Norwegians is a product of unequal control of public spaces and, hence, of the differential possibilities of signifying marked and unmarked identities in these locations (41). In public spaces, where Sami and Norwegians interact, the dominant code for conduct is Norwegian. The marginalization and stigmatization of Sami identity is secured by its privatization (p. 46). By contrast, hooks examines the ethnic and gender politics of private spaces by focusing on the difficulties faced by African-American women, many of them domestic workers in the employ of whites, in constructing their own "homeplaces." She shows how the hierarchical opposition between private and public spaces is put into question by these women who redefine home as a healing refuge and site for collective and personal resistance (72:33–49).

Anthropological research on the relationship between representations of space and place and identity formation is somewhat more developed than that on the politics of spatial organization. Subnational conflations of race, culture, and social group presuppose a notion of boundaries that differentiate inside from outside in absolute terms. These boundaries are often imagined through tropes of differential origin according to place. For example, representations of the Trinidadian nation as "populated by a set of codified and reified, collective characters" differentiate these "raced-classes" according to their origin in distinct ancestral lands—Africa, Europe, and India (108:14). Likewise, ethnic differentiation can be construed according to location within national territory: "The Indian national anthem...sequentially names the different regions (hence, languages, cultures, religions, histories) that are all distinctive parts of the united Indian nation," simultaneously proclaiming homogenity while accenting difference (60:72). Calagione shows how a vision that locates ethnic boundaries in different ancestral homelands has shaped urban planning in New York City, fomenting a "naturalized version of ethnic identity as spatially bounded enclave" (24:2), and spatializing a hierarchy of civility.

How do nationalisms construct the displaced, those whose mobility denaturalizes identifications of state, nation, and territory? The "sendentarist metaphysic" of nationalism "enables a vision of territorial displacement as pathological," as a "loss of moral bearings" that makes the uprooted the antithesis of "honest citizens" (83:31–32). How does the state manage the "pathology" of the displaced (36b, 43, 53)? Daniel (368) argues that as the national past became increasingly unavailable (in the Heideggerian sense) to Sri Lankan Tamil immigrants to the United Kingdom, who had fled ethnicism at home only to encounter it abroad, they became cynical about the nation and about the state. This break with territorialized community and with the law had wide-reaching consequences for their everyday practices, including the creation of home places. Moreover, as the links between people and place became denaturalized for these immigrants, their sense of national and ethnic identity shifted. Not only did they begin to view Tamils as a deterritorialized community of people, but they also began to form alliances with other ethnically oppressed groups. Anthropological perspectives on immigrants' and states' politics of displacement are needed particularly today as peoples from the periphery move to the metropole.

Calagione has remarked that United States government functionaries frequently use water imagery to represent Third World immigrants (personal communication). This imagery is prevalent in the media. Whereas the central place of the descendants of immigrants of European ancestry in the imagined community is signified through the adjective mainstream, the marginality of recent Third World immigrants is signified through the visual trope "waves of newcomers" (127:20), which represents the marginal as a threat to the "water-tightness" of national borders. Not surprisingly, Mexican illegal aliens are called "wetbacks." The passage of the North American Free Trade Agreement coincides with the United States government's increasing militarization of its border with Mexico and the expenditure of tax dollars in attempts to "stem the tide" by constructing giant steel walls.

Another topic that merits more research is the politics of representation of heterogenity and homogeneity in public spaces. Friedlander has analyzed how the Mexican state's ideology of *mestizo* nationalism is objectified in space through monuments such as those found in Mexico City's Plaza of the Three Cultures[2]: "an Aztec pyramid, a sixteenth-century Catholic church, and a recently constructed government building" (50:xiii). The Spanish conquest of the Aztecs is memorialized as "the painful birth of the Mestizo people," Mexico's national race, embodied and represented by the state as signified by the government building (p. xiv). The exclusiveness of this apparent form of inclusion is effected through the internal hierarchy articulated in the category of *mestizo*. The European and Indian racial and cultural components of the *mestizo* (note the erasure of African-Mexicans' contributions) are rendered distinct and ranked in relation to each other: The former is identified with progress; the latter with tradition. This transformist strategy is used all over Latin America (18, 36, 88, 122; S Rivera Cusicanqui, unpublished observations); moreover, internal hierarchy characterizes the category of *mulato* as well as that of *mestizo* (145).

Substantialization, Aestheticization, and Commodification

The above example illustrates the inequality that subsists even in polygenetic and multicultural representations of national origins in states characterized by transformist hegemonies: Race and culture are conflated, and the state as hybrid *paterfamilias* accords itself a privileged role in building community out of difference. The tropes of kinship and descent used to substantialize the nation are also invoked to substantialize the categorical identities of ethnicity. Semanticized by a tropology of blood, color, and descent, the "cultural stuff" held to characterize low-status identities is represented as inert, homogeneous tradition—something akin to *Time*'s "psychic genes" (127). Through an analogy with folk notions of biological reproduction, the transmission of this cultural heritage becomes envisioned as an endless, static process of mimesis, denying ethnically subordinated subjects any agency or creativity (126). Once endowed with misplaced concreteness, the ethnic heritage of low status subjects is then aestheticized and commodified by the state.

Anthropologists have produced some excellent accounts of this process of aestheticization and commodification of the ethnic heritage of subordinated groups (e.g. 12, 137). A substantial body of work deals with folklorization and

2

This plaza was the site of the massacre of hundreds of people by state forces in 1968.

Indian-State relations in Latin America (e.g. 50, 51, 67, 68, 84a, 96, 129). Friedlander's work shows how the Mexican state's selective glorification of elements of Indian culture has simultaneously enabled the incorporation of Indians into the nation while maintaining their low-status identity and class position (50:129). Ironically, an image of Indian authenticity as eternal mimesis is produced through this ethnicized form of commodity fetishism.

Once commodified, the charisma of "Indianess" can be appropriated by the non-Indian elite: Conspicuous consumption of these signifers of alterity by the "national race" legitimates relations of ruling vis-a-vis national and international audiences by objectifying claims to autochthony and populist pretensions (50). Hendrickson's analysis of the all *Ladino* Miss Guatemala contest, whose winner wears indigenous *traje* when representing her country in the world competition, illustrates this point (67). McAllister demonstrates that the parallel, state organized *Rabín Ahau* beauty pageant, in which only indigenous women participate, is not about beauty but about an aestheticized Indian authenticity (84a). Hill's work on "junk Spanish" (69, 70) shows how, under the guise of aesthetic openess, elite "Anglos," including government personnel, simultaneously construct themselves as good citizens and "Hispanics" as inferior alters through the pejorative borrowing of Spanish morphological material and the conspicuous consumption of "Hispanic" commodities (70:12). Vélez-Ibáñez analyzes the negative consequences that the creation of such a commodity identity has had for United States Mexicans (132).

The subordinated also engage in the mimesis of alterity through ethnic commodity fetishism,[3] but it has very different consequences for ethnically dominant versus subordinated subjects. For the Indians of Hueyapan, Hispanicization is achieved through participation in nationalist rituals and consumption of commodities that are indexes of a *mestizo* style of life (50:71); hence, *mestizo* nationalism also promotes the development of an internal market. However, the exploited class position of most Indians ensures that many of these commodities will be out of their reach. In addition, as the non-Indian "elite redefines its own identity, it demotes characteristics previously associated with its prestigious high status to the low level...of Indianess" (p. 71). In this case, the privileging of style of life over somatic indexes of ethnicity does not promote a greater status mobility or ethnic fluidity. Moreover, subordinated alters who engage in conspicuous consumption "may (and most often do) stand to be accused of riding to the pinnacle of civilization on the coattails of its real producers" (140:30) or of losing their authenticity (96:169). This points to another paradox of the politics of ethnicity substantialized as descent.

3

For a discussion of ethnic commodity fetishism, gender regionalism, and nationalism in rural northern Mexico, see reference 5a. The role of the market in commodifying ethnicity in the southwest is analyzed in reference 138.

On the one hand, tradition is held to be transmitted in the blood or handed down from one generation to the next; on the other hand, when defined as patrimony, tradition can be lost. This is because the essence of the ethnically subordinated is fixed through spatial and temporal distancing: Any departure from a mimetic performance of an invented past can be construed as loss of original substance.

Temporalization

Transformist strategies of temporalization particularize ethnic identities and differentiate their contributions and places in the nation. State constructed past-present relations distinguish subjects according to location vis-a-vis the time of national origin versus the time of the national future. Ecuadorian (36, 88, 122), Mexican (4, 50, 51, 90), and Trinidadian (108) nationalisms are good illustrations of the political character of strategies of temporalization. In Ecuador, state strategies of temporalization fossilize indigenous peoples, identifying them with an epic past rather than a national future, as well as reducing their contributions to the nation to folklore while erasing contemporary realities of exploitation and domination (36, 88). One of the effects of the Ecuadorian national pastoral is to turn land—a key means of production—into heritage, into a national patrimony whose privileged custodian, the state, secures proprietorship of the past by erasing the genealogy of property (36:54; see 17).

Yet indigenous cultural production and collective action in Ecuador is exceeding the frame implied by folklore and is challenging the state (36, 88). Hegemony is the result of a dialectic of struggle, and relations of forces in society shape the policies, routines, and practices of states (53, 56, 62, 91, 139). However, within a transformist hegemony, resistance takes place under conditions of inequality that limit the power of subordinated subjects to redefine their status and their place in and contributions to the imagined national community. This point is made painfully clear by Menchú's reflections on indigenous resistance in Guatemala (22). Research on resistance that focuses on oppositional culture without considering the political and economic power available to subordinated subjects and the possibilities for institutionalizing and inscribing popular alternatives risks becoming a form of wishful thinking.

Indigenous Resistance in Latin America

To what extent do indigenous people accept, reformulate or reject hegemonic cultures of ethnic domination? This question has received a lot of attention in the literature (e.g. 22, 50, 77, 96, 115, 121, 125, 131, 133a). According to Friedlander, the people of Hueyapan have "internalized the Hispanic elite's view of their own Indianess" (50:72), although they use everyday strategies to protect themselves from discrimination and exploitation. By contrast, Warren's study of Mayas' views of ethnic domination in Guatemala demonstrates the heterogeneity of cultures of resistance while highlighting "striking attempts by Indians to reformulate their ethnic identity and the symbolism of subordination" through counter-hegemonic mythology (133a:ix). Similarly, Menchú's analysis of the dialectic between Mayas' struggles and state repression stresses the importance of an oppositional selective tradition, expressed in ritual and narrative, in collective resistance (22). Rappaport's research in Colombia highlights the centrality of oppositional strategies of spatialization and temporalization in the reframing of dominant legal discourse by indigenous militants (96). Other work focuses on paradoxes of simultaneous contestation and reproduction of cultures of domination, arguing nonetheless that the selective incorporation by indigenous people of dominant forms also entails their reinterpretation (e.g. 1, 11, 66, 68). Overall, recent research emphasizes the importance of understanding indigenous perspectives and responses historically in terms of the conjunctural and organic dimensions of an internal dialectic and a dialectic of articulation (30) between indigenous communities, nation-states, and the international order (e.g. 3, 73, 114, 116, 134).

Harvey argues that in the current conjuncture of time-space compression, globalization of capitalism, and resurgence of aetheticized nationalism, social movements "are relatively empowered to organize in place but disempowered when it comes to organizing over space" (65:303). Privileging place-identities, social movements are highly localized and regionalized; hence, they are limited in their abilities to form broader coalitions. In this regard, the anthropology of transnational subaltern groups, diasporas, and border peoples might offer more cause for optimism (e.g. 60, 61, 82, 83). For example, Kearney concludes that "transnational communities…escape the power of the nation-state to inform their sense of collective identity" and represent a potent challenge to the spatial-temporal matrix of nationalism (77:59). Mixtec ethnicity has emerged as an alternative to nationalist consciousness and has resulted in the formation of grass-roots organizations in both the United States and Mexico "that seek to defend their members as workers, migrants, and 'aliens'" (77:63). Another topic that merits more attention is the emergence of broad, heterogeneous coalitions in the Americas in the wake of the Quincentenary, in which indigenous people play an important role. Ruiz, for example, highlights the transformative potential of the coalition that organized the Third Continental Encounter of Indigenous, Black, and Popular Resistance Movements, an event that took place in Managua in October 1992, bringing together people from "26 countries without distinction of race, language or culture" to "'generate a broad, pluralistic, multi-ethnic and democratic movement' to work for a new international economic, social, political and environmental order" (103:7). Likewise, Stavenhagen writes that a Pan-Indian consciousness has emerged in the New World since the 1970s, leading to the formation of organizations, such as the World Council of Indigenous Peoples, which act at regional, national, and international levels, calling for self-determination, autonomy, and ethnodevelopment (121). The study of such non-national movements can provide anthropologists a critical vantage point from which "the 'naturalness' of the nation can be radically called into question" (60:64)

CONCLUSION

Calling the naturalness of nationalism and the primordialness of ethnicity into question involves a critique of the impact of the precepts of nationalism and colonialism on the concept of culture (140), focusing on how anthropologists have reproduced dominant strategies of spatialization, substantialization, aestheticization, and temporalization in their work (44, 61, 64, 83, 99, 118). Such a critique is one point of departure for a renewed concept of culture that "refers less to a unified entity...than to the mundane practices of everyday life" and that focuses on the border zones within and between putatively homogeneous communities (99:217). Such a concept of culture puts into question the radical separation between Us and Them, which has underpinned much anthropology and, hence, enables an exploration of "the processes of production of difference in a world of culturally, socially, and economically interconnected and interdependent spaces" traversed by relations of inequality (61:14). Though the relatively recent inclusion of the state as an analytical category and ethnographic focus in mainstream sociocultural anthropology is a welcome move, a critical perspective also entails going beyond the nation-state, developing a global vision even as we continue to focus on the micropractices of everyday life.

If, as Harvey argues, the postmodern condition contains both liberatory and reactionary possibilities (65), further reflection on the political role of anthropologists in the contemporary world is needed. Although the critique of anthropological complicity with colonialism has been a necessary step, we should not let this blind us to the discipline's "continuing dependence on state power" (57:9) nor should we let "our discipline's flawed history" (p. 10) prevent us from acknowledging the emancipatory possibilities of critical anthropological projects (57, 77). Such a task, Scott reminds us, entails "a continuous internal labour of criticism" as well as a "continuous unlearning of...privilege" (107:388).

ACKNOWLEDGMENTS

Thanks to Daniel Nugent for the references, substantive comments, and editorial assistance he provided. Thanks to my research assistants D Goldstein and S Adrian. Thanks to J Hill, D Killick, E Krause, A Smith, B Williams, and D Woodson for providing references.

Literature Cited

1. Abercrombie T. 1991. To be Indian, to be Bolivian: "ethnic" and "national" discourses of identity. See Ref. 131, pp. 95–130
2. Abrams P. 1988. Notes on the difficulty of studying the state (1977). *J. Hist. Sociol.* 1(1):58–89
3. Adams RN. 1990. Strategies of ethnic survival in Central America. See Ref. 115, pp. 181–206
4. Alonso AM. 1988. The effects of truth: representations of the past and the imagining of community. *J. Hist. Sociol.* 1(1):33–57
5. Alonso AM. 1991. *Reflections on gender, violence and politics.* Presented at Gender, Violence and Society in Mexico & Latin Am. Conf., Univ. Texas Mexican Cent., Austin
5a. Alonso AM. 1992. Work and *gusto*: gender and recreation in a North Mexican Pueblo. In *Workers' Expressions: Beyond Accommodation and Resistance,* ed. J Calagione, D Francis, D Nugent, pp. 164–85. New York: State Univ. NY Press
6. Althusser L. 1971. *Lenin and Philosophy.* New York: Monthly Review
7. Anderson B. 1991. *Imagined Communities: Reflections on the Origin and Spread of Nationalism.* New York: Verso
8. Anthias F, Yuval-Davis N. 1989. Introduction. See Ref. 146, pp. 1–15
9. Anzaldúa G. 1987. *Borderlands/La Frontera: The New Mestiza.* San Francisco: Spinsters/Aunt Lute
10. Appiah KA. 1990. Racisms. See Ref. 54, pp. 3–17
11. Arias A. 1990. Changing Indian identity: Guatemala's violent transition to modernity. See Ref. 115, pp. 230–57
12. Babadzan A. 1988. Kastom and nation building in the South Pacific. See Ref. 59, pp. 199–228
13. Bakhtin MM. 1981. *The Dialogic Imagination.* Transl. C Emerson, M Holquist. Austin: Univ. Texas Press
14. Deleted in proof
15. Balibar E. 1990. Paradoxes of universality. See Ref. 54, pp. 283–94
16. Barth F. 1969. Introduction. In *Ethnic Groups and Boundaries: The Social Organization of Culture Difference,* ed. F Barth, pp. 9–38. Boston: Little Brown
17. Bommes M, Wright P 1982. 'Charms of Residence': the public and the past. In *Making Histories: Studies in History Writing and Politics,* ed. R Johnson, G McLennan, B Schwarz, D Sutton, pp. 253–302. Minneapolis: Univ. Minn. Press
18. Bourricaud F. 1975. Indian, mestizo, and cholo as symbols in the Peruvian system of stratification. In *Ethnicity: Theory and Experience,* ed. N Glazer, DP Moynihan, pp. 350–87. Cambridge: Harvard Univ. Press
19. Boyarin J. 1992. *Storm from Paradise: The Politics of Jewish Memory.* Minneapolis: Univ. Minn. Press
20. Brow J. 1990. Notes on community, hegemony, and the uses of the past. *Anthropol. Q.* 63(1):1–6
21. Brow J. 1990. The incorporation of a marginal community within the Sinhalese nation. *Anthropol. Q.* 63(1):7–17
22. Burgos-Debray E, ed. 1984. *I...Rigoberta Menchú: An Indian Woman in Guatemala.* Transl. A Wright. New York: Verso
23. Cain M. 1983. Gramsci, the state and the place of law. In *Legality, Ideology and the State,* ed. D Sugarman. London: Academic
24. Calagione JP. 1992. *The periphery at the center: the heart of whiteness.* Presented at Annu. Meet. Am. Anthropol. Assoc., 91st, San Francisco
25. Cashmore EE. 1984. *Dictionary of Race and Ethnic Relations.* London: Routledge & Kegan Paul
26. Chatarjee P. 1986. *Nationalist Thought and the Colonial World: A Derivative Discourse.* London: Zed
27. Chatarjee P. 1993. *The Nation and Its Fragments: Colonial and Postcolonial Histories.* Princeton, NJ: Princeton Univ. Press
28. Cohen R. 1993. Conclusion: ethnicity, the state, and moral order. In *Ethnicity and the State,* ed. J Toland, pp. 231–58. New Brunswick, NJ: Transaction
29. Collier JF, Yanagisako SJ, eds. 1987. *Gender and Kinship: Essays Toward a Unified Analysis.* Stanford, CA: Stanford Univ. Press
30. Comaroff J. 1982. Dialectical systems, history, and anthropology: units of study and questions of theory. *J. S. Afr. Hist.* 8(2):143–72
31. Comaroff J. 1992. Of totemism and ethnicity. In *Ethnography and the Historical*

Imagination, ed. J Comaroff, J Comaroff, pp. 49–67. Boulder: Westview

32. Cooper F, Stoler AL. 1989. Tensions of empire: colonial control and visions of rule. *Am. Ethnol.* 16(4):609–21

33. Corrigan P. 1987. Race/ethnicity/gender/culture: embodying differences educationally: an argument. In *Breaking the Mozaic: Ethnic Idenities in Canadian Schooling,* ed. J Young, pp. 20–30. Toronto: Garamond

34. Corrigan P. 1991. Viewpoint: power/difference. *Sociol. Rev.* May

35. Corrigan P, Sayer D. 1985. *The Great Arch: English State Formation as Cultural Revolution.* Oxford: Blackwell

36. Crain M. 1990. The social construction of national identity in highland Ecuador. *Anthropol. Q.* 63(1):43–59

36a. Daniel EV. 1993. Tea talk: violent measures in the discursive practices of Sri Lanka's estate Tamils. *Comp. Stud. Soc. Hist.* 35(3):568–600

36b. Daniel EV. 1994. *Charred Lullabies: Chapters in an Anthropography of Violence.* Princeton, NJ: Princeton Univ. Press

36c. Das V. 1994. *Critical Events.* Delhi: Oxford Univ. Press

37. Davin A. 1978. Imperialism and motherhood. *Hist. Workshop* 5:9–66

38. Domínguez VR. 1986. *White by Definition: Social Classification in Creole Louisiana.* New Brunswick, NJ: Rutgers Univ. Press

39. Domínguez VR. 1989. *People as Subject, People as Object: Selfhood and Peoplehood in Contemporary Israel.* Madison: Univ. Wisc. Press

40. Eagleton T. 1991. *Ideology: An Introduction.* London: Verso

41. Eidheim H. 1969. When ethnic identity is a social stigma. In *Ethnic Groups and Boundaries: The Social Organization of Culture Difference,* ed. F Barth, pp. 39–57. Boston: Little Brown

41a. Eller JD, Coughlan RM. 1993. The poverty of primordialism: the demystification of ethnic attachments. *Ethnic Racial Stud.* 16(2):183–202

42. Enloe C. 1989. *Bananas, Beaches and Bases: Making Feminist Sense of International Politics.* Berkeley: Univ. Calif. Press

43. Essed P. 1990. *Everyday Racism: Reports From Women of Two Cultures.* Transl. C Jaffeac. Claremont, CA: Hunter House

44. Fabian J. 1983. *Time and the Other: How Anthropology Makes its Object.* New York: Columbia Univ. Press

45. Fanon F. 1990. The fact of blackness. See Ref. 54, pp. 108–26

46. Fox RG, ed. 1990. *Nationalist Ideologies and the Production of National Cultures.* Am. Ethnol. Soc. Monogr. Ser., No. 2

47. Fox RG. 1990. Introduction. See Ref. 46, pp. 1–14

48. Foucault M. 1982. The subject and power. *Crit. Inq.* 8(4):775–95

49. Foucault M. 1984. *The Foucault Reader,* ed. P Rabinow. New York: Pantheon

50. Friedlander J. 1975. *Being Indian in Hueyapan: A Study of Forced Identity in Contemporary Mexico.* New York: St. Martin's

51. García Canclini N. 1993. *Transforming Modernity: Popular Culture in Mexico.* Transl. L Lozano. Austin: Univ. Texas Press

52. Gellner E. 1983. *Nations and Nationalism.* Ithaca, NY: Cornell Univ. Press

53. Gilroy P. 1987. *'There Ain't No Black in the Union Jack': The Cultural Politics of Race and Nation.* London: Hutchinson

54. Goldberg DT, ed. 1990. *Anatomy of Racism.* Minneapolis: Univ. Minn. Press

55. Gómez-Peña G. 1993. *Warrior for Gringostroika.* St. Paul, MN: Graywolf

56. Gramsci A. 1971. *Selections from the Prison Notebooks.* Transl. Q Hoare, GN Smith. New York: International

57. Grimshaw A, Hart K. 1993. *Anthropology and the Crisis of the Intellectuals.* Prickly Pear Pamphlet 1. Cambridge, UK: Prickly Pear

58. Guidieri R, Pellizzi F. 1988. Introduction: "smoking mirrors"—modern polity and ethnicity. See Ref. 59, pp. 7–38

59. Guidieri R, Pellizzi F, Tambiah SJ, eds. 1988. *Ethnicities and Nations: Processes of Interethnic Relations in Latin America, Southeast Asia, and the Pacific.* Austin: Univ. Texas Press

60. Gupta A. 1992. The song of the nonaligned world: transnational identities and the reinscription of space in late capitalism. *Cult. Anthropol.* 7(1):63–79

61. Gupta A, Ferguson J. 1992. Beyond "culture": space, identity and the politics of difference. *Cult. Anthropol.* 7(1):6–23

62. Hall S. 1986. Gramsci's relevance for the study of race and ethnicity. *J. Commun. Inq.* 10(2):5–27

63. Handler R. 1988. *Nationalism and the Politics of Culture in Quebec.* Madison: Univ. Wisc. Press

64. Hannerz U. 1992. *Cultural Complexity: Studies in the Social Organization of Meaning.* New York: Columbia Univ. Press

65. Harvey D. 1989. *The Condition of Postmodernity.* Oxford: Blackwell

66. Hendricks J. 1991. Symbolic counterhegemony among the Ecuadorian Shuar. See Ref. 131, pp. 53–71

67. Hendrickson C. 1991. Images of the Indian in Guatemala: the role of indigenous dress in Indian and Ladino constructions. See Ref. 131, pp. 286–306

68. Hill J. 1991. In neca gobierno de Puebla: Mexicano penetrations of the Mexican state. See Ref. 131, pp. 72–94

69. Hill J. 1993. Hasta la vista, baby: Anglo Spanish in the American Southwest. *Crit. Anthropol.* 13:145–76
70. Hill J. 1994. *Junk Spanish, Anglo identity, and the Forces of Desire.* Presented at Symp. Hispanic Lang. Soc. Ident., Albuquerque, NM
71. Hobsbawm EJ. 1990. *Nations and Nationalism Since 1780: Programme, Myth, Reality.* Cambridge: Cambridge Univ. Press
72. hooks B. 1990. *Yearning: Race, Gender, and Cultural Politics.* Boston: South End
73. Howe J. 1991. An ideological triangle: the struggle over San Blas Kuna Culture, 1915–1925. See Ref. 131, pp. 19–52
74. Joseph G, Nugent D, eds. 1994. *Everyday Forms of State Formation: Revolution and the Negotiation of Rule in Modern Mexico.* Durham, NC: Duke Univ. Press
75. Joseph G, Nugent D. 1994. Popular culture and state formation in revolutionary Mexico. See Ref. 74, pp. 3–23
76. Kapferer B. 1988. *Legends of People, Myths of State.* Washington, DC: Smithsonian Inst. Press
77. Kearney M. 1991. Borders and boundaries of state and self at the end of empire. *J. Hist. Sociol.* 4(1):52–74
77a. Kemper S. 1991. *The Presence of the Past: Chronicles, Politics, and Culture in Sinhala Life.* Ithaca, NY: Cornell Univ. Press
78. Krause EL. 1993. Forward vs. reverse gear: the politics of proliferation and resistance in the Italian fascist state. *Ariz. Anthropol.* 10:1–21
79. Laclau E, Mouffe C. 1985. *Hegemony and Socialist Strategy: Towards a Radical Democratic Politics.* Transl. W Moore, P Cammack. London: Verso
80. Lefebre H. 1991. *The Production of Space.* Transl. D Nicholson-Smith. Oxford: Blackwell
81. Macdonald S, Holden P, Ardener S, eds. 1987. *Images of Women in Peace and War: Cross-Cultural and Historical Perspectives.* Madison: Univ. Wisc. Press
82. Malkki L. 1990. Context and consciousness: local conditions for the production of historical and national thought among Hutu refugees in Tanzania. See Ref. 46, pp. 32–62
83. Malkki L. 1992. National geographic: the rooting of peoples and the territorialization of national identity among scholars and refugees. *Cult. Anthropol.* 7(1):24–44
84. Manthei J. 1994. *Art of becoming: representations of national identities in Brazilian comic books.* MA thesis. Univ. Ariz., Tucson
84a. McAllister C. 1994. *This pageant which is not won: the Rabín Ahau, Maya women, and the Guatemalan nation.* MA thesis. Univ. Ariz., Tucson
85. Mitchell T. 1989. *The effect of the state.* Presented at SSRC/ACLS Comm. Near Middle East Workshop, Istanbul
86. Mohanty CT, Russo A, Torres L, eds. 1991. *Third World Women and the Politics of Feminism.* Bloomington: Ind. Univ. Press
87. Mosse GL. 1985. *Nationalism and Sexuality: Middle-Class Morality and Sexual Norms in Modern Europe.* Madison: Univ. Wisc. Press
88. Muratorio B. 1993. Nationalism and ethnicity: images of Ecuadorian Indians and the imagemakers at the turn of the nineteenth century. In *Ethnicity and the State,* ed. J Toland. New Brunswick, NJ: Transaction
89. Norton R. 1984. Ethnicity and class: a conceptual note with reference to the politics of post-colonial societies. *Ethnic Racial Stud.* 7(3):426–34
90. Nugent D, Alonso AM. 1994. Multiple selective traditions in agrarian reform and agrarian struggle: popular culture and state formation in the *ejido* of Namiquipa, Chihuahua. See Ref. 74, pp. 209–46
91. Omi M, Winant H. 1986. *Racial Formation in the United States: From the 1960s to the 1980s.* New York: Routledge & Kegan Paul
92. Ong A. 1990. State versus Islam: Malay families, women's bodies, and the body politic in Malaysia. *Am. Ethnol.* 17(2):258–76
93. Parker A, Russo M, Sommer D, Yaeger P, eds. 1992. *Nationalisms and Sexualities.* New York: Routledge
94. Parker A, Russo M, Sommer D, Yaeger P. 1992. Introduction. See Ref. 93, pp. 1–20
95. Poulantzas N. 1978. *State, Power, Socialism.* Transl. P Camiller. London: Verso
96. Rappaport J. 1994. *Cumbe Reborn: An Andean Ethnography of History.* Chicago: Univ. Chicago Press
97. Rex J, Mason D, eds. 1986. *Theories of Race and Ethnic Relations.* Cambridge: Cambridge Univ. Press
98. Richards M. 1984. *Cosmopolitan worldview and counterinsurgency in Guatemala.* Presented at Annu. Meet. Am. Anthropol. Assoc., 83rd, Denver
99. Rosaldo R. 1989. *Culture and Truth: The Remaking of Social Analysis.* Boston: Beacon
100. Rosaldo R. 1990. Others of invention: ethnicity and its discontents. *Voice Lit. Suppl.* 82:27–29
101. Roseberry W. 1989. *Anthropologies and Histories: Essays in Culture, History, and Political Economy.* New Brunswick, NJ: Rutgers Univ. Press
102. Roseberry W. 1994. Hegemony and the language of contention. See Ref. 74, pp. 355–78
103. Ruiz L. 1993. *Towards a new radical imaginary: notes on the construction of*

transformative cultural practices. Presented at WOMP Conf., Kadoma, Zimbabwe

104. Runte A. 1979. *National Parks: The American Experience.* Lincoln: Univ. Neb. Press

105. Schneider DM. 1969. *Kinship, nationality and religion in American culture.* Proc. 1969 Annu. Meet. Am. Ethnol. Soc.

106. Scott D. 1990. The demonology of nationalism: on the anthropology of ethnicity and violence in Sri Lanka. *Econ. Soc.* 19(4): 491–510

107. Scott D. 1992. Criticism and culture: theory and post-colonial claims on anthropological disciplinarity. *Crit. Anthropol.* 12(4): 371–94

108. Segal DA. 1994. Living ancestors: nationalism and the past in post-colonial Trinidad and Tobago. In *Space, Time and the Politics of Memory,* ed. J Boyarin. Minneapolis: Univ. Minn. Press. In press

109. Segal DA, Handler R. 1992. How European is nationalism? *Soc. Anal.* 32:1–15

110. Shanklin E. 1994. *Anthropology and Race.* Belmont, CA: Wadsworth

111. Simon R. 1987. Being ethnic/doing ethnicity: a response to Corrigan. In *Breaking the Mozaic: Ethnic Identities in Canadian Schooling,* ed. J Young, pp. 31–43. Toronto: Garamond

112. Smith AD. 1987. *The Ethnic Origins of Nations.* Oxford: Blackwell

113. Smith AL. 1992. *Social memory and Germany's immigration crisis: a case of collective forgetting.* MA thesis. Univ. Ariz., Tucson

114. Smith CA. 1990. Conclusion: history and revolution in Guatemala. See Ref. 115, pp. 258–86

115. Smith CA, ed. 1990. *Guatemalan Indians and the State: 1540 to 1988.* Austin: Univ. Texas Press

116. Smith CA. 1990. Introduction: social relations in Guatemala over time and space. See Ref. 115, pp. 1–34

117. Smith G. 1989. *Livelihood and Resistance: Peasants and the Politics of Land in Peru.* Berkeley: Univ. Calif. Press

118. Smith RT. 1993. *On the disutility of the notion of 'ethnic group' for understanding status struggles in the modern world.* Presented at Univ. Guadalajara Conf., Jalisco

119. Sollors W, ed. 1989. *The Invention of Ethnicity.* New York: Oxford Univ. Press

119a. Spencer J, ed. 1990. *Sri Lanka: History and the Roots of Conflict.* New York: Routledge

120. Spillers HJ, ed. 1991. *Comparative American Identities: Race, Sex and Nationality in the Modern Text.* New York: Routledge

121. Stavenhagen R. 1984. Los movimientos etnicos indigenas y el estado nacional en America Latina. *Rev. Paraguaya Sociol.* 59:7–22

122. Stutzman R. 1981. El mestisaje: an all inclusive ideology of exclusion. In *Cultural Transformations and Ethnicity in Modern Ecuador,* ed. NE Whitten Jr, pp. 45–93. New York: Harper & Row

123. Sweedenburg T. 1990. The Palestinian peasant as national signifier. *Anthropol. Q.* 63(1):18–30

124. Szwed J. 1975. Race and the embodiment of culture. *Ethnicity* 2(1):19–33

125. Tambiah SJ. 1988. Ethnic fratricide in Sri Lanka: an update. See Ref. 59, pp. 293–319

126. Taussig M. 1993. *Mimesis and Alterity: A Particular History of the Senses.* New York: Routledge

127. *Time.* 1993. The new face of America: how immigrants are shaping the world's first multicultural society. 142(21) (Special issue)

128. Trouillot M-R. 1990. *Haiti: State Against Nation: The Origins and Legacy of Duvalierism.* New York: Monthly Review

129. Turino T. 1991. The state and Andean musical production in Peru. See Ref. 131, pp. 259–85

130. Turner V. 1967. *The Forest of Symbols: Aspects of Ndembu Ritual.* Ithaca, NY: Cornell Univ. Press

131. Urban G, Sherzer J, eds. 1991. *Nation-States and Indians in Latin America.* Austin: Univ. Texas Press

132. Vélez-Ibáñez C. 1992. *The emergence of the commodity identity of the Mexican population of the U.S. in cultural perspective.* Presented at Annu. Meet. Am. Anthropol. Assoc., 91st, San Francisco

133. Verdery K. 1990. The production and defense of "the Romanian nation," 1900 to World War II. See Ref. 46, pp. 81–111

133a. Warren K. 1989. *The Symbolism of Subordination: Indian Identity in a Guatemalan Town.* Austin: Univ. Texas Press

134. Watanabe JM. 1990. Enduring yet ineffable community in the western periphery of Guatemala. See Ref. 115, pp. 183–204

135. Weber M. 1978. *Economy and Society.* Transl. E Fischoff, ed. Roth G, Wittich C. Berkeley: Univ. Calif. Press

136. West C. 1988. Marxist theory and the specificity of Afro-American oppression. In *Marxism and the Interpretation of Culture,* ed. C Nelson, L Grossberg, pp. 17–29. Urbana: Univ. Ill. Press

137. Wetherell M, Potter J. 1992. *Mapping the Language of Racism: Discourse and the Legitimation of Exploitation.* New York: Harvester Wheatsheaf

138. Wilder JC, ed. 1990. Inventing the Southwest. *J. Southwest* 32(4).7 (Special issue)

139. Williams BF. 1989. A class act: anthropology and the race to nation across ethnic terrain. *Annu. Rev. Anthropol.* 18:401–44

140. Williams BF. 1991. *Stains on My Name, War in My Veins: Guyana and the Politics*

of *Cultural Struggle.* Durham, NC: Duke Univ. Press
141. Williams R. 1977. *Marxism and Literature.* Oxford: Oxford Univ. Press
142. Woost MD. 1990. *Developing a nation of villages: development and the formation of community on Sri Lanka's frontier.* PhD thesis. Univ. Texas, Austin
143. Woost MD. 1993. Nationalizing the local past in Sri Lanka: histories of nation and development in a Sinhalese village. *Am. Ethnol.* 20(3):502–21
144. Worsley P. 1984. *The Three Worlds: Cul-*

ture and World Development. Chicago: Univ. Chicago Press
145. Wright WR. 1990. *Café Con Leche: Race, Class, and National Image in Venezuela.* Austin: Univ. Texas Press
146. Yuval-Davis N, Anthias F, eds. 1989. *Woman—Nation—State.* New York: MacMillan
147. Zukin S. 1991. *Landscapes of Power: From Detroit to Disney World.* Berkeley: Univ. Calif. Press

Annu. Rev. Anthropol. 1994. 23:407–34

SPIRIT POSSESSION REVISITED:
Beyond Instrumentality

Janice Boddy

Department of Anthropology, University of Toronto, Division of Social Sciences, Scarborough Campus, 1265 Military Trail, Scarborough, Ontario M1C 1A4 Canada

KEY WORDS: gender, body, religious movements, cultural resistance, healing

INTRODUCTION

Spirit possession commonly refers to the hold exerted over a human being by external forces or entities more powerful than she. These forces may be ancestors or divinities, ghosts of foreign origin, or entities both ontologically and ethnically alien. Some societies evince multiple spirit forms. Depending on cultural and etiological context such spirits may be exorcised, or lodged in relatively permanent relationship with their host (or medium), occasionally usurping primacy of place in her body (even donning their own clothes and speaking their own languages) during bouts of possession trance. *Possession,* then, is a broad term referring to an integration of spirit and matter, force or power and corporeal reality, in a cosmos where the boundaries between an individual and her environment are acknowledged to be permeable, flexibly drawn, or at least negotiable. Recent studies (e.g. 39, 114, 173, 210) suggest that spirit possession rests on epistemic premises quite different from the infinitely differentiating, rationalizing, and reifying thrust of global materialism and its attendant scholarly traditions. Because it appears dramatically and intransigently exotic, unrecognizable to those so schooled (but see 1, 34, 79, 103, 104; also 147:132), possession continues to hold the anthropological gaze despite heroic attempts to tame it, render it harmless or understood. In contrast to anthropological accounts of the body (145) or of time (162), spirit possession has long been an explicit topic of inquiry; it has rarely missed a theoretical beat. Discourse on the subject is thematic for the discipline as a whole in its confrontation with the Other, continuously affirming our identity as anthropologists (eg. 48:15, see also 61).

In the revision of his influential book *Ecstatic Religion: A Study of Shamanism and Spirit Possession,* Lewis (138:14) responded to critics of the first edition (135) by asking, "How else can we understand 'other cultures' except comparatively in terms of our own concepts, constructs and language?" His remark is telling, commonsensical, and marks a good point of departure for this review. The recognition that scholars are inextricably embedded in cultural frameworks is welcome, though too frequently obscured in ethnographic writing (73), too often reserved for defense of problematic interpretations in later editions. When spirit possession is at issue, the need to demystify analytical terms and resist being seduced into thinking that they dispassionately reflect reality is especially keen. The Otherness of the phenomenon demands explanation. Yet the very categories that describe the field are inescapably ideological and preconstructed (27:189; 38a), freighted with cultural meanings and valuations, and laden with traces of their repeated reformulations as a subject for scientific investigation over time. Although it may be necessary to work with such categories in the interests of comparison, it is not necessary to concede that they transparently capture an essence, an autonomous human behavior.

Several recent studies (eg. 20, 37, 38a, 39, 93, 114, 118, 123, 124, 173, 203, 212) have tried to break through prior restrictions to examine possession on its own terms in the societies where it is found. These studies locate it in wider social and historical contexts, describing how it acts as a prism through which naturalized constructs (e.g. of person, gender, or body) are refracted or undone. This review places such developments in context, traces some principal trajectories in the field, and suggests where they might be going. The literature clusters around salient issues and does not parcel out into neat subdivisions of concern. I present the issues accordingly, risking an impression of scholarly integration that may not in fact exist. Recent reviews on shamanism (8) and the body (145) inevitably complement the topics and literatures addressed here.

PARAMETERS

This review covers mainly English language sources, and I am convinced it would be possible to write a rather different review citing only sources in French (cf 51; see 189), German (114), or Portuguese (see references in 35, 212). Though found in many societies, phenomena glossed as possession and/or possession trance (30, 31, a distinction critiqued in 121) are manifestly different in each; we do well to remember this when tempted to ascribe to them a unitary character.

In distribution, possession cuts a broad swath through Asia, Africa, Afro-America, and Latin America, with some incidence in Oceania and historical and contemporary (chiefly Mediterranean) Europe. As Karp has noted, "a single researcher would have difficulty in reviewing the literature on spirit possession in Africa alone" (99:91). Africa is therefore a good place to start; see references 4, 13, 18, 20, 39, 43, 48, 60, 62, 63, 75–77, 90, 93, 99, 107, 118, 123, 124, 126, 134, 139, 140, 150, 161, 163, 164, 193, 196, 203, 211, 217, 220. Some of the better known African cults or terms for spirits are *bori, zar, sheitani, ngoma, hauka, mhondoro,* and *mzimu.* As in other regions, terms if not pantheons often overlap and interpenetrate (77, 93, 140). Possession forms similar to and even historically continuous with those in northern Africa are found in the Levant, Arabia, and Iran (7, 43, 94). In the Americas, mainly in Brazil and the Caribbean where African influence has been considerable, better known varieties are Vodou, Umbanda, Candomblé, Shango, Kardecismo (see 35–37, 58, 82, 87, 92, 99a, 99b, 112, 115, 144, 176, 209, 212, 213). For Asia, see references 3, 38a, 68, 81, 88, 98, 153, 160, 165, 168, 171, 173, 174, 180, 191, 198, 201. In East Asia spirit mediumship is usually described as shamanism (86, 101, 111; see 8:318–319). Examples from Oceania are reference 192 and *Pacific Spirits,* a forthcoming collection edited by A Howard & J Mageo. For southern Europe, see references 15 and 179. Possession narratives have in some cases eclipsed the possession experience (179; see also 45). On Catholic Pentecostalism and charismatic healing, see references 50 and 52–55.

An assumption, now widely disputed, that spirit possession constitutes an independent category of behavior or natural field of inquiry has predictably spawned some influential typologies seeking to transcend folk epistemologies and provide an objective framework for analysis. Lewis (135, 137, 138) encompasses shamanism and possession under the rubric *ecstatic religion,* but distinguishes between main or central morality cults and peripheral ones that are incidental to a society's moral system. De Heusch (56) differentiates between exorcism, which expels intrusive spirits, and adorcism, which accommodates and establishes them in a medium. He further distinguishes shamanism from possession, each of which has an authentic or ideal type corresponding to one of these treatment vectors. The result is a complex "geometry of the soul" (56:158), a four-part structure in which each form is a cultural, historical, or logical transformation of the other. Bourguignon (30, 31) has found correlations between type of social organization and the presence of possession or possession trance, with simpler, more individualistic societies less likely to evince possession trance than are those in which strong social hierarchies exist (59, 194; see also 44, 144). Kramer's (114) recent permutation of the center-periphery model distinguishes between charismatic cults that generalize meanings and foster social unity, and acephalous cults that emphasize social differentiation; instead of morality per se, personal and political identity are the salient issues here (see also 190).

Typologies, of course, are achieved at the expense of context and inevitably reflect the interests, values, and fascinations of the analyst's society. Though heuristic, they are often mistaken for explanation or interpretation when applied, and using them as predictors can blind researchers to the complexities of the situations they describe. Indeed, Janzen recently argued that the foregrounding of possession trance in studies of sub-Saharan African therapeutics has greatly exaggerated its significance there (93:140).

THERAPY, RELIGION, AND COMMUNICATION

Spirit possession research has been characterized by a fundamental tension between reductive, naturalizing or rationalizing approaches on the one hand and contextualizing, more phenomenological approaches on the other. Studies constructed along lines of the former are more readily amenable to comparison, but insofar as they render phenomena in Western commonsense or scientific terms, they suspend epistemological inquiry of those terms (221) and are at best incomplete, at worst culturally solipsistic.

Csordas (51) tracks the rationalizing tendency by charting a progressive medicalization of possession in the Anglo-American literature. He suggests that, in contrast to the majority of studies in French (eg. 14, 129, 157, 159, 187, 189), the religious, aesthetic, and quotidian significances of possession were repeatedly eschewed in deference to its function as group therapy (64, 102, 156, 183), even when informants described their experiences as religious (46, 182).

Lewis's (135, 138) cross-cultural account lent sociological support to the medical tack by distinguishing central possession cults, where possession is a positive experience involving spirits who uphold the moral order (ancestors, culture heroes) and typically speak through men, from peripheral ones, where possession by amoral spirits is locally regarded as a form of illness that typically afflicts women and other individuals of marginal or subordinate status. This model and its assumptions guided a generation of scholarship in which peripheral possession signaled personal or social pathology, eclipsing investigation of its wider social, cultural, and aesthetic significances (38a, 51), and preventing possession systems from being discussed on their own terms (121). Instead, attention was directed to instrumental, strategic uses of consensual beliefs by socially disadvantaged (so-called status-deprived) individuals who, in claiming to be seized by spirits, indirectly brought public attention to their plight and potentially achieved some redress (eg. 78).

With Ward (214, 215) religion fades into the background and all forms of possession are reduced to medical terms. She argues that central possession is a ritually-induced therapeutic defense, while peripheral possession is "induced by individuals' stress" (214:158) and provides a cultural explanation for psychopathology. The road of rationalization heads deeper into the individual and now physiochemical body with Kehoe & Giletti's (100) calcium deficiency hypothesis and its subsequent refinement (185; for responses see 33, 136). Reductive tendencies culminated in a recent, if culturally sensitive, proposal to include Trance and Possession Disorder in the official nosology of the American Psychiatric Association (DSM-IV), based on a reified center-periphery scheme in which peripheral possession indexes aberrance requiring therapeutic intervention (see 38; for responses see 5, 22, 32, 105, 109, 113, 122, 141).

The cumulative direction of these models owes much to their sometimes unacknowledged concern with understanding trance rather than possession (i.e. behavior rather than belief). Yet few researchers regard trance as inherently pathological (9, 38, 216, 219; see 8). Lambek (121), echoing Csordas (51) in a plea for more contextually appropriate, balanced, open-ended accounts of possession and arguing for firmer recognition that trance, too, is culturally mediated and socially tuned, pithily compared the relationship between them to that between marriage (a social institution) and sex (the behavior it legitimizes) (p.46; see also 16, 69). Rouget's (189) cross-cultural analysis of the role of music and rhythm in inducing trance points to socially learned aesthetic cueing, thus, challenging Neher's (166) auditory-driving hypothesis. Even viewing trance as unconscious protest invokes an idealistic, agentive concept of self that some say cannot be presumed (e.g. 212). Moreover, because the body is both the existential ground of belief and the locus of engagement with the spirit world, it is not surprising that possession is often expressed in physical terms, as somatic change or illness (20, 40, 47, 98, 118, 121, 170, 171). The fact that possession [or pre-possession (203, see also 29)] is phrased as illness does not imply that these states are fully transitive, nor should it foreclose our questioning the meanings of illness, possession, or spirits in specific local contexts (20, 51, 123). It should not blind us to how religion and medicine subtly interweave (51, 93, 161).

Studies of Brazilian cults deemed peripheral (vis-a-vis Christianity) have largely eschewed a medical focus in favor of a religious one (e.g. 14, 125, 127, 213). Several factors are probably relevant here: significant middle class and professional participation in these cults; their importance, in part through the legitimating efforts of anthropologists, in shaping Brazilian nationalism (hence their doubtful marginality); their text-based cosmologies; and their historical links to the Catholic Church which, from the nineteenth century, exercised weak control over urban slave populations mainly through voluntary brotherhoods organized on the basis of race and ethnic affiliation (35). These conditions provided an environment in which African religious practices were maintained under a cloak of Christianity and became merged with Catholic belief. Alhough religious interpretations would seem consonant with Brazilian realities, healing and spirituality are in fact reciprocal in Candomblé (212), Kardecismo (82), and Umbanda (35). In the last this takes a biomedical idiom: Umbanda mediums wear nurses uniforms; spirits acting through their mediums hold clinics for spiritual healing; and if biomedical attention is required, spirits help to arrange it (35).

Publication of Crapanzano & Garrison's collection *Case Studies in Spirit Possession* (49) reflected a change in English-language studies, a waning of medicalized and individualized paradigms and a shift toward more context replete accounts. When Leacock (128) chastised the volume's emphasis on ethnopsychological rather than religious elucidations of possession, Garrison & Crapanzano (71) responded, "Why limit it to a form of religious behavior? What indeed is the virtue of placing it in a Western category at all? What is important is to understand its multiple significance within the particular contexts in which it occurs" (71:424). In his introductory essay, Crapanzano (47) suggested that possession be viewed as "an idiom for articulating a certain range of experience" (47:10; see also 12, 170). Seeing possession as an idiom of communication enjoins consideration of how the idiom is constructed and used in specific societies; it requires acknowledgement of the existence of spirits in the believer's world and asserts that possession is about meaning. The move echoes a discipline swing away from positivist, decontextualizing approaches (including structuralism in its epistemological guise) toward cultural interpretation (eg. 72).

Crapanzano's poignant interactive biography of Tuhami, a Moroccan man married to a she-demon whose victims seek healing from the Hamadsha, a popular Islamic brotherhood (48), requires him to question the ethnopsychological validity of notions such as projection and the presumed boundedness of the self. Where spirits are consensually understood to enter human bodies, it may be more appropriate to speak of introjection (47). Crapanzano suggests that Tuhami is afforded a "shift of responsibility...from self to Other" (48:20) through the possession idiom; he is able to objectify his feelings "in terms that transcend him"; yet the result of his demonic relationship is a "frozen identity," not curative transformation (48:86, 151; see also 179).

Obeyesekere's (171) sophisticated study of Sri Lankan ascetics possessed by ghosts and avatars of deities in the Hindu-Buddhist pantheon grapples with how cultural symbols inform and are informed by individual experience. Adopting a psychoanalytic perspective (as much to place himself in reciprocal idiomatic relationship to his informants as to universalize their problems), he demonstrates how matted hair, a sign of the god's favor (possession), is a locally meaningful idiom for articulating travail; yet, it is created anew by each who avails herself of it, and continues to have practical significance only as long as this is the case. Here the possessed are indeed unwell, and mainly subordinate women, but the analysis surpasses a static relative-status model to emphasize the flexibility and ambiguity of the spirit idiom, its capacity to enable personal growth, and the optional, manipulable nature of "personal symbols": socially and emotionally meaningful at once. These insights relieve what in less able hands might have been a reductive analysis insensitive to local concerns; instead, Obeyesekere demonstrates the potential congruity of psychoanalytic and religious interpretations.

Obeyesekere and Crapanzano focus on those who are clearly troubled. Lambek (117–121, 123), on the other hand, shows how in Mayotte possession operates as a system of communication whether or not one is, by Western definitions, distressed (see also 3, 86, 90). Lambek regards Mayotte possession as a complex semi-independent cultural domain that, lacking direct equivalent in the Euro-American West, should not be reduced to naturalized Western forms. He productively likens it to a text or genre with its own interpretive conventions. An emphasis on analytic form rather than categorical substance links his approach firmly with those of Crapanzano and Obeyesekere. And Lambek takes seriously Crapanzano's point (47) that an adequate account of possession must grant the spirits' existence in lives of their hosts. Spirits, he notes, are social beings who interact with their hosts and hosts' families not just during public ceremonies, but in everyday domestic life as well, where their presence enriches and modulates human relationships, contributing to health (117, 118, 120; see also 63). Moreover, because spirits' identities and behaviors contrast with those normative for Mayotte, they furnish an implicit commentary on human order and morality. Possession intersects with numerous cultural domains including medicine and religion, but is itself reducible to none.

Kapferer's (96, 98) analysis of demonic exorcism in Buddhist Sri Lanka is rooted firmly in the context of colonial history and social class. Sinhalese Buddhism is premised on an elaborate, coherent cosmos with humans situated between superordinate deities and subordinate demons. As a legacy of colonial revision and rationalization, the middle class devote themselves to the deities, key symbols of cosmic power and domination. Practices of working-class and peasants, however, "address the pantheon in its hierarchical totality" (98:48). Demonic attack contradicts the order of the cosmos in which demons are subjugated and restrained; it represents the unleashed hidden power of the lower orders, and is thus "metacommunicative of the dynamics of class" (98:51). Kapferer shows how the intricate rites of exorcism give external form to the victim's existential state of solitude and fear. Through music, song, dance, masked drama, and possession trance, the demonic temporarily manifests itself in the human world, gradually drawing the audience into the victim's experience. Having linked their perceptions, the ritual shifts to a comic mode that, in lampooning the quotidian world (including bureaucracy and social hierarchy), cleverly traps the demons, reasserts cultural order, and leads victim and audience back into the world of shared understandings (cf 208). Kapferer highlights the role of cultural aesthetics in effecting personal transformation (see also 81, 165, 186), without losing sight of wider political, economic, religious, or healing dimensions of the rite.

Anthropological accounts of spirit possession are no longer dominated by a few linked master narratives that endeavor to make sense of it by reducing it to behavior explicable in (largely unexamined) universal and substantially medical terms, to discover its presumed logical basis as folk psychiatry or status compensation. If loss of faith in structural and functionalist models is attributed to their limitation in enabling ethnographers to grasp the whole of what they've observed, or to a general postmodern malaise, the result is the same. Reductive models ultimately fail to comprehend phenomena that, as imaginative productions, evade all rational containment (23, also 39:263). Cults and the spirits within them continuously reinvent themselves (eg. 20, 106–108, 150, 151). By heeding cultural logics and attending to histories, the literature discussed below implicitly takes an extensive or expansive approach compatible or homologous with possession's own epistemological and etiological vectors, whose elusive dynamic was neatly captured in Matsuoka's study of fox possession in Japan (153). In these studies possession takes shape as a form of cultural knowledge and a means of knowing and healing, whose direction is both extensive and incorporative. Unlike biomedicine, which collapses into the body,[1] possession widens out from the body and self into other domains of knowledge and experience—other lives, societies, historical moments, levels of cosmos, and religions—catching these up and embodying them. Their direction ensures that possession cults are flexible and continuously transformative. It enables adherents to explore multiple refractions of order and morality; to distill the lessons of history; to sift, evaluate, and situate external influences; and to respond. Phenomena we bundle loosely as possession are part of daily experience, not just dramatic ritual. They have to do with one's relationship to the world, with selfhood—personal, ethnic, political, and moral identity. In several societies they have much to do with gender and subordination, though in less instrumental ways than were formerly supposed.

---

[1]
But see 149 on the ambiguous relationship between the body and the world in electron micrographs, or 148 on social entities within the body depicted in immunological research reports. And an extensive direction does not characterize all forms of 'ecstatic' healing (see 116).

GENDER, POWER, EMBODIMENT, AND RESISTANCE

Conflict models depicting possession as women's indirect claim for redress (135, 138, 139, 218) tacitly depend for their authority on the perspectives of socially dominant men and the assumptions of an androcentric anthropology (20, 199). They leave much to be explained: By whose evaluation are women marginal? Does economic or political subordination fully determine women's positions in other spheres of life? Most importantly, what do women and men themselves think possession is about? And how are we to make sense of possession forms, of spirits themselves?

Concern for context has meant attending to gender imagery and dynamics in the search to understand why women preponderate in possession cults. Taking seriously the givenness of spirits in the everyday lives of their hosts entails consideration of women's and men's cosmological statuses, their culturally attributed abilities, vulnerabilities, and constraints (20, 26, 98, 118, 123, 158, 165, 167, 180, 195, 198). Kapferer points out that because Sinhalese women are considered more firmly attached than men to relationships of the human world, their femininity culturally prefigures them as being prone to demonic attack (98:140; see also 20). Elsewhere such prefiguring depicts women as stronger than men, more capable of enduring hardship, taking responsibility, suffering the privations that spirits exact (37, 131). In Islamic societies where traffic with spirits is formally discouraged, men's public religiosity may require them to handle possession via exorcism instead of mollification, or refrain from acknowledging themselves to be possessed (20, 118, 123). The idea that possession is a sex-war salvo implies that the genders are homogeneous groups. Yet researchers find considerable disagreement among various concatenations of the religious and those they consider impious, women and men, old and young, over how to cope with intrusive spirits (20, 26, 77, 123, 150, 197, 198). Not long ago Lewis (137:106) wondered whether *zar* possession and Islam in north-east Africa might be gender complementary domains of religious responsibility. This has been confirmed to a degree (20, 40, 106, 107). However, the relationship of Islam to *zar* and other forms of possession—as of Christianity to Vodou or Candomblé (37, 212)—is subtle and historically complex (4, 20, 75–77, 123, 137, 146, 150), and it would be unwise to polarize them as gender distinct domains of knowledge or activity (cf also 152, 181).

Several studies describe how possession's instrumental and articulatory dimensions interlace, emphasizing the benefits of membership in a group or the idiom's flexibility in shifting between rural and urban milieux. Zebola possession in rural Zaire is family focused, with afflicting spirits likely to be ancestral and symptoms well-patterned and interpretable; but in Kinshasa, where maintenance of extended kinship is curtailed, spirits are more autonomous, oriented to individual needs, and symptoms are more diffuse (44). Cult membership can provide not only health care but also important social networks for women, enabling them to glean information and practical support that is particularly valuable in urban settings where kin are not close by (41, 106–108, 130, 131). Spring (199) shows how a women's possession cult among the Luvale (Zambia) positively addresses ailments affecting their fertility and responsibilities as mothers; healing rituals are occasions when matrilineal kinswomen otherwise separated by virilocality can learn from each others' expertise. Some authors note the use of kin terms to describe cult leaders or address fellow participants (35, 37, 39, 92, 106, 107, 212), which suggests that such groups are, in a sense, reconstituted families. In Brazil the role of spirit healer has been considered an extension of women's domestic service into the public domain, financially more rewarding than housewifery, and entailing less dependence on men (131; see also 37). The issue that some possessed women go on to become healers who attract large and sometimes lucrative followings has been raised frequently (17, 42, 86, 101, 107, 197). Still, leadership roles in possession cults are sometimes filled by men (4, 35, 106–108, 131, 212), and DG Brown's (35) observation that male leaders in Umbanda are nodes of articulation between the cult and the wider polity evokes a domestic-public gender dichotomy familiar to Euro-American societies.

If we focus on what women do, rather than what they cannot, we find them working in the spiritual realm on behalf of themselves, their families, households, or communities, channeling spirits' assistance or heading off their wrath, protecting future generations, even protesting injustice. Here so-called peripheral possession is concerned with social domains for which women are typically assigned primary responsibility: the maintenance of kin ties and family health, the social reproduction of their communities, often in the face of radical social change and erosion of prior supports (4, 20, 37, 42, 99, 117, 120, 165). It is about morality and social identity. Scholars responsive to the insights of feminist anthropology bracket the issue of instrumentality without denying the relevance of subordination per se, and endeavor to situate women's possession in wider social discourses and practices of power (19, 20, 37, 86, 101, 161, 173, 174, 196, 197).

My own work on the *zar* cult in an endogamous Sudanese village stresses the relationship between the informal logic of everyday life and that of possession as a subordinate (or subaltern) discourse (19–21, 24). Drawing on Bourdieu's (27) elaboration of the concept of *habitus*, but also on the insights of Gramsci (80) and Foucault (65–67), I point to a fundamental relationship between women's embodiment of gender-appropriate dispositions—most patently instilled through pharaonic circumcision—and the proclivity to become possessed. Women's bodies are both metonyms and icons of the enclosed, fertile, moral village, repositories of its salient values and more vulnerable than men to their rupture. A threat to women's fertility is a serious threat to their gendered sense of self, but also to the community as a whole (see also 42). Women are responsible for ceremonies and practices ensuring the continuity of social life. Men are responsible for those that extend beyond the village—to other groups, places, and the afterlife assured by Islam. Gender relations are thus both complementary and politically asymmetrical.

Zar spirits are incorporeal social creatures. They are culturally foreign, often the parallels of historical humans, and always contradictory, but firmly of this world, thus, the province of women to treat. And it is women whom spirits most afflict, mainly with fertility problems, in a bid to gain access to the material world through rituals of appeasement. There they descend into their hosts, dramatizing their Otherness, playfully and frighteningly opening a space for reflection and ambiguity by decentering or reshaping accepted meanings. The possessed learn a spirit anti-language that metaphorically alters quotidian terms (20, 21; cf 85; see also 132). The rite is patterned on the local wedding and burlesques its assertions of gender propriety and morality. Participants are engaged bodily, emotionally, and intellectually. They are expected to acquire a visceral sense of the spirits' distinctiveness from themselves, yet to recall their experiences during trance and the messages of spirits manifest in other women's bodies. *Zar* is at once a healing rite and a parodical means to domesticate male and alien powers, an ambiguous metacommentary on local morality, and a history and anthropology of life in colonial and post-colonial Sudan. I accent its comedic and aesthetic dimensions by comparing it to satirical allegory, where the historical consciousness of the village is vividly dramatized in challenging but also reinvigorating its embodied, engendered, moral order (19–21, 26).

A similar concern for community, commentary, and morality informs KM Brown's account of a Vodou priestess and her family in Haiti and New York (37). Juxtaposing analysis, narrative, and fictionalized distillations of stories told about the family's forebearers, KM Brown convincingly portrays Vodou religion as experienced, as "embedded in the vicissitudes of particular lives" (37:14, 15), including her own. She disputes the view that Vodou *lwa* are amoral, observing that, like humans, they are willful beings capable of good and evil, "larger than life but not other than life," whose benevolence demands human attention and care (37:6; see also 20, 217). Here more clearly perhaps than in *zar,* women, but also men, live with and through the spirits. Everyday acts are given meaning by the spirits' insistence on being served, and their ministering of guidance, healing, and protection in return. A helpful spirit might spontaneously assume the place of its host in a disempowering situation. Like *zar* spirits in Sudan, *lwa* condense and represent in their complex, contradictory personalities the lessons of history, but in Haiti these are the hard and bitter lessons of slavery, hunger, perennial violence. Spirits "bind up the wounds" of social change (37:37) and evolve in tandem with it. KM Brown's portrait of Vodou as subtle wisdom and practical activity linking humans to powers beyond themselves engages fully with its multiplicity and its morality. Other recent accounts of spirit possession affirm it to be a gendered moral activity in specific locales. Werbner (217) points out that among the Kalanga of Zimbabwe, virilocally married kinswomen offer themselves to be possessed by "lions" (capricious, wild, and predatory demons) in order to thwart danger and cleanse the domestic domain. Skultans (198) writes about a healing temple in Maharashtra, India, where women enter therapeutic but painful trance on behalf of their possessed kin, thus shifting to themselves the direction of spirit attack (see also 180). In Korea, women's shamanic rituals ensure family well-being by appeasing household gods lodged in the structure of the house itself. These rituals are, as Kendall claims, religiously crucial if less accessible than men's ancestral rites (101; see also 86). In these cases, disorder is circum-vented or transformed by female kin through what has been called peripheral possession. On the other side of the ledger, cremations in Hindu Nepal that fail to transform a suicide's spirit are reperformed by inducing the spirit to possess a close male agnate who, dancing entranced on the coals of a sacrificial fire, effects the spirit's transition to ancestorhood and rebirth (81). The first three cases here differ from the last not on the grounds of moral centrality but on those of gender and gendered domains of concern; apropos of this, Kendall notes that the few Korean men who become shamans must wear female dress to perform their work (101:26 ff)

Zar spirits in Sudan are often inherited matrilineally. Their movement from one relative to the next charts an embodied woman-centered history opposed to regnant patrilineality, echoing local conditions before the coming of Islam, and affirming current realities of labor emigration (20, 24; cf 220). KM Brown likewise finds parallel spirit matrilines buried beneath official kin structures among practitioners of Haitian Vodou (37:16). Korean data suggest that im-portant links between generations of in-marrying women are formed through their relationships with household gods (101, 86), although wives' own ances-tral spirits might also afflict their children and husbands' kin (101). Pandolfi's (177–179) insightful accounts of the discourse of women's suffering in south-ern Italy are germane to these observations. Tarantula possession (tarantism), which Pandolfi observed in the 1960s, no longer happens to rural women; nonetheless, it is still expressed in narrative accounts of their bodies in which iconic language links "a heritage of symptoms in the maternal line" (177:264). What Pandolfi describes is a kind of verbalized possession of women by other women, their history, and the history of the village as a whole (179). It is a politics of presence, of individualized yet also generalized resistance to domi-nation on a number of levels at once. Here the shift from active to verbal possession mirrors the extension of state hegemony, such that bodies immersed-in-the-world become bodies increasingly fragmented, bounded, and controlled; bodies that have partially internalized a reifying biomedical idiom (see also 208).

Indeed, a view now widely held is that possession is an embodied critique of colonial, national, or global hegemonies whose abrasions are deeply, but not exclusively, felt by women. Morsy (161), writing of northern Egypt, links changes in the epidemiology of spirit possession to the context of "dependent capitalist development and unequal exchange" (161:207) in which growing participation in the international petroleum labor market is transforming gender dynamics and kin-based property relations. Ong (173, 174) investigates the case of young women employed by multinational electronics firms who periodically experience possession trance on the factory floor (see also 3, 195). Mass possessions express muted opposition to inequitable, inhumane treatment and are the spiritual consequences of violating moral boundaries of gender. Managers who concede the spirits' reality by exorcising factory buildings persist in rationalizing the incidents as only, for example, psychiatric or dietary disorders, thus reproducing the logic of global capitalism as it intersects with local beliefs in producing a possession response (174).

Comaroff's subtle, historically-grounded account of Tshidi Zionists in South Africa (39) documents how profoundly Tshidi categories of subjectivity and practice—time, space, gender, person, and productivity—have been transformed in interaction with those of the white elite. Zionist practice attempts to reverse colonial reifications by subjecting such symbols and values "to indigenously derived notions of practical control" (39:193). Colonial and precolonial Tshidi concepts are combined with the body language of European oppression—uniforms, mitres, staffs, and insignia—in an imaginative but acutely serious bricolage. Christian pentecostalism resonates with indigenous views of pragmatic spirit force (39:186). During ceremonies, adherents possessed by the Holy Spirit channel its power toward the healing of bodies personal and social. This process is not unambiguous. Those who enter Zion undergo a "holistic transformation of personal identity" (39:221), but do not fully image themselves anew. Hierarchies of gender in the wider society are, for instance, reproduced in possession forms. Yet Comaroff challenges utilitarian views that depict symbolic resistance as ineffectual. She asserts that Zionism and similar iconoclastic movements are both politically and imaginatively engaged with the wider society in "commenting upon relations of inequality both local and more global, and communicating [their] message of defiance beyond [their] own limited confines" (39:262; cf 193). Together such movements constitute "a second global culture, lying in the shadow of the first" (39:254).

Most would agree that possession cults are or have become historically sensitive modes of cultural resistance (see also 36, 202, 203); others document their potential for violent praxis. Echard (60) reminds us that *bori* spirits led a revolt against the colonial regime in Niger in 1926. Involvement of Shona hero-ancestor spirits in nationalist movements that defied white settler rule is well documented (69, 70, 74, 184), as is the relationship between Zimbabwe's guerrilla forces and spirit mediums during the subsequent civil war (124, 184). Lan (124), like Comaroff, illustrates how spiritually-reformed bodily practice is an assertion of power and identity. Speaking through their mediums, Shona ancestors offered protection to the guerrillas if the latter followed a dietary and behavioral regimen that identified them simultaneously with the precolonial ancestral past and the wild. Spiritual endorsement was crucial to the legitimacy popularly accorded the guerrillas' violent roles.

That spirit movements are often suppressed or subject to strict political controls should dispel any doubt that states perceive them as subversive (see 26, 35, 86, 126, 134, 164, 203). In reshaping lives and communities, engendering a sense of identity, cohesion, and self-respect, and shattering naturalized categories, such movements threaten the reproduction and maintenance of docile bodies, work and gender disciplines, and the like. Their charismatic nature confronts and confounds established power relations (39:186). Their elusiveness is also structural. Parodical spirits appear or historically shift identity with the vagaries of domination (20, 106, 134, 150, 151, 196, 202–204, 212). And as Masquelier observes, they may even resist being objectified by their human hosts (151).

Although some possession cults are recent and several may be spreading (35, 106, 133, 134, 146), others seem to be waning, curtailed less, perhaps, by overt suppression than by the quiet revolution of capitalist reification and the contradictory marginalizing and homogenizing pressures of pluralistic states. Sharp (197), for instance, analyzes Sakalava women possessed by royal ancestors who seek to dispossess themselves because of the hardship and expense that mediumship entails. Avenues open to them are psychiatry and Protestant exorcism, both of which enjoin repudiation of Sakalava identity. Yet the latter is more effective because it does not deny the reality of their original experience and, through conversion, provides a plausible alternate life. Steedly (200, 201), taking her lead from Jameson, discusses the effects of religious rationalization in urban Sumatra where, under Indonesian state policy, *adat* is separated from *belief* and reduced to secular custom. Those who continue to venerate ancestors or placate spirits must do so under the aegis of an officially sanctioned monotheistic faith. Given Sumatra's religious pluralism, spirit healers cannot rely on support from the patient's full range of kin, which jeopardizes ritual efficacy. Social and cultural integration is now a nostalgic goal of these rites. Instead, Steedly claims, they have begun to work reductively, to contain social and cultural tensions. Symbols and spirit offerings shorn of their contingent, kin contextual significances become "self-contained moral objects" (200:850), moral fetishes. The flow of experience fragmented into its component parts is thereby rendered manageable (200:850). For Afro-America both Littlewood (144) and DG Brown (35) have noted a gradual and official disaggregation of religion from healing as the latter has been naturalized and spirits absorbed into the Christian pantheon as deities or devils (cf 83). Similar changes have occurred in Sudan. Kenyon (107) describes a successful woman healer possessed by a male spirit whose characteristics are similar to those of a well-known *zar,* but who speaks as a servant of Allah. And following the 1983 declaration of Islamic law, *zar* itself began a gradual transformation. In the late 1980s several urban cults distanced themselves from Islam by registering as national folk theater groups (89; cf 35, 93, 126, 212, 213) or professionalizing under the leadership of a male healer (108). After seizing power in 1989 the current Islamist regime banned possession ceremonies as heretical and superstitious (26; cf 77). But in Toronto, *zar* has surfaced among the regime's female refugees as part of a conscious strategy to create an African, not Islamic, national identity (26).

Still, fragmenting and objectifying trends do not go unopposed. During rituals Kalanga women possessed by "lions" wear store-bought cloths with lion designs or *LION* printed on them. Werbner (217) suggests that such semantic conversions (217:69) deobjectify trade goods and help countermand the threat commodity relations pose to domestic morality (cf 45). Masquelier (151) notes the emergence of a new group of spirits in Niger who contrast with the avaricious *bori* in stoically rejecting Western goods and modern conveniences. In Madagascar, spirits of royal Sakalava ancestors impose tastes and taboos on their mediums that effectively bar their participation in the exploitative plantation economy (62, 196). Shona mediums hearkening to ancestral ways revile commodities produced by the white-dominated industrial establishment, whetting people's consciousness of the oppression it has brought (124). In short, spirit practices and narratives often interrupt the extension of Western hegemonies by refusing to endorse the naturalization of the commodity form (see also 45, 173, 174, 191, 209, 210).

Comaroff's insight that iconoclastic movements form a global subculture "lying in the shadow of the first" (39: 254) needs to be taken seriously. It is here that gender and subaltern resistances intersect. Possession cults are embedded in local contexts that are never only local and are always complex. With other spiritual philosophies (cf 209), they provide ways of understanding, trying out, coming to terms with, and contesting modernity, colonialism, capitalism, and religious and other hegemonies. They allow the implicit synthesis of the foreign with the local and historically relevant while reshaping all in the process. They heal and they teach; they are intellectually empowering (e.g. 193). They may pave the way for overt political struggle (207:319); yet, they might also (re)insert disaffected individuals into the very structures of domination they contest (20, 200; cf 97, 208). A spirit's host or medium is a malleable metonym for her society, both expressing and embodying its moral conundrums (19, 20, 39, 195, 196). It is hardly surprising that some spirits should fetishize the past in resisting an inequitable present or conventionalizing what is new or that others should abhor change, and still others be hedonistic and enamored of novelty. Because possession is about morality, it is crucial that neither they nor their hosts be *indifferent* to novelty (20, 118, 124, 151, 160, 176, 200, 203, 204; cf 114).

SELF AND OTHER: IDENTITY, AESTHETICS, MIMESIS, AND EMBODIMENT (AGAIN)

An issue threading throughout the literature is that of selfhood or identity: how possession creatively resituates individuals in a profoundly alienating or confusing world (19, 20, 29, 37, 38a, 39, 48, 117, 118, 120, 121, 123, 167, 171, 203, 204). Taking the givenness of spirits as a matter of salience, three parties of variable inclusiveness are implicated in any possession episode: a self, other humans, and external powers. The ritual reordering of their relationships is a process of self-construction and healing that takes place on several planes at once.

Kapferer (95, 98) provisionally mobilizes Mead's theory of social dynamics to analyze how the experience of demonic possession in Sri Lanka is culturally understood. He suggests that the reciprocity of perspectives constituting the victim's identity is disrupted by her illness, dissolved or negated by pain and the social isolation that intimations of demonic agency entail. Such conditions impel loss of the ability to treat herself as an object (95:116). As the mutual interpenetration of self with social other that comprises the *me* abates, a demonically overdetermined *I* takes hold; this is both experienced and objectified during ritual demonic trance. A successful exorcism distances *I* from *me* and reconstitutes the dynamics of self and now social, not demonic, Other.

Although Mead's model is derived from Euro-American templates of contestable universality (and Kapferer's analysis must be held to the same account), its terms are ambiguous enough to encourage consideration of how the parameters of selfhood might shift or be constituted differently in societies other than the anthropologist's own. My analysis of *zar* possession in Sudan uses a similar heuristic (19, 20), noting that instead of overwhelming subjectivity, what seems problematic for women there is a culturally overdetermined sense of self, an inherently fertile, objectified, yet fully embodied self-image that the vicissitudes of life make it impossible for them to sustain. In contrast to the exorcised Sri Lankan, the *zar* victim acquires a pantheon of spirits who permanently attend her self. And unlike her equally well socialized kin, the spirits are ineluctably Other; they form a non-self component of her person that continuously affirms the veracity of her self by providing it negative ground and assuming some blame for its violation. De Heusch's distinction between exorcistic and adorcistic possession is relevant here (56).

Several authors remark on how possession thickens interpersonal ties. Many spirits have coherent public identities and, as social actors, mediate among kin. Lambek, for instance, broadens the self-other dialogue in Mayotte to include domestic interactions between spirits and the spouses of their hosts (117, 118, 123). Elsewhere he notes that a spirit who possesses two generations of kin both articulates social continuity and becomes a reciprocally internalized third party enabling them to negotiate their self-constitutive interaction or maintain it when separated by distance or even death (120, 123). In rural Sudan, where the density of localized kin ties is pronounced, possession by the same or different spirits enables kinswomen to open up convoluted, overlapping relationships produced by endogamous intermarriages (20, 24). Spirit inheritance often defies politically dominant forms or furnishes alternative genealogical connections by which to map out or modify effective alignments of kin (13, 20, 24, 37, 69, 77, 94, 106, 107, 120, 123). Among Kel Fadey Twareg, however, women's spirits validate a dominant yet threatened matrilineal ideology (220); and Songhay spirits reiterate patrilineal sociality (203). Whether possession clarifies, modulates, or obfuscates kin ties, it invariably denaturalizes them, and undermines their givenness.

Spirit assertions of difference or identity are metastatements: coded moral and political acts of the humans they possess, derived from thinking about one's relationships to others by thinking through the Other writ large. This point accommodates a widening of perspective from specific spirits to their imagined worlds, which are in various and subtle ways alien to their hosts'. To some investigators spirit mythologies constitute reservoirs of cultural knowledge, about illnesses and medicines (eg. 169, 175, 203), but also about ethnicity, history, domination, social propriety, and caprice (20, 37, 92, 118, 176, 196, 202, 203, 212). During possession rites when human and spirit realities most obviously interpenetrate—or fuse, as Stoller suggests (203)—this knowledge is momentarily embodied, expressed indirectly via the images and antics of the alien performance, and undoubtedly changed. Without denying their seriousness to participants, possession ceremonies have been described in aesthetic terms as theater, allegory, satire, and burlesque (20, 37, 98, 118, 129, 203), as witty and historically perceptive metacommentaries on the human world.

Inspired by Bakhtin (10, 11), Wafer (212) extends this analogy, claiming that spirits in Brazilian Candomblé display elements of the carnivalesque. In that these spirits are images of what Bakhtin calls "the grotesque body," they challenge the dominant social order and regime of truth. Unlike the "bourgeois body," which Wafer describes as atomized, completed, and the locus of social control, reductive analysis, and fixed meanings,[2] "the grotesque body" is open to the world. It goes out to the world through its appendages, allowing the world to enter via its apertures and convexities (212:59); it is unrestrained and unbounded. Candomblé spirits, like those in other cults, are variations on the grotesque. Some are embodied (and thus behave) as unsocialized children, others are socialized but perverse, and still others are oxymoronic, naive, and only incipiently social (212:62 ff). Wafer suggests that Candomblé plays with and across social, spiritual, and physical boundaries. And it resists formal analysis, for one can never stand outside its game; it is "an interplay of identities that are constantly being tested, circulated, transformed" (212:182; see also 20, 37, 118, 123, 203).

From the evidence above it is clear that aesthetic and performance dimensions of possession are inseparable from its spirituality, its capacity to reformulate identity or to heal. This observation leads to a consideration of what may be the most important but potentially most problematic addition to our current understanding of possession, the newly reinvigorated concept of mimesis or quotation.

In a recently translated work on possession and art in Africa, Kramer (114) explodes the category spirit possession as conventionally portrayed. His approach is comparative but not universalizing. Rather than presume a naturally bounded subject matter, he begins with an image found in several African possession cults, the red fez—one of the details of colonial habit and dress that was seized upon as crystallizing Europeanness (cf. 143), and is still commonly requested by spirits in possession rites throughout the continent. Kramer notes that just as Europeans use images of the Other in articulating their sense of self, so do Africans (114:2). The point is hardly news. Yet in following this lead while staying close to cultural logics, Kramer productively links phenomena that anthropologists usually keep distinct: ancestor reverence, popular culture, secular dance, religious masquerade, rules governing the status of strangers, spirit mediumship and possession, and forms of art.

Kramer's book is a rich compendium of materials and ideas that deals with issues of identity, of social differentiation via the Other. More novel is Kramer's view that possession and other indigenous aesthetic genres are not just forms of knowledge; they are also ways of knowing. Such epistemic styles have been subordinated, rendered illegitimate by Western scholarly paradigms, and depicted as exotic, even aberrant, as we've seen. Despite this they persist. Unlike globally dominant positive science, they presume no Archi-

---

2
   This is not to say, of course, that all societies in which the image of an atomized body prevails are bourgeois. In India, for example, a different concept of atomization based on the significances of the humors has its own implications for possession beliefs and experiences. I am grateful to EV Daniel for suggesting this clarification.

medean point; rather, both knower and known are engaged in a reciprocal and reversible relationship. The knower, implicated in the subject of her knowledge, is moved by it, to the extent of being bodily possessed by it (114:60; see 25). Kramer does not imply some essential cultural or physical difference between African and European, but points to a Western rationalization of holistic human experience, a separation of "cosmology from psychology in their entireties" (114:59), elsewhere described as reification.

Kramer builds on Lienhardt's (142) concept of *passiones,* the self as being acted upon and affected by unwilled experience [an idea to which others have been drawn as well (46, 103, 123, 172)]. He suggests that "unfamiliarity with the other can overwhelm" and "compel" to mimesis (114:251). Compulsion notwithstanding, mimesis, then, is the human faculty by which *passiones* are expressed. By replicating an experience in gesture and art, the experience becomes known and familiar, incorporated by the individual and her society. But it is also interpreted and thereby transformed.

Mimesis as a pedagogical process, both embodiment of knowledge and bodying forth of knowledge, has been more discerningly depicted by Taussig (210) and to a lesser extent, by Bourdieu (28). Mimetic actors do not lack agency. We are all mimetic actors insofar as mimesis is the way in which the *habitus* is learned, through profound identification, and made self (28, 210). It is thus that social convention acquires its quotidian naturalness (210:xvi–xiii). Mimesis is a two-layered notion, Taussig suggests, "a copying, or imitation, and a palpable, sensuous, connection between the very body of the perceiver and the perceived" (p. 21). Thus, knowing is at once an intimate corporeal act, the ability to "yield into and become Other" (210:xiii), and an ideational activity, a trying out of perceptions (210:46). Mimesis is dependent on alterity, the existence of an Other (114, 210); hence, there always exists the possibility of what Taussig (210) calls second contact, seeing one's own ethnic group, material objects, and personal traits, in the images produced by others (eg. 20:359, 188, 206). This is the basis of allegory and quotation, the synoptic principles behind possession performances where, among others, white colonial officials appear as they were observed.

The notion of mimesis could well enable us to recognize and analyze with greater clarity the multidimensioned resistances possession cults evince to Enlightenment myths of context-free Reason, the mischief they work with capitalist reifications, their iconoclastic interpretations of commodities and bodily disciplines (cf.210:133), and the morality of their aesthetics. It surely affords increased insight into possession forms. Perhaps most relevant, however, is its role in destabilizing scholarly assumptions about objectivity and rationality, and in challenging intellectual categories. It provides no harbor for the analyst outside of the processes she studies. Being possessed by possession is symptomatic of the interpenetration of realities that it is possession's task to make clear. Taussig impassions us to welcome the vertigo that acknowledging mimesis entails, to resist appropriating it by means of explanation (210:237), to remain, as it were, possessed, and to let that condition work its effects. He has a point. Like trance before it, mimesis is in danger of becoming a reductive behaviorist explanation for possession, which would neutralize its power to disconcert (cf 206) and depoliticize it by categorical fiat. Instead of collapsing possession into a generalized human body, we need better to understand embodiment as a contextually nuanced project.

Two recent attempts to do so return us to more familiar terrain. Lambek (123) takes a classical social constructionist approach in addressing the dialectics of embodiment and objectification in three domains of knowledge in Mayotte. He suggests that in any form of knowledge, one part of this dialectic will be privileged over the other. Possession privileges embodiment, yet not to the exclusion of objectification, because manifest possession—active embodiment—produces objectified knowledge of spirits, and of their implicit or emphatic commentaries, for hosts and observers alike (also 20; cf 2, 205). This in turn becomes part of the host's lived experience of her body when, for example, she conforms to spirits' demands to eat or abstain from certain foods (123:305–309), or walk rather than ride in a car (124, 151). If the body is the ground for legitimating objective knowledge, internalizing it, and making it experientially real [or originating it (cf 171)], objectification is the process of rendering embodied knowledge graspable by others through performance and conversation (see also 45, 191). Mimesis encompasses both, but Lambek's argument enables us to see the process as contextually variable and potentially reflexive.

Csordas draws from Bourdieu's account of the socially informed body and Merleau-Ponty's focus on the pre-objective act of perception (154, 155) in constructing a sophisticated provisional model of embodiment (53–55). He suggests the term "somatic modes of attention" to specify the various culturally elaborated ways in which we attend to, attend with, and objectify our bodies "in surroundings that include the embodied presence of others" (55:138), and looks to the healing practices of Puerto Rican spirit mediums and Anglo-American Catholic Charismatics for clues to the phenomenology of religious therapeutic transformation (52–55). Csordas is analytically rigorous and mindful of his model's indeterminacies. Still, his concepts of intersubjective embodiment and somatic modes of attention echo Taussig's and Kramer's invocations of the mimetic faculty and suggest directions for its theoretical and pragmatic elucidation (see also 57, 91, 110, 145).

Yet do we not, even here, in attending so fully to embodiment, risk denying the whole of the possession experience, which our informants insist is embodied and disembodied at one and the same time?

CONCLUSION

The literature on spirit possession has changed direction in the past twenty years, as concern for behavioral and psychological rationalization gave way to increased attention to local contexts, cultural logics, human imagination, and creativity. To be sure, rationalist reduction was a humanizing enterprise, an attempt to render familiar what had seemed to be so strange. Deeper realization of the situatedness of knowledge, our loss of Olympian privilege, has led many scholars here reviewed to eschew it as dehumanizing; ironically, the projects were not dissimilar in intent.

There has also been a gradual dismantling of the category spirit possession as an autonomous subject of inquiry. Where the 1960s and 1970s saw several collections (e.g. 16, 30a, 49), the field is now dominated by finely situated ethnographies in which possession figures, yet not exclusively (but see 140, 216). Researchers currently locate possession in wider spheres of human endeavor, as speaking to quotidian issues of selfhood and identity, challenging global political and economic domination, and articulating an aesthetic of human relationship to the world. And whether central or peripheral, possession has been shown to be about morality, kinship, ethnicity, history, and social memory—the touchstones of social existence. Here morality and resistance are one.

It is too soon to gauge how the recent revival of mimesis and its history will influence analysis. The development merits careful thought but its potential for misuse as evolutionary rhetoric means we would be unwise to install it as a new master narrative. Yet it is undeniably provocative. It shifts the question from "How is it that other peoples believe the self to be permeable by forces from without?" to "How is it that Western models have repeatedly denied such permeability?" This gives new relevance to Kenny's (103, 104) important observations on the relationship between spirit possession and Multiple Personality Disorders burgeoning in North America today (see also 6, 84). It requires us to rethink Western cultural assumptions of an integral self, sheds new light on religious and psychiatric iatrogenesis, and pathological forms of embodied aesthetics like anorexia nervosa. If, as Taussig (210:20) suggests, modernity's technologies offer new schooling for our mimetic powers, then possession, which has ever foregrounded them, can perhaps provide some sense of this process.

ACKNOWLEDGMENTS

I am grateful to Ronald Wright, Michael Lambek, and E. Valentine Daniel for carefully reading the manuscript and providing sound advice on short notice. Thanks also to Carole Tuck, Audrey Glasbergen, the staff of Bladen Library, and my students for their patience.

Literature Cited

1. Abdalla HI. 1991. Neither friend nor foe: the malam practitioner—*yan bori* relationship in Hausaland. See Ref. 140, pp. 37–48

2. Abu-Lughod L. 1993. Review of *Wombs and Alien Spirits. Am. Ethnol.* 20(2):425–26

3. Ackerman S, Lee R. 1981. Communication and cognitive pluralism in a spirit possession event in Malaysia. *Am. Ethnol.* 8(4):789–99

4. Alpers EA. 1984. 'Ordinary household chores': ritual and power in a 19th-century Swahili women's spirit possession cult. *Int. J. Afr. Hist. Stud.* 17(4):677–702

5. Antze P. 1992. Possession trance and multiple personality: psychiatric disorders or idioms of distress? *Transcult. Psychiatr. Res. Rev.* 29(4):319–23

6. Antze P. 1992. *Being multiple together: conversational narratives in a support group for persons with Multiple Personality Disorder.* Presented at Annu. Meet. Can. Anthropol. Soc., 19th, Montreal

7. Ashkanani Z. 1991. Zar in a changing world: Kuwait. See Ref. 140, pp. 219–29

8. Atkinson JM. 1992. Shamanisms today. *Annu. Rev. Anthropol.* 21:307–30

9. AvRuskin TL. 1988. Neurophysiology and the curative possession trance: the Chinese case. *Med. Anthropol. Q.* 2(3):286–302

10. Bakhtin M. 1981. *The Dialogic Imagination,* ed. M Holquist. Transl. C Emerson, M Holquist. Austin: Univ. Texas Press

11. Bakhtin M. 1984. *Rabelais and His World.* Transl. H Iswolsky. Bloomington: Univ. Ind. Press

12. Balandier G. 1966. *Ambiguous Africa.* London: Chatto & Windus

13. Bastian M. 1993. *Married in the water: returning children, water spirits and modern problems in urban Nigeria.* Presented at Annu. Meet. Am. Anthropol. Assoc., 92nd, Washington, DC

14. Bastide R. 1978. *The African Religions of Brazil.* Transl. H Sebba. Baltimore: Johns Hopkins Univ. Press

15. Bax M. 1992. Female suffering, local power relations, and religious tourism: a case study from Yugoslavia. *Med. Anthropol. Q.* 6(2):114–27

16. Beattie J, Middleton J, eds. 1969. *Spirit Mediumship and Society in Africa.* London: Routledge & Kegan Paul

17. Berger I. 1976. Rebels or status seekers? Women as spirit mediums in East Africa. In *Women in Africa,* ed. NJ Hafkin, EG Bay, pp. 157–81. Stanford, CA: Stanford Univ. Press

18. Besmer FE. 1983. *Horses, Musicians, and Gods: The Hausa Cult of Possession-Trance.* South Hadley, MA: Bergin & Garvey

19. Boddy J. 1988. Spirits and selves in northern Sudan: the cultural therapeutics of possession and trance. *Am. Ethnol.* 15(1):4–27

20. Boddy J. 1989. *Wombs and Alien Spirits: Women, Men, and the Zar Cult in Northern Sudan.* Madison: Univ. Wisc. Press

21. Boddy J. 1991. Anthropology, feminism and the postmodern context. *Culture* 11(1–2):125–33

22. Boddy J. 1992. Comment on the proposed DSM-IV criteria for Trance and Possession Disorder. *Transcult. Psychiatr. Res. Rev.* 29(4):323–30

23. Boddy J. 1992. Review of *Women's Medicine: The Zar-Bori Cult in Africa and Beyond. Man* 27(3):678–79

24. Boddy J. 1993. Subversive kinship: the role of spirit possession in negotiating social place in rural northern Sudan. *POLAR: Pol. Legal Anthropol. Rev.* 16(2):29–37

25. Boddy J. 1994. Review of *The Red Fez. Times Literary Suppl.* In press

26. Boddy J. 1994. Managing tradition: "superstition" and the making of national identity among Sudanese women refugees. In *Religious and Cultural Certainties,* ed. W James. ASA Monogr. London: Routledge. In press

27. Bourdieu P. 1977. *Outline of a Theory of Practice.* Transl. R Nice. Cambridge: Cambridge Univ. Press

28. Bourdieu P. 1990. *The Logic of Practice.* Transl. R Nice. Cambridge: Polity

29. Bourguignon E. 1965. The self, the behavioral environment, and the theory of spirit possession. In *Context and Meaning in Cultural Anthropology,* ed. ME Spiro, pp. 39–60. New York: Free Press

30. Bourguignon E. 1973. Introduction: a framework for the comparative study of

altered states of consciousness. See Ref 30a, pp. 3–35
30a. Bourguignon E, ed. 1973. *Religion, Altered States of Consciousness, and Social Change.* Columbus: Ohio State Univ. Press
31. Bourguignon E. 1976. *Possession.* San Francisco: Chandler & Sharp
32. Bourguignon E. 1992. The DSM-IV and cultural diversity. *Transcult. Psychiatr. Res. Rev.* 29(4):330–32
33. Bourguignon E, Bellisari A, McCabe S. 1983. Women, possession trance cults, and the extended nutrient-deficiency hypothesis. *Am. Anthropol.* 85(2):413–16
34. Braude SE. 1991. *First Person Plural: Multiple Personality and the Philosophy of Mind.* London: Routledge
35. Brown DG. 1986. *Umbanda: Religion and Politics in Urban Brazil.* Ann Arbor, MI: Univ. Mich. Res. Press
36. Brown DG, Bick M. 1987. Religion, class and context: continuities and discontinuities in Brazilian Umbanda. *Am. Ethnol.* 14(1):73–93
37. Brown KM. 1991. *Mama Lola: A Vodou Priestess in Brooklyn.* Berkeley: Univ. Calif. Press
38. Cardeña E. 1992. Trance and possession as dissociative disorders. *Transcult. Psychiatr. Res. Rev.* 29(4):287–300
38a. Claus PJ. 1984. Medical anthropology and the ethnography of spirit possession. *Contr. Asian Stud.* 18(1):60–72
39. Comaroff J. 1985. *Body of Power, Spirit of Resistance: The Culture and History of a South African People.* Chicago: Univ. Chicago Press
40. Constantinides P. 1977. "Ill at ease and sick at heart": symbolic behavior in a Sudanese healing cult. In *Symbols and Sentiments,* ed. IM Lewis, pp. 61–83. New York: Academic
41. Constantinides P. 1982. Women's spirit possession and urban adaptation in the Muslim northern Sudan. In *Women United, Women Divided,* ed. P Caplan, D Bujra, pp. 185–205. Bloomington: Univ. Ind. Press
42. Constantinides P. 1985. Women heal women: spirit possession and sexual segregation in a Muslim society. *Soc. Sci. Med.* 21(6):685–92
43. Constantinides P. 1991. The history of *zar* in the Sudan: theories of origin, recorded observation and oral tradition. See Ref. 140, pp. 83–99
44. Corin E. 1979. A possession psychotherapy in an urban setting: Zebola in Kinshasa. *Soc. Sci. Med.* 13B(4):327–38
45. Crain MM. 1991. Poetics and politics in the Ecuadorean Andes: women's narratives of death and devil possession. *Am. Ethnol.* 18(1):67–89
46. Crapanzano V. 1973. *The Hamadsha: A Study in Moroccan Ethnopsychiatry.* Berkeley: Univ. Calif. Press
47. Crapanzano V. 1977. Introduction. See Ref. 49, pp. 1–39
48. Crapanzano V. 1980. *Tuhami: Portrait of a Moroccan.* Chicago: Univ. Chicago Press
49. Crapanzano V, Garrison V, eds. 1977. *Case Studies in Spirit Possession.* New York: Wiley
50. Csordas TJ. 1983. The rhetoric of transformation in ritual healing. *Cult. Med. Psychiatr.* 7:333–75
51. Csordas TJ. 1987. Health and the holy in African and Afro-American spirit possession. *Soc. Sci. Med.* 24(1):1–11
52. Csordas TJ. 1988. Elements of charismatic persuasion and healing. *Med. Anthropol. Q.* 2(2):121–42
53. Csordas TJ. 1990. Embodiment as a paradigm for anthropology. *Ethos* 18:5–47
54. Csordas TJ. 1993. *The Sacred Self: A Cultural Phenomenology of Charismatic Healing.* Berkeley: Univ. Calif. Press
55. Csordas TJ. 1993. Somatic modes of attention. *Cult. Anthropol.* 8(2):135–56
56. De Heusch L. 1971. *Why Marry Her? Society and Symbolic Structures.* Transl. J Lloyd. Cambridge: Cambridge Univ. Press
57. Desjarlais R. 1992. *Body and Emotion: The Aesthetics of Illness and Healing in the Nepal Himalayas.* Philadelphia: Univ. Penn. Press
58. Dobbin JD. 1986. *The Jombee Dance of Montserrat: A Study of Trance Ritual in the West Indies.* Columbia: Ohio State Univ. Press.
59. Douglas M. 1973. *Natural Symbols.* Harmondsworth, UK: Penguin
60. Echard N. 1991. The Hausa bori possession cult in the Ader region of Niger: its origins and present-day function. See Ref. 140, pp. 64–80
61. Fabian J. 1983. *Time and the Other: How Anthropology Makes Its Object.* New York: Columbia Univ. Press
62. Feeley-Harnick G. 1984. The political economy of death: communication and change in Malagasy colonial history. *Am. Ethnol.* 11(1):1–19
63. Feeley-Harnick G. 1991. *A Green Estate: Restoring Independence in Madagascar.* Washington, DC: Smithsonian Inst. Press
64. Field MJ. 1960. *Search for Security: An Ethnopsychiatric Study of Rural Ghana.* London: Faber & Faber
65. Foucault M. 1972. *The Archaeology of Knowledge.* Transl. AMS. Smith. London: Tavistock
66. Foucault M. 1980. *Power/Knowledge,* ed. C Gordon. Transl. C Gordon, L Marshall, J Mepham, K Soper. New York: Pantheon
67. Foucault M. 1982. The subject and power. In *Michel Foucault: Beyond Structuralism and Hermenuetics,* ed. HL Dreyfus, P Rabi-

now, pp. 208–26. New York: Harvester Wheatsheaf

68. Freed RS, Freed SA. 1990. Ghost illness in a North Indian village. *Soc. Sci. Med.* 30(5):617–23

69. Fry P. 1976. *Spirits of Protest: Spirit-Mediums and the Articulation of Consensus among Zezuru of Southern Rhodesia (Zimbabwe).* Cambridge: Cambridge Univ. Press

70. Garbett K. 1977. Disparate regional cults and a unitary field in Zimbabwe. In *Regional Cults,* ed. RP Werbner, pp. 55–92. ASA Monogr. No. 16. London: Academic

71. Garrison V, Crapanzano V. 1978. Comment on Leacock's review of *Case Studies in Spirit Possession. Rev. Anthropol.* 5:420–25

72. Geertz C. 1973. *The Interpretation of Cultures.* New York: Basic

73. Geertz C. 1988. *Works and Lives: The Anthropologist as Author.* Stanford, CA: Stanford Univ. Press

74. Gelfand M. 1959. *Shona Ritual.* Cape Town: Juta

75. Giles L. 1987. Possession cults of the Swahili Coast: a re-examination of theories of marginality. *Africa* 57(2):234–58

76. Giles L. 1989. The dialectic of spirit production: a cross-cultural dialogue. *Mankind Q.* 29(3):243–65

77. Giles L. 1992. *Socio-cultural change and spirit possession on the Swahili Coast of East Africa.* Presented at Annu. Meet. Central States Anthropol. Soc., Cleveland, OH

78. Gomm R. 1975. Bargaining from weakness: spirit possession on the south Kenya coast. *Man* 10:530–43

79. Graham H. 1976. The social image of pregnancy: pregnancy as spirit possession. *Sociol. Rev.* May:291–308

80. Gramsci A. 1971. *Selections from the Prison Notebooks,* ed./transl. Q Hoare, GN Smith. New York: International

81. Gray JN. 1987. Nayu Utarnu: ghost exorcism and sacrifice in Nepal. *Ethnology* 26:179–99

82. Greenfield SM. 1992. Spirits and spiritist therapy in southern Brazil: a case study of an innovative, syncretic healing group. *Cult. Med. Psychiatr.* 16:23–51

83. Haar GT, Ellis S. 1988. Spirit possession and healing in modern Zambia: an analysis of letters to Archbishop Milingo. *Afr. Affairs* 87:185–206

84. Hacking I. 1992. Multiple Personality Disorder and its hosts. *Hist. Hum. Sci.* 5(2):3–31

85. Halliday M. 1976. Anti-languages. *Am. Anthropol.* 78:570–84

86. Harvey KS. 1980. Possession sickness and women shamans in Korea. In *Unspoken Worlds: Women's Religious Lives in Non-*

Western Cultures, ed. NA Falk, RM Gray, pp. 41–52. San Francisco: Harper & Row

87. Harwood A. 1987. *Rx: Spiritist as Needed: A Study of a Puerto Rican Community Mental Health Resource.* Ithaca, NY: Cornell Univ. Press

88. Hitchcock JT, Jones RL, eds. 1976. *Spirit Possession in the Nepal Himalayas.* Warminster, UK: Aris & Phillips

89. Hurreiz S. 1991. Zar as ritual psychodrama: from cult to club. See Ref. 140, pp. 147–55

90. Irvine JT. 1982. The creation of identity in spirit mediumship and possession. In *Semantic Anthropology,* ed. D Parkin, pp. 241–60. ASA Monogr. No. 22. London: Academic

91. Jackson M. 1989. *Paths Toward a Clearing: Radical Empiricism and Ethnographic Enquiry.* Bloomington: Univ. Ind. Press

92. Jacobs CF. 1989. Spirit guides and possession in the New Orleans black spiritual churches. *J. Am. Folklore* 102(Jan–Mar): 45–67

93. Janzen J. 1992. *Ngoma: Discourses of Healing in Central and Southern Africa.* Berkeley: Univ. Calif. Press

94. Kahana Y. 1985. The zar spirits, a category of magic in the system of mental health care in Ethiopia. *Int. J. Soc. Psychiatr.* 31(Summer):125–43

95. Kapferer B. 1979. Mind, self and other in demonic illness: the negotiation and reconstruction of self. *Am. Ethnol.* 6(1):110–33

96. Kapferer B. 1986. Performance and the structure of meaning and experience. In *The Anthropology of Experience,* ed. VW Turner, EM Bruner, pp. 188–206. Chicago: Univ. Ill. Press

97. Kapferer B. 1988. The anthropologist as hero. *Crit. Anthropol.* 8(2):77–104

98. Kapferer B. 1991. *A Celebration of Demons: Exorcism and Healing in Sri Lanka.* Washington, DC: Smithsonian Inst. Press. 2nd ed.

99. Karp I. 1989. Power and capacity in rituals of possession. In *Creativity of Power: Cosmology and Action in African Societies,* ed. W Arens, I Karp, pp. 91–109. Washington, DC: Smithsonian Inst. Press

99a. Kearney M. 1977. Oral performance by Mexican spiritualists in possession trance. *J. Latin Am. Lore* 3(2):309–28

99b. Kearney M. 1978. Spiritualist healing in Mexico. In *Culture and Curing,* ed. P Morley, R Wallis, pp. 19–39. London: Owen

100. Kehoe AB, Giletti DH. 1981. Women's preponderance in possession cults: the calcium deficiency hypothesis extended. *Am. Anthropol.* 83(3):549–61

101. Kendall L. 1985. *Shamans, Housewives, and Other Restless Spirits: Women in Ko-*

rean Ritual Life. Honolulu: Univ. Hawaii Press

102. Kennedy JG. 1967. Nubian *zar* ceremonies as psychotherapy. *Hum. Org.* 26(4):185–94

103. Kenny MG. 1981. Multiple personality and spirit possession. *Psychiatry* 44(Nov): 337–58

104. Kenny MG. 1986. *The Passion of Ansel Bourne: Multiple Personality in American Culture*. Washington, DC: Smithsonian Inst. Press

105. Kenny MG. 1992. Notes on the proposed revisions of the dissociative disorders section of DSM-III-R. *Transcult. Psychiatr. Res. Rev.* 29(4):337–41

106. Kenyon SM. 1991. The story of a tin box: *zar* in the Sudanese town of Sennar. See Ref. 140, pp. 100–17

107. Kenyon SM. 1991. *Five Women of Sennar: Culture and Change in Central Sudan*. Oxford: Clarendon

108. Kenyon SM. 1992. *Social change and ecstatic experience: zar as modernization in contemporary Sudan*. Presented at Annu. Meet. Central States Anthropol. Soc., Cleveland, OH

109. Kirmayer L. 1992. Editorial: taking possession of trance. *Transcult. Psychiatr. Res. Rev.* 29(4):283–6

110. Kirmayer L. 1992. The body's insistence on meaning: metaphor as presentation and representation in illness experience. *Med. Anthropol. Q.* 6(4):323–46

111. Kleinman A. 1980. *Patients and Healers in the Context of Culture*. Berkeley: Univ. Calif. Press

112. Koss-Chioino JD. 1992. *Women as Healers, Women as Patients: Mental Health Care and Traditional Healing in Puerto Rico*. Boulder, CO: Westview

113. Koss-Chioino JD. 1992. Possession/trance and psychopathology: mismatched conceptual constructs. *Transcult. Psychiatr. Res. Rev.* 29(4):343–45

114. Kramer F. 1993. *The Red Fez: Art and Spirit Possession in Africa*. Transl. MR Green. London: Verso

115. Krippner SK. 1989. A call to heal: entry patterns in Brazilian mediumship. See Ref. 216, pp. 186–206

116. Laderman C. 1991. *Taming the Wind of Desire: Psychology, Medicine and Aesthetics in Malay Shamanistic Performance*. Berkeley: Univ. Calif. Press

117. Lambek M. 1980. Spirits and spouses: possession as a system of communication among Malagasy speakers of Mayotte. *Am. Ethnol.* 7(2):318–31

118. Lambek M. 1981. *Human Spirits: A Cultural Account of Trance in Mayotte*. Cambridge: Cambridge Univ. Press

119. Lambek M. 1988. Graceful exits: spirit possession as personal performance in Mayotte. *Culture* 8(1):59–70

120. Lambek M. 1988. Spirit possession/spirit succession: aspects of social continuity among Malagasy speakers in Mayotte. *Am. Ethnol.* 15(4): 710–31

121. Lambek M. 1989. From disease to discourse: remarks on the conceptualization of trance and spirit possession. See Ref. 216, pp. 36–61

122. Lambek M. 1992. Discreteness or discretion? *Transcult. Psychiatr. Res. Rev.* 29(4): 345–47

123. Lambek M. 1993. *Knowledge and Practice in Mayotte: Local Discourses of Islam, Sorcery, and Spirit Possession*. Toronto: Univ. Toronto Press

124. Lan D. 1985. *Guns and Rain: Guerrillas and Spirit Mediums in Zimbabwe*. London: Currey

125. Landes R. 1947. *The City of Women*. New York: Macmillan

126. Last M. 1991. Spirit possession as therapy: bori among non-Muslims in Nigeria. See Ref. 140, pp. 49–63

127. Leacock S, Leacock R. 1972. *Spirits of the Deep: A Study of an Afro-Brazilian Cult*. Garden City, NY: Doubleday

128. Leacock S. 1978. Trance and psychopathology. *Rev. Anthropol.* 5:399–409

129. Leiris M. 1958. *La possession et ses aspects théâtraux chez les Ethiopiens de Gondar*. Paris: Plon

130. Lerch B. 1980. Spirit mediums in Umbanda Evangelizada of Porto Alegre Brazil. In *A World of Women*, ed. E Bourguignon, pp. 129–59. New York: Praeger

131. Lerch B. 1982. An explanation for the predominance of women in the Umbanda cults of Porto Alegre, Brazil. *Urban Anthropol.* 11(2):237–61

132. Leslau W. 1949. An Ethiopian argot of people possessed by a Spirit. *Africa* 19:204–12

133. Lewis H. 1983. Spirit possession in Ethiopia: an essay in interpretation. In *Ethiopian Studies*, ed. S Segert, AJ Bodrogligeti, pp. 466–80. Wiesbaden, Germany: Harrassowitz

134. Lewis H. 1990. *Spirit mediums, social control, and the moral order among the Oromo of western Ethiopia*. Presented at Int. Colloq. Afr. Ritual Relig., 6th, Satterthwaite, UK

135. Lewis IM. 1971. *Ecstatic Religion: An Anthropological Study of Spirit Possession and Shamanism*. Harmondsworth, UK: Penguin

136. Lewis IM. 1983. Spirit possession and biological reductionism: a rejoinder to Kehoe and Giletti. *Am. Anthropol.* 85(2):412–13

137. Lewis IM. 1986. *Religion in Context: Cults and Charisma*. Cambridge: Cambridge Univ. Press

138. Lewis IM. 1989. *Ecstatic Religion: A Study of Spirit Possession and Shamanism*. London: Routledge. 2nd ed.

139. Lewis IM. 1991. *Zar* in context: the past, the present and future of an African healing cult. See Ref. 140, pp. 1–16

140. Lewis IM, Al-Safi A, Hurreiz S, eds. 1991. *Women's Medicine: The Zar-Bori Cult in Africa and Beyond.* Edinburgh: Edinburgh Univ. Press

141. Lewis-Fernández R. 1992. The proposed DSM-IV Trance and Possession Disorder category: potential benefits and risks. *Transcult. Psychiatr. Res. Rev.* 29(4):301–17

142. Lienhardt G. 1961. *Divinity and Experience: The Religion of the Dinka.* Oxford: Clarendon

143. Lipps JE. 1966. *The Savage Hits Back.* New York: University Books. 2nd ed.

144. Littlewood R. 1988. From vice to madness: the semantics of naturalistic and personalistic understandings in Trinidadian local medicine. *Soc. Sci. Med.* 27(2):129–48

145. Lock M. 1993. Cultivating the body: anthropology and epistemologies of bodily practice and knowledge. *Annu. Rev. Anthropol.* 22:133–55

146. Makris GP, Al-Safi A. 1991. The tumbura spirit possession cult of the Sudan. See Ref. 140, pp. 118–36

147. Martin E. 1987. *The Woman in the Body.* Boston: Beacon

148. Martin E. 1990. Toward an anthropology of immunology: the body as nation state. *Med. Anthropol. Q.* 4(4):410–26

149. Martin E. 1993. *Interpreting electron micrographs.* Presented at ASA Decennial Conf., 4th, Oxford

150. Masquelier A. 1993. *Ritual economies, historical mediations: the poetics and power of bori among the Mawri of Niger.* PhD thesis. Univ. Chicago

151. Masquelier A. 1993. *The invention of antitradition: Dodo spirits in southern Niger.* Presented at Annu. Meet. Am. Anthropol. Assoc., 92nd, Washington, DC

152. Matory JL. 1991. *Rival empires: Islam and the religions of spirit possession among the Oyo-Yoruba.* Presented at Conf. Afr. Spirit Possess. Univ. Relig., June, Harvard Univ., Cambridge, MA

153. Matsuoka E. 1991. The interpretations of fox possession: illness as metaphor. *Cult. Med. Psychiatr.* 15:453–77

154. Merleau-Ponty M. 1962. *Phenomenology of Perception.* Transl. C Smith. London: Routledge

155. Merleau-Ponty M. 1964. *The Primacy of Perception*, ed. JM Edie. Evanston, IL: Northwestern Univ. Press

156. Messing SD. 1958. Group therapy and social status in the *zar* cult of Ethiopia. *Am. Anthropol.* 60(6):1120–26

157. Métraux A. 1959. *Voodoo in Haiti.* Oxford: Oxford Univ. Press

158. Middleton J. 1991. *Spirit possession among the Swahili.* Presented at Conf. Afr. Spirit Possess. Univ. Relig., June, Harvard Univ., Cambridge, MA

159. Monfouga-Nicolas J. 1972. *Ambivalence et culte de possession.* Paris: Editions Anthropos

160. Morris R. 1993. *Eternal returns: spirit mediumship, nostalgia, and postmodernity in Chiang Mai, northern Thailand.* Presented at Annu. Meet. Am. Anthropol. Assoc., 92nd, Washington, DC

161. Morsy S. 1991. Spirit possession in Egyptian ethnomedicine: origins, comparison and historical specificity. See Ref. 140, pp. 189–208

162. Munn N. 1992. The cultural anthropology of time: a critical essay. *Annu. Rev. Anthropol.* 21:93–123

163. Natvig R. 1987. Oromos, slaves, and the *zar* spirits: a contribution to the history of the *zar* cult. *Int. J. Afr. Hist. Stud.* 20(4):669–89

164. Natvig R. 1991. Some notes on the history of the *zar* cult in Egypt. See Ref. 140, pp. 178–88

165. Neff DL. 1987. Aesthetics and power in Pambin Tullal: a possession ritual of rural Kerala. *Ethnology* 26:63–71

166. Neher A. 1962. A physiological explanation of unusual behavior in ceremonies involving drums. *Hum. Biol.* 34:151–60

167. Nelson C. 1971. Self, spirit possession and world view: an illustration from Egypt. *Int. J. Soc. Psychiatr.* 17(1):194–209

168. Nuckolls CW. 1991. Becoming a possession-medium in South India: a psychocultural account. *Med. Anthropol. Q.* 5(1):63–77

169. Obeyesekere G. 1969. The ritual drama of the Sanni demons: collective representations of disease in Ceylon. *Comp. Stud. Soc. Hist.* 11(2):174–216

170. Obeyesekere G. 1970. The idiom of demonic possession. *Soc. Sci. Med.* 4:97–111

171. Obeyesekere G. 1981. *Medusa's Hair: An Essay on Personal Symbols and Religious Experience.* Chicago: Univ. Chicago Press

172. Okazaki A. 1992. *Standing up to dreams: an aspect of healing rituals among the Gâmk of Sudan.* Presented at Int. Colloq. Afr. Ritual Relig., 8th, Satterthwaite, UK

173. Ong A. 1987. *Spirits of Resistance and Capitalist Discipline: Factory Women in Malaysia.* Albany: State Univ. NY Press

174. Ong A. 1988. The production of possession: spirits and the multinational corporation in Malaysia. *Am. Ethnol.* 15(1):28–42

175. Onwuejeogwu M. 1969. The cult of the *bori* spirits among the Hausa. In *Man in Africa*, ed. M Douglas, P Kaberry, pp. 279–305. London: Tavistock

176. Palmié S. 1993. *Against syncretism: Afri-*

canizing and Cubanizing discourses in North American òrìsá worship. Presented at ASA Decennial Conf., 4th, Oxford

177. Pandolfi M. 1990. Boundaries inside the body: women's sufferings in southern peasant Italy. *Cult. Med. Psychiatr.* 14: 255–73

178. Pandolfi M. 1991. Memory within the body: women's narrative and identity in a southern Italian village. In *Anthropologies of Medicine,* ed. B Pfleiderer, G Bibeau, pp. 59–65. Heidelberg: Vieweg

179. Pandolfi M. 1992. *The expanded body and the fragmented body: inside and beyond narrative.* Presented at Annu. Meet. Can. Anthropol. Soc., 19th, Montreal

180. Pfleiderer B. 1988. The semiotics of ritual healing in a north Indian Muslim shrine. *Soc. Sci. Med.* 5:417–24

181. Pressel E. 1980. Spirit magic in the social relations between men and women (São Paulo, Brazil). In *A World of Women,* ed. E Bourguignon, pp. 107–28. New York: Praeger

182. Prince RH. 1974. The problem of "spirit possession" as a treatment for psychiatric disorders. *Ethos* 2:315–33

183. Prince R, ed. 1968. *Trance and Possession States.* Montreal: RM Bucke Mem. Soc.

184. Ranger T. 1982. The death of Chaminuka: spirit mediums, nationalism and the guerrilla war in Zimbabwe. *Afr. Affairs* 81:349–69

185. Raybeck D, Shoobe J, Grauberger J. 1989. Women, stress, and participation in possession cults: a reexamination of the calcium deficiency hypothesis. *Med. Anthropol. Q.* 3(2):139–61

186. Roseman M. 1988. The pragmatics of performance: the performance of healing among the Senoi Temiar. *Soc. Sci. Med.* 27(8):811–18

187. Rouch J. 1960. *La religion et la magie Songhay.* Paris: Presses Univ. France

188. Rouch J. 1978. On the vicissitudes of the self: the possessed dancer, the magician, the sorcerer, the filmmaker, the ethnographer. *Stud. Anthropol. Vis. Commun.* 5(Fall):2–8

189. Rouget G. 1985. *Music and Trance: A Theory of the Relations between Music and Possession.* Transl. B Biebuyck, G Rouget. Chicago: Univ. Chicago Press

190. Salisbury R. 1966. Possession among the Siane (New Guinea). *Transcult. Psychiatr. Res. Rev.* 3:108–16

191. Schattschneider E. 1993. *Mountains of memory: spirit mediumship and the work of narrative in northern Japan.* Presented at Annu. Meet. Am. Anthropol. Assoc., 92nd, Washington, DC

192. Schieffelin EL. 1985. Performance and the cultural construction of reality. *Am. Ethnol.* 12(4):707–24

193. Schmoll P. 1991. *Searching for Health in a World of Dis-Ease.* PhD thesis. Univ. Chicago

194. Shaara L, Strathern A. 1992. A preliminary analysis of the relationship between altered states of consciousness, healing, and social structure. *Am. Anthropol.* 94(1):145–60

195. Sharp LA. 1990. Possessed and dispossessed youth: spirit possession of school children in northwest Madagascar. *Cult. Med. Psychiatr.* 14:339–64

196. Sharp LA. 1993. *The Possessed and the Dispossessed: Spirits, Identity, and Power in a Madagascar Migrant Town.* Berkeley: Univ. Calif. Press

197. Sharp LA. 1994. Exorcists, psychiatrists, and the problems of possession in northwest Madagascar. *Soc. Sci. Med.* 38(4): 525–42

198. Skultans V. 1987. The management of mental illness among Maharashtrian families: a case study of a Mahanubhav healing temple. *Man* 22:661–79

199. Spring A. 1978. Epidemiology of spirit possession among the Luvale of Zambia. In *Women in Ritual and Symbolic Roles,* ed. J Hoch-Smith, A Spring, pp. 165–90. New York: Plenum

200. Steedly MM. 1988. Severing the bonds of love: a case study in soul loss. *Soc. Sci. Med.* 27(8):841–56

201. Steedly MM. 1993. *Hanging Without a Rope: Narrative Experience in Colonial and Postcolonial Karoland.* Princeton, NJ: Princeton Univ. Press

202. Stoller P. 1984. Horrific comedy: cultural resistance and the Hauka movement in Niger. *Ethos* 12(2):165–88

203. Stoller P. 1989. *Fusion of the Worlds: An Ethnography of Possession among the Songhay of Niger.* Chicago: Univ. Chicago Press

204. Stoller P. 1989. Stressing social change and Songhay possession. See Ref. 216, pp. 267–84

205. Stoller P. 1992. Embodying cultural memory in Songhay spirit possession. *Arch. Sci. Soc. Relig.* 79(July–Sept):53–68

206. Stoller P. 1993. *Diplomacy on a dune: embodiment, power and the Hauka movement in Niger.* Presented at Annu. Meet. Am. Anthropol. Assoc., 92nd, Washington, DC

207. Sundkler BGM. 1976. *Zulu Zion and Some Swazi Zionists.* London: Oxford Univ. Press

208. Taussig MT. 1980. Reification and the consciousness of the patient. *Soc. Sci. Med.* 14B:3–13

209. Taussig M. 1987. *Shamanism, Colonialism, and the Wild Man: A Study in Terror and Healing.* Chicago: Univ. Chicago Press

210. Taussig M. 1993. *Mimesis and Alterity: A Particular History of the Senses.* New York: Routledge

211. Van Binsbergen W. 1981. *Religious Change in Zambia.* London: Routledge & Kegan Paul

212. Wafer J. 1991. *The Taste of Blood: Spirit Possession in Brazilian Candomblé.* Philadelphia: Univ. Penn. Press

213. Walker S. 1990. Everyday and esoteric reality in the Afro-Brazilian Candomblé. *Hist. Relig.* 30(Nov):103–28

214. Ward C. 1980. Spirit possession and mental health: a psycho-anthropological perspective. *Hum. Relat.* 33(3):149–63

215. Ward CA. 1989. Possession and exorcism: psychopathology and psychotherapy in a magico-religious context. See Ref. 216, pp. 125–44

216. Ward CA, ed. 1989. *Altered States of Consciousness and Mental Health: A Cross-Cultural Perspective.* Newbury Park, CA: Sage

217. Werbner R. 1989. *Ritual Passage, Sacred Journey: The Process and Organization of Religious Movement.* Washington, DC: Smithsonian Inst. Press

218. Wilson P. 1967. Status ambiguity and spirit possession. *Man* (NS) 2:366–78

219. Winkelman M. 1986. Trance states: a theoretical model and cross-cultural analysis. *Ethos* 14:174–204

220. Worley B. 1993. *Construction of power, identity, and female-centered cultural memory in Kel Fadey Twareg spirit possession.* Presented at Annu. Meet. Am. Anthropol. Assoc., 92nd, Washington, DC

221. Young A. 1982. The anthropologies of illness and sickness. *Annu. Rev. Anthropol.* 11:257–85

Annu. Rev. Anthropol. 1994. 23:435–55

LEGAL LANGUAGE: Pragmatics, Poetics, and Social Power

Elizabeth Mertz

American Bar Foundation and Northwestern University School of Law, Chicago, Illinois 60611

KEY WORDS: law, language structure, contextualization, politics of discourse, social construction of legal categories

INTRODUCTION

Recent work in linguistic anthropology has generated new and exciting perspectives on the vital role of contextualization in language meaning and function. At the same time, scholarship on legal language has begun to develop a more social and constructionist vision of the way linguistic processes affect the workings of the law at many levels. This review places some of the scholarship on legal language within the context of current linguistic-anthropological understandings of language use and contextualization, to develop a framework for further work on language and law. It also draws on work in legal scholarship that has illuminated the politics of legal discourse, to demonstrate how this kind of approach can enliven anthropological understandings of the social grounding of language.

SOCIAL GROUNDING AND LANGUAGE STRUCTURE: PRAGMATICS, POETICS, AND SEMANTICS IN CONTEXT

Recent work by anthropologists, linguists, and sociolinguists has moved our understanding of language to more social and contextual levels. In contrast with traditions that concentrate on language as an abstract system (giving little attention to its actual use as a medium of social exchange), and with approaches that focus on how language effects social ends (without much consideration of linguistic systems as structures with dynamics of their own), linguistic anthropologists and sociolinguists have been developing a more integrative way of understanding language as a structure-in-use (e.g. 6, 81, 84, 100–102, 110, 116, 117, 210, 213, 217, 218). To an understanding of language as formal grammatical structure (206) and a concern with instrumentalist functions of language, this work adds a further insight: language also embodies social creativity (5, 82, 213, 221). This insight can be viewed as supplementing, rather than contradicting, other perspectives. There are certainly internal dynamics that are an important part of how language works, and language sometimes functions as a reflection or implementation of social dynamics. But current work has just begun to explore the systematic ways in which language performs a creative role in the dynamics of social change, connection, and rupture—and in the ongoing constitution of social epistemologies (4, 18, 22, 23, 25, 28, 36, 64, 74, 75, 82, 86, 87, 103, 104, 133, 134, 154, 155, 161, 165, 213, 216, 217, 220, 240).

Further, this social-linguistic creativity is not random, but rather is implicated deeply in language structure (see especially 217, 221, 223), a discovery with broad implications for those seeking to understand social interaction in general. If language is the key medium through which social exchange and understanding are accomplished—and if, furthermore, this does not occur in haphazard fashion but in a deeply structured way—then it becomes vital to develop a thorough analysis of the linguistic channeling and structuring of social life. This is particularly important in the domain of law, which is so often (particularly in Western capitalist societies) a key locus of institutionalized linguistic channeling (123, 235) of social power (see 7, 31, 108, 121; for particular arguments and examples, see 33, 35, 43–45, 71, 149, 150, 154, 155, 158, 237).

The line between language as an instrument or reflection of social dynamics and language as an active participant in social construction is a fine one. On the one hand, we know that minute details of linguistic variation often reflect divisions of gender, race, class, ethnicity, and other socially-salient categories (e.g. 27, 29, 61, 119, 145, 146, 183, 192, 197, 225, 227, 234). On the other hand, much of the power of sociolinguistic analysis lies in its ability to map convincingly the ways in which language use not only conveys information (semantic meaning), but also expresses and reflects social divisions and inequalities (pragmatic or contextual meaning). Language here serves as a reflection or mirror of social structure and process, a particularly fine-tuned diagnostic of social morphology.

Similarly, instrumentalist approaches see language as a tool used more or less transparently by actors to effect social ends. These social goals can be defined narrowly, posed in terms of micro-contexts of speaking [for example, a speaker can use linguistic devices such as tropes, repetition, and imagery to maintain audience interest (see 224)], or they can encompass the broader social contexts in which more global battles over social power are enacted (see 66). An instrumentalist analysis focuses on the role of language as a vehicle for the reproduction and contestation of existing social divisions. This approach highlights the social sources and shaping of inequalities and resistance, while linguistic forms become a focus only as resources to be manipulated in service of reproduction and contestation.

Both reflectionist and instrumentalist approaches to language-and-society capture important aspects of language function. In both cases, language is important because it provides a window on social process; it is viewed as an expression of social context and contest. Language can also be understood as an integral part of the constitution of social contexts and contests [what can be called, adapting from Silverstein (215a), the "language-as-society" approach]—and as nontransparent, with dynamics of its own that contribute to social results (113, 114, 217). At the same time, language is integrally structured by its contexts of use, strongly and inherently social in character (see 4, 5, 59, 82, 114, 153, 221). Thus a nontransparent view of language can still avoid linguistic determinism, by stressing the social grounding and nature of language structure and use.

Context in the Structure of Discourse

A number of recent articles and volumes evidence the renewed vigor with which linguists are pursuing the study of the contextual organization and operation of language (e.g. 5, 17, 20, 22–24, 28, 36, 37a, 57–59, 64, 65, 74, 86, 87, 89, 92, 93, 95, 103, 112, 133, 134, 160, 173, 177, 179, 191, 208, 209, 213, 221, 222, 223, 240). A focus on indexical (181) and metapragmatic structuring; concern with performance, recontextualizations, and audience; interest in the interlinguistic contexts of poetic and co-textual structuring; and studies integrating linguistic detail with broad social currents all exemplify this trend. However, although anthropologists and linguists are returning to a focus on the social and contextual structuring of discourse in recent years, our understanding of pragmatic and poetic structure as central to language has roots in the scholarship of the Prague School and of Jakobson, Whorf, and Sapir, among others (e.g. 5, 86, 133a, 214, 221). Gal (74), Irvine (103), Philips (191), and Woolard (240, 242) further direct our attention to the ways in which contextual understandings of language can be integrated with social theoretic traditions.

In contrast with instrumentalist views of language function, which focus on the purposive use of language to attain social goals, this structured and contextualist vision of language takes into account the unpredictability or lack of transparency that results from the complicated social structuring of language.

One can focus on how a particular set of linguistic forms (e.g. a working-class dialect, political oratory, or repetition) can be mobilized relatively predictably to achieve certain goals (e.g. to reproduce class structure, to resist hegemonic forces, or to keep an audience's attention). But purposive usage may be limited in its capacity to achieve the intended effects by complex, deeply rooted, socially-responsive, and creative aspects of language structure—aspects of language that go beyond surface awareness and encode the multifaceted, always shifting, shared understandings of communities across time (see 113, 114, 217). Social actions and events, both purposive and unintended, impact language use and structure, producing results that reflect both the original social impulse and its channeling through language. A re-regimenting process occurs that is socially motivated but also responsive to a peculiarly linguistic systematicity. This systematicity is not entirely language-internal or asocial, because even the systematicity of language is socially grounded in crucial ways. However, the new form of linguistic analysis envisions a different kind of social function for language, one that includes a moment of linguistic creativity.

How do we understand the social grounding of the systematicity of language? We can find examples of the newly emerging approach to this issue in Bauman and others' concern with performance, Gumperz's conception of contextualization cues, and Silverstein's theories regarding pragmatic and metapragmatic structure (but also see the many sources cited above). In each case, there is a reversal of the common emphasis on decontextual semantic and syntactic structuring as the core or dominant feature of language. It is perhaps not surprising that many scholars have privileged this referential aspect of language, because it is an aspect that is arguably more accessible to conscious reflection than are pragmatic structural features (see 215). The ability to use grammatical structure to convey semantic information may also be what renders human language "unique among natural semiotic systems" (see 135:174; see also discussion in 153).

And yet, the social-expressive function of language is what structures and makes possible the expression of semantic meaning (221). The translation of language into use in speech inescapably implicates an indexical structuring that is not merely a happenstance quality of individual situational use, but rather resounds through the very system of grammar itself. From the vantage of language as it is actually used in human interactions, indexicality is primary, and expressing semantic meaning is one of the many functions language fulfills while performing in context. Thus, semantic meaning can be seen as a special subset of pragmatic function, rather than pragmatics being a problematic wrinkle in the transmission of semantic information. Observations on the grammatically "founding" character of deictic categories (114), and on the primacy of aesthetic over referential function (109, 169), support such an approach.

Silverstein has located a number of key principles underlying the structuring of indexical meaning (213, 214, 221). First, language operates against a backdrop of presupposed social knowledge that is variously encoded and enacted in indexical usage. Second, language use is continuously socially creative in its ongoing operation against that backdrop—deploying and rupturing expectations, playing with categories and generating ambiguities, expressing and forming the fluid polyphony of social interaction. Finally, another key aspect of language is its ability to represent and refer to itself—its meta-level capacity. Thus a speaker can in multiple ways characterize the speaking that is under way as a type (or multiple types) of speech. In the move to this meta-level of speech, a process of typification occurs that gives coherence to ongoing speech as it anchors and reanchors sounds and meanings in contexts—contexts that the ongoing speech is also, at least partially, creating and changing (221, 222). Current work on the crucial role of language ideology and meta-pragmatics in linking language and social structure further demonstrates the powerful role of meta-level representations of language in creating and altering social meanings (25, 26, 37, 65, 86, 94, 105, 112, 134, 156, 157, 176, 180, 191, 209, 214, 221, 233, 242).

Gumperz has similarly stressed the contextual anchoring of the structure of language:

> …[the] channelling of interpretation is effected by conversational implicatures based on conventionalized co-occurrence expectations between content and surface style. That is, constellations of surface features of message form are the means by which speakers signal and listeners interpret what the activity is, how semantic content is to be understood and how each sentence relates to what precedes or follows. These features are referred to as *contextualization cues* (82:131).

Gumperz explores the centrality of contextual structuring not only for effective communication but also for production of grammatical utterances. In other words, grammatical structure, the indexical structuring of language use, and the social act of communication are intertwined inextricably. Similarly, Bauman's insistence that we examine oral narrative as performed "in the totality of all its events" (4:114; see also 5, 6) pushes us toward an integrative vision of language use, structure, and context. Bauman, Briggs (23, 25, 27, 28), Brenneis (17, 18, 19, 21), Irvine (102, 104, 105), and others concerned with performance and the role of the audience in communication have uncovered the social dimensions of language forms and traditions often understood primarily in terms of semantic content or abstract structure (e.g. as contrastive typologies of variants of stories). Pioneering work on language socialization by Ochs and Schieffelin (176a, 177, 208, 210), and on child language by

Hickmann (92, 93), among others, is providing us with a fuller picture of the contextual character of language as children first learn to use it—another argument for the primacy of pragmatics in language structure. As anthropologists and linguists have turned their attention to contextual structuring, a renewed emphasis on poetics (28, 91), gesture (58), and prosody and musical aspects of speech (27, 226) has emerged, generating evermore socially grounded analyses of language.

Thus, the current focus on contextualization has opened some exciting avenues for future work. Such work promises to integrate the study of a broad range of linguistic and communicative levels—poetics, pitch and intonation, gesture, indexicals of other kinds, grammar, metalanguage, and ideology—with a more social kind of analysis than scholars of language structure have attempted previously. And, as if that were not enough, there is more to be done, as we consider how to integrate semantic and content-focused analyses with the emergent focus on context.

Social-Linguistic Creativity

If language is structured in important ways by context, this contextually-organized language is also socially creative. As Duranti & Goodwin note, "Instead of viewing context as a set of variables that statically surround strips of talk, context and talk are now argued to stand in a mutually reflexive relationship to each other, with talk, and the interpretive work it generates, shaping context as much as context shapes talk" (59:31). In a sense, sociolinguists were already moving to this understanding of the relationship of context and talk when they analyzed ways in which ongoing usage delineating speakers of differing social statuses continually recreated and reinforced social difference (e.g. 81, 116, 117).

If the newer work charts a different direction, that direction is in part toward an examination of the less predictable consequences of language use, places in which language does more than reinforce or maintain—often ambiguous, uncertain, or difficult social-linguistic moments, moments of possibility. For example, Herzfeld takes us through the details of a Cretan funeral in which a young woman deploys the poetics of a lament to protest "the categorical definition of herself as a woman limited by her gender" (91:251). Her redefinition of herself and the situation, in a contextualized discourse, opens up new possibilities; she is able to escape the difficult bind within which she was left when her father died before she was married. Yet, Herzfeld also warns us that we cannot understand this as an unambiguously successful contestation of the hegemonic order, for the woman remains in many ways marginalized. Similarly, Hill (94) traces the ambiguously counter-hegemonic role of language ideology for Mexicano speakers. The high-status men most likely to speak hispanized Mexicano wax nostalgic for former linguistic purity, while women and low-status men whose speech is more "pure" attack such nostalgia. This debate obscures the "most obvious function of Spanish loan words, which is to mark elevated Mexicano registers in which the discourses of power in the communities are conducted" (94:278).

In these analyses, language is understood as a central medium of social exchange and connection between people, a link that forges shared cultural understanding, a process in which social structures—and legal systems—express their changing and unchanging characters (see 14, 16, 18, 25, 33, 36, 59, 75, 80, 147, 159, 162–164, 170, 191, 228, 241). This is an approach to language that fairly demands an accompanying social theory. How can this theory of meaning and its social construction, of language structure and speakers' awareness, be informed by current work on social and psychological processes? Interestingly, scholarship from the language-and-law field may provide some valuable links.

LEGAL LANGUAGE: AT THE CROSSROADS

In legal language can be found a crucial "crossroads" where social power and language interact. Law is, in effect, the locus of a powerful act of linguistic appropriation, where the translation of everyday categories into legal language effects powerful changes. Through legal language, the state imposes its interpretations and its appropriations (of physical and symbolic power), and social actors struggle to shift existing power relations. For this reason, legal language affords a key site for advancing the social-linguistic project of unpacking the social and creative character of language use and structure. Legal scholars, with typically acute ears for the nuances of language and power, have already begun work that has affinities with anthropological-linguistic scholarship. Sociolinguists and anthropologists studying legal discourse have also in some ways converged on a contextual and nontransparent approach to language.

Law, Power, and Language

Recent years have witnessed the development in legal anthropology of a sophisticated discourse about the role of law in reproducing and contesting relations of power and of colonial domination (see 151; see also 15a, 38, 39, 44, 45, 55a, 107, 120, 121, 148, 165, 167, 191, 243). A searching examination of the mutually-implicated constitution of legal power and cultural meaning is also under way (e.g. 43, 78a, 79, 80, 149, 150, 198–200). These emphases represent something of a shift from an earlier focus on the cross-cultural study of dispute processing.

Critical legal scholars from different schools of thought, including Critical Legal Studies, Legal Feminism, and Critical Race Theory, have been similarly concerned about the role of law as a site for struggle over social power (e.g. 8,

42, 54, 70, 71, 108, 139–141, 166). In recent years, work in critical race theory and legal feminist theory in particular has generated sensitive treatments of the place of legal language in that struggle. Matsuda writes of the transformative force of language in legal arenas:

> [Frederick] Douglass' skill in transforming the standard text of American political life into a blueprint for fundamental social change is instructive. He chose to believe in the Constitution, but at the same time refused to accept a racist Constitution. In his hands, the document grew to become greater than some of its drafters had intended. Douglass' reconstructed Constitution inspired black readers to endure the tremendous personal costs of resistance. Martin Luther King, Jr.'s reconstructed Constitution produced the same effect in the twentieth century.
> This ability to adopt and transform standard texts and mainstream consciousness is an important contribution of those on the bottom. Black Americans...have turned the Bible and the Constitution into texts of liberation....
> Those who lack material wealth or political power still have access to thought and language.... In poetry, the most concentrated form of language, black women have employed words to criticize and transform existing assumptions (139:334–36).

Although this literature could gain from anthropological insights about the power of detailed and systematic aspects of language structure, it could also contribute to anthropological visions a more stringent sensibility about the relations of language, ideology, and power—particularly from the perspective of the disenfranchised. Increasingly, feminist legal and critical race theory scholars are turning to look more empirically at aspects of legal language. Fineman, for example, looks in detail at the language of legal and political texts that locate indigent "single mothers" as the source of a variety of social ills (71; see also 70).

These traditions also urge careful attention to the ways in which the form of our own language shapes and limits our messages, working with alternative forms of discourse and voicing in order to contest the normal order of academic texts (e.g. 8, 237). This, of course, has been a concern of anthropologists as well. For example, in a thoughtful attempt to overcome the removed voice of academic writing, Feldman's treatment of violence has suggested how the pragmatics of our own presentation might make certain topics difficult to represent without massive dislocation and distortion (67; see also 46, 47). Contesting the exclusion of voices through diversification of the people allowed to speak in academic texts, which has long been central to critical-race and feminist legal theorists (see 53a), is beginning to emerge in anthropology as well (e.g. 85).

In a somewhat different (but similarly language-sensitive) vein, legal scholars drawing on literary theory have advocated deconstructionist and other approaches to legal language (see 3). White, an important pioneer of law-and-literature studies, has argued that law is a process of translation in which legal texts shape and create reflective and responsive communities of discourse about central issues in our society (235). Cunningham approaches the attorney as a translator for and to clients (48, 49; see also 236). Drawing on literary, linguistic, and critical theory, a number of legal scholars have analyzed the stories told in the language of the law. Some have urged that storytelling is a counter-hegemonic form, a discursive structure suited to oppositionalists seeking to disrupt the existing power structure as it is reproduced in legal language (e.g. 54, 136, 207). More empirically oriented work on storytelling has pointed out that juries use story structures in reaching decisions, and that attorneys use story-telling and narrative in attempts to win juries over to their versions of the truth (1, 9, 129, 182). As legal scholars increasingly examine the empirical details of language use, they might benefit from the overarching framework afforded by anthropological linguistics in understanding the systematic connections among those details.

Social Construction in Legal Language

Few realms of scholarship are better surveyed and summarized than are language-and-law studies. Levi has provided overviews of the broad range of work in this area (124–127), and there have been other reviews (20, 50, 172) and a number of collected essays in the area [cf 52, 55 (section on law), 128]. With these excellent resources as a backdrop, this review eschews repetition and proceeds with a narrow and selective focus on the treatment of language structure and context in language-and-law studies. Perhaps because the socially powerful effects of language are highlighted in legal arenas, an awareness of the formative effects of language pragmatics came early in the development of language-and-law studies. Work by psycholinguists demonstrated that legal outcomes can be very much affected by seemingly minor variations in language usage (see 32, 62, 131, 132). For example, in a study of the effects of language on eyewitness reports, Loftus found that subjects were more likely to report seeing a nonexistent object if asked "Did you see *the* broken headlight?" than if asked "Did you see *a* broken headlight?" Linguistically, the difference between *the* and *a* is in the presupposing indexical meanings of the two terms; *the* presupposes a previously introduced referent, whereas *a* does not.

At a more systemic level, anthropologists and psychologists examining the effects of speech style on credibility found that variation in clusters of pragmatic features contributed to differential weighting of testimony (see 41, 63, 172, 173). Thus speakers who used a powerless speech style (i.e. associated with frequent use of intensifiers, hedges, hesitation forms, gestures, questioning intonation, tag questions, and politeness forms) were less likely to be believed than were speakers who used a powerful speech style (i.e. characterized by an absence of those forms) (41, 63, 172, 173).

The question of powerful versus powerless speech styles leads us to the next challenge: how to analyze more systematically the social foundations linking language and law. The powerless speech style, associated originally with women's speech (119), was found to characterize the speech of both men and women occupying more powerless social statuses (173). Conley & O'Barr have further posited a link between differential use of speech styles, deployment of different discourses (rule-oriented vs relational), and different legal ideologies (law as constraint vs law as enabling) (40). They suggest that even in informal courts that are purportedly designed to empower the layperson, upper-status and business people have an advantage because they 1. often use powerful speech styles, 2. tend toward a deductive discourse oriented around legal rules, and 3. generally maintain an ideology of the legal system that views law not as a broad social enablement, but as a limited-purpose, constraining system. Thus, ironically, small claims courts serve the interests of business people and experienced repeat players in the legal system better than they do those of the inexperienced consumer (40). Conley & O'Barr's study complicates these broad categories, showing us that not all judges are rule-oriented, and that occasionally litigants who focus more on social relationships than on rules in their stories meet their matches in relationally-oriented judges. However, they conclude that the overall tendency in the system is toward a powerful, professional, business-friendly, rule-oriented language that further disenfranchises people who are at the lower end of the socioeconomic scale (and they note that this would have race and gender, as well as class, implications).

Conley & O'Barr's work demonstrates that studies of legal language have potential for linking the details of pragmatic structure with the content of legal discourse and with broader socioeconomic considerations. This kind of analysis suggests the ways in which language structure in the courtroom can exert a power of its own, becoming a crucial way in which the hegemonic order reasserts itself in an institutional structure supposedly designed to work against that order. At the same time, there is room for contestation and resistance, and both judges and litigants make use of that opening from time to time—a conclusion supported by Merry's work on working-class citizens' use of the courts (148). Although Conley & O'Barr's sample is not large enough for such generalizations, their results indicate that the entry of women into the judiciary may be opening the courtroom to more social and relational and powerless discourses. A study examining the effects of powerful and powerless speech styles on undergraduates, sitting judges, and practicing mediators further supports a non-determinist and complex view. Although both undergraduates' and sitting judges' assessments of credibility were affected by speech style, mediators' were not (168). In that study, Morrill & Facciola returned to the sociolinguistic concept of the speech community in an attempt to understand what linguistic norms and practices might insulate mediators (in their institutional communities) from the effects of speech style.

Thus several questions, also raised by the social-linguistic framework outlined at the outset, emerge from language-and-law studies: 1. How do systematic aspects of language structure and use impact and mediate the social conflicts with which (legal) institutions deal? 2. How are both imposition of hegemony and moments of resistance made possible in, through, and by (legal) language? 3. In a related vein, how do we understand the complex and nondeterminist embodiment of social epistemologies in (legal) language? and 4. What is the role of ideology and meta-language in the (legal) institutional regimentation and sedimentation of language—and in the linguistic regimentation and sedimentation of (legal) institutions?

LANGUAGE STRUCTURE AND SOCIAL CONFLICT   How do systematic aspects of language structure and use impact and mediate the social conflicts with which legal institutions deal? We can broadly distinguish two levels at which this question has been addressed in the literature: first, the way in which language operates situationally within legal contexts, and second, the broader social and cultural levels at which legal language works. Brenneis has elaborated a distinction between process-oriented and ethnography-of-speaking approaches that maps this difference fairly closely (20). Process-oriented work has focused on the immediate dynamics of the linguistic interactions in legal settings, combining ethnomethodological (34, 76) and conversational analytic (201) techniques in analyzing how participants in these interactions contest, manage, understand, and create social and legal realities in language (e.g. 1, 51, 53, 56, 90, 115, 118, 143, 144, 193, 194). Scholars building from ethnography-of-speaking and other traditions have focused on semantic and discourse-level phenomena as well, to link the workings of legal language with broader social aspects of conflict (e.g. 17–19, 22, 57, 69, 77, 204).

Detailed work on situational usage in legal settings (and then subsequent renditions of that situational usage in legal texts) indicates that legal language operates in subtle and structured ways to constrain or translate litigants' and witnesses' speech—at times in a fashion not uniquely legal, and at times in quite distinctively legal modes (e.g. 10, 13, 30, 83, 111, 185–188, 190, 194–196, 230, 231, 238, 239). Philips finds less copy of the question in response and more elaboration in responses from higher-status participants in courtroom discourse than from lower-status participants. This demonstrates the subtle level at which language structure instantiates and recreates social structure within a legal setting purportedly designed to neutralize such nonlegal effects (185). At the same time, the interactional process is a fluid one in which the power and relevance of certain kinds of linguistic usage (i.e. descriptors) are constantly in flux, as the conversation helps to create its own ongoing context (194).

At a wider level, legal language can be understood as culturally and socially constitutive as it forms an integral part of a culture's dispute process (see 19–22, 57, 77, 98, 99, 170). Brenneis, for example, suggests that dispute language is integral to the constitution of egalitarian as opposed to hierarchical social systems (18, 19). Greenhouse (79) and Rosen (198–200) suggest a deeply intertwined relationship between discourses dealing with conflict and the worldviews and social situations of entire communities (see also 11, 12, 22, 102, 170). This brings us to the next set of questions posed above.

POWER RELATIONS, EPISTEMOLOGY, AND LEGAL LANGUAGE   How are both imposition of hegemony and moments of resistance made possible in, through, and by legal language? And how do we understand the complex and nondeterminist embodiment of social epistemologies in legal language? Work on legal language is increasingly linking an understanding of microlinguistic processes with analysis of wider social change (see 10, 33, 78, 80, 88, 96, 97, 106, 138, 159, 163, 174–176). Much of the previous work in this area focused on the role of language in maintaining existing power relations, but attention is now beginning to focus as well on the openness of legal and linguistic practice to resistance, instability, and change—joining a wider trend in current social thought (see 15, 36, 38, 39, 44, 72, 75, 120, 121, 211, 237, 240).

Some scholarship concentrates on the interplay of hegemony and resistance in the individualized interactions of judges, lawyers, and clients with one another. Sarat and Felstiner analyze the ways in which the translation of clients' concerns into legal language—and of the legal system to clients— channels and tames clients' demands, while also permitting a process of co-construction in which some play is possible (69, 202–205). Mather & Yngvesson (137) and Felstiner et al (68) provide broad outlines of the process by which legal language channels social conflict. Cunningham (49) performs a detailed and sensitive analysis of lawyer-client interactions, arguing for the interesting step of cross-checking interpretive analysis with the subject of that analysis. This approach examines the ways in which microlinguistic channeling of citizens' grievances reflects and effects the wider position of law in social conflict (see also 20, 31, 35, 60, 142, 148, 149, 152, 167, 175, 212).

A similar picture emerges from attempts to link the details of linguistic structure in courtroom interactions with wider social processes (see 9, 40). Frohmann (73), Hirsch (96, 97), and Matoesian (138) discuss how patriarchal norms are imposed and contested in gendered discourse both within courts and with the courts' gatekeepers. Courts also serve as linguistic fora for struggles over the imposition of colonialist and racist discourses (see 45, 78, 154).

Alternatively, some analyses look to the epistemologies, cultural under-standings, and social prerogatives broadly embodied in legal texts and dis-courses for an understanding of the links between legal language and society (see 16, 80, 154, 155, 158, 159, 164, 165, 184, 229, 233). This level of analysis often requires some attention to the role of ideology.

IDEOLOGY AND META-LANGUAGE   What is the role of ideology and meta-lan-guage in the legal institutional regimentation and sedimentation of language—and in the linguistic regimentation and sedimentation of legal institutions? This is an appropriate question with which to conclude the discussion, as it points to an area of inquiry just beginning to be explored—and so permits us to finish by pointing to the future (a favored finale in this genre). Explorations of lay ideologies of the law have uncovered a fascinating tendency on the part of litigants to rationalize the system even when they are dissatisfied with the result or process they received (see 40, 148; see also 130). This not-quite-conscious process strongly resembles the process described by linguists for other kinds of discourse, in which key meanings are conveyed by features of discourse of which speakers are only dimly aware (215).

Initial applications of linguistic work on ideology to law have revealed that legal doctrines are shaped by and responsive to semiotic processes and linguis-tic ideologies (159, 178, 180, 219, 220). At the same time, these processes and ideologies do not arise sui generis, but are themselves the products of the complicated interplay of social contexts and actors, groups and patterned language use. As linguistic anthropologists are opening up the study of this process more generally (e.g. 95, 112, 134, 154, 156, 214, 242), we can antici-pate further applications of their findings to legal language.

CONCLUSION

There is an exciting convergence among a number of disciplines on the role of legal language as socially creative and constitutive in the struggle over power in and through law. Anthropological linguists have developed a framework that permits detailed consideration of the contextual structuring of language to be linked with analysis of wider social change and reproduction. Legal anthro-pologists and critical legal theorists have outlined the ways in which law serves as a site for struggle and the imposition of hegemony. Legal theorists focusing sensitively on language from critical race theory, feminist, and de-constructionist perspectives add a dynamic, daring, and vivid understanding of the impact of legal language in these struggles, also challenging academic writers to think more reflexively and carefully about the impact and shape of their own semiotic product. Scholars from the language-and-law tradition have for some time been investigating the formative role of language pragmatics in legal results and epistemologies.

The framework developed by linguistic anthropologists, outlined at the beginning of this review, offers a useful template for merging the concerns of these various schools, providing an approach to language that unites details of grammar with contexts of many kinds. This should not be too difficult for language-and-law scholars, who have been at work for some time on this combination of detailed linguistic and social contextual analyses. Work on legal language from social science and the legal academy can provide a more acute understanding of the political dimensions of legal language and, reflexively, of the texts that analyze legal language. We can best achieve a well-grounded understanding of the power of legal language, I would argue, through an analysis that systematically combines precise observation of the details of linguistic structure-in-use with consideration of the wider political and social forces at issue. Because legal language crystallizes the interplay of pragmatics, poetics, and social power with such clarity, it affords a crucial crucible for the formulation of social-linguistic theory.

Literature Cited

1. Amsterdam A, Hertz R. 1992. An analysis of closing arguments to a jury. *New York Law Sch. Law Rev.* 37:55–122
2. Atkinson JM, Drew P. 1979. *Order in the Court.* Atlantic Highlands, NJ: Humanities
3. Balkin JM. 1987. Deconstructive practice and legal theory. *Yale Law J.* 96:743–86
4. Bauman R. 1986. *Story, Performance, and Event: Contextual Studies of Oral Narrative.* Cambridge: Cambridge Univ. Press
5. Bauman R, Briggs C. 1990. Poetics and performance as critical perspectives on language and social life. *Annu. Rev. Anthropol.* 19:59–88
6. Bauman R, Sherzer J, eds. 1974. *Explorations in the Ethnography of Speaking.* Cambridge: Cambridge Univ. Press
7. Beirne P, Quinney R. 1982. *Marxism and Law.* New York: Wiley
8. Bell D. 1987. *And We Are Not Saved.* New York: Basic
9. Bennett L, Feldman M. 1981. *Reconstructing Reality in the Courtroom.* New Brunswick, NJ: Rutgers Univ. Press
10. Berk-Seligson S. 1990. *The Bilingual Courtroom: Court Interpreters in the Judicial Process.* Chicago: Univ. Chicago Press
11. Bloch M. 1975. *Political Language and Oratory in Traditional Societies.* New York: Academic
12. Bloch M. 1975. Introduction. See Ref. 11, pp. 1–28
13. Bogoch B, Danet B. 1984. Challenge and control in lawyer-client interactions: a case study in an Israeli legal aid office. *Text* 4:259–75
14. Borneman J. 1993. Uniting the German nation: law, narrative, and historicity. *Am. Ethnol.* 20:288–311
15. Bourdieu P. 1977. *Outline of a Theory of Practice.* Cambridge: Cambridge Univ. Press
15a. Bourdieu P. 1987. The force of law: toward a sociology of the juridical field. *Hastings Law J.* 38:201–48
16. Bowen J. 1992. On scriptural essentialism and ritual variation: Muslim sacrifice in Sumatra and Morocco. *Am. Ethnol.* 19: 656–71

17. Brenneis D. 1984. Grog and gossip in Bhatgaon: style and substance in Fiji Indian conversation. *Am. Ethnol.* 11:487–506
18. Brenneis D. 1984. Straight talk and sweet talk: political discourse in an occasionally egalitarian community. See Ref. 22, pp. 69–84
19. Brenneis D. 1987. Performing passions: aesthetics and politics in an occasionally egalitarian community. *Am. Ethnol.* 14:236–50
20. Brenneis D. 1988. Language and disputing. *Annu. Rev. Anthropol.* 17:221–37
21. Brenneis D. 1990. Telling troubles: narrative, conflict, and experience. See Ref. 24, pp. 279–91
22. Brenneis D, Myers F, eds. 1984. *Dangerous Words: Language and Politics in the Pacific.* New York: New York Univ. Press
23. Briggs C. 1986. *Learning How to Ask: A Sociolinguistic Appraisal of the Role of the Interview in Social Science Research.* Cambridge: Cambridge Univ. Press
24. Briggs C, ed. 1990. Narrative Resources for the Creation and Mediation of Conflict. Special Issue of *Anthropol. Linguist.* 30
25. Briggs C. 1990. Disorderly dialogues in ritualized impositions of order: the role of metapragmatics in Warao dispute mediation. See Ref. 24, pp. 448–91
26. Briggs C. 1992. Linguistic ideologies and the naturalization of power in Warao discourse. See Ref. 112, pp. 387–404
27. Briggs C. 1993. Personal sentiments and polyphonic voices in Warao women's ritual wailing: music and poetics in a critical and collective discourse. *Am. Anthropol.* 95:929–57
28. Briggs C, Bauman R. 1992. Genre, intertextuality, and social power. *J. Linguist. Anthropol.* 2:131–72
29. Brown P. 1980. Why and how women are more polite: some evidence from a Mayan community. See Ref. 146, pp. 111–36
30. Caesar-Wolf B. 1984. The construction of 'adjudicable' evidence in a West German civil hearing. *Text* 4:193–224
31. Cain M, Harrington C, eds. 1994. *Lawyers in a Postmodern World: Translation and Transgression.* Buckingham, UK: Open Univ. Press
32. Charrow R, Charrow V. 1979. Making legal language understandable: a psycholinguistic study of jury instructions. *Columbia Law Rev.* 79:1306–74
33. Chock P. 1991. "Illegal aliens" and "opportunity": myth-making in congressional testimony. *Am. Ethnol.* 18:279–94
34. Cicourel A. 1974. *Cognitive Sociology: Language and Meaning in Social Interactions.* New York: Free Press
35. Cobb, S, Rifkin J. 1991. Practice and paradox: deconstructing neutrality in mediation. *Law Soc. Inq.* 16:35–62
36. Collins J. 1988. *Hegemonic practice: literacy and standard language in public education.* Work. Pap. Proc. Cent. Psychosoc. Stud. 21. Chicago: Cent. Psychosoc. Stud.
37. Collins J. 1992. Our ideologies and theirs. See Ref. 112, pp. 405–16
38. Comaroff J. 1985. *Body of Power, Spirit of Resistance: The Culture and History of a South African People.* Chicago: Univ. Chicago Press
39. Comaroff J, Comaroff J. 1991. *Of Revelation and Revolution: Christianity, Colonialism, and Consciousness in South Africa,* Vol. I. Chicago: Univ. Chicago Press
40. Conley J, O'Barr W. 1990. *Rules Versus Relationships: The Ethnography of Legal Discourse.* Chicago: Univ. Chicago Press
41. Conley J, O'Barr WM, Lind A. 1978. The power of language: presentational style in the courtroom. *Duke Law J.* 78:1375–99
42. Coombe R. 1989. Room for manoeuver: toward a theory of practice in critical legal studies. *Law Soc. Inq.* 14:69–121
43. Coombe R. 1991. Objects of property and subjects of politics: intellectual property laws and democratic dialogue. *Texas Law Rev.* 69:1853–80
44. Coombe R. 1991. Contesting the self: negotiating subjectivities in nineteenth century Ontario defamation trials. *Stud. Law Polit. Soc.* 11:3–40
45. Coombe R. 1993. The properties of culture and the politics of possessing identity: Native claims in the cultural appropriation controversy. *Can. J. Law Jurisprud.* 6:249–85
46. Crapanzano V. 1980. *Tuhami.* Chicago: Univ. Chicago Press
47. Crapanzano V. 1992. *Hermes' Dilemma and Hamlet's Desire.* Cambridge, MA: Harvard Univ. Press
48. Cunningham C. 1989. A tale of two clients: thinking about law as language. *Mich. Law Rev.* 87:2459–94
49. Cunningham C. 1992. The lawyer as translator, representation as text: towards an ethnography of legal discourse. *Cornell Law Rev.* 77:1298–1387
50. Danet B. 1980. Language in the legal process. *Law Soc. Rev.* 14:445–564
51. Danet B. 1984. The magic flute: a prosodic analysis of binomial expressions in legal Hebrew. *Text* 4:143–72
52. Danet B. 1984. Introduction. *Text* 4:1–8
53. Danet B, Hoffman K, Kermish N, Rafn HJ, Stayman D. 1980. An ethnography of questioning. In *Language Use and the Uses of Language,* ed. R Shuy, A Shnukal, pp. 222–34. Washington, DC: Georgetown Univ. Press
53a. Delgado R. 1984. The imperial scholar:

reflections on a review of civil rights literature. *Univ. Penn. Law Rev.* 132:561–78

54. Delgado R. 1989. Storytelling for oppositionalists and others: a plea for narrative. *Mich. Law Rev.* 87:2411–41

55. DiPietro R, ed. 1982. *Linguistics and the Professions.* Norwood, NJ: ABLEX

55a. Domínguez V. 1989. *People as Subject, People as Object.* Madison: Univ. Wisc. Press

56. Drew P. 1990. Analyzing language in legal settings. See Ref. 128, pp. 39–64

57. Duranti A. 1984. Lauga and Talanoaga: two speech genres in a Samoan political event. See Ref. 22, pp. 217–37

58. Duranti A. 1992. Language and bodies in social space: Samoan ceremonial greetings. *Am. Anthropol.* 94:657–91

59. Duranti A, Goodwin C, ed. 1992. *Rethinking Context.* Cambridge: Cambridge Univ. Press

60. Edelman L, Abraham S, Erlanger H. 1992. Professional construction of law: the inflated threat of wrongful discharge. *Law Soc. Rev.* 26:47–84

61. Eidheim H. 1969. When ethnic identity is a social stigma. In *Ethnic Groups and Boundaries,* ed. F Barth, pp. 39–57. Boston: Little, Brown

62. Elwork A, Sales B, Alfini J. 1982. *Making Jury Instructions Understandable.* Charlottesville, VA: Bobbs-Merrill

63. Erickson B, Lind EA, Johnson B, O'Barr W. 1978. Speech style and impression formation in a court setting: the effects of "powerful" and "powerless" speech. *J. Exp. Soc. Psychol.* 14:266–79

64. Errington J. 1988. *Structure and Style in Javanese: A Semiotic View of Linguistic Etiquette.* Philadelphia: Univ. Penn. Press

65. Errington J. 1992. On the ideology of Indonesian language development: the state of a language of state. See Ref. 112, pp. 417–26

66. Fairclough N. 1989. *Language and Power.* London: Longman

67. Feldman A. 1991. *Formations of Violence: The Narrative of the Body and Political Terror in Northern Ireland.* Chicago: Univ. Chicago Press

68. Felstiner W, Abel R, Sarat A. 1980–1981. The emergence and transformation of disputes: naming, blaming and claiming. *Law Soc. Rev.* 15:631–55

69. Felstiner W, Sarat A. 1992. Enactments of power: negotiating reality and responsibility in lawyer-client interactions. *Cornell Law Rev.* 77:1447–98

70. Fineman M. 1991. *The Illusion of Equality: The Rhetoric and Reality of Divorce Reform.* Chicago: Univ. Chicago Press

71. Fineman M. 1991. Images of mothers in poverty discourses. *Duke Law J.* 1991: 274–74

72. Foucault M. 1980. *Power/Knowledge: Selected Interviews and Other Writings.* New York: Pantheon

73. Frohmann L. 1991. Discrediting victims' allegations of sexual assault. *Soc. Prob.* 38:213–26

74. Gal S. 1989. Language and political economy. *Annu. Rev. Anthropol.* 18:345–67

75. Gal S. 1991. Bartok's funeral: representations of Europe in Hungarian political rhetoric. *Am. Ethnol.* 18:440–58

76. Garfinkel H. 1967. *Studies in Ethnomethodology.* Englewood Cliffs, NJ: Prentice-Hall

77. Goldman L. 1983. *Talk Never Dies: The Language of Huli Disputes.* London: Tavistock

78. Gooding S. 1993. *"But I wouldn't want to disappoint either of my parents": legal constraints on the layering of kinship and polity among the Colville tribes.* Presented at Annu. Meet. Law Soc. Assoc., Chicago

78a. Greenhouse C. 1986. *Praying for Justice: Faith, Order and Community in an American Town.* Ithaca, NY: Cornell Univ. Press

79. Greenhouse C. 1988. Courting difference: issues of interpretation and comparison in the study of legal ideologies. *Law Soc. Rev.* 22:687–709

80. Greenhouse C. 1989. Just in time: temporality and the cultural legitimation of law. *Yale Law J.* 98:1631–51

81. Gumperz J. 1964. Linguistic and social interaction in two communities. *Am. Anthropol.* 66:137–53

82. Gumperz J. 1982. *Discourse Strategies.* Cambridge: Cambridge Univ. Press

83. Gumperz J. 1982. Fact and inference in courtroom testimony. In *Language and Social Identity,* ed. J Gumperz, pp. 163–95. Cambridge: Cambridge Univ. Press

84. Gumperz J, Hymes D, eds. 1972. *Directions in Sociolinguistics.* New York: Holt, Rinehart & Winston

85. Hajj, the, Lavie S, Rouse F. 1993. Notes on the fantastic journey of the Hajj, his anthropologist, and her American Passport. *Am. Ethnol.* 20:363–84

86. Hanks W. 1989. Text and textuality. *Annu. Rev. Anthropol.* 18:95–127

87. Hanks W. 1990. *Referential Practice: Language and Lived Space among the Maya.* Chicago: Univ. of Chicago Press

88. Haviland J. 1989. *Mixtecs, migrants, multilingualism, and murder.* Work. Pap. Proc. Cent. Psychosoc. Stud. 25. Chicago: Cent. Psychosoc. Stud.

89. Haviland J. 1990. "We want to borrow your mouth": Tzotzil marital squabbles. See Ref. 24, pp. 395–447

90. Hayden R. 1987. Turn-taking, overlap, and

the task at hand: ordering speaking turns in legal settings. *Am. Ethnol.* 14:251–70
91. Herzfeld M. 1993. In defiance of destiny: the management of time and gender at a Cretan funeral. *Am. Ethnol.* 20:241–55
92. Hickmann M. 1980. Creating referents in discourse: a developmental analysis of discourse cohesion. In *Papers from the Sixteenth Regional Meeting of the Chicago Linguistic Society: Parasession on Anaphora*, pp. 192–203. Chicago: Chicago Linguist. Soc.
93. Hickmann M. 1985. Metapragmatics in child language. See Ref. 161, pp. 177–201
94. Hill J. 1992. "Today there is no respect": nostalgia, "respect" and oppositional discourse in Mexicano (Nahuatl) language ideology. See Ref. 112, pp. 263–80
95. Hill J, Irvine J, eds. 1993. *Responsibility and Evidence in Oral Discourse.* Cambridge: Cambridge Univ. Press
96. Hirsch S. 1989. *Asserting male authority, recreating female experience: gendered discourse in coastal Kenyan Muslim courts.* Am. Bar Found. Work. Pap. Ser. 8906. Chicago: Am. Bar Found.
97. Hirsch S. 1990. *Gender and disputing: insurgent voices in coastal Kenyan Islamic courts.* PhD thesis. Duke Univ.
98. Hutchins E. 1980. *Culture and Inference: A Trobriand Case Study.* Cambridge, MA: Harvard Univ. Press
99. Hutchins E. 1981. Reasoning in Trobriand discourse. In *Language, Culture and Cognition,* ed. R Casson, pp. 481–89. New York: Macmillan
100. Hymes D. 1972. Models of the interaction of language and social life. See Ref. 84, pp. 35–71
101. Hymes D. 1974. *Foundations in Sociolinguistics.* Philadelphia: Univ. Penn. Press
102. Irvine J. 1979. Formality and informality in communicative events. *Am. Anthropol.* 81: 773–90
103. Irvine J. 1989. When talk isn't cheap: language and political economy. *Am. Ethnol.* 16:248–67
104. Irvine J. 1992. *Implicated dialogues: structures of participation in discourse.* Work. Pap. Proc. Cent. Psychosoc. Stud. 51. Chicago: Cent. Psychosoc. Stud.
105. Irvine J. 1992. Ideologies of honorific language. See Ref. 112, pp. 251–62
106. Jackson B. 1988. *Law, Fact, and Narrative Coherence.* Robey, UK: Charles
107. Jacquemet M. 1992. Namechasers. *Am. Ethnol.* 19:733–48
108. Kairys D, ed. 1982. *The Politics of Law: A Progressive Critique.* New York: Pantheon
109. Jakobson R. 1960. Linguistics and poetics. In *Style in Language,* ed. T Sebeok, pp. 350–77. Cambridge, MA: MIT Press
110. Keenan E. 1975. A sliding sense of obligatoriness. See Ref. 11, pp. 93–112
111. Kevelson R. 1982. Language and legal speech acts. See Ref. 55, pp. 121–32
112. Kroskrity P, Schieffelin B, Woolard K, eds. 1992. Language ideologies. Special Issue of *Pragmatics* 2(3):235–435
113. Kurylowicz J. 1945–1949. La nature des proces dits 'analogiques'. *Acta Linguist.* 5:121–38
114. Kurylowicz J. 1972. The role of deictic elements in linguistic evolution. *Semiotica* 5:174–83
115. Kurzon D. 1984. Themes, hyperthemes, and the discourse structure of British legal texts. *Text* 4:31–56
116. Labov W. 1964. Phonological correlates of social stratification. *Am. Anthropol.* 66: 164–75
117. Labov W. 1966. *The Social Stratification of English in New York City.* Washington, DC: Cent. Appl. Linguist.
118. Labov W. 1988. The judicial testing of linguistic theory. In *Linguistics and Context,* ed. D Tannen, pp. 159–82. Norwood, NJ: ABLEX
119. Lakoff R. 1975. *Language and Woman's Place.* New York: Harper & Row
120. Lazarus-Black M. 1991. *Slaves, masters, and magistrates: law and the politics of resistance in the British Caribbean, 1736–1834.* Am. Bar Found. Work. Pap. Series 9124 Chicago: Am. Bar Found.
121. Lazarus-Black M, Hirsch S, eds. 1994. *Contested States: Law, Hegemony, and Resistance.* New York: Routledge
122. Deleted in proof
123. Levi E. 1949. *An Introduction to Legal Reasoning.* Chicago: Univ. Chicago Press
124. Levi J. 1982. *Linguistics, Language and the Law: A Topical Bibliography.* Bloomington, IN: Ind. Univ. Linguist. Club
125. Levi J. 1986. Applications of linguistics to the language of legal interactions. In *The Real-World Linguist: Applications of Linguistics in the 1980s,* ed. PC Bjarkman, V Raskin, pp. 230–65. Norwood, NJ: ABLEX
126. Levi J. 1990. The study of language in the judicial process. See Ref. 128, pp. 3–35
127. Levi J. 1994. *Language and Law: A Bibliographic Guide to Social Science Research in the U.S.A.* Chicago: Am. Bar Assoc.
128. Levi J, Walker AG, eds. 1990. *Language in the Judicial Process.* New York: Plenum
129. Liebes-Plesner T. 1984. Rhetoric in the service of justice: the sociolinguistic construction of stereotypes in an Israeli rape trial. *Text* 4:193–224
130. Lind EA, Maccoun R, Ebener P, Felstiner W, Hensler D, et al. 1990. In the eye of the beholder: tort litigants' evaluations of their experiences in the civil justice system. *Law Soc. Rev.* 24:953–96
131. Loftus E. 1975. Leading questions and the eyewitness report. *Cogn. Psychol.* 7:560–72

132. Loftus E. 1979. *Eyewitness Testimony.* Cambridge, MA: Harvard Univ. Press

133. Lucy J. 1992. *Grammatical Categories and Cognition: A Case Study of the Linguistic Relativity Hypothesis.* Cambridge: Cambridge Univ. Press

133a. Lucy J. 1992. *Language Diversity and Thought: A Reformulation of the Linguistic Relativity Hypothesis.* Cambridge: Cambridge Univ. Press

134. Lucy J, ed. 1993. *Reflexive Language: Reported Speech and Metapragmatics.* Cambridge: Cambridge Univ. Press

135. Lyons J. 1977. *Semantics,* Vol. I. London: Cambridge Univ. Press

136. Massaro T. 1989. Empathy, legal storytelling, and the rule of law: new words, old wounds. *Mich. Law Rev.* 87:2099–127

137. Mather L, Yngvesson B. 1980–1981. Language, audience, and the transformation of disputes. *Law Soc. Rev.* 15:775–821

138. Matoesian G. 1993. *Reproducing Rape.* Chicago: Univ. Chicago Press

139. Matsuda M. 1987. Looking to the bottom: critical legal studies and reparations. *Harvard Civil-Rights Civil Liberties Law Rev.* 22:323–99

140. Matsuda M. 1989. Public response to racist speech: considering the victim's story. *Mich. Law Rev.* 2320–81

141. Matsuda M. 1991. The voices of America: accent, antidiscrimination law, and a jurisprudence for the last reconstruction. *Yale Law J.* 100:1329–407

142. May M, Stengel D. 1990. Who sues their doctors? How patients handle medical grievances. *Law Soc. Rev.* 24:105–20

143. Maynard D. 1984. *Inside Plea Bargaining: The Language of Negotiation.* New York: Plenum

144. Maynard D. 1990. Narratives and narrative structure in plea bargaining. See Ref. 128, pp. 65–96

145. McConnell-Ginet S. 1983. Intonation in a man's world. See Ref. 225, pp. 69–88

146. McConnell-Ginet S, Borker R, Furman N, eds. 1980. *Women and Language in Literature and Society.* New York: Praeger

147. Mehan H. 1987. Language and power in organizational process. *Discourse Process.* 10:291–301

148. Merry S. 1990. *Getting Justice and Getting Even: Legal Consciousness among Working-Class Americans.* Chicago: Univ. Chicago Press

149. Merry S. 1990. The discourses of mediation and the power of naming. *Yale J. Law Humanit.* 2:1–36

150. Merry S. 1992. Culture, power, and the discourse of law. *New York Law Sch. Rev.* 1/2:209–26

151. Merry S. 1992. Anthropology, law, and transnational processes. *Annu. Rev. Anthropol.* 1992:357–79

152. Merry S, Silbey S. 1984. What do plaintiffs want? Reexamining the concept of dispute. *Justice Syst. J.* 9:151–78

153. Mertz E. 1985. Beyond symbolic anthropology: introducing semiotic mediation. See Ref. 161, pp. 1–19

154. Mertz E. 1988. The uses of history: language, ideology and law in the United States and South Africa. *Law Soc. Rev.* 22:661–85

155. Mertz E. 1990. Consensus and dissent in U.S. legal opinions: narrative control and social voices. See Ref. 24, pp. 369–94

156. Mertz E. 1992. Linguistic ideology and praxis in U.S. law school classrooms. See Ref. 112, pp. 325–34

157. Mertz E. 1993. Learning what to ask: metapragmatic factors and methodological reification. See Ref. 134, pp. 159–74

158. Mertz E. 1994. Social/semiotic frames in the language of the law. *Polit. Legal Anthropol. Rev.* In press

159. Mertz E. 1994. Linguistic constructions of difference and history in the U.S. law school classroom. In *Difference and History,* ed. C Greenhouse, D Greenwood. In press

160. Mertz E. 1994. Recontextualization as socialization: text and pragmatics in the law school classroom. In *Natural Histories of Discourse,* ed. M Silverstein, G Urban. In press

161. Mertz E, Parmentier R, eds. 1985. *Semiotic Mediation: Sociocultural and Psychological Perspectives.* New York: Academic

162. Messick B. 1983. Legal documents and the concept of 'restricted literacy.' *Int. J. Sociol. Lang.* 4:41–52

163. Messick B. 1986. The Mufti, the text, and the world: legal interpretation in Yemen. *Man (NS)* 21:102–19

164. Messick B. 1987. Subordinate discourse: women, weaving, and gender relations in North Africa. *Am. Ethnol.* 14:210–25

165. Messick B. 1988. Kissing hands and knees: hegemony and hierarchy in Shari'a discourse. *Law Soc. Rev.* 22:637–61

166. Minow M. 1990. *Making All the Difference: Inclusion, Exclusion, and American Law.* Ithaca, NY: Cornell Univ. Press

167. Moore SF. 1992. Treating law as knowledge: telling colonial officers what to say to Africans about running "their own" native courts. *Law Soc. Rev.* 26:11–46

168. Morrill C, Facciola P. 1992. The power of language in adjudication and mediation: institutional contexts as predictors of social evaluation. *Law Soc. Inq.* 17:191–212

169. Mukarovsky J. 1964. Standard language and poetic language. In *A Prague School Reader on Esthetics, Literary Structure, and Style,* ed. P Garvin, pp. 17–30. Washington, DC: Georgetown Univ. Press

170. Myers F. 1986. Reflections on a meeting:

structure, language, and the polity in a small-scale society. *Am. Ethnol.* 13:430–47
171. O'Barr W. 1981. The language of the law. In *Language in the USA,* ed. C Ferguson, CB Heath, pp. 386–406. Cambridge: Cambridge Univ. Press
172. O'Barr W. 1982. *Linguistic Evidence: Language, Power, and Strategy in the Courtroom.* New York: Academic
173. O'Barr W, Atkins B. 1980. Women's language or powerless language? See Ref. 146, pp. 93–110
174. O'Barr W, Conley J. 1985. Litigant satisfactions versus legal adequacy in small claims court narratives. *Law Soc. Rev.* 19: 661–701
175. O'Barr W, Conley J. 1988. Lay expectations of the civil justice system. *Law Soc. Rev.* 22:137–61
176. O'Barr W, Conley J. 1990. Ideological dissonance in the American legal system. See Ref. 24, pp. 345–68
176a. Ochs E, Schieffelin B, eds. 1979. *Developmental Pragmatics.* New York: Academic
177. Ochs E, Schieffelin B, eds. 1983. *Acquiring Communicative Competence.* London: Routledge & Kegan Paul
178. Parmentier R. 1986. *Puffery and pragmatics, regulation and reference.* Work. Pap. Proc. Cent. Psychosoc. Stud. 4. Chicago: Cent. Psychosoc. Stud.
179. Parmentier R. 1987. *The Sacred Remains.* Chicago: Univ. Chicago Press
180. Parmentier R. 1993. The political function of reported speech: a Belauan example. See Ref. 134, pp. 261–86
181. Peirce CS. 1974. *Collected Papers of Charles Sanders Peirce,* Vol. II. Cambridge, MA: Harvard Univ. Press
182. Pennington N, Hastie R. 1991. A cognitive theory of juror decision making: the story model. *Cardozo Law Rev.* 13:519–57
183. Philips S. 1980. Sex differences and language. *Annu. Rev. Anthropol.* 9:523–44
184. Philips S. 1982. The language socialization of lawyers: acquiring the 'cant'. In *Doing the Ethnography of Schooling,* ed. G Spindler, pp. 177–209. New York: Holt, Rinehart, & Winston
185. Philips S. 1984. The social organization of questions and answers in courtroom discourse. *Text* 4:25–248
186. Philips S. 1984. Contextual variation in courtroom language use: noun phrases referring to crimes. *Int. J. Sociol. Lang.* 49: 29–50
187. Philips S. 1985. Strategies of clarification in judges' use of language: from the written to the spoken. *Discourse Process.* 8:421–36
188. Philips S. 1986. Reported speech as evidence in an American trial. In *Languages and Linguistics: The Interdependency of*

Theory, Data, and Application, ed. D Tannen, J Alatis, pp. 154–70. Washington, DC: Georgetown Univ. Press
189. Philips S. 1993. Evidentiary standards for American trials. See Ref. 95, pp. 248–59
190. Philips S. 1992. The routinization of repair in courtroom discourse. See Ref. 59, pp. 311–22
191. Philips S. 1992. A Marx-influenced approach to ideology and language: comments. See Ref. 112, pp. 377–85
192. Philips S, Steele S, Tanz C, eds. 1987. *Language, Gender & Sex in Comparative Perspective.* Cambridge: Cambridge Univ. Press
193. Pomerantz A. 1978. Attributions of responsibility: blamings. *Sociology* 12:115–21
194. Pomerantz A, Atkinson J. 1984. Ethnomethodology, conversational analysis, and the study of courtroom interaction. In *Psychology and the Law,* ed. D Muller, D Blackmun, A Chapman, pp. 283–97. Chichester, UK: Wiley
195. Prince E. 1984. Language and the law: reference, stress, and context. In *Meaning, Form, and Use in Context: Linguistic Applications,* ed. D Schiffrin, pp. 240–52. Washington, DC: Georgetown Univ. Press
196. Prince E. 1990. On the use of social conversation as evidence in a court of law. See Ref. 128, pp. 279–89
197. Quay LC, Mathews M, Schwarzmuller B. 1977. Communication encoding and decoding in children from different socioeconomic and racial groups. *Dev. Psychol.* 13: 415–16
198. Rosen L. 1984. *Bargaining for Reality.* Chicago: Univ. Chicago Press
199. Rosen L. 1989. Responsibility and compensatory justice in Arab culture and law. In *Semiotics, Self and Society,* ed. B Lee, G Urban, pp. 101–20. Berlin: Mouton
200. Rosen L. 1989. *The Anthropology of Justice: Law as Culture in Islamic Society.* Cambridge: Cambridge Univ. Press
201. Sacks H, Schegloff E, Jefferson G. 1974. A simple systematics for the organization of turn-taking in conversation. *Language* 50: 696–735
202. Sarat A, Felstiner W. 1986. Law and strategy in the divorce lawyer's office. *Law Soc. Rev.* 20:93–134
203. Sarat A, Felstiner W. 1988. Law and social relations: vocabularies of motive in lawyer/client interaction. *Law Soc. Rev.* 22: 737–69
204. Sarat A, Felstiner W. 1989. Lawyers and legal consciousness: law talk in the divorce lawyer's office. *Yale Law J.* 98:1663–88
205. Sarat A, Felstiner W. 1990. Legal realism in lawyer-client communication. See Ref. 128, pp. 133–51
206. Saussure F. 1959. *Course in General Linguistics.* New York: McGraw-Hill

207. Scheppele K. 1989. Foreword: telling stories. *Mich. Law Rev.* 87:2073–98

208. Schieffelin B. 1990. *The Give and Take of Everyday Life: Language Socialization of Kaluli Children.* Cambridge: Cambridge Univ. Press

209. Schiefflin B, Charlier Doucet R. 1992. The "real" Haitian Creole: metalinguistics and orthographic choice. See Ref. 112, pp. 427–44

210. Schieffelin B, Ochs E. 1986. *Language Socialization across Cultures.* Cambridge: Cambridge Univ. Press

211. Scott J. 1988. *Gender and the Politics of History.* New York: Columbia Univ. Press

212. Silbey S, Merry S. 1986. Mediator settlement strategies. *Law Soc. Pol.* 8:7–32

213. Silverstein M. 1976. Shifters, linguistic categories, and cultural description. In *Meaning in Anthropology,* ed. K Basso, H Selby, pp. 11–55. Albuquerque: Univ. N. Mex. Press

214. Silverstein M. 1979. Language structure and linguistic ideology. In *The Elements: A Parasession on Linguistic Units and Levels,* ed. P Clyne, W Hanks, C Hofbauer, pp. 193–247. Chicago: Chicago Linguist. Soc.

215. Silverstein M. 1981. *The limits of awareness.* Work. Pap. Sociolinguist. 84. Austin, TX: Southwest Educ. Dev. Lab.

215a. Silverstein M. 1981. *Implications of (models of) culture for language.* Presented at SSRC Conf. "Conceptions of Culture and its Acquisitions," New York City, May 8–10

216. Silverstein M. 1984. On the pragmatic "poetry" of prose: parallelism, repetition, and cohesive structure in the time course of dyadic conversation. In *Meaning, Form, and Use in Context: Linguistic Applications,* ed. D Schiffrin, pp. 181–99. Washington, DC: Georgetown Univ. Press

217. Silverstein M. 1985. Language and the culture of gender: at the intersection of structure, usage, and ideology. See Ref. 161, pp. 219–59

218. Silverstein M. 1987. The three faces of "function": preliminaries to a psychology of language. In *Social and Functional Approaches to Language and Thought,* ed. M Hickmann, pp. 17–38. Orlando, FL: Academic

219. Silverstein M. 1990. *The skin of our teeth: registers, poetics, and the first amendment.* Presented at 89th Annu. Meet. Am. Anthropol. Assoc., New Orleans

220. Silverstein M. 1992. *U.S. linguistic pluralism: constitutionalism, culturalism, and the monoglot imagination of the public good.* Presented at 91st Annu. Meet. Am. Anthropol. Assoc., San Francisco

221. Silverstein M. 1993. Metapragmatic discourse and metapragmatic function. See Ref. 134, pp. 33–58

222. Silverstein M. 1993. The indeterminacy of contextualization: when is enough enough? In *The Contextualization of Language,* ed. A DiLuzio, P Auer, pp. 55–76. Amsterdam: Benjamins

223. Silverstein M. 1993. *A minimax approach to verbal interaction: invoking 'culture' in realtime discursive practice.* Presented at Conf. Lang. Cult. Cogn., Fundacio Catalana per a la Recerca, Barcelona, Spain

224. Tannen D. 1989. *Talking Voices: Repetition, Dialogue and Imagery in Conversational Discourse.* Cambridge: Cambridge Univ. Press

225. Thorne B, Kramarae C, Henley N, eds. 1983. *Language, Gender, and Society.* Cambridge, MA: Newbury House

226. Urban G. 1988. Discourse, affect, and social order: ritual wailing in Amerindian Brazil. *Am. Anthropol.* 90:385–400

227. Van der Broeck J. 1977. Class differences in syntactic complexity in the Flemish town of Maaseik. *Lang. Soc.* 6:149–81

228. Van Luong H. 1988. Discursive practices and power structure. *Am. Ethnol.* 15:239–53

229. Vargas D. 1984. Two types of legal discourse: transitivity in American appellate opinions and casebooks. *Text* 4:9–30

230. Walker AG. 1982. Patterns and implications of cospeech in a legal setting. See Ref. 55, pp. 101–12

231. Walker AG. 1990. Language at work in the law: the customs, conventions, and appellate consequences of court reporting. See Ref. 128, pp. 203–46

232. Deleted in proof

233. Weissbourd B, Mertz E. 1985. Rule-centrism versus legal creativity: the skewing of legal ideology through language. *Law Soc. Rev.* 19:623–59

234. West C, Zimmerman D. 1983. Small insults: a study of interruptions in cross-sex conversations between unacquainted persons. See Ref. 225, pp. 103–17

235. White JB. 1990. *Justice as Translation.* Chicago: Univ. Chicago Press

236. White L. 1992. Seeking "…the faces of otherness…." *Cornell Law Rev.* 77:1499–511

237. Williams P. 1991. *The Alchemy of Race and Rights: Diary of a Law Professor.* Cambridge, MA: Harvard Univ. Press

238. Wodak R. 1980. Discourse analysis and courtroom interaction. *Discourse Process.* 3:369–80

239. Wodak R. 1985. The interaction between judge and defendant. In *Handbook of Discourse Analysis,* ed. T Van Dijk, pp. 181–91. New York: Academic

240. Woolard K. 1985. Language variation and cultural hegemony: toward an integration of sociolinguistic and social theory. *Am. Ethnol.* 12:738–48

241. Woolard K. 1989. *Double Talk: Bilingualism and the Politics of Ethnicity.* Stanford, CA: Stanford Univ. Press
242. Woolard K. 1992. Language ideology: issues and approaches. See Ref. 112, 235–49

243. Yngvesson B. 1993. *Virtuous Citizens, Disruptive Subjects: Order and Complaint in a New England Court.* New York: Routledge

Annu. Rev. Anthropol. 1994. 23:457–82

NON-INSULIN DEPENDENT DIABETES MELLITUS AMONG ABORIGINAL NORTH AMERICANS

Emőke J.E. Szathmáry

Office of the Provost and Vice-President (Academic), McMaster University, Hamilton, Ontario, L8S 4K9 Canada

KEY WORDS: Native American diabetes epidemiology, etiology, genes, obesity

INTRODUCTION

West (157) observed in 1974 that extraordinarily high rates of adult-onset diabetes occur in many populations of the New World, that is, regions discovered by Europeans during their age of exploration. In contrast were other indigenous groups, especially in North America, whose rates of morbidity were below that of European- or African-derived citizenry. Yet, regardless of the current frequency of disease, diabetes was virtually unknown among Amerindian peoples before 1940 (157).

Since the mid-1960s numerous surveys have noted the increasing incidence of diabetes among Native Americans (44, 124, 139, 171), Micronesians and Polynesians (173), Australian Aborigines (102), and the peoples of Papua New Guinea (84). In most localities, the prevalence rates among indigenous inhabitants are higher than among other citizens.

We know now that diabetes is not a single disease, and different factors are responsible for the onset of its two common forms—insulin dependent diabetes mellitus (IDDM) and non-insulin dependent diabetes mellitus (NIDDM) (7, 172). Regardless of disease type, the long-term consequences (19) are similar. They include cardiovascular disease, end-stage renal disease, retinopathy leading to blindness, and gangrene of the extremities (161, 163). Approximately 6% of the United States population aged 40–59 exhibits NIDDM (7); hence, understanding the epidemiology and etiology of NIDDM is scientifically and socially important.

Most research on diabetes among Native Americans has focused on disease prevalence, and studies addressing other topics are relatively few. Exceptions include the studies on diabetes etiology, epidemiology, and complications among Pima Indians of Gila River, Arizona, which have been ongoing for 30 years (60, 64, 89). Only in a handful of other communities has longitudinal investigation been attempted, and then over a shorter time period, on a more restricted range of topics than among the Pima (53, 136, 141). Concerns about innate susceptibility or resistance to diabetes among specific Amerindian people (98) have led to the postulation of a variety of etiological and evolutionary explanations (50, 64, 115, 139, 154, 173). The cultural diversity among the peoples affected also has spurred exploration of indigenous perspectives on health and illness, appropriate disease treatment, and disease prevention (59, 151). Because the literature on diabetes mellitus is voluminous, my focus here is on biological and some cultural aspects of NIDDM in North American aboriginal peoples. Readers interested in beliefs and cultural knowledge concerning diabetes should consult the relevant chapters in references 59 and 168.

Diagnosis of Diabetes Mellitus

Diabetes mellitus is characterized by the presence of higher than normal levels of glucose in the blood (hyperglycemia). Until 1980 there was no universal agreement on the level of glucose that constituted abnormality, so diagnostic standards varied nationally and internationally (160). Not only was there a real possibility that people were wrongly classified as diabetics (125), but advances in understanding the pathophysiology of this heterogeneous disease were also limited.

The situation began to change in 1979 when the United States National Diabetes Data Group (NDDG) defined several categories of diabetic states (93). The World Health Organization (WHO) subsequently accepted the definitions and diagnostic benchmarks, albeit in modified form (164, 165). The term diabetes includes IDDM, NIDDM, gestational diabetes (GDM), and diabetes associated with certain rare inherited syndromes or other disease states. In IDDM (called type-1 diabetes) the β cells of the pancreas fail to produce insulin, which is essential for life. Without exogenous insulin, diabetic acidosis (ketosis) results, and death follows in a matter of days. In contrast, in NIDDM (called type-2 diabetes or maturity onset diabetes) hyperglycemia is accompanied by excess levels of insulin (7), ketosis does not occur, and insulin is not required for treatment. However, in NIDDM conversion to insulin dependence is possible through increasing impairment of insulin secretion (24, 27, 110). In such cases provision of insulin may be necessary.

The diabetic threshold of plasma glucose for non-pregnant adults in the fasting state is 7.8 mmol/l (140 mg/dl). Diabetes is also present if one random plasma glucose measure of 11.1 mmol/l (200 mg/dl) or more is accompanied by the classic signs of the disease (e.g. excessive thirst, urination, hunger with weight loss). Unfortunately, symptoms of NIDDM do not appear for many years until after the initial onset of the disease (7). Thus, unsuspecting individuals often learn of their condition from the outcome of a fasting oral glucose tolerance test (OGTT). The test involves a fasting venipuncture, followed by ingestion of a 75 g glucose solution and two subsequent venipunctures at timed intervals. One is drawn two hours after the fasting venipuncture, and the other is taken at any time (commonly at hour-1) between the fasting and hour-2 samples. Diagnosis of diabetes does not require that the fasting glucose level be at or above the threshold value. Thus, the fasting value may be normal, but if the hour-2 level is 11.1 mmol/l (200 mg/dl) or higher on two different OGTTs, diabetes is indicated (93). The WHO (164, 165) does not require a second independent OGTT for diagnosis, but accepts that diabetes is manifest when the hour-2 glucose level and the sample drawn between the fasting and hour-2 venipunctures is also 11.1 mmol/l (200 mg/dl) or higher.

To facilitate participation in epidemiological surveys of NIDDM prevalence, the NDDG (93) and the WHO (164, 165) accept the use of one abbreviated OGTT, involving only two venipunctures: fasting and/or hour-2. The plasma glucose criteria are unchanged from those in the standard OGTT.

Do the differences among the cut-off criteria used in epidemiologic surveys and those recommended by the NDDG (93) and WHO (165) lead to false classifications? False positives inflate diabetic prevalence rates, and false negatives underestimate them. This certainly is of clinical and epidemiological significance, but it also has ramifications for studies on the etiology of NIDDM. If single screen prevalence rates are unreliable, our ability to recognize factors that trigger NIDDM onset in Native Americans is compromised. Formerly, when plasma glucose criteria were lower, reversion to normal glucose levels on a second OGTT screen were observed frequently (93). Unfortunately, even with the more rigorous standards, instability of identification occurs among some Indians (139, 141). A careful comparison has revealed that epidemiological surveys that use a single, modified OGTT screen overestimate the prevalence of diabetes by 16% (130).

Epidemiology of NIDDM Among Indigenous Peoples of North America

Although the prevalence of NIDDM in American Indians was called an epidemic (7, 157, 158) two decades ago, the absence of uniform diagnostic methods, and a lower plasma glucose criterion than is used currently for diagnosis, made it difficult to verify this claim. Of the 65 studies examined by Sievers & Fisher (124), for example, only two used the 11.1 mmol/l at hour-2 threshold. Rates of diabetes reported from hospital-based studies were about half the rates based on surveys conducted before 1979 (139).

Prior to 1940 diabetes was virtually unknown among Native Americans (16, 157, 159, 170). By 1984, among properly diagnosed American Indian, Eskimo, and Aleut diabetic outpatients, 98% suffered from NIDDM, while the remainder exhibited IDDM (44). Evidence now shows that NIDDM is extraordinarily common in some tribes (8, 16, 60, 65) and some regions of the United States (39, 44, 71), but in others prevalence is still lower than the United States national average (2.47% in 1980) (e.g. Alaskan Eskimos, Alaskan Athapaskan-speaking Indians; 120). Low NIDDM rates were also reported for Navajos of Arizona and New Mexico as recently as 1984 (44). By 1986, however, the NIDDM rate in one Navajo community exceeded the United States national average (53, 131). By 1987, out of 11 Indian Health Service Areas examined, only Alaska had an age-adjusted prevalence in persons 15 and over that was lower than the United States average (16). In all groups morbidity continues to increase (119, 170). Prevalence rates often vary by sex, with a higher rate among women than men (14, 16, 28, 60), although peak rates are attained earlier by men than by women (60).

Among Canadian indigenous people, the epidemiology of diabetes resembles that in the United States (169), with two notable differences. The rise in the Canadian aboriginal diabetes rate became noticeable only in the last 15 years, and considerable variability exists in tribal and regional prevalence rates (140, 169, 170). Latitude is a significant predictor of diabetes in Canada, with the highest prevalences recorded in the south, where the bulk of the Euro-Canadian population resides. Age-standardized diabetes rates are lower than the national average (around 2%) in British Columbia, the Yukon Territory, and the Northwest Territories (171). New data from regions not covered in the national survey (171), for example, the Cree area of Quebec (149), show that the age-standardized prevalence of NIDDM among people 20 years and older was 6.6% in 1989, and IDDM accounted for approximately 1% of the detected cases (14). Females exhibit higher prevalence rates than do males, and female prevalence rates peak later than do those of males (14, 169). Finally, among Canadian aboriginal peoples, indigenous ethnicity affects the distribution of NIDDM (171). Although such differences were also noted in the United States (98), current data show that only in Alaska are indigenous ethnic differences in NIDDM prevalence still manifest (119).

Age-adjusted diabetes mortality rates indicate that NIDDM has become a lethal problem among aboriginal peoples of North America. For United States Native Americans, Gohdes (44) estimated the mortality rate from diabetes at

19.9 per 100,000, or twice the rate in all other peoples of the United States. Among Canadian Indians, the risk of death from diabetes is 2–4 times that in Euro-Canadian men and women, respectively (170).

At one time diabetes was thought to be a benign biochemical anomaly in Amerindians (60, 117). Now we know that vascular and neuropathic complications do occur (59, 119, 155, 161). Diabetic sequelae take years to develop; hence, their absence from the 1960s–1970s literature on Amerindian diabetes is not surprising. Published data on complications in Amerindians is sparse, but it is clear that some sequelae occur more commonly in this population than in others (59, 170). Kidney failure is an example (16, 170). In some Amerindian populations 88% of all lower extremity amputations (LEA) are also related to diabetes (15, 44). The Native American rate across the United States is around 50% (16). Even for first amputations the incidence rate among diabetics is high—18.0/1000 person-years for LEA in Oklahoma Indians (73), a rate higher than among the Pimas. In these populations, LEA incidence was significantly higher in men than in women, and the sex-adjusted rate was much higher than in non-Indian diabetics (73).

The frequency of another common complication of diabetes, proliferative diabetic retinopathy (PDR), was 18.6% among Oklahoma Indians (72) and 18% among Pimas (97). These rates again are significantly higher than those found in other Americans. PDR is more common in both Amerindian populations with increasing age and duration of NIDDM. Independent risk factors for PDR include hypertension, hypercholesterolemia, and insulin treatment in the Pima (97), and systolic blood pressure, cholesterol level, and therapeutic regimen in Oklahoma Indians (72). A distressing finding that is not widely appreciated is that insulin therapy is a significant risk factor for PDR in American and Canadian Indians (170).

Finally, NIDDM also seems to increase the risk of cardiovascular disease in Native Americans. Over 60% of Canadian Mohawk diabetics had at least one of the following complications: ischemic heart disease, stroke, or peripheral vascular disease (170). However, diabetic Pima aged 50–79 years exhibited less than half the fatal coronary heart disease (CHD) found in the United States population studied in Framingham (97). CHD is an uncommon disease in nondiabetic Pimas (96), and among Native Americans age-adjusted cardiovascular mortality rates generally are lower than in the aggregate United States population (74). Thus, although cardiovascular mortality and morbidity rates seem to be variably increasing among Native Americans (74), the role NIDDM plays in these changes is not fully known. In aboriginal Americans, unknown factors may modify the detrimental impact of NIDDM that is observed in other populations.

BODY FUEL METABOLISM AND NIDDM PATHOPHYSIOLOGY

Sustenance of life requires energy, and in humans, glucose is the preferred fuel. A complex interplay of hormones, namely insulin, its antagonists glucagon and growth hormone, as well as cortisol and epinephrine (adrenalin), ensure glucose homeostasis. The primary source of glucose is ingested carbohydrates. However, in a process called gluconeogenesis, glucose is also produced by the liver from specific amino acid precursors (69, 148).

Carbohydrate digestion in the gut yields glucose and minor amounts of other monosaccharides, all of which are absorbed into the blood. From the blood, glucose must pass through cell walls to be of use, because energy metabolism takes place within cells. However, glucose can pass through the cell walls of most tissues only with the assistance of insulin. Accordingly, as blood glucose level rises, the β cells in the pancreas secrete insulin, which after binding to cell surface receptors (104), facilitate cellular glucose uptake. Insulin also enables the storage of glucose, mainly in the liver but also in muscle, in the form of glycogen. Provided no more carbohydrate is ingested, insulin-mediated glucose transport and glycogen storage proceed until basal circulating glucose levels are reached (148).

Most meals include carbohydrates, fats, and proteins. After these substances are broken down into their constituents, insulin plays other essential roles involving protein and fat synthesis. In lipid metabolism, for example, insulin is required for the transport of triglycerides across the cell membrane of adipose tissue, where storage of triglycerides (neutral fat) takes place (148).

The energy needs of the body continue even in nonfed periods, for example, during sleep. As glucose level falls, so does insulin, because its secretion is regulated through a feedback mechanism between blood glucose concentration and the β cell. Simultaneously, other feedback mechanisms ensure that glucose levels do not fall too low, given the brain's dependence on glucose for fuel. Thus, as glucose level decreases, the α cells of the pancreas release glucagon, and epinephrine acts on the liver to release stored glucose from the liver. Glucagon rapidly promotes glycogenolysis, stimulates gluconeogenesis, blocks formation of lipids, and promotes the breakdown of stored fat (148). In this way glucose is made available to the organism, and fat is released into the circulation in the form of free fatty acids (FFA), which can also be oxidized in hepatic and peripheral tissues (but not the brain) for use as fuel (148). To replenish the energy supply, hunger stimulates food consumption, and the cycle begins anew.

Clearly, a set of interrelated, simultaneously ongoing processes regulated by hormonal and neural feedback systems regulate energy metabolism. The development of NIDDM involves disruption of these normal processes.

Pathophysiology of NIDDM

The pathophysiology of IDDM is straightforward, but considerable debate surrounds the basic defect in NIDDM (110). The normal coordination of glucose homeostasis involves insulin secretion; glucose uptake by liver, gut, and peripheral tissues; and suppression of glucose production in the liver (27). DeFronzo (27) suggested that in lean NIDDM patients, the primary defect involves the β cell, which is incapable of producing adequate insulin. However, in the majority of NIDDM patients, the presence of obesity suggests that their basic problem is muscle and liver insensitivity to insulin. In DeFronzo's view, both diminished insulin secretion and insulin resistance are required for NIDDM onset, and continuing hepatic glucose production is important only in the development of fasting hyperglycemia.

The inability to suppress hepatic glucose production in the severe hyperglycemia of NIDDM is not disputed (24). However, recent overviews of the true pathophysiology of NIDDM argue that the primary deficit is resistance to insulin-mediated glucose uptake by muscle (110) and/or liver tissues (27), and that impaired insulin secretion is a secondary development that leads to fasting hyperglycemia (27, 110). The latter may enhance FFA release, which stimulates hepatic glucose production despite the presence of hyperglycemia (110).

ETIOLOGY OF NIDDM

NIDDM is a complex disease, with both genetic and environmental factors involved in its onset (37). The specific mechanisms involved in the pathophysiology of NIDDM are presumed to operate in all humans. Populations may vary in the genes encoded at the loci involved with these mechanisms—for example, genes that govern transport and receptor proteins in different tissues, cellular components, and enzymes involved in carbohydrate metabolism. Some of the genes, tractable to molecular identification and analysis, may constitute the hypothesized susceptibility genes that lead to population differences in NIDDM morbidity. Alternatively, susceptibility may derive from still other genes that have been suggested by complex biometric analysis (37).

Because nutrition provides the input variable in carbohydrate metabolism, and because human culture governs access to food, environmental involvement in NIDDM has long been recognized. Cultural variables also influence human energy expenditures. These two environmental phenomena are commonly subsumed under the label of lifestyle. Thus, the current burden of NIDDM among aboriginal peoples of the New World is explained by lifestyle changes since World War II that favored the emergence of NIDDM in genetically susceptible individuals (40, 59, 64, 136, 173). The widespread and excessive diabetes morbidity suggests not only that lifestyle changes have been extreme over the last half century, but also that the susceptibility gene or genes must be widely distributed across aboriginal population boundaries.

Biological Basis: Evolutionary Models and Causal Hypotheses

Over 30 years ago the geneticist James V. Neel (94) asked why a gene with such debilitating consequences as diabetes was not eliminated from human populations through natural selection. He reasoned that a gene that is deleterious today might actually have been preserved because of some selective advantage under specific environmental conditions of the past. Thus, without knowing whether one or many genes were involved in diabetes onset, without knowing that diabetes was genetically heterogeneous, and without current understanding of the pathophysiology of NIDDM, Neel formulated the first and still predominant evolutionary explanation for diabetes: the thrifty gene hypothesis. To date, three other evolutionary models have been suggested to explain the prevalence of diabetes in Native American populations specifically. These models all propose that the genes predisposing Native Americans to NIDDM today were selectively advantageous in their pre-modern environments.

THRIFTY GENE HYPOTHESIS   Neel's original thrifty gene model (94) postulated that genes promoting rapid insulin response to a plasma glucose stimulus prevented energy loss by converting excess glucose to stored fat. Without such storage, glucose homeostasis requires that excess glucose be excreted in the urine. For our hunter-gatherer ancestors, excess glucose was not a regular condition, but occurred periodically, under feasting conditions. Once stored as fat, the energy could be released when food availability became restricted (i.e. in fasting conditions). In such situations, bearers of "thrifty genes" had a selective advantage, and the genes spread. However, the cultural and environmental changes that produced a continuous and ample food supply made the quick insulin response maladaptive. The altered conditions led to the development of hyperinsulinemia and obesity, and the excess insulin was responsible for provoking insulin antagonists that eventually produced β-cell exhaustion (94). The new version of the thrifty gene model (95) keeps the basic aspects of the original, but proposes new pathways based on current understanding of the pathophysiology of diabetes. One of these pathways, believed to operate in the Pima Indians (64), is the existence of a genetically determined greater than normal difference in the insulin sensitivity of glucose and lipid metabolic pathways. In this case, some peripheral tissues might be more resistant to the entry of insulin-mediated glucose (e.g. skeletal muscle), while others are not (e.g. adipose tissue). Again, the result would be hyperglycemia and obesity, both of which provoke hyperinsulinemia.

Hyperinsulinemia, characteristic of NIDDM without regard to race, is present even in nondiabetic Pima Indians (2, 64). However, fasting hyperinsulinemia has not been described to date in seven groups of nondiabetic Native Americans whose insulin levels have been published (135, 138). Such observations question the common assumption that hyperinsulinemia is a racial characteristic of Amerindians (49). What is unusual among some Amerindians compared to Caucasians is the insulin response to oral glucose. In Navajo (113) and Dogrib people (138) insulin response during an OGTT is massive. Attempts to link the hypothesized thrifty genotype with the three migration models for the colonization of the Americas (156) disregard problems with the migratory wave model itself (142). Furthermore, the claimed Amerind susceptibility is belied by the current epidemiology of NIDDM in the descendants of the supposed second and third migratory waves from Asia (53, 119, 140, 171).

THE NEW WORLD SYNDROME   Neel's thrifty gene hypothesis (94, 95) applied to all human populations. A population-specific evolutionary model for NIDDM, the New World Syndrome, was proposed subsequently (154). This model postulated a genetically controlled alteration of the pathways involved in lipid synthesis and regulation of lipid level. The advantage again would lie in the ability to store fat when food was plentiful and release it when food was scarce. The latter is particularly important for pregnant women and nursing mothers. Women who were efficient in fat storage and fat release under particular food-availability conditions would survive and reproduce, while their genetically less-fortunate relatives would not. The New World Syndrome, therefore, links lipid and carbohydrate metabolism, and is based on the observation that NIDDM, obesity, and gallbladder disease—all of which are new conditions in Native Americans—tend to occur together in people with Amerindian ancestry (98, 154).

ADAPTATION TO A LOW CARBOHYDRATE, COLD ENVIRONMENT   A third model, involving adaptation to a low carbohydrate, cold environment was suggested by Szathmáry (139), who noted that Neel's thrifty gene hypothesis presupposed a nutritional environment that produced carbohydrate in excess of daily energy requirements. This was not the nutritional milieu of the arctic and subarctic (29), in which the original ancestors of modern Native Americans resided before the southward movement of their colonizing descendants. Meat and fat constituted the only available foods in the Arctic and Subarctic for most of the year. High protein and fat intake, accompanied by carbohydrate restriction in a low temperature environment in which heavy physical activity is demanded, would promote survival of individuals in whom gluconeogenesis (46, 69, 148) and free fatty acid release and utilization (36, 51, 55) were enhanced (139).

Gluconeogensis is promoted by glucagon, epinephrine, and glucocorticoids, all insulin antagonists (69). Plasma glucagon increases in normal individuals on low carbohydrate diets, and exercise triples glucagon levels (55). In experimental animals, gluconeogensis increases in a cold environment (92). Because glucose homeostasis is regulated through a complex interplay of counter-regulatory hormones and neural stimuli, it is worth emphasizing that the metabolic responses of target tissues depend on relative amounts of different hormones. If selection favored genes that enhanced gluconeogenesis and promoted FFA release and utilization, and if these persisted in the descendants of the first North Americans, then in the carbohydrate-rich environment of the Westernized diet, this adaptation could lead to NIDDM today (139).

NORTHERN HUNTING ADAPTATION   Ritenbaugh & Goodby (115) linked Szathmáry's low carbohydrate adaptation model with that of the New World Syndrome (154) in their Northern Hunting Adaptation hypothesis. They suggested that genetically controlled adaptations could have occurred in several different enzymatically mediated pathways involving glucose and lipid metabolism. Glucose sparing in the arctic environment of the first North Americans would have been beneficial, they argue, and glucose sparing is the effect of the glucose fatty-acid cycle (109), which operates as follows.

After glucose is taken up by cells, it is either stored as glycogen or is broken down (glycolysis) to release energy for the cell. More than 90% of glycolysis involves glucose oxidation through a series of stepwise reactions mediated by different enzymes (46). Less than 10% involves an anaerobic process that yields a metabolite called lactate (27). The glucose fatty-acid cycle refers to the biochemical pathway through which the excessive oxidation of free fatty acids yields compounds that inhibit oxidative glycolysis in skeletal muscle. Eventually, the accumulation of glucose-6-phosphate—the first break-down product after glucose is taken into the cell—inhibits glucose uptake. As a result, glycogen cannot be synthesized for storage in muscle cells. In the liver, meanwhile, FFA oxidation directly inhibits glycogen synthase, the key enzyme involved in glycogen synthesis (although it is not known if the same direct effect occurs in muscle; 27). The net effect of the inhibition of glucose oxidation, glucose uptake, and glycogen synthesis is an increase of circulating glucose. The latter is further enhanced because the lactate produced through anaerobic glycolysis diffuses into the circulation and reaches the liver, where lactate is a preferred gluconeogenic precursor. The result is the hepatic production of still more glucose (25).

To Ritenbaugh & Goodby (115) increased lactate production in Indians may indicate the existence of the Northern Hunting Adaptation. Kashiwagi et al (61) found a 67% increase in lactate production after short-term overfeeding of Pima Indians, an increase that is large in comparison to output in Caucasians. C Ritenbaugh (unpublished observations) also found that after glucose challenge, lactate levels in Amerindian students rose compared to the Caucasians in the control group. Her samples were small, but the directions of these changes suggest that the ingested glucose was being cycled into lactate in the Indians, as would occur under conditions of glucose sparing. Further testing of this model is warranted.

Biological Basis: Evidence of Genetic Involvement in NIDDM

In 1987 Szathmáry (136) reviewed the evidence on genetic factors involved with the onset of NIDDM in Native Americans. More recent reviews (37) have considered the role of genetic factors without population restriction. Many note the almost 100% concordance of identical twins for NIDDM (26, 45, 121) and also observe that the genetics of NIDDM remain poorly understood. Strategies are needed to elucidate the genetics of NIDDM and to secure multidisciplinary cooperation in this endeavor (26, 45). The biometric approach also remains useful (112), especially in Indians (10, 21), for whom a strong genetic propensity to NIDDM is suggested. Chakraborty and others (see 129) have demonstrated that the proportion of Amerindian ancestry increases with the rate of NIDDM in some populations. They translate this as a possible manifestation of the genetic risk for NIDDM in Indians. If so, the risk can be masked when only the average differences in Amerindian ancestry are compared between diabetics and their nondiabetic controls. Among Mohawk Indians, for example, a case-control study found no differences in the proportion of Amerindian ancestry (140).

GENETIC CONTROL OF GLUCOSE LEVEL   Several attempts have been made to determine the transmission pattern of NIDDM in Indians, assuming this involves control of plasma glucose level. The mode of inheritance of this phenomenon has not been identified to general satisfaction (136) because conflicting claims have been made. Initial studies on the Pima suggested that a model of autosomal recessive inheritance should be tested (128). Subsequently, a major gene, transmitted as an autosomal dominant, was reported in an abstract that provided the conclusions of segregation analysis (167). In Oklahoma Seminole Indians, a major gene seems involved, although its transmission pattern is unclear. Elston et al (33) favored recessive inheritance. No major gene effect could be determined in Florida Seminoles (33). Among Dogrib Indians the suspected inheritance pattern is complex and multifactorial, involving many genes, some dominant, along with an intragenerational environmental effect (134). This pattern is similar to one proposed for Michigan Caucasians (4).

Biometrical studies of the sort described have not yet revealed the locations of putative genes, although methods to detect linkage between a genetic locus and a quantitative marker—such as plasma glucose level—do exist. Not all population studies link the same genetic marker and diabetes. Nevertheless, in people with Amerindian heritage, NIDDM has been linked to loci on four different chromosomes: 1 (Rh blood groups), 4 (Gc, or vitamin-D-binding protein), 6 (HLA [human leukocyte antigens] and GLO [glyoxalase]), and 16 (Hp [haptoglobin] and PGP [phosphoglycolate phosphatase]) (136).

GENETIC CONTROL OF INSULIN LEVEL   Advances in molecular biology have permitted examination of genes that are believed to be implicated in NIDDM onset. A sequence of DNA at one end of the insulin gene (the 5′-flanking region) was believed (116) to convey susceptibility in American whites, blacks, and Pima Indians by influencing expression of the gene. This polymorphism was later found not to be involved in NIDDM onset in the Pima (67), although it might influence diabetes severity.

The metabolically active form of vitamin D, $1,25\text{-}(OH)_2D_3$, is involved in the regulation of insulin level (43, 100). Szathmáry (137) found that genotypes of the vitamin-D–binding protein locus, Gc, have significant impact on fasting insulin level after adjustment for adiposity. In her total sample as well as a reduced sample of normoglycemics, and in a reduced sample that excluded first-degree relatives, homozygotes for *Gc 1F-1F* had the lowest levels of fasting insulin. Because the elevation of fasting insulin is a portender of NIDDM, quantitative variation of basal insulin by genotype may indicate that some genotypes are more at risk for hyperinsulinemia than are others.

The Gc locus is located on chromosome 4q. Prochazka et al (107) reported linkage between each of three other markers in the region of 4q26 and maximal insulin action in Pima Indians. It is possible that these authors and Szathmáry (137) detected the effect of the same gene, albeit by very different methods.

GENETICS OF INSULIN ACTION   NIDDM and impaired glucose tolerance in Pima Indians are characterized by insulin resistance (80). Insulin action (in vivo insulin-mediated glucose disposal) is familial in nondiabetic Pimas (81), and its distribution is trimodal (11), suggesting a mixture of three distributions controlled by three genotypes that can result from codominant inheritance of a pair of alleles. Total insulin concentration, manifest as hyperinsulinemia, is also familial in Mexican Americans (48), a group known to have variable degrees of Amerindian ancestry. A site on chromosome 4q, probably between 4q11 and 4q26, may encode the gene responsible for insulin action in Pima (107) and Dogrib Indians (137).

INSULIN RECEPTOR   Insulin resistance, thought to have a central role in NIDDM (5), can be brought about in a variety of ways. Insulin receptor abnormalities, from mutation (101) to deletion (146) of the tyrosine kinase domain of the gene, have been associated with insulin-resistant diabetes in two Japanese families. Restriction fragment length polymorphism of the insulin receptor has also been identified in different populations (86), including Mexican Americans. In the latter, homozygosity of the so-called C allele was twice as likely in NIDDM patients than in controls (108). However, the genotype association was not found in blacks, whites, or Pima Indians (30). Attempts to establish linkage of the insulin receptor locus to NIDDM in a set of white pedigrees also was unsuccessful (31). Direct sequencing of the insulin receptor in cells from Pima NIDDM patients and healthy individuals (90) showed no differences. The insulin receptor may, nevertheless, be implicated in NIDDM in some populations. In Chinese Americans, the insulin receptor and apolipoprotein B loci, as well as the apolipoprotein A1/C3/A4 gene cluster, were found to contribute to the development of NIDDM (166). The insulin receptor may contain protective haplotypes that resist NIDDM onset, while both the apolipoprotein B locus and the apolipoprotein A1/C3/A4 gene cluster increase the risk of diabetes in normal-weight and obese persons.

INSULIN RESISTANCE   If insulin receptor defects are not the cause of insulin resistance in Pima Indians, then post-receptor anomalies are possible. One example is low basal glycogen synthase activity in skeletal muscle, accompanied by a possible defect in glycogen synthase that reduces its response to insulin stimulus (62). Further investigation of the enzymes involved in the activation of glycogen synthase and glycogen synthase phosphatase eliminated casein kinase II (CKII) as the post-receptor defect. The latter enzyme activates the phosphatase after CKII is activated by insulin. In Pima Indians, CKII response to insulin is normal, so the defect that causes insulin resistance must occur in a different pathway (82).

INSULIN-RESPONSIVE GLUCOSE TRANSPORTER   Insulin resistance in NIDDM may be caused by a variety of post-receptor binding defects (41). Li et al (76) reported that the frequency of the X1 allele was elevated significantly in NIDDM patients relative to normal controls in each of three different populations. The locus (now called GLUT1 for glucose transporter) demonstrated no association with NIDDM in the Chinese American study reported above (166). No associations of either the *GLUT1* or the *GLUT2* gene were observed in Utah whites (32). Hope has diminished (37) that the identification and chromosomal localization of these and three other glucose-transporter protein loci (GLUT1–5) would show involvement in producing insulin resistance (42) in the different tissues in which the glucose transporters are expressed (6). The *GLUT4* gene expressed in muscle and fat, for example, has been sequenced in one diabetic Pima Indian, but it was normal (18a). Sequence variation was found in non-Indian diabetic and nondiabetic subjects, but the polymorphisms are not associated with NIDDM. Nevertheless, normal fasting glucose level is associated with *GLUT4* mRNA and also GLUT4 protein in skeletal muscle (34), and a decrease was observed in the plasma membranes of skeletal muscle in lean diabetic European patients (153). GLUT5 protein seems to be a monosaccharide sugar transporter in several tissues, but its contribution to fructose and glucose transport in the brain and insulin-dependent tissues needs to be clarified (122).

Environmental Basis: Evidence of the Roles of Diet, Physical Activity, Obesity, and Stress

Lifestyle changes in diet, obesity, body-fat patterning, physical activity, and psychosocial stress (57, 136) form the environment for the emergence of NIDDM phenotype in individuals with the requisite (if unknown) genotype. In general, the sequence of possible changes could be increasing sedentism, diminishment of physical exercise, increase in total caloric intake and/or possibly specific nutrients, shift in the distribution of body fat, and development of obesity. It is highly likely that the earlier the decreased physical activity/increased caloric intake/obesity triad impacts in a life, the greater the risk of NIDDM. Thus, children who live under the altered lifeways, whether modern Native American (132) or Australian Aborigine (103), are at great risk for NIDDM. Conversely, evidence from Australian aborigines with NIDDM shows that with a reverse shift in lifeways, that is, consumption of traditional foods and increase in physical activity, plasma glucose and insulin levels can be normalized (59, 102).

A novel hypothesis has been proposed for the environmental induction of NIDDM: the thrifty phenotype hypothesis (50). Inadequate early nutrition may impair the development of the endocrine functions of the pancreas, thereby greatly increasing NIDDM susceptibility. The hypothesis proposes that fetal and infant nutrition are critical to the development of an appropriate supply of pancreatic β cells. Protein insufficiency in utero inhibits β cell number, and perhaps function (50). This may not cause problems in the first decades, but in mid-adulthood, NIDDM would result from either insulin deficiency, or altered function. The inverse relationship between rates of aboriginal Canadian diabetes and latitude (14, 171), with lower prevalence manifest in locations in which protein intake exceeds Euro-Canadian norms (145), fits with predictions of the thrifty phenotype hypothesis. The model certainly bears investigation.

DIET   Dietary change includes shifts in the proportions of macronutrients consumed (e.g. percent protein, fat, and carbohydrate), deficiency of specific nutrients (e.g. chromium or zinc), and increase in specific food items (e.g. refined sugar) and total caloric consumption. Studies on Pima (111) and Dogrib Indians (145) found no association between any dietary factor and NIDDM. A study of over 84,000 United States women also failed to find any association between risk of NIDDM and intakes of total calories, carbohydrate, fiber, sucrose, or protein after controlling for previous weight change, body mass index, and alcohol consumption (22). This result contradicts international studies that show protein and fat intake posing risks for NIDDM, while carbohydrate intake does not (22). On the other hand, one prospective study among the Pima showed a significantly higher NIDDM rate among those women, who in their nondiabetic days had consumed more total carbohydrates (170). Individual dietary components [e.g. chromium decrease (1)] impair glucose metabolism and induce insulin resistance. Varying rates of absorption of starchy foods from the gut indicate that plasma glucose levels are altered at different rates (150). This also applies to many aboriginally utilized vegetable foods (13). These observations all suggest that the role played by dietary changes in the onset of NIDDM in aboriginal Americans still warrants investigation. Certainly the Pima diet has changed since the baseline provided by the 1968 nutrition survey (126). Furthermore, experimental work among the Pima (61) suggests that dietary shifts have an impact on insulin secretion.

Short-term overnutrition (in moderately overweight, nondiabetic Pima Indians), without shifts in macronutrient composition, produced a 58% increase in the average fasting insulin concentration (61). Although not conclusive, this result suggests that overnutrition could induce hyperinsulinemia in healthy individuals. Increased caloric intake is one type of dietary change found among Indians (145). It is unknown whether hyperinsulinemia could be produced over a long-term period of overfeeding, or in the presence of more moderate degrees of overnutrition. On the other hand, differences in daily caloric intakes between Pima women of Arizona (3164 calories in 1988) (126) and Dogrib Indian women of the Northwest Territories (1843 calories in 1985) (145) parallel differences in fasting insulin levels between them (135).

High-fat diets and dietary sucrose increase insulin resistance (57), but whether changes in the ingestion of these substances are implicated directly in the onset of NIDDM in Native Americans has not been demonstrated.

With reference to protein consumption and the thrifty phenotype hypothesis (50), no study has compared the fetal and postnatal protein intake of Native American infants and the NIDDM rate during their adulthood. Differences exist in protein intakes of adults from different tribes. For example, among Dogrib people 31% of the calories are derived from protein, in comparison to the scant 11% among Pima women (126). Protein intake has declined among the Standing Rock Sioux, from an estimated 37% of the daily energy intake aboriginally, to 24% on reservation in 1877, to a likely 16%, as among other Americans in 1985 (57). Protein consumption among Alaskan Eskimos and Indians has also decreased (99, 119). Thus, although Dogrib people have a very low prevalence of NIDDM today, at one time they had none, and increasing NIDDM morbidity characterizes both Alaska Natives and the Sioux of

Standing Rock, South Dakota (16). Investigation of the protein malnutrition aspects of the thrifty phenotype hypothesis among Native North Americans would be useful.

PHYSICAL ACTIVITY DECLINE AND OBESITY   Generalized obesity, measured most often by the body mass index (BMI) (93), is now common in Amerindians (17, 66, 71, 170). Inuit are an exception (170), although among Alaska Natives (Aleut, Eskimos, and Indians) obesity is increasing (91, 119). Among Pima Indians a variety of metabolic differences accompany obesity (56). Despite a significant genetic dimension to obesity (12), in its simplest conceptualization obesity develops when caloric intake is excessive relative to the level of physical activity (87); hence, obesity is also secondarily associated with age (162).

   Without doubt, physical activity has decreased in the transition from aboriginal to modern lifeways (16, 53, 136). Because insulin excess accompanies obesity even in nondiabetics, and because obesity generally precedes the onset of NIDDM, obesity is thought to be diabetogenic (7, 159). But obesity alone cannot explain NIDDM (129). Among the environmental variables, reduced physical activity independent of obesity may also constitute a risk factor for NIDDM, given the well-demonstrated effects of exercise on glucose and insulin metabolism (68).

   Physical fitness can be measured precisely by exercise physiologists in laboratory settings, but few studies on aboriginal North Americans have actually done so (136, 170). Culture-specific instruments of activity assessment are preferable in field situations (85). The NIDDM rate was elevated among those Pima who reported low levels of leisure-time physical activity in their past, and diabetics reported low rates of both current and past physical activity (70).

   Other evidence also suggests a role for physical activity in NIDDM. Higher rates of diabetes have been found in sedentary Melanesian and Indian men living in Fiji, compared to physically active ones (147). In diabetics, habitual physical activity can improve glucose tolerance and insulin sensitivity, and high aerobic capacity improves glycemic control (152).

   A recent review (3) identified six remaining problem areas regarding the relationship between obesity and NIDDM worldwide. Young (170) noted that this is an underestimate for Native North Americans, among whom most studies of obesity and NIDDM have been cross-sectional, and information on the relationship between NIDDM and obesity is scant. The exception, again, is the Pima Indians, among whom several aspects of the relationship between NIDDM and obesity have been explored. Duration of obesity is a risk factor for NIDDM among Pimas (35). Weight loss also occurs among Pima diabetics, apparently because of a greater metabolic rate among those with NIDDM than those without (38).

Attempts to thwart the onset of NIDDM in Native American communities, separate from treatment of NIDDM, are beginning to focus on weight loss through exercise regimens. Physical activity benefits glucose and insulin metabolism independently of weight loss. Accordingly, attention needs to be paid to cultural conceptualizations of large body mass (59, 114, 127); otherwise, considerable resistance may greet instructions to decrease body mass and shape. Obesity prevention indubitably has several dimensions (58, 88). Experience shows that community effort and support is essential, and that Amerindian success stories exist. For example, obese Zuni diabetics whose weight loss was obtained through regular physical exercise also exhibited a fall in plasma glucose and a reduced need for hypoglycemic medication in comparison to nonexercising diabetic controls (54).

OBESITY, INSULIN RESISTANCE, AND LOCATION OF BODY FAT   The contrast between aboriginally lean Indians and their modern obese counterparts (157) and the link between obesity and NIDDM have led to the view that obesity by itself is diabetogenic (159). Hyperinsulinemia accompanies obesity; hence, a great deal of work has been done among the Pima to clarify the relationships between NIDDM, insulin resistance, and obesity. These studies have shown (77) that insulin resistance has three components:

1. Insulin resistance also involves fat-free tissue. The biophysical properties of muscle are altered in obesity, as the fat-free mass is characterized by hypertrophy of skeletal muscle and changed capillary density (greater space between capillaries in muscle) (77, 78). These biophysical alterations seem to impair insulin's ability to penetrate muscle (77, 78); thus they are partly responsible for the insulin resistance found in obese people.

2. Glucose storage, the major aspect of glucose disposal during insulin resistance, is dependent on the enzyme glycogen synthase. The latter is activated by glucose 6-phosphate (83). Increase in glycogen synthase activity requires decrease in the activity of glucose 6-phosphate, which in turn is dependent on insulin (83). Insulin resistance may arise from a genetic defect regulating the step between the insulin receptor and the activation of glycogen synthase (77).

3. On the basis of new evidence (174), which contradicts initial findings (79), insulin resistance in obese Pima Indians does not appear to result from inhibition of glucose metabolism through the glucose fatty-acid cycle (77).

It is worth noting that this new evidence (174) is an abstract (which does not deal directly with the issue of the role of the glucose fatty-acid cycle, and cannot, in any case, be evaluated without more detail than is currently available). Pedersen (105) takes a different view, discussing evidence that supports a link between the enhanced lipolysis found in the abdominal obesity typical of NIDDM and the glucose fatty-acid cycle (109).

The deposition of fat in humans differs by location, with some depots larger than others (9). Sex differences exist in fat patterning, at least in Caucasians (75). Abdominal obesity, sometimes called upper body obesity, central adiposity, or centripetality, is predictive of NIDDM (63). It can be measured by the simple ratio of waist to hip circumference. Centripetal obesity has been observed in Dogrib Indians with hyperglycemia (144), in other Native Canadians with unambiguous NIDDM (170), in Navajo (52) and Pima Indians (66), and in the different Indian groups of Oklahoma (71). A prospective study on Mexican Americans (47) has demonstrated that the incidence of NIDDM is predicted by central adiposity, and that this form of obesity predicts NIDDM in women significantly better than it does in men. Studies on French Canadian men show that accumulation of thigh fat may protect against the disease consequences of abdominal obesity (106).

The cause of centralized obesity has not been identified, but studies have implicated adreno-pituitary hormones (151a). Cortisol, a known stress hormone, is an adreno-pituitary hormone, and stress may have a role in the onset of centralized obesity that is predictive of future NIDDM (9, 144).

STRESS AS A DIMENSION OF CULTURE CHANGE   A variety of studies (133, 136) suggest that psychosocial stress affects glucose homeostasis. Glycemic control in IDDM is affected by stress under some conditions (20), and it may be a factor in the advent of NIDDM in Western Samoa (173).

Physical and psychological stress produce increased adrenocorticotropin secretion from the anterior pituitary gland, adrenalin from the adrenal medulla, glucocorticoids from the adrenal cortex, and noradrenalin from the sympathetic nerves (15). Of this array, the powerful insulin antagonists are the glucocorticoids and the catecholamines. Bjorntorp (9) has detailed how sustained elevation of cortisol could be involved in the production of abdominal obesity and hyperinsulinemia. No studies of NIDDM and stress have been carried out among Native Americans. Significant elevations in centripetal obesity were found in the most acculturated Dogrib community, in which long-term circulating plasma glucose levels and fasting triglyceride levels were significantly higher than in outlying settlements (143). Szathmáry & Ferrell (143) suggested that acculturation-induced stress might be the cause of the difference. Certainly in animal models of disease genesis, social factors have an impact on adrenal physiology and related physiology. For example, in one nonhuman primate species (*Macaca fascicularis*), subordinate animals had higher plasma glucose levels, while dominant animals had worsened atherosclerosis under certain conditions (123). Lipid and carbohydrate metabolism, therefore, are linked in human and nonhuman primates, and stress may also influence these processes.

Formal studies of NIDDM and stress in humans are rare. Bruce et al (18) reported that psychological stress significantly increased pulse, blood pressure, and FFA level in both NIDDM patients and their nondiabetic controls, without any increase in plasma glucose in either the diabetics or the controls. On the other hand, infusion of noradrenaline significantly increased liver glucose production in the same diabetic subjects. Bruce et al (18) observed that chronic psychological stress in NIDDM might produce continuous FFA elevation that could hamper glucose metabolism as predicted by the glucose fatty-acid cycle, reduce sensitivity of target cells to insulin, and lead to glucose intolerance (18). Patients with NIDDM exhibited either a greater activity of the sympathetic nervous system or an increased sensitivity of the catecholamine receptor mechanisms (18).

Scheder (118) has studied one of the enzymes, dopamine-beta-hydroxylase (DBH), that elevates catecholamine level during stress. Her studies on Mexican migrant laborers showed that DBH activity was correlated positively with stressful life events, demarcated diabetic and nondiabetic women, was higher in nondiabetic women than nondiabetic men, and was a better predictor of diabetes than was BMI. Other studies are needed to substantiate these observations. Studies on Native Americans undergoing cultural transition would be most useful in clarifying the role of stress (133) in NIDDM onset.

CONCLUSIONS

Understanding the etiology of NIDDM in North American Native peoples is a challenge. Although much is known about prevalence and specific environmental risk factors, a great deal remains to be elucidated in both the genetic and environmental spheres of NIDDM causation. An enormous amount of what is known about NIDDM pathophysiology, the factors that contribute to its onset, and evolutionary explanations for its appearance have been gleaned through studies on the Pima people of Arizona. The accumulating evidence in that population favors Neel's thrifty gene hypothesis as the explanation for the appearance of NIDDM. However, the Pima people constitute only one population of the many in North America, and the precise mechanisms that are involved elsewhere in Native American diabetes susceptibility might be different from those in the Pima and related tribes, given the extent of genetic differences among Native Americans (115, 136, 171). Many more in-depth investigations of diabetes, including longitudinal ones, need to be conducted among aboriginal North Americans. Candidate genes in carbohydrate and lipid metabolism need to be investigated as much as environmental variables such as dietary change, obesity in its varied forms, and the role of psychosocial stress factors. No aboriginal North American population is immune from the ravages of this disease. NIDDM is increasing even in the Arctic and Subarctic culture areas, although the extent of the problem in these regions still lags behind that in other parts of North America. Fortunately, NIDDM prevention remains possible everywhere in North America. But the effectiveness of prevention strategies would be enhanced if the factors responsible for NIDDM onset were known precisely, and if culturally appropriate methods for prevention were developed for the diverse aboriginal populations of North America.

Literature Cited

1. Anderson RA, Polansky MM, Bryden NA, Canary JJ. 1991. Supplemental-chromium effects on glucose, insulin, glucagon, and urinary chromium losses in subjects consuming controlled low-chromium diets. *Am. J. Clin. Nutr.* 54:909–16
2. Aronoff SL, Bennett PH, Gorden P, Rushforth N, Miller M. 1977. Unexplained hyperinsulinemia in normal and prediabetic Pima Indians compared with normal Caucasians. *Diabetes* 26:827–40
3. Barrett-Connor E. 1989. Epidemiology, obesity, and non-insulin-dependent diabetes mellitus. *Epidemiol. Rev.* 11:172–81
4. Beaty TH, Neel JV, Fajans SS. 1982. Identifying risk factors for diabetes in first degree relatives of non-insulin dependent diabetic patients. *Am. J. Epidemiol.* 115:380–97
5. Beck-Nielsen H. 1989. Insulin-resistance: a scientific and clinical challenge. *Diabet. Metab. Rev.* 5:529–30
6. Bell GI, Murray JC, Nakamura Y, Kayano T, Eddy RL, et al. 1989. Polymorphic human insulin-responsive glucose-transporter gene on chromosome 17p13. *Diabetes* 38:1072–75
7. Bennett PH. 1982. The epidemiology of diabetes mellitus. In *Diabetes Mellitus and Obesity*, ed. BN Blodoff, SI Bleicher, pp. 387–99. Baltimore: Williams & Wilkins
8. Bennett PH, Rushforth NB, Miller M, LeCompte DM. 1976. Epidemiologic studies of diabetes in the Pima Indians. *Recent Prog. Horm. Res.* 32:333–75
9. Bjorntorp P. 1988. Possible mechanisms relating fat distribution and metabolism. In *Fat Distribution During Growth and Later Health Outcomes*, ed. C Bouchard, FE Johnson, pp. 175–92. New York: Liss

10. Bogardus C, Lillioja S. 1992. Pima Indians as a model to study the genetics of NIDDM. *J. Cell. Biochem.* 48:337–43
11. Bogardus C, Lillioja S, Nyomba BL, Zurlo F, Swinburn B, et al. 1989. Distribution of in vivo insulin action in Pima Indians as mixture of three normal distributions. *Diabetes* 38:1423–32
12. Bouchard C. 1993. Genes and body fat. *Am. J. Hum. Biol.* 5:425–32
13. Brand JC, Snow BJ, Nabhan GP, Truswell AS. 1990. Plasma glucose and insulin responses to traditional Pima Indian meals. *Am. J. Clin. Nutr.* 51:416–20
14. Brassard P, Robinson E, Lavallee C. 1992. Prevalence of diabetes mellitus among the James Bay Cree of northern Quebec, Canada. *Can. Med. Assoc. J.* 149:303–7
15. Bratush-Marrain PR. 1983. Insulin-counteracting hormones: their impact on glucose metabolism. *Diabetologia* 24:74–79
16. Brosseau JD. 1993. Diabetes and Indians: a clinician's perspective. See Ref. 58a, pp. 41–67
17. Broussard BA, Johnson A, Himas JH, Story M, Fichtner R, et al. 1991. Prevalence of obesity in American Indians and Alaska Natives. *Am. J. Clin. Nutr.* 53:1535–42
18. Bruce DG, Chisholm DJ, Storlien LH, Kraeger EW, Smythe GA. 1992. The effects of sympathetic nervous system activation and psychological stress on glucose metabolism and blood pressure in subjects with Type 2 (non-insulin-dependent) diabetes mellitus. *Diabetologia* 35:835–43
18a. Buse JB, Yasuda K, Lay TP, Seo TS, Olson AL, et al. 1992. Human GLUT4/muscle-fat glucose-transporter gene. *Diabetes* 41:1436–45

19. Carter Center of Emory University. 1985. Closing the gap: the problem of diabetes mellitus in the United States. *Diabet. Care* 8:391–406
20. Carter WR, Gonder-Frederick LA, Cox DJ, Clarke WL, Scott D. 1985. Effect of stress on blood glucose in IDDM. *Diabet. Care* 8:411–12
21. Chakraborty R, Szathmáry EJE, eds. 1985. *Diseases of Complex Etiology in Small Populations: Ethnic differences and Research Approaches.* New York: Liss
22. Colditz GA, Manson JAE, Stampfer MJ, Rosner B, Willett WC, et al. 1992. Diet and risk of clinical diabetes in women. *Am. J. Clin. Nutr.* 55:1018–23
23. Cole SA, Szathmáry EJE, Ferrell RE. 1989. Gene and gene product variation in the apolipoprotein A-I/C-III/A-IV cluster in the Dogrib Indians of the Northwest Territories. *Am. J. Hum. Genet.* 44:835–43
24. Consoli A. 1992. Role of liver in pathophysiology of NIDDM. *Diabet. Care* 15: 430–41
25. Consoli A, Nurjhan N, Capani F, Gerich J. 1989. Predominant role of gluconeogenesis in increased hepatic glucose production in NIDDM. *Diabetes* 38:550–57
26. Cook JTE, Page RCL, O'Rahilly S, Levy J, Holman R, et al. 1993. Availability of Type II diabetic families for detection of diabetes susceptibility genes. *Diabetes* 42: 1536–43
27. DeFronzo RA. 1992. Pathogenesis of Type 2 (non-insulin dependent) diabetes mellitus: a balanced overview. *Diabetologia* 35: 389–97
28. Doeblin TD, Evans K, Ingall GB, Dowling K, Chilcote ME, et al. 1969. Diabetes and hyperglycemia in Seneca Indians. *Hum. Hered.* 19:613–27
29. Draper HH. 1978. Nutrition studies: the aboriginal Eskimo diet—a modern perspective. In *Eskimos of Northwestern Alaska,* ed. PL Jamison, SL Zegura, FA Milan, pp. 139–44. Stroudsburg, PA: Dowden, Hutchinson & Ross
30. Elbein SC, Corsetti L, Ullrich A, Permutt MA. 1986. Multiple restriction length polymorphisms at the insulin receptor locus: a highly informative marker for linkage analysis. *Proc. Natl. Acad. Sci. USA* 83: 5223–27
31. Elbein SC, Hoffman MD, Matsutani A, Permutt MA. 1992. Linkage analysis of GLUT1 (HepG2) and GLUT2 (liver/islet) genes in familial NIDDM. *Diabetes* 41: 1660–67
32. Elbein SC, Sorensen LK, Taylor M. 1992. Linkage analysis of insulin-receptor gene in familial NIDDM. *Diabetes* 41:648–56
33. Elston RC, Namboodiri KK, Nino HV, Pollitzer WS. 1974. Studies on blood and urine glucose in Seminole Indians: implications for segregation of a major gene. *Am. J. Hum. Genet.* 26:13–34
34. Eriksson J, Koranyi L, Bourey R, Schalin-Jantti C, Widen E, et al. 1992. Insulin resistance in Type 2 (non-insulin-dependent) diabetic patients and their relatives is not associated with a defect in the expression of the insulin-responsive glucose transporter (GLUT-4) gene in human skeletal muscle. *Diabetologia* 35:143–47
35. Everhart JE, Pettitt DJ, Bennett PH, Knowler WC. 1992. Duration of obesity increases the incidence of NIDDM. *Diabetes* 41:235–40
36. Feldman SA, Ho K, Lewis LA, Middelson B, Taylor CB. 1972. Lipid and cholesterol metabolism in Alaskan arctic Eskimos. *Arch. Pathol.* 94:42–58
37. Ferrell RE, Iyengar S. 1993. Molecular studies of the genetics of non-insulin-dependent diabetes mellitus. *Am. J. Hum. Biol.* 5:415–24
38. Fontvieille AM, Lillioja S, Ferraro RT, Schulz LO, Rising R, et al. 1992. Twenty-four-hour energy expenditure in Pima Indians with Type 2 (non-insulin-dependent) diabetes mellitus. *Diabetologia* 35: 753–59
39. Freeman WL, Hosey GM, Diehr P, Gohdes D. 1989. Diabetes in American Indians of Washington, Oregon, and Idaho. *Diabet. Care* 12:282–88
40. Friedman JM, Fialkow PJ. 1980. The genetics of diabetes mellitus. *Prog. Med. Genet.* 4:199–232
41. Galton DJ. 1989. DNA polymorphisms of the human insulin and receptor genes in Type 2 diabetes mellitus. *Diabet. Metab. Rev.* 5:443–53
42. Garvey WT, Huecksteadt TPO, Birnbaum MJ. 1989. Pretranslational suppression of an insulin-responsive glucose transporter in rats with diabetes mellitus. *Science* 245: 60–63
43. Gedik O, Akalin S. 1986. Effects of vitamin D deficiency and repletion on insulin and glucagon secretion in man. *Diabetologia* 29:142–45
44. Gohdes DM. 1986. Diabetes in American Indians: a growing problem. *Diabet. Care* 609–13
45. Granner DK, O'Brien RM. 1992. Molecular physiology and genetics of NIDDM. *Diabet. Care* 15:369–95
46. Guyton AC. 1971. *Basic Human Physiology: Normal Function and Mechanisms of Disease.* New York: Saunders
47. Haffner SM, Mitchell BD, Hazuda HP, Stern MP. 1991. Greater influence of central distribution of adipose tissue on incidence of non-insulin dependent diabetes in women than in men. *Am. J. Clin. Nutr.* 53:1312–17
48. Haffner SM, Stern MP, Hazuda HP,

Mitchell BD, Patterson JK. 1988. Increased insulin concentrations in nondiabetic off-spring of diabetic parents. *New Engl. J. Med.* 319:1297–301

49. Haffner SM, Stern MP, Hazuda HP, Pugh JA, Patterson JK. 1986. Hyperinsulinemia in a population at high risk for non-insulin dependent diabetes mellitus. *New Engl. J. Med.* 315:220–24

50. Hales CN, Barker DJP. 1992. Type 2 (non-insulin-dependent) diabetes mellitus: the thrifty phenotype hypothesis. *Diabetologia* 35:595–601

51. Hall SE, Wastney ME, Bolton TM, Braaten JT, Berman M. 1984. Ketone body kinetics in humans: the effects of insulin-dependent diabetes, obesity and starvation. *J. Lipid Res.* 25:1184–94

52. Hall TR, Hickey ME, Young TB. 1991. The relationship of body fat distribution to non-insulin-dependent diabetes mellitus in a Navajo community. *Am. J. Hum. Biol.* 3:119–26

53. Hall TR, Hickey ME, Young TB. 1992. Evidence for recent increases in obesity and non-insulin-dependent diabetes mellitus in a Navajo community. *Am. J. Hum. Biol.* 4:547–53

54. Heath GW, Wilson RH, Smith J, Leonard BE. 1991. Community-based exercise and weight control: diabetes risk reduction and glycemic control in Zuni Indians. *Am. J. Clin. Nutr.* 53:1642S-46S

55. Hochachka PW, Somero GN. 1984. *Biochemical Adaptation.* Princeton, NJ: Princeton Univ. Press

56. Howard BV, Bogardus C, Ravussin E, Foley JE, Lillioja S, et al. 1991. Studies on the etiology of obesity in Pima Indians. *Am. J. Clin. Nutr.* 53:1577S-85S

57. Jackson MY. 1993. Diet, culture and diabetes. See Ref. 58a, pp. 381–407

58. Jackson MY, Proulx JM, Pelican S. 1991. Obesity prevention. *Am. J. Clin. Nutr.* 53:1625S-30S

58a. Joe JR, Young RS, eds. 1993. *Diabetes as a Disease of Civilization.* Berlin: Mouton de Gruyter

59. Joe JR, Young RS. 1993. Introduction. See Ref. 58a, pp. 1–18

60. Justice JW. 1993. The history of diabetes in the Desert People. See Ref. 58a, pp. 69–128

61. Kashiwagi A, Mott D, Bogardus C, Lillioja S, Reaven GM, et al. 1985. The effects of short-term overfeeding on adipocyte metabolism in Pima Indians. *Metabolism* 34:364–70

62. Kida Y, Esposito-Del Puente A, Bogardus C, Mott DM. 1990. Insulin resistance is associated with reduced fasting and insulin-stimulated glycogen synthase phosphatase activity in human skeletal muscle. *J. Clin. Invest.* 85:476–81

63. Kissebah AH, Vydelingum N, Murray R,

Evans DJ, Hartz AJ, et al. 1982. Relation of body fat distribution to the metabolic complications of obesity. *J. Clin. Endocrinol. Metab.* 54:254–60

64. Knowler WC, Pettitt DJ, Bennett PH, Williams RC. 1983. Diabetes mellitus in the Pima Indians: genetic and evolutionary considerations. *Am. J. Phys. Anthropol.* 62:107–14

65. Knowler WC, Pettitt DJ, Bennett PH, Williams RC. 1990. Diabetes mellitus in the Pima Indians: incidence, risk factors and pathogenesis. *Diabet. Metab. Rev.* 6:1–27

66. Knowler WC, Pettitt DJ, Saad MF, Charles MA, Nelson RG, et al. 1991. Obesity in the Pima Indians: its magnitude and relationship with diabetes. *Am. J. Clin. Nutr.* 53:1543S-51S

67. Knowler WC, Pettitt DJ, Vasquez B, Rotwein PS, Andreone T, et al. 1984. Polymorphism in the 5' flanking region of the insulin gene. *J. Clin. Invest.* 74:2129–35

68. Koivisto VA, Yki-Jarvinen H, DeFronzo RA. 1986. Physical training and insulin sensitivity. *Diabet. Metab. Rev.* 1:445–81

69. Kraus-Friedmann N. 1984. Hormonal regulation of hepatic gluconeogenesis. *Physiol. Rev.* 64:170–259

70. Kriska AM, LaPorte RE, Pettitt DJ, Charles MA, Nelson RG, et al. 1993. The association of physical activity with obesity, fat distribution and glucose intolerance in Pima Indians. *Diabetologia* 36:863–69

71. Lee ET, Anderson PS Jr, Bryan J, Bahr C, Coniglione T, et al. 1985. Diabetes, parental diabetes, and obesity in Oklahoma Indians. *Diabet. Care* 8:107–13

72. Lee ET, Lee VS, Lu M, Russell D. 1992. Development of proliferative retinopathy in NIDDM. A follow-up of American Indians in Oklahoma. *Diabetes* 41:359–67

73. Lee ET, Welty TK, Fabsitz R, Cowan LD, Le N-A, et al. 1990. The strong heart study. A study of cardiovascular disease in American Indians: design and methods. *Am. J. Epidemiol.* 132:1141–55

74. Lee JS, Lu M, Lee VS, Russell D, Bahr C, Lee ET. 1993. Lower-extremity amputation. Incidence, risk factors and mortality in the Oklahoma Indian diabetes study. *Diabetes* 42:876–82

75. Lemieux S, Prud'Homme D, Bouchard C, Tremblay A, Despres JP. 1993. Sex differences in the relation of visceral adipose tissue accumulation to total body fatness. *Am. J. Clin. Nutr.* 58:463–67

76. Li SR, Oelbaum RS, Baroni MG, Stock J, Galton DJ. 1988. Association of genetic variant of the glucose transporter with non-insulin-dependent diabetes mellitus. *Lancet* 2:368–70

77. Lillioja S, Bogardus C. 1988. Obesity and

insulin resistance: lessons learned from the Pima Indians. *Diabet. Metab. Rev.* 4:517–40

78. Lillioja S, Bogardus C. 1988. Insulin resistance in Pima Indians. *Acta Med. Scand. Suppl.* 723:103–19

79. Lillioja S, Bogardus C, Mott DM, Kennedy AL, Knowler WC, et al. 1985. Relationship between insulin-mediated glucose disposal and lipid metabolism in man. *J. Clin. Invest.* 75:1106–15

80. Lillioja S, Mott DM, Howard BV, Bennett PH, Yki-Jarvinen H, et al. 1988. Impaired glucose tolerance as a disorder of insulin action: longitudinal and cross-sectional studies in Pima Indians. *New Engl. J. Med.* 318:1217–25

81. Lillioja S, Mott DM, Zawadzki JK, Young AA, Abbott WGH, et al. 1987. In vivo insulin action is a familial characteristic in nondiabetic Pima Indians. *Diabetes* 36:1329–35

82. Maeda R, Raz I, Zurlo F, Sommercorn J. 1991. Activation of skeletal muscle casein kinase II by insulin is not diminished in subjects with insulin resistance. *J. Clin. Invest.* 87:1017–22

83. Mandarino LJ. 1989. Regulation of skeletal muscle pyruvate dehydrogenase and glycogen synthase in man. *Diabet. Metab. Rev.* 5:475–86

84. Martin FIR, Griew AR, Haurahelia M, Higginbotham L, Wyatt GB. 1980. Diabetes mellitus in urban and rural communities in Papua New Guinea. Studies of prevalence and plasma insulin. *Diabetologia* 18:369–74

85. Mayer EJ, Alderman BW, Regensteiner JG, Marshall JA, Haskell WL, et al. 1991. Physical-activity-assessment measures compared in a biethnic rural populations: the San Luis Valley Diabetes Study. *Am. J. Clin. Nutr.* 53:812–20

86. McClain DA, Henry RR, Ullrich A, Olefsky JM. 1988. Restriction-fragment-length polymorphism in insulin-receptor gene and insulin resistance in NIDDM. *Diabetes* 37:1071–75

87. McGarvey ST. 1991. Obesity in Samoans and a perspective on its etiology in Polynesians. *Am. J. Clin. Nutr.* 53:1586S-94S

88. McGinnis JM, Ballard-Barbash RM. 1991. Obesity in minority populations: policy implications of research. *Am. J. Clin. Nutr.* 53:1512S-4S

89. Miller M, Bennett PH, Burch TA. 1968. Hyperglycemia in Pima Indians: a preliminary appraisal of its significance. In *Biomedical Challenges Presented by the American Indian,* PAHO Sci. Publ. No. 165, pp. 89–104. Washington, DC: World Health Org.

90. Moller DE, Yokota A, Flier JS. 1989. Normal insulin-receptor cDNA sequence in Pima Indians with NIDDM. *Diabetes* 38:1496–500

91. Murphy NJ, Schraer CD, Bulkow LR, Boyko EJ, Lanier AP. 1992. Diabetes mellitus in Alaskan Yup'ik Eskimos and Athabascan Indians after 25 yr. *Diabet. Care* 15:1390–91

92. Nagai K, Nakagawa H. 1973. Cold adaptation. III. Effects of catecholamines and thyroid hormone on induction of liver phosphoenolpyruvate carboxykinase on cold-exposure. *J. Biochem.* 74:873–79

93. National Diabetes Data Group. 1979. Classification and diagnosis of diabetes mellitus and other categories of glucose intolerance. *Diabetes* 28:1039–57

94. Neel JV. 1962. Diabetes mellitus: a "thrifty" genotype rendered detrimental by progress? *Am. J. Hum. Genet.* 14:353–62

95. Neel JV. 1982. The thrifty genotype revisited. In *The Genetics of Diabetes Mellitus,* ed. J Kobberling, R Tattersall, pp. 283–93. New York: Academic

96. Nelson RG, Sievers ML, Knowler WC, Swinburn BA, Pettitt DJ, et al. 1990. Low incidence of fatal coronary heart disease in Pima Indians despite high prevalence on non-insulin-dependent diabetes. *Circulation* 81:987–95

97. Nelson RG, Wolfe JA, Horton MB, Pettit DJ, Bennett PH, Knowler WC. 1989. Proliferative retinopathy in NIDDM: incidence and risk factors in Pima Indians. *Diabetes* 38:435–40

98. Niswander J. 1968. Discussion. In *Biomedical Challenges Presented by the American Indian,* PAHO Sci. Publ. No. 165, pp. 133–36. Washington, DC: World Health Org.

99. Nobman ED, Byers T, Lanier AP, Hankin JH, Jackson MY. 1992. The diet of Alaska Native adults: 1987–1988. *Am. J. Clin. Nutr.* 55:1024–32

100. Nyomba BL, Auwerx J, Bormans V, Peeters TL, Petelmans W, et al. 1986. Pancreatic secretion in man with subclinical vitamin D deficiency. *Diabetologia* 29:34–38

101. Odawara M, Kadowaki T, Yamamoto R, Shibasaki Y, Tobe K, et al. 1989. Human diabetes associated with a mutation in tyrosine kinase domain of the insulin receptor. *Science* 245:66–68

102. O'Dea K. 1991. Westernization, insulin resistance and diabetes in Australian Aborigines. *Med. J. Aust.* 155:258–64

103. O'Dea K, Patel M, Kubisch D, Hopper J, Traianedes K. 1993. Obesity, diabetes and hyperlipidemia in a central Australian aboriginal community with a long history of acculturation. *Diabet. Care* 16:1004–10

104. Olefsky JM. 1990. Perspectives in diabetes. The insulin receptor: a multifunctional protein. *Diabetes* 39:1009–15

105. Pedersen O. 1989. The impact of obesity on the pathogenesis of non-insulin-dependent diabetes mellitus: a review of current hypotheses. *Diabet. Metab. Rev.* 5:495–509

106. Pouliot MC, Despres JP, Nadeau A, Moorjani S, Prud'Homme D, et al. 1992. Visceral obesity in men. *Diabetes* 41:826–34

107. Prochazka M, Lillioja S, Knowler WC, Tait J, Bogardus C. 1992. Confirmation of genetic linkage between markers on chromosome 4q and a gene for insulin resistance in obese Pima Indians. *Diabetes* 41(Suppl. 1):94a

108. Raboudi SH, Mitchell BD, Stren MP, Eifler CW, Haffner SM, et al. 1989. Type II diabetes mellitus and polymorphism of insulin-receptor gene in Mexican Americans. *Diabetes* 38:975–80

109. Randle PJ, Garland PB, Hales CN, Newsholme EA. 1963. The glucose fatty-acid cycle. Its role in insulin sensitivity and the metabolic disturbances of diabetes mellitus. *Lancet* 1:785–89

110. Reaven GM. 1993. Role of insulin resistance in the pathophysiology of non-insulin dependent diabetes mellitus. *Diabet. Metab. Rev.* 9(Suppl. 1):5S-12S

111. Reid JM, Fullmer SD, Pettigrew KD, Burch TA, Bennett PH, et al. 1971. Nutrient intake of Pima Indian women: relationships to diabetes mellitus and gallbladder disease. *Am. J. Clin. Nutr.* 4:1281–89

112. Rich SS. 1990. Mapping genes in diabetes. *Diabetes* 39:1315–19

113. Rimoin DL. 1969. Ethnic variability in glucose tolerance and insulin secretion. *Arch. Int. Med.* 124:695–700

114. Ritenbaugh C. 1982. Obesity as a culture-bound syndrome. *Cult. Med. Psychiatry* 6:347–61

115. Ritenbaugh C, Goodby C-S. 1989. Beyond the thrifty gene: metabolic implications of prehistoric migrations into the New World. *Med. Anthropol.* 11:227–37

116. Rotwein P, Chyn R, Chirgwin J, Cordell B, Goodman HM, et al. 1981. Polymorphism in the 5'-flanking region of the human insulin gene and its possible relation to type 2 diabetes. *Science* 213:1117–20

117. Saiki JH, Rimoin DL. 1968. Diabetes mellitus among the Navajo. I. Clinical features. *Arch. Int. Med.* 122:1–5

118. Scheder J. 1988. A sickly-sweet harvest: farmworker diabetes and social equality. *Med. Anthropol. Q.* 2:251–77

119. Schraer CD. 1993. Diabetes among the Alaska Natives—the emergence of a chronic disease with changing life-styles. See Ref. 58a, pp. 169–95

120. Schraer CD, Lanier AP, Boyko EJ, Gohdes D, Murphy NJ. 1988. Prevalence of diabetes mellitus in Alaskan Eskimos, Indians and Aleuts. *Diabet. Care* 11:693–700

121. Schumacher MC, Hasstedt SJ, Hunt SC, Williams RR, Elbein SC. 1992. Major gene effect for insulin levels in familial NIDDM pedigrees. *Diabetes* 41:416–23

122. Shepherd PR, Gibbs EM, Wesslau C, Gould GW, Kahn B. 1992. Human small intestine fructose/glucose transporter (GLUT5) is also present in insulin-responsive tissues and brain. *Diabetes* 41:1360–65

123. Shively C, Kaplan J. 1984. Effects of social factors on adrenal weight and related physiology of *Macaca fascicularis*. *Physiol. Behav.* 33:777–82

124. Sievers ML, Fisher JR. 1985. Diabetes in North American Indians. In *Diabetes in America,* ed. MI Harris, RF Hamman, 11:1–20. Bethesda, MD: DHHS, NIH

125. Sipperstein MD. 1975. The glucose tolerance test: a pitfall in the diagnosis of diabetes mellitus. *Ann. Int. Med.* 20:297–323

126. Smith CJ, Manahan EM, Pablo SG. 1993. Food habit and cultural changes among the Pima Indians. See Ref. 58a, pp. 407–34

127. Sobal J. 1991. Obesity and socioeconomic status: a framework for examining relationships between physical and social variables. *Med. Anthropol.* 13:231–47

128. Steinberg AG, Rushforth NB, Bennett PH, Burch TA, Miller M. 1970. On the genetics of diabetes mellitus. In *The Pathogenesis of Diabetes Mellitus,* ed. E Cerasi, R Luft, pp. 237–60. New York: Wiley

129. Stern MP, Gonzalez C, Mitchell BD, Villalpando E, Haffner SM, et al. 1992. Genetic and environmental determinants of type II diabetes in Mexico City and San Antonio. *Diabetes* 41:484–92

130. Stern MP, Valdez RA, Haffner SM, Mitchell BD, Hazuda HP. 1993. Stability over time of modern diagnostic criteria for Type II diabetes. *Diabet. Care* 16:978–83

131. Sugarman J, Percy C. 1989. Prevalence of diabetes in a Navajo Indian community. *Am. J. Public Health* 79:511–13

132. Sugarman JR, White LL, Gilbert TJ. 1990. Evidence for a secular change in obesity, height and weight among Navajo Indian schoolchildren. *Am. J. Clin. Nutr.* 52:960–66

133. Surwit RS, Feinglos MN. 1988. Stress and the autonomic nervous system in Type II diabetes. *Diabet. Care* 11:83–85

134. Szathmáry EJE. 1985. Search for genetic factors controlling plasma glucose levels in Dogrib Indians. In *Diseases of Complex Etiology in Small Populations,* ed. R Chakraborty, EJE Szathmáry, pp. 199–226. New York: Liss

135. Szathmáry EJE. 1986. Diabetes in arctic and subarctic populations undergoing acculturation. *Coll. Anthropol.* 10:145–48

136. Szathmáry EJE. 1987. Genetic and environmental risk factors. See Ref. 168, pp. 27–66

137. Szathmáry EJE. 1987. The effect of Gc genotype on fasting insulin level in Dogrib Indians. *Hum. Genet.* 75:368–72
138. Szathmáry EJE. 1989. The impact of low carbohydrate consumption on glucose tolerance, insulin concentration and insulin response to glucose challenge in Dogrib Indians. *Med. Anthropol.* 11:329–50
139. Szathmáry EJE. 1990. Diabetes in Amerindian populations: the Dogrib studies. In *Disease in Populations in Transition,* ed. AC Swedlund, GJ Armelagos, pp. 75–103. South Hadley, MA: Bergin & Garvey
140. Szathmáry EJE. 1993. Application of our understanding of genetic variation in Native North America. In *Individual, Family and Population Variability,* ed. CF Sing, CL Hanis, pp. 213–38. New York: Oxford Univ. Press
141. Szathmáry EJE. 1993. Factors that influence the onset of diabetes in Dogrib Indians of the Canadian Northwest Territories. See Ref. 58a, pp. 229–68
142. Szathmáry EJE. 1993. Invited editorial. *Am. J. Hum. Genet.* 53:793–99
143. Szathmáry EJE, Ferrell RE. 1990. Glucose level, acculturation and glycosylated hemoglobin: an example of biocultural interaction. *Med. Anthropol. Q.* 4:315–41
144. Szathmáry EJE, Holt N. 1983. Hyperglycemia in Dogrib Indians of the Northwest Territories, Canada: association with age and a centripetal distribution of body fat. *Hum. Biol.* 55:493–515
145. Szathmáry EJE, Ritenbaugh C, Goodby C-S. 1989. Dietary change and plasma glucose levels in an Amerindian population undergoing cultural transition. *Soc. Sci. Med.* 24:791–804
146. Taira M, Taira M, Hashimoto N, Shimada F, Suzuki Y, et al. 1989. Human diabetes associated with a deletion of the tyrosine kinase domain of the insulin receptor. *Science* 245:63–66
147. Taylor R, Ram P, Zimmer P, Raper LR, Ringrose H. 1984. Physical activity and prevalence of diabetes in Melanesian and Indian men in Fiji. *Diabetologia* 27:578–82
148. Tepperman J. 1980. *Metabolic and Endocrine Physiology.* Chicago: Year Book Medical. 4th ed.
149. Thouez JP, Ekoe JM, Foggin P, Verdy M, Nadeau M, et al. 1990. Obesity, hypertension, hyperuricemia and diabetes mellitus among the Cree and Inuit of northern Quebec. *Arct. Med. Res.* 49:180–88
150. Trout DL, Behall KM, Osilesi O. 1993. Prediction of glycemic index for starchy foods. *Am. J. Clin. Nutr.* 58:973–78
151. Urdaneta ML, Krehbiel R. 1989. Introduction. Anthropological perspectives on diabetes mellitus type II. *Med. Anthropol.* 11:221–27
151a.Vague J, Combes R, Tramoni M, Angeletti S, Rubin P, et al. 1979. Clinical features of diabetogenic obesity. In *Diabetes and Obesity,* ed. J Vague, PH Vague, FJG Ebling, pp. 127–47. Amsterdam: Excerpta Medica
152. Vanninen E, Uusitupa M, Siitonen O, Laitinen J, Jansimies E. 1992. Habitual physical activity, aerobic capacity and metabolic control in patients with newly diagnosed Type 2 (non-insulin dependent) diabetes mellitus: effect of 1-year diet and exercise intervention. *Diabetologia* 35:340–46
153. Vogt B, Mullbacker C, Carrascosa J, Obermaier-Kusser B, Seffer E, et al. 1991. Subcellular distribution of GLUT4 in the skeletal muscle of lean Type 2 (non-insulin dependent) diabetic patients in the basal state. *Diabetologia* 35:456–63
154. Weiss KM, Ferrell RE, Hanis CL. 1984. A New World syndrome of metabolic diseases with a genetic and evolutionary basis. *Yearb. Phys. Anthropol.* 27:153–78
155. Weiss KM, Ulbrecht JS, Cavanagh PR, Buchanan AV. 1989. Diabetes mellitus in American Indians: characteristics, origins and preventive health care implications. *Med. Anthropol.* 11:283–304
156. Wendorf M, Goldfine ID. 1991. Archaeology of NIDDM. *Diabetes* 40:161–65
157. West KM. 1974. Diabetes in American Indians and other native populations of the New World. *Diabetes* 23:841–55
158. West KM. 1978. Diabetes in American Indians. *Adv. Metab. Disord.* 9:29–48
159. West KM. 1978. *Epidemiology of Diabetes and its Vascular Lesions.* New York: Elsevier
160. West KM, Kalbfeisch JM. 1971. Sensitivity and specificity of five screening tests for diabetes in ten countries. *Diabetes* 20:289–96
161. Wetterhall SH, Olson DR, DiStefano F, Steenson JM, Ford ES, et al. 1992. Trends in diabetes and diabetic complications, 1980–1987. *Diabet. Care* 15:960–67
162. Wideman DW. 1989. Adiposity or longevity: Which factor accounts for the increase in Type II diabetes mellitus when populations acculturate to an industrial technology? *Med. Anthropol.* 11:237–54
163. Wingard DL, Barrett-Connor EL, Scheidt-Have C, McPhillips JB. 1993. Prevalence of cardiovascular and renal complications in older adults with normal or impaired glucose tolerance of NIDDM. *Diabet. Care* 16:1022–25
164. World Health Organization. 1980. *WHO Expert Committee on Diabetes Mellitus. Second Report.* Tech. Rep. Ser. 646. Geneva: WHO
165. World Health Organization. 1985. *Diabetes Mellitus. Report of a WHO Study Group.* Tech. Rep. Ser. 727. Geneva: WHO
166. Xiang K-S, Cox NJ, Sanz N, Huang P,

Karam JH, et al. 1989. Insulin-receptor and apolipoprotein genes contribute to development of NIDDM in Chinese Americans. *Diabetes* 38:17–23

167. Yamashita T, Mackay W, Rushforth NB, Bennett P, Houser H. 1984. Pedigree analyses of non-insulin dependent diabetes mellitus (NIDDM) in the Pima Indians suggest autosomal dominant mode of inheritance. *Am. J. Hum. Genet.* 36:183S

168. Young TK, ed. 1987. *Diabetes in the Canadian Native Population: Biocultural Perspectives.* Toronto: Canadian Diabetes Assoc.

169. Young TK. 1993. Diabetes among Canadian Indians and Inuit: an epidemiological overview. See Ref. 58a, pp. 21–40

170. Young TK. 1993. Diabetes mellitus among Native Americans in Canada and the United States: an epidemiological overview. *Am. J. Hum. Biol.* 5:399–414

171. Young TK, Szathmáry EJE, Evers S, Wheatley B. 1990. Geographic distribution of diabetes among the native population of Canada: a national survey. *Soc. Sci. Med.* 31:129–39

172. Zimmet P. 1982. Type 2 (non-insulin-dependent) diabetes—an epidemiological overview. *Diabetologia* 22:399–411

173. Zimmet P, Dowse G, Finch C, Sargentson S, King H. 1990. The epidemiology and natural history of NIDDM—lessons from the South Pacific. *Diabet. Metab. Rev.* 6:91–124

174. Zurlo F, Bogardus C, Freymond D, Lillioja S, Boyce V, et al. 1988. Daily formation of energy substrate oxidation (respiratory quotient) in man: a familial trait independent of the degree of obesity. *Lipid Res.* 36:360A

Annu. Rev. Anthropol. 1994. 23:483–508

ALTERNATIVE INTERPRETATIONS OF THE LATE UPPER PALEOLITHIC IN CENTRAL EUROPE

Anta Montet-White

Department of Anthropology, University of Kansas, Lawrence, Kansas 66045

KEY WORDS: Gravettian, Epigravettian, Last Glacial Maximum

INTRODUCTION

The sector of Central Europe considered in this review extends from southern Poland to the Balkans and encompasses the Carpathian Basin, the Middle Danube, and its tributaries (Figure 1). The region corresponds in size to the Atlantic provinces from the Loire to the Pyrenees. It is vast enough to permit the discussion of faunal distribution and hunting strategies, as well as territoriality, population shift, and settlement organization (4, 8, 27, 28, 36). The Upper Paleolithic history of this sector of Central Europe derived originally from a few classic sites. Willendorf, for its long stratigraphic sequence broadly comparable to that of Pataud, and Dolni Vestonice, Predmosti, and Pavlov, for the abundance and variety of the materials they contained, dominated research in the region much as the rock shelters of Les Eyzies did in Western Europe. The series of meetings held since 1976 helped promote a change of perspective and contributed to the development of regional and interregional studies (44, 45, 53, 55). The broader approach has shown the pitfalls of interpretations based on classic sites and, as research continues to expand in neighboring areas, the Gravettian of the Pavlov hills no longer appears as the only significant cultural manifestation in the region between 28,000 and 20,000 B.P. (26, 44). It is better understood as a chapter, albeit an important one, in the complex and long

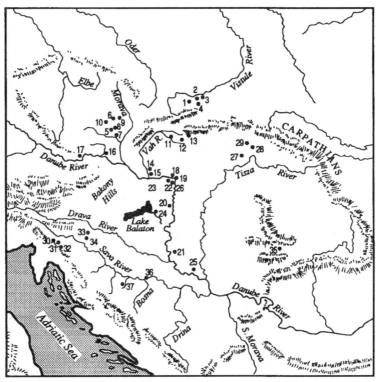

1. Mamutova	13. Kasov	25. Szeged
2. Spadzista	14. Moravany	26. Zebegeny
3. Wojcice	15. Nitra	27. Arka
4. Wolowice	16. Grubraben	28. Bodrogkerestur
5. D. Vestonice	17. Willendorf	29. Hidasnemeti
6. Kulna	18. Dios	30. Luplanska
7. Milovice	19. Domos	31. Ovca Jama
8. Pavlov	20. Dunafoldavar	32. Zupanov Spodmol
9. Pod Hradem	21. Madaras	33. Veternica
10. Stranska Skala	22. Pilismarot	34. Vindjia
11. Vedrovice	23. Pilisszanto	35. Temnata
12. Cejkov	24. Sagvar	36. Kadar
		37. Zobiste

Figure 1 Map of Central Europe showing the location of major sites discussed in the text: 1. Mamutova, 2. Spadzista, 3. Wojcice, and 4. Wolowice, north of the Carpathian mountains; 5. Dolni Vestonice and 8. Pavlov, near the Pavlov hills; 18. Dios, 19. Domos, 22. Pilismarot, and 26. Zebegeny, at the Danube bend; 27. Arka, 28. Bodrogkerestur, and 29. Hidasnemeti, south of the Carpathian mountains; 33. Veternica and 34. Vindjia, in the Croatian Karst; and 30. Luplanska, 31. Ovca Jama, and 32. Zupanov Spodmol, in the Slovenian Karst.

history of hunter-gatherer settlements of Central Europe at the end of the Pleistocene. And, in a somewhat similar way, the extension of research in adjacent provinces helps place Les Eyzies rock shelters in a broader perspective (49).

The processes of adaptation and change undergone by human populations between 28,000 and 15,000 years ago have been the focus of discussions (55) and field research (45) in recent years. New understandings of the nature and impact of the climatic changes of this period have emerged. The Last Glacial Maximum is understood to have had profound effects on animal populations, which in turn forced the displacement of human settlements. Moreover, recent finds (13, 14, 35, 40, 57) have challenged the commonly accepted view that the glacial advance forced human populations out of north Central Europe into more favorable niches (e.g. the Perigord and Cantabria to the west, the Russian uplands to the east). This review focuses on a complex situation marked by a series of climatic ameliorations during which animal and other natural resources were sufficient to support human groups in different sections of the Central European Basin. The economic base went from the opportunistic foraging of a diverse local fauna (26) to more specialized forms of horse and reindeer herd exploitation (32). The processes of adaptation and change these Central European groups underwent are in many ways comparable to the ones that took place in Western Europe. The similarities in economy and technology would be even more apparent if it were not for the resurgence of bifacial technology that produced the large leaf-shaped points characteristic of the Solutrean in the Franco-Cantabrian region. The relatively short-lived development (21,000–19,000 B.P.) of large projectile points that may have been associated with a special type of spear has no equivalent in Central Europe. But, the Badgoulian, the cultural phase that follows the Solutrean at Laugerie Haute and other sites of central and southwestern France, is characterized by technological innovations (56, 60) that are comparable to those seen in the Epigravettian of Central Europe after 19,000 B.P. Population movements and especially east-west migrations have been viewed traditionally as the mechanism explaining cultural change and the spread of new technologies into Western Europe (26, 44, 46), whereas Central Europe is viewed alternatively as a reservoir of new inventions (46) or as a region periodically emptied of human populations (13). The latter view has been reinforced by numerous gaps that still impair the Paleolithic record. A review of the material suggests that at the time of Last Glacial Maximum (20,000–15,000 B.P.), human groups became increasingly mobile and shifted between valley systems while maintaining their hunting territories and raw material procurement networks.

THE ARCHAEOLOGICAL RECORD

Research Bias

In Central Europe, as anywhere else, sampling bias remains a major handicap of regional studies. Blanks on Paleolithic maps often reflect a lack of systematic research and/or publications that field programs of the 1980s and 1990s have begun to fill. Dobosi's survey (14) of loess covered areas between the Upper Tisza (sites 27 and 29 in Figure 1) and the Danube bend group (sites 18 and 19 in Figure 1) of northern Hungary, for example, brought the discovery of Epigravettian sites, which invalidates the view that extreme conditions would have made the area uninhabitable to human groups during the late Pleistocene and that, if there were sites, they would be too deeply buried to be found. But the area south of Lake Balaton and north of the Drava (Figure 1) remains an almost complete blank. The lack of information reinforces the view that the Carpathian Basin and the northern Balkans formed two distinct and unrelated cultural areas during the late Pleistocene and that east-west migrations were of greater importance than were north-south shifts. Sampling bias takes other, more insidious forms. Cave sites have been excavated at the exclusion of open-air sites in Slovenia and Croatia, whereas field work in northern Bosnia has focused on open-air hilltop sites. And known, classic sites continue to attract attention even when they are almost exhausted, while little attention is given to the testing of new sites.

Stratigraphic Hiatus

The attention of quaternary geologists has turned recently to questions relating to discontinuities in sedimentary sequences. The problems were clearly outlined by Campy (6), who identified several disconformities in the stratigraphic sequence at La Baume de Gigny, a cave in the French Jura, which he attributes to a series of erosional episodes. He generalizes that as much as 70% or 80% of cave deposits were destroyed by natural processes. The amplitude of erosional activities during the last stages of the Pleistocene varied from site to site and region to region. The longest hiatus is registered in the Slovenian caves where Epigravettian layers directly overlay Mousterian occupations (41–43). In the Croatian Karst caves, a probable gap separates layers containing early Aurignacian assemblages with Mladec points from the Gravettian and Epigravettian levels (33). This gap signals an erosional phase that corresponds to that described at Temnata (site 35 in Figure 1), a cave of the Karlukovo Karst in Bulgaria (29), where early Gravettian layers (dated between 28,000 and 29,000 B.P.) are separated, directly overlaid by a late Gravettian layer (dated between 23,000 and 21,000 B.P.), a gap of at least 5000 years. At the Kulna Cave in Moravia (61) the remnants of a Gravettian level are found underneath a Magdalenian level dated at 12,000 B.P. (a gap of some 10,000 years) and overlying a series of Mousterian layers (a gap of 15,000–20,000 years). The erosion phenomena that affected karstic caves from the Jura to the Carpathians and the Dinaric Alps are in sharp contrast to the relatively stable sedimentation processes of the Perigord rock shelters and some of the Cantabrian sites that provide an almost continuous record of human occupations. It should be noted, however, that at la Baume de Gigny, for example, the remnants of late Wurm deposits contain no traces of human occupation. Distinguishing between archaeologically sterile deposits and stratigraphic gaps has obvious implications for the interpretation and reconstruction of human settlements.

Episodes of soil formation and erosions affected the loam series that cover the bluff tops along the Sava River Valley. A major erosional phase preceded the deposition of Late Glacial sediments containing Epigravettian industries and, later, an early Holocene erosion destroyed the Late Glacial deposits at Kadar, Londza, and Zobiste (38). The best preserved record is found in the loess series of the northern part of the Basin (20, 21), where sedimentation processes were more regular. Multicomponent loess sites include several series of occupations within a 2000 to 3000 year period indicative of the repeated use of a locality over prolonged periods of times. Such is the case at Vestonice (24, 58), Spadzista (25, 30), and a number of other lesser known sites like Moravany and Nitra (2). The 10,000 year time span that the Willendorf sequence encompasses is an exception (17, 21). The record from open-air sites of Central Europe has some similarities to that of the Aquitaine Basin, where multicomponent sites like Solvieux are few (50).

Occupation layers at open-air sites are separated by sterile deposits. Therefore, in contrast to rock shelters like Laugerie Haute, where there is at least an appearance of continuity, each archaeological layer represents a moment of human presence that is not immediately related to earlier or later episodes of occupation. Such is the case at Willendorf, although the site provides the best single series of Aurignacian and Gravettian layers in Central Europe and is still used as a model for the reconstruction of cultural change in the region (46). In short, natural and man-made conditions contributed to the unbalanced perception of the Paleolithic settlement of the Central European Basin. As it is, the number of well documented sites remains low. Dobosi (13) deplores that there are about 50 sites within a 93,000 km^2 area to reconstruct some 30,000 years of Upper Paleolithic history in northern Hungary. The number is even lower in the southern section of the Basin. And in many areas, a record of the middle phases of the Upper Paleolithic is simply not there.

The C^{14} Evidence

Tables of available C^{14} dates illustrate trends in the distribution of human settlements within all sectors of Central Europe. Early Gravettian sites dated around 28,000 B.P. are distributed in clusters scattered along the periphery of the Central European Basin from the Moravian Plateau to Willendorf on the Danube (Figure 2) and in the Upper Tisza area of northern Hungary (Bodrogkerestur, Figure 3). Between 28,000 and 24,000 B.P. settlements concentrated in Moravia and the nearby stretch of the Danube Valley (Willendorf) but there is little evidence of occupation in other parts of Central Europe, especially in the southern sector, as a result of the major erosional phase noted above. Moravia continued to be occupied regularly until about 19,000 B.P. A 6000 year gap then separates the last Epigravettian occupation at Stranska

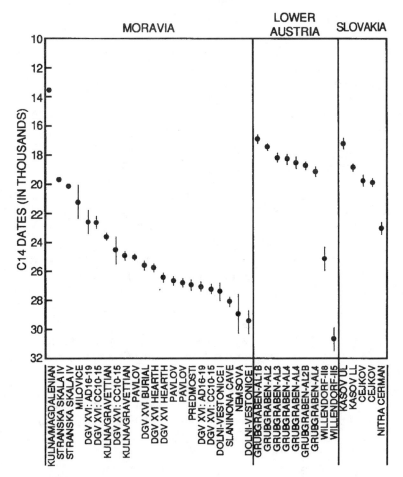

Figure 2   C[14]dates from groups of Moravian sites, where a gap occurred between occupation levels at Stranska Skala and Kulna, and sites from Austria and Slovakia, where there are a series of occupations between 20,000 and 16,000 B.P.

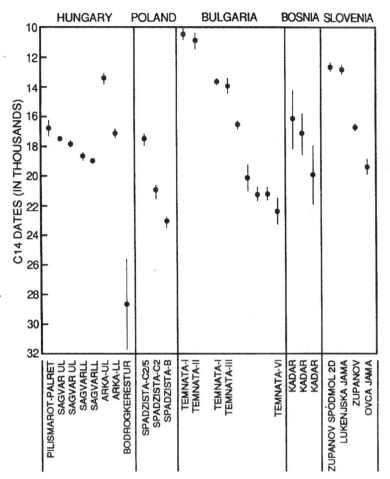

Figure 3 C[14] dates from other regions of Central Europe (Hungary, southern Poland, Bulgaria, Bosnia, and Slovenia) showing human occupations between 23,000 and 16,000 B.P., between 14,000 and 13,000 B.P., and between 11,000 and 10,000 B.P.

Skala from the Magdalenian at Kuhlna. But, a number of sites in Lower Austria, Slovakia, Hungary, Slovenia, and Bosnia fall within the 19,000– 16,000 B.P. time period. Epigravettian phases posterior to the major erosional phase are relatively well represented. However, when the region is taken as a whole, there is evidence of continued human presence before and during the Last Glacial Maximum between 28,000 and 15,000 B.P., with indications of shift in settlement location through time. Questions concerning the nature of these shifts, and their economic or cultural bases, generated a number of research programs in the region in the last ten years.

ENVIRONMENT AND NATURAL RESOURCES

According to Valoch (62), the climatic oscillations that preceded the Glacial Maximum between 33,000 and 25,000 B.P. were well represented at the Pod Hradem Cave and several open-air sites around Brno including Bohunice, Stranska Skala III, and Vedrovice II and V, where faunal remains include mostly horse and mammoth. Charcoal and pollen evidence indicate that a grass steppe with local clusters of fir dominated the landscape. However, the charred wood remains recovered from these sites exhibit narrow annual rings, which Valoch attributes to overall cold temperatures. A complex of paleosols (fossil soils) was identified at Spadzista layer 7 and at Stranska Skala III layer 3, where it is dated at about 32,000 B.P., and at Dolni Vestonice and Milovice (21, 40), where it is dated at 30,000 B.P.

Valoch estimates the beginning of the glacial advance at around 27,000 B.P. Its earliest phases are marked in central Moravia by a steppe vegetation that supported a broad range of animal populations. Pine and fir charcoal fragments and the remains of a relatively temperate, forest-steppe, faunal assemblage are associated with the Kulna Cave Gravettian (61). The level is interpreted as representing a mild oscillation between 23,000 and 22,000 B.P. A paleosol evidenced at Spadzista corresponds to the main phase of occupation at the site dated around 23,000 B.P. (25). Conditions in the Lower Vistula Basin were cold and humid, supporting mammoth, arctic fox, wolf, arctic hare, and some reindeer. A similar environment marked the lower Vah and Nitra Basins, where a concentration of sites indicates an area of major settlement (2). The Willendorf sequence of 5 Gravettian levels dated between 28,000 and 23,000 B.P. indicate that the Wachau, a section of the Danube Valley, was occupied by a variety of animal species including bovids, horse, mammoth, cervids, but also ibex (wild mountain goats), fox, and hare during most of the Gravettian. The site occupied an ecotone between plain, valley, and uplands, which gave it strategic advantage as a hunting camp.

The lower loess series at Grubgraben that underlies and therefore antedates the humic horizon dated between 19,000 and 18,500 B.P. is associated with relatively humid conditions and a steppe vegetation as indicated by both the mollusc (20) and pollen (A Leroi-Gourhan, personal communication) records. A soil horizon dated between 19,000 and 18,000 B.P. is associated with the lower archaeological level at Sagvar near Lake Balaton in the west-central section of the Central European Basin (18, 19). The soil horizon at Pilismarot (10, 16), a loess site near the Danube bend, and the lower humic horizon at Grubgraben, which contained pollens of pine, juniper, sedges, and grass (A Leroi-Gourhan personal communication), are attributed to the same episode that appears to have affected the whole northwest sector of the Basin. A soil horizon of the same date was recorded at Madaras in southern Hungary (11).

And the episodes of sediment alteration that affected level 2 at Kadar, where the pollen spectrum included grass, sedges, and small percentages of linden, pine, and juniper, show that similar climatic conditions extended to the Sava River (38). Charcoal fragments of pine, linden, beech, birch, and ash were recovered from the two Epigravettian levels at Zupanov Spodmol (41). The climatic episode that corresponds to the Laugerie episode in the west affected the sediments, vegetation, and fauna of the whole region from north to south.

A second humic horizon dated between 17,500 and 17,000 B.P. was recorded at Sagvar, where it is associated with the upper archaeological level, and with level 2 at Grubgraben. The degree of soil formation during that second phase varies from site to site, suggesting variability in the relative intensity of the climatic fluctuation that corresponds to the Lascaux episode in the west. Pine, beech, and ash are still present in Slovenia around 17,000 B.P. (37). The situation in the whole Pannonian Basin between 16,000 and 14,000 B.P. appears to have been one of localized and shifting, relatively humid niches within a generally drier region. More humid conditions were reestablished on a regional scale between 14,000 and 13,000 B.P., as indicated in the stratigraphic sequence at Arka in northern Hungary (63), Kulna in Moravia (61), and Lupljanska in Slovenia (43). In short, the region was affected by a series of climatic fluctuations that correlate in broad terms with the mild oscillations noted in the west. The Laugerie, Lascaux, and Angles episodes are well marked in the sedimentological record of Central Europe. Vegetation maps derived from pollen sequences for the time period around 13,000 B.P. show the Pannonian Basin west of the Danube as a large bioclimatic region (23).

There is, however, a notable scarcity of record for the colder periods of the Pleniglacial. The fact is largely attributable to stratigraphic hiatuses in cave sites. Small scatters of artifacts occur in loess series, in level 5 at Spadzista, for example, which indicates that human groups frequented the region, but there were no major sites. The hiatuses mean that the understanding of human adaptations to cold episodes of the final Pleistocene remains incomplete. There again, the rock shelters of Western Europe encapsulate a unique record of human occupations during cold episodes, with no direct parallel in Central Europe.

Mammoth herds were well established in Moravia between 28,000 and 25,000 B.P., and in Slovakia, in the Vah and Nitra area between 25,000 and 23,000 B.P. They are found again in Moravia around 23,000 B.P. The significant reduction in body size noted at Spadzista (69) suggests that between 24,000 and 23,000 B.P. conditions north of the Carpathians became less favorable and, as a result, mammoth herds were subjected to stress. The Glacial Maximum was marked by the arrival of northern fauna in the southern sector of Central Europe. The presence of mammoth was recorded at loess sites in the Vojvodina and as far as the southern Morava Valley (3) that is attributed to the

Gravettian sensu lato. The hypothesis of a migration along the Danube-Tisza interfluve at the time of the Glacial Maximum may explain the presence of mammoth in the southern region. The Glacial Maximum was also a period of expansion for horse and reindeer herds, which spread west of the Danube from Hungary to Croatia, Slovenia, and into the north Adriatic Basin. Marmots hibernated in the karstic caves of Slovenia and Croatia and were easy prey to carnivores and humans (34). The faunal assemblage at Temnata (Bulgaria) was not affected by the intrusion of cold-adapted species during the final stages of the Pleistocene (29), when there was a marked difference between the eastern and western sectors of the southern Central European Basin. Regional variation in faunal assemblages may in turn account for variability in Epigravettian hunting tool kits (37).

ECONOMY AND SETTLEMENTS

Kozlowski (26) categorizes Gravettian hunting strategies on the basis of the relative proportion of mammoth bones in the total faunal assemblage. He identifies a first group where mammoth accounts for 80–90% of the total faunal count, a second group where the proportion is down to about 20%, and a third group where mammoth is absent or scarce. Spadzista (25, 68, 69) and Milovice (40) fall into the first group. Both sites belong to a late Gravettian phase dated between 24,000 and 22,000 B.P. When new excavations are completed, other sites of the late Gravettian phase including the Nitra and Moravany stations may prove to belong to the same group.

The earlier Gravettian sites, Pavlov and Dolni Vestonice, belong to the second group, where a wide variety of game including bovids, deer and elk, and horse and reindeer complemented the resource base. Mammoth meat and fat may have contributed the greater proportion of the food supply at these sites, but the additional resources may have allowed human groups to remain for longer periods of time at a single site, accounting for the relative stability of these settlements. Willendorf levels 5 to 8 and the Kulna Cave fall within the third group, which is marked by a variety of game.

The contrast between Middle Upper Paleolithic and Late Upper Paleolithic faunal assemblages is well illustrated at the Kulna Cave. Bovids, elk, deer, and horse dominated the Gravettian faunal assemblage at this site (dated between 21,000 and 23,000 B.P.), with only 8% reindeer, whereas the Magdalenian assemblage included 70% reindeer and 17% horse. Faunal evidence from Sagvar (65), Pilisszanto (15), Pilismarot-Palret (16), and Grubgraben (32) indicates that the change to specialized reindeer hunting was in place at the beginning of the Epigravettian. The redistribution of animal herds during the Glacial Maximum, as mammoth and bovids moved out of the Carpathian Basin and horse and reindeer herds expanded in the area, probably triggered the change in hunting tactics. A different situation prevailed south of the Drava, where reindeer was added to the varied local fauna. Available faunal lists from Slovenian and Croatian caves suggest that the diversified procurement pattern that existed in the Gravettian of north Central Europe remained in practice in the southern region during the more recent Epigravettian. Gravettian groups of the Perigord relied on the exploitation of red deer, reindeer, horse, ibex, and chamois. Elaborate scheduling of hunting parties and selection of best animals allowed occupants of Pataud and other shelters to remain at the site from early fall to late spring (5, 48). The stable settlements of the Late Perigordian were supported by the high concentration of medium-sized game (deer) in the Vezere Valley, and high-yield game (mammoth and bovids) supported the prolonged occupation of sites in Moravia during the Gravettian. In contrast, the strategy used by Epigravettian groups in north Central Europe is better adapted to the low density of medium-sized game that resulted from the redistribution of animal resources after 22,000 B.P. Comparable situations may have existed in other areas of the French Massif Central, where game density may have been much lower than in the lower Vezere Valley (e.g. at the Abri Fritch; 60).

Animal Use

Most of the available data comes from sites of the northern sector. Little information has come from the southern section of Central Europe.

IBEX   When present, ibex is no more than an occasional addition to the diet, represented by one individual at a number of sites and no more than four or five individuals at a few sites (Figure 4, top). The pattern is constant regardless of the total MNI (minimum number of individuals) at the sites. Ibex were hunted for their meat and coats, and their long, lower limb bones, especially metapodials, were used for weapon manufacture. A split metapodial, a partially worked splinter, and a spear point were the only faunal elements attributed to ibex at Grubgraben AL1 (70). The specialized and limited nature of the elements present suggests that the metapodials were retrieved from animals killed and butchered elsewhere and carried into the site as raw materials for tool manufacture.

FUR-BEARING ANIMALS   Hunting of fur-bearing animals was more commonly practiced in the early and later phases of the Gravettian. Foxes were well represented at Dolni Vestonice (24), but they were the predominant game at Willendorf level 9 (59). The total of 29 individuals of red and arctic fox recovered at that level exceeds by far the number of individuals from other sites of the Carpathian Basin and identifies Willendorf 9 as a specialized fur procurement site. Spadzista is an interesting case. In most areas of the site, fox is either

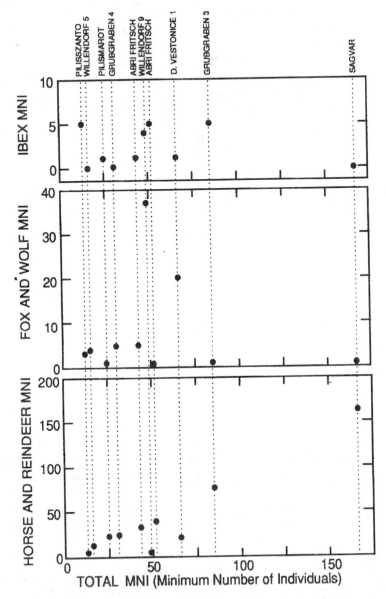

Figure 4 Faunal distribution of Gravettian and Epigravettian sites. Horse and reindeer are the main sources of food at Epigravettian sites as well as at the Abri Fritsch, as shown by the diagonal line formed when horse and reindeer MNI are plotted against total faunal assemblage. This is not the case at Willendorf 9 and Dolni Vestonice. The distribution of fox, wolf, and ibex (low priority items) is independent of the total number of individuals as shown by the horizontal pattern displayed on the graph. Willendorf 9 is an exception.

absent or represented by a few bone elements, but a concentration of 14 individuals was found in one area. West (68) has argued that fox elements from this area were typical of carcasses processed for fur. The list of elements included in the Willendorf 9 assemblage (59) could be interpreted in the same manner. Fur animals are rare in Epigravettian assemblages except for Pilisszanto, where they account for 5% of the assemblage (15).

MAMMOTH   Hunting, scavenging, and bone collecting were practiced in turn by Gravettian groups. The number of mammoths killed at Spadzista was first estimated at 60 (25). Soffer (55) questioned whether all the mammoth bones at Spadzista were the result of kills, and she suggested that the accumulation of young and sub-adult bones was procured from natural death sites. Haynes (22a) came to a similar conclusion. West (68, 69) concluded from her taphonomic study of postcranial elements that about 17 animals were deliberately ambushed and killed at or near the site while another 30 or so skulls were collected as construction material. She noted the presence of knee caps and small toe bones, which because of their size are not likely to have been used as construction material, but they could have been taken back to the site still attached to the long leg bones. Green bone fracture and spalling of limb bones indicated to her the disarticulation of carcasses and subsequent fracturing of long bones for marrow.

Topographic features at Spadzista, Milovice, or Dolni Vestonice may have been used to facilitate the capture of large game. At Willendorf, however, where so few elements are represented, a case could be made for scavenging. Ivory continued to be collected throughout the Late Upper Paleolithic. Between 28,000 and 23,000 B.P., the Carpathian Basin was within, and probably at the limits of, the territory where mammoth were exploited for food and construction materials.

REINDEER   Vörös (65) identified different kinds of butchering and storing stations in the Epigravettian, which indicates that different forms of animal use were in place at the time. Whole carcasses were carried in at Domos, Pilismarot Palret (16), and at Grubgraben (31, 32, 70). At the latter site, however, apendicular elements far outnumber axial elements, which suggests that in some cases leg quarters, skulls, and hides were brought back to the site. Transport of quartered carcasses after an initial butchering at the kill site was the most common tactic at the Pilisszanto shelter (15). The practice, noted at this site, of breaking long bones above the articulation would have kept sinews intact to facilitate transport. A different form of butchering was used at Sagvar, where legs were broken at or just above the metapodials (65). The large observed MNI at Sagvar suggests that game drives were used to procure a large number of animals (Figure 4). The site is considered to be a winter camp. Hunting and butchering practices seen at the site may relate to cold-season hunts and/or the special kind of hunting strategy used by the site's occupants.

An abundance of long bone splinters was found clustered around the hearths and work areas at Grubgraben (39), a site tentatively attributed to cold-season occupations. The cracking of mandibles as well as long bones for fat and marrow extraction may be a sign of stress induced by long winters and limited animal resources. The situation at Grubgraben was probably very different from that of Gravettian occupants of Dolni Vestonice or Willendorf. It is in marked contrast to the selective hunting and gourmet butchering attributed to the late Perigordian occupants at Pataud (48). More comparable forms of exhaustive use of limited resources would be expected at Badgoulian sites that are largely contemporaneous to the Central European Epigravettian, and especially at sites in less protected areas (e.g. Abri Fritch; 60).

Current data is insufficient to ascertain whether the observed differences in butchering techniques relate to seasonality, hunting strategies, settlement types, or other factors. The evidence supports the view that Epigravettian groups pursued single or small numbers of animals. The more organized capture of larger groups of reindeer that became prevalent in the Magdalenian began to appear in the Epigravettian context, perhaps as a kind of winter hunt.

HORSE   Two kinds of horse butchering techniques apparently were used during the Gravettian and the Epigravettian. At Sagvar, for example, cranial elements were introduced into the camp along with dry limbs and foot bones. At other sites, such as Willendorf and Grubgraben, the recovery of skull fragments, back legs, front legs, and shoulder blades indicates that quartered sections of carcasses were introduced at the site after butchering at the kill site. Vörös's interpretation is corroborated by the discovery of a kill and butchering station at Stranska Skala IV (57). The site located at the foot of a limestone cliff is in many ways comparable to Solutré, where game was driven along the foot of the cliff. Svoboda (57) reported that long bones and skull fragments were in very small proportion at the site and suggested that the meaty quarters had been transported away from the kill site.

The picture that emerges from the still limited taphonomic studies of faunal assemblages remains incomplete (54). Broad-based foraging appears to have been the most common form of game procurement during the Gravettian. Specialized mammoth hunting may have developed within that context in sectors of Central Europe and especially along an axis extending from the Krakov Jura to the Vah River during the late Gravettian phase, before disappearing with the mammoth sometime before 20,000 B.P. Specialized fox hunting is also evidenced during that period. Epigravettian groups of the Carpathian Basin became horse and reindeer hunters as a result of the redistribution of animal resources at the Glacial Maximum. They used game drive and foraging as means of game procurement.

HUNTING EQUIPMENT

A variety of armatures appeared in Western and Central Europe between 28,000 and 15,000 B.P. (9). But straight-backed points were the predominant elements used to tip spears in Central Europe. Other forms include a series of large point types such as the pointed blades, the unifacial points, and the shouldered points, as well as a variety of small armatures (backed bladelet elements, truncated bladelets and rectangles, and small retouched bladelets or flechettes). According to Otte (46) flechettes were part of the initial Gravettian hunting kit (30,000–28,000 B.P.). A second phase (28,000–25,000 B.P.) was marked by the presence of pointed blades; and more specialized weaponry was found in the later phase of the Gravettian with the development of the larger shouldered points (25,000–23,000 B.P.). The seriation was based on small artifact frequencies that make it inapplicable on a large regional scale. According to the data collated by Kozlowski (26), flechettes occurred in the Willendorf level 5 assemblage (dated at 28,000 B.P.) as well as in level 8 (24,000 B.P.). Unifacial points and shouldered points were represented each by one specimen in the level 5 and level 7 assemblages. Both forms occurred together in much larger numbers at Kostienki I layer 1, Kostienki 18, and Avdeevo. The validity of armature seriation in the Upper Paleolithic has been questioned in recent years (49). Straus underlined that the Solutrean point seriation based on the Laugerie Haute sequence is not generally applicable and added that there does not appear to be any clear association between armature types and game (56).

However, a case can be made here for the association of large shouldered points and the form of hunting associated with the capture of mammoth. The larger shouldered points (Kostienki points) share several metrical and formal attributes, especially stem (hafting element) dimensions. Limited experiments with use wear showed that specimens from Spadzista exhibited distal impact fractures, confirming their use as projectile points (B Adams, personal communication). The Kostienki points disappeared from the Carpathian Basin along with the mammoth and the particular hunting economy characteristic of the late Gravettian. Other shouldered points from Central Europe, those of Willendorf and Hidasnemeti (51), are more comparable to the ones from Kadar and the Slovenian sites (37). They tend to be smaller with shorter stems and were resharpened extensively. These lighter points appear to have been associated with the capture of a broad range of medium-sized animals in the mountainous or dissected terrains of the Dinaric Alps and the Slovenian Karst. Early Epigravettian bone or antler points are short with round cross-sections.

Table 1 Seriation of Central European sites according to tool counts and total artifact counts. The lower left block includes assemblages with less than 50 tools and 200 artifacts (briefly occupied hunting stations); the lower right block includes assemblages with less than 50 tools but much higher numbers of artifacts (workshops); and the upper block includes assemblages with higher tool and artifact counts (camp sites).

Tool counts	Assemblage total					
	<100	<200	<600	<1200	<2200	<4000
>300				Willendorf 8	Willendorf 9	Wojicice
<300			Vestonice Lower	Grubgraben 4 Spadzista B Kadar IE Kadar IW	Vestonice I	Kasov
<150		Ovca Lama LL Pilismarot	Ovca Lama UL Grubgraben 3 Willendorf 7 Willendorf 5 Willendorf 6	Dios	Bodrogkerestur	Spadzista C3
<90						
<50	Dunafoldvar Szeged Nogradevoce Zebegeny Zakajeni Spodmol Parska G Zupanov D	Zupanov C Szob	Spadzista C2 Palret Matzajeve K Zupanov A/B	Korlat II Hidasnemeti LL	Korlat Hidasnemeti UL Spadzista B5	

Longer bone points with quadrangular cross-sections and double bevelled bases appeared at Grubgraben level 1, which has an estimated date of 16,500 B.P. These bone points were later found in middle Magdalenian assemblages dated between 15,000 and 14,000 B.P. The Epigravettian appears to have been a period of economic adjustment and a time of experimentation with new technologies. Recent analyses of Upper Paleolithic armatures from the Perigord show patterns of association between weaponry and hunting strategies (47) that are comparable to what is seen in Central Europe. In the Carpathian Basin, there appears to be a clearer association between armature types and hunting strategies. Larger points were replaced by lighter weapons armed with small-backed elements and finely retouched bladelets as the subsistence base switched from broad-based foraging to the more specialized forms of reindeer and horse hunting. The mode of propulsion for the lighter weapons is still unknown. The scarcity of atlatl and harpoons in Central Europe may reflect an early appearance of the bow in association with the development of the lighter armatures (47).

SETTLEMENT TYPES

Attempts to identify patterning in settlement variability may include estimates of site size, faunal data, and the presence of hearths and other remnants of site architecture (22, 66, 67), but they rely primarily on tool and artifact counts, which remain the most commonly available measure of site use. A survey of Gravettian and Epigravettian sites from Central Europe uncovered 18 sites with less than 50 tools, including 13 with less that 25 tools; 8 sites with 100–150 tools; 12 with 150–300 tools; and 6 with 400 or more tools. Additional information is obtained when the level of processing activities as measured by tool counts is compared to flint knapping and artifact production as measured by total artifact counts. Such a comparison provides a measure of intensity of artifact use in relation to level of artifact manufacture (Table 1).

A series of small sites characterized by low tool and artifact counts belong to the Epigravettian. Cave occurrences from the Slovenian Karst and open-air localities from the Danube-Tisza interfluve and the Danube Valley signal the presence of small groups within a large territory. These small artifact scatters, often associated with hearths and some faunal material, are the remnants of a limited range of tasks performed during single, brief stays at a locality. At Parska Golobina, the assemblage contained used or retouched blades and backed points (i.e. the knives and armatures of a hunting-butchering tool kit). Burins, the chisel-like tools used to make or repair spear shafts and bone artifacts, were found together with knives and armatures at Dunafoldvar, Szeged, and Zebegeny (18). And a different tool kit made of blades and scrapers, perhaps used for hide working, came from the site at Szob, associated

with an unusually large number of fossil shells. Tool clusters of blades-arma-
tures, burins-blades-armatures, and blades-scrapers(-perforators) were found
spatially segregated at Kadar (38), Grubgraben 1 (39), and other camp sites
where a wider range of tasks were performed during longer stays. The repeated
occurrence of tool clusters at single occupation sites strengthens their interpretation as tool kits associated with the performance of specific tasks.

Low tool counts and high density of tool-making debris characterize the
workshop-camps at Wojcice and Spadzista (28), Hidasnemeti and Korlat (51),
and Kasov (1). These sites were located near raw material sources, which in
Central Europe tended to occur at the periphery of territories occupied by
Paleolithic groups.

Camp sites exhibit a relatively high level of tool use and a constant level of
proportion between the numbers of tools and flaking debris. Detailed comparisons between Gravettian and Epigravettian camps are still lacking. Tool frequency tables suggest that the larger sites belong to the Gravettian. Gravettian
camp sites like Dolni Vestonive, which contain thousands of artifacts as a
result of recurring episodes of site use over long periods of time, attest to the
stability of settlement patterns during the early phase of the Gravettian. Recent
excavations at Dolni Vestonice II revealed discrete clusters of artifacts, bones,
and features assumed to represent single or a series of single occupations (58).
Similar patterns continued into the later Gravettian phase at Nitra and
Moravany. Epigravettian sites like Grubgraben, Sagvar, or Kadar represent
similar patterns of recurring occupations, although the smaller quantity of
materials they contain indicates shorter stays and/or smaller group size.
Smaller seasonal camps and briefly occupied hunting camps signal the increased mobility of Epigravettian groups. A comparable change in settlement
size and organization may have taken place in the Perigord. A sharp drop in
artifact and tool frequencies distinguishes the early Magdalenian (Badgoulian)
from the Solutreau levels at Laugerie Haute.

RAW MATERIAL PROCUREMENT NETWORKS

The study of lithic raw materials has met with considerable success in Central
Europe. More importantly, the subject has been investigated from both ends of
the sequence: the extraction points and workshops from which materials origi-
nated and the camp sites where materials were expanded.

Raw Material Sources

The systematic identification of raw material sources is a major research
objective in Moravia, Poland (28), and Hungary (4). The *Lithoteka* located at
Budapest contains the most extensive series of well documented samples from
sources exploited in prehistoric times. So far no quarrying pit has been se-

curely attributed to Gravettian or Epigravettian context. Workshops were identified at Piekary, Wojcice, and Spadzista (28). The Spadzista workshops are the most informative to date. A series of artifact clusters characterized by an abundance of trimming flakes, pre-cores, and core preparation flakes, as well as a few blades and tools, surrounded the main camp and the fox hide processing area. But there is no evidence of extraction pits. Presumably, nodules were collected with minimal efforts from the detritic clay visible at several spots along the bluff.

The earlier evidence of quarry pits found in the Krakow Jura is associated with the Swiderian and perhaps the final Magdalenian at Wolowice (52). The Wolowice quarry was used over a long period with a first phase of exploitation dated at about 12,000 B.P. and a second phase around 11,000 B.P. The extraction pits and piles of debris are assumed to be the work of groups who occupied camps at some distance along the Vistula River (52). The evidence from the Krakow Jura suggests that the use of quarries located at some distance from the camp sites began in the final stages of the Paleolithic.

The emergence of quarries marks a major transformation of raw material economy resulting from population expansion and increased demand for raw materials. To date there is no evidence that the density of human populations and the demand for raw materials were sufficient during the Gravettian and Epigravettian to necessitate the expenditure of time and energy that the Wolowice quarry represents or to support the kind of social organization that craft specialization demands. Examples of Epigravettian workshops were found at Kasov where Carpathian obsidian was the main material to be processed (1). The site consists of a series of artifact scatters centered around a hearth forming features 2–3 m in diameter. Intensive flint knapping activities were reported at Arka (63) and other sites (12). But as at Gravettian sites, lithic procurement and tool making were done along with other tasks at these Epigravettian camps. Gravettian groups frequented Spadzista to obtain flint, ivory, fox pelts, and meat. The Kasov clusters were both workshops and camp sites. In contrast, flint extraction and initial core preparation were the only activities recorded at Wolowice.

Many late Magdalenian workshops have been identified in the Perigord (8), in the Paris Basin (1a), and in the French Jura (7), which, like Wolowice, were located at some distance from the camp sites. In addition, detailed analysis of workshop debris demonstrated the high level of skill achieved by some flint knappers in late Magdalenian camp sites (1a). But there is no evidence of deep quarry pits in the final Paleolithic of Western Europe. It appears that lithic procurement remained an embedded activity until the LUP and developed into a specialized form of economic activity during the Magdalenian in northern as well as in Western Europe.

RAW MATERIAL NETWORKS   The flow of raw material across the Carpathians and through the Danube Basin followed different routes: (*a*) the Morava and the Moravian Gate between the Vienna Basin and Silesia, (*b*) the Vah and across to the Upper Vistula, west of the Tatra mountains, between western Slovakia and the Krakow Jura, (*c*) east of the Tatra between the Upper Tisza and southern Poland, or (*d*) along the Danube and across the Transdanubian hills to the south. Links between sources and sites along these routes describe procurement networks that reflect the territory used by human groups at different time periods.

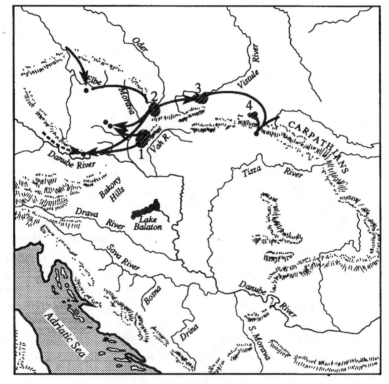

Early Gravettian Network

Figure 5   Network of raw materials distribution during the early Gravettian. Shaded areas indicate major sources of 1. radiolarite from the White Carpathians, 2. glacial moraines of the Upper Oder, 3. flint of the Krakow Jura, and 4. obsidian from the Carpathians. The dotted arrow indicates possible but unconfirmed transport of raw materials along the Danube. Dots indicate sites to which materials were transported.

EARLY GRAVETTIAN NETWORKS   Data from Dolni Vestonice and Willendorf (27, 28) indicate that a majority of raw materials were imported from long-distance sources, including the moraine (also known as Nordic) flint from the Upper Oder at the Moravian gate and perhaps pieces of Krakow flint. Lesser quantities of radiolarian flint came from the Little Carpathians and the Vah. Small percentages of local materials completed the assemblage. The procurement network extended along the Morava River to the north and to the Little Carpathians and the Vah to the northeast (Figure 5). Some of the material was transported farther south to Willendorf along the Danube.

Two northeast Hungarian sites, Hidasnemeti (site 29 in Figure 1; 51) and Bodrogkeresztur (site 28 in Figure 1; 64), belong to the early Gravettian. The latter site included obsidian from the Tokai-Presov mountains in Slovakia, opalite and porphyry from the Bukk mountains, Swieciechow flint from southern Poland, and some transparent Vohynian flint from the Dniestr Basin (4). Evidence of these long-distance transports at a site of the upper Tisza drainage indicates use of pathways through the eastern Carpathians across Slovakia into the Vistula Valley and farther east to the Ukraine. There is no apparent link between the western (Morava) and the eastern (Tisza) segments of the network except perhaps in the Upper Vistula area.

THE LATER GRAVETTIAN NETWORK   Transport of northern flint from the Silesian moraines continued along the Morava and into the Danube Valley as evidenced from Willendorf (Figure 6). But the main axis of transport was along the Vah Valley between the Krakow area and the sites situated along the Nitra and Vah Rivers (1, 27). There are no site known for that period in eastern Hungary.

THE EPIGRAVETTIAN NETWORK   The Epigravettian network is the most extensive (Figure 7). It extended (a) from the Carpathians to the Danube bend following axes formed by the Morava, the Vah, and the Tisza Rivers (4, 35), (b) from the Danube bend to the Bakony hills and Lake Balaton (4, 12), and (c) from the Mecsek mountains in southern Hungary to Lake Balaton (11). The network probably continued south and across the Drava River into Croatia. Assemblages from the Croatian caves contained nonlocal materials but their origin has not been traced (33). They contain radiolarites, which may have come from Lake Balaton, the Mecsek, or from northern Bosnia.

THE MAGDALENIAN OR LUP NETWORK   Little attention has been given recently to the final stages of the Paleolithic. Arka (site 27 in Figure 1) is the only site of northern Hungary to fall within the appropriate time period (63). A few sites cluster in Bohemia, Moravia (61), and lower Austria. The greater concentration of sites is in southern Germany (66, 67) and north and west of the Carpathians and Sudettes mountains, indicating a recolonization of territories

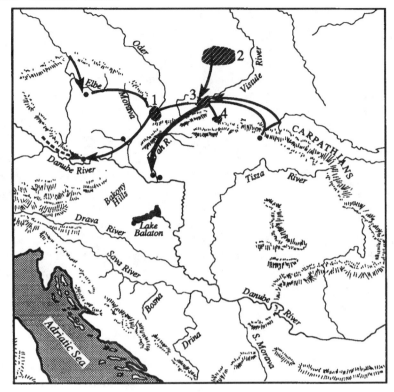

Late Gravettian Network
24-22,000

Figure 6   Network of raw materials distribution during the late Gravettian. Shaded areas indicate major sources of 1. glacial moraines of the Upper Oder (northern flint), 2. flints from the Krakow Jura, 3. radiolarite from the Vah, and 4. obsidian from the Carpathians. The dotted arrow indicates a possible but unconfirmed route. Dots indicate sites to which materials were transported.

that probably followed the northern migration of reindeer and horse herds at the end of the Last Glacial. There is a marked increase in the number of sites in the southern section of the Central European Basin and especially along the Adriatic coast at the time (37). But the raw materials used at these sites were of local origin.

CONCLUSION

Recent excavations have reemphasized the importance of the 5000-year period of the Epigravettian phase in Central Europe. Major changes in hunting strategies and in weaponry took place during that time. Winter camps, seasonal camp sites, small hunting stations, and workshops give a measure of the com-

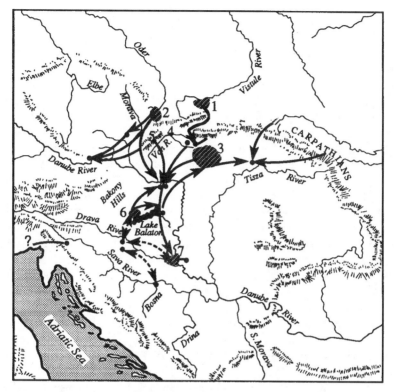

Epigravettian Network
19,000-16,000

Figure 7   Network of raw materials distribution during the Epigravettian. Shaded areas indicate major sources of 1. flints from the Krakow Jura, 2. glacial moraines of the Upper Oder (northern flint), 3. quartzite and radiolarite from northern Hungary, 4. radiolarite from the Vah, 5. radiolarite from the White Carpathians, 6. radiolarite from the Bakony hills, and 7. chert from the Mecsek hills. Dotted arrows indicate possible but unconfirmed routes. Dots indicate sites to which materials were transported.

plexity of the settlement system. Reliance on two animal species, reindeer and horse, which may have had differently scheduled behavior through the yearly cycle, would account for longer stays at base camps like Sagvar and perhaps Grubgraben. These larger sites where game drives were probably practiced may have functioned as aggregation sites. The widely scattered, small hunting camps and the extensive raw material network show that human groups dispersed within a wide territory that extended north to south through the western side of the Pannonian Basin. There are clear similarities between the Epigravettian and the Badgoulian of Western Europe. The transformation of hunting equipment went through the same stages as the development of light armatures, perhaps associated with bows and arrows. Processing tools in both regions include chunky scrapers, carinates, and transverse burins on tabular flakes. Badgoulian sites include a range of settlement types, open-air camps like Solvieux, brief occupations marked by small artifact assemblages at Laugerie Haute and other sites of the Perigord, and artifact scatters in the Entre-deux-mers, which may be the remains of hunting stations. The distribution of Badgoulian manifestations differs notably from that of the Late Perigordian.

Hunting strategies and equipment of the Epigravettian vary markedly from that of the late Gravettian mammoth hunters who occupied southern Moravia, western Slovakia, and southern Poland. However, the occupants of Willendorf levels 8 and 9 used a more diversified hunting strategy, exploiting medium-sized animals. Such diversified hunting may have led to the progressively more specialized types of hunting of the Epigravettian. Unfortunately, data on the late Gravettian remains scarce, mostly as a result of widespread erosional phenomena that eradicated the record at many Central European sites.

A lack of data impedes a study of relationships between the northern and southern sectors of the Central European Basin. Little is known of the Gravettian manifestations in the southern sector. The Epigravettian raw material network extends well into the southern region, indicating that reindeer and horse hunters of the northern sector were in contact with, or were part of the same group as, the foragers of the south. If this is true, the vast region stretching from the Adriatic to the Middle Danube could be considered one large cultural area. The pattern of low population density, settlement mobility, specialized hunting, and intensive use of food resources that characterized the late Paleolithic groups of Central Europe at the Glacial Maximum appears when a large region is considered. Badgoulian sites, when considered on a larger regional scale, may display some of the same traits, showing similar responses to environmental constraints.

Literature Cited

1. Banesz L, Kozlowski JK, Sobcyzk K. 1992. Le Site de Plein Air du Paléolithique supérieur de Kasov I en Slovaquie orientale. *Slov. Archeol.* XL 1:5–28

1a. Audouze F. 1987. The Paris Basin in Magdalenian times. See Ref. 53, pp. 183–200

2. Barta J. 1980. *Importants sites paléolithiques de la Slovaquie Centrale et Occidentale.* Nitra: Inst. Archéol. Acad. Slov. Sci. 69 pp.

3. Basler D, ed. 1979. *Praistoija Jugoslavenski Zemalja,* Vol. I. Sarajevo: Akad. Nauka Bone Hercegovine. 452 pp.

4. Biro K. 1988. Distribution of lithic raw materials on prehistoric sites, an interim report. *Acta Arch. Acad. Sci. Hung.* 40:251–74

5. Boyle KV. 1993. Upper Palaeolithic procurement and processing strategies. See Ref. 47, pp. 151–62

6. Campy M, Chaline J, Vuillemet M. 1989. *La Baume de Gigny, Jura.* XXVII Suppl. Gallia Préhist. Paris: Editions du CNRS. 262 pp.

7. Cupillard C, Richard A. 1991. *Silex à fleur de sol, L'exploitation de la matière première dans la région d'Etrelles (Haute Saône).* Besançon: Cent. Rég. Doc. Archéol. 84 pp.

8. Demars PY. 1982. *L'utilisation du silex au Paléolithique supérieur: choix, approvisionnement, circulation. L'éxemple du Bassin de Brive.* Cah. Quat. 5. Paris: Edit. CNRS

9. Demars PY, Laurent P. 1989. *Types d'outils lithiques du Paléolithique supérieur en Europe.* Cah. Quat. 14. Paris: Edit. CNRS

10. Dobosi V. 1981. Pilismarot-Dios: uj oskokori telep. *Commun. Arch. Acad. Hung.* 8:9–27

11. Dobosi V. 1989. Felsopaleolit telep Madaras-Teglavetoben. *Cumania* 11:9–66

12. Dobosi V. 1991. Economy and raw materials. A case study of 3 Upper Paleolithic sites in Hungary. See Ref. 36, pp. 192–204

13. Dobosi V. 1991. Discontinuity in the Upper Paleolithic of Hungary. In *Les Bassins du Rhin et du Danube au Paleolithique supérieur,* ed. A Montet-White, pp. 17–26. ERAUL 43. Liège: Univ. Liège. 137 pp.

14. Dobosi V. 1991. Upper Paleolithic excavations in Hungary 1986–1990. See Ref. 45, pp. 79–86

15. Dobosi V, Vörös I. 1986. Chronological revision of the Pilisszanto rock-shelter. *Folia Arch.* XXXVII:25–45

16. Dobosi V, Vörös I, Krolopp E, Szabo J, Ringer A, Schweitzer F. 1983. Upper Paleolithic settlement in Pilismarot-Palret. *Acta Arch. Acad. Hung.* 22:3–11

17. Felgenhauer F. 1956–1959. *Willendorf in der Wachau.* Monogr. palaolith. Fundstelle I–VII. Vienna: Rohrer. 217 pp.

18. Gabori M, Gabori V. 1957. Etudes archéologiques et stratigraphiques dans les stations de loess paléolithiques de Hongrie. *Acta Arch. Acad. Sci. Hung.* 8:1–118

19. Gabori-Csank V. 1978. Une oscillation climatique à la fin du Wurm en Hongrie. *Acta Arch. Acad. Sci. Hung.* 30:3–11

20. Haesaerts P. 1990. Stratigraphy of the Grubgraben loess sequence. See Ref. 35, pp. 25–36

21. Haesaerts P. 1990. Nouvelles recherches au gisement de Willendorf (Basse Autriche). *Bull. Int. R. Sci. Nat. Belgique* 60:203–18

22. Hahn J. 1987. Aurignacian and Gravettian settlement patterns in Central Europe. See Ref. 53, pp. 251–61

22a. Haynes G. 1991. *Mammoths, Mastodons, and Elephants: Biology, Behavior, and the Fossil Record.* Cambridge: Cambridge Univ. Press

23. Huntley H, Birks E. 1983. *An Atlas of Past and Present Pollen Maps for Europe: 0–13,000 Years Ago.* Cambridge: Cambridge Univ. Press

24. Klima B. 1981. Stredni Cast Paleoliticke Stanice u Dolnich Vestonic. *Pamatky Archeol.* LXXII:5–92

25. Kozlowski JK, ed. 1974. Upper Paleolithic site with dwellings of mammoth bones. *Folia Quat.* 44. Krakow: Jagiellonian Univ.

26. Kozlowski JK. 1986. The Gravettian in Central and Eastern Europe. *Adv. World Archaeol.* 5(3):131–200

27. Kozlowski JK. 1986. Changes in the raw material economy of the Gravettian technocomplex in Northcentral Europe. In *Int. Conf. Prehist. Flint Mining and Lithic Raw Material Identification in the Carpathian Basin,* ed. K Takacs-Biro, pp. 65–80. Budapest: Magyar Nemzeti Mus. 294 pp.

28. Kozlowski JK. 1991. Les techniques de débitage dans le Gravettien de la Partie septentrionale de l'Europe Centrale. In *25 ans d'études technologiques en préhistoire, XIe Rencontres Internationales d'Archeologie et d'Histoire d'Antibes,* pp. 289–304. Juan les Pines: Edit. APDCA

29. Kozlowski JK, Laville H, Gunter B, eds. 1992. *Temnata Cave Excavations in Karlukovo Karst Area, Bulgaria.* Krakow: Jagellonian Univ. Press. 501 pp.

30. Kozlowski JK, Sobczyk K. 1984. The Upper Paleolithic site Krakow-Spadzista Street C2, 1980 excavations. *Prace Archeol.* 42. Krakow: Jagiellon Univ. 98 pp.

31. Logan B. 1990. The hunted of Grubgraben: an analysis of faunal remains. See Ref. 35, pp. 65–92

32. Logan B. 1990. *The changing game: Gravettian-Epigravettian hunting strategies in the Middle Danube.* Presented at Int. Symp. Chasse Préhist., Treignes, Belgium

33. Malez M. 1979. Nalazista Paleolitskog i Mezolitskog doba u Hrvatskoj. See Ref. 3, pp. 227–76

34. Mirade P. 1991. Carnivore dens or carnivore hunts? *Rad HAZU* (Zagreb) 458:193–219

35. Montet-White A, ed. 1990. *The Epigravettian site of Grubgraben, the 1986–87 excavations.* ERAUL 40. Liège: Univ. Liège. 171 pp.

36. Montet-White A, Holen S. 1991. *Raw Material Economies Among Hunter-Gatherers.* Publ. Anthropol. 19. Lawrence: Univ. Kansas. 414 pp.

37. Montet-White A, Kozlowski JK. 1983. Les industries à pointes à dos dans les Balkans. *Riv. Sci. Prehist.* 1–2:371–99

38. Montet-White A, Laville H, Lézine AM. 1986. Le Paléolithique en Bosnie du nord:

chronologie, environnement et préhistoire. *L'Anthropologie* 90:29–88

39. Montet-White A, Williams J. 1992. *Spatial organization at a winter campsite of the Last Glacial Maximum.* Presented at Annu. Meet. Soc. Am. Arch., Pittsburgh

40. Oliva M. 1989. Excavations in the Paleolithic site of Milovice I, southern Moravia, in the year 1988. *Anthropologie (Brno)* 27: 265–71

41. Osole F. 1971. Zupanov Spodmol, station paléolithique. *Proc. VIIIe. Congrès UISPP,* pp. 238–41. Beograd

42. Osole F. 1977. Matjazeve Kamre, Paleolotsko Jamsko Najdbisce. *Archeol. Vestnik* XXVII:13–41

43. Osole F. 1983. Epigravettien iz Lukenjske Jame pri Precni. *Poricilo o raziskovanju paleolita v Sloveniji* XI:7–25

44. Otte M. 1981. *Le Gravettian en Europe Centrale.* Diss. Archaeol. Gandenses, XX. Brugges: De Tempel

45. Otte M, ed. 1991. *Le Paléolithique supérieur européen, Bilan Quinquennal, UISPP, Commission VII.* ERAUL 52 Liège: Univ. Liège. 369 pp.

46. Otte M. 1991. Révision de la séquence de Willendorf. In *Les Bassins du Rhin et du Danube au Paléolithique supérieur,* ed. A Montet-White. pp. 45–60. ERAUL 43. Liège: Derouaux Ordina. 133 pp.

47. Peterkin GL, Bricker H, Mellars P, eds. 1993. *Hunting and animal exploitation in the Later Palaeolithic and Mesolithic of Eurasia.* Arch. Pap. Am. Anthropol. Assoc. 4. 249 pp.

48. Pike Tay AS, Bricker HM. 1993. Hunting in the Gravettian: an examination of the evidence from SW France. See Ref. 47, pp. 127–44

49. Rigaud JP, Simek J. 1987. "Arms too short to box with Gods." Problems and prospects for Paleolithic prehistory in Dordogne, France. See Ref. 53, pp. 47–60

50. Sackett JR. 1988. The Neuvic Group. Upper Paleolithic open-air sites in the Perigord. In *Upper Pleistocene Prehistory of Western Eurasia,* ed. H Dibble, A Montet-White, pp. 61–84. Univ. Mus. Monogr. 54. Philadelphia: Univ. Penn.

51. Siman K. 1989. Hidasnemeti, Upper Paleolithic Site in the Hernad Valley, NE Hungary. *Acta Arch. Carpathica* XXVIII:5–24

52. Sobczyk K. 1993. The Late Paleolithic flint workshops at Brzoskowinia-Krzemionki near Krakow. *Prace Archeol.* 55. Krakow: Jagiellonian Univ. 85 pp.

53. Soffer O, ed. 1987. *The Pleistocene Old World: Regional Perspectives.* New York: Plenum. 380 pp.

54. Soffer O. 1991. Upper Paleolithic huntergatherers in Europe: studies of subsistence practices and settlement systems 1986–1990. See Ref. 45, pp. 321–40

55. Soffer O, Praslov N. 1993. *From Kostienki to Clovis: Upper Paleolithic Paleoindian Adaptations.* New York: Penum

56. Straus LG. 1993. Upper Paleolithic hunting tactics and weapons in Western Europe. See Ref. 47, pp. 83–94

57. Svoboda J. 1989. Czechoslovakia at the Last Pleniglacial in the World at 18,000 BP, ed. O Soffer, C Gamble, 1:20–31. London: Hyman

58. Svoboda J, ed. 1991. *Dolni Vestonice II, Western Slope.* ERAUL 54. Liège: Univ. Liège. 102 pp.

59. Thenius E. 1956–1959. Die jungpleistozäne Wirbeltierfauna von Willendorf. See Ref. 17, pp. 133–70

60. Trotignon F, Poulain T, Leroi-Gouirhan A. 1984. *Etudes sur l'Abri Fritsch.* XXe Suppl. Gallia Préhist. Paris: Edit. CNRS. 122 pp.

61. Valoch K. 1989. *Die Erforshung der Kulna Höhle. Anthropos* 24 (NS 16). BRNO: Moravske Muzeum.

62. Valoch K. 1989. Settlement and climatic changes in the last Ice Age in Moravia. *Acta Mus. Moraviae* LXXIV:7–34

63. Vertes L. 1964–65. Das Jungpaläolithikum von Arka in Nord Ungarn. *Quärtar* 15–16:79–132

64. Vertes L. 1966. The Upper Paleolithic Site on Mt-Henye at Bodrogkeresztur. *Acta Arch. Acad. Sci. Hung.* 18:3–14

65. Vörös I. 1982. Faunal remains from the Gravettian reindeer hunter campsite at Sagvar. *Folio Arch.* 33:43–71

66. Weniger GC. 1991. Uberlegungen zur Mobilitat Jägerischer Gruppen in Jungpaläolithikum. *Saeculum* 42(1):82–103

67. Weniger GC. 1987. Magdalenian settlement pattern and subsistence in Central Europe, the southwestern and central Germany cases. See Ref. 53, pp. 201–14

68. West D. 1990. *Preliminary results of a taphonomic analysis of fox and mammoth bones from Spadzista, Poland.* Presented at Int. Symp. Chasse Préhist., Treignes, Belgium

69. West D. 1993. Mammoth hunters or mammoth collectors: the controversy over megafauna procurement in the Old World. *Kansas Work. Pap. Anthropol.,* pp. 1–36. Lawrence: Univ. Kansas, Dept. Anthropol.

70. Whitney PL. 1992. *A faunal analysis of Grubgraben AL1.* Masters thesis. Univ. Kansas

Annu. Rev. Anthropol. 1994. 23:509–26

THE EPIDEMIOLOGY OF HIV TRANSMISSION: Trends, Structure and Dynamics[1]

Kathleen M. MacQueen

Division of HIV/AIDS, National Center for Infectious Diseases, Centers for Disease Control and Prevention, Atlanta, Georgia 30333

KEY WORDS: dynamic models, networks, AIDS, risk behavior

INTRODUCTION

This review summarizes dynamic processes in human immunodeficiency virus (HIV) transmission. A brief overview of current trends in the HIV epidemic is followed by a discussion of the basic components of HIV transmission. Several epidemiologic models are then described that seek to delineate how HIV transmission is structured by human relationships and the implications of those structural relationships for the evolving epidemic.

RECENT TRENDS IN THE HIV EPIDEMIC

Acquired immunodeficiency syndrome (AIDS) was first recognized in 1981 among men who have sex with men (MSM) in the United States, and shortly thereafter in populations of injecting drug users (IDUs), hemophiliacs and blood transfusion recipients, Haitians and Africans, and infants of women with AIDS. The identification of these diverse risk groups provided epidemiologists with their first clues about the nature of the disease (67). By 1983 the

---

[1]

viral cause of AIDS had been discovered (eventually named human immunodeficiency virus or HIV) and the basic modes of transmission established:
sexual transmission, parenteral exposure to blood and blood products, and
perinatal transmission (27).

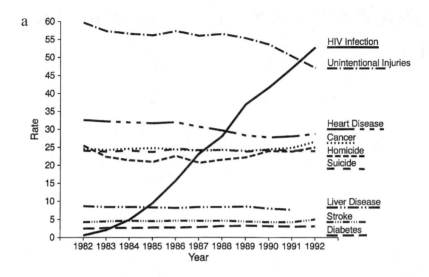

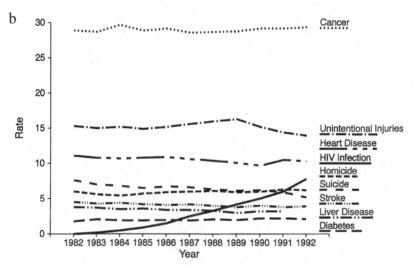

Figure 1   Death rates per 100,000 population for leading causes of death in persons aged 25–44
years, by year—United States, 1982–1992. Rates are national vital statistics based on underlying
cause of death, using final data for 1982–1991 and provisional data for 1992 (13). Figure 1a shows
death rates in men; figure 1b shows death rates in women.

Because HIV is primarily a sexually transmitted disease (STD), its spread reflects the social patterning of human sexual relationships. This characteristic has led to oversimplifications of the risk group concept (an important heuristic device in epidemiology) and to popular notions that social identity is a good measure of a person's risk of infection. However, the risks for HIV are common to all social groups, and few (if any) groups are sufficiently isolated to avoid all chance of the virus being introduced. Some 13 years since it was first recognized, AIDS has become the leading cause of death in 64 cities in the United States for men aged 25–44 years and in 9 cities for similarly aged women. For the nation as a whole, AIDS is the second leading cause of death for young adult men and the sixth leading cause for young adult women (66; see also Figures 1a,b). Among children aged 1–4 years, AIDS was the ninth leading cause of death in 1988 (15a) and is currently estimated to be the eighth leading cause (S Chu, personal communication). By the end of 1993, the number of reported AIDS cases in the United States totaled 361,509, and 218,052 people had died of the disease (14). Official estimates of the number of people currently infected with HIV in the United States are around 1 million (12), although these estimates are being reassessed.

Gay and bisexual men constitute 54% of the total number of reported AIDS cases in the United States (14). The epidemic appears to have leveled off or even declined somewhat among gay and bisexual men in some metropolitan areas (e.g. New York City, Los Angeles, and San Francisco; 15, 40, 87), but more new AIDS cases are reported each year among MSM than for any other group (14). AIDS incidence rates continue to increase among black and Hispanic MSM (15, 40), and recent evidence suggests that HIV prevalence is higher than previously thought among young gay men in San Francisco (47).

Injecting drug users constitute 24% of reported AIDS cases, with another 7% attributable to male IDUs who have also reported sex with another man (14). The number of new AIDS cases among all IDUs in the northeastern United States, where drug users were most affected in the early years of the epidemic, has leveled off since 1989 (54). In New York City, HIV prevalence rates among IDUs have been stable since approximately 1993 (18, 19), although at a high rate. The number of AIDS cases among IDUs is increasing in the south and among female, black, and Hispanic IDUs nationally (54).

The number of AIDS cases in heterosexuals, particularly women and teenagers, has increased steadily in recent years (15). Heterosexual contact now accounts for 35% of United States AIDS cases in women (14). Seroprevalence rates among childbearing women are generally highest among black women and lowest among white women; rates among Latina women vary by geographic region and are highest among women of Puerto Rican descent (28).

As heterosexual transmission increases, so does perinatal transmission. It is estimated that 7000 children were born each year to HIV-infected women in

1991 and 1992 (14a). Based on observed rates of perinatal transmission (28), between 1000 and 2000 of these children are estimated to have been infected perinatally in each of those years.

Regional differences in the prevalence and incidence of HIV and AIDS among gay men, IDUs, and minority women to some extent reflect differences in underlying behavioral patterns within these broadly defined groups. For example, the higher prevalence of injecting drug use among Puerto Ricans in New York City compared to Mexican Americans in Texas has resulted in different rates of HIV infection in these Hispanic groups (15). Among populations experiencing similar patterns of behavioral risk, such as gay men in urban centers, regional differences in prevalence and incidence may reflect differences in the timing of the introduction of HIV into specific communities (73).

The epidemic in Europe has shown trends similar to those in the United States. Transmission has been greatest among MSM and IDUs in the early years, with the number and proportion of AIDS cases in women increasing recently. As in the United States, most of the infections in women result from injecting drug use or sexual contact with an IDU (38). Newly reported AIDS cases among heterosexuals now exceed those reported for IDUs in the United Kingdom, and HIV prevalence rates are 1–2% among non-IDU heterosexuals attending STD clinics in France, Germany, Italy, Spain, and Switzerland (4).

In Latin America, HIV appeared first among MSM and IDU populations and then spread to commercial sex workers and women generally. Bisexual men seem to have been an important bridge group for this process (38). Considerable variation occurs throughout Latin America, with MSM transmission prevalent in the Andean and Southern Cone countries of South America, while heterosexual transmission predominates in Central America and the Caribbean. IDU transmission is also important in the Southern Cone countries, Brazil, and Mexico City (68).

Throughout Africa, the epidemic continues to expand as heterosexual intercourse accounts for more than 80% of infections (60). High rates of heterosexual transmission in Africa appear to result in part from a synergistic relationship between HIV and other STDs (61). High rates of heterosexual transmission, in turn, fuel an epidemic among infants and children of infected mothers. A smaller but nonetheless substantial contributor to continuing HIV transmission in Africa is the unintentional use of infected blood in transfusions (24).

HIV appeared later in Asia than in North America or Africa, but it is spreading with unprecedented speed (38). As recently as 1987 few cases of AIDS were reported anywhere in the region. In 1988 HIV surveillance in Thailand indicated a dramatic increase in the number of infections among IDUs in Bangkok, from 1% to more than 30% of those receiving methadone treatment. In 1989 a similar increase in HIV prevalence was noted among brothel-based prostitutes in northern Thailand. By 1991 prevalence was clearly increasing among sexually active heterosexual men and non-prostitute heterosexual women (84). Genetic analyses of the virus indicate that HIV entered Thailand in two separate waves of infection, the first among IDUs and the second among female prostitutes and their male clients (85, 57).

The spread of HIV in India and Myanmar is following a pattern similar to that of Thailand and includes both IDU and sexual transmission. Significant rates of IDU-related transmission have occurred throughout the heroin-producing Golden Triangle region and its environs, including Thailand, Myanmar, China, and India (85).

The epidemics in various continents and among subpopulations in particular areas are not fully distinct. Keenlyside and colleagues (38) note that sexual partnerships with non-European men from countries where heterosexual transmission predominates account for a significant proportion of heterosexually acquired HIV among European women. Similarly, increases in the heterosexual transmission of HIV in Japan reflect the presence of Thai prostitutes in Japan and Japanese patronage of prostitutes in Thailand (85). Such patterns underscore the fact that the sexual transmission of HIV encompasses more than individual decisions about the use of condoms or the appropriateness of abstinence. Complex social, political, and economic factors are operating as well.

HIV TRANSMISSION

Basic Components of Transmission

The transmission of HIV is the result of four interacting factors: 1. the infectiousness of the person with HIV, 2. the susceptibility of the uninfected person to infection, 3. the efficiency of the mode of transmission, and 4. the infectivity of the viral strain. Evidence suggests that infectiousness is high in the first weeks or months after infection, during what is commonly called the window period between initial infection and the production of detectable HIV antibodies (16). Infectiousness then declines, remaining low as long as immune functioning is stable and the viral load in the blood is low. As immune functioning declines, viral load and infectiousness again rises (33). Infectiousness in the context of sexual transmission also appears to be affected by the presence of other STDs, especially those that cause genital ulcers such as chancroid, syphilis, and herpes simplex virus type 2 (7, 33, 83).

Susceptibility to HIV infection similarly appears to be influenced by STDs, particularly genital ulcerative diseases that may facilitate HIV transmission in the genital tract. Susceptibility may also be subject to a wide range of other factors including vaginal or rectal bleeding and trauma during sexual intercourse, lack of circumcision in men, and possibly human genetic variation in immune response (33). The type of sexual behavior engaged in by the infected and uninfected partners has an important effect on susceptibility. Receptive anal sex presents the greatest risk of sexual transmission for an uninfected partner, whether the receptive partner is a man or woman. Transmission to an uninfected insertive male partner is generally less efficient during anal intercourse. During penile-vaginal sex, transmission from an infected male to an uninfected female appears to be more efficient than from an infected female to an uninfected male, in the absence of STDs or other enhancing factors (1). There is evidence of HIV transmission during oral sex, especially where an infected male partner has ejaculated into the mouth of an uninfected partner (48, 62), although transmission without ejaculation may also be possible (1). Such oral transmission appears to be relatively inefficient, but inefficiency must be balanced against the frequency at which exposure to the virus is occurring. Every low-risk exposure is an opportunity for transmission; the number of times HIV transmission occurs as a result of low-risk exposures will be, on average, a product of the transmission efficiency and the number of opportunities. Of course, there is no way to predict whether a particular individual will become infected after a single exposure or remain uninfected after several thousand exposures, regardless of efficiency.

Within each of the three basic modes of HIV transmission (parenteral, sexual, and perinatal) transmission efficiency is affected by a variety of factors. Parenteral transmission through transfusion of blood or blood products can be extremely efficient as evidenced by the rapid early spread of HIV among hemophiliacs and blood transfusion recipients. More than 95% of individuals transfused with HIV-infected blood or blood products subsequently become infected (68). At the other extreme, HIV-contaminated needlestick injuries result in transmission in less than 1% (approximately 0.4%) of exposed health care workers (68). Instances of HIV transmission have been established among children in Eastern Europe resulting from the reuse of needles and syringes in a health care setting (68), but such transmission is uncommon. Sharing of needles, syringes, and other drug paraphernalia that may result in the injection of small amounts of blood has led to very high rates of HIV transmission among IDUs (25, 26, 54). The high number of potential exposures resulting from repeated sharing of equipment contributes to these high rates.

Although there is still much uncertainty regarding the mechanics of perinatal transmission, about one quarter to one third of infants born to HIV-infected mothers are themselves infected (28). Evidence suggests that transmission can occur during pregnancy, at delivery, and during breastfeeding (especially when colostrum is being produced) (46). Several maternal factors have been associated with increased risk of perinatal transmission, including more advanced maternal HIV disease and placental membrane inflammation (69).

Sexual transmission is less efficient than parenteral and perinatal transmission of HIV. For example, the per act probability of transmission from an infected man to an uninfected woman is about 0.2% (33). However, this lack of efficiency must be balanced against the frequency of sexual exposure, the rate of exposure to multiple partners, and the infectiousness of each partner.

HIV is highly variable and mutates easily, but the epidemiologic significance of these characteristics for infectivity is poorly understood (33). Ewald (23) notes population-level among between the rapid spread of HIV, higher virulence of the strains transmitted, and disruptive social conditions such as warfare. He argues that virulence and infectivity are inherently linked and that it is erroneous to assume that an infectious agent such as HIV will evolve toward decreased virulence as long as high infectivity leads to continued propagation of the virus in uninfected populations or groups. In Thailand, different strains of HIV are associated with sexual and IDU transmission, but each strain is relatively homogenous because of the recency of the virus' introduction to the area and, hence, the limited time for strain variability to evolve. Detailed studies of HIV in this setting should provide important insights into the relationships between virus characteristics, transmission, and virulence (57, 85). Molecular epidemiologic studies also represent a critical component of the search for effective HIV vaccines, and our understanding of infectivity and virulence will undoubtedly increase as a result of on-going efforts in this area.

In sum, epidemiologists have successfully sketched the major components and some of the finer details about how HIV is transmitted from one individual to another. Based on this knowledge, a wide range of HIV prevention programs have been implemented worldwide, focusing on techniques for encouraging individuals to change particular behaviors known to be causally related to HIV transmission. Yet despite some important successes, HIV continues to spread at high rates in many populations (39). In response, recent research on the determinants of HIV-related risk behavior has led to a greater focus on the role of social support and peer norms (31, 58, 72). Similarly, there is increasing interest in the community as a social and cultural context for human behavior (52, 65, 88). Such research is important, but there is a parallel need for basic epidemiologic research that is socially informed. We need to understand how HIV spreads within and between populations, and how HIV transmission is structured by human relationships.

Structure of Transmission

Understanding why HIV continues to spread, despite our clear understanding of the direct causal factors leading to transmission, has led to a consideration of the structure of human relationships. This concept of structure is derived from a number of distinct perspectives that use mathematical terms to describe structures as systems of constraints or selective forces that shunt the probability of particular outcomes away from randomness. These outcomes, in turn, may generate consequences that feed back on the system to either reinforce it or destabilize it. It may help to think of structure in terms of a tree rather than a building. The structure of a tree may appear static at any given moment when it is observed, but the structure is in fact dynamic. Concepts of dynamic structure can be found in HIV-related writings of ecological epidemiologists (71), biological anthropologists (8, 63, 64), network modelers (53), mathematical epidemiologists (4a, 29, 44, 45), and evolutionary epidemiologists (22, 23).

Although both mathematical and statistical models are inherently numeric, mathematical descriptions of the dynamic aspects of structures are not equivalent to statistical descriptions of those structures. In fact, a mathematical model may provide a qualitative description that is more important than the quantitative results. For example, the exact number of HIV infections projected by a model may be of less interest than the fact that small changes in a single parameter lead to a drastic reduction in the projected number of infections (37). The numeric projection tells us how important it is to intervene, but the dynamic structural picture helps us figure out what needs to go into an effective intervention. For example, Pinkerton & Abramson (59) developed a model to assess the relative contributions of consistent condom use and reduction in the number of sexual partners to HIV risk reduction, concluding that "in many cases condom usage results in a greater reduction in the probability of infection than would be achieved by eliminating 1,000 one-night stands" (p. 523). Although it would be inappropriate to use the results of a computer model as the sole basis for deciding how to design an intervention or target prevention resources, models can be effective tools for exploring options and for testing the plausibility of the assumptions underlying a planned intervention.

The models reviewed here are those used primarily as tools for exploring the dynamic interaction of complex factors, where direct observation of the interaction process and/or measurement of key aspects of that process are difficult or impossible (5, 10, 32, 37, 59). A key strength of the mathematical modeling approach is its ability to include the impact of environmental factors in the assessment of HIV transmission. For example, an individual's risk for HIV infection is partially dependent on the prevalence of HIV in his or her risk network (i.e. those individuals with whom he or she engages in risk behavior). But it is impossible to include this effect when using statistical models to measure individual-level risk because prevalence is not an individual-level measure. It is a group-level measure that impacts both the individual likelihood of infection and the population likelihood of epidemic spread (71). Similarly, population-level measures of risk (e.g. incidence rate ratios and other measures of relative risk among subgroups) are often biased because the likelihood that one individual will be infected is dependent on the likelihood of infection among other individuals (29, 44). Koopman and colleagues (44) make a particularly convincing argument against the use of risk assessment strategies that fail to take into account the lack of independence in the outcome measure.

Accurate prediction of dependent outcomes requires historical data because the likelihood that person A will get infected depends on whether person B has already been infected. The historical development of the spread of HIV in a particular area is thus another example of a non–individual-level factor relevant to epidemiologic investigations of HIV transmission. In areas where HIV has become well established, risk assessment is particularly fraught with problems if one fails to consider historical factors such as fluctuations in local population composition, the stability of risk networks, and behavioral changes related to the impact of the epidemic (26). In contrast, an historically informed epidemiologic analysis can provide important insights. For example, Des Jarlais and colleagues combined data from HIV prevalence surveys conducted among IDUs in New York City in 1984 and 1990–1992 with information on trends in routes of drug administration, levels of drug purity, and factors influencing the sharing of injection equipment to identify "reasonable public health goals" (19:126).

The demographic structure of a population is also relevant to a full understanding of the epidemiology of HIV. An exploratory analysis of AIDS mortality curves for five-year birth cohorts in New York City uncovered a consistent age-specific pattern of mortality for all cohorts, although the height of the mortality curve varied by gender, race, and birth cohort (70). The authors hypothesize that the apparent stability of HIV prevalence in New York City is the composite result of historically high but subsequently declining incidence in older cohorts and lower but still increasing incidence in younger cohorts. Such results underscore the importance of both historical specificity and cross-cutting patterns.

TRANSMISSION MODELS

Mathematical Epidemiology

Most of the HIV transmission models developed by mathematical epidemiologists look at transmission dynamics in hypothetical populations of gay men (6, 35, 51, 63), although IDU (10, 36) and heterosexual populations (20, 51) have also been modeled. In a comprehensive effort, Hethcote & Van Ark (32) modeled transmission dynamics both within and among all of these populations in the United States.

Each mathematic epidemiologic model includes a set of parameters that are varied in order to evaluate the effect of each parameter on the spread of HIV in a population over a long period of time, generally until prevalence is stable. Patterns of increase, decrease, and stability in HIV incidence and prevalence constitute the outcome of analytic interest. Background parameters are primarily demographic and usually limited to the size of the initial population and the rate at which individuals enter or leave the population. HIV transmission parameters include the rate at which individuals have intercourse with new partners, the probability that an individual will engage in a particular sex act (e.g. unprotected receptive anal intercourse), the probability that a given sex act will transmit HIV (if the partner is infected), and the probability that the partner is infected. Some modelers also include an AIDS staging parameter (49, 50) that reflects time-dependent changes in infectiousness, so that transmission is more likely to occur in either the early weeks of a partner's infection or after the onset of AIDS-defining illness. Structural parameters are used to divide the population into groups that differ systematically from each other, usually in terms of key transmission parameters. For example, a hypothetical population of gay men may include one group with high rates of partner turnover and a second with low rates.

Several models have found that the amount of mixing between individuals engaging in different levels of risk behavior is important (5, 10, 44). Anderson & May (5) summarize findings from studies that suggest the greatest overall spread of infection results from random mixing among all individuals in a population. With nonrandom (assortative) mating, the epidemic moves in waves through linked subgroups, but the epidemic peak is lower in those groups with lower risk profiles, and prevalence stabilizes at a lower level than when mixing is random. Anderson & May note that the variance in risk behavior is particularly important for understanding the rate at which HIV is transmitted within a community. Individuals engaging in extremely high rates of risk behavior influence the likelihood that an HIV epidemic will occur in the community. On the other hand, the likelihood that the epidemic will spread throughout the community is determined by the average level of risk activity taking place.

Koopman and colleagues (34, 43–45, 63, 64) introduced so-called mixing parameters in order to systematically investigate the impact of nonrandom partnership formation on HIV spread. The concept of *selective mixing* was formulated to explore the impact of variation in factors such as sexual need and the acceptability of potential sex partners (i.e. individual-level constraints on partnership formation) (34, 43–45). *Structured mixing* (also called preferred mixing) permits the exploration of group-level constraints by defining average rates of participation of groups in the social or geographical settings where partnership formation occurs (44, 45) or by defining the proportion of sexual contacts that are endogamous (64). *Random mixing* is used to assess the effect of average rates of partnership formation within groups without regard to selectivity.

Koopman and his colleagues have used the mixing parameters to explore both epidemic trends and the utility of epidemiologic measures of relative risk for assessing the riskiness of particular behaviors. The results indicate that structured mixing ultimately lowers prevalence but has a limited effect on incidence unless endogamy is extreme (44, 64). When both selective and structured mixing are operating, they generate significant biases in cross-sectional assessments of the relative risk of specific behaviors (44, 45). These biases can mask the extent to which some behaviors constitute a risk for transmission. In a model incorporating two types of sexual risk behaviors, one of which was four times as likely to transmit HIV as the other, the underlying relative risk of the two behaviors was greatly distorted when assessed using standard epidemiologic measures. The high-risk behavior appeared to be 10–15 times as likely to transmit HIV in the first 20 years of the simulated epidemic when assessed using incidence rate ratios, and as much as 35 times as likely to transmit HIV when assessed using odds ratios (44).

The relationship between selectivity and structure in the real world is undoubtedly more complex than mathematical epidemiologic models suggest. For example, Koopman and colleagues (43) postulate that structure might emerge as a result of changes in selectivity, if these changes led subgroups to form on the basis of behavioral similarity. The emergence of a high-risk subgroup could then set the stage for rapid epidemic spread within that group. Although the models allow for an assessment of dependent outcomes, they have not been used to explore these types of emergent phenomena.

The mathematical epidemiology models described above use population or subpopulation averages to evaluate the impact of variability in partnership formation rates and levels of risk behavior on disease spread. The actual interaction between individuals within populations or groups is not modeled. Sattenspiel (63) has proposed the use of migration matrices such as those originally developed by population geneticists to assess the effect of within-group variability; however, this approach has not yet been attempted. Others (20, 21, 74) have developed models that use pairs of individuals (dyads) as the basic unit of analysis in order to better understand the effect of steady partnerships on the likely spread of disease. These dyadic models tend to project lower HIV prevalence than equivalent models that do not explicitly consider pair formation.

Both migration matrix models and dyadic models require large numbers of parameters, even when they are highly simplified. A more manageable and highly promising approach to both within-group variability and relationship effects is network theory (2, 42, 53). It has also been noted (4a, 5, 10) that sexual network data are potentially useful for assessing the extent to which subgroups with different risk profiles are linked to each other through individuals engaging in risk behavior within both groups (5, 10).

Networks

The classic empirical demonstration of the importance of networks for the spread of HIV is the so-called Patient Zero cluster of original AIDS cases among gay men in both New York and California (9, 17). Using standard methods of contact tracing developed for use with other STDs, Darrow and colleagues were able to demonstrate the role that one geographically mobile individual played in linking otherwise distinct sexual networks. Although this individual's historic role in the epidemic has been overstated by some (67), the potential contribution of the analysis for understanding the dynamics of the epidemic has been largely ignored. In one of the few exceptions to this trend, Altmann (3) explicitly references this early analysis as inspiration for his refinements in the measurement of a given individual's centrality in a network.

The Colorado Springs study (41, 42) was among the first to attempt a true network analysis of HIV transmission. Rather than assess the extent to which HIV transmission had already occurred within the community, this study sought to evaluate the potential risk of epidemic spread that could result from sexual behavior and drug use behavior within the community if HIV were present. The results of the study indicate that a network approach is feasible, but the model itself is oversimplified in that it equates risk- and nonrisk-based relationships (e.g. individuals linked by a sexual relationship are indistinguishable from those linked by friendship).

The importance of distinguishing risk networks from other types of social networks is demonstrated by Neaigus et al's work (53) among ethnically diverse IDUs in New York City. Of particular importance is their identification of the role of anonymous risk relationships between individuals, such as the "renting" of previously used syringes in shooting galleries. Neaigus et al describe such relationships as "an institutional form of a risk network" and draw parallels with the anonymous sexual partnering commonly found in gay bathhouses. Similar parallels could be drawn with some types of prostitute-client relationships, for example, in brothels where there is frequent turnover among the sex workers. These types of institutional networks create situations similar to those of the random mixing models discussed above and that invariably result in the highest HIV transmission rates.

Trotter and colleagues (71a) have developed a network typology for IDUs, based on empirical research among drug users in a small southwestern city. They found higher HIV infection rates in networks that were open (i.e. those that allowed new members to join the network), but found higher rates of drug-related HIV risk behavior in closed networks. In this situation, the spread of HIV throughout the drug-using community will depend on the number of individuals who belong to both open and closed networks.

A somewhat different approach to the role of networks has been used in research in non-Western settings (3a, 11, 30, 55, 56). These studies place greater emphasis on describing the types of people with whom one has relationships (e.g. spouses, brothel-based sex workers) than on the structure of those relationships. The studies provide rich descriptions of contextual factors (e.g. historical, economic, cultural) that foster multiple sexual relationships.

Sociogeographic Models

Wallace (75–82) has modeled the impact of emergent social phenomena on the spread of HIV. Beginning with an analysis of the impact of a reduction in municipal services in the Bronx, New York City, Wallace describes statistical and geographic patterns that link urban burnout or desertification with intentional violent death, substance abuse, and AIDS mortality (75, 76). He then postulates that the link between urban desertification and its associated plagues is found in the disintegrating social networks of neighborhood residents. Using a network model of social and geographic interaction, he investigates the potential role of sociogeographic networks as mediating structures in the epidemic spread of HIV (77–79). The model suggests that a synergistic relationship exists between the susceptibility of an individual community to disease spread and the probability of disease transmission between communities. When the level of susceptibility and the probability of intercommunity transmission are related (e.g. if social disintegration encourages outmigration or if susceptibility is structurally associated with transience; 78), then the rate of transmission is enhanced substantially.

More recent articles by Wallace and colleagues (80–82) continue to explore the social, political, and economic dimensions of HIV transmission from a sociogeographic perspective. Building on the concepts developed in their urban models, they are now exploring the potential for the spread of HIV and other infectious diseases from urban to suburban settings.

Evolutionary Epidemiology

The models developed by Wallace and his colleagues are ecological models with a twist. Humans are in the ecosystem they describe, but more importantly, they *are* the ecosystem as expressed in the concept of sociogeographic interaction. This perspective is akin to Darwinian or evolutionary epidemiology (22, 23, 86) in that both assess the role of humans as pathogenic environments rather than assessing pathogens as an element in the human environment.

Ewald (23) has introduced the concept of cultural vectors, which he describes as "amalgams of culture, human behavior and the physical environment that allow pathogens to be transmitted" (p. 88). Drawing on the lessons we are learning from our experiences with multi-drug resistant strains of tuberculosis, *Escherichia coli,* and other pathogens, Ewald argues that HIV prevention policies should actively seek to foster the selection of less virulent strains of HIV, although how this might be done is unclear. A more salient example of the need for consideration of evolutionary factors might be found in the current search for a vaccine to prevent HIV infection (30a, 47a). The challenges facing HIV vaccinologists are many, and it seems likely that initial vaccines will not be fully protective against infection. Because HIV exhibits a high degree of genetic variability, the possibility that partially effective vaccines could operate as selective forces on HIV may warrant consideration and may constitute another area where a modeling approach can provide insight into the dynamics of HIV transmission.

CONCLUSION: ANTHROPOLOGY AND HIV EPIDEMIOLOGY

Anthropologists engaged in HIV/AIDS research generally have focused on HIV transmission either from an applied interventionist perspective (e.g. 71a), from a critical theory standpoint (e.g. 10a), or occasionally from both (e.g. 34a,b). The epidemiologic perspective has generally elicited less interest, much of it critical (e.g. 24a, 27a). HIV epidemiologic theory is moving toward complex levels of analysis incorporating a wide range of social, cultural, and ecological issues that parallel those traditionally studied by anthropologists. Clearly, there is much that anthropologists and epidemiologists can learn from each other in their common struggle to halt the spread of HIV.

ACKNOWLEDGMENTS

I would like to thank Scott Holmberg for his generous input during the writing of this paper, as well as Lynda Doll, Martha Rogers, Michael Little, and Carole Hill for their helpful review and comments. I am also grateful to Brad Bartholow, Susan Chu, Susan Davis, Richard Selik, and Dawn Smith for sharing their expertise, and to George Lemp, Mark Lobato, Robert Trotter II, and Bruce Weniger for providing me with manuscripts that were not yet in press.

Literature Cited

1. AIDS Institute. 1993. Expert panel on sexual transmission of HIV. *Summary of Proceedings.* The AIDS Inst., NY State Dept. Health
2. Alperin S, Needle R. 1989. *Social network analysis: an approach to understanding intravenous drug users.* Presented at Annu. Natl. AIDS Demonstration Res. Conf., 1st, Rockville, MD
3. Altmann M. 1993. Reinterpreting network measures for models of disease transmission. *Soc. Netw.* 15:1–17
3a. Anarfi J. 1991. Sexual networking in selected communities in Ghana and the sexual behavior of Ghanian female migrants in Abidjan, Côte D'Ivoire. In *Sexual Behavior and Networking: Anthropological and Socio-Cultural Studies on the Transmission of HIV,* ed. T Dyson, pp. 233–47. Liege, Belgium: IUSSP
4. Anderson RM. 1993. AIDS: trends, predictions, controversy. *Nature* 363:393–94
4a. Anderson RM. 1991. The transmission dynamics of sexually transmitted diseases: the behavioral component. In *Sexual Behavior and Networking: Anthropological and Socio-Cultural Studies on the Transmission of HIV,* ed. T Dyson, pp. 23–48. Liege, Belgium: IUSSP
5. Anderson RM, May RM. 1992. Understanding the AIDS pandemic. *Sci. Am.* 85: 58–66
6. Anderson RM, Medley GF, May RM, Johnson AM. 1986. A preliminary study of the transmission dynamics of the human immunodeficiency virus (HIV), the causative agent of AIDS. *IMA J. Math. Appl. Med. Biol.* 3:229–63
7. Aral SO. 1993. Heterosexual transmission of HIV: the role of other sexually transmitted infections and behavior in its epidemiology prevention and control. *Annu. Rev. Public Health* 14:451–67
8. Armelagos GJ, Ryan M, Leatherman T. 1990. Evolution of infectious disease: a biocultural analysis of AIDS. *Am. J. Hum. Biol.* 2:253–63
9. Auerbach DM, Darrow WW, Jaffe HW, Curran JW. 1984. Cluster of cases of the acquired immune deficiency syndrome. *Am. J. Med.* 76:487–92
10. Blower S, Medley G. 1992. Epidemiology, HIV and drugs: mathematical models and data. *Br. J. Addict.* 87:371–79
10a. Bolton R. 1992. AIDS and promiscuity: muddles in the models of HIV prevention. *Med. Anthropol.* 14:145–223
11. Caldwell JC, Caldwell P, Orubuloye IO. 1992. The family and sexual networking in sub-Saharan Africa: historical regional differences and present-day implications. *Popul. Stud.* 46:385–410
11a. Castillo-Chavez C, ed. 1989. *Mathematical and Statistical Approaches to AIDS Epidemiology. Lecture Notes in Biomathematics,* Vol. 83. Berlin: Springer-Verlag
12. Centers for Disease Control and Prevention. 1990. HIV prevalence estimates and AIDS case projections for the United States: report based upon a workshop. *MMWR* 39 (No. RR-16)
13. Centers for Disease Control and Prevention. 1993. Update: mortality attributable to HIV/AIDS among persons aged 25–44 years—United States, 1990 and 1991. *MMWR* 42:481–86
14. Centers for Disease Control and Prevention. 1994. *HIV/AIDS Surveillance Report,* 5(4). Atlanta, GA: US Dept. Health Human Serv.
14a. Centers for Disease Control and Prevention. 1994. *National HIV Serosurveillance Summary: Results through 1992,* Vol. 3. Atlanta, GA: US Dept. Health Human Serv.
15. Chu SY, Berkelman RL, Curran JW. 1992. Epidemiology of HIV in the United States. In *AIDS Etiology, Diagnosis, Treatment and Prevention,* ed. VT DeVita, S Hellman, SA Rosenberg, pp. 99–109. Philadelphia: Lippincott. 3rd ed.
15a. Chu SY, Buehler JW, Oxtoby MJ, Kilbourne BW. 1991. Impact of the human immunodeficiency virus epidemic on mortality in children, United States. *Pediatrics* 87(6):806–10
16. Clark SJ, Saag MS, Decker WD, Campbell-Hill S, Roberson JL, et al. 1991. High titers of cytopathic virus in plasma of patients with symptomatic primary HIV-1 infection. *N. Engl. J. Med.* 324(14):954–64
17. Darrow WW, Gorman EM, Glick BP. 1986. The social origins of AIDS: social change, sexual behavior, and disease trends. In *The Social Dimensions of AIDS: Method and Theory,* ed. DA Feldman, TM Johnson, pp. 95–107. New York: Praeger
18. Des Jarlais DC, Friedman SR, Novick D, Sotheran JL, Kreek MJ, et al. 1989. HIV-1 infection among intravenous drug users in Manhattan. *J. Am. Med. Assoc.* 261:1008–12
19. Des Jarlais DC, Friedman SR, Sotheran JL, Wenston J, Marmor M, et al. 1994. Continuity and change within an HIV epidemic: injecting drug users in New York City, 1984 through 1992. *J. Am. Med. Assoc.* 271(2): 121–27
20. Dietz K. 1988. On the transmission dynamics of HIV. *Math. Biosci.* 90:397–414
21. Dietz K, Hadeler KP. 1988. Epidemiologi-

cal models for sexually transmitted diseases. *J. Math. Biol.* 26:1–25

21a. Essex M, Mboup S, Kanki PJ, Kalengayi MR, eds. 1994. *AIDS in Africa*. New York: Raven

22. Ewald PW. 1993. *Evolution of Infectious Disease*. Oxford: Oxford Univ. Press

23. Ewald PW. 1993. The evolution of virulence. *Sci. Am.* 86:86–93

24. Francis HL, Quinn TC. 1994. Bloodborne transmission of HIVs in Africa. See Ref. 21a, pp. 237–49

24a. Frankenberg RJ. 1994. The impact of HIV/AIDS on concepts relating to risk and culture within British community epidemiology: candidates or targets for prevention. *Soc. Sci. Med.* 38(10):1325–35

25. Friedland G. 1989. Parenteral drug users. In *The Epidemiology of AIDS*, ed. RA Kaslow, DP Francis, pp. 153–78. New York: Oxford Univ. Press

26. Friedman SR, Des Jarlais DC, Jose B, Neaigus A, Goldstein M. 1994. Seroprevalence, seroconversion, and the history of the HIV epidemic among drug injectors. In *HIV Epidemiology*, ed. A Nicolosi, pp. 137–50. New York: Raven

27. Fultz P. 1989. The biology of human immunodeficiency viruses. In *The Epidemiology of AIDS*, ed. RA Kaslow, DP Francis, pp. 3–17. New York: Oxford Univ. Press

27a. Glick-Schiller N, Crystal S, Lewellen D. 1994. Risky business: the cultural construction of AIDS risk groups. *Soc. Sci. Med.* 38(10):1337–46

28. Gwinn M, Pappaioanou M, George JR, Hannon WH, Wasser SC, et al. 1991. Prevalence of HIV infection in childbearing women in the United States: surveillance using newborn blood samples. *J. Am. Med. Assoc.* 265(13):1704–8

29. Halloran ME, Struchiner CJ. 1991. Study designs for dependent happenings. *Epidemiology* 2(5):331–38

30. Havanon N, Bennett A, Knodel J. 1993. Sexual networking in provincial Thailand. *Stud. Fam. Plan.* 24(1):1–17

30a. Haynes BF. 1993. Scientific and social issues of human immunodeficiency virus vaccine development. *Science* 260:1279–86

31. Hays RB, Kegeles SM, Coates TJ. 1990. High HIV risk-taking among young gay men. *AIDS* 4:901–7

32. Hethcote HW, Van Ark JW. 1992. *Modeling HIV transmission and AIDS in the United States. Lecture Notes in Biomathematics*, Vol. 95. Berlin: Springer-Verlag

33. Holmberg SD, Horsburgh CR Jr, Ward JW, Jaffe HW. 1989. Biologic factors in the sexual transmission of human immunodeficiency virus. *J. Infect. Dis.* 160(1):116–25

34. Jacquez JA, Simon CP, Koopman J. 1989. Structured mixing: heterogeneous mixing by the definition of activity groups. See Ref. 11a, pp. 301–15

34a. Kane S. 1991. HIV, heroin and heterosexual relations. *Soc. Sci. Med.* 32(9):1037–50

34b. Kane S. 1991. Sexual transmission of HIV in drug users' networks: the social context and implications for intervention. *AIDS Health Promot. Exch.* 21:3–15

35. Kaplan EH. 1989. What are the risks of risky sex? Modeling the AIDS epidemic. *Oper. Res.* 37(2):198–209

36. Kaplan EH. 1989. Needles that kill: modeling human immunodeficiency virus transmission via shared drug injection equipment in shooting galleries. *Rev. Infect. Dis.* 11(2):289–98

37. Kaplan EH. 1990. An overview of AIDS modeling. In *Evaluating AIDS Prevention: Contributions of Multiple Disciplines*, ed. LC Leviton, AM Hegedus, A Kubrin, pp. 23–36. San Francisco: Jossey-Bass

38. Keenlyside RA, Johnson AM, Mabey DCW. 1993. The epidemiology of HIV-1 infection and AIDS in women. *AIDS* 7(Suppl. 1):S83–S90

39. Kelly JA, Murphy DA, Sikkema KJ, Kalichman SC. 1993. Psychological interventions to prevent HIV infection are urgently needed. *Am. Psychol.* 48(10):1023–34

40. Kingsley LA, Shou SYJ, Bacellar H, Rinaldo CR Jr, Chmiel J, et al. 1991. Temporal trends in human immunodeficiency virus type 1 seroconversion 1984–1989. *Am. J. Epidemiol.* 134(4):331–39

41. Klovdahl AS. 1985. Social networks and the spread of infectious diseases: the AIDS example. *Soc. Sci. Med.* 21:1203–16

42. Klovdahl AS, Potterat JJ, Woodhouse DE, Muth JB, Muth SQ, Darrow WW. 1993. Social networks and infectious disease: the Colorado Springs Study. *Soc. Sci. Med.* 38(1):79–88

43. Koopman J, Simon C, Jacquez J, Joseph J, Sattenspiel L, Park T. 1988. Sexual partner selectiveness effects on homosexual HIV transmission dynamics. *J. Acquir. Immune Defic. Syndr.* 1:486–504

44. Koopman JS, Longini IM, Jacquez JA, Simon CP, Ostrow DG, et al. 1991. Assessing risk factors for transmission of infection. *Am. J. Epidemiol.* 133(12):1199–1209

45. Koopman JS, Simon CP, Jacquez JA, Park TS. 1989. Selective contact within structured mixing with an application to HIV transmission risk from oral and anal sex. See Ref. 11a, pp. 316–48

46. Lallemant MJ, Lallemant-Le Coeur S, Nzingoula S. 1994. Perinatal transmission of HIV in Africa. See Ref. 21a, pp. 211–36

47. Lemp GF, Hariozawa AM, Givertz D, Nieri BA, Anderson L, et al. 1994. HIV seroprevalence and risk behaviors among young gay and bisexual men: the San Fran-

cisco/Berkeley Young Men's Study. *J. Am. Med. Assoc.* In press

47a. Letvin NL. 1993. Vaccines against human immunodeficiency virus—progress and prospects. *N. Engl. J. Med.* 329(19):1400–5

48. Lifson AR, O'Malley PM, Hessol NA, Buchbinder SP, Cannon L, Rutherford GW. 1990. HIV seroconversion in two homosexual men after receptive oral intercourse with ejaculation: implications for counseling concerning safe sexual practices. *Am. J. Public Health* 80:1509–11

49. Longini IM, Clark WS, Gardner LI, Brundage JF. 1991. The dynamics of CD4+ T-lymphocyte decline in HIV-infected individuals: a Markov modeling approach. *J. Acquir. Immune Defic. Syndr.* 4:1141–47

50. Longini IM, Clark WS, Haber M, Horsburgh R Jr. 1989. The stages of HIV infection: waiting times and infection transmission probabilities. See Ref. 11a, pp. 111–37

51. May RM, Anderson RM. 1987. Transmission dynamics of HIV infection. *Nature* 326:137–42

52. Morales ES, Fullilove MT. 1992. 'Many are called...': participation by minority leaders in an AIDS intervention in San Francisco. *Ethn. Dis.* 2:389–401

53. Neaigus A, Friedman SR, Curtis R, Des Jarlais DC, Furst RT, et al. 1993. The relevance of drug injectors' social and risk networks for understanding and preventing HIV infection. *Soc. Sci. Med.* 38(1):67–78

54. Nwanyanwu OC, Chu SY, Green TA, Buehler JW, Berkelman RL. 1993. Acquired immunodeficiency syndrome in the United States associated with injecting drug use, 1981–1991. *Am. J. Drug Alcohol Abuse* 19(4):399–408

55. Orubuloye IO, Caldwell JC, Caldwell P. 1991. Sexual networking in the Ekiti District of Nigeria. *Stud. Fam. Plan.* 22(2):61–73

56. Orubuloye IO, Caldwell JC, Caldwell P. 1992. Diffusion and focus in sexual networking: identifying partners and partners' partners. *Stud. Fam. Plan.* 23(6):343–51

57. Ou C-Y, Takebe Y, Weniger BG, Luo C-C, Kalish ML, et al. 1993. Independent introduction of two major HIV-1 genotypes into distinct high-risk populations in Thailand. *Lancet* 341:1171–74

58. Peterson JL, Coates TJ, Catania JA, Middleton L, Hilliard B, Hearst N. 1992. High risk sexual behavior and condom use among gay and bisexual African-American men. *Am. J. Public Health* 82(11):1490–94

59. Pinkerton SD, Abramson PR. 1993. Evaluating the risks: a Bernoulli process model of HIV infection and risk reduction. *Eval. Rev.* 17(5):504–28

60. Piot P, Goeman J, Laga M. 1994. The epidemiology of HIV and AIDS in Africa. See Ref. 21a, pp. 157–71

61. Plummer FA, Tyndall MW, Ndinya-Achola JO, Moses S. 1994. Sexual transmission of HIVs and the role of sexually transmitted diseases. See Ref. 21a, pp. 195–209

62. Samuel MC, Hessol N, Shiboski S, Engel RR, Speed TP, Winkelstein W. 1993. Factors associated with human immunodeficiency virus seroconversion in homosexual men in three San Francisco cohort studies, 1984–1989. *J. Acquir. Immune Defic. Syndr.* 6:303–12

63. Sattenspiel L. 1989. The structure and context of social interactions and the spread of HIV. See Ref. 11a, pp. 242–59

64. Sattenspiel L, Koopman J, Simon C, Jacquez J. 1989. The effects of population structure on the spread of HIV infection. *Am. J. Phys. Anthropol.* 82:421–29

65. Schilling RF, Schinke SP, Nichols SE, Zayas LH, Miller SO, et al. 1989. Developing strategies for AIDS prevention research with black and Hispanic drug users. *Public Health Rep.* 104(1):2–11

66. Selik RM, Chu SY, Buehler JW. 1993. HIV infection as leading cause of death among young adults in US cities and states. *J. Am. Med. Assoc.* 269(23):2991–94

67. Shilts R. 1987. *And the Band Played On.* New York: Penguin

68. Smith DK, Curran JW. 1994. The international epidemiology of HIV infection. In *Blood, Blood Products and AIDS,* ed. R Madhok, CD Forbes, BL Evatt, pp. 1–37. London: Chapman & Hall Medical. 2nd ed.

69. St. Louis ME, Kamenga M, Brown C, Nelson AM, Manzila T, et al. 1993. Risk for perinatal HIV-1 transmission according to maternal immunologic, virologic, and placental factors. *J. Am. Med. Assoc.* 269(22):2853–59

70. Stoneburner RL, Lessner L, Fordyce EJ, Bevier P, Chiasson MA. 1993. Insight into the infection dynamics of the AIDS epidemic: a cohort analysis of New York City AIDS mortality. *Am. J. Epidemiol.* 138(12):1093–1104

71. Susser M. 1994. The logic in ecological. In *HIV Epidemiology: Models and Methods,* ed. A Nicolosi, pp. 161–74. New York: Raven

71a. Trotter RT II, Bowen AM, Potter JM Jr. 1994. Network models for HIV outreach and prevention programs for drug users. In *Social Network Analysis, HIV Prevention and Drug Abuse.* NIDA Monogr. Ser. Bethesda, MD: Natl. Inst. Drug Abuse. In press

72. Valdiserri RO, ed. 1989. *Preventing AIDS: The Design of Effective Programs.* New Brunswick, NJ: Rutgers Univ. Press

73. van Griensven GJP, Hessol NA, Koblin BA, Byers RH, O'Malley PM, et al. 1993.

Epidemiology of human immunodeficiency virus type 1 infection among homosexual men participating in hepatitis B vaccine trials in Amsterdam, New York City, and San Francisco, 1978–1990. *Am. J. Epidemiol.* 137(8):909–15

74. Waldstätter R. 1989. Pair formation in sexually-transmitted diseases. See Ref. 11a, pp. 260–74

75. Wallace R. 1988. A synergism of plagues: 'planned shrinkage,' contagious housing destruction and AIDS in the Bronx. *Environ. Res.* 47:1–33

76. Wallace R. 1990. Urban desertification, public health and public order: 'planned shrinkage', violent death, substance abuse and AIDS in the Bronx. *Soc. Sci. Med.* 31(7):801–13

77. Wallace R. 1991. Traveling waves of HIV infection on a low dimensional 'socio-geographic' network. *Soc. Sci. Med.* 32(7):847–52

78. Wallace R. 1991. Social disintegration and the spread of AIDS: thresholds for propagation along 'sociogeographic' networks. *Soc. Sci. Med.* 33(10):1155–62

79. Wallace R. 1993. Social disintegration and the spread of AIDS—II: meltdown of sociogeographic structure in urban minority neighborhoods. *Soc. Sci. Med.* 37(7):887–96

80. Wallace R, Fullilove M, Fullilove R, Gould P, Wallace D. 1994. Will AIDS be contained within U. S. minority urban populations? *Soc. Sci. Med.* In press

81. Wallace R, Wallace D. 1993. Inner-city disease and public health of the suburbs: the sociogeographic dispersion of point-source infection. *Environ. Plan. A* 25:1707–23

82. Wallace R, Wallace D. 1993. The coming crisis of public health in the suburbs. *Milbank Q.* 71(4):543–64

83. Wasserheit JN. 1992. Epidemiological synergy: interrelationships between human immunodeficiency virus infection and other sexually transmitted diseases. *Sex. Transm. Dis.* 19(2):61–77

84. Weniger BG, Limpakarnjanarat K, Ungchusak K, Thanprasertsuk S, Choopanya K, et al. 1991. The epidemiology of HIV infection and AIDS in Thailand. *AIDS* 5(Suppl. 2):S71-S85

85. Weniger BG, Takebe Y, Ou C-Y, Yamazaki S. 1994. The molecular epidemiology of HIV in Asia. *AIDS* 8(Suppl. 2):In press

86. Williams GC, Nesse RM. 1991. The dawn of Darwinian medicine. *Q. Rev. Biol.* 66(1):1–22

87. Winkelstein W, Wiley JA, Padian NS, Samuel M, Shiboski S, et al. 1988. The San Francisco Men's Health Study: continued decline in HIV seroconversion rates among homosexual/bisexual men. *Am. J. Public Health* 78:1472–74

88. Wright JW. 1993. African-American male sexual behavior and the risk for HIV infection. *Human Organ.* 52(4):421–31

AUTHOR INDEX

A

Aarsleff H, 60, 67, 68
Abasiekong EM, 356
Abbott E, 348, 360
Abbott WGH, 468
Abbruzzi W, 99
Abdalla HI, 259, 407
Abel R, 446
Abercrombie N, 116
Abercrombie T, 399
Abraham S, 446
Abrahams RD, 332–35
Abrahams RG, 365
Abramovitch H, 40
Abrams P, 109, 116, 117, 379, 380
Abramson PR, 516
Abruzzi WS, 318
Abu-Lughod JL, 39, 161
Abu-Lughod L, 25, 31, 41, 42, 426
Achenbaum WA, 144
Acheson JM, 358
Acheson SR, 215, 216, 218, 222, 224
Ackerly N, 88
Ackerman RE, 216, 218
Ackerman S, 409, 413, 419
Adair LS, 268
Adams A, 366
Adams E, 99, 100
Adams KL, 63
Adams REW, 189, 191
Adams RMcC, 160, 167, 173, 190
Adams RN, 391, 399
Adams WM, 366
Adamu M, 359, 362
Adeniyi PO, 352
Adler M, 97
Agawu VK, 31, 39
AGHA A, 277–302; 60, 286, 288, 292, 294
Aguayo S, 114
Agurcia R, 195
Ahlstrom R, 88
Ahmed S, 267
Ajuwon B, 39
Akalin S, 468
Akhtar Y, 240, 242
Akinnaso FN, 60, 63
Albright NL, 243
Albright TE, 243
Alcock S, 165, 167, 168, 171, 173
Alderman BW, 472
Alexiou M, 39

Alfini J, 443
Algaze G, 161, 162
Allaire L, 220
Allan W, 348
Allaway S, 239
Allen H, 268
Allen HA, 268
Allen M, 161
Alleyne M, 329
Allsen TT, 162, 163
Almagor U, 149
ALONSO AM, 379–405; 116, 382, 385, 386, 389, 398
Alperin S, 519
Alpers EA, 409, 415, 416
Alrabaa S, 279
Al-Safi A, 409, 415, 420, 427
Althusser L, 381, 397
Altmann M, 520
Altschul J, 90
Alvarez C, 61, 64
Alvarez S, 125
Alvarez-Cáccamo C, 61, 64
Ambrose SH, 311, 312, 315, 316
AMES KM, 209–29; 209, 212, 213, 215, 217, 219, 220
Amin S, 161
Amoss PT, 137
Amsterdam A, 443
Anagnost A, 116
Anarfi J, 521
Andersen MA, 120
Anderson B, 65, 109, 116, 118, 352, 379, 382, 384, 387
Anderson DG, 116, 358
Anderson DJ, 239
Anderson EA, 286, 288, 294
Anderson L, 511
Anderson PS Jr, 460, 472, 474
Anderson RA, 471
Anderson RM, 512, 516, 517, 519
Anderson TJ, 348
Andreone T, 468
Andresen J, 67
Andrews AP, 185
Andrews EW IV, 184
Andrews EW V, 183–85, 189, 191–93
Angeletti S, 474
Ann TB, 266
Annamalai E, 278
Annis S, 186

Anschuetz K, 98
Anthias F, 385
Antonov-Ovseyenko A, 114
Antonovsky A, 242
Antze P, 411, 427
Anzalduá G, 392
Aponte WL, 339
Appadurai A, 119, 350
Appiah KA, 391
Apter D, 258, 260, 261, 264
Aral SO, 513
Ardener S, 354, 360
Arensburg B, 222
Arias A, 399
Armelagos G, 95
Armelagos GJ, 516
Armillas P, 172
Armstrong N, 124
Arnaud CD, 247
Arndt H, 284, 285
Arnould E, 354, 355
Aronoff SL, 465
Aronowitz S, 120
Asad T, 57, 58, 62
Asaro F, 185
Asch RH, 259
Asher C, 170
Ashkanani Z, 409
Ashmore W, 182, 188, 193, 195
Asiwaju AI, 352
Asselain B, 261
Atieno-Odhiambo ES, 351, 352, 361, 368
Atkins B, 437, 443, 444
Atkins L, 235
Atkinson JM, 408, 409, 411, 445, 446
Attali J, 43
Attinasi JJ, 61
Attridge D, 69
Audouze F, 501
Auerbach DM, 520
Auerbach S, 42
Aunger R, 304, 308, 318
Auroux S, 67
Austerlitz R, 28
Austin JL, 59
Austin S, 260, 267
Auwerx J, 468
Aveni AF, 196
Avis NE, 232, 242, 246
AvRuskin TL, 411

B

Baars J, 139
Babadzan A, 396

‌

SUBJECT INDEX

A

Aboriginal North Americans
  non-insulin-dependent diabetes mellitus
    and, 457–76
Abortion
  age at menopause and, 241
Acculturation, 126
Acephalous cults, 410
Acheulian techno-complex, 14
Acquired immunodeficiency syndrome
  See AIDS
Acquisition
  ancient empires and, 165–66
Actualistic data, 12
Addison's disease
  anti-ovarian antibodies and, 239
Addressee honorifics, 292
Address forms, 278–81
Administration
  ancient empires and, 164–65
Adorcism, 409
Adrar Bous, 13
Aesthetic cueing, 411
Aestheticization
  ethnicity and nationalism and, 396–98
Aesthetics
  language and, 56
  social and cultural significance
    music and, 34
  spirit possession and, 422–26
Affect
  language ideology and, 60
Affinal kinship
  hunter-farmer social interaction and, 308
Africa
  age group systems, 149
  archaeological research, 1–22
  commodities exchange, 305
  See also Tropical Africa
African American English, 325–39
  African American attitudes and, 336–38
  discourse and verbal genres, 332–34
  features, 330–32
  identity and, 338–39
  language and gender, 334–36
  language ideology and, 327–28
  theories of origins, 329–30
  vernacular speech, 328–29
African Islam
  land tenure and, 362
African languages
  honorific registers, 286
Age
  female fecundity and, 256–64
  female reproductive physiology and, 258–60
  follicular atresia and, 244
  land inequality and, 350

  menopause and, 240–41
  natural fertility and, 256–58
  ovarian function and, 260–64
  social indexing through speech and song
    and, 31
  state formation and, 380
  status in state societies and, 391
Age grading
  rights in land and, 349
Age group systems, 149–50
Age inequality
  gender-specific, 150
Age sequencing
  fertility of land and, 361–62
Age stratification theory, 148–51
Agha A, 277–96
Aging
  female reproductive, 233
  hermeneutics, 154–55
  menopause and, 232
  phenomenologies, 152
  rationalities, 152–54
  See also Old age
Agnatic lineages, 353
Agricultural commitment
  in Southwest United States, 93–95
Agricultural labor
  demographic growth and, 355
Agriculture
  in ancient empires, 172
  Maya, 188–90
  prehistoric in Southwest United States, 83–102
  in Southwest United States, 88–90
Agropastoralists
  hunter-gatherers and, 316
Agta, 304
Agta-Palanan food exchange, 310
AID
  See Artificial insemination by donor
AIDS
  epidemiology, 509–22
Air massif, 13
Akbar, 163
Akkadian empire, 162
Aleut
  diabetes mellitus and, 460
  obesity and, 472
Alonso AM, 379–400
Alopecia
  early menopause and, 239
Altar de Sacrificios, 184
Ambiguity
  old age and, 143–46
Amenorrhea, 231, 240
  postpartum
    lactation and, 267
American Anthropological Association
  (AAA), 140

mobility, sedentism, and commitment, 93–95
prehistoric desert farmers, 83–102
resource depletion, 91–92
scales of analysis, 95–100
Sovereignty
territorial integrity and, 127
Spadzista, 492–93, 495, 497, 500
Spatialization
ethnicity and, 393–96
state formation and, 382–84
Spatial symbolics, 360–61
Speaker stereotypes, 291
Speaking
ethnography, 27–28, 59–60
Specialization
Northwest Coast, 212–13, 219–20
Speech
boundaries, 30–31
refiguring, 35–39
sung, 30–31
vernacular
African American, 328–29
Western view, 65
Speech act theory, 59–60
Speech art, 32
Speech level, 292
Speech-level stratification, 292–93
Speech-song interactions, 35–39
Speech style
powerful versus powerless, 444
Spielmann KA, 303–20
Spirit possession, 407–27
gender, power, embodiment, resistance and, 415–22
parameters, 408–10
self and other and, 422–26
therapy, religion, communication and, 410–14
Spiritual sanction
access to land and, 348
Sprechgesang, 30–31
Sprechstimme, 31, 36
State, 116–17
conflict theory and, 116
conformity and, 109
hegemony and, 117, 381, 389–90
ideal, 109
misplaced concreteness and, 380–90
social contract theory and, 123
violence and, 109–29
Statecraft
Maya, 196–97
State formation, 379–400
ethnogenesis and, 391
nationalism and, 391
spatialization and territorialization, 382–84
substantialization, 384–87
temporalization and memory, 387–90
State-idea, 380
State-system, 380
Status
honorific phenomena and, 293–96
STD
See Sexually transmitted disease

Steroids
follicular atresia and, 244
Stigmatization
privatization and, 394
Stone Age, 7, 10
Stone monuments
Maya, 183
Storage
Northwest Coast, 212–13, 217–18
Stranska Skala III, 490
Stratification
Northwest Coast, 221–23
Stress
glucose homeostasis and, 474
non-insulin-dependent diabetes mellitus and, 474–75
Subordination
symbolic violence and, 111
Sub-Saharan Africa
hunter-gatherer kinship systems, 307–8
Subsistence
Northwest Coast, 210, 215–19
Substantialization
ethnicity and nationalism and, 396–98
state formation and, 384–87
Sulu sultanate
slaves, 112
Sundanese language
honorific registers, 286
speech levels, 294
Sung speech, 30–31
Sung-texted-weeping, 39, 43
Sutton Hoo, 3
Swahili
colonial linguistics and, 68
Swidden farming
hunter-gatherer labor and, 306
labor organization and, 355
Swiderian, 501
Swiss yodel, 31
Syllabic song, 35
Symbiosis
hunter-farmer relations and, 309
Syntax
honorific, 287
Syphilis
HIV transmission and, 513–14
Systemic lupus erythematosus (SLE)
early menopause and, 239
Száthmáry EJE, 457–76
Szeged, 499

T

Tagalog, 68
Talk
as self-reflexive action, 59
Tamang, 262, 265
Tamil, 114, 390, 395
Tamil-Paliyan interactions, 307–8
Tarahumara
residential movement, 94
Tarantism, 418
Taxation
ancient empires and, 165

CUMULATIVE INDEXES

CONTRIBUTING AUTHORS, VOLUMES 16–23

CHAPTER TITLES, VOLUMES 16–23

Economics, Ecology, Technology, and Development

Social and Political Relationships